CLASSICAL THERMODYNAMICS OF NONELECTROLYTE SOLUTIONS
With Applications to Phase Equilibria

McGraw-Hill Chemical Engineering Series

Editorial Advisory Board

BUILDING THE LITERATURE OF A PROFESSION

Fifteen prominent chemical engineers first met in New York more than 50 years ago to plan a continuing literature for their rapidly growing profession. From industry came such pioneer practitioners as Leo H. Baekeland, Arthur D. Little, Charles L. Reese, John V. N. Dorr, M. C. Whitaker, and R. S. McBride. From the universities came such eminent educators as William H. Walker, Alfred H. White, D. D. Jackson, J. H. James, Warren K. Lewis, and Harry A. Curtis. H. C. Parmelee, then editor of *Chemical and Metallurgical Engineering*, served as chairman and was joined subsequently by S. D. Kirkpatrick as consulting editor.

After several meetings, this committee submitted its report to the McGraw-Hill Book Company in September 1925. In the report were detailed specifications for a correlated series of more than a dozen texts and reference books which have since become the McGraw-Hill Series in Chemical Engineering and which became the cornerstone of the chemical engineering curriculum.

From this beginning there has evolved a series of texts surpassing by far the scope and longevity envisioned by the founding Editorial Board. The McGraw-Hill Series in Chemical Engineering stands as a unique historical record of the development of chemical engineering education and practice. In the series one finds the milestones of the subject's evolution: industrial chemistry, stoichiometry, unit operations and processes, thermodynamics, kinetics, and transfer operations.

Chemical engineering is a dynamic profession, and its literature continues to evolve. McGraw-Hill and its consulting editors remain committed to a publishing policy that will serve, and indeed lead, the needs of the chemical engineering profession during the years to come.

THE SERIES

Bailey and Ollis: *Biochemical Engineering Fundamentals*
Bennett and Myers: *Momentum, Heat, and Mass Transfer*
Beveridge and Schechter: *Optimization: Theory and Practice*
Carberry: *Chemical and Catalytic Reaction Engineering*
Churchill: *The Interpretation and Use of Rate Data—The Rate Concept*
Clarke and Davidson: *Manual for Process Engineering Calculations*
Coughanowr and Koppel: *Process Systems Analysis and Control*
Danckwerts: *Gas Liquid Reactions*
Finlayson: *Nonlinear Analysis in Chemical Engineering*
Gates, Katzer, and Schuit: *Chemisty of Catalytic Processes*
Harriott: *Process Control*
Holland: *Fundamentals of Multicomponent Distillation*
Johnson: *Automatic Process Control*
Johnstone and Thring: *Pilot Plants, Models, and Scale-up Methods in Chemical Engineering*
Katz, Cornell, Kobayashi, Poettmann, Vary, Elenbaas, and Weinaug: *Handbook of Natural Gas Engineering*
King: *Separation Processes*
Klinzing: *Gas-Solid Transport*
Knudsen and Katz: *Fluid Dynamics and Heat Transfer*
Lapidus: *Digital Computation for Chemical Engineers*
Luyben: *Process Modeling, Simulation, and Control for Chemical Engineers*
McCabe and Smith, J. C.: *Unit Operations of Chemical Engineering*
Mickley, Sherwood, and Reed: *Applied Mathematics in Chemical Engineering*
Nelson: *Petroleum Refinery Engineering*
Perry and Chilton (Editors): *Chemical Engineers' Handbook*
Peters: *Elementary Chemical Engineering*
Peters and Timmerhaus: *Plant Design and Economics for Chemical Engineers*
Probstein and Hicks: *Synthetic Fuels*
Ray: *Advanced Process Control*
Reed and Gubbins: *Applied Statistical Mechanics*
Reid, Prausnitz, and Sherwood: *The Properties of Gases and Liquids*
Resnick: *Process Analysis and Design for Chemical Engineers*
Rodriguez: *Principles of Polymer Systems*
Satterfield: *Heterogeneous Catalysis in Practice*
Sherwood, Pigford, and Wilke: *Mass Transfer*
Slattery: *Momentum, Energy, and Mass Transfer in Continua*
Smith, B. D.: *Design of Equilibrium Stage Processes*
Smith, J. M.: *Chemical Engineering Kinetics*
Smith, J. M., and Van Ness: *Introduction to Chemical Engineering Thermodynamics*
Thompson and Ceckler: *Introduction to Chemical Engineering*
Treybal: *Mass Transfer Operations*

CLASSICAL THERMODYNAMICS OF NONELECTROLYTE SOLUTIONS

With Applications to Phase Equilibria

Hendrick C. Van Ness

Michael M. Abbott

Department of Chemical and Environmental Engineering
Rensselaer Polytechnic Institute

McGraw-Hill Book Company

New York   St. Louis   San Francisco   Auckland   Bogotá   Hamburg
Johannesburg   London   Madrid   Mexico   Montreal   New Delhi
Panama   Paris   São Paulo   Singapore   Sydney   Tokyo   Toronto

This book was set in Times Roman. The editor was Diane D. Heiberg;
the production supervisor was Leroy A. Young.
Fairfield Graphics was printer and binder.

CLASSICAL THERMODYNAMICS OF NONELECTROLYTE SOLUTIONS
With Applications to Phase Equilibria

1 2 3 4 5 6 7 8 9 0 F G F G 8 9 8 7 6 5 4 3 2 1

Library of Congress Cataloging in Publication Data

Van Ness, H. C. (Hendrick C.)
    Classical thermodynamics of nonelectrolyte solutions.

    (McGraw-Hill chemical engineering series)
    Includes bibliographical references and index.
    1. Thermodynamics.   2. Solution (Chemistry)
I. Abbott, Michael M.   II. Title.   III. Series.
QD505.V36   541.3'69   81–5996
ISBN 0–07–067095–1   AACR2

CONTENTS

PREFACE

Our purpose in this work is to present a systematic and comprehensive development of that part of classical thermodynamics applicable to solutions of non-electrolytes. Even so circumscribed a subject has a vast literature and a wide range of practical use in the chemical and petroleum industries. We here develop known theory through concise derivation, making every effort to expose the structure and to illustrate the utility of the subject; ultimately, we focus its power on problems of phase equilibrium in fluid systems.

Although we assume the reader well versed in the basic principles of classical thermodynamics, we include an introductory chapter which reviews and summarizes the fundamentals. Chapters 2 and 3 deal with the thermodynamic properties of pure fluids and their mixtures, presenting definitions, fundamental equations, and basic ideas. The volumetric properties of fluids are given detailed consideration in Chap. 4, where correlations of data based on the corresponding-states principle and on equations of state are described. Chapter 5 treats the special functions and methods appropriate to the thermodynamics of liquid solutions. In Chap. 6 we present a comprehensive, though by no means exhaustive, discussion of phase equilibria, illustrating the practical application of subject matter from preceding chapters.

Thermodynamics is useless without data or correlations intended to approximate data. We have indicated from place to place sources of such information, to which reference may be made. However, new data and improved correlations appear regularly in the literature, allowing ever more effective application of the principles and methods of thermodynamics.

The computer has made possible rapid solution of rigorously formulated problems that formerly could be treated only through unrealistic simplification. This is particularly true where multicomponent phase equilibrium is involved. We presume availability of an adequate computer, and suggest where its use is appropriate, but we are not here concerned with details of programming. Rather, we present the thermodynamic foundation on which intelligent exploitation of computer capability is based.

The material is appropriate for a graduate-level course in chemical-engineering thermodynamics and for professional reference. The inclusion of numerous examples, figures, and summarizing tables is intended to promote understanding and to make use of the book as a reference particularly convenient.

A book of manageable proportions must necessarily be limited in scope, and the decision of what to omit is clearly arbitrary. Among the topics of possible interest that we have excluded are chemical-reaction equilibrium, statistical thermodynamics, and molecular thermodynamics. Nor have we provided a detailed treatment of high-pressure phase equilibria. These topics are of unquestioned interest, and some are the subject of problems (with references) in App. I. They are, however, topics either already well developed in other books or are topics not sufficiently understood to allow definitive treatment.

We wish to thank Gary P. Brown for development of the computer programs required for the equation-of-state calculations of Sec. 6-4. Our appreciation also goes to Robert V. Mrazek (Oregon State University) and to Peter Rasmussen (Danmarks tekniske Højskole) for providing critical reviews of the manuscript.

Hendrick C. Van Ness
Michael M. Abbott

ONE

FUNDAMENTAL BASIS OF THERMODYNAMICS

Classical thermodynamics is a network of equations, developed through the formal logic of mathematics from a very few fundamental postulates and leading to a great variety of useful deductions. In the sense that mathematics is an exact system of logic, thermodynamics is an exact science. However, as with any deductive procedure, the derived conclusions are conditioned by the limitations imposed by the fundamental postulates and depend for validity upon the truth of these postulates within the imposed limitations. One might trace the historical development of the concepts necessary to the formulation of the fundamental postulates, but this is not appropriate to our purpose. Rather, we take advantage of the considerable benefit of hindsight, and present these concepts in such a way that they lead most directly to the basic postulates of classical thermodynamics.

1-1 THE NATURE OF A FUNCTION

A variable F is said to be a *function* of x and y, that is $F = f(x, y)$, if for every pair of values (x, y) there exists a value for F. The function F may, of course, depend on more than two independent variables, but its general nature is the same regardless of the number of variables. An equation connecting F with x and y may or may not be known. The functional relationship may equally well be given graphically, for the nature of a function $F = f(x, y)$ is obviously such that a definite value of the function F is associated with each point on a y-x plane.

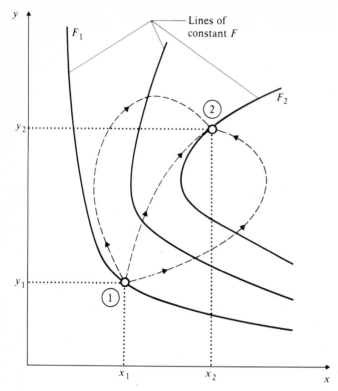

Figure 1-1 F represented as a function of x and y.

The simplest means of representation is to show lines of constant F on a y-x plot, as illustrated in Fig. 1-1. For a given point (x_1, y_1) there is a particular value of F, namely F_1, and for another point (x_2, y_2) there is also a particular value of F, namely F_2. For a change in the variables x and y from (x_1, y_1) to (x_2, y_2), no matter how accomplished, there is a particular change in F, given by $\Delta F = F_2 - F_1$. This constancy of ΔF for a pair of points 1 and 2, regardless of the path connecting these points on a y-x plane, is a distinguishing characteristic which marks F as a function of x and y whether or not an equation relating F to x and y is known.

A simple example is evident if we regard Fig. 1-1 as a contour map; F then represents elevation, and x and y are the position coordinates. Clearly, if one travels from position 1 to position 2, the net change in elevation ΔF is independent of the path taken. This immediately marks the elevation F as a function of the position coordinates x and y.

We recognize through experience the functional dependence of elevation on position coordinates. Were we interested in mathematics only, we could write a limitless number of equations expressing F as various functions of x and y, or alternatively we could draw any number of "contour maps" giving similar arbitrary relationships, and we might study their properties. But the problem of science and technology is to detect characteristics of our material world which are expressible as functions of measurable variables and to express these functional relationships in graphical, tabular, or equation form. The characteristic of elevation above a datum (sea level) is easily recognized, and has long been expressed as a function of position coordinates by means of contour maps.

1-2 PROPERTIES OF FLUIDS

Our applications of classical thermodynamics are concerned with the macroscopic properties of fluids and their relation to the measurable conditions of temperature, pressure, and composition. Experimentation leads us to believe that there is a large class of homogeneous fluids (both liquid and gas) whose properties depend solely on these variables. We observe, for example, that the density of pure liquid acetone is constant for a given temperature and pressure, regardless of the past history of the experimental sample. Similarly, we find the specific volume of an equimolar mixture of gaseous oxygen and nitrogen to be fixed for a given temperature and pressure. For given *changes* in temperature and pressure, no matter how accomplished, we find fixed changes in these properties. Such observations are quite general for single-phase fluids.

However, we note that in setting up experiments we carefully avoid the introduction of extraneous influences. We do not carry out experiments in the presence of a strong magnetic or electrostatic field. Our samples of material are small enough that the effect of the earth's gravitational field is not detected in a variation of properties from top to bottom. The sample is stationary, not subject to shear stresses, and is not subdivided into small droplets or bubbles that make surface effects important.

Under these circumstances we find that the specific or molar volumes of our fluids are functions of just temperature, pressure, and composition, and we characterize the fluids as existing in *PVT systems*. The equations we write to describe the behavior of fluids then apply only to such systems. As a practical matter, these equations are in fact used in cases where extraneous influences are not entirely absent, but where their effects are considered negligible or secondary.

This discussion has been preliminary to the statement of our first fundamental postulate:

> The macroscopic properties of homogeneous fluids in equilibrium states are functions of temperature, pressure, and composition only.

One must keep in mind that this is a postulate which contributes to the basis upon which our network of equations is founded, and is not a law of nature. Thus the ensuing equations are restricted to applications where this postulate is essentially valid, i.e., to fluids in PVT systems.

1-3 THE SPECIAL FUNCTIONS OF THERMODYNAMICS

We have taken temperature, pressure, and composition as basic thermodynamic variables for homogeneous fluids. These are not regarded primarily as properties of fluids but as *conditions* imposed on them, or manifested by them by virtue of their direct measurability. They serve as our principle *thermodynamic coordinates*. What *are* the properties that we recognize as being functions of temperature, pressure, and composition? Specific or molar volume is certainly one; we know this from experience. For any homogeneous fluid of constant composition and existing in equilibrium in a PVT system we can write

$$V = V(T, P)$$

We know this functional relationship to exist, but its expression for a given fluid by means of a table, a graph, or an equation must be based on careful experimental measurements. Equations which provide this relationship are called *PVT equations of state*.

What other functions of constant-composition, homogeneous fluids can be expressed in terms of temperature and pressure? We could define *arbitrarily* any number of functions of T and P. For example, we might *define* a function X as

$$X = \frac{3P^2}{VT}$$

We could give this function a name; call it *Xtropy*. We sould show lines of constant Xtropy on a T-P plane for the given fluid. We could compute the value of ΔX for the fluid which would result from given changes in T and P. The function X would satisfy all the mathematical requirements of a property of the fluid. But from the scientific, as opposed to the purely mathematical, point of view, is X to be regarded as a *useful* property of the fluid? The scientist or engineer requires an affirmative answer to one or both of the following questions:

(*a*) Is X directly measurable, like specific volume, and thus capable of adding to our experimental knowledge of the fluid?

(*b*) Is X an *essential* function in that some generalization can be made concerning it which allows the prediction of the behavior of material systems? For example, are there common processes which occur at constant Xtropy?

Since X was arbitrarily defined, the answer to both questions is probably negative, and we are not likely to consider the function X a useful property of the fluid.

The only way to avoid arbitrary definitions of properties is to base their recognition on observations of the behavior of real fluids. The most fundamental concept to arise from such observations is that of *energy*. The development of this concept took many centuries, and eventually led to one of the great generalizations of science: the law of conservation of energy. All this is discussed in detail in other books, and will not be further elaborated here. We merely list as postulates those principles pertinent to this work:

(a) There exists a form of energy, known as *internal energy*, U, which for homogeneous fluids existing at equilibrium in PVT systems is a property of the material and a function of temperature, pressure, and composition.

(b) The *total* energy of a system *and* its surroundings is conserved; energy may be transferred from a system to its surroundings and vice versa, it may be transformed from one form to another, but the total quantity remains constant.

The first of these postulates is requisite to the second, which through its universal acceptance has come to be known as the first law of thermodynamics. Its domain of validity has been circumscribed by the discovery of nuclear reactions in which mass is converted into energy and vice versa. Nevertheless, it remains a law valid for all other processes.

A number of thermodynamic properties are *extensive* in nature. The numerical value of an extensive property for a system is proportional to the amount of fluid present, with the proportionality factor given by the molar or specific value of the property. Temperature, pressure, and composition are not extensive (they are *intensive* thermodynamic coordinates), but volume and internal energy are. We therefore find it convenient to introduce a notation which distinguishes between the molar or specific property of a fluid and the *total* property of a system. For this purpose we often use a superscript t to signal a total property. Thus, U^t is the *total* internal energy of a system. If the system contains n moles of fluid, then $U^t = nU$, where U is the *molar* internal energy of the fluid. Similarly, if U is the *specific* internal energy of the fluid, then $U^t = mU$, where m is the mass of fluid in the system. Clearly, if $n = 1$ or $m = 1$, then the total property of a system is numerically equal to the molar or specific property of the fluid.

The total extensive property of a multiphase system is simply the sum of the property values of the phases. Thus for the internal energy

$$U^t = n^\alpha U^\alpha + n^\beta U^\beta + \cdots + n^\pi U^\pi = \sum n^p U^p$$

where the superscripts α, β, and π identify particular phases, and p is the general designation. If the basic relation $U^t = nU$ is applied to such systems, then the overall molar internal energy U must be a weighted average over the phases:

$$U = \frac{\sum n^p U^p}{n}$$

with $n = \sum n^p$.

Heat is a word used to denote energy in transit as the result of a temperature gradient or difference. In thermodynamics a quantity of heat Q represents an amount of energy that is transferred ("flows") between a system and its surroundings, and is not a property of the system.

Work is again energy in transit between a system and its surroundings, but resulting from the displacement of an external force acting on the system. A quantity of work W represents an amount of energy transferred between system and surroundings, and again is not a property of the system.

As applied to systems of constant mass (closed systems) and for which internal energy is the only form of energy to experience change, the first law of thermodynamics is expressed as:

$$\Delta U^t = Q + W$$

The numerical values of Q and W are both taken as positive when they represent energy transfer *to* the system.

This equation cannot be regarded as giving an explicit *definition* of internal energy. In fact, no such definition is known. However, the postulated existence of internal energy as a property can be tested through the use of this equation as applied to experiments with homogeneous fluids.

Consider, then, the performance of a series of experiments with *one mole* or a *unit mass* of a constant-composition homogeneous fluid in a piston-and-cylinder assembly. Temperature and pressure are taken as the independent variables. Changes are brought about by alteration of temperature and pressure. This is accomplished by the addition or extraction of heat and by displacement of the piston within the cylinder. In all experiments the temperature and pressure are changed from T_1 and P_1 to T_2 and P_2, so that the properties of the system are altered by constant amounts. However, the *path* of the change, i.e., the relation between T and P during the process, is varied arbitrarily from run to run.

It is implicit in these discussions that there *be* a single value of P and a single value of T for the entire system at each stage of every process. The moment we write P and T for the system, we imply uniformity of temperature and pressure throughout the system. The only way we can ensure this uniformity during the course of our experiments is to carry them out slowly so as to avoid the generation of pressure waves in our fluids and so as to allow time for the thermal diffusivity of the system to smooth out even minute temperature variations. A system *within which* there are no nonuniformities which act as driving forces for change is said to be in a state of internal equilibrium. Processes that proceed so that displacements from internal equilibrium are always infinitesimal are said to be internally reversible. To carry out such processes in practice, we find it necessary also to keep the system very nearly in equilibrium with its surroundings. Processes that proceed so that displacements from both external and internal equilibrium are infinitesimal are called completely reversible, or more simply reversible. The term arises from the fact that such processes can be reversed by a differential change in external conditions.

The experiments we are discussing are therefore conducted essentially reversibly. For each experiment we keep a careful account of the volume V of the system, of the amount of heat Q_{rev} added or extracted, and of the work W_{rev} done on or by the system up to each intermediate set of conditions T and P. We emphasize the restriction to processes that are reversible by writing Q_{rev} and W_{rev}.

We then examine the data, trying various combinations of the measured values and performing various numerical operations, to see what order, if any, can be brought out of the apparently disconnected sets of numbers.

For one mole or a unit mass of fluid of given composition changed along various paths from a particular initial condition (T_1, P_1) to a particular final condition (T_2, P_2), we first note, as expected, that $\Delta V = V_2 - V_1$ is constant regardless of path. This serves to confirm our earlier observation that the volume of a given amount of a homogeneous fluid (or its specific or molar volume) is a function of temperature, pressure, and composition.

Our next observation is that for the same set of experiments $Q_{rev} + W_{rev}$ is constant for the overall change regardless of path. This result is expected provided our postulates regarding the existence of internal energy as a property and the conservation of energy are valid. This observation provides at least partial confirmation of these postulates, for $Q_{rev} + W_{rev}$ is seen to be the *measure* of a property change which has already been designated ΔU. The restriction of reversibility here comes about from the nature of the experiments being considered, and not as a consequence of any limitation imposed by the basic postulates. The result obtained that $\Delta U = Q_{rev} + W_{rev}$ is merely a special case of the more general equation for closed systems, $\Delta U = Q + W$, which applies for any two equilibrium states whether the process connecting them is reversible or not.

A further examination of the experimental data is then made to determine whether the existence of any additional properties is indicated. Certainly none is obvious, but if we evaluate the integral $-\int_1^2 dW_{rev}/P$ for each experiment we find it to be constant and equal to ΔV. Thus

$$\Delta V = -\int_1^2 \frac{dW_{rev}}{P}$$

This is actually a well-known equation, far more easily found from the definition of work. As a result of this definition it is immediately deduced for a reversible expansion or compression of a fluid in a PVT system that

$$dW_{rev} = -P\,dV$$

Hence

$$dV = \frac{-dW_{rev}}{P}$$

or

$$\Delta V = -\int_1^2 \frac{dW_{rev}}{P}$$

The point here is that we *could* establish the existence of the property V as a result of integrations of our experimental data as indicated. Once it is shown that a single value of the integral results, regardless of the path, for given initial and final states, it becomes clear that the integral is the measure of a property change. In this case we immediately recognize the property as already known through much more direct observations.

A similar integral is $\int_1^2 dQ_{rev}/T$. If we evaluate this integral for each of our experiments, we again find a single value for all paths. Again we have evidence of the existence of a property. However, in this instance it is not recognized as being known. Nevertheless, once the existence of a property is indicated, it is natural to give it a symbol and a name. Thus we write

$$\Delta S = \int_1^2 \frac{dQ_{rev}}{T}$$

where S is called the *entropy*. This result leads to an additional basic postulate:

There exists a property called entropy S which for homogeneous fluids existing at equilibrium in PVT systems is a function of temperature, pressure, and composition.

Just as the equation $\Delta U = Q + W$ does not explicitly define the property internal energy, so the equations

$$\Delta V = - \int_1^2 \frac{dW_{rev}}{P} \quad \text{and} \quad \Delta S = \int_1^2 \frac{dQ_{rev}}{T}$$

do not give explicit definitions of volume and entropy. But implicit in these three equations is the existence of three extensive properties. This is obvious in the case of volume, for which an explicit definition in terms of directly measurable distances is known. With regard to internal energy and entropy, the situation is quite different. Classical thermodynamics furnishes no explicit definitions of these properties.

We have dealt with *homogeneous* fluids in PVT systems because the state of such a system is fixed when the conditions of temperature, pressure, and composition are established. For *heterogeneous* systems made up of several phases, each in itself a PVT system existing in equilibrium with the others, the state of the system depends on its temperature and pressure, on the composition of each of the phases, and on the relative amounts of the phases. It is clear that the total property of such a system is the sum of its parts. Thus one can ascribe a complete set of total properties to any equilibrium state of the system, and for a change in a closed system between two equilibrium states a unique set of property changes must result regardless of the path of the process connecting the two states. Experiments carried out on such systems yield exactly the same results as described for homogeneous fluids. It is simply more difficult to identify unique states of the system. The point of this is to generalize the equations presented for homogeneous fluids to apply to heterogeneous systems.

Thus for *any* closed PVT system of arbitrary extent, we may write the fundamental equation:

$$\Delta U^t = Q + W$$

and, as a special case,

$$\Delta U^t = Q_{rev} + W_{rev}$$

In differential form, this last equation is written:

$$dU^t = dQ_{rev} + dW_{rev} \tag{1-1}$$

For reversible processes

$$dW_{rev} = -P \, dV^t \tag{1-2}$$

and entropy changes are given by

$$\Delta S^t = \int_1^2 \frac{dQ_{rev}}{T}$$

It follows immediately that

$$dS^t = \frac{dQ_{rev}}{T}$$

or

$$dQ_{rev} = T \, dS^t \tag{1-3}$$

The methods of classical thermodynamics for the calculation of property values are based ultimately on Eqs. (1-1) through (1-3). This is not to suggest that direct use is commonly made of these equations for this purpose. Accurate measurements of heat and work effects in experiments such as those described are in fact very difficult. The actual methods used are described in subsequent chapters.

1-4 THE FIRST AND SECOND LAWS OF THERMODYNAMICS

The volume is an important thermodynamic property because it is directly measurable and can be used to provide experimental information about a system. Internal energy and entropy, on the other hand, can be determined only by indirect means. Nevertheless, these properties are essential to the science of thermodynamics, for without recognition of their existence the two great generalizations on which this science is based would be impossible.

The law of conservation of energy or the first law of thermodynamics could not be formulated without a prior postulate affirming the existence of internal energy as a property of materials. And internal energy is regarded as a property precisely for the reason that it allows this generalization to be made.

Once the existence of the entropy is postulated, it becomes necessary to determine whether any broad generalization based on this property is possible. Thus one calculates the entropy changes associated with various processes and examines the results to see whether some pattern emerges. The particular processes considered are not important, for one finds in every case that for reversible processes the *total* entropy change in system *and* surroundings resulting from the process is zero and for irreversible processes it is positive. Thus one is led to conclude that this is in general true, and we have for our final postulate a statement that has come to be known as the second law of thermodynamics:

> All processes proceed in such a direction that the *total* entropy change caused by the process is positive; the limiting value of zero is approached for processes which approach reversibility. Mathematically this is expressed as

$$\Delta S_{\text{total}} \geq 0$$

It is one of the major triumphs of nineteenth-century science to have developed a principle, unsurpassed in conciseness of statement, that describes at once the directions of all processes in this vastly complex world.

The basic postulates upon which we built the science of thermodynamics are here recapitulated for convenience.

Postulate 1.1 The macroscopic properties of homogeneous fluids existing at equilibrium in PVT systems are functions of temperature, pressure, and composition.

Postulate 1.2 One such property is a form of energy known as internal energy.

Postulate 1.3 Energy is conserved.

Postulate 1.4 There exists a property called entropy. Changes in this property are calculable by the equation $dS^t = dQ_{\text{rev}}/T$.

Postulate 1.5 The *total* entropy change resulting from any real process is positive and approaches zero as the process approaches reversibility.

These postulates form the foundation for the development of a vast network of equations. All that is needed is definition and deduction. The deduction process is purely mathematical. This deductive process and the postulates upon which it is based are ultimately subject to two tests. The network of equations which results must be internally consistent, and the consequences predicted must be in reality observed without exception. If these tests are met, then the system of logic employed and the postulates upon which it is based must be considered valid. Such tests have been applied for more than a century with complete success. As with all such postulates, the proof of their validity lies in the absence of disproof, in the absence of contrary experience.

TWO

THERMODYNAMIC PROPERTIES OF FLUIDS

Any change in the equilibrium state of a PVT system is reflected by changes in the thermodynamic properties of the fluid within the system. As a consequence of the first and second laws of thermodynamics, a fundamental equation relates the changes which occur in the primary thermodynamic properties U, V, and S. For convenience, alternative sets of primary thermodynamic properties are created by definition, and these lead to alternative forms of the fundamental relationship. These fundamental property relations are derived in this chapter, and are further developed to yield a number of equations useful for the calculation of property changes in systems of constant composition.

2-1 THE FUNDAMENTAL PROPERTY RELATION

It was shown in the preceding chapter that for *closed* systems comprised of phases which are themselves PVT systems the following equations apply for any infinitesimal change of state of the system resulting from a reversible process:

$$dU^t = dQ_{rev} + dW_{rev} \tag{1-1}$$

$$dW_{rev} = -P\,dV^t \tag{1-2}$$

$$dQ_{rev} = T\,dS^t \tag{1-3}$$

Hence

$$\boxed{dU^t = T\,dS^t - P\,dV^t}$$ (2-1)

This is the basic differential equation relating the three thermodynamic properties considered so far. These properties depend on state alone, and not on the kind of process that produces the state. Although *derived* for a reversible process, Eq. (2-1) is therefore *not* limited in application to reversible processes. Thus it applies to *any* process in a *closed* PVT system that results in a differential change from one *equilibrium* state to another. Composition changes as a result of chemical reaction or mass transfer between phases are by no means excluded, provided equilibrium with respect to these processes obtains at the end states.

If M^t is taken as the general designation of any of the total properties U^t, S^t, and V^t in Eq. (2-1), then each may be written as nM, where n is the total number of moles present in the system, and M is the *overall* molar property of the fluid in the system. Equation (2-1) then becomes

$$d(nU) = T\,d(nS) - P\,d(nV)$$ (2-2)

Like Eq. (2-1), it applies to the general closed multiphase system. However, we may consider its application to the special case of a *single-phase* closed system in which *no chemical reactions occur*, i.e., a system in which all mole numbers are necessarily constant. Since Eq. (2-2) is an exact differential expression (see App. A-1), we can make the identifications:

$$\left[\frac{\partial(nU)}{\partial(nS)}\right]_{nV,\,n} = T$$ (2-3)

$$\left[\frac{\partial(nU)}{\partial(nV)}\right]_{nS,\,n} = -P$$ (2-4)

where U, S, and V are molar properties of the phase, and the subscript n indicates that *all* mole numbers n_i are held constant.

We are now in a position to consider the more general case of a single-phase system in which the n_i vary, either by virtue of the interchange of matter with the surroundings for an open system or because of chemical reaction within the system or both. In this case we assume that the internal energy nU is a function of the n_i as well as of nS and nV:

$$nU = f(nS,\,nV,\,n_1,\,n_2,\,n_3,\,\ldots)$$

The total differential of nU is then

$$d(nU) = \left[\frac{\partial(nU)}{\partial(nS)}\right]_{nV,\,n} d(nS) + \left[\frac{\partial(nU)}{\partial(nV)}\right]_{nS,\,n} d(nV) + \sum \left[\frac{\partial(nU)}{\partial n_i}\right]_{nS,\,nV,\,n_j} dn_i$$

(2-5)

where the summation is over all chemical species present in the system, and the subscript n_j indicates that all mole numbers are held constant except the ith. Equations (2-3) and (2-4), together with the definition

$$\mu_i \equiv \left[\frac{\partial(nU)}{\partial n_i} \right]_{nS, \, nV, \, n_j} \tag{2-6}$$

allow us to write Eq. (2-5) as

$$\boxed{d(nU) = T \, d(nS) - P \, d(nV) + \sum \mu_i \, dn_i} \tag{2-7}$$

This equation is the *fundamental property relation* connecting the primary thermodynamic variables for single-phase PVT systems, either open or closed. All other equations relating the properties of such systems derive from it. The quantity μ_i is called the *chemical potential* of component i. We will see that a difference or gradient in chemical potential is the driving force for chemical change in the same way that a temperature gradient is the driving force for heat transfer, and force imbalance is the driving force for mechanical change. We can no more give a word definition for chemical potential than we can for temperature or force.

2-2 CHEMICAL AND PHASE EQUILIBRIA

Consider a closed, single-phase, PVT system comprised of chemically reactive species. When reaction equilibrium is attained in such a system, both Eqs. (2-2) and (2-7) must apply. Comparison of these two equations shows that for both to be valid, we must have

$$\sum \mu_i \, dn_i = 0 \tag{2-8}$$

This equation therefore represents a general criterion for chemical-reaction equilibrium in a single-phase, closed PVT system, and is the basis for development of working equations for solution of reaction-equilibrium problems through equilibrium constants. It means that equilibrium with respect to reactive chemical species is established at that state for which differential reaction displacements cause mole-number changes in accord with Eq. (2-8).

Consider now a closed PVT system consisting of two phases in equilibrium. Although the entire system is closed, each of the two phases may be considered a single-phase open system to which Eq. (2-7) applies. With superscripts α and β identifying the two phases we may therefore write for differential changes at the equilibrium state:

$$d(nU)^\alpha = T \, d(nS)^\alpha - P \, d(nV)^\alpha + \sum \mu_i^\alpha \, dn_i^\alpha$$

$$d(nU)^\beta = T \, d(nS)^\beta - P \, d(nV)^\beta + \sum \mu_i^\beta \, dn_i^\beta$$

where we presume equilibrium to imply uniformity of T and P throughout both phases. The total internal-energy change of the entire system is given by the sum of these two equations:

$$dU^t = T \, dS^t - P \, dV^t + \sum \mu_i^\alpha \, dn_i^\alpha + \sum \mu_i^\beta \, dn_i^\beta \tag{A}$$

where (with U^t, S^t, and V^t represented by M^t) we have expressed each total property of the system by

$$M^t = (nM)^\alpha + (nM)^\beta$$

Comparison of Eq. (A) with Eq. (2-1), which must also be valid for the entire (closed) system, shows that at equilibrium we must have:

$$\sum \mu_i^\alpha \, dn_i^\alpha + \sum \mu_i^\beta \, dn_i^\beta = 0$$

For changes dn_i^α and dn_i^β resulting from mass transfer between the phases, mass conservation requires that

$$dn_i^\alpha = - dn_i^\beta$$

Thus

$$\sum (\mu_i^\alpha - \mu_i^\beta) \, dn_i^\alpha = 0$$

Since the dn_i^α are independent and arbitrary, this equation can in general be satisfied for an N-component system only when

$$\mu_i^\alpha = \mu_i^\beta \qquad (i = 1, 2, 3, \ldots, N) \tag{B}$$

For more than two phases, successive application of Eq. (B) to pairs of phases leads to the generalization for π phases:

$$\boxed{\mu_i^\alpha = \mu_i^\beta = \cdots = \mu_i^\pi} \qquad (i = 1, 2, 3, \ldots, N) \tag{2-9}$$

This equation provides a general criterion for equilibrium with respect to mass transfer between phases. Equilibrium requires the chemical potential for each species to be uniform throughout the system.

2-3 ADDITIONAL PRIMARY THERMODYNAMIC FUNCTIONS

A natural basis for definition of other thermodynamic functions arises from the following treatment. Introducing the mole fraction

$$x_i \equiv n_i/n$$

we can write Eq. (2-7) as

$$d(nU) - T \, d(nS) + P \, d(nV) - \sum \mu_i \, d(x_i n) = 0$$

Expansion of the differentials and collection of like terms gives

$$(dU - T \, dS + P \, dV - \sum \mu_i \, dx_i)n + (U - TS + PV - \sum x_i \mu_i) \, dn = 0$$

Table 2-1 Primary functions related to the internal energy

Primary grouping	Symbol	Name	Alternative grouping
U	U	Internal energy	$TS - PV + \sum x_i \mu_i$
$U + PV$	H	Enthalpy	$TS + \sum x_i \mu_i$
$U - TS$	A	Helmholtz function†	$-PV + \sum x_i \mu_i$
$U + PV - TS$	G	Gibbs function†	$\sum x_i \mu_i$
$U - \sum x_i \mu_i$	X		$TS - PV$
$U + PV - \sum x_i \mu_i$	Y	Unnamed	TS
$U - TS - \sum x_i \mu_i$	Z		$-PV$
$U + PV - TS - \sum x_i \mu_i$		"Zero function"	

† These functions are sometimes given other names. Both have been called free energy: A, the Helmholtz free energy; G, the Gibbs free energy. Another terminology designates A the free energy and G the free enthalpy.

Since n and dn are independent and arbitrary, the terms in parentheses must separately be zero. Thus

$$dU = T\, dS - P\, dV + \sum \mu_i\, dx_i \qquad (2\text{-}10)$$

and

$$U = TS - PV + \sum x_i \mu_i \qquad (2\text{-}11)$$

Equations (2-7) and (2-10) are similar, but there is an important difference between them. Equation (2-7) applies to a system of n moles, where n may vary, whereas Eq. (2-10) applies to a system where n is always unity. Thus Eq. (2-10) is constrained by the relations, $\sum x_i = 1$ and $\sum dx_i = 0$, and the mole *fractions* x_i cannot be treated as independent variables. The mole *numbers* n_i are not so constrained.

Equation (2-11) suggests possible combinations of terms that may be defined as additional primary thermodynamic functions, each related to U and having units of energy per mole. Provided the summation $\sum x_i \mu_i$ is treated as a single term, there are but eight distinct combinations, and these are shown in Table 2-1. Several examples of their use follow.

Example 2-1 The definitions of new functions in Table 2-1 are based on U as the primitive energy variable. One can of course substitute for U as a result of the definition of one of the new functions. For example, by the definition of the enthalpy H we have

$$U = H - PV$$

The Helmholtz function A can then be expressed as

$$A = H - PV - TS$$

However, this is no simplification of the original definition. The Gibbs function, on the other hand, can be written

$$G = H - TS$$

and this *is* a shorter expression for G. The following are the preferred working definitions for the three functions H, A, and G:

$$H \equiv U + PV \tag{2-12}$$

$$A \equiv U - TS \tag{2-13}$$

$$G \equiv H - TS \tag{2-14}$$

Example 2-2 The potential utility of the enthalpy function is easily illustrated. Consider a closed single-phase PVT system. If the system undergoes a reversible process, then for each mole of fluid we have by Eqs. (1-1) and (1-2)

$$dQ_{rev} = dU + P \, dV$$

Since

$$U = H - PV$$

and

$$dU = dH - P \, dV - V \, dP$$

we find

$$dQ_{rev} = dH - V \, dP$$

If the process occurs at constant pressure (an *isobaric* process), then

$$\left. \begin{matrix} dQ_{rev} = dH \\ Q_{rev} = \Delta H \end{matrix} \right| \text{(const } P)$$

and

Thus for a reversible, constant-pressure process in a closed PVT system, the heat transferred equals the enthalpy change of the system.

Example 2-3 The equations of Sec. 2-2 indicate the importance of the chemical potential to the theory of chemical and phase equilibria. From the entries of the fourth row of Table 2-1, we have

$$G = \sum x_i \mu_i$$

where G is the Gibbs function of a *mixture* of species identified by subscript i. This equation, giving G as the mole-fraction-weighted sum of the chemical potentials of the constituent species, suggests an interpretation of the chemical potential as the contribution of a species to the mixture property G, i.e., as the Gibbs function of species i *in solution*. A pure material is a special case of a solution for which one mole fraction is unity and all others are zero. If it is the particular species k for which $x_k = 1$, then the equation for G reduces to

$$G_k = \mu_k$$

where G_k is the Gibbs function for pure k, and represents a limiting value for the chemical potential of species k.

2-4 ALTERNATIVE FORMS OF THE FUNDAMENTAL PROPERTY RELATION

The working definitions of H, A, and G given by Eqs. (2-12) through (2-14) allow development of expressions alternative to Eq. (2-7), the fundamental property relation. We demonstrate the procedure for the enthalpy H. Multiplication of Eq. (2-12) by n gives

$$nH = nU + P(nV)$$

from which

$$d(nH) = d(nU) + P\,d(nV) + (nV)\,dP$$

Substitution of Eq. (2-7) for $d(nU)$ then gives a general expression for the total differential $d(nH)$ for a single-phase, PVT system, either closed or open:

$$d(nH) = T\,d(nS) + (nV)\,dP + \sum \mu_i\,dn_i \qquad (2\text{-}15)$$

The total differentials $d(nA)$ and $d(nG)$ are found similarly. They are:

$$d(nA) = -(nS)\,dT - P\,d(nV) + \sum \mu_i\,dn_i \qquad (2\text{-}16)$$

$$d(nG) = -(nS)\,dT + (nV)\,dP + \sum \mu_i\,dn_i \qquad (2\text{-}17)$$

These important equations, along with those for the total differentials of the remaining functions from Table 2-1, are summarized in Table 2-2.

Since Eqs. (2-15) through (2-17) derive from Eq. (2-7) simply as the result of definition, the four equations are equivalent. However, inspection of the right-hand sides of these equations reveals that each of the functions nU, nH, nA, and nG is associated with a different set of independent variables. These are the *canonical* variables for the function. Thus the canonical variables for nU are nS, nV, and the n_i; those for nG are T, P, and the n_i.

Table 2-2 Alternative forms of the fundamental property relation

Total differential of the primary function	Canonical variables for the primary function
$d(nU) = T\,d(nS) - P\,d(nV) + \sum \mu_i\,dn_i$	$nS,\ nV,\ n_i$
$d(nH) = T\,d(nS) + (nV)\,dP + \sum \mu_i\,dn_i$	$nS,\ P,\ n_i$
$d(nA) = -(nS)\,dT - P\,d(nV) + \sum \mu_i\,dn_i$	$T,\ nV,\ n_i$
$d(nG) = -(nS)\,dT + (nV)\,dP + \sum \mu_i\,dn_i$	$T,\ P,\ n_i$
$d(nX) = T\,d(nS) - P\,d(nV) - \sum n_i\,d\mu_i$	$nS,\ nV,\ \mu_i$
$d(nY) = T\,d(nS) + (nV)\,dP - \sum n_i\,d\mu_i$	$nS,\ P,\ \mu_i$
$d(nZ) = -(nS)\,dT - P\,d(nV) - \sum n_i\,d\mu_i$	$T,\ nV,\ \mu_i$
$0 = -(nS)\,dT + (nV)\,dP - \sum n_i\,d\mu_i$	$T,\ P,\ \mu_i$

The significance of the canonical variables is intimately connected with the theory of *Legendre transformations;* the functions defined in Table 2-1 are in fact examples of Legendre transformations of the internal energy nU. The special properties of Legendre transformation functions are treated in App. A-3.

A set of equations similar to that in Table 2-2 can be developed from Eq. (2-10). This set can also be written directly from the equations of Table 2-2 by imposition of the constraints $n = 1$, $n_i = x_i$, and $dn_i = dx_i$. Thus for example Eq. (2-17) becomes

$$dG = -S\,dT + V\,dP + \sum \mu_i\,dx_i \qquad (2\text{-}18)$$

The two sets are related exactly as Eq. (2-7) is related to Eq. (2-10). The equations written for $n = 1$ are of course less general than those of Table 2-2. In fact they are of limited practical use, because in applications to open systems they yield only *part* of the total property change. If we want, for example, the change in the Gibbs function for an open system, we can write:

$$d(nG) = n\,dG + G\,dn$$

Equation (2-18) provides only an expression for dG in the first term on the right, whereas Eq. (2-17) yields directly the desired result. In addition, in equations such as Eq. (2-18) the x_i are not independent, and this precludes certain mathematical operations which *are* entirely proper for equations such as Eq. (2-17). According to Eq. (2-18)

$$G = G(T, P, x_1, x_2, \ldots, x_N)$$

The total differential of G is then given by

$$dG = \left(\frac{\partial G}{\partial T}\right)_{P,\,x} dT + \left(\frac{\partial G}{\partial P}\right)_{T,\,x} dP + \sum \left(\frac{\partial G}{\partial x_i}\right)_{T,\,P,\,x_j} dx_i$$

where the subscript x indicates constant composition. This equation and Eq. (2-18) both express G as functions of the same variables. However, term-by-term comparison of the coefficients of the dx_i is not allowed, because the x_i are not independent. Since T and P are independent of the x_i, it is correct to write:

$$\left(\frac{\partial G}{\partial T}\right)_{P,\,x} = -S \quad \text{and} \quad \left(\frac{\partial G}{\partial P}\right)_{T,\,x} = V$$

However,

$$\left(\frac{\partial G}{\partial x_i}\right)_{T,\,P,\,x_j} \neq \mu_i$$

Example 2-4 The equations of Table 2-2 are readily reduced to forms appropriate to *constant-composition* solutions. One procedure is first to set $n = 1$, yielding an equation such as Eq. (2-18). If composition is constant, then $dx_i = 0$ for all i, and Eq. (2-18) becomes:

$$dG = -S\,dT + V\,dP$$

an expression which applies to each mole of a constant-composition solution.

An alternative procedure, which does not require the arbitrary assignment $n = 1$, is based for example on Eq. (2-17). Since $n_i = x_i n$, we have for constant composition that $dn_i = x_i\, dn$. Thus we can write Eq. (2-17) as

$$d(nG) = -nS\, dT + nV\, dP + \sum x_i \mu_i\, dn$$

Expanding the differential $d(nG)$ and rearranging, we find

$$n\, dG = -nS\, dT + nV\, dP + \left(\sum x_i \mu_i - G\right) dn$$

Entries of the fourth row in Table 2-1 show that the quantity in parentheses is zero. Thus

$$n\, dG = -nS\, dT + nV\, dP$$

from which, as before,

$$dG = -S\, dT + V\, dP$$

Since a *pure material* is a special case of a constant-composition solution, this equation for pure species k becomes

$$dG_k = -S_k\, dT + V_k\, dP$$

where G_k, S_k, and V_k are the molar properties of pure k.

Example 2-5 The definition of the chemical potential μ_i by Eq. (2-6) led from Eq. (2-5) to the concise statement of the fundamental property relation given by Eq. (2-7). Since Eqs. (2-15) through (2-17) are equivalent to Eq. (2-7), and since μ_i appears in each, alternative expressions for μ_i are possible. For example, inspection of Eq. (2-15) yields the identification

$$\mu_i = \left[\frac{\partial(nH)}{\partial n_i}\right]_{nS,\, P,\, n_j} \tag{2-19}$$

Similarly, we find from Eqs. (2-16) and (2-17) that

$$\mu_i = \left[\frac{\partial(nA)}{\partial n_i}\right]_{T,\, nV,\, n_j} \tag{2-20}$$

and

$$\mu_i = \left[\frac{\partial(nG)}{\partial n_i}\right]_{T,\, P,\, n_j} \tag{2-21}$$

In a development based on Eq. (2-15), (2-16), or (2-17) as the fundamental property relation, Eq. (2-19), (2-20), or (2-21) would serve as the *definition* of μ_i. Equation (2-21) is in fact the preferred working definition of μ_i, because T and P are the most useful experimental thermodynamic coordinates by virtue of the ease of their measurement and control.

Equations (2-7) and (2-15) through (2-17), the fundamental property relation and its alternative forms, were developed for differential changes in the equilibrium state of a single-phase PVT system. They are readily extended to apply to multiphase systems. We have presumed that equilibrium implies uniformity of T and P throughout any PVT system, and Eq. (2-9) requires like uniformity of the chemical potentials. Thus the property relations as written for the separate phases are readily added.

For a multiphase system, where superscript p identifies a phase, Eq. (2-7) becomes

$$\sum_p d(nU)^p = T \sum_p d(nS)^p - P \sum_p d(nV)^p + \sum_i \left(\mu_i \, d \sum_p n_i^p \right)$$

which may be written

$$dU^t = T \, dS^t - P \, dV^t + \sum \mu_i \, dn_i^t \qquad (2\text{-}22)$$

where the superscript t indicates a total value for the entire multiphase system. This equation holds for both open and closed systems. However, for a *closed* system Eq. (2-22) must agree with Eq. (2-1), and this requires the final term to be zero:

$$\sum \mu_i \, dn_i^t = 0$$

This result is the extension to multiphase systems of the criterion for chemical-reaction equilibrium given by Eq. (2-8).

The alternative forms of the fundamental property relations are extended in similar fashion to apply to multiphase systems, either open or closed. The resulting equations follow:

$$dH^t = T \, dS^t + V^t \, dP + \sum \mu_i \, dn_i^t \qquad (2\text{-}23)$$

$$dA^t = -S^t \, dT - P \, dV^t + \sum \mu_i \, dn_i^t \qquad (2\text{-}24)$$

$$dG^t = -S^t \, dT + V^t \, dP + \sum \mu_i \, dn_i^t \qquad (2\text{-}25)$$

As with Eq. (2-22) the last term must be zero in each of these equations when applied to closed systems. Thus for changes between equilibrium states in multiphase, *closed*, PVT systems, whether or not the species are chemically reactive, we have four basic property relations:

$$dU^t = T \, dS^t - P \, dV^t$$

$$dH^t = T \, dS^t + V^t \, dP$$

$$dA^t = -S^t \, dT - P \, dV^t$$

$$dG^t = -S^t \, dT + V^t \, dP$$

For these closed systems the following functional relationships are always valid:

$$U^t = U^t(S^t, V^t)$$

$$H^t = H^t(S^t, P)$$

$$A^t = A^t(T, V^t)$$

$$G^t = G^t(T, P)$$

The fact that these functional relationships are valid in general does not exclude the existence of other functional relationships for particular systems. Indeed, one of our basic postulates affirms that for *homogeneous* fluids of constant composition all the thermodynamic properties are functions of temperature and pressure. But this is not true for heterogeneous or reacting systems. The general functional relationships, however, *are* valid for such systems. For example, a system made up of a pure liquid in equilibrium with its vapor at a given temperature exists at a particular pressure, and the internal energy of the system depends not only on these conditions but also upon the relative amounts of vapor and liquid present. Temperature and pressure in no way reflect this. However, entropy and volume do, and the relationship $U^t = U^t(S^t, V^t)$ is entirely valid. On the other hand, the Gibbs function is in general a function of temperature and pressure, $G^t = G^t(T, P)$; thus it is fixed for a given T and P regardless of the relative amounts of the phases.

2-5 SOME BASIC EQUATIONS FOR CONSTANT-COMPOSITION FLUIDS

For a homogeneous fluid of *constant composition*, the methods of Example 2-4 applied to Eqs. (2-7) and (2-15) through (2-17) yield

$$dU = T\, dS - P\, dV \tag{2-26}$$

$$dH = T\, dS + V\, dP \tag{2-27}$$

$$dA = -S\, dT - P\, dV \tag{2-28}$$

$$dG = -S\, dT + V\, dP \tag{2-29}$$

From these it is seen that

$$T = \left(\frac{\partial U}{\partial S}\right)_V = \left(\frac{\partial H}{\partial S}\right)_P \tag{2-30}$$

$$P = -\left(\frac{\partial U}{\partial V}\right)_S = -\left(\frac{\partial A}{\partial V}\right)_T \tag{2-31}$$

$$V = \left(\frac{\partial H}{\partial P}\right)_S = \left(\frac{\partial G}{\partial P}\right)_T \tag{2-32}$$

$$S = -\left(\frac{\partial A}{\partial T}\right)_V = -\left(\frac{\partial G}{\partial T}\right)_P \tag{2-33}$$

Equations (2-30) through (2-33) provide vital links between the natural independent variables T, P, V, and S and the energy-related principal functions U, H, A, and G.

Equations (2-26) through (2-29) relate thermodynamic properties only; hence they are *exact* differential expressions. Application of the reciprocity relation for exact differential expressions (see App. A-1) to these equations yields the *Maxwell equations* for a constant-composition PVT system:

$$\left(\frac{\partial T}{\partial V}\right)_S = -\left(\frac{\partial P}{\partial S}\right)_V \qquad (2\text{-}34)$$

$$\left(\frac{\partial T}{\partial P}\right)_S = \left(\frac{\partial V}{\partial S}\right)_P \qquad (2\text{-}35)$$

$$\left(\frac{\partial S}{\partial V}\right)_T = \left(\frac{\partial P}{\partial T}\right)_V \qquad (2\text{-}36)$$

$$\left(\frac{\partial S}{\partial P}\right)_T = -\left(\frac{\partial V}{\partial T}\right)_P \qquad (2\text{-}37)$$

The last two Maxwell equations are particularly useful for equation-of-state applications, for they allow replacement of derivatives of the entropy (which is not a measurable quantity) by derivatives of the observable coordinates P and V.

A pure material is of course a special case of a constant-composition fluid, one whose mole fraction in one species is unity. Thus, all equations written for a constant-composition fluid apply to pure-species fluids.

Example 2-6 Equations (2-30) through (2-33) and (2-34) through (2-37) can be derived *directly* from Eqs. (2-7) and (2-15) through (2-17). By this procedure, additional relationships are obtained. We illustrate the technique for Eq. (2-17):

$$d(nG) = -(nS)\,dT + (nV)\,dP + \sum \mu_i\,dn_i \qquad (2\text{-}17)$$

Inspection of the coefficients of the differentials on the right-hand side of this equation reveals that

$$nS = -\left[\frac{\partial(nG)}{\partial T}\right]_{P,\,n} \qquad (A)$$

$$nV = \left[\frac{\partial(nG)}{\partial P}\right]_{T,\,n} \qquad (B)$$

and

$$\mu_i = \left[\frac{\partial(nG)}{\partial n_i}\right]_{T,\,P,\,n_j} \qquad (C)$$

The subscript n denotes that *all* mole numbers, and hence composition, are held constant. Thus, for example, Eq. (A) yields

$$nS = -n\left(\frac{\partial G}{\partial T}\right)_{P,\,n}$$

or

$$S = -\left(\frac{\partial G}{\partial T}\right)_P \qquad \text{(constant composition)}$$

This is just part of Eq. (2-33). Similarly, Eq. (B) is equivalent to part of Eq. (2-32). Equation (C) is Eq. (2-21), already presented in Example 2-5.

Maxwell-type equations are found by application of the reciprocity relation:

$$\left[\frac{\partial(nS)}{\partial P}\right]_{F,\,n} = -\left[\frac{\partial(nV)}{\partial T}\right]_{P,\,n} \tag{D}$$

$$\left(\frac{\partial \mu_i}{\partial T}\right)_{P,\,n} = -\left[\frac{\partial(nS)}{\partial n_i}\right]_{T,\,P,\,n_j} \tag{E}$$

$$\left(\frac{\partial \mu_i}{\partial P}\right)_{T,\,n} = \left[\frac{\partial(nV)}{\partial n_i}\right]_{T,\,P,\,n_j} \tag{F}$$

$$\left(\frac{\partial \mu_k}{\partial n_l}\right)_{T,\,P,\,n_{j\neq l}} = \left(\frac{\partial \mu_l}{\partial n_k}\right)_{T,\,P,\,n_{j\neq k}} \tag{G}$$

Because of the restriction to constant composition, Eq. (D) is equivalent to Eq. (2-37); the remaining equations are new.

2-6 ENTHALPY AND ENTROPY AS FUNCTIONS OF T AND P

At constant composition the molar thermodynamic properties of homogeneous fluids are functions of temperature and pressure (Postulate 1.1). Thus

$$dH = \left(\frac{\partial H}{\partial T}\right)_P dT + \left(\frac{\partial H}{\partial P}\right)_T dP \tag{2-38}$$

and

$$dS = \left(\frac{\partial S}{\partial T}\right)_P dT + \left(\frac{\partial S}{\partial P}\right)_T dP \tag{2-39}$$

The obvious next step is to eliminate the partial derivatives in favor of measurable quantities.

For this purpose the *constant-pressure molar heat capacity* is defined as

$$\boxed{C_P \equiv \left(\frac{\partial H}{\partial T}\right)_P} \tag{2-40}$$

Clearly, C_P is a *property of a fluid* and a function of temperature, pressure, and composition. Equation (2-27) may first be divided by dT and restricted to constant P, and second be divided by dP and restricted to constant T, yielding the two equations

$$\left(\frac{\partial H}{\partial T}\right)_P = T\left(\frac{\partial S}{\partial T}\right)_P$$

and

$$\left(\frac{\partial H}{\partial P}\right)_T = T\left(\frac{\partial S}{\partial P}\right)_T + V$$

In view of Eq. (2-40), the first of these becomes

$$\left(\frac{\partial S}{\partial T}\right)_P = \frac{C_P}{T} \qquad (2\text{-}41)$$

and in view of Eq. (2-37) the second becomes

$$\left(\frac{\partial H}{\partial P}\right)_T = V - T\left(\frac{\partial V}{\partial T}\right)_P \qquad (2\text{-}42)$$

Combination of Eqs. (2-38), (2-40), and (2-42) gives

$$dH = C_P\, dT + \left[V - T\left(\frac{\partial V}{\partial T}\right)_P\right] dP \qquad (2\text{-}43)$$

and combination of Eqs. (2-39), (2-41), and (2-37) gives

$$dS = \frac{C_P}{T}\, dT - \left(\frac{\partial V}{\partial T}\right)_P dP \qquad (2\text{-}44)$$

Equations (2-43) and (2-44) are general equations expressing the enthalpy and entropy of homogeneous fluids *at constant composition* as functions of T and P. The coefficients of dT and dP are expressed in terms of measurable quantities.

Example 2-7 The *Joule-Thomson coefficient*

$$\mu \equiv \left(\frac{\partial T}{\partial P}\right)_H \qquad (2\text{-}45)$$

is an experimentally accessible quantity, related to C_P and to the volumetric properties of a fluid. This relationship is most easily developed through Eq. (2-43), which becomes for constant H

$$0 = C_P\, dT + \left[V - T\left(\frac{\partial V}{\partial T}\right)_P\right] dP \qquad (\text{const } H)$$

from which

$$\mu = \left(\frac{\partial T}{\partial P}\right)_H = \frac{T(\partial V/\partial T)_P - V}{C_P} \qquad (2\text{-}46)$$

An alternative and equivalent procedure is to start with the mathematical relationship (see App. A-2)

$$\left(\frac{\partial T}{\partial P}\right)_H = -\left(\frac{\partial T}{\partial H}\right)_P\left(\frac{\partial H}{\partial P}\right)_T = -\left(\frac{\partial H}{\partial T}\right)_P^{-1}\left(\frac{\partial H}{\partial P}\right)_T$$

Combination of this result with Eqs. (2-40) and (2-42) yields Eq. (2-46).

2-7 INTERNAL ENERGY AND ENTROPY AS FUNCTIONS OF T AND V

It is frequently more convenient to take T and V as independent variables rather than T and P. Because at constant composition V is related to T and P through an equation of state, this is clearly permissible. In this case, it is conventional to work with the internal energy and the entropy, for which

$$dU = \left(\frac{\partial U}{\partial T}\right)_V dT + \left(\frac{\partial U}{\partial V}\right)_T dV \tag{2-47}$$

and

$$dS = \left(\frac{\partial S}{\partial T}\right)_V dT + \left(\frac{\partial S}{\partial V}\right)_T dV \tag{2-48}$$

The procedure is now analogous to that of the preceding section. Define the *constant-volume molar heat capacity* by

$$\boxed{C_V \equiv \left(\frac{\partial U}{\partial T}\right)_V} \tag{2-49}$$

Thus, C_V is a property of a fluid and a function of temperature, pressure, and composition.

Two relations follow immediately from Eq. (2-26):

$$\left(\frac{\partial U}{\partial T}\right) = T\left(\frac{\partial S}{\partial T}\right)_V$$

$$\left(\frac{\partial U}{\partial V}\right) = T\left(\frac{\partial S}{\partial V}\right)_T - P$$

As a result of Eq. (2-49), the first of these becomes

$$\left(\frac{\partial S}{\partial T}\right)_V = \frac{C_V}{T} \tag{2-50}$$

and as a result of Eq. (2-36) the second becomes

$$\left(\frac{\partial U}{\partial V}\right)_T = T\left(\frac{\partial P}{\partial T}\right)_V - P \tag{2-51}$$

Combination of Eqs. (2-47), (2-49), and (2-51) gives

$$\boxed{dU = C_V\, dT + \left[T\left(\frac{\partial P}{\partial T}\right)_V - P\right] dV} \tag{2-52}$$

and combination of Eqs. (2-48), (2-50), and (2-36) gives

$$\boxed{dS = \frac{C_V}{T}\, dT + \left(\frac{\partial P}{\partial T}\right)_V dV}$$

(2-53)

Equations (2-52) and (2-53) are general equations expressing the internal energy and entropy of homogeneous fluids *at constant composition* as functions of temperature and molar volume. The coefficients of dT and dV are expressed in terms of measurable quantities.

> **Example 2-8** Equations from this and the preceding section allow one to find the dependence of any of the principal thermodynamic functions on either T and P or T and V. Suppose that an expression is required for the T and V dependence of the enthalpy of a constant-composition fluid. By definition, $H = U + PV$, and therefore
>
> $$dH = dU + P\, dV + V\, dP$$
>
> But, at constant composition,
>
> $$dP = \left(\frac{\partial P}{\partial T}\right)_V dT + \left(\frac{\partial P}{\partial V}\right)_T dV$$
>
> Combination of these two equations with Eq. (2-52) gives the required result
>
> $$dH = \left[C_V + V\left(\frac{\partial P}{\partial T}\right)_V\right] dT + \left[T\left(\frac{\partial P}{\partial T}\right)_V + V\left(\frac{\partial P}{\partial V}\right)_T\right] dV$$
>
> The coefficients of dT and dV are expressed in terms of measurable quantities.

> **Example 2-9** It is convenient for some applications to treat S as a function of P and V. The required expression for dS can be determined from equations of this section and the preceding one. At constant composition, $S = S(P, V)$. Thus
>
> $$dS = \left(\frac{\partial S}{\partial P}\right)_V dP + \left(\frac{\partial S}{\partial V}\right)_P dV$$
>
> But
>
> $$\left(\frac{\partial S}{\partial P}\right)_V = \left(\frac{\partial S}{\partial T}\right)_V\left(\frac{\partial T}{\partial P}\right)_V$$
>
> and
>
> $$\left(\frac{\partial S}{\partial V}\right)_P = \left(\frac{\partial S}{\partial T}\right)_P\left(\frac{\partial T}{\partial V}\right)_P$$
>
> The temperature derivatives of the entropy are given by Eqs. (2-41) and (2-50). Combination of these equations with the above three gives the desired result:
>
> $$\boxed{dS = \frac{C_V}{T}\left(\frac{\partial T}{\partial P}\right)_V dP + \frac{C_P}{T}\left(\frac{\partial T}{\partial V}\right)_P dV}$$
>
> (2-54)

It is noted that Eqs. (2-44), (2-53), and (2-54) are *equivalent*; their differences merely reflect the different choices of independent variables.

2-8 HEAT-CAPACITY RELATIONSHIPS

In Eqs. (2-43) and (2-52) both dH and dU are exact differentials, and application of the reciprocity relation leads to

$$\left(\frac{\partial C_P}{\partial P}\right)_T = -T\left(\frac{\partial^2 V}{\partial T^2}\right)_P \qquad (2\text{-}55)$$

and

$$\left(\frac{\partial C_V}{\partial V}\right)_T = T\left(\frac{\partial^2 P}{\partial T^2}\right)_V \qquad (2\text{-}56)$$

Thus the pressure or volume dependence of the heat capacities may be determined from PVT data. The *temperature* dependence of the heat capacities is, however, determined empirically, most often for ideal gases and for liquids at atmospheric pressure.

Equations (2-44) and (2-53) both provide expressions for dS, which must be equal for the same change of state. Equating them and solving for dT gives

$$dT = \frac{T}{C_P - C_V}\left(\frac{\partial V}{\partial T}\right)_P dP + \frac{T}{C_P - C_V}\left(\frac{\partial P}{\partial T}\right)_V dV$$

However, at constant composition, $T = T(P, V)$. Thus,

$$dT = \left(\frac{\partial T}{\partial P}\right)_V dP + \left(\frac{\partial T}{\partial V}\right)_P dV$$

Equating coefficients of either dP or dV in these two expressions gives

$$C_P - C_V = T\left(\frac{\partial V}{\partial T}\right)_P\left(\frac{\partial P}{\partial T}\right)_V \qquad (2\text{-}57)$$

Thus the *difference* between the two heat capacities may be determined from PVT data.

The *ratio* of these heat capacities is obtained by division of Eq. (2-41) by Eq. (2-50)

$$\frac{C_P}{C_V} = \frac{(\partial S/\partial T)_P}{(\partial S/\partial T)_V}$$

or

$$\frac{C_P}{C_V} = \frac{(\partial S/\partial V)_P(\partial V/\partial T)_P}{(\partial S/\partial P)_V(\partial P/\partial T)_V}$$

But

$$\frac{(\partial S/\partial V)_P}{(\partial S/\partial P)_V} = \left(\frac{\partial S}{\partial V}\right)_P\left(\frac{\partial P}{\partial S}\right)_V = -\left(\frac{\partial P}{\partial V}\right)_S$$

and
$$\frac{(\partial V/\partial T)_P}{(\partial P/\partial T)_V} = \left(\frac{\partial V}{\partial T}\right)_P \left(\frac{\partial T}{\partial P}\right)_V = -\left(\frac{\partial V}{\partial P}\right)_T$$

Thus
$$\gamma = \left(\frac{\partial V}{\partial P}\right)_T \left(\frac{\partial P}{\partial V}\right)_S \qquad (2\text{-}58)$$

where
$$\gamma \equiv \frac{C_P}{C_V} \qquad (2\text{-}59)$$

is the symbol commonly used to represent the heat-capacity ratio.

2-9 EQUATIONS FOR IDEAL GASES

Use of equations developed in Secs. 2-5 through 2-8 requires the availability of PVT data, or, equivalently, of a PVT *equation of state*. Strictly, any algebraic equation for a single-phase constant-composition PVT system relating one state variable to two others can be considered an equation of state. However, the phrase is commonly taken to mean an equation relating temperature, pressure, and molar volume. Equations of state are treated in some detail in Chap. 4.

The simplest PVT equation of state is that for an *ideal gas*:

$$PV = RT \qquad (2\text{-}60)$$

Here, R is a universal constant, values for which are given in App. B. The molecular picture of an ideal gas is one of molecules which have no volume, and which exert no influence upon one another: intermolecular forces are absent. No real fluid conforms to this model, or to Eq. (2-60). Nevertheless, the concept of an ideal gas is useful, for it leads to simple equations frequently applicable as good approximations to the behavior of real gases at low pressures. Moreover, it serves as the basis for the definition of certain auxiliary functions which are used for the description of real-fluid behavior. These auxiliary functions are treated in Secs. 2-10 and 2-11.

The following partial derivatives are obtained from Eq. (2-60):

$$\left(\frac{\partial P}{\partial T}\right)_V = \frac{R}{V} = \frac{P}{T}$$

$$\left(\frac{\partial^2 P}{\partial T^2}\right)_V = 0$$

$$\left(\frac{\partial V}{\partial T}\right)_P = \frac{R}{P} = \frac{V}{T}$$

$$\left(\frac{\partial^2 V}{\partial T^2}\right)_P = 0$$

$$\left(\frac{\partial P}{\partial V}\right)_T = -\frac{P}{V}$$

The general equations for constant-composition fluids derived in the preceding sections reduce to very simple forms when the relations for an ideal gas are substituted into them:

$$\left(\frac{\partial S}{\partial V}\right)_T = \frac{R}{V} \qquad (2\text{-}36 \; ideal)$$

$$\left(\frac{\partial S}{\partial P}\right)_T = -\frac{R}{P} \qquad (2\text{-}37 \; ideal)$$

$$\left(\frac{\partial H}{\partial P}\right)_T = 0 \qquad (2\text{-}42 \; ideal)$$

$$dH = C_P \, dT \qquad (2\text{-}43 \; ideal)$$

$$dS = \frac{C_P}{T} \, dT - \frac{R}{P} \, dP \qquad (2\text{-}44 \; ideal)$$

$$\mu \equiv \left(\frac{\partial T}{\partial P}\right)_H = 0 \qquad (2\text{-}46 \; ideal)$$

$$\left(\frac{\partial U}{\partial V}\right)_T = 0 \qquad (2\text{-}51 \; ideal)$$

$$dU = C_V \, dT \qquad (2\text{-}52 \; ideal)$$

$$dS = \frac{C_V}{T} \, dT + \frac{R}{V} \, dV \qquad (2\text{-}53 \; ideal)$$

$$dS = \frac{C_V}{P} \, dP + \frac{C_P}{V} \, dV \qquad (2\text{-}54 \; ideal)$$

$$\left(\frac{\partial C_P}{\partial P}\right)_T = 0 \qquad (2\text{-}55 \; ideal)$$

$$\left(\frac{\partial C_V}{\partial V}\right)_T = 0 \qquad (2\text{-}56 \; ideal)$$

$$C_P - C_V = R \qquad (2\text{-}57 \; ideal)$$

$$\gamma \equiv \frac{C_P}{C_V} = -\left(\frac{\partial \ln P}{\partial \ln V}\right)_S \qquad (2\text{-}58 \; ideal)$$

Several important qualitative features of the ideal-gas model follow from these equations. First, we note by Eqs. (2-42 *ideal*), (2-51 *ideal*), (2-55 *ideal*), and (2-56 *ideal*) that H, U, C_P, and C_V for a constant-composition ideal gas are functions of temperature only, independent of P and V. Second, we see from Eq. (2-57 *ideal*) that although C_P and C_V for an ideal gas may separately depend upon T, their *difference* is always constant. Finally, inspection of the entropy equations reveals that S for an ideal gas, unlike H and U, depends upon *both T* and *P*, or upon *both T* and *V*.

Example 2-10 One mole of an ideal gas *with constant heat capacities* undergoes a reversible, adiabatic change of state. We wish to determine equations for this process which relate the pairs of variables P and V, T and V, and T and P.

If the process is *adiabatic*, then the only entropy change is that experienced by the gas. Moreover, since the process is *reversible*, then $\Delta S_{\text{total}} = \Delta S_{\text{gas}} = 0$. Thus the gas undergoes an *isentropic* change of state. The simplest route to a solution is direct integration of Eq. (2-58 *ideal*); this is straightforward because constancy of the heat capacities implies constancy of γ. The result is

$$\ln P = -\gamma \ln V + \text{constant}$$

or

$$PV^\gamma = k \qquad (2\text{-}61a)$$

where k is a constant. Equations relating the other pairs of variables are most easily found by elimination of P or V in favor of T and V or T and P by Eq. (2-60). The results are

$$TV^{\gamma-1} = k' \qquad (2\text{-}61b)$$

and

$$TP^{-[(\gamma-1)/\gamma]} = k'' \qquad (2\text{-}61c)$$

Here, k' and k'' are also constants, related to k by $k' = k/R$ and $k'' = k^{1/\gamma}/R$.

Alternative derivations of Eqs. (2-61) are possible. For example, one can proceed from Eqs. (2-54 *ideal*), (2-53 *ideal*), and (2-44 *ideal*), restricting each to an isentropic change of state $(dS = 0)$. In these derivations, the following identities, valid for an ideal gas only, prove useful:

$$\frac{C_P}{R} = \frac{\gamma}{\gamma-1}$$

and

$$\frac{C_V}{R} = \frac{1}{\gamma-1}$$

2-10 VOLUMETRIC AUXILIARY FUNCTIONS

The volumetric properties of fluids are frequently reported and correlated in terms of certain auxiliary functions, related by definition to V or its derivatives. Two such functions are the *volume expansivity* β, and the *isothermal compressibility* κ. By definition

$$\beta \equiv \frac{1}{V}\left(\frac{\partial V}{\partial T}\right)_P \qquad (2\text{-}62)$$

$$\kappa \equiv -\frac{1}{V}\left(\frac{\partial V}{\partial P}\right)_T \qquad (2\text{-}63)$$

Since

$$\left(\frac{\partial P}{\partial T}\right)_V = -\left(\frac{\partial P}{\partial V}\right)_T\left(\frac{\partial V}{\partial T}\right)_P = -\left(\frac{\partial V}{\partial P}\right)_T^{-1}\left(\frac{\partial V}{\partial T}\right)_P$$

we can write

$$\left(\frac{\partial P}{\partial T}\right)_V = \frac{\beta}{\kappa} \tag{2-64}$$

For a constant-composition fluid, $V = V(T, P)$. Thus,

$$dV = \left(\frac{\partial V}{\partial T}\right)_P dT + \left(\frac{\partial V}{\partial P}\right)_T dP$$

Elimination of the partial derivatives in favor of β and κ yields the equivalent expression

$$dV = \beta V\, dT - \kappa V\, dP \tag{2-65}$$

The equations for constant-composition fluids derived in Secs. 2-5 through 2-8 may be recast in terms of β, κ, and their derivatives. We summarize below these restatements of Eqs. (2-43), (2-44), (2-52), (2-53), and (2-57):

$$dH = C_P\, dT + V(1 - \beta T)\, dP \tag{2-66}$$

$$dS = \frac{C_P}{T}\, dT - \beta V\, dP \tag{2-67}$$

$$dU = C_V\, dT + \frac{1}{\kappa}(\beta T - \kappa P)\, dV \tag{2-68}$$

$$dS = \frac{C_V}{T}\, dT + \frac{\beta}{\kappa}\, dV \tag{2-69}$$

$$C_P - C_V = \frac{\beta^2 V T}{\kappa} \tag{2-70}$$

Although appropriate for any fluid, Eqs. (2-65) through (2-70) find greatest application to the calculation of property changes of liquids. One advantage to the use of β and κ is that for liquids their T and P dependence is often weak, and they may therefore sometimes be treated as approximately constant.

Example 2-11 An idealized model of liquid-phase behavior is the *constant-β, κ fluid*, a substance for which both β and κ are constants, independent of T and P. For such a fluid, integration of Eq. (2-65) yields the equation of state

$$\ln V = \beta T - \kappa P + \text{const}$$

The usual application of this equation is in the calculation of *changes* in T, P, or V. Noting that

$$\frac{V_2}{V_1} \equiv 1 + \frac{V_2 - V_1}{V_1}$$

we can write

$$\ln\left(1 + \frac{V_2 - V_1}{V_1}\right) = \beta(T_2 - T_1) - \kappa(P_2 - P_1)$$

If the relative change of volume $(V_2 - V_1)/V_1$ is *small*

$$\ln\left(1 + \frac{V_2 - V_1}{V_1}\right) \simeq \frac{V_2 - V_1}{V_1}$$

from which

$$V_2 - V_1 \simeq V_1[\beta(T_2 - T_1) - \kappa(P_2 - P_1)]$$

This last equation is the integrated version of Eq. (2-65) commonly used as an approximation.

The equation of state for an ideal gas, Eq. (2-60), applies to a *model* substance, and is inappropriate in general for precise representation of molar volumes of real fluids. However, *ideal-gas* volumes V' computed from Eq. (2-60) serve as the basis for the definition of auxiliary functions. There are two obvious choices for such functions:

$$Z \equiv V/V' \tag{2-71}$$

$$\Delta V' \equiv V' - V \tag{2-72}$$

Equation (2-71) defines the *compressibility factor* Z; it is the *ratio* of the actual molar volume to that given by the equation for an ideal gas at the same T and P. Equation (2-72) defines the *residual volume* $\Delta V'$; it is the *difference* between the molar volume of an ideal gas and the molar volume of the real fluid at the same T and P. Since by Eq. (2-60) $V' = RT/P$, expressions alternative to the above definitions are

$$Z = \frac{PV}{RT} \tag{2-73}$$

$$\Delta V' = \frac{RT}{P} - V \tag{2-74}$$

Clearly, the two functions are related. For example, the molar volume may be eliminated in favor of Z in Eq. (2-74), giving

$$\Delta V' = \frac{RT}{P}(1 - Z) \tag{2-75}$$

Both Z and $\Delta V'$ are functions of T and P for a constant-composition fluid.

Equations presented in Secs. 2-5 through 2-8 may be written in terms of Z or $\Delta V'$ and their derivatives.

In the limit as P approaches zero, real-gas behavior in many respects approaches ideal-gas behavior. In particular, for constant-composition gases it is known that

$$\lim_{P \to 0} Z = 1 \qquad (\text{const } T) \tag{2-76}$$

However, it is *not* generally true that $\Delta V'$ tends to zero in the zero-pressure limit; Eqs. (2-75) and (2-76) show that $\Delta V'$ becomes *indeterminate* (i.e., approaches 0/0) as $P \to 0$. The indeterminacy is resolved by application of l'Hôpital's rule, which gives

$$\lim_{P \to 0} \Delta V' = -RT \lim_{P \to 0} \left(\frac{\partial Z}{\partial P} \right)_T \tag{2-77}$$

Thus, provided that $(\partial Z/\partial P)_T$ remains finite as $P \to 0$, $\Delta V'$ has a finite zero-pressure limit. Experiment shows this limit to be generally nonzero.

Figures 2-1 and 2-2 show plots of Z and $\Delta V'$ versus P for nitrogen at several temperatures. It is to be noted that while $\Delta V'$ can assume an enormous range of values (most of the liquid portion of the saturation curve is off-scale on Fig. 2-2), the compressibility factor Z for the pressure range shown is order of magnitude unity. Moreover, as P tends to zero, Z for the vapor portion of *any* isotherm tends to unity, while the zero-pressure limit of $\Delta V'$ is different for different isotherms.

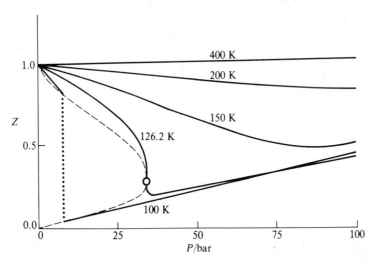

Figure 2-1 Compressibility factor Z versus P for nitrogen. Solid lines are isotherms for single-phase regions; dotted line represents states of two-phase equilibrium at 100 K. Dashed line represents states of saturation, and the open circle is the critical point.

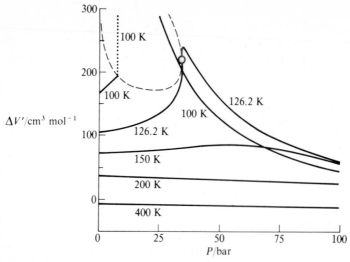

Figure 2-2 Residual volume $\Delta V'$ versus P for nitrogen. (See legend of Fig. 2-1 for description of curves.)

Example 2-12 Expression of the general equations of Secs. 2-5 through 2-8 in terms of the compressibility factor Z requires equations relating derivatives of P and V to those involving Z. Since by definition $PV = ZRT$, we have for a general change in state that

$$P\,dV + V\,dP = RT\,dZ + ZR\,dT$$

Dividing this equation by dV and restricting the result to constant T, we find

$$P + V\left(\frac{\partial P}{\partial V}\right)_T = RT\left(\frac{\partial Z}{\partial V}\right)_T$$

Elimination of P in favor of Z and rearrangement gives

$$\left(\frac{\partial P}{\partial V}\right)_T = \frac{RT}{V}\left[\left(\frac{\partial Z}{\partial V}\right)_T - \frac{Z}{V}\right] \tag{2-78}$$

By similar procedures we obtain the following useful equations:

$$\left(\frac{\partial P}{\partial T}\right)_V = \frac{RT}{V}\left[\left(\frac{\partial Z}{\partial T}\right)_V + \frac{Z}{T}\right] \tag{2-79}$$

$$\left(\frac{\partial V}{\partial P}\right)_T = \frac{RT}{P}\left[\left(\frac{\partial Z}{\partial P}\right)_T - \frac{Z}{P}\right] \tag{2-80}$$

$$\left(\frac{\partial V}{\partial T}\right)_P = \frac{RT}{P}\left[\left(\frac{\partial Z}{\partial T}\right)_P + \frac{Z}{T}\right] \tag{2-81}$$

Equations (2-80) and (2-81) permit expression of β and κ in terms of Z and its derivatives. Thus, by Eqs. (2-62) and (2-81), we find

$$\beta = \frac{RT}{PV}\left[\left(\frac{\partial Z}{\partial T}\right)_P + \frac{Z}{T}\right]$$

or

$$\beta = \frac{1}{T}\left[1 + \frac{T}{Z}\left(\frac{\partial Z}{\partial T}\right)_P\right] \qquad (2\text{-}82)$$

Similarly, from Eqs. (2-63) and (2-80), we find

$$\kappa = \frac{1}{P}\left[1 - \frac{P}{Z}\left(\frac{\partial Z}{\partial P}\right)_T\right] \qquad (2\text{-}83)$$

The simplest equation for Z is that for an ideal gas, for which $Z = 1$ at all T and P. For this special case, Eqs. (2-82) and (2-83) give

$$\beta = 1/T \qquad (2\text{-}82 \; ideal)$$

and

$$\kappa = 1/P \qquad (2\text{-}83 \; ideal)$$

2-11 RESIDUAL FUNCTIONS

An important application of the material of Sec. 2-6 is to the calculation of the effect of pressure on the enthalpy and entropy of real gases. Suppose that a constant-composition fluid undergoes an isothermal change of state from initial pressure P_1 to final pressure P_2. If an equation of state is available for the fluid, then the changes in enthalpy and entropy may be computed by integration of Eqs. (2-43) and (2-44):

$$\Delta H = \int_{P_1}^{P_2}\left[V - T\left(\frac{\partial V}{\partial T}\right)_P\right]dP \qquad (\text{const } T)$$

and

$$\Delta S = -\int_{P_1}^{P_2}\left(\frac{\partial V}{\partial T}\right)_P dP \qquad (\text{const } T)$$

Although this procedure is straightforward in principle, there exists a more convenient technique, based on the use of *residual functions*. One advantage of the residual-function technique is that it allows particularly simple evaluation of temperature dependence.

We have already seen in the preceding section one example of a residual function: the residual volume

$$\Delta V' \equiv V' - V$$

All residual functions are defined in like fashion:

$$\boxed{\Delta M' \equiv M' - M} \qquad (2\text{-}84)$$

where the M's represent molar values for any extensive thermodynamic property. In particular, M is the true value of the property of a fluid at given T and P, and M' is the value for the fluid in its *ideal-gas state* at the same T and P.

The ideal-gas state of a fluid is hypothetical, except in the limit of zero pressure, where the ideal-gas equation holds; for this real ideal-gas state

$$PV = RT$$

If it is imagined that this equation retains its validity for the fluid as pressure increases, then the fluid remains in the ideal-gas state, and its properties in this state are represented by M'.

Real fluids at zero pressure have properties that reflect their individuality, and this is true also for their ideal-gas states. Thus, for example, heat capacities of fluids in their ideal-gas states (e.g., C_P') are different for different fluids, and they vary with temperature. These differences depend on the characteristics of the molecules and not on their interactions. Residual functions, representing the difference between ideal and real behavior, do depend on molecular interactions and on molecular configuration. Thus they represent *configurational properties*. Since the ideal-gas model presumes the absence of molecular interactions, the deviations from ideality represented by Eq. (2-84) characterize molecular interactions alone.

For the calculation of values of a thermodynamic property M (such as H or S), Eq. (2-84) is written

$$M = M' - \Delta M'$$

This divides the calculation into two parts: first, the calculation of the ideal-gas value M', which can be accomplished with the equations of Sec. 2-9; and second, the calculation of $\Delta M'$, which has the nature of a correction to the ideal-gas value and which depends on PVT data, or on the equation of state. The equations for H and S which arise out of this procedure are developed in the following paragraphs.

Differentiation of Eq. (2-84) with respect to P at constant T and composition gives

$$\left(\frac{\partial \Delta M'}{\partial P}\right)_T = \left(\frac{\partial M'}{\partial P}\right)_T - \left(\frac{\partial M}{\partial P}\right)_T$$

For a change in state at constant T and composition, this may be written

$$d\Delta M' = \left[\left(\frac{\partial M'}{\partial P}\right)_T - \left(\frac{\partial M}{\partial P}\right)_T\right] dP$$

Integration from some arbitrary pressure P^* to the actual pressure P yields, on rearrangement

$$\Delta M' = (\Delta M')^* + \int_{P*}^{P} \left[\left(\frac{\partial M'}{\partial P}\right)_T - \left(\frac{\partial M}{\partial P}\right)_T\right] dP \qquad (\text{const } T, x)$$

When $P^* \to 0$, $(\Delta M')^*$ becomes the zero-pressure limit of $\Delta M'$. In practice, it is found that the values of certain thermodynamic properties approach their ideal-gas values as P approaches zero. When this is the case

$$(\Delta M')^* = 0$$

It was stated in the preceding section that this result is *not* valid for $\Delta M' \equiv \Delta V'$. On the other hand, experimental evidence shows that this assumption *is* valid when $\Delta M' \equiv \Delta H'$ and when $\Delta M' \equiv \Delta S'$. These are the two cases we wish to consider, and for them we have

$$\Delta M' = \int_0^P \left[\left(\frac{\partial M'}{\partial P} \right)_T - \left(\frac{\partial M}{\partial P} \right)_T \right] dP \qquad (\text{const } T, x)$$

When $\Delta M' \equiv \Delta H'$, the required derivatives are given by Eqs. (2-42 *ideal*) and (2-42), and substitution for them in the foregoing equation yields

$$\Delta H' = \int_0^P \left[T \left(\frac{\partial V}{\partial T} \right)_P - V \right] dP \qquad (\text{const } T, x) \qquad (2\text{-}85)$$

Similarly, when $\Delta M' \equiv \Delta S'$, the appropriate derivatives are provided by Eqs. (2-37 *ideal*) and (2-37), and we obtain

$$\Delta S' = \int_0^P \left[\left(\frac{\partial V}{\partial T} \right)_P - \frac{R}{P} \right] dP \qquad (\text{const } T, x) \qquad (2\text{-}86)$$

Knowing $\Delta V'$, $\Delta H'$, and $\Delta S'$, one can easily determine residual functions corresponding to other extensive properties. Consider for example the internal energy U. Since $U = H - PV$, we have also that $U' = H' - PV'$. Thus

$$\Delta U' \equiv U' - U = (H' - PV') - (H - PV)$$

or

$$\Delta U' = \Delta H' - P \, \Delta V' \qquad (2\text{-}87)$$

Similarly, we find that

$$\Delta A' = \Delta H' - P \, \Delta V' - T \, \Delta S' \qquad (2\text{-}88)$$

and

$$\Delta G' = \Delta H' - T \, \Delta S' \qquad (2\text{-}89)$$

Although the zero-pressure limit of $\Delta V'$ is generally nonzero for a real gas, it is finite. Thus the product $P \, \Delta V'$ becomes zero in the limit, and all of the functions $\Delta U'$, $\Delta A'$, and $\Delta G'$ approach zero as $P \to 0$.

2-12 CALCULATION OF PROPERTY CHANGES OF CONSTANT-COMPOSITION PHASES

We consider in this section use of residual functions in the calculation of property changes of *single-phase, constant-composition* fluids for an arbitrary change of state. The actual change of state, in which the fluid passes from initial conditions T_1, P_1 to final conditions T_2, P_2, is indicated by the dashed line on Fig. 2-3. As a result of this change of state, thermodynamic property M undergoes a change $\Delta M = M_2 - M_1$. It is ΔM which we wish to calculate.

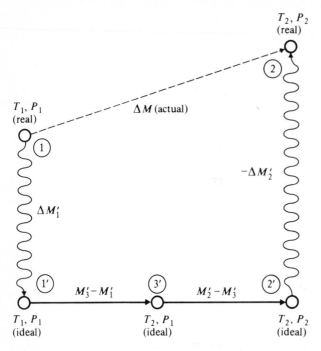

Figure 2-3 Calculational path for determination of property change ΔM (actual) by use of residual functions.

The property M is a state function, and for purposes of calculating its change we can replace the actual path $1 \rightarrow 2$ by any combination of hypothetical steps taking the fluid from its *actual* initial equilibrium state to its *actual* final equilibrium state. Otherwise, we are free to choose them any way we wish. In practice, the choice is dictated by calculational convenience.

The set of four steps shown on Fig. 2-3 constitutes a convenient basis for the use of residual functions in the calculation of ΔM. Step $1 \rightarrow 1'$ represents a hypothetical process as a result of which the fluid passes from its real state at T_1, P_1 to the ideal-gas state at the same conditions. Step $1' \rightarrow 3'$ is an isobaric process, in which the fluid in its ideal-gas state undergoes a change in temperature from T_1 to T_2, at constant pressure P_1. Step $3' \rightarrow 2'$ represents an isothermal process, again for the ideal-gas state, in which the pressure of the fluid changes from P_1 to P_2, at constant temperature T_2. Finally, the process represented by step $2' \rightarrow 2$ takes the fluid from the ideal-gas state at final conditions T_2, P_2 to the real state at the same conditions. The actual property change ΔM is just the sum of the property changes for the four steps:

$$\Delta M = (M_1' - M_1) + (M_3' - M_1') + (M_2' - M_3') + (M_2 - M_2')$$

The first and last of the groups in parentheses may be replaced by residual functions:

$$M_1' - M_1 = \Delta M_1'$$

and

$$M_2 - M_2' = -\Delta M_2'$$

Combination of these three equations gives

$$\Delta M = \Delta M_1' + (M_3' - M_1') + (M_2' - M_3') - \Delta M_2' \qquad (2\text{-}90)$$

Application of Eq. (2-90) requires the availability of PVT information for the *real* fluid for evaluation of $\Delta M_1'$ and $\Delta M_2'$, and of *ideal-gas* heat capacities C_P' for the evaluation of the first group in parentheses. We illustrate the procedure for the enthalpy and for the entropy.

For $M \equiv H$, the expressions for ideal gases, Eqs. (2-43 *ideal*) and (2-42 *ideal*) give

$$M_3' - M_1' = H_3' - H_1' = \int_{T_1}^{T_2} C_P' \, dT$$

and

$$M_2' - M_3' = H_2' - H_3' = 0$$

and thus Eq. (2-90) becomes

$$\Delta H = \Delta H_1' + \int_{T_1}^{T_2} C_P' \, dT - \Delta H_2' \qquad (2\text{-}91)$$

Similarly, for $M \equiv S$, Eq. (2-44 *ideal*) gives

$$M_3' - M_1' = S_3' - S_1' = \int_{T_1}^{T_2} \frac{C_P'}{T} \, dT$$

and

$$M_2' - M_3' = S_2' - S_3' = -R \ln \frac{P_2}{P_1}$$

and Eq. (2-90) becomes

$$\Delta S = \Delta S_1' + \int_{T_1}^{T_2} \frac{C_P'}{T} \, dT - R \ln \frac{P_2}{P_1} - \Delta S_2' \qquad (2\text{-}92)$$

Given an equation of state for the fluid, one calculates the residual functions from Eqs. (2-85) and (2-86), or their equivalents. The integrals involving C_P' are evaluated from empirical expressions for the temperature dependence of the ideal-gas heat capacities.

Ideal-gas heat capacities depend upon temperature, composition, and the identities of the chemical species present. For a pure fluid, the temperature dependence is commonly expressed by a few terms from the empirical formula

$$C_P' = C_0 + C_1 T + C_2 T^2 + C_3 T^3 + \frac{C_4}{T} + \frac{C_5}{T^2} \qquad (2\text{-}93)$$

Here, parameters C_0 through C_5 are empirical constants, different for different fluids. They are determined by analysis of experimental measurements, and are often reported in compilations of thermodynamic data. Substitution of Eq. (2-93) into the integrals appearing in Eqs. (2-91) and (2-92) yields on integration

$$\int_{T_1}^{T_2} C_P \, dT = C_0(T_2 - T_1) + \frac{C_1}{2}(T_2^2 - T_1^2) + \frac{C_2}{3}(T_2^3 - T_1^3)$$

$$+ \frac{C_3}{4}(T_2^4 - T_1^4) + C_4 \ln(T_2/T_1) + C_5\left(\frac{T_2 - T_1}{T_1 T_2}\right) \quad (2\text{-}94)$$

and

$$\int_{T_1}^{T_2} \frac{C_P'}{T} \, dT = C_0 \ln(T_2/T_1) + C_1(T_2 - T_1) + \frac{C_2}{2}(T_2^2 - T_1^2)$$

$$+ \frac{C_3}{3}(T_2^3 - T_1^3) + C_4\left(\frac{T_2 - T_1}{T_1 T_2}\right) + \frac{C_5}{2}\left(\frac{T_2^2 - T_1^2}{T_1^2 T_2^2}\right) \quad (2\text{-}95)$$

If C_P' is a constant, independent of T (as it is for monatomic gases and approximately for diatomic gases at moderate temperatures), then Eqs. (2-94) and (2-95) reduce to the expressions

$$\int_{T_1}^{T_2} C_P \, dT = C_0(T_2 - T_1) = C_P'(T_2 - T_1)$$

and

$$\int_{T_1}^{T_2} \frac{C_P'}{T} \, dT = C_0 \ln(T_2/T_1) = C_P' \ln(T_2/T_1)$$

The simple form of these results suggests the definition of quantities called *mean heat capacities*. We define two useful kinds of mean heat capacities:

$$C_{P_{mh}}' \equiv \frac{\int_{T_1}^{T_2} C_P' \, dT}{T_2 - T_1} \quad (2\text{-}96)$$

and

$$C_{P_{ms}}' \equiv \frac{\int_{T_1}^{T_2} \dfrac{C_P'}{T} \, dT}{\ln(T_2/T_1)} \quad (2\text{-}97)$$

Expressions for mean heat capacities follow directly when Eqs. (2-94) and (2-95) are combined with Eqs. (2-96) and (2-97). The simplest statement of these results is obtained in terms of three average temperatures. Thus we define the *arithmetic-mean temperature* T_{am}, the *geometric-mean temperature* T_{gm}, and the *logarithmic-mean temperature* T_{lm}:

$$T_{am} \equiv \frac{T_1 + T_2}{2} \quad (2\text{-}98a)$$

$$T_{gm} \equiv (T_1 T_2)^{1/2} \qquad (2\text{-}98b)$$

$$T_{lm} \equiv \frac{T_2 - T_1}{\ln (T_2/T_1)} \qquad (2\text{-}98c)$$

The mean heat capacities are then given as:

$$C'_{P_{mh}} = C_0 + C_1 T_{am} + \frac{C_2}{3} (4T_{am}^2 - T_{gm}^2) + C_3 (2T_{am}^2 - T_{gm}^2) T_{am} + \frac{C_4}{T_{lm}} + \frac{C_5}{T_{gm}^2}$$

$$(2\text{-}99)$$

and

$$C'_{P_{ms}} = C_0 + C_1 T_{lm} + C_2 T_{am} T_{lm} + \frac{C_3}{3} (4T_{am}^2 - T_{gm}^2) T_{lm} + C_4 \frac{T_{lm}}{T_{gm}^2} + C_5 \frac{T_{am} T_{lm}}{T_{gm}^4}$$

$$(2\text{-}100)$$

Once values for mean heat capacities are calculated, evaluation of the integrals giving isobaric ideal-gas enthalpy and entropy changes is carried out with equations that are simple rearrangements of Eqs. (2-96) and (2-97):

$$\int_{T_1}^{T_2} C'_P \, dT = C'_{P_{mh}} (T_2 - T_1) \qquad (2\text{-}101)$$

and

$$\int_{T_1}^{T_2} \frac{C'_P}{T} \, dT = C'_{P_{ms}} \ln (T_2/T_1) \qquad (2\text{-}102)$$

One advantage of this two-step procedure is that values of mean heat capacities, the intermediate results, are far more readily judged for reasonableness than are final values of enthalpy and entropy changes. In addition, the calculation of mean heat capacities from mean temperatures permits efficient programming for electronic calculators and computers.

The mean-heat-capacity formulas, developed here in particular for ideal gases, are of course equally valid for evaluation of isobaric changes in H and S for any fluid for which C_P is given by the empirical relation of Eq. (2-93).

Example 2-13 For generality, the temperature dependence of C'_P as given by Eq. (2-93) combines terms from several commonly used expressions. In a particular application, the pertinent equation does not likely include all terms. The constants C_i for those omitted are then set equal to zero. If C'_P is linear in T, then

$$C'_P = C_0 + C_1 T$$

In this event, Eq. (2-99) becomes

$$C'_{P_{mh}} = C_0 + C_1 T_{am}$$

and the mean heat capacity in Eq. (2-101) is the heat capacity evaluated at the arithmetic mean of the temperature limits. Similarly, Eq. (2-100) becomes

$$C'_{P_{ms}} = C_0 + C_1 T_{lm}$$

and the appropriate mean heat capacity in Eq. (2-102) is the heat capacity evaluated at the logarithmic mean of the temperature limits.

THREE

SYSTEMS OF VARIABLE COMPOSITION

The individuality of a given chemical species is evident not only in its thermodynamic properties as a pure material but also in its influence on the properties
of mixtures of which it is a constituent. The contribution of a given constituent to
a particular property of a mixture is accounted for by a defined thermodynamic
function called a partial property. In this chapter we rationalize this definition,
and develop the relationships between mixture properties and partial properties
and among the partial properties themselves. We also introduce the fugacity and
fugacity coefficient, auxiliary thermodynamic functions of great utility in the
treatment of phase equilibria. Although not partial properties themselves, they
are directly related to functions of this kind.

3-1 PARTIAL MOLAR PROPERTIES

Postulate 1.1 of Chap. 1 affirms that the macroscopic properties of homogeneous
fluids existing at equilibrium in PVT systems are functions of temperature,
pressure, and composition. Mathematically, we may express the functional
dependence of property M by

$$M = M(T, P, x_1, x_2, \ldots)$$

These properties are, of course, *intensive*, independent of the total amount of
fluid present. Although the x_i's are not all independent, they are independent of
T and P. If n_i represents the mole number of chemical species i for the entire

system and if $n = \sum n_i$, then $x_i = n_i/n$, and we can express the product nM as a function of the independent variables:

$$nM = m(T, P, n_1, n_2, \ldots)$$

The quantity nM is clearly proportional to n, and is therefore *extensive*. The symbol M may stand for any intensive thermodynamic property of a solution (excluding, of course, temperature, pressure, and composition, the conditions which fix M). For example, M can represent any of the molar properties V, U, H, C_V, C_P, S, A, and G; it can also represent such properties as the compressibility factor Z, the isothermal compressibility κ, the volume expansivity β, and density ρ.

In view of the functional dependence of nM, we can write its total differential as

$$d(nM) = \left[\frac{\partial(nM)}{\partial T}\right]_{P, n} dT + \left[\frac{\partial(nM)}{\partial P}\right]_{T, n} dP + \sum \left[\frac{\partial(nM)}{\partial n_i}\right]_{T, P, n_j} dn_i \quad (3\text{-}1)$$

Since the subscript n signifies constancy of *all* mole numbers, and hence of composition, Eq. (3-1) may also be written:

$$d(nM) = n\left(\frac{\partial M}{\partial T}\right)_{P, x} dT + n\left(\frac{\partial M}{\partial P}\right)_{T, x} dP + \sum \left[\frac{\partial(nM)}{\partial n_i}\right]_{T, P, n_j} dn_i \quad (3\text{-}2)$$

Here, subscript x denotes *constant composition*; thus the derivatives with respect to T and P are of a kind treated in the preceding chapter. Derivatives like those in the summation also arose in Examples 2-5 and 2-6; they are clearly important to the thermodynamic treatment of solutions of variable composition and extent. These derivatives, taken with respect to a mole number *at constant temperature and pressure*, are called partial molar properties, denoted by $\bar{M}_i$:

$$\boxed{\bar{M}_i \equiv \left[\frac{\partial(nM)}{\partial n_i}\right]_{T, P, n_j}} \quad (3\text{-}3)$$

Substitution into Eq. (3-2) gives an expression for the total differential $d(nM)$ of any extensive function for a *homogeneous* fluid:

$$\boxed{d(nM) = n\left(\frac{\partial M}{\partial T}\right)_{P, x} dT + n\left(\frac{\partial M}{\partial P}\right)_{T, x} dP + \sum \bar{M}_i \, dn_i} \quad (3\text{-}4)$$

This equation, valid for an equilibrium phase, either closed or open, attributes variations in the function nM to changes in temperature and pressure and to changes in the mole numbers resulting from mass transfer and chemical reaction.

Since the properties represented by M are intensive and at given T and P functions of composition, they depend only on the *relative* amounts of the chemical species making up the system. Thus, if the mole numbers n_i of all species are increased by the same factor (e.g., all doubled), the values of these properties are unchanged. Such properties are characterized mathematically as *homogeneous functions of zero degree in the mole numbers.* On the other hand, the quantities represented by nM depend on both composition and the amount of fluid present. If the mole numbers of all species are increased by the same factor, the values of these quantities all increase by this factor. They are characterized as *homogeneous functions of first degree in the mole numbers.*

As discussed in App. A-4, application of Euler's theorem on homogeneous functions either to the properties M or to the quantities nM leads to the relation:

$$nM = \sum n_i \bar{M}_i \qquad (3\text{-}5)$$

Upon division by n, this becomes

$$M = \sum x_i \bar{M}_i \qquad (3\text{-}6)$$

These equations are mathematical consequences of experimental observations regarding the nature of thermodynamic properties. One sees by inspection of Eq. (3-6) that since M is an intensive property and a homogeneous function of zero degree in the mole numbers, the $\bar{M}_i$ must be of the same nature. Thus, the $\bar{M}_i$ are also intensive properties and homogeneous functions of zero degree in the mole numbers. Moreover, since M depends as well on T and P, so do the $\bar{M}_i$. In summary, the $\bar{M}_i$ are functions of T, P, and composition for a homogeneous fluid at equilibrium in a PVT system.

Equations for partial molar properties apply as well to partial *specific* properties, where the basis is a unit of mass rather than a mole. In this case, m replaces n, and the x_i become mass fractions.

Equation (3-6) suggests that the solution property M is a simple sum of the properties of its constituent species, each weighted in proportion to the quantity present. The partial property $\bar{M}_i$ is then interpreted as the value of the property of species i as it exists in solution. However, each species in a solution is an intimate part of the solution, and cannot actually have identifiable separate properties of its own. Nevertheless, we may view Eq. (3-3), which defines $\bar{M}_i$, as a formula which also defines how a solution property is *apportioned* among its constituent species, and on this basis treat partial properties as though they represent values of properties of the individual species in solution. Partial properties lend themselves completely to this interpretation, and one can always reason logically to correct conclusions from this point of view.

As the result of experiment, we know that the partial property $\bar{M}_k$ for species k in solution is not in general equal to M_k, the property of k as a pure fluid at the temperature and pressure of the solution. However, for the limiting case of a solution for which x_k, the mole fraction of species k, becomes unity, Eq. (3-6) becomes

$$M_k = \bar{M}_k \qquad \text{(pure } k\text{)}$$

and the equality of the two properties is established for $x_k = 1$.

Example 3-1 The fundamental interpretation of $\bar{M}_i$ is based on the definition of Eq. (3-3). To be specific, we deal with a particular property, the volume. Consider an open beaker containing an equimolar mixture of ethanol (e) and water (w). This mixture occupies a total volume $V^t = nV$ at room temperature T and atmospheric pressure P. Now add to this solution a drop of pure water, also at T and P, containing Δn_w moles, and mix it thoroughly into the solution, allowing sufficient time for heat exchange so that the contents of the beaker return to the initial temperature. What is the volume change of the solution in the beaker?

One might expect the volume to increase by an amount equal to the volume of water added, i.e., by $V_w \Delta n_w$, where V_w is the molar volume of pure water at T and P. If this were true, we would have

$$\Delta(nV) = V_w \Delta n_w$$

However, we find by experiment that the actual change in volume $\Delta(nV)$ is somewhat less than given by this equation. Evidently, the *effective* molar volume of the added water *in solution* is less than the molar volume of pure water at the same T and P. Designating this effective molar volume by $\bar{V}_w$, we can write

$$\Delta(nV) = \bar{V}_w \Delta n_w$$

or

$$\bar{V}_w = \frac{\Delta(nV)}{\Delta n_w} \tag{A}$$

If the effective molar volume $\bar{V}_w$ is to represent a characteristic property of the original equimolar solution, it must be based on data for a solution of *this* composition. However, in the process described a *finite* drop of water added to the equimolar solution causes a small but *finite* change in composition. We may, however, consider the limiting case for which $\Delta n_w \to 0$. Then Eq. (A) becomes

$$\bar{V}_w = \lim_{\Delta n_w \to 0} \frac{\Delta(nV)}{\Delta n_w} = \frac{d(nV)}{dn_w}$$

Since T, P, and n_e (the number of moles of ethanol) are constant, this equation is more appropriately written

$$\bar{V}_w = \left[\frac{\partial(nV)}{\partial n_w} \right]_{T, P, n_e}$$

which for $M = V$ is a particular case of Eq. (3-3), the definition of a partial molar property. Thus the partial molar volume is the rate of change of total solution volume with n_w at constant T, P, and n_e. More generally, the partial molar property $\bar{M}_i$ is the rate of change of the quantity nM with n_i at constant T and P, for constant values of all other mole numbers n_j.

Since the intensive thermodynamic properties of solutions, represented by M, are usually expressed as functions of mole (or mass) fractions, the direct application of Eq. (3-3), which defines a partial property in terms of n and n_i (or m and m_i) is not always convenient. We need an equation which relates $\bar{M}_i$ to the solution property M and to the mole (or mass) fractions. Several such expressions are developed in the following paragraphs.

Expansion of the derivative of Eq. (3-3) yields

$$\bar{M}_i = M + n\left(\frac{\partial M}{\partial n_i}\right)_{T, P, n_j} \tag{3-7}$$

For evaluation of the derivative in this equation, we recall that at constant temperature and pressure M is a function of the mole fractions:

$$M = M(x_1, x_2, \ldots, x_k, \ldots, x_N)$$

where k is the general identifying index running over *all* chemical species. At constant T and P, the total differential dM is therefore given by

$$dM = \sum \left(\frac{\partial M}{\partial x_k}\right)_{T, P, x_j} dx_k \tag{3-8}$$

where x_j indicates that all mole fractions are held constant except the particular x_k in the derivative. We have retained all mole fractions as variables, even though they are not all independent; this in no way compromises the validity of Eq. (3-8). Division by dn_i and restriction to constant n_j $(j \neq i)$ gives

$$\left(\frac{\partial M}{\partial n_i}\right)_{T, P, n_j} = \sum \left(\frac{\partial M}{\partial x_k}\right)_{T, P, x_j} \left(\frac{\partial x_k}{\partial n_i}\right)_{n_j}$$

where subscript i identifies a particular species included in the set k. Since

$$x_k \equiv n_k/n$$

where $n = \sum n_k$, we have

$$\left(\frac{\partial x_k}{\partial n_i}\right)_{n_j} = \frac{1}{n}\left(\frac{\partial n_k}{\partial n_i}\right)_{n_j} - \frac{n_k}{n^2}\left(\frac{\partial n}{\partial n_i}\right)_{n_j}$$

Clearly, $(\partial n/\partial n_i)_{n_j} = 1$, and the equation becomes

$$\left(\frac{\partial x_k}{\partial n_i}\right)_{n_j} = \frac{1}{n}\left[\left(\frac{\partial n_k}{\partial n_i}\right)_{n_j} - x_k\right]$$

Substitution into the equation for $(\partial M/\partial n_i)_{T, P, n_j}$ yields

$$\left(\frac{\partial M}{\partial n_i}\right)_{T, P, n_j} = \frac{1}{n}\sum \left(\frac{\partial M}{\partial x_k}\right)_{T, P, x_j} \left[\left(\frac{\partial n_k}{\partial n_i}\right)_{n_j} - x_k\right]$$

or

$$n\left(\frac{\partial M}{\partial n_i}\right)_{T, P, n_j} = \sum \left(\frac{\partial M}{\partial x_k}\right)_{T, P, x_j} \left(\frac{\partial n_k}{\partial n_i}\right)_{n_j} - \sum x_k\left(\frac{\partial M}{\partial x_k}\right)_{T, P, x_j}$$

Since the n_k are independent variables, the derivative $(\partial n_k/\partial n_i)_{n_j}$ in the first summation is zero for all terms except the one for which $k = i$, in which case it is unity. Therefore

$$n\left(\frac{\partial M}{\partial n_i}\right)_{T, P, n_j} = \left(\frac{\partial M}{\partial x_i}\right)_{T, P, x_j} - \sum x_k\left(\frac{\partial M}{\partial x_k}\right)_{T, P, x_j}$$

and Eq. (3-7) becomes

$$\bar{M}_i = M + \left(\frac{\partial M}{\partial x_i}\right)_{T, P, x_j} - \sum x_k \left(\frac{\partial M}{\partial x_k}\right)_{T, P, x_j} \tag{3-9}$$

The summation in Eq. (3-9) is over *all* constituents including i, and the partial derivatives are taken with all mole fractions held constant except the particular mole fraction with respect to which differentiation is performed. Physically, of course, it is impossible to vary just one mole fraction, because $\sum x_k = 1$. Nevertheless, this equation does have mathematical significance; if one has an equation expressing M as a function of the mole fractions, the mathematical operations represented by the derivatives are entirely proper. Because of its symmetry, Eq. (3-9) is most convenient for analytical treatment of data. Moreover, it is especially suitable for efficient computer programming.

Equation (3-9) may, however, be written in forms which take account of the relation $\sum x_k = 1$. Thus, we may write

$$\left(\frac{\partial M}{\partial x_i}\right)_{T, P, x_j} = \left(\frac{\partial M}{\partial x_i}\right)_{T, P, x_j} \sum x_k = \sum x_k \left(\frac{\partial M}{\partial x_i}\right)_{T, P, x_j}$$

and Eq. (3-9) becomes

$$\bar{M}_i = M + \sum x_k \left[\left(\frac{\partial M}{\partial x_i}\right)_{T, P, x_j} - \left(\frac{\partial M}{\partial x_k}\right)_{T, P, x_j}\right]$$

where the summation is over *all* species. However, for the particular species $k = i$, the quantity in brackets is zero, and we can equally well write:

$$\bar{M}_i = M + \sum_{k \neq i} x_k \left[\left(\frac{\partial M}{\partial x_i}\right)_{T, P, x_j} - \left(\frac{\partial M}{\partial x_k}\right)_{T, P, x_j}\right] \tag{3-10}$$

The interdependence of the mole fractions is still not recognized in the derivatives of this equation. The appropriate expression is found from Eq. (3-8). If this equation is applied to the particular case where all mole fractions are held constant except for x_i and a *specific* x_k, it reduces to

$$dM = \left(\frac{\partial M}{\partial x_i}\right)_{T, P, x_j} dx_i + \left(\frac{\partial M}{\partial x_k}\right)_{T, P, x_j} dx_k$$

Division by dx_k under the same restrictions gives

$$\left(\frac{\partial M}{\partial x_k}\right)_{T, P, x_{j \neq i,k}} = \left(\frac{\partial M}{\partial x_i}\right)_{T, P, x_j} \left(\frac{dx_i}{dx_k}\right) + \left(\frac{\partial M}{\partial x_k}\right)_{T, P, x_j}$$

in which dx_i/dx_k remains an ordinary derivative, because x_i depends only upon x_k with all other mole fractions constant. In fact, $dx_i/dx_k = -1$, and

$$\left(\frac{\partial M}{\partial x_k}\right)_{T, P, x_{j \neq i,k}} = - \left[\left(\frac{\partial M}{\partial x_i}\right)_{T, P, x_j} - \left(\frac{\partial M}{\partial x_k}\right)_{T, P, x_j}\right]$$

The term in brackets appears in Eq. (3-10), which may therefore be written:

$$\bar{M}_i = M - \sum_{k \neq i} x_k \left(\frac{\partial M}{\partial x_k}\right)_{T, P, x_{j \neq i,k}} \tag{3-11}$$

Example 3-2 Application of Eq. (3-11) to a binary solution containing species designated 1 and 2 yields particularly simple expressions for the partial molar properties. For such a system, index k can have but a single value, since $k \neq i$. Thus for $i = 1$, $k = 2$, and Eq. (3-11) becomes

$$\bar{M}_1 = M - x_2 \left(\frac{\partial M}{\partial x_2}\right)_{T, P, x_{j \neq 1,2}}$$

Similarly, for $i = 2$, $k = 1$, and

$$\bar{M}_2 = M - x_1 \left(\frac{\partial M}{\partial x_1}\right)_{T, P, x_{j \neq 2,1}}$$

Implicit in these equations is the relation $x_1 + x_2 = 1$. Thus, *at constant T and P* there is but a single independent variable, and the two partial derivatives can be written as ordinary derivatives. Moreover, they are related, because $dx_2 = -dx_1$. Therefore

$$\left(\frac{\partial M}{\partial x_1}\right)_{x_{j \neq 2,1}} = \frac{dM}{dx_1}$$

and

$$\left(\frac{\partial M}{\partial x_2}\right)_{x_{j \neq 1,2}} = \frac{dM}{dx_2} = -\frac{dM}{dx_1}$$

and the equations for $\bar{M}_1$ and $\bar{M}_2$ become

$$\bar{M}_1 = M + x_2 \frac{dM}{dx_1} \tag{3-12a}$$

$$\text{(const } T, P\text{)}$$

$$\bar{M}_2 = M - x_1 \frac{dM}{dx_1} \tag{3-12b}$$

Equations (3-12) are valid for any intensive property M in a binary system.

Example 3-3 Suppose for a given T and P that the composition dependence of M in a binary system is given by

$$M = x_1 M_1 + x_2 M_2 + A x_1 x_2 \tag{A}$$

where M_1 and M_2 are the values of M for pure chemical species 1 and 2 and A is a parameter independent of composition. We wish to develop the expressions for $\bar{M}_1$ and $\bar{M}_2$ which result from Eq. (A).

Since $x_1 + x_2 = 1$, Eq. (A) may be written in various equivalent forms. For example, we may eliminate either x_2 or x_1, yielding the two equations:

$$M = x_1 M_1 + (1 - x_1)M_2 + A x_1(1 - x_1) \tag{B}$$

$$M = (1 - x_2)M_1 + x_2 M_2 + A(1 - x_2)x_2 \tag{C}$$

One may always start with any one of Eqs. (A), (B), or (C).

First, consider direct application of the definition of a partial molar property as given by Eq. (3-3). We choose to start with Eq. (A); to get an expression for nM, we multiply through by n, noting that $n_1 = nx_1$ and $n_2 = nx_2$. Eliminating *all* x_i, one finds

$$nM = n_1 M_1 + n_2 M_2 + A \frac{n_1 n_2}{n} \tag{D}$$

Equation (3-3) with $i = 1$ and $j = 2$ and for constant T and P becomes:

$$\bar{M}_1 = \left[\frac{\partial(nM)}{\partial n_1} \right]_{n_2}$$

Since $n = n_1 + n_2$ and $(\partial n / \partial n_1)_{n_2} = 1$, differentiation of Eq. (D) yields:

$$\bar{M}_1 = M_1 + A n_2 \left(\frac{1}{n} - \frac{n_1}{n^2} \right) = M_1 + A \frac{n_2}{n} \left(1 - \frac{n_1}{n} \right)$$

or

$$\bar{M}_1 = M_1 + A x_2 (1 - x_1) = M_1 + A x_2^2 \tag{E}$$

Similar application of Eq. (3-3) for $i = 2$ and $j = 1$ gives

$$\bar{M}_2 = M_2 + A x_1^2 \tag{F}$$

An alternative means for development of these equations is application of Eqs. (3-12). Again we choose to start with Eq. (A); differentiation gives:

$$\frac{dM}{dx_1} = M_1 + M_2 \frac{dx_2}{dx_1} + A \left(x_2 + x_1 \frac{dx_2}{dx_1} \right)$$

Since $x_1 + x_2 = 1$, $dx_2 / dx_1 = -1$, and we have

$$\frac{dM}{dx_1} = M_1 - M_2 + A(x_2 - x_1) \tag{G}$$

Substitution in Eqs. (3-12) for M by Eq. (A) and for dM/dx_1 by Eq. (G) leads again to Eqs. (E) and (F).

Example 3-4 We illustrate application of Eq. (3-9) by considering a ternary system comprised of species 1, 2, and 3. Suppose that a property M for the solution is given by

$$M = x_1 x_2 A_{12} + x_1 x_3 A_{13} + x_2 x_3 A_{23} + x_1 x_2 x_3 C \tag{A}$$

where A_{12}, A_{13}, A_{23}, and C are parameters independent of the x_i. The summation term in Eq. (3-9) is the same for all values of i; representing this term by Σ, we have for constant T and P:

$$
\left.
\begin{aligned}
\bar{M}_1 &= M + \left(\frac{\partial M}{\partial x_1} \right)_{x_2, x_3} - \Sigma \\[2mm]
\bar{M}_2 &= M + \left(\frac{\partial M}{\partial x_2} \right)_{x_1, x_3} - \Sigma \\[2mm]
\bar{M}_3 &= M + \left(\frac{\partial M}{\partial x_3} \right)_{x_1, x_2} - \Sigma
\end{aligned}
\right\} \tag{B}
$$

where

$$\Sigma = x_1\left(\frac{\partial M}{\partial x_1}\right)_{x_2,\,x_3} + x_2\left(\frac{\partial M}{\partial x_2}\right)_{x_1,\,x_3} + x_3\left(\frac{\partial M}{\partial x_3}\right)_{x_1,\,x_2}$$

We first find expressions for the three partial derivatives from Eq. (A):

$$\left(\frac{\partial M}{\partial x_1}\right)_{x_2,\,x_3} = x_2 A_{12} + x_3 A_{13} + x_2 x_3 C$$

$$\left(\frac{\partial M}{\partial x_2}\right)_{x_1,\,x_3} = x_1 A_{12} + x_3 A_{23} + x_1 x_3 C$$

$$\left(\frac{\partial M}{\partial x_3}\right)_{x_1,\,x_2} = x_1 A_{13} + x_2 A_{23} + x_1 x_2 C$$

From these we find:

$$\Sigma = 2[x_1 x_2 A_{12} + x_1 x_3 A_{13} + x_2 x_3 A_{23} + x_1 x_2 x_3 C] + x_1 x_2 x_3 C$$

or

$$\Sigma = 2M + x_1 x_2 x_3 C$$

Substitution for the derivatives and for Σ in Eqs. (B) leads to:

$$\bar{M}_1 = x_2 A_{12} + x_3 A_{13} + x_2 x_3(1 - x_1)C - M$$

$$\bar{M}_2 = x_1 A_{12} + x_3 A_{23} + x_1 x_3(1 - x_2)C - M$$

$$\bar{M}_3 = x_1 A_{13} + x_2 A_{23} + x_1 x_2(1 - x_3)C - M$$

The same results can of course be obtained when one starts with Eq. (3-11), which for a ternary system at constant T and P provides

$$\bar{M}_1 = M - x_2\left(\frac{\partial M}{\partial x_2}\right)_{x_3} - x_3\left(\frac{\partial M}{\partial x_3}\right)_{x_2}$$

$$\bar{M}_2 = M - x_1\left(\frac{\partial M}{\partial x_1}\right)_{x_3} - x_3\left(\frac{\partial M}{\partial x_3}\right)_{x_1}$$

$$\bar{M}_3 = M - x_1\left(\frac{\partial M}{\partial x_1}\right)_{x_2} - x_2\left(\frac{\partial M}{\partial x_2}\right)_{x_1}$$

These equations include six different derivatives, and in their evaluation use *must* be made of the equation $x_1 + x_2 + x_3 = 1$. Thus, for example,

$$\left(\frac{\partial x_3}{\partial x_1}\right)_{x_2} = -1 \quad \text{and} \quad \left(\frac{\partial x_3}{\partial x_2}\right)_{x_1} = -1$$

We consider here only $\bar{M}_1$; differentiation of Eq. (A) provides the required derivatives:

$$\left(\frac{\partial M}{\partial x_2}\right)_{x_3} = (x_1 - x_2)A_{12} - x_3 A_{13} + x_3 A_{23} + x_3(x_1 - x_2)C$$

$$\left(\frac{\partial M}{\partial x_3}\right)_{x_2} = -x_2 A_{12} + (x_1 - x_3)A_{13} + x_2 A_{23} + x_2(x_1 - x_3)C$$

Substitution into the equation for $\bar{M}_1$ with some algebraic rearrangement gives:

$$\bar{M}_1 = M - x_2(x_1 - x_2 - x_3)A_{12} - x_3(x_1 - x_3 - x_2)A_{13}$$
$$- 2x_2 x_3 A_{23} - x_2 x_3 (2x_1 - x_2 - x_3)C$$

Since $-x_2 - x_3 = x_1 - 1$, this reduces to

$$\bar{M}_1 = M - 2x_1 x_2 A_{12} + x_2 A_{12} - 2x_1 x_3 A_{13}$$
$$+ x_3 A_{13} - 2x_2 x_3 A_{23} - 3x_1 x_2 x_3 C + x_2 x_3 C$$

which with Eq. (A) easily transforms into the expression obtained before.

Data for ternary mixtures are often taken in experiments wherein one starts with a binary mixture of two of the species and adds to it increments of the third species. For example, we might start with a binary mixture of species 1 and 2 and add species 3 to it. Since the quantities of species 1 and 2 do not change during the experiment, the *ratio* of their mole fractions is constant:

$$\frac{n_1}{n_2} = \frac{n_1/n}{n_2/n} = \frac{x_1}{x_2} \equiv r$$

We now develop an expression for $\bar{M}_3$ which is appropriate to this experimental procedure.

For a ternary solution at constant T and P, Eq. (3-4) becomes

$$d(nM) = \bar{M}_1 \, dn_1 + \bar{M}_2 \, dn_2 + \bar{M}_3 \, dn_3$$

For 1 mole of solution, $n = 1$ and $n_i = x_i$; then

$$dM = \bar{M}_1 \, dx_1 + \bar{M}_2 \, dx_2 + \bar{M}_3 \, dx_3 \qquad (C)$$

where we must have

$$x_1 + x_2 + x_3 = 1$$

and

$$dx_1 + dx_2 + dx_3 = 0 \qquad (D)$$

Dividing Eqs. (C) and (D) by dx_3 and restricting the results to constant $r \equiv x_1/x_2$, we get

$$\left(\frac{\partial M}{\partial x_3}\right)_r = \bar{M}_1\left(\frac{\partial x_1}{\partial x_3}\right)_r + \bar{M}_2\left(\frac{\partial x_2}{\partial x_3}\right)_r + \bar{M}_3 \qquad (E)$$

and

$$\left(\frac{\partial x_1}{\partial x_3}\right)_r + \left(\frac{\partial x_2}{\partial x_3}\right)_r + 1 = 0 \qquad (F)$$

From the constraint, $x_1 = rx_2$, it follows that

$$\left(\frac{\partial x_1}{\partial x_3}\right)_r = r\left(\frac{\partial x_2}{\partial x_3}\right)_r \qquad (G)$$

Equations (F) and (G) together yield

$$\left(\frac{\partial x_2}{\partial x_3}\right)_r = \frac{-1}{r+1}$$

and

$$\left(\frac{\partial x_1}{\partial x_3}\right)_r = \frac{-r}{r+1}$$

Substituting $r \equiv x_1/x_2$ in these two equations, we get

$$\left(\frac{\partial x_2}{\partial x_3}\right)_r = \frac{-x_2}{1-x_3}$$

and

$$\left(\frac{\partial x_1}{\partial x_3}\right)_r = \frac{-x_1}{1-x_3}$$

These equations in combination with Eq. (E) give

$$\left(\frac{\partial M}{\partial x_3}\right)_r = \bar{M}_1\left(\frac{-x_1}{1-x_3}\right) + \bar{M}_2\left(\frac{-x_2}{1-x_3}\right) + \bar{M}_3$$

or

$$\left(\frac{\partial M}{\partial x_3}\right)_r = \bar{M}_3 - \frac{x_1\bar{M}_1 + x_2\bar{M}_2}{1-x_3} \tag{H}$$

By Eq. (3-6) for a ternary mixture, we have

$$M = x_1\bar{M}_1 + x_2\bar{M}_2 + x_3\bar{M}_3$$

or

$$x_1\bar{M}_1 + x_2\bar{M}_2 = M - x_3\bar{M}_3$$

Substitution for this expression in Eq. (H) gives

$$\left(\frac{\partial M}{\partial x_3}\right)_r = \bar{M}_3 - \frac{M - x_3\bar{M}_3}{1-x_3}$$

or

$$\bar{M}_3 = M + (1-x_3)\left(\frac{\partial M}{\partial x_3}\right)_r \tag{I}$$

Recalling that $r \equiv x_1/x_2$ and that we have taken T and P constant, we write the more explicit equation:

$$\bar{M}_3 = M + (1-x_3)\left(\frac{\partial M}{\partial x_3}\right)_{T,\,P,\,x_1/x_2} \tag{J}$$

This may be generalized to apply to any of the three species:

$$\bar{M}_i = M + (1-x_i)\left(\frac{\partial M}{\partial x_i}\right)_{T,\,P,\,x_j/x_k}$$

The two constraints, $x_1 = rx_2$ and $x_1 + x_2 + x_3 = 1$, combine to yield

$$x_1 = \frac{r(1-x_3)}{1+r} \tag{K}$$

and

$$x_2 = \frac{1 - x_3}{1 + r} \tag{L}$$

Elimination of x_1 and x_2 from Eq. (A) gives an expression for M as a function of the single independent variable x_3:

$$M = \left(\frac{1 - x_3}{1 + r}\right)\left[\frac{rA_{12}(1 - x_3)}{1 + r} + rA_{13}x_3 + A_{23}x_3 + \frac{rC(x_3 - x_3^2)}{1 + r}\right] \tag{M}$$

If we let Y represent the quantity in brackets, this equation becomes

$$M = \left(\frac{1 - x_3}{1 + r}\right)Y$$

and

$$\left(\frac{\partial M}{\partial x_3}\right)_r = \left(\frac{1 - x_3}{1 + r}\right)\left(\frac{\partial Y}{\partial x_3}\right)_r - \frac{Y}{1 + r}$$

Equation (I) now becomes

$$\bar{M}_3 = \left(\frac{1 - x_3}{1 + r}\right)Y + \frac{(1 - x_3)^2}{1 + r}\left(\frac{\partial Y}{\partial x_3}\right)_r - \frac{(1 - x_3)Y}{1 + r}$$

or

$$\bar{M}_3 = \frac{(1 - x_3)^2}{1 + r}\left(\frac{\partial Y}{\partial x_3}\right)_r \tag{N}$$

Taking the derivative of Y, the term in brackets in Eq. (M), we get

$$\left(\frac{\partial Y}{\partial x_3}\right)_r = -\frac{rA_{12}}{1 + r} + rA_{13} + A_{23} + \frac{rC}{1 + r}(1 - 2x_3)$$

and Eq. (N) becomes

$$\bar{M}_3 = \frac{(1 - x_3)}{1 + r}$$

$$\times \left[-\frac{r(1 - x_3)A_{12}}{1 + r} + r(1 - x_3)A_{13} + (1 - x_3)A_{23} + \frac{r(1 - x_3)C}{1 + r}(1 - 2x_3)\right]$$

Eliminating $r(1 - x_3)/(1 + r)$ by Eq. (K) and $(1 - x_3)/(1 + r)$ by Eq. (L) and setting $r \equiv x_1/x_2$, we get

$$\bar{M}_3 = x_2\left[-x_1 A_{12} + \frac{x_1}{x_2}(1 - x_3)A_{13} + (1 - x_3)A_{23} + x_1(1 - 2x_3)C\right]$$

or

$$\bar{M}_3 = -x_1 x_2 A_{12} + x_1 A_{13} - x_1 x_3 A_{13} + x_2 A_{23} - x_2 x_3 A_{23} + x_1 x_2(1 - 2x_3)C$$

Combining this result with Eq. (A), we get finally

$$\bar{M}_3 = x_1 A_{13} + x_2 A_{23} + x_1 x_2(1 - x_3)C - M$$

the same result previously obtained.

We now make explicit the general system of notation that has been adopted. Since solutions are of primary interest, we represent their molar (or unit-mass) properties by the unadorned symbol M. Solutions are mixtures of chemical species, and their molar (or unit-mass) properties as pure materials are often needed. These pure-species properties are identified by a subscript, and we write M_i. Finally, the symbols for partial molar (or partial specific) properties of species in solution carry an overbar as well as a subscript: $\bar{M}_i$. In summary, we have three kinds of properties:

Solution properties	M:	V, U, H, S, G, etc.
Pure-species properties	M_i:	V_i, U_i, H_i, S_i, G_i, etc.
Partial properties	$\bar{M}_i$:	$\bar{V}_i, \bar{U}_i, \bar{H}_i, \bar{S}_i, \bar{G}_i$, etc.

Equations (3-12) of Example 3-2 are the basis for the classical graphical technique for determination of the $\bar{M}_i$ for a binary system from measurements of M for the mixture. We develop the method by reference to Fig. 3-1, a representative plot of M versus x_1. Here, values of the derivative dM/dx_1 are given by the slopes of lines drawn tangent to the curve of M versus x_1. One such line drawn tangent at a particular value of x_1 is shown on the figure. Its intercepts with the boundaries of the figure at $x_1 = 1$ and $x_1 = 0$ are labeled I_1 and I_2 respectively. It is seen from the figure that two equivalent expressions can be written for the slope of this line:

$$\frac{dM}{dx_1} = \frac{M - I_2}{x_1 - 0} = \frac{M - I_2}{x_1} \quad \text{and} \quad \frac{dM}{dx_1} = \frac{I_1 - I_2}{1 - 0} = I_1 - I_2$$

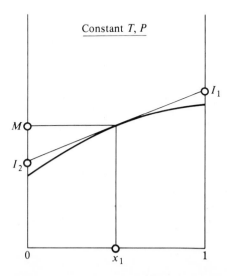

Constant T, P

Figure 3-1 Illustration of the method of tangent intercepts for determination of the partial molar properties $\bar{M}_i$ in a binary solution. By construction, $I_1 = \bar{M}_1$ and $I_2 = \bar{M}_2$.

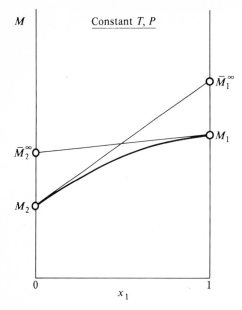

Figure 3-2 Limiting values of the partial molar properties of a binary solution, as given by the method of tangent intercepts. The $\bar{M}_i^\infty$ are partial molar properties at infinite dilution.

Solving for I_1 and I_2, we obtain

$$I_1 = M + (1 - x_1)\frac{dM}{dx_1} \quad \text{and} \quad I_2 = M - x_1\frac{dM}{dx_1}$$

Comparison of these two equations with Eqs. (3-12) gives

$$I_1 = \bar{M}_1 \quad \text{and} \quad I_2 = \bar{M}_2$$

Thus the tangent intercepts give directly the values of the two partial properties. These intercepts of course shift as the point of tangency moves along the curve, and the limiting values are indicated by the constructions shown on Fig. 3-2. The tangent drawn at $x_1 = 0$ (pure component 2) gives $\bar{M}_2 = M_2$, consistent with our earlier conclusion regarding the partial property of a pure material. The opposite intercept gives $\bar{M}_1 = \bar{M}_1^\infty$, the partial property of component 1 when it is present at *infinite dilution* ($x_1 = 0$). Similar comments apply to the tangent drawn at $x_1 = 1$ (pure component 1). In this case $\bar{M}_1 = M_1$ and $\bar{M}_2 = \bar{M}_2^\infty$, since it is component 2 that is present at infinite dilution ($x_2 = 0$).

3-2 THE GIBBS-DUHEM EQUATION

Equation (3-5) is a general expression for nM, valid for any homogeneous PVT system in an equilibrium state:

$$nM = \sum n_i \bar{M}_i \tag{3-5}$$

Differential changes in nM resulting from alteration of T, P, or the n_i are given by the total differential $d(nM)$:

$$d(nM) = \sum \bar{M}_i \, dn_i + \sum n_i \, d\bar{M}_i \qquad (3\text{-}13)$$

Equation (3-4) is an alternative general expression for $d(nM)$. Comparison of these two equations shows that they can both be generally true only if

$$n\left(\frac{\partial M}{\partial T}\right)_{P,x} dT + n\left(\frac{\partial M}{\partial P}\right)_{T,x} dP - \sum n_i \, d\bar{M}_i = 0 \qquad (3\text{-}14)$$

which, after division by n, becomes

$$\boxed{\left(\frac{\partial M}{\partial T}\right)_{P,x} dT + \left(\frac{\partial M}{\partial P}\right)_{T,x} dP - \sum x_i \, d\bar{M}_i = 0} \qquad (3\text{-}15)$$

Equation (3-15) is the most general form of the *Gibbs-Duhem equation*, valid for any molar thermodynamic property M in a homogeneous phase. For example, if M is taken to be the molar enthalpy H, then combination of Eqs. (2-40) and (2-42) with Eq. (3-15) yields the general relation

$$C_p \, dT + \left[V - T\left(\frac{\partial V}{\partial T}\right)_P\right] dP - \sum x_i \, d\bar{H}_i = 0$$

Similar equations are readily derived when M takes on other identities.

The Gibbs-Duhem equation is one of the most important relations of classical solution thermodynamics, for it constrains the allowable composition dependencies of the partial properties. This is most readily seen by examination of the constant-T, P form of Eq. (3-15):

$$\boxed{\sum x_i \, d\bar{M}_i = 0} \qquad \text{(const } T, P) \qquad (3\text{-}16)$$

At constant temperature and pressure, the only variations in the $\bar{M}_i$ are those resulting from changes in composition. Equation (3-16) asserts that these variations are *not independent*, and therefore that $\bar{M}_1$, $\bar{M}_2$, ... are related. Consider for example a binary solution at constant T and P. Equation (3-16) becomes

$$x_1 \, d\bar{M}_1 + x_2 \, d\bar{M}_2 = 0 \qquad \text{(const } T, P) \qquad (3\text{-}17)$$

from which

$$d\bar{M}_2 = -\frac{x_1}{x_2} \, d\bar{M}_1$$

This equation may also be written

$$d\bar{M}_2 = -d\left(\frac{x_1}{x_2}\bar{M}_1\right) + \bar{M}_1 \, d\left(\frac{x_1}{x_2}\right)$$

Expanding the differential of the last term and noting that $x_1 + x_2 = 1$ and $dx_1 = -dx_2$, we get

$$d\bar{M}_2 = -d\left(\frac{x_1}{x_2}\bar{M}_1\right) - \frac{\bar{M}_1}{x_2^2}\,dx_2$$

Integration from $x_2 = 1$, where $x_1 = 0$ and $\bar{M}_2 = M_2$, to any value $0 < x_2 < 1$ yields

$$\bar{M}_2 = M_2 - \frac{x_1}{x_2}\bar{M}_1 - \int_1^{x_2}\frac{\bar{M}_1}{x_2^2}\,dx_2 \tag{3-18}$$

Equation (3-18) illustrates *explicitly* how $\bar{M}_1$ and $\bar{M}_2$ are related for a binary solution at constant T and P. It shows that one cannot arbitrarily impose expressions for the composition dependence of both $\bar{M}_1$ and $\bar{M}_2$; given an expression for one, the other follows from integration of the Gibbs-Duhem equation.

Example 3-5 For a binary system, suppose that

$$\bar{M}_1 = M_1 + Ax_2^2$$

Equation (3-18) is applied to find the corresponding expression for $\bar{M}_2$:

$$\bar{M}_2 = M_2 - \frac{x_1}{x_2}(M_1 + Ax_2^2) + \int_{x_2}^1\frac{M_1 + Ax_2^2}{x_2^2}\,dx_2$$

Integration and reduction lead to

$$\bar{M}_2 = M_2 + Ax_1^2$$

In addition we may find an expression for the solution property M by application of Eq. (3-6):

$$M = x_1\bar{M}_1 + x_2\bar{M}_2 = x_1(M_1 + Ax_2^2) + x_2(M_2 + Ax_1^2)$$

This readily reduces to

$$M = x_1 M_1 + x_2 M_2 + Ax_1 x_2$$

We illustrate several other features of the composition dependence of the $\bar{M}_i$ as imposed by the Gibbs-Duhem equation on a binary solution at constant T and P. For this case there is but a single independent variable, which we take as x_1. Division of Eq. (3-17) by dx_1 gives

$$x_1\frac{d\bar{M}_1}{dx_1} + x_2\frac{d\bar{M}_2}{dx_1} = 0 \tag{3-19}$$

Since the pure-component properties M_1 and M_2 are independent of x_1, and therefore constant for constant T and P, Eq. (3-19) may also be written

$$x_1\frac{d(\bar{M}_1 - M_1)}{dx_1} + x_2\frac{d(\bar{M}_2 - M_2)}{dx_1} = 0 \tag{3-20}$$

We deal with Eq. (3-20), because partial properties for binary systems at constant T and P are most often represented graphically by plots of $\bar{M}_i - M_i$ versus x_1. Equation (3-20) places important restrictions on the shapes that the curves may assume.

First, we note that Eq. (3-20) provides a mathematical relation between the *slopes* of the curves. In particular, since x_1 and x_2 are always positive quantities, it shows that the slopes must be of opposite sign. This feature is satisfied by the representative curves sketched in Fig. 3-3.

The composition extremes $x_1 = 0$ and $x_1 = 1$ are of special interest. First, we note that since $\bar{M}_i = M_i$ for $x_i = 1$, then $\bar{M}_i - M_i = 0$ at this limiting composition. Thus each curve goes to zero as x_i goes to unity. Furthermore, if $d\bar{M}_1/dx_1$ is finite at $x_1 = 0$, then from Eqs. (3-19) and (3-20),

$$\frac{d\bar{M}_2}{dx_1} = \frac{d(\bar{M}_2 - M_2)}{dx_1} = 0 \qquad \text{at } x_1 = 0$$

Similarly, if $d\bar{M}_2/dx_2$ is finite at $x_2 = 0$, i.e., if $d\bar{M}_2/dx_1$ is finite at $x_1 = 1$, then

$$\frac{d\bar{M}_1}{dx_1} = \frac{d(\bar{M}_1 - M_1)}{dx_1} = 0 \qquad \text{at } x_1 = 1$$

For nonelectrolyte solutions, the limiting derivatives $d\bar{M}_i/dx_i$ at $x_i = 0$ *are* finite for most properties M, and for these cases the last two equations require that the $\bar{M}_i - M_i$ curves become tangent to the composition axis at $x_i = 1$. The two curves in Fig. 3-3 conform to this requirement.

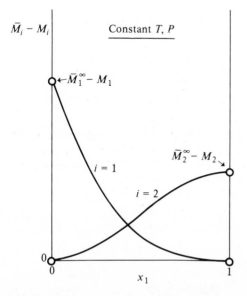

Figure 3-3 Representative plot of $\bar{M}_i - M_i$ versus x_1 for the two species in a binary solution. For the case shown, $\bar{M}_i \geq M_i$ for both species.

A further property of the $\bar{M}_i - M_i$ plot follows from the Gibbs-Duhem equation. Consider the function ΔM, defined as

$$\Delta M \equiv M - x_1 M_1 - x_2 M_2$$

(We will see in Chap. 5 that ΔM is a *property change of mixing.*) Since for a binary solution Eq. (3-6) becomes

$$M = x_1 \bar{M}_1 + x_2 \bar{M}_2$$

this equation may be written:

$$\Delta M = x_1(\bar{M}_1 - M_1) + x_2(\bar{M}_2 - M_2)$$

The total differential of ΔM is

$$d\Delta M = x_1\, d(\bar{M}_1 - M_1) + (\bar{M}_1 - M_1)\, dx_1 + x_2\, d(\bar{M}_2 - M_2) + (\bar{M}_2 - M_2)\, dx_2$$

But $dx_2 = -dx_1$ and, by Eq. (3-20),

$$x_1\, d(\bar{M}_1 - M_1) + x_2\, d(\bar{M}_2 - M_2) = 0$$

Combination of the last two equations gives

$$d\Delta M = [(\bar{M}_1 - M_1) - (\bar{M}_2 - M_2)]\, dx_1$$

Now $\Delta M = 0$ at $x_1 = 0$ and $x_1 = 1$; as a result, we obtain on integrating the last equation from $x_1 = 0$ to $x_1 = 1$ that

$$\int_0^1 [(\bar{M}_1 - M_1) - (\bar{M}_2 - M_2)]\, dx_1 = 0 \qquad (3\text{-}21)$$

or, equivalently,

$$\int_0^1 (\bar{M}_1 - M_1)\, dx_1 = \int_0^1 (\bar{M}_2 - M_2)\, dx_1 \qquad (3\text{-}22)$$

Equation (3-22) requires that the areas under the two $(\bar{M}_i - M_i)$-versus-x_i curves be *equal*, while Eq. (3-21) requires that the net area under a plot of $[(\bar{M}_1 - M_1) - (\bar{M}_2 - M_2)]$ versus x_1 be *zero*.

Equations (3-19) through (3-22) are examples of *thermodynamic consistency requirements* for the partial molar properties $\bar{M}_i$. Such requirements constitute necessary, but not sufficient, conditions for the validity of thermodynamic data. Thus, if both $\bar{M}_1$ and $\bar{M}_2$ are determined for a binary solution at constant T and P, they may be subjected to a "slope test" [Eq. (3-19) or (3-20)] or to an "area test" [Eq. (3-21) or (3-22)]. If data do not satisfy one or more of these tests, they are inconsistent and therefore incorrect. Even if data prove consistent, however, they are not necessarily valid.

Example 3-6 Although independently measured sets of *data* for partial properties may prove inconsistent with respect to the Gibbs-Duhem equation, *expressions* for the $\bar{M}_i$ derived by the methods of Sec. 3-1 from an expression for M must necessarily satisfy this equation. We illustrate this for a binary system at constant T and P.

Equation (3-12) provides expressions for the $\bar{M}_i$:

$$\bar{M}_1 = M + x_2 \frac{dM}{dx_1}$$

$$\bar{M}_2 = M - x_1 \frac{dM}{dx_1}$$

and we wish to show that these expressions satisfy Eq. (3-19):

$$x_1 \frac{d\bar{M}_1}{dx_1} + x_2 \frac{d\bar{M}_2}{dx_1} = 0$$

Performing the differentiations, we find

$$\frac{d\bar{M}_1}{dx_1} = \frac{dM}{dx_1} - \frac{dM}{dx_1} + x_2 \frac{d^2M}{dx_1^2} = x_2 \frac{d^2M}{dx_1^2}$$

$$\frac{d\bar{M}_2}{dx_1} = \frac{dM}{dx_1} - \frac{dM}{dx_1} - x_1 \frac{d^2M}{dx_1^2} = -x_1 \frac{d^2M}{dx_1^2}$$

from which

$$x_1 \frac{d\bar{M}_1}{dx_1} + x_2 \frac{d\bar{M}_2}{dx_1} = x_1 x_2 \frac{d^2M}{dx_1^2} - x_2 x_1 \frac{d^2M}{dx_1^2} = 0$$

as required by the Gibbs-Duhem equation.

Example 3-7 It is possible to define functions $\mathscr{M}_k$ which satisfy the equation

$$M = \sum x_k \mathscr{M}_k \qquad \text{(A)}$$

but which are *not* partial properties with respect to M. If $\mathscr{M}_k$ is a partial property it must of course conform to the definition given by Eq. (3-3). We develop here an alternative criterion which, when satisfied, guarantees that $\mathscr{M}_k = \bar{M}_k$.

Multiplication of Eq. (A) by n and differentiation with respect to a particular mole number n_i in accord with Eq. (3-3) gives

$$\bar{M}_i \equiv \left[\frac{\partial(nM)}{\partial n_i} \right]_{T, P, n_j} = \left[\frac{\partial}{\partial n_i} \left(\sum n_k \mathscr{M}_k \right) \right]_{T, P, n_j}$$

or

$$\bar{M}_i = \mathscr{M}_i + \sum n_k \left(\frac{\partial \mathscr{M}_k}{\partial n_i} \right)_{T, P, n_j} \qquad \text{(B)}$$

If the Gibbs-Duhem equation holds for the functions $\mathscr{M}_k$, we can write

$$\sum n_k \, d\mathscr{M}_k = 0 \qquad \text{(const } T, P)$$

or equivalently

$$\sum n_k \left(\frac{\partial \mathscr{M}_k}{\partial n_i} \right)_{T, P, n_j} = 0$$

But this summation also appears on the right-hand side of Eq. (B), and if it is zero, $\bar{M}_i = \mathscr{M}_i$. Thus we conclude that the $\mathscr{M}_k$ of Eq. (A) can be identified as partial properties only when they satisfy the Gibbs-Duhem equation.

Consider the particular functions for the components of a binary solution defined by

$$\mathscr{M}_1 = M_1 + Ax_2(3x_2 - 1)$$

$$\mathscr{M}_2 = M_2 + Ax_1(3x_1 - 1)$$

Here, A is an empirical constant, and M_1 and M_2 are molar properties of the pure components. For $x_k = 1$, these functions yield $\mathscr{M}_k = M_k$, a necessary attribute of partial molar properties. Moreover, Eq. (A) gives a perfectly reasonable expression for M for a binary mixture (see Example 3-3):

$$\sum x_k \mathscr{M}_k = x_1 M_1 + x_2 M_2 + Ax_1 x_2 \tag{C}$$

However, the $\mathscr{M}_k$ are *not* partial molar properties. An appropriate form of the Gibbs-Duhem equation is given by Eq. (3-19):

$$x_1 \frac{d\bar{M}_1}{dx_1} + x_2 \frac{d\bar{M}_2}{dx_1} = 0$$

Taking derivatives of $\mathscr{M}_1$ and $\mathscr{M}_2$, we get

$$\frac{d\mathscr{M}_1}{dx_1} = -A(6x_2 - 1)$$

and

$$\frac{d\mathscr{M}_2}{dx_1} = A(6x_1 - 1)$$

from which

$$x_1 \frac{d\mathscr{M}_1}{dx_1} + x_2 \frac{d\mathscr{M}_2}{dx_1} = A(x_1 - x_2)$$

The right-hand side of this equation is identically zero for all x_1, as required by Eq. (3-19), *only* for the trivial case $A = 0$. There is only *one* set of partial molar properties consistent with Eq. (C); their derivation was treated in Example 3-3.

Example 3-8 Application of the Gibbs-Duhem equation to solutions containing more than two species becomes progressively more complex as the number of components increases. Consider a ternary solution comprised of species 1, 2, and 3. Equation (3-15) for constant T and P becomes:

$$x_1 \, d\bar{M}_1 + x_2 \, d\bar{M}_2 + x_3 \, d\bar{M}_3 = 0 \tag{A}$$

Since

$$x_1 + x_2 + x_3 = 1$$

the mole fractions are not independent. We can however choose any pair of them as our independent variables. If the choice is x_1 and x_2, we can write:

$$d\bar{M}_1 = \left(\frac{\partial \bar{M}_1}{\partial x_1}\right)_{x_2} dx_1 + \left(\frac{\partial \bar{M}_1}{\partial x_2}\right)_{x_1} dx_2$$

$$d\bar{M}_2 = \left(\frac{\partial \bar{M}_2}{\partial x_1}\right)_{x_2} dx_1 + \left(\frac{\partial \bar{M}_2}{\partial x_2}\right)_{x_1} dx_2$$

$$d\bar{M}_3 = \left(\frac{\partial \bar{M}_3}{\partial x_1}\right)_{x_2} dx_1 + \left(\frac{\partial \bar{M}_3}{\partial x_2}\right)_{x_1} dx_2$$

Substitution of these total differentials into Eq. (A) and rearrangement gives

$$\left[x_1\left(\frac{\partial \bar{M}_1}{\partial x_1}\right)_{x_2} + x_2\left(\frac{\partial \bar{M}_2}{\partial x_1}\right)_{x_2} + x_3\left(\frac{\partial \bar{M}_3}{\partial x_1}\right)_{x_2}\right] dx_1$$

$$+ \left[x_1\left(\frac{\partial \bar{M}_1}{\partial x_2}\right)_{x_1} + x_2\left(\frac{\partial \bar{M}_2}{\partial x_2}\right)_{x_1} + x_3\left(\frac{\partial \bar{M}_3}{\partial x_2}\right)_{x_1}\right] dx_2 = 0$$

Since dx_1 and dx_2 are independent and arbitrary, each of the terms in brackets must be zero; thus

$$\sum x_i\left(\frac{\partial \bar{M}_i}{\partial x_1}\right)_{x_2} = 0$$

and   (B)

$$\sum x_i\left(\frac{\partial \bar{M}_i}{\partial x_2}\right)_{x_1} = 0$$

Similar pairs of equations result for alternative choices of the independent variables. If x_1 and x_3 are taken to be independent, we get

$$\sum x_i\left(\frac{\partial \bar{M}_i}{\partial x_1}\right)_{x_3} = 0$$
                                                                                         (C)
$$\sum x_i\left(\frac{\partial \bar{M}_i}{\partial x_3}\right)_{x_1} = 0$$

and for x_2 and x_3 independent:

$$\sum x_i\left(\frac{\partial \bar{M}_i}{\partial x_2}\right)_{x_3} = 0$$
                                                                                         (D)
$$\sum x_i\left(\frac{\partial \bar{M}_i}{\partial x_3}\right)_{x_2} = 0$$

The Gibbs-Duhem equation is satisfied only when *all* three pairs of equations, Eqs. (B), (C), and (D), prove valid.

In Examples 3-3 and 3-5 we illustrated the application of very simple expressions for the behavior of solution properties, and found the partial properties for binary solutions to be given by

$$\bar{M}_1 = M_1 + Ax_2^2$$

$$\bar{M}_2 = M_2 + Ax_1^2$$

One might propose an extension of these equations to make them applicable to ternary systems; the following set appears reasonable:

$$\bar{M}_1 = M_1 + A_{12}x_2^2 + A_{13}x_3^2$$

$$\bar{M}_2 = M_2 + A_{12}x_1^2 + A_{23}x_3^2$$

$$\bar{M}_3 = M_3 + A_{13}x_1^2 + A_{23}x_2^2$$

Is the Gibbs-Duhem equation satisfied? The first of Eqs. (B) is applied as follows:

$$\left(\frac{\partial \bar{M}_1}{\partial x_1}\right)_{x_2} = 2A_{13}x_3\left(\frac{\partial x_3}{\partial x_1}\right)_{x_2} = -2A_{13}x_3$$

$$\left(\frac{\partial \bar{M}_2}{\partial x_1}\right)_{x_2} = 2A_{12}x_1 + 2A_{23}x_3\left(\frac{\partial x_3}{\partial x_1}\right)_{x_2} = 2A_{12}x_1 - 2A_{23}x_3$$

$$\left(\frac{\partial \bar{M}_3}{\partial x_1}\right)_{x_2} = 2A_{13}x_1$$

and

$$\sum x_i\left(\frac{\partial \bar{M}_i}{\partial x_1}\right)_{x_2} = -2A_{13}x_1x_3 + 2A_{12}x_1x_2 - 2A_{23}x_2x_3 + 2A_{13}x_1x_3$$

$$= 2x_2(A_{12}x_1 - A_{23}x_3)$$

Since this cannot in general be zero, except for the trivial case of $A_{12} = A_{23} = 0$, the Gibbs-Duhem equation is not satisfied, and the original expressions for the $\bar{M}_i$ cannot be valid. No purpose is served by checking the other equations which must also be satisfied.

3-3 THE PARTIAL MOLAR GIBBS FUNCTION

It was shown in Examples 2-5 and 2-6 that the chemical potential μ_i, originally defined as

$$\mu_i \equiv \left[\frac{\partial(nU)}{\partial n_i}\right]_{nS,\, nV,\, n_j} \tag{2-6}$$

could also be given the alternative interpretation

$$\mu_i = \left[\frac{\partial(nG)}{\partial n_i}\right]_{T,\, P,\, n_j} \tag{2-21}$$

But, according to Eq. (3-3), the derivative on the right-hand side of Eq. (2-21) is just the *partial molar Gibbs function* $\bar{G}_i$. Thus we make the important identification that

$$\mu_i \equiv \bar{G}_i \tag{3-23}$$

Referring to Table 2-1, we see that the fourth entry can be written

$$G = \sum x_i\mu_i = \sum x_i\bar{G}_i$$

and, therefore,

$$nG = \sum n_i \bar{G}_i$$

These are, of course, just special cases of Eqs. (3-6) and (3-5); they confirm our earlier interpretation (see Example 2-3) of the chemical potential as representing the contribution of a species to G for a mixture. In addition, Eq. (2-17) and the last entry of Table 2-2 with $\bar{G}_i$ substituted for μ_i become special cases of Eqs. (3-4) and (3-15):

$$\boxed{d(nG) = -nS\,dT + nV\,dP + \sum \bar{G}_i\,dn_i} \qquad (3\text{-}24)$$

and

$$-nS\,dT + nV\,dP - \sum n_i\,d\bar{G}_i = 0$$

Division by n gives

$$\boxed{-S\,dT + V\,dP - \sum x_i\,d\bar{G}_i = 0} \qquad (3\text{-}25)$$

Equation (3-25) is a commonly encountered form of the Gibbs-Duhem equation.

Application of the reciprocity relation for an exact differential to Eq. (3-24) yields Maxwell-type equations, as in Example 2-6, where it was shown that two resulting expressions are

$$\left(\frac{\partial \mu_i}{\partial T}\right)_{P,\,n} = -\left[\frac{\partial(nS)}{\partial n_i}\right]_{T,\,P,\,n_j}$$

$$\left(\frac{\partial \mu_i}{\partial P}\right)_{T,\,n} = \left[\frac{\partial(nV)}{\partial n_i}\right]_{T,\,P,\,n_j}$$

We recognize the derivatives on the right-hand sides of these equations as partial properties. Also, constancy of all mole numbers implies constant composition, and we may write:

$$\left(\frac{\partial \mu_i}{\partial T}\right)_{P,\,x} = -\bar{S}_i \qquad (3\text{-}26)$$

$$\left(\frac{\partial \mu_i}{\partial P}\right)_{T,\,x} = \bar{V}_i \qquad (3\text{-}27)$$

In a *constant-composition solution*, μ_i is a function of T and P. Thus

$$d\mu_i \equiv d\bar{G}_i = \left(\frac{\partial \mu_i}{\partial T}\right)_{P,\,x} dT + \left(\frac{\partial \mu_i}{\partial P}\right)_{T,\,x} dP$$

or, by Eqs. (3-26) and (3-27),

$$d\bar{G}_i = -\bar{S}_i\,dT + \bar{V}_i\,dP \qquad (3\text{-}28)$$

Comparison of Eq. (3-28) with Eq. (2-29)

$$dG = -S\,dT + V\,dP \tag{2-29}$$

provides an example of the parallelism that exists between the equations for constant-composition solutions and for the *components* in a constant-composition solution. This parallelism is developed more fully in the next section.

The Gibbs function can be nondimensionalized by dividing it by RT. Not only is G/RT dimensionless, but it is also a useful thermodynamic property and a function of temperature, pressure, and composition. The function standing in relation to G/RT as a partial molar property is $\bar{G}_i/RT$, or μ_i/RT. Thus Eq. (3-6) applied to these functions becomes

$$\frac{G}{RT} = \sum x_i \frac{\mu_i}{RT} \tag{3-29}$$

In addition Eqs. (3-4) and (3-15) may be written for these functions once the partial derivatives are expressed in terms of measurable quantities. By definition, $G = H - TS$. Thus

$$\frac{G}{RT} = \frac{H}{RT} - \frac{S}{R}$$

Differentiation gives

$$\left[\frac{\partial(G/RT)}{\partial T}\right]_{P,\,x} = \frac{1}{RT}\left(\frac{\partial H}{\partial T}\right)_{P,\,x} - \frac{H}{RT^2} - \frac{1}{R}\left(\frac{\partial S}{\partial T}\right)_{P,\,x}$$

Substitution for $(\partial H/\partial T)_{P,\,x}$ by Eq. (2-40) and for $(\partial S/\partial T)_{P,\,x}$ by Eq. (2-41) reduces this to

$$\boxed{\left[\frac{\partial(G/RT)}{\partial T}\right]_{P,\,x} = -\frac{H}{RT^2}} \tag{3-30}$$

Equation (3-30) is an example of a *Gibbs-Helmholtz equation*. The pressure derivative of G/RT is found similarly. We have

$$\left[\frac{\partial(G/RT)}{\partial P}\right]_{T,\,x} = \frac{1}{RT}\left(\frac{\partial H}{\partial P}\right)_{T,\,x} - \frac{1}{R}\left(\frac{\partial S}{\partial P}\right)_{T,\,x}$$

Substitution for the two derivatives on the right by Eqs. (2-42) and (2-37) reduces this to

$$\left[\frac{\partial(G/RT)}{\partial P}\right]_{T,\,x} = \frac{V}{RT} \tag{3-31}$$

Equations (3-4) and (3-15), with $M \equiv G/RT$, now assume the particular forms

$$\boxed{d\left(\frac{nG}{RT}\right) = -\frac{nH}{RT^2}\,dT + \frac{nV}{RT}\,dP + \sum \frac{\mu_i}{RT}\,dn_i} \tag{3-32}$$

and

$$-\frac{H}{RT^2}\,dT + \frac{V}{RT}\,dP - \sum x_i\,d\!\left(\frac{\mu_i}{RT}\right) = 0 \qquad\qquad (3\text{-}33)$$

Equations (3-32) and (3-33) are *alternatives* to Eqs. (3-24) and (3-25). The utility of such general equations is that they represent most concisely a considerable amount of information. They are easily reduced to specialized cases and provide required partial derivatives and reciprocal relations by visual inspection. For example, applied to a constant-composition solution or to a pure material Eq. (3-32) becomes

$$d\!\left(\frac{G}{RT}\right) = -\frac{H}{RT^2}\,dT + \frac{V}{RT}\,dP \qquad\qquad (3\text{-}34)$$

from which we can recover Eqs. (3-30) and (3-31) by inspection.

3-4 RELATIONS AMONG PARTIAL MOLAR PROPERTIES FOR CONSTANT-COMPOSITION SOLUTIONS

In Chap. 2 we developed a large number of equations relating the molar properties of a constant-composition solution. Analogs of many of these equations exist for the partial properties of a component in a constant-composition solution. In this section we present examples illustrating the development of these analogous equations.

Equation (2-12) provides a definition of the enthalpy H:

$$H \equiv U + PV \qquad\qquad (2\text{-}12)$$

Multiplication by n gives

$$nH = nU + P(nV)$$

and differentiation with respect to n_i at constant T, P, and n_j yields

$$\left[\frac{\partial(nH)}{\partial n_i}\right]_{T,P,n_j} = \left[\frac{\partial(nU)}{\partial n_i}\right]_{T,P,n_j} + P\left[\frac{\partial(nV)}{\partial n_i}\right]_{T,P,n_j}$$

According to Eq. (3-3), the derivatives may be identified with $\bar{H}_i$, $\bar{U}_i$, and $\bar{V}_i$. Thus

$$\bar{H}_i = \bar{U}_i + P\bar{V}_i \qquad\qquad (3\text{-}35)$$

which may be compared with Eq. (2-12). Similar operations on Eqs. (2-13) and (2-14), the defining equations for A and G, yield

$$\bar{A}_i = \bar{U}_i - T\bar{S}_i \qquad\qquad (3\text{-}36)$$

and

$$\bar{G}_i = \bar{H}_i - T\bar{S}_i \tag{3-37}$$

The constant-pressure heat capacity C_P was defined as

$$C_P \equiv \left(\frac{\partial H}{\partial T}\right)_{P,\,x} \tag{2-40}$$

For n moles of constant-composition solution

$$nC_P = \left[\frac{\partial(nH)}{\partial T}\right]_{P,\,x}$$

Differentiation with respect to n_i at constant T, P, and n_j gives

$$\left[\frac{\partial(nC_P)}{\partial n_i}\right]_{T,\,P,\,n_j} = \left|\frac{\partial[\partial(nH)/\partial T]_{P,\,x}}{\partial n_i}\right|_{T,\,P,\,n_j}$$

Since the order of differentiation is immaterial, we may equally well write

$$\left[\frac{\partial(nC_P)}{\partial n_i}\right]_{T,\,P,\,n_j} = \left|\frac{\partial[\partial(nH)/\partial n_i]_{T,\,P,\,n_j}}{\partial T}\right|_{P,\,x}$$

or

$$\bar{C}_{P_i} = \left(\frac{\partial \bar{H}_i}{\partial T}\right)_{P,\,x} \tag{3-38}$$

which may be compared with Eq. (2-40). In a similar fashion it follows from the definition of the constant-volume heat capacity C_V that

$$\bar{C}_{V_i} = \left(\frac{\partial \bar{U}_i}{\partial T}\right)_{V,\,x} \tag{3-39}$$

which may be compared with Eq. (2-49).

We showed in Sec. 3-3 for a constant-composition solution that

$$d\bar{G}_i = -\bar{S}_i \, dT + \bar{V}_i \, dP \tag{3-28}$$

But, by Eqs. (3-35) and (3-37),

$$\bar{G}_i = \bar{U}_i + P\bar{V}_i - T\bar{S}_i$$

from which

$$d\bar{G}_i = d\bar{U}_i + P \, d\bar{V}_i + \bar{V}_i \, dP - T \, d\bar{S}_i - \bar{S}_i \, dT$$

Combination of this expression with Eq. (3-28) gives

$$d\bar{U}_i = T \, d\bar{S}_i - P \, d\bar{V}_i \tag{3-40}$$

Similar elimination of $d\bar{G}_i$ in Eq. (3-28) by Eq. (3-37), and of $d\bar{U}_i$ in Eq. (3-40) by Eq. (3-36), yields the equations

$$d\bar{H}_i = T \, d\bar{S}_i + \bar{V}_i \, dP \tag{3-41}$$

$$d\bar{A}_i = -\bar{S}_i \, dT - P \, d\bar{V}_i \tag{3-42}$$

Equations (3-40), (3-41), (3-42), and (3-28) are analogs of Eqs. (2-26) through (2-29).

The compressibility factor is defined as

$$Z = \frac{PV}{RT} \tag{2-73}$$

For n moles

$$nZ = \frac{P}{RT}(nV)$$

from which

$$\left[\frac{\partial(nZ)}{\partial n_i}\right]_{T,P,n_j} = \frac{P}{RT}\left[\frac{\partial(nV)}{\partial n_i}\right]_{T,P,n_j}$$

Thus

$$\bar{Z}_i = \frac{P\bar{V}_i}{RT} \tag{3-43}$$

which may be compared with Eq. (2-73). The partial compressibility factor is useful for characterizing the volumetric behavior of a component in a gas mixture.

These examples illustrate the fact that many equations relating thermodynamic properties for a *constant-composition* solution have as counterparts analogous equations relating the corresponding partial properties for any component in the solution. Recognition of this parallelism allows us to write down by inspection many equations that relate partial properties. The analogy is valid whenever the solution properties in the parent equation are related *linearly* (in the algebraic sense). The following example treats a thermodynamic relationship for which this is *not* true.

Example 3-9 Consider the *molar density* ρ, defined as the reciprocal of the molar volume V:

$$\rho \equiv \frac{1}{V} \tag{A}$$

Multiplication by n gives

$$n\rho = \frac{n}{V} = \frac{n^2}{nV} \tag{B}$$

We now *define* the partial molar density $\bar{\rho}_i$:

$$\bar{\rho}_i \equiv \left[\frac{\partial(n\rho)}{\partial n_i}\right]_{T,P,n_j} \tag{C}$$

from which, by operation on Eq. (B), we obtain

$$\bar{\rho}_i = \frac{2n}{nV} - \frac{n^2}{(nV)^2}\left[\frac{\partial(nV)}{\partial n_i}\right]_{T,P,n_j}$$

or

$$\bar{\rho}_i = \frac{1}{V}\left(2 - \frac{\bar{V}_i}{V}\right) \qquad (D)$$

Thus the partial molar density, defined by Eq. (C), is related to the partial molar volume $\bar{V}_i$ *and* to the molar volume of the mixture. However,

$$\bar{\rho}_i \neq \frac{1}{\bar{V}_i}$$

as one would obtain by analogy to Eq. (A). The reason is that ρ, by definition, is not related *linearly* to the molar volume V. The density of a mixture is however the mole-fraction-weighted sum of the $\bar{\rho}_i$:

$$\sum x_i \bar{\rho}_i = \frac{1}{V}\left(2 - \frac{\sum x_i \bar{V}_i}{V}\right) = \frac{1}{V}\left(2 - \frac{V}{V}\right) = \frac{1}{V} = \rho$$

This is to be expected, because the quantity $n\rho \equiv n/V$ is a special case of nM and is a homogeneous function of first degree in the mole numbers.

3-5 FUGACITY AND FUGACITY COEFFICIENT: DEFINITIONS

The Gibbs function G is of particular importance in classical thermodynamics because of its unique relation to temperature and pressure through the equation

$$dG^t = -S^t\, dT + V^t\, dP$$

Applied to one mole of a single-phase pure fluid i, this equation becomes

$$dG_i = -S_i\, dT + V_i\, dP$$

and restriction to constant T gives

$$dG_i = V_i\, dP \qquad (\text{const } T) \qquad (3\text{-}44)$$

For an ideal gas, $V_i = V_i' = RT/P$. Thus

$$dG_i' = \frac{RT}{P}\, dP \qquad (\text{const } T)$$

or

$$dG_i' = RT\, d \ln P \qquad (\text{const } T) \qquad (3\text{-}45)$$

Equation (3-45) provides an expression for the effect of pressure on the Gibbs function of an ideal gas. Although valid only for an ideal gas, the simplicity of form of the equation suggests that it would be convenient to replace the pressure P by a new function, which by definition makes the equation *universally* valid. Thus we write

$$dG_i = RT\, d \ln f_i \qquad (\text{const } T) \qquad (3\text{-}46)$$

where f_i, called the *fugacity* of pure i, is a property of i with dimensions of pressure.

Equation (3-46) provides only a partial definition of f_i, for it allows calculation of isothermal *changes* in $\ln f_i$ but not of absolute values. Completion of the definition is realized as follows. For an *isothermal* change of state, Eqs. (3-44) and (3-46) are both valid expressions for dG_i. Equating the right-hand sides of these expressions, we obtain

$$d \ln f_i = \frac{V_i}{RT} dP \qquad (\text{const } T) \qquad (3\text{-}47)$$

Subtraction of the quantity $dP/P \ (\equiv d \ln P)$ from both sides of Eq. (3-47) yields on rearrangement

$$d \ln (f_i/P) = -\frac{1}{RT}\left(\frac{RT}{P} - V_i\right) dP \qquad (\text{const } T)$$

The quantity RT/P is just the ideal-gas molar volume V_i', and the group in parentheses on the right is the *residual volume* $\Delta V_i' \ (\equiv V_i' - V_i)$. Thus we have

$$d \ln (f_i/P) = -\frac{\Delta V_i'}{RT} dP \qquad (\text{const } T) \qquad (3\text{-}48)$$

Integration at constant T from an arbitrary, fixed reference pressure P^* to the actual pressure P gives

$$\ln (f_i/P) = \ln (f_i/P)^* - \frac{1}{RT}\int_{P^*}^{P} \Delta V_i' \, dP \qquad (\text{const } T)$$

The only remaining step is to specify the reference pressure P^* and the value of $\ln (f/P)^*$ at this pressure. The simplest procedure is to set $P^* = 0$ and $(f_i/P)^* = 1$, or $\ln (f_i/P)^* = 0$. Thus we *define*

$$\lim_{P \to 0} (f_i/P) = 1 \qquad (3\text{-}49)$$

as a result of which

$$\ln (f_i/P) = -\frac{1}{RT}\int_{0}^{P} \Delta V_i' \, dP \qquad (\text{const } T) \qquad (3\text{-}50)$$

Equations (3-46) and (3-49) together constitute the *definition* of the fugacity f_i of a pure fluid i, and Eq. (3-50) prescribes how numerical values of f_i may be computed from PVT information for the fluid. The dimensionless group f_i/P is seen to arise naturally in the development of the definition of fugacity; hence it is given a special name and symbol. Thus we define the *fugacity coefficient* ϕ_i of pure i:

$$\phi_i \equiv f_i/P \qquad (3\text{-}51)$$

The residual volume $\Delta V_i'$ of a pure *ideal gas* is identically zero for all temperatures and pressures. Hence, by Eqs. (3-50) and (3-51),

$$\left.\begin{array}{l} f_i = P \\ \phi_i = 1 \end{array}\right\} \quad \text{(ideal gas)} \tag{3-52}$$

Values of f_i and ϕ_i, calculated from experimental data for nitrogen by Eqs. (3-50) and (3-51), are plotted versus pressure in Figs. 3-4 and 3-5, which display several isotherms. Note that, in conformance with Eq. (3-49), f_i approaches the line $f_i = P$ at low pressures, while ϕ_i approaches the limit of unity.

Definitions analogous to that for a pure material can be made for a *solution* and for *a component in solution*. For a solution, one merely deletes the subscript i on f and ϕ:

$$dG = RT \, d \ln f \quad \text{(const } T) \tag{3-53}$$

$$\lim_{P \to 0} (f/P) = 1 \tag{3-54}$$

$$\phi \equiv f/P \tag{3-55}$$

For a component i in solution, we write

$$d\bar{G}_i = RT \, d \ln \hat{f}_i \quad \text{(const } T) \tag{3-56}$$

$$\lim_{P \to 0} (\hat{f}_i / x_i P) = 1 \tag{3-57}$$

$$\hat{\phi}_i \equiv \hat{f}_i / x_i P \tag{3-58}$$

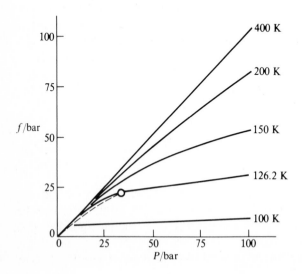

Figure 3-4 Fugacity f versus P for nitrogen. Dashed line is the saturation curve, and the open circle is the critical point.

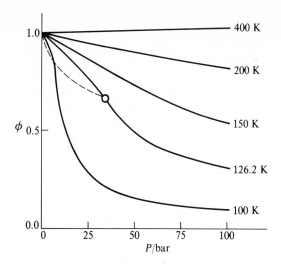

Figure 3-5 Fugacity coefficient ϕ versus P for nitrogen. Curves correspond to those of Fig. 3-4.

In Eqs. (3-56) through (3-58), a special notation designates values of f and ϕ for species in solution: subscript i identifies the component, and the circumflex (ˆ) distinguishes them from pure-fluid properties. An *overbar* is not used here, because, as will be shown, $\hat{f}_i$ and $\hat{\phi}_i$ are not partial properties with respect to f or ϕ.

Equation (3-57), which completes the definition of fugacity for a species in solution, is in some sense analogous to Eq. (3-49), to which it must reduce for the special case of $x_i = 1$. This it clearly does, but so do other expressions, such as $\hat{f}_i/x_i^2 P$ or $\hat{f}_i/P^{x_i}$. Many equations of solution thermodynamics depend on this definition, and its justification is found in the fact that these equations reduce for ideal gases to expressions known to be correct, as is shown in Example 3-10.

The defining equations for the three cases treated are formally similar, and they can be concisely represented by a generalized Gibbs function $\mathscr{G}$, fugacity $\mathscr{F}$, "partial pressure" $\mathscr{P}$, and fugacity coefficient φ. Thus

$$d\mathscr{G} = RT\, d \ln \mathscr{F} \qquad (\text{const } T) \tag{3-59}$$

$$\lim_{P \to 0} (\mathscr{F}/\mathscr{P}) = 1 \tag{3-60}$$

$$\varphi \equiv \mathscr{F}/\mathscr{P} \tag{3-61}$$

The appropriate forms of Eqs. (3-59) through (3-61) are recovered for the three special cases by selection of particular expressions for the generalized variables from Table 3-1.

According to Eqs. (3-60) and (3-61), φ for a real fluid approaches unity in the limit as P approaches zero:

$$\lim_{P \to 0} \varphi = 1 \tag{3-62}$$

Table 3-1 Special cases of the generalized variables appearing in Eqs. (3-59) through (3-64)

Generalized variable	Special case for		
	Pure i	Mixture	i in solution
$\mathscr{G}$	G_i	G	$\bar{G}_i\ (\equiv \mu_i)$
$\mathscr{F}$	f_i	f	$\hat{f}_i$
$\mathscr{P}$	P	P	$x_i P$
φ	ϕ_i	ϕ	$\hat{\phi}_i$

Moreover, we stipulate as a generalization of Eq. (3-52) that φ be *identically* unity for an ideal gas. Thus

$$\left. \begin{array}{r} \mathscr{F} = \mathscr{P} \\ \varphi = 1 \end{array} \right\} \quad \text{(ideal gas)} \tag{3-63}$$

With respect to Eq. (3-59) and its specializations, the restriction to constant temperature must never be overlooked. Within this restriction, the equation merely provides a change of variable, and general integration *at constant T* always gives

$$\Delta \mathscr{G} = RT\ \Delta \ln \mathscr{F} \quad \text{(const } T)$$

or

$$\mathscr{G}(\text{final}) - \mathscr{G}(\text{initial}) = RT \ln \frac{\mathscr{F}(\text{final})}{\mathscr{F}(\text{initial})} \quad \text{(const } T) \tag{3-64}$$

Equation (3-64) is of considerable utility; it allows for both pressure and composition changes, and for changes of physical state.

Example 3-10 The seemingly arbitrary definitions summarized in Eqs. (3-59) and (3-60) and in the entries of Table 3-1 are in fact not arbitrary at all. They are designed to yield as limiting cases expressions known from experiment to be valid for real gases and real-gas mixtures at low pressures. Since the ideal-gas model in many ways approximates real-gas behavior at such conditions, it is useful at this point to apply the results of this and preceding sections to the special case of an ideal-gas mixture. We proceed by first deriving an expression for the partial molar Gibbs function $\bar{G}_i\ (\equiv \mu_i)$ of a species in an ideal-gas mixture.

Integration of Eq. (3-56) at constant T and P from the state of pure i to the state of i in solution gives

$$\bar{G}_i = G_i + RT \ln (\hat{f}_i/f_i) \tag{3-65}$$

Here, we have made the identification for pure i that

$$\hat{f}_i = f_i$$

for, if Eq. (3-56) is to be valid for arbitrary composition, then it must reduce to Eq. (3-46) for $x_i = 1$. Equation (3-65) holds for species i in *any* mixture; restriction to the case of an ideal-gas mixture yields

$$\bar{G}'_i = G'_i + RT \ln \left(\hat{f}'_i / f'_i \right)$$

But by Eq. (3-63) we have that $\hat{f}'_i = x_i P$ and $f'_i = P$. Thus the last equation becomes

$$\bar{G}'_i = G'_i + RT \ln x_i \qquad (A)$$

An expression for $\bar{S}'_i$, the partial molar entropy of a species in an ideal-gas mixture, can be found by application of Eq. (3-26) to Eq. (A). Thus

$$\bar{S}'_i = -\left(\frac{\partial \bar{G}'_i}{\partial T} \right)_{P,\,x} = -\left(\frac{\partial G'_i}{\partial T} \right)_P - R \ln x_i$$

which in view of Eq. (2-33) becomes

$$\bar{S}'_i = S'_i - R \ln x_i \qquad (B)$$

The partial molar enthalpy $\bar{H}'_i$ is found from Eqs. (A) and (B) via Eq. (3-37):

$$\bar{H}'_i = \bar{G}'_i + T\bar{S}'_i = G'_i + RT \ln x_i + TS'_i - RT \ln x_i$$

or

$$\bar{H}'_i = G'_i + TS'_i$$

or

$$\bar{H}'_i = H'_i \qquad (C)$$

Finally, the partial molar volume $\bar{V}'_i$ is found by use of Eq. (3-27) with Eq. (A):

$$\bar{V}'_i = \left(\frac{\partial \bar{G}'_i}{\partial P} \right)_{T,\,x} = \left(\frac{\partial G'_i}{\partial P} \right)_T$$

which, by Eq. (2-32), becomes

$$\bar{V}'_i = V'_i \qquad (D)$$

Equations (A) through (D) provide expressions for partial molar properties of a species in an ideal-gas mixture. Significantly, the partial molar enthalpy and the partial molar volume are equal to the corresponding molar ideal-gas properties for *pure i* at the same temperature and pressure. The same can be shown to be true for the internal energy and the heat capacities. However, even for ideal gases, the partial molar entropy and other quantities related to it by definition depend upon composition.

Expressions for the molar properties of ideal-gas *mixtures* are found by application of Eq. (3-6). Thus, multiplication of Eq. (A) by x_i and summation over all species i gives

$$G' = \sum x_i G'_i + RT \sum x_i \ln x_i \qquad (E)$$

Similarly, we find

$$S' = \sum x_i S_i' - R \sum x_i \ln x_i \tag{F}$$

$$H' = \sum x_i H_i' \tag{G}$$

$$V' = \sum x_i V_i' \tag{H}$$

These equations are known to be valid for ideal gases. Their derivation here depends on the definitions of fugacity, and we therefore conclude that these definitions are justified.

3-6 EQUALITY OF FUGACITIES AS A CRITERION OF PHASE EQUILIBRIUM

In Sec. 2-2 we found that the criterion for phase equilibrium for PVT systems of uniform T and P could be concisely stated by equality of the chemical potentials:

$$\mu_i^\alpha = \mu_i^\beta = \cdots = \mu_i^\pi \qquad (i = 1, 2, \ldots, N) \tag{2-9}$$

Equation (2-9) holds for each component i of an N-component system containing π phases at equilibrium. The relationship between the fugacity $\hat{f}_i$ and the chemical potential μ_i expressed in the definition of Eq. (3-56) allows us to derive an alternative criterion for phase equilibrium which is often of greater practical utility than Eq. (2-9).

We proceed by applying Eq. (3-64) to each component i in each phase p, letting $\mathscr{G} = \bar{G}_i \equiv \mu_i$ and $\mathscr{F} = \hat{f}_i$:

$$\mu_i^p(\text{final}) - \mu_i^p(\text{initial}) = RT \ln \frac{\hat{f}_i^p(\text{final})}{\hat{f}_i^p(\text{initial})} \tag{3-66}$$

Since Eq. (3-66) is valid both for changes in composition and for changes in physical state, we can without loss of generality let the "initial" state be the same for all phases, namely that of component i as it exists in the πth phase at equilibrium conditions. Thus, for $i = 1, 2, \ldots, N$

$$\mu_i^p(\text{initial}) = \mu_i^\pi$$

$$\hat{f}_i^p(\text{initial}) = \hat{f}_i^\pi$$

and Eq. (3-66) yields the following equations for μ_i in each of the phases α through $\pi - 1$:

$$\mu_i^\alpha = \mu_i^\pi + RT \ln \left(\hat{f}_i^\alpha / \hat{f}_i^\pi\right)$$

$$\mu_i^\beta = \mu_i^\pi + RT \ln \left(\hat{f}_i^\beta / \hat{f}_i^\pi\right)$$

$$\vdots \qquad \vdots$$

$$\mu_i^{\pi-1} = \mu_i^\pi + RT \ln \left(\hat{f}_i^{\pi-1} / \hat{f}_i^\pi\right)$$

Substitution of these equations in Eq. (2-9) and rearrangement gives

$$\ln\left(\hat{f}_i^{\alpha}/\hat{f}_i^{\pi}\right) = \ln\left(\hat{f}_i^{\beta}/\hat{f}_i^{\pi}\right) = \cdots = \ln\left(\hat{f}_i^{\pi-1}/\hat{f}_i^{\pi}\right) = 0$$

from which we obtain

$$\boxed{\hat{f}_i^{\alpha} = \hat{f}_i^{\beta} = \cdots = \hat{f}_i^{\pi}} \qquad (i = 1, 2, \ldots, N) \qquad (3\text{-}67)$$

Thus the fugacity $\hat{f}_i$ of a component in a multicomponent, multiphase system must be the same in all phases in which it is present at equilibrium. Equation (3-67) constitutes a major justification for the introduction of the fugacity as a thermodynamic variable, and will be the starting point for many of the applications considered in later chapters.

As an example of a specific application of Eq. (3-67), consider the vapor (v)/liquid (l) equilibrium of a single pure component i. Since for a pure component $\hat{f}_i = f_i$, Eq. (3-67) becomes

$$f_i^l = f_i^v \qquad (3\text{-}68)$$

Now f_i is a property of a pure material, and it depends upon temperature and pressure, which must be uniform throughout both phases at equilibrium. Designating the vapor/liquid equilibrium ("saturation") pressure of pure i by the symbol P_i^{sat}, we can rewrite Eq. (3-68) in the form

$$f_i^l(T, P_i^{\text{sat}}) = f_i^v(T, P_i^{\text{sat}}) \qquad (3\text{-}69)$$

which displays the T and P dependence explicitly. Equation (3-69) is the equation for the *vapor-pressure* curve of a pure substance, and the basis for calculation of vapor/liquid saturation pressures from equations of state.

Example 3-11 We illustrate for pure nitrogen at 100 K the calculation of f and ϕ. For simplicity in this example we omit the usual subscript i. The pressure range considered is from 0 to 25 bar; since the vapor pressure P^{sat} is 7.78 bar for nitrogen at 100 K, the calculations involve both the vapor and liquid states.

The basis for the vapor-phase calculations is Eq. (3-50):

$$\ln\left(f^v/P\right) = \ln \phi^v = -\frac{1}{RT}\int_0^P \Delta V'\, dP \qquad (\text{const } T)$$

An alternative form of this expression, incorporating the compressibility factor Z rather than the residual volume $\Delta V'$, is found from Eq. (2-75):

$$\Delta V' = \frac{RT}{P}(1 - Z)$$

Combination of the last two equations gives

$$\boxed{\ln \phi^v = \int_0^P (Z - 1)\frac{dP}{P}} \qquad (3\text{-}70)$$

Evaluation of $\ln \phi^v$ by Eq. (3-70) requires the availability of a PVT equation of state. The volumetric behavior of nitrogen vapor at 100 K is adequately described by a three-term polynomial in pressure:

$$Z = 1 + B'P + C'P^2$$

Substitution of the equation of state into Eq. (3-70) and integration yields

$$\ln \phi^v = B'P + \frac{C'}{2}P^2 \tag{A}$$

from which, since $f = \phi P$,

$$\ln f^v = \ln P + B'P + \frac{C'}{2}P^2 \tag{B}$$

At 100 K, B' and C' for nitrogen are approximately:

$$B' = -2.01 \times 10^{-2} \text{ bar}^{-1}$$

$$C' = -3.5 \times 10^{-4} \text{ bar}^{-2}$$

Use of these numerical values with Eqs. (A) and (B) provides values for ϕ and f for the vapor phase.

The above procedure takes us to $P^{sat} = 7.78$ bar, above which pressure nitrogen is liquid at 100 K. According to Eq. (3-69), at the saturation conditions of 100 K and 7.78 bar,

$$f^l(T, P^{sat}) = f^v(T, P^{sat}) = f^{sat}$$

and similarly

$$\phi^l(T, P^{sat}) = \phi^v(T, P^{sat}) = \phi^{sat}$$

Thus the vapor and liquid branches of the ϕ-versus-P and f-versus-P curves are *continuous* at P^{sat}, and f^{sat} and ϕ^{sat} calculated for the vapor phase can be used as reference values for calculation of liquid-phase quantities. For this purpose, it is conventional to use Eq. (3-47):

$$d \ln f^l = \frac{V^l}{RT} dP \qquad (\text{const } T)$$

from which, integrating between P^{sat} and P, we obtain

$$\boxed{\ln (f^l/f^{sat}) = \frac{1}{RT} \int_{P^{sat}}^{P} V^l \, dP} \tag{3-71}$$

Again we require an equation of state, this time for the liquid phase. At 100 K, molar volumes for liquid nitrogen up to about 100 bar are adequately represented by a three-term polynomial in pressure:

$$V^l = a + bP + cP^2$$

Here, a, b, and c are empirical constants:

$$a = 40.87 \text{ cm}^3 \text{ mol}^{-1}$$

$$b = -3.47 \times 10^{-2} \text{ cm}^3 \text{ mol}^{-1} \text{ bar}^{-1}$$

$$c = 8.84 \times 10^{-5} \text{ cm}^3 \text{ mol}^{-1} \text{ bar}^{-2}$$

Substitution of this equation into Eq. (3-71) gives on integration:

$$\ln f^l = \ln f^{sat} + \frac{1}{RT}\left\{ a(P - P^{sat}) + \frac{b}{2}[P^2 - (P^{sat})^2] \right.$$

$$\left. + \frac{c}{3}[P^3 - (P^{sat})^3] \right\}$$
(C)

The fugacity coefficient is then found from

$$\phi^l = f^l/P$$
(D)

The values calculated from Eqs. (A), (B), (C), and (D) are plotted as functions of P in Fig. 3-6. For comparison, three common approximations are indicated by dashed lines. The first, labeled $\phi^v = 1$ and $f^v = P$, represents the assumption of an ideal gas. For nitrogen vapor at 100 K, this leads to increasing error with increasing pressure up to the saturation pressure, where it is about 18 percent.

The second approximation, which is a natural extension of the first to the liquid state, is based on the assumption that $f^l = P^{sat}$ at the saturation pressure and at all higher pressures. For the pressure range considered here, this leads to errors between 10 and 18 percent in both f^l and ϕ^l.

The third common approximation rests on the assumption that $f^l = f^{sat}$ at the saturation pressure and at all higher pressures. This assumption leads to much smaller errors than the second, giving in this case a maximum error of seven percent at 25 bar. With respect to Eq. (3-71), this assumption is realized by taking the liquid molar volume equal to zero. A much better approximation is to take V^l equal to its

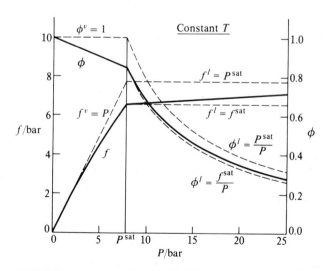

Figure 3-6 Fugacity and fugacity coefficient for nitrogen at 100 K and moderate pressure. Dashed lines represent various approximations to true behavior. (See Example 3-11 for discussion.)

value at saturation, not only at P^{sat}, but at all higher pressures. For the present case, V^l at saturation is 40.61 cm^3 mol^{-1}, and use of this value with the equation

$$\ln (f^l/f^{sat}) = \frac{V^l(sat)}{RT}(P - P^{sat})$$

results in a maximum error in f^l of only 0.1%, at 25 bar.

3-7 DEPENDENCE OF MIXTURE FUGACITY AND FUGACITY COEFFICIENT ON T, P, AND COMPOSITION

Fugacity and fugacity coefficient are thermodynamic properties, and thus depend on temperature, pressure, and composition. Moreover, it is apparent from the material of the preceding section that the *natural logarithms* of f and ϕ, rather than f and ϕ themselves, are the thermodynamically significant functions of these properties. We therefore develop in this section general expressions of the form of Eqs. (3-4) and (3-15), with $M = \ln f$ and $M = \ln \phi$. What is required are expressions for the temperature and pressure derivatives of $\ln f$ and $\ln \phi$, and identification of what quantities stand in relation to $\ln f$ and $\ln \phi$ as partial molar properties. We treat the last item first.

By Eq. (3-53), for a mixture,

$$dG = RT\, d \ln f \quad \text{(const } T)$$

Integration at constant T, P, and composition from the ideal-gas state (for which $f = f' = P$) to the state of the real fluid gives

$$G - G' = RT \ln f - RT \ln P \tag{3-72}$$

For n moles of fluid

$$nG - nG' = RT(n \ln f) - nRT \ln P$$

Differentiation with respect to n_i at constant T, P, and n_j then yields

$$\left[\frac{\partial(nG)}{\partial n_i}\right]_{T,P,n_j} - \left[\frac{\partial(nG')}{\partial n_i}\right]_{T,P,n_j} = RT\left[\frac{\partial(n \ln f)}{\partial n_i}\right]_{T,P,n_j} - RT \ln P$$

or

$$\bar{G}_i - \bar{G}_i' = RT\left[\frac{\partial(n \ln f)}{\partial n_i}\right]_{T,P,n_j} - RT \ln P \tag{3-73}$$

An alternative expression for $\bar{G}_i - \bar{G}_i'$ is found by direct integration of Eq. (3-56) from the ideal-gas state (for which $\hat{f}_i = \hat{f}_i' = x_i P$) to the state of species i in the real solution:

$$\bar{G}_i - \bar{G}_i' = RT \ln \hat{f}_i - RT \ln x_i P$$

or

$$\bar{G}_i - \bar{G}_i' = RT \ln (\hat{f}_i/x_i) - RT \ln P \tag{3-74}$$

Comparison of Eqs. (3-73) and (3-74) shows that

$$\ln \frac{\hat{f}_i}{x_i} = \left[\frac{\partial (n \ln f)}{\partial n_i} \right]_{T, P, n_j} \tag{3-75}$$

The right-hand side of Eq. (3-75) is recognized as defining a partial molar property. *Thus* $\ln (\hat{f}_i/x_i)$ *stands in relation to* $\ln f$ *as a partial molar property.* Obviously, $\hat{f}_i$ cannot also be related to f as a partial molar property; hence we use the circumflex on $\hat{f}_i$. Since $\bar{M}_i = \ln (\hat{f}_i/x_i)$ for $M = \ln f$, we can write immediately by Eq. (3-6) that

$$\ln f = \sum x_i \ln \frac{\hat{f}_i}{x_i} \tag{3-76}$$

Equations analogous to Eqs. (3-75) and (3-76) are readily determined for the fugacity coefficient. By the definitions of ϕ and $\hat{\phi}_i$, Eqs. (3-55) and (3-58), we have

$$n \ln f = n \ln \phi P = n \ln \phi + n \ln P$$

and

$$\ln (\hat{f}_i/x_i) = \ln \hat{\phi}_i P = \ln \hat{\phi}_i + \ln P$$

Substitution of the last two expressions into Eq. (3-75) gives

$$\ln \hat{\phi}_i = \left[\frac{\partial (n \ln \phi)}{\partial n_i} \right]_{T, P, n_j} \tag{3-77}$$

Thus $\ln \hat{\phi}_i$ *stands in relation to* $\ln \phi$ *as a partial molar property.* Equation (3-6) then becomes, with $M = \ln \phi$ and $\bar{M}_i = \ln \hat{\phi}_i$,

$$\ln \phi = \sum x_i \ln \hat{\phi}_i \tag{3-78}$$

We now seek expressions for the temperature and pressure derivatives of $\ln f$ and $\ln \phi$. Solution of Eq. (3-72) for $\ln f$ gives

$$\ln f = \frac{G}{RT} - \frac{G'}{RT} + \ln P$$

from which

$$\left(\frac{\partial \ln f}{\partial T} \right)_{P, x} = \left[\frac{\partial (G/RT)}{\partial T} \right]_{P, x} - \left[\frac{\partial (G'/RT)}{\partial T} \right]_{P, x}$$

By the Gibbs-Helmholtz equation, Eq. (3-30), this becomes

$$\left(\frac{\partial \ln f}{\partial T} \right)_{P, x} = - \frac{H}{RT^2} + \frac{H'}{RT^2}$$

or, introducing the residual enthalpy $\Delta H' \equiv H' - H$,

$$\left(\frac{\partial \ln f}{\partial T}\right)_{P,x} = \frac{\Delta H'}{RT^2} \tag{3-79}$$

Since $\ln \phi = \ln f - \ln P$, a similar equation holds for the fugacity coefficient:

$$\left(\frac{\partial \ln \phi}{\partial T}\right)_{P,x} = \frac{\Delta H'}{RT^2} \tag{3-80}$$

The pressure derivatives are most easily found from the defining equation for f, Eq. (3-53). For a constant-composition solution

$$dG = RT \, d \ln f \quad (\text{const } T, x)$$

But by Eq. (2-29) we can also write

$$dG = V \, dP \quad (\text{const } T, x)$$

Combination of these two equations gives

$$d \ln f = \frac{V}{RT} \, dP \quad (\text{const } T, x)$$

from which

$$\left(\frac{\partial \ln f}{\partial P}\right)_{T,x} = \frac{V}{RT} \tag{3-81}$$

Since $\ln \phi = \ln f - \ln P$, we then have for the fugacity coefficient

$$\left(\frac{\partial \ln \phi}{\partial P}\right)_{T,x} = \frac{V}{RT} - \frac{d \ln P}{dP} = \frac{V}{RT} - \frac{1}{P} = -\frac{1}{RT}\left(\frac{RT}{P} - V\right)$$

But RT/P is just the ideal-gas molar volume V'. Thus

$$\left(\frac{\partial \ln \phi}{\partial P}\right)_{T,x} = -\frac{\Delta V'}{RT} \tag{3-82}$$

When applied to the special case of a pure species, Eqs. (3-81) and (3-82) are equivalent to Eqs. (3-47) and (3-48).

We are now able to write down the specializations of Eq. (3-4) appropriate for $M = \ln f$ and $M = \ln \phi$. By Eqs. (3-79) and (3-81), with $\bar{M}_i = \ln (\hat{f}_i/x_i)$, we find

$$\boxed{d(n \ln f) = \frac{n\Delta H'}{RT^2} \, dT + \frac{nV}{RT} \, dP + \sum \left(\ln \frac{\hat{f}_i}{x_i}\right) dn_i} \tag{3-83}$$

Similarly, by Eqs. (3-80) and (3-82), with $\bar{M}_i = \ln \hat{\phi}_i$,

$$\boxed{d(n \ln \phi) = \frac{n\Delta H'}{RT^2} \, dT - \frac{n\Delta V'}{RT} \, dP + \sum (\ln \hat{\phi}_i) \, dn_i} \tag{3-84}$$

Specializations of the Gibbs-Duhem equation, Eq. (3-15), also follow immediately. Thus, for $M = \ln f$,

$$\frac{\Delta H'}{RT^2} dT + \frac{V}{RT} dP - \sum x_i \, d \ln \frac{\hat{f}_i}{x_i} = 0 \qquad (3\text{-}85a)$$

Since

$$\sum x_i \, d \ln \frac{\hat{f}_i}{x_i} = \sum x_i \, d \ln \hat{f}_i - \sum x_i \, d \ln x_i$$

and since

$$\sum x_i \, d \ln x_i = \sum x_i \left(\frac{dx_i}{x_i} \right) = 0$$

an alternative form of Eq. (3-85a) is

$$\frac{\Delta H'}{RT^2} dT + \frac{V}{RT} dP - \sum x_i \, d \ln \hat{f}_i = 0 \qquad (3\text{-}85b)$$

For $M = \ln \phi$, the Gibbs-Duhem equation becomes

$$\frac{\Delta H'}{RT^2} dT - \frac{\Delta V'}{RT} dP - \sum x_i \, d \ln \hat{\phi}_i = 0 \qquad (3\text{-}86)$$

For a *constant-composition solution*, the methods of Example 2-4 applied to Eqs. (3-83) and (3-84) yield the expressions

$$d \ln f = \frac{\Delta H'}{RT^2} dT + \frac{V}{RT} dP \qquad (3\text{-}87)$$

and

$$d \ln \phi = \frac{\Delta H'}{RT^2} dT - \frac{\Delta V'}{RT} dP \qquad (3\text{-}88)$$

Reference to Sec. 3-4 reveals that Eqs. (3-87) and (3-88) are of a form which permits the writing down by inspection of analogous equations for the partial molar properties $\ln (\hat{f}_i/x_i)$ and $\ln \hat{\phi}_i$. Thus, analogous to Eq. (3-87), we have for species i in a constant-composition solution

$$d \ln \frac{\hat{f}_i}{x_i} = \frac{\overline{\Delta H_i'}}{RT^2} dT + \frac{\overline{V}_i}{RT} dP$$

But if composition is constant, then $d \ln (\hat{f}_i/x_i) = d \ln \hat{f}_i$. Moreover,

$$\overline{\Delta H_i'} = \overline{H}_i' - \overline{H}_i$$

and, as shown in Example (3-10), $\bar{H}_i = H'_i$. Therefore, for a *constant-composition solution*,

$$d \ln \frac{\hat{f}_i}{x_i} = d \ln \hat{f}_i = \frac{H'_i - \bar{H}_i}{RT^2} dT + \frac{\bar{V}_i}{RT} dP \tag{3-89}$$

Similarly, since $\overline{\Delta V'_i} = \bar{V}'_i - \bar{V}_i$ and $\bar{V}'_i = V'_i$, we have analogous to Eq. (3-88) for a *constant-composition solution* that

$$d \ln \hat{\phi}_i = \frac{H'_i - \bar{H}_i}{RT^2} dT - \frac{V'_i - \bar{V}_i}{RT} dP \tag{3-90}$$

Given Eqs. (3-89) and (3-90), one may determine by inspection expressions for the temperature and pressure derivatives of $\ln \hat{f}_i$ and $\ln \hat{\phi}_i$. Thus we find from Eq. (3-89) that

$$\left[\frac{\partial \ln (\hat{f}_i/x_i)}{\partial T} \right]_{P, x} = \left(\frac{\partial \ln \hat{f}_i}{\partial T} \right)_{P, x} = \frac{H'_i - \bar{H}_i}{RT^2} \tag{3-91}$$

$$\left[\frac{\partial \ln (\hat{f}_i/x_i)}{\partial P} \right]_{T, x} = \left(\frac{\partial \ln \hat{f}_i}{\partial P} \right)_{T, x} = \frac{\bar{V}_i}{RT} \tag{3-92}$$

and from Eq. (3-90) that

$$\left(\frac{\partial \ln \hat{\phi}_i}{\partial T} \right)_{P, x} = \frac{H'_i - \bar{H}_i}{RT^2} \tag{3-93}$$

$$\left(\frac{\partial \ln \hat{\phi}_i}{\partial P} \right)_{T, x} = - \frac{V'_i - \bar{V}_i}{RT} \tag{3-94}$$

3-8 COMPOSITION DEPENDENCE OF FUGACITY: THERMODYNAMIC INSIGHTS

A major use of fugacity is in the formulation and solution of problems in phase- and chemical-reaction equilibria. In such problems, it is often the *composition* of an equilibrium phase that is sought; this obviously requires knowledge of the functional dependence of the component fugacities $\hat{f}_i$ on composition of the phase. Although any such detailed knowledge must ultimately come from experiment, thermodynamics does impose constraints on the nature of the composition dependence. Our purpose here is to develop these constraints and to present some qualitative features of the composition dependence of the $\hat{f}_i$ that lead in later chapters to the definition of additional functions, such as the *activity coefficient* and the *excess Gibbs function*, which greatly facilitate the treatment of experimental data.

For simplicity, we consider here only a binary solution at constant temperature and pressure. Figures 3-1 and 3-2 illustrate the composition dependence of the general property M for such systems. As shown in the preceding section, when $M = \ln f$, $\bar{M}_i = \ln (\hat{f}_i/x_i)$, and then the tangent intercepts of Figs. 3-1 and 3-2 represent $\ln (\hat{f}_i/x_i)$. Consider in particular the limiting tangent drawn at $x_1 = 0$ on Fig. 3-2. Here

$$\lim_{x_1 \to 0} \bar{M}_1 = \bar{M}_1^{\infty}$$

which for the fugacity becomes

$$\lim_{x_1 \to 0} \ln \frac{\hat{f}_1}{x_1} = \ln k_1$$

where the limiting intercept $\bar{M}_1^{\infty}$ is represented by $\ln k_1$. We may equally well write

$$\lim_{x_1 \to 0} \left(\frac{\hat{f}_1}{x_1} \right) = k_1$$

Since an analogous equation applies to component 2 in a binary solution, we have

$$\lim_{x_i \to 0} \left(\frac{\hat{f}_i}{x_i} \right) = k_i \qquad (i = 1, 2)$$

If, as indicated by experiment, k_i is finite when $x_i \to 0$, then we must also have $\hat{f}_i \to 0$ when $x_i \to 0$. Thus, the ratio $(\hat{f}_i/x_i)$ is indeterminate in this limit, and application of l'Hôpital's rule yields

$$\lim_{x_i \to 0} \left(\frac{\hat{f}_i}{x_i} \right) = \left(\frac{d\hat{f}_i}{dx_i} \right)_{x_i=0} = k_i \tag{3-95}$$

Equation (3-95) states *Henry's law*, and k_i is known as *Henry's constant*. It expresses the thermodynamic requirement that $\hat{f}_i$ become zero at $x_i = 0$ and establishes the limiting slope of a $\hat{f}_i$-versus-x_i curve as k_i.

Consider now the limiting tangent drawn at $x_1 = 1$ in Fig. 3-2, for which

$$\lim_{x_1 \to 1} \bar{M}_1 = M_1$$

For the fugacity, this becomes

$$\lim_{x_1 \to 1} \ln \frac{\hat{f}_1}{x_1} = \ln f_1$$

or

$$\lim_{x_1 \to 1} \left(\frac{\hat{f}_1}{x_1} \right) = f_1$$

An additional requirement applying at the limiting composition $x_1 \to 1$ follows from the Gibbs-Duhem equation. At constant T and P Eq. (3-85b) written for a binary solution and divided through by dx_1 becomes

$$x_1 \frac{d \ln \hat{f}_1}{dx_1} + x_2 \frac{d \ln \hat{f}_2}{dx_1} = 0 \tag{3-96}$$

or

$$\frac{d\hat{f}_1}{dx_1} = -\frac{x_2 \hat{f}_1}{x_1 \hat{f}_2} \frac{d\hat{f}_2}{dx_1}$$

Substituting $dx_1 = -dx_2$ on the right, we get

$$\frac{d\hat{f}_1}{dx_1} = \frac{(\hat{f}_1/x_1)}{(\hat{f}_2/x_2)} \frac{d\hat{f}_2}{dx_2}$$

In the limit as $x_1 \rightarrow 1$ and $x_2 \rightarrow 0$, we have

$$\left(\frac{d\hat{f}_1}{dx_1}\right)_{x_1=1} = \frac{\lim_{x_1 \to 1}(\hat{f}_1/x_1)}{\lim_{x_2 \to 0}(\hat{f}_2/x_2)}\left(\frac{d\hat{f}_2}{dx_2}\right)_{x_2=0}$$

As a result of Eq. (3-95) applied to component 2, this becomes

$$\left(\frac{d\hat{f}_1}{dx_1}\right)_{x_1=1} = \lim_{x_1 \to 1}\left(\frac{\hat{f}_1}{x_1}\right) = f_1$$

Since an analogous derivation holds for component 2 in a binary solution, we write

$$\left(\frac{d\hat{f}_i}{dx_i}\right)_{x_i=1} = \lim_{x_i \to 1}\left(\frac{\hat{f}_i}{x_i}\right) = f_i \tag{3-97}$$

Equation (3-97) states what is known as the *Lewis-Randall rule*. It expresses the thermodynamic requirement that both $\hat{f}_i$ and its derivative with respect to x_i become equal to the fugacity of pure i in the limit as $x_i \rightarrow 1$.

Equations (3-95) and (3-97) are formally similar, but k_i and f_i are experimentally determined values, generally found not to be equal. Both equations, if assumed valid over the entire composition range instead of just at the appropriate limit, represent straight lines on a plot of $\hat{f}_i$ versus x_i, and are shown as dashed lines on Fig. 3-7. The thermodynamic constraints just developed require the $\hat{f}_i$-versus-x_i curve for a fluid to become tangent to these two lines as shown in the figure. The nature of the curve between these limits must be found by experiment. We note, however, that owing to the logarithmic functionality in the defining equations, fugacities are always positive. Moreover, there is a thermodynamic requirement, presented in Sec. 6-10, that the slope $d\hat{f}_i/dx_i$ be everywhere positive for any stable fluid.

The straight (dashed) lines of Fig. 3-7, representing Henry's law and the Lewis-Randall rule, may be expressed in equation form as

$$\boxed{\hat{f}_i(HL) = k_i x_i} \tag{3-98}$$

and

$$\boxed{\hat{f}_i(LR) = f_i x_i} \tag{3-99}$$

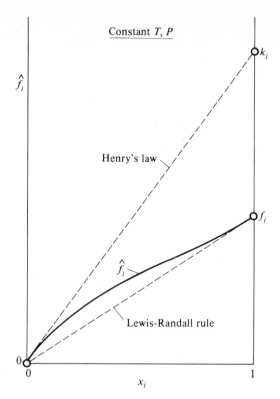

Figure 3-7 Composition dependence of $\hat{f}_i$ for species i in a binary solution.

These *idealizations* clearly do not in general provide accurate representations of the composition dependence of $\hat{f}_i$ over a wide range of mole fractions. However, they are satisfactory approximations for solutions sufficiently dilute or concentrated in species i. Moreover, we will see in Chap. 5 that the concept of an *ideal solution*, inspired by Eqs. (3-98) and (3-99), plays a central role in development of methods for concise representation of the properties of real solutions.

The $\hat{f}_i$-versus-x_i curve of Fig. 3-7 may have various shapes within the thermodynamic constraints described. The value of k_i may be less than that of f_i, in which case the $\hat{f}_i$-versus-x_i curve would be concave upward at the left end. However, once the curve is fixed for one component in a binary solution at constant T and P, then the composition dependence of $\hat{f}_i$ for the other component can be determined to within an additive constant by the Gibbs-Duhem equation. Thus if the curve of Fig. 3-7 holds for species 1 ($i = 1$), the corresponding curve for species 2 must follow from it, given a value for the constant f_2.

Example 3-12 The $\hat{f}_i$-versus-x_i curve of Fig. 3-7 actually represents the $\hat{f}_1$-versus-x_1 relation generated from the equation

$$\hat{f}_1 = x_1 \exp\,(0.25 + 0.75x_2^2) \tag{A}$$

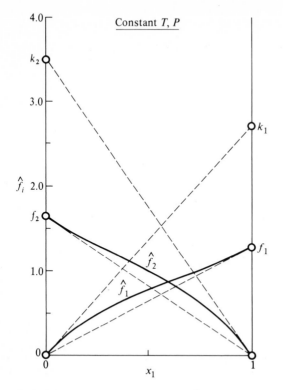

Figure 3-8 Composition dependence of $\hat{f}_i$ for the two species in a binary solution. The basis for the numerical values is described in Example 3-12.

and this relation is reproduced in Fig. 3-8 as the curve for species 1. Numerical values for k_1 and f_1 are found by application of Eqs. (3-95) and (3-97):

$$k_1 = \lim_{x_1 \to 0} \frac{\hat{f}_1}{x_1} = \exp(1.00) = 2.72$$

$$f_1 = \lim_{x_1 \to 1} \frac{\hat{f}_1}{x_1} = \exp(0.25) = 1.28$$

No particular units are presumed here, but k_1, f_1, and $\hat{f}_1$ all have dimensions of pressure, and could well be bars.

We wish now to find the expression for $\hat{f}_2$ corresponding to Eq. (A) through integration of the Gibbs-Duhem equation as given by Eq. (3-96), which may be written

$$\frac{d \ln (\hat{f}_2/x_2)}{dx_1} = \frac{x_1}{x_2} \frac{d \ln (\hat{f}_1/x_1)}{dx_2} \tag{B}$$

By Eq. (A)

$$\ln (\hat{f}_1/x_1) = 0.25 + 0.75x_2^2$$

and

$$\frac{d \ln \left(\hat{f}_1/x_1\right)}{dx_2} = 1.50x_2$$

Substitution in Eq. (B) gives

$$\frac{d \ln \left(\hat{f}_2/x_2\right)}{dx_1} = 1.50x_1$$

and integration yields

$$\ln \left(\hat{f}_2/x_2\right) = 0.75x_1^2 + \text{const}$$

The constant of integration is found from the value of $\ln \left(\hat{f}_2/x_2\right)$ at $x_2 = 1$ and $x_1 = 0$:

$$\text{const} = \lim_{x_2 \to 1} \ln \left(\hat{f}_2/x_2\right) = \ln f_2$$

and one must have an experimental value for f_2. For purposes of this example, we arbitrarily set $f_2 = 1.65$, which makes the integration constant 0.50. Thus for species 2

$$\ln \left(\hat{f}_2/x_2\right) = 0.50 + 0.75x_1^2$$

and

$$\hat{f}_2 = x_2 \exp \left(0.50 + 0.75x_1^2\right) \tag{C}$$

The curve of Fig. 3-8 for species 2 represents Eq. (C). Henry's constant k_2 is evaluated by Eq. (3-95):

$$k_2 = \lim_{x_2 \to 0} \frac{\hat{f}_2}{x_2} = \exp \left(1.25\right) = 3.49$$

Given expressions for $\hat{f}_1$ and $\hat{f}_2$, one can also find the expression for the mixture fugacity f. By Eq. (3-76)

$$\ln f = x_1 \ln \frac{\hat{f}_1}{x_1} + x_2 \ln \frac{\hat{f}_2}{x_2} \tag{D}$$

Combination of Eqs. (A), (C), and (D) gives, after reduction,

$$\ln f = 0.25x_1 + 0.50x_2 + 0.75x_1 x_2$$

This example is just an illustration for a specific property of the treatment given in Example 3-5.

FOUR

BEHAVIOR OF REAL FLUIDS

The previous chapters were devoted to the development of a large number of definitions and equations. The ultimate application of these results is to the analysis and design of chemical and physical processes. However, *numbers* are required for practical calculations, and classical thermodynamics provides no numerical values for thermodynamic properties. Such values must come from experiment, or from the correlated results of experimental measurements. We therefore describe in this chapter some methods used for representation of real-fluid volumetric behavior, and illustrate by example the determination of derived properties from PVT equations of state. The emphasis is on the properties of pure fluids and of mixtures of gases; Chap. 5 deals with methods used for representation of the properties of liquid solutions.

4-1 SOLIDS, LIQUIDS, GASES, VAPORS, AND FLUIDS

The relationship of specific or molar volume to temperature and pressure for a pure substance in equilibrium states can be represented by a PVT surface in three dimensions, as shown in Fig. 4-1. This figure, not drawn to scale, is representative of substances which expand on melting. Portions of the surface labeled S, L, and G correspond to states of *single-phase* equilibrium of solid, liquid, or gas. Portions of the surface labeled with a pair of letters (S/L, S/G, and L/G) are regions of coexistence of *two* phases in equilibrium. Heavy lines separate the various regions and form boundaries of the parts of the surface representing individual phases. The heavy curve passing through points *A*, *B*, and *C*

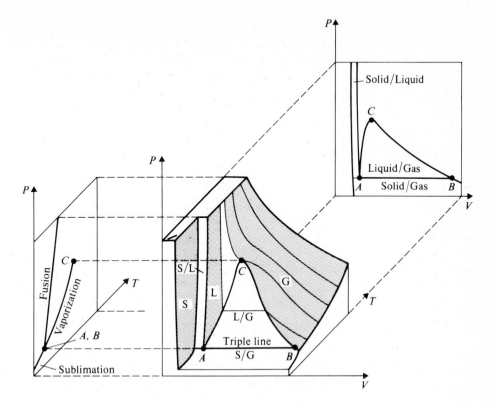

Figure 4-1 PVT surface for a substance which expands on melting.

delineates the region of vapor/liquid equilibrium, designated L/G. Point C, the *gas/liquid critical point*, marks the terminus of this region. The heavy, straight line passing through points A and B marks the intersections of the three two-phase regions; it is the *triple line*, along which solid, liquid, and gas phases exist in three-phase equilibrium.

Two-dimensional representations of the PVT surface are obtained by projection of the surface onto planes. Shown on Fig. 4-1 are constructions yielding the *PT diagram* and the *PV diagram* of a pure substance. The *PT* projection of Fig. 4-1 is shown to a larger scale in Fig. 4-2, and the liquid and gas regions of the *PV* projection are shown in more detail in Fig. 4-3.

With reference to Figs. 4-1 and 4-2, we see that the two-phase regions project as *lines* on a *PT* diagram; this is a consequence of the uniformity of temperature and pressure for phase equilibrium in a PVT system. Thus, corresponding to the regions S/L, S/G, and L/G on the surface of Fig. 4-1, we have three *saturation curves* on Fig. 4-2, labeled on Fig. 4-2*a* as the *fusion curve*, the *sublimation curve*, and the *vaporization curve*. The triple line and the gas/liquid critical point project as points (t and C) on the PT diagram, and define the limits of the vaporization curve. Although the vaporization curve ends at the critical

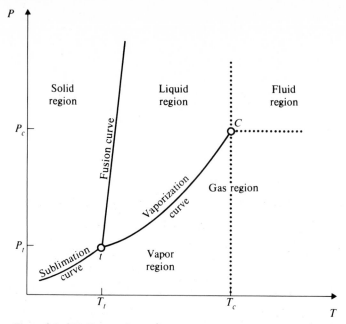

Figure 4-2a PT diagram for a substance which expands on melting.

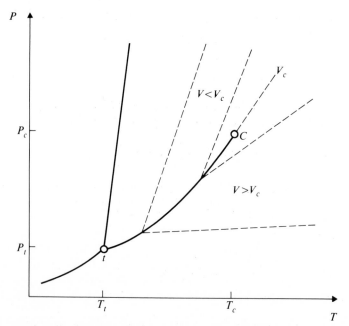

Figure 4-2b The same, showing qualitative behavior of isochores.

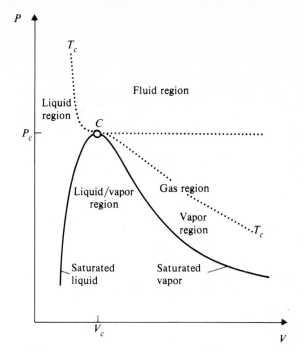

Figure 4-3a PV diagram for the fluid regions of a substance.

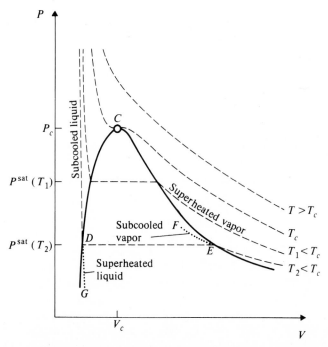

Figure 4-3b The same, showing qualitative behavior of isotherms.

point, the fusion curve continues upward indefinitely, or until it intercepts another solid/solid or solid/liquid saturation curve.

Because of the abrupt termination of the vaporization curve at the critical point, there is some arbitrariness in the assignment of names to the nonsolid equilibrium phases of a substance; the labels on Fig. 4-2a serve as well as any. Thus, a *vapor* is a gas phase that can be condensed both by an isothermal increase of pressure and by an isobaric decrease of temperature. The term *fluid* designates any nonsolid phase; in particular, it can be used as a label for the region for which both $T > T_c$ and $P > P_c$, where the terms *liquid* and *gas* seem inappropriate.

The dashed lines on Fig. 4-2b are *isochores*, lines of constant V. Isochores intersecting the vaporization curve from above ($V < V_c$) are for the liquid phase, and those from below ($V > V_c$) for the vapor phase. The dashed line labeled V_c is the *critical isochore*; it is colinear with the vaporization curve at the critical point. The isochores are drawn as straight lines on Fig. 4-2b; however they actually show some small curvature.

It is clear from Fig. 4-1 that two-phase regions of the PVT surface project as *areas* on a PV diagram. On Fig. 4-3 the area corresponding to vapor/liquid equilibrium is separated from regions of single-phase equilibrium by a dome-shaped curve. The left segment of this curve (for $V < V_c$) represents states of *saturated liquid* and the right segment (for $V > V_c$) represents states of *saturated vapor*. The two segments join smoothly at the critical point, and thus at the critical state the liquid and vapor phases in equilibrium become identical.

On the PV diagram of Fig. 4-3b, isotherms are shown by dashed lines. For very high temperatures, these curves approach the shape of rectangular hyperbolas, given by the ideal-gas equation

$$P = \frac{RT}{V}$$

As temperature decreases, deviations from the ideal-gas equation become more pronounced, until the critical temperature is reached. The critical isotherm, labeled T_c, exhibits a singular behavior; it has a horizontal inflection at the critical point, implying the two mathematical conditions

$$(\partial P/\partial V)_{T:\,cr} = 0 \qquad (4\text{-}1a)$$

$$(\partial^2 P/\partial V^2)_{T:\,cr} = 0 \qquad (4\text{-}1b)$$

where subscript cr denotes the critical state.

Subcritical isotherms ($T < T_c$) consist of three branches. The left branch corresponds to states of *subcooled liquid*; because liquids are relatively incompressible, this branch is steep. The right branch represents states of *superheated vapor*. Connecting these two branches is the third section of the isotherm, a horizontal line representing states of vapor/liquid equilibrium. The intersections of the horizontal segment with the liquid and vapor branches of the isotherm define the states of saturated liquid and saturated vapor. The *pressure* corresponding to this horizontal section is the vapor/liquid saturation pressure, or *vapor pressure*, P^{sat}. It is a single point on the vaporization curve of Fig. 4-2. As noted in Sec. 3-6, the condition which establishes the value of P^{sat} for a particular T is the equality of fugacity for the equilibrium liquid and vapor phases.

The surface of Fig. 4-1 portrays only the stable equilibrium states of a pure substance. It is possible under certain conditions to maintain a pure liquid at a temperature *greater* than its saturation temperature, or a pure vapor at a temperature *less* than its saturation temperature; such states are *metastable*. Thus states of *superheated liquid* are shown on Fig. 4-3b by the dotted line segment *DG*; states of *subcooled vapor* are shown by the dotted line segment *EF*.

4-2 VAPOR/LIQUID EQUILIBRIUM OF A PURE FLUID

It is evident from Fig. 4-3 that the molar or specific volumes are different for liquid and vapor phases in equilibrium. The same is true of most other thermodynamic properties, and it is convenient to give these differences a special name and symbol. Thus we define a *property change of vaporization* ΔM_i^{lv} as

$$\boxed{\Delta M_i^{lv} \equiv M_i^{v} - M_i^{l}}$$
(4-2)

Here, M_i^{v} and M_i^{l} are the values of property M for the saturated vapor and the saturated liquid of pure i at a given value of T. Since the vapor pressure P_i^{sat} of a pure material depends upon T only, the properties ΔM_i^{lv} can equally well be regarded as functions of T only or of P only.

Important special cases of Eq. (4-2) are the *volume change of vaporization*, the *enthalpy change of vaporization* (or *latent heat of vaporization*), and the *entropy change of vaporization*:

$$\Delta V_i^{lv} \equiv V_i^{v} - V_i^{l}$$

$$\Delta H_i^{lv} \equiv H_i^{v} - H_i^{l}$$

$$\Delta S_i^{lv} \equiv S_i^{v} - S_i^{l}$$

One might also define a *Gibbs function change of vaporization*:

$$\Delta G_i^{lv} \equiv G_i^{v} - G_i^{l}$$

However, as shown in Example 2-3, $G_i = \mu_i$ for a pure species i; moreover, by Eq. (2-9),

$$\mu_i^{l} = \mu_i^{v}$$

for vapor/liquid equilibrium. Thus, for a pure material in vapor/liquid equilibrium,

$$G_i^{l} = G_i^{v}$$

or

$$\Delta G_i^{lv} = 0$$
(4-3)

Thus the Gibbs function change of vaporization is *zero* for a pure material. Equation (4-3) is important, for it implies a relationship between ΔH_i^{lv} and ΔS_i^{lv}. Since, by definition, $G \equiv H - TS$, we can write

$$G_i^v = H_i^v - TS_i^v$$

and

$$G_i^l = H_i^l - TS_i^l$$

For phase equilibrium, the temperature is uniform; thus subtraction of the last two equations gives

$$G_i^v - G_i^l = (H_i^v - H_i^l) - T(S_i^v - S_i^l)$$

or

$$\Delta G_i^{lv} = \Delta H_i^{lv} - T\,\Delta S_i^{lv}$$

But by Eq. (4-3) $\Delta G_i^{lv} = 0$. Thus we obtain the expression

$$\boxed{\Delta H_i^{lv} = T\,\Delta S_i^{lv}} \tag{4-4}$$

Another important relationship can be shown to hold between ΔS_i^{lv} and ΔV_i^{lv}. For a differential change in the equilibrium state, we can write, by Eq. (2-29),

$$dG_i^v = -S_i^v\,dT + V_i^v\,dP$$

and

$$dG_i^l = -S_i^l\,dT + V_i^l\,dP$$

from which

$$d(G_i^v - G_i^l) = -(S_i^v - S_i^l)\,dT + (V_i^v - V_i^l)\,dP$$

or

$$d\,\Delta G_i^{lv} = -\Delta S_i^{lv}\,dT + \Delta V_i^{lv}\,dP$$

But, by Eq. (4-3), $\Delta G_i^{lv} = 0$ for *any* state of vapor/liquid equilibrium; therefore

$$d\,\Delta G_i^{lv} = 0$$

for a differential change in the equilibrium state. Identification of the pressure P with P_i^{sat} and combination of the last two equations then gives

$$\frac{dP_i^{sat}}{dT} = \frac{\Delta S_i^{lv}}{\Delta V_i^{lv}} \tag{4-5}$$

Other expressions of Eq. (4-5) are possible. For example, elimination of ΔS_i^{lv} in favor of ΔH_i^{lv} by Eq. (4-4) gives

$$\boxed{\frac{dP_i^{sat}}{dT} = \frac{\Delta H_i^{lv}}{T\,\Delta V_i^{lv}}} \tag{4-6}$$

The volume change of vaporization may be written in terms of the compressibility factor change of vaporization ΔZ_i^{lv}:

$$\Delta Z_i^{lv} \equiv Z_i^v - Z_i^l$$

Since, for saturation conditions, $Z_i = P_i^{sat} V_i / RT$, the last equation yields

$$\Delta Z_i^{lv} = \frac{P_i^{sat}}{RT} \Delta V_i^{lv}$$

Combination with Eq. (4-6) gives, on rearrangement,

$$\frac{d \ln P_i^{sat}}{d(1/T)} = - \frac{\Delta H_i^{lv}}{R \, \Delta Z_i^{lv}} \tag{4-7}$$

Equations (4-5) through (4-7) are all forms of the *Clapeyron equation*. This useful expression permits the calculation of heats of vaporization from vapor-pressure and volumetric data or, conversely, it enables the rationalization of algebraic forms for the vapor-pressure equation from the observed temperature dependence of the group appearing on the right-hand side of Eq. (4-7).

Although presented specifically for the case of vapor/liquid equilibrium, all of the definitions and equations of this section apply for any of the common (first-order) phase transitions experienced by a pure material. Thus, for equilibrium between any pair of phases α and β, correct expressions are obtained by the substitutions $l = \alpha$ and $v = \beta$ and by appropriate reinterpretation of P_i^{sat}. For example, Eqs. (4-2), (4-4), and (4-6) become

$$\Delta M_i^{\alpha\beta} \equiv M_i^{\beta} - M_i^{\alpha} \tag{4-8}$$

$$\Delta H_i^{\alpha\beta} = T \, \Delta S_i^{\alpha\beta} \tag{4-9}$$

and

$$\frac{dP_i^{sat}}{dT} = \frac{\Delta H_i^{\alpha\beta}}{T \, \Delta V_i^{\alpha\beta}} \tag{4-10}$$

Example 4-1 The basis for our derivation of the Clapeyron equation was Eq. (4-3), a consequence of the equality of chemical potentials for phase equilibrium. An alternative but equivalent derivation is based on Eq. (3-68):

$$f_i^l = f_i^v$$

or

$$\ln \left(f_i^v / f_i^l \right) = 0$$

For a differential change in the equilibrium state

$$d \ln \left(f_i^v / f_i^l \right) = 0 \tag{A}$$

Equation (3-87) provides the following expression for $d \ln f_i$:

$$d \ln f_i = \frac{H_i^* - H_i}{RT^2} dT + \frac{V_i}{RT} dP \tag{B}$$

For a differential change in the equilibrium state, Eq. (B) may be written separately for the vapor and liquid phases. Noting that H_i' is the same in both of these expressions, we get on subtraction

$$d \ln (f_i^v/f_i^l) = -\left(\frac{H_i^v - H_i^l}{RT^2}\right) dT + \left(\frac{V_i^v - V_i^l}{RT}\right) dP \qquad \text{(C)}$$

But the quantities $H_i^v - H_i^l$ and $V_i^v - V_i^l$ are just property changes of vaporization. Combination of Eqs. (A) and (C) then gives

$$-\frac{\Delta H_i^{lv}}{RT^2} dT + \frac{\Delta V_i^{lv}}{RT} dP = 0 \qquad \text{(4-11)}$$

Equation (4-11) is a special case of the *coexistence equation* which is developed in Sec. 6-6. Identification of P with P_i^{sat} in Eq. (4-11) gives, on rearrangement,

$$\frac{dP_i^{sat}}{dT} = \frac{\Delta H_i^{lv}}{T \, \Delta V_i^{lv}}$$

which is Eq. (4-6).

Example 4-2 The vapor pressure P_i^{sat} is usually represented as a function of T by an empirical formula. We illustrate in this example how the Clapeyron equation is used for the derivation of vapor-pressure equations, and how it serves as a vehicle for comparison of the capabilities of rival equations; a comprehensive treatment of this topic is given by Reid, Prausnitz, and Sherwood (1977).

Equation (4-7) may be written as

$$\frac{d \ln P^{sat}}{d(1/T)} = -\Omega \qquad \text{(A)}$$

where

$$\Omega \equiv \frac{\Delta H^{lv}}{R \, \Delta Z^{lv}} \qquad \text{(B)}$$

and subscript i is deleted for simplicity. Quantity Ω depends on T only, through the two property changes of vaporization. These are plotted against temperature for nitrogen on Fig. 4-4. Both ΔH^{lv} and ΔZ^{lv} are strong functions of T, decreasing in magnitude from their values at the triple point to zero at the critical point. Their *ratio*, however, depends less strongly on T, and moreover is finite and nonzero at the critical temperature. This is illustrated by Fig. 4-5, a plot of Ω versus T for nitrogen, derived from the values of ΔH^{lv} and ΔZ^{lv} on Fig. 4-4.

Although the values of Ω for nitrogen vary by no more than 10 percent, there are clear trends with T, and any equation intended for the precise representation of vapor pressures must be capable of reproducing these trends. This is assured if one *starts* with an appropriate expression for Ω and obtains the vapor-pressure equation by integration of Eq. (A). The simplest polynomial expression of sufficient generality for the temperature dependence of Ω is

$$\Omega = B + DT + ET^m \qquad \text{(C)}$$

where B, D, E, and m are empirical constants. Equation (C) is chosen because it is capable of reproducing a minimum in Ω; the exponent m might arbitrarily be fixed,

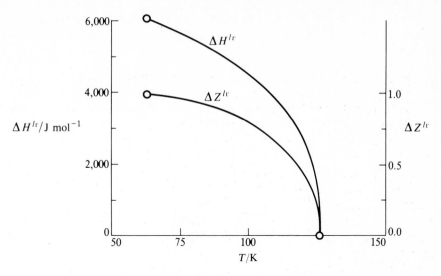

Figure 4-4 ΔH^{lv} and ΔZ^{lv} versus T for nitrogen.

but is here treated as an adjustable parameter. Substitution of Eq. (C) into Eq. (A) and integration gives

$$\ln P^{\text{sat}} = A - \frac{B}{T} + D \ln T + FT^n \tag{D}$$

where $n \equiv m - 1$, $F \equiv E/n$, and A is a constant of integration. Equation (D) yields as special cases several popular equations for the vapor pressure; Eq. (C) and Fig. 4-5 permit comparison of their capabilities.

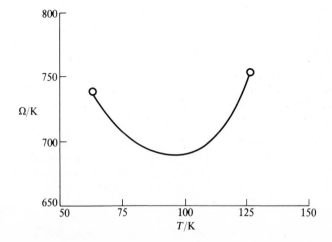

Figure 4-5 Plot of $\Omega(\equiv \Delta H^{lv}/R \, \Delta Z^{lv})$ versus T for nitrogen.

The simplest nontrivial equation for P^{sat} is obtained from Eq. (D) by the assignments $D = F = 0$, giving

$$\ln P^{sat} = A - \frac{B}{T} \qquad (4\text{-}12)$$

Equation (4-12) is sometimes called the *Clausius-Clapeyron vapor-pressure equation*; according to Eq. (C), it implies that Ω is a constant, independent of T. Figure 4-5 shows that Ω *is* a function of T; therefore Eq. (4-12) cannot precisely represent the vapor-pressure curve. On the other hand, if constants A and B are chosen judiciously, the equation never provides absurd values for vapor pressures. For this reason, plus the fact that it contains only two adjustable parameters, Eq. (4-12) is often used for rough calculations and in applications where trends of P^{sat} with T are important but where high accuracy is not required.

If we set $F = 0$ in Eq. (D), then there results the *Kirchhoff equation*:

$$\ln P^{sat} = A - \frac{B}{T} + D \ln T \qquad (E)$$

By Eq. (C), this implies a linear approximation to the T dependence of Ω and, by Fig. 4-5, there should obtain an improvement in fit to P^{sat} data over Eq. (4-12) for limited ranges of T. However, if the *entire* liquid range is of interest, Eq. (E) offers little advantage over Eq. (4-12). Figure 4-5 suggests that the best overall linear approximation to Ω is something very close to a horizontal line for nitrogen, whose behavior is typical of many substances.

Equation (D) in its complete form is capable of reasonably accurate description of the entire vapor-pressure curve. Various values of n have been proposed; the choice $n = 6$ (i.e., $m = 7$) produces the four-parameter *Riedel equation*, an expression favored by many investigators.

One final vapor-pressure formula deserves mention: the three-parameter *Antoine equation*

$$\ln P^{sat} = A - \frac{B}{T + C} \qquad (4\text{-}13)$$

Equation (4-13) is essentially an empirical modification of Eq. (4-12); differentiation with respect to $1/T$ yields the following expression for Ω:

$$\Omega = \frac{BT^2}{(T + C)^2} \qquad (F)$$

The nonlinear temperature dependence given by Eq. (F) makes the Antoine equation more accurate than the three-parameter Kirchhoff equation over limited ranges of temperature. The Antoine equation is the most widely used of all the empirical expressions for P^{sat}, and values of Antoine constants A, B, and C are reported in many compilations of thermodynamic data.

4-3 CORRESPONDING-STATES CORRELATIONS

A particular application of the material of previous chapters may require the availability of thermodynamic property data for many different fluids over a wide range of temperatures and pressures. Often as not, such data are not available for all of the fluids, or for all conditions of interest. In such cases, one must make judicious interpolations or extrapolations from existing information; this procedure is greatly facilitated if one has methods for simultaneous correlation of data on many different fluids. The search for such *generalized correlations* has occupied the attention of scientists and engineers for a century, and has led to some remarkable successes; a critical survey is given by Reid, Prausnitz, and Sherwood (1977).

The basis for the generalized correlation of volumetric properties of fluids is the *theorem of corresponding states*. This theorem may be rationalized by molecular considerations, by equation-of-state arguments, or by the observation that data for different fluids exhibit considerable uniformity when the thermodynamic coordinates are expressed in a suitable dimensionless or *reduced* form. In one of its simplest expressions, the theorem of corresponding states asserts that the compressibility factor Z is for all pure fluids a universal function of the *reduced temperature* T_r and the *reduced pressure* P_r. Hence

$$Z = Z(T_r, P_r) \qquad \text{all fluids} \qquad (4\text{-}14)$$

where T_r and P_r are, by definition,

$$T_r \equiv \frac{T}{T_c}$$

$$P_r \equiv \frac{P}{P_c}$$

and T_c and P_c are the critical temperature and critical pressure. In other words, *the compressibility factors of all fluids are the same when compared at the same values of T_r and P_r*. The approximate validity of this assertion for gases is illustrated in Fig. 4-6.

Corresponding-states correlations based on Eq. (4-14) are called *two-parameter* correlations, because they require the use of the two reducing parameters T_c and P_c. Two-parameter correlations provide excellent representations of the behavior of the class of *simple fluids* (Ar, Kr, and Xe). However, systematic deviations are noted for other substances; generally, the magnitude of the deviations increases with increasing complexity of the intermolecular force field, as determined by such factors as molecular shape, polarity, and tendencies to form quasi-chemical intermolecular bonds. While not especially pronounced on a plot such as Fig. 4-6, such deviations are very evident in the derived properties (e.g., the residual functions), particularly at low reduced temperatures and high reduced pressures.

The shortcomings of the two-parameter approach have prompted the development of extensions of the corresponding states principle. An obvious extension of Eq. (4-14) is a *three-parameter* theorem of corresponding states:

$$Z = \mathscr{Z}(T_r, P_r; \pi) \qquad \text{all fluids} \qquad (4\text{-}15)$$

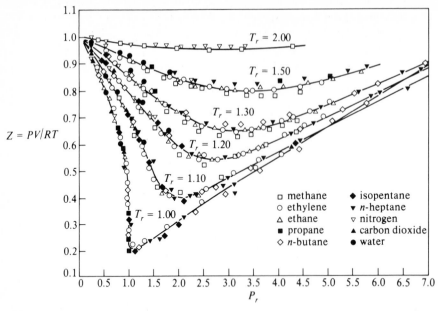

Figure 4-6 Two-parameter corresponding-states correlation of the compressibility factor Z [from Su (1946)].

Here, π is a dimensionless parameter characteristic of a fluid. According to Eq. (4-15), compressibility factors of all fluids *having the same value of parameter π* are the same when compared at the same values of T_r and P_r.

Three-parameter corresponding-states correlations have proved capable of unifying to a considerable degree the PVT behavior of nonpolar, nonassociating fluids. The choice of the third correlating parameter π is clearly critical. It must be a true constant for a given fluid, not correlated solely with T_c and P_c; it should be capable of accurate experimental determination with a minimum of effort; and differences in π from one substance to another should in fact represent differences in the intermolecular forces. These criteria are met more or less well by characteristics of the vapor-pressure curve evaluated at a specific T_r. The most popular three-parameter correlations are those incorporating *Pitzer's acentric factor ω* as a third parameter. By definition

$$\omega \equiv -1 - \log_{10}\left(P_r^{\text{sat}}\right)_{T_r=0.7} \qquad (4\text{-}16)$$

The argument of the logarithm is the reduced vapor pressure P^{sat}/P_c evaluated at a reduced temperature of 0.7. For the three simple fluids Ar, Kr, and Xe, the acentric factor is approximately zero; for most other substances it is a positive number less than unity. Values of ω for selected substances are given in App. D.

Example 4-3 Some of the considerations which lead to the choice of a third corresponding-states parameter may be illustrated by example. Suppose that the vapor pressures of all fluids could be represented by Eq. (4-12):

$$\ln P^{sat} = A - \frac{B}{T} \tag{4-12}$$

where A and B are specific to individual fluids. Now the critical point is a point on the vapor-pressure curve: $P^{sat} = P_c$ for $T = T_c$. At the critical point, Eq. (4-12) becomes

$$\ln P_c = A - \frac{B}{T_c} \tag{A}$$

and subtraction of Eq. (A) from Eq. (4-12) yields on rearrangement a *reduced* form of the vapor-pressure equation:

$$\ln P_r^{sat} = \frac{B}{T_c}\left(1 - \frac{1}{T_r}\right)$$

or

$$\log_{10} P_r^{sat} = b\left(1 - \frac{1}{T_r}\right) \tag{B}$$

If the two-parameter theorem of corresponding states were valid for gases and for liquids, then P_r^{sat} would be a universal function of T_r; if *in addition* Eq. (4-12) were valid, then, according to Eq. (B), parameter b would be a universal constant, independent of T_r, and the same for all substances. This however is *not* the case; Fig. 4-7 shows plots of parameter b, evaluated from vapor-pressure data by the equation

$$b = -\left(\frac{T_r}{1 - T_r}\right)\log_{10} P_r^{sat} \tag{C}$$

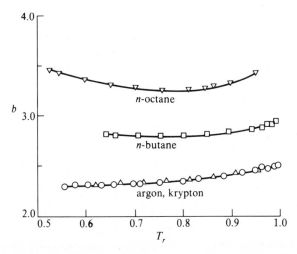

Figure 4-7 Plot of $b\{\equiv -[T_r/(1 - T_r)]\log_{10} P_r^{sat}\}$ versus T_r for several fluids. (See Example 4-3.)

and plotted against T_r for several substances. Two things may be noted from these plots. First, the values of b for a given substance show small but regular trends with T_r. This reflects the fact, discussed in Example 4-2, that Eq. (4-12) is incapable of *precise* description of the vapor-pressure curve.

The second feature of the curves is their distinct separation from one substance to another. Were the two-parameter theorem of corresponding states valid, all of the data would fall on a single curve, for by Eq. (C) parameter b would be at most a function of T_r only. The fact that Ar and Kr *do* fall on a single curve merely confirms the observation made earlier that the simple fluids conform to the two-parameter theorem of corresponding states. The magnitudes of the separations of the curves for *n*-butane and *n*-octane from that for the simple fluids provide quantitative measures of the departures of these substances from the theorem.

The curves of Fig. 4-7 provide one basis for the definition of Pitzer's acentric factor. If we search for a rational measure of the differences in magnitude of b from one substance to another, it is clear that we must specify the value of T_r at which the differences are reckoned, for the curves are not conformal. Call this fixed value of reduced temperature T_r^*. We then define a third parameter π as *proportional* to Δb^*, the difference between b for any fluid and b for simple fluids, both evaluated at T_r^*.

$$\pi \equiv K \, \Delta b^* = K(b^* - b_{SF}^*)$$

where K is a constant of proportionality and subscript SF refers to the simple fluid. But, by Eq. (C),

$$b^* = -\left(\frac{T_r^*}{1 - T_r^*}\right) \log_{10} (P_r^{sat})_{T_r^*}$$

and the last two equations give

$$\pi = -K\left(\frac{T_r^*}{1 - T_r^*}\right)[\log_{10} (P_r^{sat})_{T_r^*} - \log_{10} (P_r^{sat})_{T_r^*}^{SF}] \qquad (D)$$

All that remains is to specify T_r^* and K. Both choices are arbitrary, and we make them primarily on the basis of convenience. Examination of the vapor-pressure data upon which Fig. 4-7 is based reveals that P_r^{sat} for simple fluids is very nearly 0.1 at $T_r^* = 0.7$. With this choice of T_r^*, $\log_{10} (P_r^{sat})_{T_r^*}^{SF} = -1$, and Eq. (D) becomes

$$\pi = -\tfrac{7}{3}K[\log_{10} (P_r^{sat})_{T_r = 0.7} + 1]$$

Finally, we set $K = \tfrac{3}{7}$, obtaining

$$\pi = -1 - \log_{10} (P_r^{sat})_{T_r = 0.7} \qquad (E)$$

which is just the definition of Pitzer's acentric factor as given by Eq. (4-16).

Clearly, the kind of argument used to develop Eq. (E) could equally well have led to the definition of countless other third parameters, each of them potentially as useful as the acentric factor. However, it should be noted that $T_r = 0.7$ is close to the normal boiling point of most substances; thus the particular choice of T_r^* adopted by Pitzer not only provides numerical simplicity, but also convenience, for vapor-pressure data are most commonly available at pressures near atmospheric.

We return to the Pitzer correlations at the end of this section. First, however, we develop equations which provide generalized correlations for derived properties from any corresponding-states correlation of the form of Eq. (4-14) or (4-15). Formulas presented in earlier chapters reveal that calculation of derived properties requires values not only for Z, but also for its derivatives with respect to T and P. Thus we assume in this and in the next section the availability of an internally consistent set of correlations for Z and for its derivatives with respect to T_r and P_r.

For the residual enthalpy $\Delta H'$, we have

$$\Delta H' = \int_0^P \left[T\left(\frac{\partial V}{\partial T}\right)_P - V \right] dP \qquad (\text{const } T, x) \qquad (2\text{-}85)$$

and for the residual entropy $\Delta S'$,

$$\Delta S' = \int_0^P \left[\left(\frac{\partial V}{\partial T}\right)_P - \frac{R}{P} \right] dP \qquad (\text{const } T, x) \qquad (2\text{-}86)$$

The compressibility factor is introduced through Eqs. (2-73) and (2-81), which give

$$V = \frac{ZRT}{P}$$

$$\left(\frac{\partial V}{\partial T}\right)_P = \frac{RT}{P}\left(\frac{\partial Z}{\partial T}\right)_P + \frac{RZ}{P}$$

Thus Eqs. (2-85) and (2-86) become

$$\Delta H' = RT^2 \int_0^P \left(\frac{\partial Z}{\partial T}\right)_P \frac{dP}{P} \qquad (4\text{-}17)$$

and

$$\Delta S' = R \int_0^P \left[T\left(\frac{\partial Z}{\partial T}\right)_P + Z - 1 \right] \frac{dP}{P} \qquad (4\text{-}18)$$

Finally, to put these equations into reduced form we introduce the relationships

$$T = T_c T_r \qquad\qquad P = P_c P_r$$
$$dT = T_c\, dT_r \qquad dP = P_c\, dP_r$$

Thus, Eqs. (4-17) and (4-18) become, on rearrangement,

$$\boxed{\frac{\Delta H'}{RT_c} = T_r^2 \int_0^{P_r} \left(\frac{\partial Z}{\partial T_r}\right)_{P_r} \frac{dP_r}{P_r}} \qquad (4\text{-}19)$$

and

$$\boxed{\frac{\Delta S'}{R} = \int_0^{P_r} \left[T_r\left(\frac{\partial Z}{\partial T_r}\right)_{P_r} + Z - 1 \right] \frac{dP_r}{P_r}} \qquad (4\text{-}20)$$

The terms on the right-hand sides of Eqs. (4-19) and (4-20) may be evaluated from generalized compressibility factors and their derivatives with respect to T_r. The values of the integrals depend only upon the upper limit P_r and on the reduced temperature at which the integrations are carried out. The dimensionless quantities $\Delta H'/RT_c$ and $\Delta S'/R$ may therefore be evaluated once and for all from a given correlation for Z.

Two other derived properties are often required for practical calculations with generalized correlations: the fugacity coefficient ϕ and the dimensionless residual constant-pressure heat capacity $\Delta C_P'/R$. For the fugacity coefficient, we find by Eq. (3-72) that

$$\ln \phi = \frac{1}{RT}(G - G') = -\frac{\Delta G'}{RT} \tag{4-21}$$

where $\Delta G'$ is the residual Gibbs function. But $G \equiv H - TS$ and therefore

$$\Delta G' \equiv G' - G = (H' - TS') - (H - TS)$$

or

$$\Delta G' = \Delta H' - T \Delta S'$$

Equation (4-21) then becomes

$$\boxed{\ln \phi = \frac{\Delta S'}{R} - \frac{\Delta H'}{RT}} \tag{4-22}$$

or, since $T = T_r T_c$,

$$\ln \phi = \frac{\Delta S'}{R} - \frac{1}{T_r}\frac{\Delta H'}{RT_c} \tag{4-23}$$

Thus generalized correlations for $\Delta S'/R$ and $\Delta H'/RT_c$, as obtained by Eqs. (4-19) and (4-20), may be combined to give a generalized correlation for $\ln \phi$.

It is known that C_P for a real gas approaches its ideal-gas value C_P' as pressure approaches zero. Moreover, by Eqs. (2-55) and (2-55 *ideal*),

$$\left(\frac{\partial C_P}{\partial P}\right)_T = -T\left(\frac{\partial^2 V}{\partial T^2}\right)_P$$

and

$$\left(\frac{\partial C_P'}{\partial P}\right)_T = 0$$

The method of Sec. 2-11 therefore provides the following expression for the residual constant-pressure heat capacity:

$$\Delta C_P' = T \int_0^P \left(\frac{\partial^2 V}{\partial T^2}\right)_P dP \qquad (\text{const } T, x) \tag{4-24}$$

The derivative in the integral must be expressed in terms of derivatives of Z. Since

$$\left(\frac{\partial V}{\partial T}\right)_P = \frac{R}{P}\left[T\left(\frac{\partial Z}{\partial T}\right)_P + Z\right] \qquad (2\text{-}81)$$

then

$$\left(\frac{\partial^2 V}{\partial T^2}\right)_P = \frac{R}{P}\left[T\left(\frac{\partial^2 Z}{\partial T^2}\right)_P + 2\left(\frac{\partial Z}{\partial T}\right)_P\right]$$

Thus

$$\Delta C_P' = RT \int_0^P \left[T\left(\frac{\partial^2 Z}{\partial T^2}\right)_P + 2\left(\frac{\partial Z}{\partial T}\right)_P\right]\frac{dP}{P} \qquad (4\text{-}25)$$

or, in terms of reduced variables,

$$\boxed{\frac{\Delta C_P'}{R} = T_r \int_0^{P_r} \left[T_r\left(\frac{\partial^2 Z}{\partial T_r^2}\right)_{P_r} + 2\left(\frac{\partial Z}{\partial T_r}\right)_{P_r}\right]\frac{dP_r}{P_r}} \qquad (4\text{-}26)$$

Equations (4-19), (4-20), (4-23), and (4-26) may be used with any corresponding-states correlation, graphical, tabular, or analytical, which gives Z and its derivatives as functions of T_r, P_r, and any number of additional dimensionless parameters. We consider now their application to correlations of the form first proposed by Pitzer and coworkers [Pitzer (1955), Pitzer et al. (1955), Pitzer and Curl (1957), Curl and Pitzer (1958)]. These authors showed that the compressibility factors of "normal" fluids (those not exhibiting strong polarity or chemical association) are well correlated by the equation

$$Z = Z^0(T_r, P_r) + \omega Z^1(T_r, P_r)$$

or, more concisely, by

$$Z = Z^0 + \omega Z^1 \qquad (4\text{-}27)$$

Equation (4-27) is a special form of Eq. (4-15), with the third parameter π equal to the acentric factor ω. Function Z^0 is the *simple-fluid* contribution to Z; it may be determined by analysis of volumetric data for the substances Ar, Kr, and Xe, whose acentric factors are essentially zero. The function Z^1 may then be found by analysis of data for *nonsimple* fluids (those with acentric factor different from zero) by use of Eq. (4-27) and the previously established correlation for Z^0.

The assumed linear dependence of Z on ω makes possible the decomposition of expressions for derived properties to a form similar to Eq. (4-27). Differentiations of Eq. (4-27) yield

$$\left(\frac{\partial Z}{\partial T_r}\right)_{P_r} = \left(\frac{\partial Z}{\partial T_r}\right)_{P_r}^0 + \omega\left(\frac{\partial Z}{\partial T_r}\right)_{P_r}^1 \qquad (4\text{-}28)$$

and

$$\left(\frac{\partial^2 Z}{\partial T_r^2}\right)_{P_r} = \left(\frac{\partial^2 Z}{\partial T_r^2}\right)_{P_r}^0 + \omega\left(\frac{\partial^2 Z}{\partial T_r^2}\right)_{P_r}^1 \tag{4-29}$$

For the residual enthalpy, we then find by Eqs. (4-19) and (4-28) that

$$\frac{\Delta H'}{RT_c} = \left(\frac{\Delta H'}{RT_c}\right)^0 + \omega\left(\frac{\Delta H'}{RT_c}\right)^1 \tag{4-30}$$

where

$$\left(\frac{\Delta H'}{RT_c}\right)^0 = T_r^2 \int_0^{P_r} \left(\frac{\partial Z}{\partial T_r}\right)_{P_r}^0 \frac{dP_r}{P_r}$$

and

$$\left(\frac{\Delta H'}{RT_c}\right)^1 = T_r^2 \int_0^{P_r} \left(\frac{\partial Z}{\partial T_r}\right)_{P_r}^1 \frac{dP_r}{P_r}$$

Similarly, Eqs. (4-20), (4-27), and (4-28) give for the residual entropy

$$\frac{\Delta S'}{R} = \left(\frac{\Delta S'}{R}\right)^0 + \omega\left(\frac{\Delta S'}{R}\right)^1 \tag{4-31}$$

where

$$\left(\frac{\Delta S'}{R}\right)^0 = \int_0^{P_r} \left[T_r\left(\frac{\partial Z}{\partial T_r}\right)_{P_r}^0 + Z^0 - 1\right] \frac{dP_r}{P_r}$$

and

$$\left(\frac{\Delta S'}{R}\right)^1 = \int_0^{P_r} \left[T_r\left(\frac{\partial Z}{\partial T_r}\right)_{P_r}^1 + Z^1\right] \frac{dP_r}{P_r}$$

Finally, expressions for $\ln \phi$ are found from Eqs. (4-23), (4-30), and (4-31), and for $\Delta C_P'/R$ from Eqs. (4-26), (4-28), and (4-29). The results are

$$\ln \phi = \ln \phi^0 + \omega \ln \phi^1 \tag{4-32}$$

and

$$\frac{\Delta C_P'}{R} = \left(\frac{\Delta C_P'}{R}\right)^0 + \omega\left(\frac{\Delta C_P'}{R}\right)^1 \tag{4-33}$$

where

$$\ln \phi^0 = \left(\frac{\Delta S'}{R}\right)^0 - \frac{1}{T_r}\left(\frac{\Delta H'}{RT_c}\right)^0$$

$$\ln \phi^1 = \left(\frac{\Delta S'}{R}\right)^1 - \frac{1}{T_r}\left(\frac{\Delta H'}{RT_c}\right)^1$$

$$\left(\frac{\Delta C_P'}{R}\right)^0 = T_r \int_0^{P_r} \left[T_r\left(\frac{\partial^2 Z}{\partial T_r^2}\right)_{P_r}^0 + 2\left(\frac{\partial Z}{\partial T_r}\right)_{P_r}^0\right] \frac{dP_r}{P_r}$$

and

$$\left(\frac{\Delta C_P'}{R}\right)^1 = T_r \int_0^{P_r} \left[T_r \left(\frac{\partial^2 Z}{\partial T_r^2}\right)^1_{P_r} + 2\left(\frac{\partial Z}{\partial T_r}\right)^1_{P_r} \right] \frac{dP_r}{P_r}$$

Pitzer's original correlations for Z and the derived properties were presented in tabular form. Since then, analytical approximations to the tables have been developed, with extended range and improved accuracy. One of the best of the current Pitzer-type correlations is that of Lee and Kesler (1975); these authors present tables for contributions to Z and the derived functions for both the liquid and vapor phases, covering the ranges $0.3 \leq T_r \leq 4.0$ and $0.01 \leq P_r \leq 10.0$. Notwithstanding the usefulness of correlations such as those of Pitzer and of Lee and Kesler, it is safe to say that new and improved versions will continue to appear. If one is to take advantage of such developments, there is no substitute for familiarity with current literature.

4-4 MIXTURE PROPERTIES FROM CORRESPONDING-STATES CORRELATIONS

Corresponding-states correlations of the type treated in the preceding section are always developed from data for pure substances. However, many applications require the calculation of properties of mixtures, or of partial molar properties of species in solution. The use of generalized correlations for such applications requires an extension to mixtures of the corresponding-states concept. Conventional practice is to assume that mixture properties are represented by the same correlations developed for pure fluids, with appropriately defined values of the corresponding-states parameters for the mixture. Thus, a three-parameter corresponding-states correlation for mixture compressibility factors is of the form

$$Z = \mathscr{Z}(T_{\mathrm{pr}}, P_{\mathrm{pr}}; \pi_p) \tag{4-34}$$

where $\mathscr{Z}$ is the *same function* given by Eq. (4-15) for the correlation of Z for pure fluids. Here T_{pr} and P_{pr} are the *pseudoreduced temperature* and *pseudoreduced pressure*, defined with respect to *pseudocritical parameters* T_{pc} and P_{pc}:

$$T_{\mathrm{pr}} \equiv \frac{T}{T_{\mathrm{pc}}}$$

and

$$P_{\mathrm{pr}} \equiv \frac{P}{P_{\mathrm{pc}}}$$

Parameter π_p is similarly a pseudovalue of the third corresponding-states parameter π, appropriate for mixture calculations.

The major assumption of this approach is that a correlation for pure fluids is indeed extendable to mixtures; this is sometimes called the "one-fluid approximation." The major practical difficulty of the approach is in the definition of suitable recipes for the pseudoparameters T_{pc}, P_{pc}, and π_p. With respect to T_{pc} and P_{pc}, one might think that the *true* critical properties of the mixture would be appropriate. However, this has been shown to be not generally so; thus the appropriate parameters for use with Eq. (4-34) are indeed "pseudo"-values.

The simplest recipes for pseudoparameters are mole-fraction-weighted sums of the pure-component values:

$$T_{pc} = \sum x_i T_{c_i} \qquad (4\text{-}35a)$$

$$P_{pc} = \sum x_i P_{c_i} \qquad (4\text{-}35b)$$

$$\pi_p = \sum x_i \pi_i \qquad (4\text{-}35c)$$

These expressions are easy to use, and they satisfy the necessary condition that the mixture parameters reduce to the pure-component values in the appropriate limits. Equations (4-35a) and (4-35b) are known as *Kay's rules* [Kay (1936)]. For mixtures of similar chemical species, Kay's rules are often adequate; for mixtures of dissimilar fluids, more elaborate recipes have been proposed. Examples are given by Reid, Prausnitz, and Sherwood (1977). Whatever the form of the equations for T_{pc} and P_{pc}, Eq. (4-35c) is almost invariably used for the third corresponding-states parameter π (e.g., for ω in the Pitzer correlations). Given a set of rules such as Eqs. (4-35), one determines mixture Z's from Eq. (4-34). Derived properties for mixtures are found similarly from corresponding-states correlations for pure fluids.

Calculation of *partial molar properties* requires differentiation with respect to composition, and the composition dependence is buried in rules for the pseudoparameters, such as those of Eqs. (4-35). We develop in the following paragraphs a general method for evaluation of partial molar properties from any three-parameter corresponding-states correlation, and illustrate its application for two important special cases.

We assume the availability of a corresponding-states correlation for property M, of the form

$$M = \mathscr{M}(T_{pr}, P_{pr}; \pi_p) \qquad (4\text{-}36)$$

where $\mathscr{M}$ is the *same function* developed for the correlation of M for pure fluids. By definition

$$\bar{M}_i \equiv \left[\frac{\partial(nM)}{\partial n_i} \right]_{T,P,n_j}$$

and thus

$$\bar{M}_i = M + n\left(\frac{\partial M}{\partial n_i}\right)_{T,P,n_j} \qquad (4\text{-}37)$$

Now M depends on composition through the pseudoparameters, which in the case of T_{pc} and P_{pc} appear as reducing parameters for T and P. Evaluation of the derivative in Eq. (4-37) therefore requires the chain rule for partial differentiation:

$$\left(\frac{\partial M}{\partial n_i}\right)_{T,P,n_j} = \left(\frac{\partial M}{\partial T_{\mathrm{pr}}}\right)_{P_{\mathrm{pr}},\,\pi_p}\left(\frac{\partial T_{\mathrm{pr}}}{\partial T_{\mathrm{pc}}}\right)_T\left(\frac{\partial T_{\mathrm{pc}}}{\partial n_i}\right)_{n_j}$$

$$+ \left(\frac{\partial M}{\partial P_{\mathrm{pr}}}\right)_{T_{\mathrm{pr}},\,\pi_p}\left(\frac{\partial P_{\mathrm{pr}}}{\partial P_{\mathrm{pc}}}\right)_P\left(\frac{\partial P_{\mathrm{pc}}}{\partial n_i}\right)_{n_j}$$

$$+ \left(\frac{\partial M}{\partial \pi_p}\right)_{T_{\mathrm{pr}},\,P_{\mathrm{pr}}}\left(\frac{\partial \pi_p}{\partial n_i}\right)_{n_j}$$

But, since $T_{\mathrm{pr}} \equiv T/T_{\mathrm{pc}}$ and $P_{\mathrm{pr}} \equiv P/P_{\mathrm{pc}}$, we have

$$\left(\frac{\partial T_{\mathrm{pr}}}{\partial T_{\mathrm{pc}}}\right)_T = -\frac{T}{T_{\mathrm{pc}}^2} = -\frac{T_{\mathrm{pr}}}{T_{\mathrm{pc}}}$$

and

$$\left(\frac{\partial P_{\mathrm{pr}}}{\partial P_{\mathrm{pc}}}\right)_P = -\frac{P}{P_{\mathrm{pc}}^2} = -\frac{P_{\mathrm{pr}}}{P_{\mathrm{pc}}}$$

Moreover, it is easily shown that

$$\left(\frac{\partial T_{\mathrm{pc}}}{\partial n_i}\right)_{n_j} = \frac{1}{n}\left\{\left[\frac{\partial(nT_{\mathrm{pc}})}{\partial n_i}\right]_{n_j} - T_{\mathrm{pc}}\right\}$$

$$\left(\frac{\partial P_{\mathrm{pc}}}{\partial n_i}\right)_{n_j} = \frac{1}{n}\left\{\left[\frac{\partial(nP_{\mathrm{pc}})}{\partial n_i}\right]_{n_j} - P_{\mathrm{pc}}\right\}$$

and

$$\left(\frac{\partial \pi_p}{\partial n_i}\right)_{n_j} = \frac{1}{n}\left\{\left[\frac{\partial(n\pi_p)}{\partial n_i}\right]_{n_j} - \pi_p\right\}$$

Combination of the last six equations with Eq. (4-37) then gives the required expression for $\bar{M}_i$:

$$\boxed{\begin{aligned}
\bar{M}_i = M &- T_{\mathrm{pr}}\left(\frac{\partial M}{\partial T_{\mathrm{pr}}}\right)_{P_{\mathrm{pr}},\,\pi_p}\left\{\frac{1}{T_{\mathrm{pc}}}\left[\frac{\partial(nT_{\mathrm{pc}})}{\partial n_i}\right]_{n_j} - 1\right\}\\
&- P_{\mathrm{pr}}\left(\frac{\partial M}{\partial P_{\mathrm{pr}}}\right)_{T_{\mathrm{pr}},\,\pi_p}\left\{\frac{1}{P_{\mathrm{pc}}}\left[\frac{\partial(nP_{\mathrm{pc}})}{\partial n_i}\right]_{n_j} - 1\right\}\\
&+ \pi_p\left(\frac{\partial M}{\partial \pi_p}\right)_{T_{\mathrm{pr}},\,P_{\mathrm{pr}}}\left\{\frac{1}{\pi_p}\left[\frac{\partial(n\pi_p)}{\partial n_i}\right]_{n_j} - 1\right\}
\end{aligned}}$$

$$(4\text{-}38)$$

Equation (4-38) applies for any partial molar property $\bar{M}_i$. Not only is M for the mixture required for evaluation of $\bar{M}_i$, but also values for the derivatives of M with respect to reduced temperature, reduced pressure, and π_p.

For practical calculations, the two most important partial molar properties are $\bar{V}_i$ and $\ln \hat{\phi}_i$. Evaluation of partial molar volumes is most easily accomplished through the compressibility factor Z. Thus, since $Z = PV/RT$, we have

$$\bar{V}_i \equiv \left[\frac{\partial(nV)}{\partial n_i}\right]_{T, P, n_j} = \frac{RT}{P}\left[\frac{\partial(nZ)}{\partial n_i}\right]_{T, P, n_j}$$

or

$$\bar{V}_i = \frac{RT}{P}\bar{Z}_i \tag{4-39}$$

To find $\bar{V}_i$, we first determine $\bar{Z}_i$ by Eq. (4-38) and then multiply the result by RT/P. Letting $M = Z$ in Eq. (4-38), we find

$$\bar{Z}_i = Z - T_{pr}\left(\frac{\partial Z}{\partial T_{pr}}\right)_{P_{pr}, \pi_p}\left\{\frac{1}{T_{pc}}\left[\frac{\partial(nT_{pc})}{\partial n_i}\right]_{n_j} - 1\right\}$$

$$- P_{pr}\left(\frac{\partial Z}{\partial P_{pr}}\right)_{T_{pr}, \pi_p}\left\{\frac{1}{P_{pc}}\left[\frac{\partial(nP_{pc})}{\partial n_i}\right]_{n_j} - 1\right\}$$

$$+ \pi_p\left(\frac{\partial Z}{\partial \pi_p}\right)_{T_{pr}, P_{pr}}\left\{\frac{1}{\pi_p}\left[\frac{\partial(n\pi_p)}{\partial n_i}\right]_{n_j} - 1\right\} \tag{4-40}$$

Combination of Eq. (4-40) with Eq. (4-39) gives the required result.

To find $\ln \hat{\phi}_i$, we let $M = \ln \phi$ in Eq. (4-38). By Eq. (3-80), we have that

$$\left(\frac{\partial \ln \phi}{\partial T}\right)_{P, x} = \frac{\Delta H'}{RT^2}$$

and thus

$$\left(\frac{\partial \ln \phi}{\partial T_r}\right)_{P_r, x} = \frac{1}{T_r^2}\frac{\Delta H'}{RT_c}$$

from which

$$\left(\frac{\partial \ln \phi}{\partial T_{pr}}\right)_{P_{pr}, \pi_p} = \frac{1}{T_{pr}^2}\mathcal{H} \tag{4-41}$$

with

$$\mathcal{H} = \mathcal{H}(T_{pr}, P_{pr}; \pi_p) \equiv \frac{\Delta H'}{RT_c} \tag{4-42}$$

Also, by Eqs. (3-82) and (2-75),

$$\left(\frac{\partial \ln \phi}{\partial P}\right)_{T, x} = -\frac{\Delta V'}{RT} = -\frac{(1 - Z)}{P}$$

from which

$$\left(\frac{\partial \ln \phi}{\partial P_r}\right)_{T_r, x} = -\frac{(1 - Z)}{P_r}$$

Therefore

$$\left(\frac{\partial \ln \phi}{\partial P_{\text{pr}}}\right)_{T_{\text{pr}},\,\pi_p} = -\frac{(1-Z)}{P_{\text{pr}}} \tag{4-43}$$

Then, by Eqs. (4-38), (4-41), and (4-43),

$$
\begin{aligned}
\ln \hat{\phi}_i = \ln \phi &- \frac{\mathscr{H}}{T_{\text{pr}}}\left\{\frac{1}{T_{\text{pc}}}\left[\frac{\partial(nT_{\text{pc}})}{\partial n_i}\right]_{n_j} - 1\right\} \\
&+ (1-Z)\left\{\frac{1}{P_{\text{pc}}}\left[\frac{\partial(nP_{\text{pc}})}{\partial n_i}\right]_{n_j} - 1\right\} \\
&+ \pi_p\left(\frac{\partial \ln \phi}{\partial \pi_p}\right)_{T_{\text{pr}},\,P_{\text{pr}}}\left\{\frac{1}{\pi_p}\left[\frac{\partial(n\pi_p)}{\partial n_i}\right]_{n_j} - 1\right\}
\end{aligned} \tag{4-44}
$$

Example 4-4 We illustrate the use of Eq. (4-44) with a concrete example: the calculation of $\ln \hat{\phi}_i$ from Pitzer's corresponding-states correlation for $\ln \phi$, which, by Eqs. (4-32) and (4-36), is written for a mixture as

$$\ln \phi = \ln \phi^0 + \omega_p \ln \phi^1 \tag{A}$$

Additionally, we assume the applicability of the rules given by Eq. (4-35) and written as

$$
\left.
\begin{aligned}
T_{\text{pc}} &= \sum x_k T_{c_k} \\
P_{\text{pc}} &= \sum x_k P_{c_k} \\
\omega_p &= \sum x_k \omega_k
\end{aligned}
\right\} \tag{B}
$$

Here, we use dummy subscript k to avoid confusing a general species with the *particular* species i. Multiplication of Eqs. (B) by n and differentiation with respect to n_i gives

$$
\left.
\begin{aligned}
\left[\frac{\partial(nT_{\text{pc}})}{\partial n_i}\right]_{n_j} &= T_{c_i} \\
\left[\frac{\partial(nP_{\text{pc}})}{\partial n_i}\right]_{n_j} &= P_{c_i} \\
\left[\frac{\partial(n\pi_p)}{\partial n_i}\right]_{n_j} &\equiv \left[\frac{\partial(n\omega_p)}{\partial n_i}\right]_{n_j} = \omega_i
\end{aligned}
\right\} \tag{C}
$$

Also, by Eq. (A),

$$\left(\frac{\partial \ln \phi}{\partial \pi_p}\right)_{T_{\text{pr}},\,P_{\text{pr}}} \equiv \left(\frac{\partial \ln \phi}{\partial \omega_p}\right)_{T_{\text{pr}},\,P_{\text{pr}}} = \ln \phi^1 \tag{D}$$

Noting that $T_{\text{pr}} T_{\text{pc}} = T$, we then have, by Eqs. (4-44), (C), and (D),

$$\ln \hat{\phi}_i = \ln \phi - \mathscr{H}\left(\frac{T_{c_i} - T_{\text{pc}}}{T}\right) + (1-Z)\left(\frac{P_{c_i} - P_{\text{pc}}}{P_{\text{pc}}}\right) + (\omega_i - \omega_p)\ln \phi^1 \tag{E}$$

with $\mathcal{H}$ defined by Eq. (4-42) and T_{pc}, P_{pc}, and ω_p given by Eqs. (B). For a *binary* mixture containing components 1 and 2, Eq. (E) yields the pair of equations

$$\ln \hat{\phi}_1 = \ln \phi + x_2 F_{12}$$

$$\ln \hat{\phi}_2 = \ln \phi - x_1 F_{12}$$

where

$$F_{12} \equiv -\mathcal{H}\left(\frac{T_{c_1} - T_{c_2}}{T}\right) + (1 - Z)\left(\frac{P_{c_1} - P_{c_2}}{x_1 P_{c_1} + x_2 P_{c_2}}\right) + (\omega_1 - \omega_2)\ln \phi^1$$

The validity of Eq. (E) is conditioned in part by the appropriateness of the simple rules for the pseudoparameters given by Eqs. (B). However, there is nothing that limits the *general* approach of this section to such rules. For example, the pseudocritical rules given by Eqs. (4-35a) and (4-35b) are sometimes replaced by the more flexible *quadratic* rules

$$T_{pc} = \sum_i \sum_j x_i x_j T_{c_{ij}}$$

and

$$P_{pc} = \sum_i \sum_j x_i x_j P_{c_{ij}}$$

Such rules merely produce more complicated expressions for the mole-number derivatives of nT_{pc} and nP_{pc} than are given in this example by Eqs. (C). In addition, the quadratic rules require recipes for evaluation of the "cross terms" $T_{c_{ij}}$ and $P_{c_{ij}}$, where $i \neq j$.

4-5 VIRIAL EQUATIONS OF STATE

The use of corresponding-states correlations for the calculation of thermodynamic properties is not always possible. For example, if a fluid is highly polar, it is not likely to conform to correlations such as Pitzer's. Even for nonpolar substances, one inevitably sacrifices some accuracy for *particular* species when developing correlations for a *class* of substances, and the accuracy obtained for properties of a particular conforming substance may not be satisfactory for all applications. Finally, the apparatus developed in the preceding section for evaluation of partial properties may be difficult to implement, particularly if the corresponding-states correlations are not available in analytical form. For these and other reasons, one often resorts to the use of *equations of state*. In this and the next section we treat a class of equations appropriate for the description of properties of gases at low to moderate densities.

At constant temperature and composition, we may consider the compressibility factor of a fluid to be a function only of the molar density ρ ($\rho \equiv 1/V$). If Z is moreover an *analytic* function of ρ, then we may represent it by a Taylor series:

$$Z = Z_0 + \sum_{n=1}^{\infty} \mathcal{B}_n(\rho - \rho_0)^n \tag{A}$$

where

$$\mathcal{B}_n = \frac{1}{n!}\left(\frac{\partial^n Z}{\partial \rho^n}\right)_{T,\,x;\,\rho_0} \tag{B}$$

In these equations, subscript 0 refers to a *reference state*, about which the series expansion is performed. The temperature and composition of the reference state are those of the fluid, but the density ρ_0 is the value at some reference pressure P_0. The reference value of the compressibility factor Z_0 is related to ρ_0 and P_0 through the definition of Z:

$$Z_0 = \frac{P_0}{\rho_0 RT} \tag{C}$$

Equation (B) provides a general recipe for the coefficient $\mathcal{B}_n$ in terms of derivatives of Z with respect to density, evaluated at the reference state.

In applying Eq. (A) to the representation of gas-phase isotherms, we choose the reference state to be that of the *real gas at zero pressure*. Thus $P_0 = 0$, $Z_0 = 1$, and, by Eq. (C), $\rho_0 = 0$. Equations (A) and (B) then become

$$Z = 1 + \sum_{n=1}^{\infty} \mathcal{B}_n \rho^n \tag{4-45}$$

and

$$\mathcal{B}_n = \frac{1}{n!}\left(\frac{\partial^n Z}{\partial \rho^n}\right)_{T,\,x;\,\rho=0} \tag{4-46}$$

Equation (4-45) is the *virial equation in density*, and Eq. (4-46) provides definitions for the *density-series virial coefficients*. Thus

$$B \equiv \mathcal{B}_1 = \left(\frac{\partial Z}{\partial \rho}\right)_{T,\,x;\,\rho=0} \tag{4-47a}$$

$$C \equiv \mathcal{B}_2 = \frac{1}{2}\left(\frac{\partial^2 Z}{\partial \rho^2}\right)_{T,\,x;\,\rho=0} \tag{4-47b}$$

$$D \equiv \mathcal{B}_3 = \frac{1}{6}\left(\frac{\partial^3 Z}{\partial \rho^3}\right)_{T,\,x;\,\rho=0} \tag{4-47c}$$

etc.

where by convention B is called the *second virial coefficient*, C the *third virial coefficient*, D the *fourth*, and so on. (By this convention, the "first" virial coefficient is unity.) According to the general definition, Eq. (4-46), the virial coefficients are functions of T and x only.

In the above development we considered Z a function of density, at constant T and x. We may equally well choose *pressure* as the independent variable and expand Z in powers of the difference $P - P_0$, where P_0 is the pressure of the reference state, obtaining as analogs of Eqs. (A) and (B):

$$Z = Z_0 + \sum_{n=1}^{\infty} \mathcal{B}'_n (P - P_0)^n \qquad \text{(D)}$$

and

$$\mathcal{B}'_n = \frac{1}{n!} \left(\frac{\partial^n Z}{\partial P^n} \right)_{T, x; P_0} \qquad \text{(E)}$$

Again picking the reference state as the real gas at zero pressure, we obtain from Eq. (D) the *virial equation in pressure*

$$\boxed{Z = 1 + \sum_{n=1}^{\infty} \mathcal{B}'_n P^n} \qquad \text{(4-48)}$$

with *pressure-series virial coefficients* given by

$$\boxed{\mathcal{B}'_n = \frac{1}{n!} \left(\frac{\partial^n Z}{\partial P^n} \right)_{T, x; P=0}} \qquad \text{(4-49)}$$

Thus

$$B' \equiv \mathcal{B}'_1 = \left(\frac{\partial Z}{\partial P} \right)_{T, x; P=0} \qquad \text{(4-50a)}$$

$$C' \equiv \mathcal{B}'_2 = \frac{1}{2} \left(\frac{\partial^2 Z}{\partial P^2} \right)_{T, x; P=0} \qquad \text{(4-50b)}$$

$$D' \equiv \mathcal{B}'_3 = \frac{1}{6} \left(\frac{\partial^3 Z}{\partial P^3} \right)_{T, x; P=0} \qquad \text{(4-50c)}$$

etc.

Here also B' is called a second virial coefficient, C' a third, etc. By Eq. (4-49), each of the pressure-series virial coefficients is a function of T and x only.

Equations (4-45) and (4-48) both provide general expressions for Z, the first in terms of ρ, T, and x, and the second in terms of P, T, and x. Since ρ and P are related through $P = \rho ZRT$, the virial coefficients in the two series are clearly also related. There are many ways of establishing these relationships; we illustrate here a procedure which makes direct use of the definitions given by Eqs. (4-47) and (4-50). For the second virial coefficients

$$B = \left(\frac{\partial Z}{\partial \rho} \right)_{T, x; \rho=0} \qquad B' = \left(\frac{\partial Z}{\partial P} \right)_{T, x; P=0}$$

and to find the relation between B and B' we need only find the relation between the two derivatives. We have

$$\left(\frac{\partial Z}{\partial P}\right)_{T,x} = \left(\frac{\partial Z}{\partial \rho}\right)_{T,x}\left(\frac{\partial \rho}{\partial P}\right)_{T,x}$$

But $\rho = P/ZRT$, and therefore

$$\left(\frac{\partial \rho}{\partial P}\right)_{T,x} = \frac{1}{ZRT}\left[1 - \frac{P}{Z}\left(\frac{\partial Z}{\partial P}\right)_{T,x}\right]$$

Combination of the last two equations and solution for $(\partial Z/\partial P)_{T,x}$ gives

$$\left(\frac{\partial Z}{\partial P}\right)_{T,x} = \frac{(\partial Z/\partial \rho)_{T,x}}{ZRT + (P/Z)(\partial Z/\partial \rho)_{T,x}}$$

from which we obtain, for $P = \rho = 0$ and $Z = 1$,

$$\left(\frac{\partial Z}{\partial P}\right)_{T,x;\,\rho=0} = \frac{1}{RT}\left(\frac{\partial Z}{\partial \rho}\right)_{T,x;\,P=0}$$

and thus

$$B' = \frac{B}{RT} \tag{4-51a}$$

Similar but more lengthy derivations yield relations among the higher coefficients. For C' and D' they are

$$C' = \frac{C - B^2}{(RT)^2} \tag{4-51b}$$

and

$$D' = \frac{D - 3BC + 2B^3}{(RT)^3} \tag{4-51c}$$

Although we have introduced the virial equations on purely empirical grounds, their real utility derives from the fact that they have a firm basis in theory. The methods of statistical mechanics allow independent derivation of these equations and moreover provide physical significance to the virial coefficients. Thus, for the expansion in density, the term $B\rho$ arises on account of interactions between pairs of molecules, the $C\rho^2$ term on account of three-body interactions, and so on. The nature and magnitude of intermolecular forces are represented through models for the intermolecular potential function, and statistical mechanics provides recipes for the calculation of B, C, etc. from such models. For our purposes, the most important result of the statistical approach is that it also yields *exact* expressions for the composition dependence of the virial coefficients for mixtures. These are used in the next section, where we apply the virial equations to calculation of mixture properties.

It has already been noted that the virial coefficients depend upon T and x

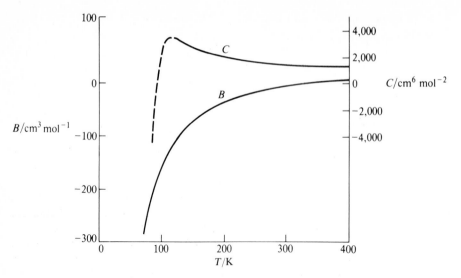

Figure 4-8 Density-series virial coefficients B and C for nitrogen. Dashed portion of C curve is computed from correlation of Chueh and Prausnitz (1967*a*).

only. Figure 4-8 illustrates the effect of temperature on the density-series coefficients B and C for nitrogen; although the numerical values given are different for other fluids, similar trends with T are observed for all substances. At low temperatures, the second virial coefficient B is negative; qualitatively, this is attributed to the preponderance of long-range *attractive* forces, which tend to reduce the pressure of a gas below that given by the ideal-gas equation. As temperature increases, molecular collisions become more energetic, increasing the contribution of short-range *repulsive* forces and causing B to become less negative. At the *Boyle temperature* (about 330 K for nitrogen), attractive and repulsive forces between pairs of molecules are approximately balanced, and B becomes zero. For higher temperatures, repulsive forces dominate, and B is positive, increasing slowly with T and eventually passing through a very flat maximum. This maximum has only been observed for fluids with very low critical temperatures (He, H_2, Ne).

The effect of T on C is qualitatively similar to that for B. However, the maximum in C occurs at a much lower temperature, and the change of C with T to the left of the maximum is very rapid. The experimental determination of values for C is in fact subject to large uncertainties, particularly at subcritical temperatures, and the low-temperature behavior indicated by the dashed line on Fig. 4-8 has been substantiated for only a few fluids.

Virtually nothing is known about the detailed behavior of virial coefficients beyond the third, except as has been determined from statistical-mechanical calculations based on models of the intermolecular potential. Such calculations suggest similar shapes for D versus T and E versus T as for the third virial coefficient.

Shown on Fig. 4-9 are the pressure-series virial coefficients B' and C' for nitrogen, determined from B and C by Eqs. (4-51a) and (4-51b). Particularly to be noted is the relative flatness of the curves, compared to those for the density-series coefficients. The biggest variations in B' and C' occur over relatively narrow ranges of temperature, and C' is effectively zero for all temperatures above about 175 K.

The virial coefficients are *defined* by Eqs. (4-46) and (4-49) as proportional to derivatives of Z with respect to ρ or P, evaluated at zero pressure, and *only* quantities determined in accordance with these prescriptions may actually be identified as virial coefficients. It is obvious that collection of data suitable for extraction of higher virial coefficients places extreme demands on the experimentalist, for his results must survive n differentiations at a condition (zero pressure) where in fact no data can actually be taken. Clearly, extrapolations are required, but the extrapolation techniques must be consistent with the definitions. We develop one such technique in the following paragraphs, and illustrate its use in Example 4-5.

The virial equation in density, Eq. (4-45), may be written

$$Z = 1 + \sum_{n=1}^{l-1} \mathscr{B}_n \rho^n + \sum_{n=l}^{\infty} \mathscr{B}_n \rho^n$$

Without the final sum, this equation would represent a truncation of the virial equation to l terms; the remaining terms are provided by the final sum. An alternative form of this equation is given by

$$Z - 1 - \sum_{n=1}^{l-1} \mathscr{B}_n \rho^n = \sum_{n=l}^{\infty} \mathscr{B}_n \rho^n = \rho^l \sum_{n=l}^{\infty} \mathscr{B}_n \rho^{n-l}$$

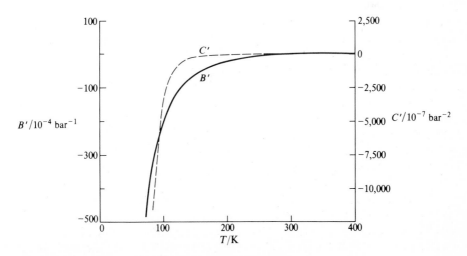

Figure 4-9 Pressure-series virial coefficients B' and C' for nitrogen.

We *define* the function ψ_l as

$$\psi_l \equiv \frac{Z - 1 - \sum\limits_{n=1}^{l-1} \mathscr{B}_n \rho^n}{\rho^l} \tag{4-52}$$

An alternative expression for this function results from the preceding equation:

$$\psi_l = \sum_{n=l}^{\infty} \mathscr{B}_n \rho^{n-l} \tag{4-53}$$

or

$$\psi_l = \mathscr{B}_l + \mathscr{B}_{l+1}\rho + \mathscr{B}_{l+2}\rho^2 + \cdots$$

In the limit as $\rho \to 0$, this becomes

$$\lim_{\rho \to 0} \psi_l = \mathscr{B}_l \tag{4-54}$$

Differentiation of Eq. (4-53) with respect to density at constant temperature and composition gives

$$\left(\frac{\partial \psi_l}{\partial \rho}\right)_{T,x} = \sum_{n=l}^{\infty} (n - l)\mathscr{B}_n \rho^{n-l-1}$$

or

$$\left(\frac{\partial \psi_l}{\partial \rho}\right)_{T,x} = \mathscr{B}_{l+1} + 2\mathscr{B}_{l+2}\rho + 3\mathscr{B}_{l+3}\rho^2 + \cdots$$

In the limit as $\rho \to 0$, this becomes

$$\lim_{\rho \to 0} \left(\frac{\partial \psi_l}{\partial \rho}\right)_{T,x} = \mathscr{B}_{l+1} \tag{4-55}$$

Equations (4-54) and (4-55) show that a plot of ψ_l versus ρ has an intercept at $\rho = 0$ of $\mathscr{B}_l$ and a slope at $\rho = 0$ of $\mathscr{B}_{l+1}$.

Calculation of values of ψ_l from Eq. (4-52) for such a plot requires a set of isothermal Z versus ρ data, plus predetermined values for virial coefficients $\mathscr{B}_{n<l}$. Thus, we must start the process with $l = 1$, in which case Eq. (4-52) becomes

$$\psi_1 \equiv \frac{Z - 1}{\rho}$$

A plot of ψ_1 versus ρ then yields the second virial coefficient $B \equiv \mathscr{B}_1$ as the intercept:

$$B = \lim_{\rho \to 0} \psi_1 = \lim_{\rho \to 0} \left(\frac{Z - 1}{\rho}\right) \tag{4-56}$$

From the same plot, an estimate of the third virial coefficient $C \equiv \mathscr{B}_2$ is given as the limiting slope at $\rho = 0$:

$$C = \lim_{\rho \to 0} \left(\frac{\partial \psi_1}{\partial \rho} \right)_{T, x} = \lim_{\rho \to 0} \left| \frac{\partial [(Z - 1)/\rho]}{\partial \rho} \right|_{T, x} \qquad (4\text{-}57)$$

With data of sufficient precision, one can obtain a better value for C by a second application of Eq. (4-54), but with $l = 2$. Equation (4-52) here becomes

$$\psi_2 \equiv \frac{Z - 1 - \mathscr{B}_1 \rho}{\rho^2} = \frac{Z - 1 - B\rho}{\rho^2}$$

where the value of B is now known. From Eq. (4-54), we have

$$\lim_{\rho \to 0} \psi_2 = \mathscr{B}_2 \equiv C$$

or

$$C = \lim_{\rho \to 0} \left(\frac{Z - 1 - B\rho}{\rho^2} \right) \qquad (4\text{-}58)$$

and by Eq. (4-55)

$$\lim_{\rho \to 0} \left(\frac{\partial \psi_2}{\partial \rho} \right)_{T, x} = \mathscr{B}_3 \equiv D$$

or

$$D = \lim_{\rho \to 0} \left| \frac{\partial [(Z - 1 - B\rho)/\rho^2]}{\partial \rho} \right|_{T, x} \qquad (4\text{-}59)$$

Thus, from a plot of ψ_2 versus ρ, we find a value for the third virial coefficient and an estimate of the fourth.

In principle, this procedure can be extended indefinitely, but in practice rarely further than has been illustrated. An advantage of the procedure is that virial coefficients found through Eq. (4-54) result from the operation of *extrapolation* rather than the more difficult operation of *differentiation* implicit in direct application of the defining equation, Eq. (4-46). The differentiation indicated by Eq. (4-55) is, in effect, of a lower order than that required by Eq. (4-46). These advantages are of course partly illusory. We see by Eq. (4-52) that ψ_1 becomes indeterminate as $\rho \to 0$; this is reflected in the fact that plots of ψ_1 versus ρ are very sensitive to any imprecisions in the data, and the scatter of data points increases in magnitude and extends to higher densities as l is increased. The inherent limitations of current experimental techniques limit the usefulness of this and equivalent procedures to the determination of B, C, and, occasionally, D. Nonetheless, one finds in data compilations tables of "virial coefficients" through the *seventh* for some fluids. Such parameters are obtained by curve-fits of volumetric data to finite polynomial equations, for example of the form

$$Z = 1 + \sum_{n=1}^{m} \mathscr{B}_n^* \rho^n$$

Except for $\mathscr{B}_1^*$ and possibly $\mathscr{B}_2^*$, the values of the $\mathscr{B}_n^*$ so obtained cannot properly be identified with the true virial coefficients $\mathscr{B}_n$; the higher $\mathscr{B}_n^*$ are merely curve-fit coefficients, which may show no regular variation with temperature and no rational trends from one substance to another.

Example 4-5 We illustrate the evaluation of virial coefficients from PVT data. The basis for this example is the set of specific volumes for water vapor at 260°C reported in the steam tables of Keenan et al. (1969). These of course are not actual data; they are values generated from a comprehensive equation of state *based* on many data. They are extremely smooth, and thus simulate a data set of very high precision.

Keenan et al. list 141 entries of specific volume V at 260°C for pressures between 0.01 bar and the saturation pressure of 46.88 bar. Values selected at reasonable intervals were converted to compressibility factors and molar densities. The corresponding values of $\psi_1 \equiv (Z - 1)/\rho$ were then computed and plotted against ρ as shown in Fig. 4-10a. The points represent pressures from 0.25 bar to 46.88 bar. On the scale of this graph, there is a substantial amount of scatter up to a ρ of about 20×10^{-5} mol cm^{-3}, but a much smoother trend at higher densities. The curve drawn through the points yields an intercept of -142.2 cm^3 mol^{-1}, and by Eq. (4-56) this is the second virial coefficient B. Depending on how the limiting tangent to the curve at $\rho = 0$ is drawn, values for C between about -6500 and -7500 cm^6 mol^{-2} are obtained.

A better estimate for C results from the ψ_2 versus ρ plot, shown in Fig. 4-10b. Very significant scatter is obtained up to a ρ of about 50×10^{-5} mol cm^{-3}, with many of the points off scale on Fig. 4-10b. Above this density, a linear trend is observed, with less scatter. At 260°C and below 50×10^{-5} mol cm^{-3}, Z for water vapor is insensitive to C within the range of values covered by the scatter; for purposes of determining the intercept an extrapolation (as shown) from higher densities is entirely satisfactory. This extrapolation gives a C of -7140 cm^6 mol^{-2}, and the slope of the line yields $D = 1.51 \times 10^6$ cm^9 mol^{-3}.

To summarize:

$$B = -142.2 \text{ cm}^3 \text{ mol}^{-1}$$

$$C = -7140 \text{ cm}^6 \text{ mol}^{-2}$$

$$D = 1.51 \times 10^6 \text{ cm}^9 \text{ mol}^{-3}$$

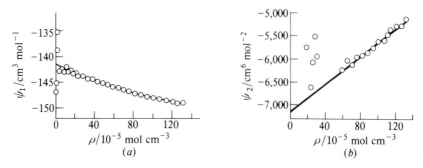

Figure 4-10 Plots of ψ_1 (a) and ψ_2 (b) for water vapor at 260°C. Values of ψ_1 and ψ_2 are determined from steam-table entries of Keenan et al. (1969). (See Example 4-5.)

Table 4-1 Contributions of terms in the virial equation to Z for water vapor at 260°C

P/bar	$B\rho$	$C\rho^2$	$D\rho^3$	Z	V(calculated)/ cm^3 g^{-1}	V(steam tables)/ cm^3 g^{-1}
0.01	-0.00003	-4×10^{-10}	2×10^{-14}	0.99997	246,046	246,046
0.1	-0.00032	-4×10^{-8}	2×10^{-11}	0.99968	24,598	24,598
1	-0.00322	-4×10^{-6}	2×10^{-8}	0.99678	2,452.6	2,453
10	-0.03318	-0.00039	0.00002	0.96645	237.80	237.8
25	-0.08816	-0.00274	0.00036	0.91193	89.511	89.51
46.88	-0.18695	-0.01234	0.00343	0.80414	42.206	42.21

for water vapor at 260°C. No indication has been given of the uncertainties in these coefficients, but it should be evident that the determination of the latter two, particularly D, is subject to rather large errors. Estimates of the higher coefficients cannot be made from the steam-table entries, but it is apparent from Fig. 4-10 that coefficients beyond D are unnecessary at this temperature.

It is instructive to compare the relative contributions to Z of the terms containing B, C, and D, and we do this in Table 4-1. Also shown are specific volumes calculated with the derived virial coefficients and the corresponding volumes from the steam tables. Up to a pressure of about 5 bar, the virial equation truncated to two terms gives essentially a perfect fit to the steam-table values, and even at 25 bar the contribution of the C and D terms to Z is only about 0.4%. This is why the extrapolation to $\rho = 0$ from higher densities in Fig. 4-10b is sufficient for determination of C. The excellent agreement between calculated and steam-table volumes illustrates the appropriateness of a four-term polynomial in ρ as a curve-fitting device for this isotherm.

Expressions for the residual functions may be found from the virial equations. We treat the virial equations in pressure first. Evaluation of $\Delta H'$, $\Delta S'$, $\ln \phi$, and $\Delta C'_P$ requires expressions for the first and second temperature derivatives of Z. Since

$$Z = 1 + \sum_{n=1}^{\infty} \mathscr{B}'_n P^n \tag{4-48}$$

we find

$$\left(\frac{\partial Z}{\partial T}\right)_P = \sum_{n=1}^{\infty} \frac{d\mathscr{B}'_n}{dT} P^n \tag{4-60}$$

and

$$\left(\frac{\partial^2 Z}{\partial T^2}\right)_P = \sum_{n=1}^{\infty} \frac{d^2 \mathscr{B}'_n}{dT^2} P^n \tag{4-61}$$

Then, by Eqs. (4-17) and (4-60),

$$\Delta H' = RT^2 \int_0^P \left(\frac{\partial Z}{\partial T}\right)_P \frac{dP}{P}$$

$$= RT^2 \int_0^P \sum_{n=1}^{\infty} \frac{d\mathscr{B}'_n}{dT} P^{n-1} \, dP$$

or

$$\Delta H' = RT^2 \sum_{n=1}^{\infty} \frac{1}{n} \frac{d\mathscr{B}'_n}{dT} P^n \qquad (4\text{-}62)$$

Similarly, we find $\Delta S'$ by combination of Eqs. (4-18), (4-48), and (4-60), obtaining

$$\Delta S' = RT \sum_{n=1}^{\infty} \frac{1}{n} \left(\frac{\mathscr{B}'_n}{T} + \frac{d\mathscr{B}'_n}{dT} \right) P^n \qquad (4\text{-}63)$$

The expression for $\ln \phi$ follows by combination of Eqs. (4-62) and (4-63) according to Eq. (4-22). The result is

$$\ln \phi = \sum_{n=1}^{\infty} \frac{1}{n} \mathscr{B}'_n P^n \qquad (4\text{-}64)$$

Finally, Eqs. (4-25), (4-60), and (4-61) yield for $\Delta C'_P$ the equation

$$\Delta C'_P = RT^2 \sum_{n=1}^{\infty} \frac{1}{n} \left(\frac{d^2\mathscr{B}'_n}{dT^2} + \frac{2}{T} \frac{d\mathscr{B}'_n}{dT} \right) P^n \qquad (4\text{-}65)$$

Equation (4-65) also follows from Eq. (4-62) by application of the exact thermodynamic formula

$$\Delta C'_P = \left(\frac{\partial \Delta H'}{\partial T} \right)_P \qquad (4\text{-}66)$$

The equations of this section apply to a gas of *constant composition*. Thus the temperature derivatives of the $\mathscr{B}'_n$ are written as ordinary derivatives, for the $\mathscr{B}'_n$ depend upon T and x only.

The virial equation in pressure is a *volume-explicit equation of state*; that is, Eq. (4-48) can be solved explicitly for V as a function of T and P:

$$V = \frac{ZRT}{P} = \frac{RT}{P} \left(1 + \sum_{n=1}^{\infty} \mathscr{B}'_n P^n \right)$$

This has practical advantages, because the intensive variables T and P are the ones normally measured and controlled in experiments, or specified in a chemical process design. Given values for T and P, calculation of volumes (or densities) and of all residual functions from a volume-explicit equation of state is straightforward, involving no iteration.

The virial equation in density, on the other hand, is a *pressure-explicit equation of state*. That is, Eq. (4-45) can be solved explicitly for P as a function of T and ρ:

$$P = Z\rho RT = \rho RT \left(1 + \sum_{n=1}^{\infty} \mathscr{B}_n \rho^n \right)$$

However, it cannot be solved explicitly for V (or ρ) as a function of T and P. Moreover, Eqs. (4-17), (4-18), and (4-25) for the residual functions cannot be used as they stand with Eq. (4-45), for they are written in a form which presumes the availability of a volume-explicit equation. This difficulty is easily circumvented, but the derivations of the required equations are tedious and we relegate them to App. C, where there is deposited a collection of formulas for evaluation of residual functions from equations of state. We merely list here the ones useful for our present purposes:

$$\Delta H' = RT^2 \int_0^\rho \left(\frac{\partial Z}{\partial T}\right)_\rho \frac{d\rho}{\rho} - RT(Z-1) \tag{4-67}$$

$$\Delta S' = RT \int_0^\rho \left(\frac{\partial Z}{\partial T}\right)_\rho \frac{d\rho}{\rho} + R \int_0^\rho (Z-1) \frac{d\rho}{\rho} - R \ln Z \tag{4-68}$$

$$\ln \phi = Z - 1 - \ln Z + \int_0^\rho (Z-1) \frac{d\rho}{\rho} \tag{4-69}$$

and

$$\Delta C_V' = RT \int_0^\rho \left[T\left(\frac{\partial^2 Z}{\partial T^2}\right)_\rho + 2\left(\frac{\partial Z}{\partial T}\right)_\rho \right] \frac{d\rho}{\rho} \tag{4-70}$$

Here, all integrations are performed at constant T and x. Note that Eq. (4-70) yields $\Delta C_V'$; this is the natural residual heat capacity for a pressure-explicit equation of state. The residual constant-*pressure* heat capacity can be found from $\Delta C_V'$ by use of exact thermodynamic methods, as described in App. C.

Since

$$Z = 1 + \sum_{n=1}^\infty \mathscr{B}_n \rho^n \tag{4-45}$$

we have

$$\left(\frac{\partial Z}{\partial T}\right)_\rho = \sum_{n=1}^\infty \frac{d\mathscr{B}_n}{dT} \rho^n \tag{4-71}$$

and

$$\left(\frac{\partial^2 Z}{\partial T^2}\right)_\rho = \sum_{n=1}^\infty \frac{d^2 \mathscr{B}_n}{dT^2} \rho^n \tag{4-72}$$

By Eqs. (4-45) and (4-67) through (4-72) we find the following expressions for residual functions implied by the virial equation in density:

$$\Delta H' = RT^2 \sum_{n=1}^\infty \left(\frac{1}{n} \frac{d\mathscr{B}_n}{dT} - \frac{\mathscr{B}_n}{T}\right) \rho^n \tag{4-73}$$

$$\Delta S' = RT \sum_{n=1}^\infty \frac{1}{n} \left(\frac{d\mathscr{B}_n}{dT} + \frac{\mathscr{B}_n}{T}\right) \rho^n - R \ln Z \tag{4-74}$$

$$\ln \phi = \sum_{n=1}^\infty \left(\frac{n+1}{n}\right) \mathscr{B}_n \rho^n - \ln Z \tag{4-75}$$

$$\Delta C_V' = RT^2 \sum_{n=1}^{\infty} \frac{1}{n} \left(\frac{d^2\mathscr{B}_n}{dT^2} + \frac{2}{T} \frac{d\mathscr{B}_n}{dT} \right) \rho^n \qquad (4\text{-}76)$$

We have now developed two parallel sets of equations: one based upon the virial expansion in pressure, and the other upon the virial equation in density. But the two virial equations are merely alternative infinite-series representations of the compressibility factor, and are presumably equivalent. One might therefore question the value of two parallel approaches. The reason is a pragmatic one: the actual representation of Z by an *infinite* series in ρ or P is a practical impossibility; moreover, values for the true virial coefficients beyond the third are rarely available. Thus one must in practice deal with *truncations* of the virial equations, and for the same number of terms these are not equivalent for the two kinds of series.

Two degrees of approximation to the virial equations are commonly used: truncations to two terms, and truncations to three terms. Thus, we have by Eqs. (4-45) and (4-48) to the first-order terms in ρ and P:

$$Z = 1 + B\rho \qquad (4\text{-}77)$$

and

$$\boxed{Z = 1 + \frac{BP}{RT}} \qquad (4\text{-}78)$$

Similarly, we obtain through the second-order terms in ρ and P:

$$\boxed{Z = 1 + B\rho + C\rho^2} \qquad (4\text{-}79)$$

and

$$Z = 1 + \frac{BP}{RT} + \frac{C - B^2}{(RT)^2} P^2 \qquad (4\text{-}80)$$

In Eqs. (4-78) and (4-80), we have eliminated B' and C' in favor of B and C by Eqs. (4-51a) and (4-51b), because the density-series virial coefficients have more direct theoretical interpretations, and are the ones normally reported in experimental studies and in data compilations.

The virial equations in pressure and in density are known to converge at different rates, and so for a given degree of truncation the two types of equations provide different degrees of approximation to the true behavior of a fluid. This is illustrated by Figs. 4-11 and 4-12, which are plots of isotherms of Z for nitrogen; on Fig. 4-11, density is the independent variable, and on Fig. 4-12, pressure. Whether compared over a fixed range of pressure or of density, the shapes of the isotherms on the two figures are markedly different. In particular, the isotherms on the Z-versus-ρ plot show less irregular behavior at high densities and low temperatures. This is reflected in the common observation that Z for dense gases is better represented by a polynomial in density than by a polynomial of the same degree in pressure. Thus Eq. (4-79) is the preferred three-term virial equation. At low densities, the situation is not so clear-cut. As shown on Figs. 4-11

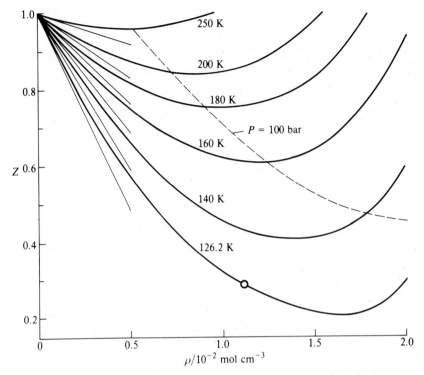

Figure 4-11 Isotherms of Z for nitrogen, with molar density as the independent variable. Straight lines are approximations provided by Eq. (4-77).

and 4-12, the straight-line approximations provided by Eqs. (4-77) and (4-78) yield deviations of comparable magnitudes up to a density of 5×10^{-3} mol cm^{-3} (about half the critical density); in fact, for the temperature range shown, Eq. (4-78) appears to be better. Because it is easier to use, Eq. (4-78) is therefore the preferred two-term virial equation for applications at low densities.

The expressions for the derived functions may now be simplified. For applications based upon the two-term equation in pressure, Eqs. (4-62) through (4-65) yield, with $\mathcal{B}'_1 \equiv B' = B/RT$,

$$\Delta H' = \left(T\,\frac{dB}{dT} - B \right) P \tag{4-81}$$

$$\Delta S' = \frac{dB}{dT}\,P \tag{4-82}$$

$$\ln \phi = \frac{BP}{RT} \tag{4-83}$$

$$\Delta C'_P = T\,\frac{d^2 B}{dT^2}\,P \tag{4-84}$$

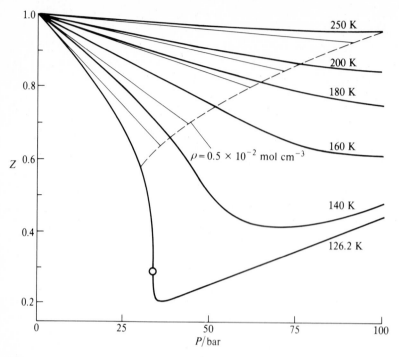

Figure 4-12 Isotherms of Z for nitrogen, with pressure as the independent variable. Straight lines are approximations provided by Eq. (4-78).

Similarly, Eqs. (4-73) through (4-76) produce, consistent with the three-term equation in density,

$$\Delta H' = RT^2 \left[\left(\frac{dB}{dT} - \frac{B}{T} \right) \rho + \left(\frac{1}{2} \frac{dC}{dT} - \frac{C}{T} \right) \rho^2 \right] \tag{4-85}$$

$$\Delta S' = RT \left[\left(\frac{dB}{dT} + \frac{B}{T} \right) \rho + \frac{1}{2} \left(\frac{dC}{dT} + \frac{C}{T} \right) \rho^2 \right] - R \ln Z \tag{4-86}$$

$$\ln \phi = 2B\rho + \tfrac{3}{2}C\rho^2 - \ln Z \tag{4-87}$$

$$\Delta C_V' = RT^2 \left[\left(\frac{d^2B}{dT^2} + \frac{2}{T} \frac{dB}{dT} \right) \rho + \frac{1}{2} \left(\frac{d^2C}{dT^2} + \frac{2}{T} \frac{dC}{dT} \right) \rho^2 \right] \tag{4-88}$$

For specified T and P, the application of Eqs. (4-81) through (4-84) is straightforward; all that is required is an expression for B as a function of T. Since $\Delta H'$, $\Delta S'$, and $\Delta C_P'$ depend upon the derivatives of B, the temperature dependence of the second virial coefficient must be known with some accuracy. Use of Eqs. (4-85) through (4-88) requires prior evaluation of Z and ρ; if T and P are given, then Eq. (4-79) must first be solved for these quantities.

Rules of thumb for the ranges of applicability of truncations of the virial equations are conventionally expressed in terms of the reduced density, or the reduced volume. Thus, the two-term expression in pressure, Eq. (4-78), is variously stated as being a good approximation up to reduced densities between 0.25 and 0.50. Similarly, the three-term equation in density, Eq. (4-79), is often claimed to be useful up to reduced densities of 0.50 to 1.0. Neither rule (however stated) should be viewed as more than a rough guideline, for the maximum density appropriate to a given degree of truncation depends also on the temperature level.

For applications at high densities (those near or greater than the critical), higher-order truncations of the virial equation are required. However, as already noted, virial coefficients beyond the third are rarely available. Moreover, there are questions as to whether the infinite virial series actually *converge* at high densities. Therefore the description of volumetric properties of dense gases is usually done with other, more empirical, equations of state.

Example 4-6 An important application of the results of this section is to the estimation of vapor-phase fugacity coefficients for phase-equilibrium calculations. Comparisons made at conditions near the critical state provide particularly severe tests of the approximations based upon truncated forms of the virial equations.

Kang et al. (1961) report isothermal volumetric data for SO_2 at its critical temperature of 157.5°C. Reduction of these data by the method illustrated in Fig. 4-10a and Example 4-5 provides the following values for the second and third virial coefficients:

$$B = -159 \text{ cm}^3 \text{ mol}^{-1} \qquad C = 9000 \text{ cm}^6 \text{ mol}^{-2}$$

Figure 4-13 shows several curves representing ϕ versus P. The curve labeled "experimental" is obtained from the data by graphical integration of Eq. (3-70):

$$\ln \phi = \int_0^P (Z - 1) \frac{dP}{P} \qquad (3\text{-}70)$$

Other curves represent various approximations to the fugacity coefficient. In addition to curves computed from Eqs. (4-83) and (4-87), there are shown two other approximations. The first is based on Eq. (4-80), the three-term virial equation in pressure, for which Eq. (4-64) reduces to

$$\ln \phi = \frac{BP}{RT} + \frac{C - B^2}{2(RT)^2} P^2 \qquad (4\text{-}89)$$

The approximation that $\phi = Z$ can be rationalized from Eqs. (4-78) and (4-83). If the two-term virial equation in pressure is valid, then these two equations imply that

$$\ln \phi = Z - 1$$

or

$$\phi = \exp (Z - 1)$$

Expanding the exponential, we obtain

$$\phi = 1 + (Z - 1) + \tfrac{1}{2}(Z - 1)^2 + \cdots$$

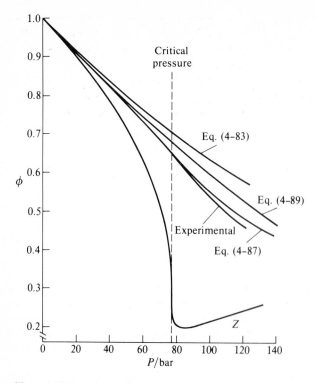

Figure 4-13 Fugacity coefficients for SO_2 at 157.5°C. (See Example 4-6.)

from which it follows, for $Z \simeq 1$, that

$$\phi \simeq Z$$

The assumptions underlying this approximation are of course severe, and it is not surprising that it compares very poorly with the experimental values, except at the lowest pressures.

Of the other approximations, the one based on the three-term virial equation in density is best, and clearly superior to Eq. (4-89). Equation (4-83), although imprecise, does not produce *gross* errors in the pressure range shown. This may seem surprising, in view of the inability of the two-term virial equation in pressure to reproduce even the qualitative features of the critical isotherm (see Fig. 4-12). The reason is that the calculation of ϕ by expressions such as Eq. (3-70) involves an integration, which tends to smooth out the peculiarities of volumetric behavior so evident on a Z-versus-P or Z-versus-ρ diagram. The effect of the rapid change in Z with P in the critical region *is* of course manifested in the behavior of ϕ, but not so dramatically.

Example 4-7 We have remarked several times that the behavior of real gases in the limit as $P \to 0$ does not in all respects approach that of the ideal gas. Material of this section provides the means for demonstrating some of the peculiarities of the "real ideal gas."

The basis for these demonstrations is the virial equation in pressure, Eq. (4-48):

$$Z = 1 + \sum_{n=1}^{\infty} \mathscr{B}'_n P^n$$

We first consider the residual volume $\Delta V'$, related to Z by Eq. (2-75):

$$\Delta V' = -\frac{RT}{P}(Z-1)$$

Combination of these two equations gives

$$\Delta V' = -RT \sum_{n=1}^{\infty} \mathscr{B}'_n P^{n-1}$$

from which

$$\lim_{P \to 0} \Delta V' = -RT\mathscr{B}'_1 = -RTB'$$

or, since $B' = B/RT$,

$$\lim_{P \to 0} \Delta V' = -B \tag{A}$$

Thus, the zero-pressure limit of $\Delta V'$ is proportional to the second virial coefficient. It is therefore nonzero except at the Boyle temperature, the single finite temperature at which $B = 0$. For simple fluids, the Boyle temperature corresponds to a reduced temperature of about $T_r = 2.7$. The behavior of $\Delta V'$ was illustrated earlier for nitrogen on Fig. 2-2.

We consider next the Joule-Thomson coefficient μ. By its definition, Eq. (2-45), we have

$$\mu \equiv \left(\frac{\partial T}{\partial P}\right)_H = -\left(\frac{\partial T}{\partial H}\right)_P \left(\frac{\partial H}{\partial P}\right)_T = -\frac{(\partial H/\partial P)_T}{(\partial H/\partial T)_P}$$

or

$$\mu = -\frac{(\partial H/\partial P)_T}{C_P}$$

As $P \to 0$, C_P for a real gas approaches its ideal-gas value C'_P. Moreover, by the definition of $\Delta H'$ and by Eq. (4-62),

$$\lim_{P \to 0}\left(\frac{\partial H}{\partial P}\right)_T = -\lim_{P \to 0}\left(\frac{\partial \Delta H'}{\partial P}\right)_T = -RT^2 \lim_{P \to 0} \sum_{n=1}^{\infty} \frac{d\mathscr{B}'_n}{dT} P^{n-1}$$

$$= -RT^2 \frac{d\mathscr{B}'_1}{dT} = -RT^2 \frac{dB'}{dT}$$

But $B' = B/RT$, and thus

$$\lim_{P \to 0}\left(\frac{\partial H}{\partial P}\right)_T = -T\left(\frac{dB}{dT} - \frac{B}{T}\right)$$

Therefore

$$\lim_{P \to 0} \mu = \frac{T}{C_P}\left(\frac{dB}{dT} - \frac{B}{T}\right) \tag{B}$$

Unlike the ideal gas, for which $\mu = 0$ everywhere, the real gas at zero pressure generally has nonzero values for μ, except, according to Eq. (B), at the single temperature for which

$$\frac{dB}{dT} = \frac{B}{T}$$

This temperature is called the *maximum inversion temperature*; it is a point on the inversion curve of a fluid, the curve representing the locus of all states for which $\mu = 0$. For simple fluids, the maximum inversion temperature corresponds to a reduced temperature of about $T_r = 5.1$.

As a final example, we consider the pressure derivative of C_P. From the definition of $\Delta C_P'$, we have

$$\lim_{P \to 0} \left(\frac{\partial C_P}{\partial P} \right)_T = -\lim_{P \to 0} \left(\frac{\partial \Delta C_P'}{\partial P} \right)_T$$

and, by Eq. (4-65), we find that

$$\lim_{P \to 0} \left(\frac{\partial \Delta C_P'}{\partial P} \right)_T = T \frac{d^2 B}{dT^2}$$

Thus

$$\lim_{P \to 0} \left(\frac{\partial C_P}{\partial P} \right)_T = -T \frac{d^2 B}{dT^2} \tag{C}$$

The pressure derivative of C_P is identically zero for an ideal gas. For a real gas at zero pressure, it is generally nonzero and positive up to very high reduced temperatures. Experimental measurements of $(\partial C_P / \partial P)_T$ provide a route to the determination of the second temperature derivative of B.

Example 4-8 Sufficient data have been collected for the second virial coefficient to allow the development of corresponding-states correlations for B. The basis for these correlations is the two-term virial equation in pressure, Eq. (4-78). Elimination of T and P in favor of reduced variables gives

$$Z = 1 + \left(\frac{BP_c}{RT_c} \right) \frac{P_r}{T_r} \tag{4-90}$$

If Z is assumed correlatable within a three-parameter corresponding-states framework, then it follows from Eqs. (4-15) and (4-90) that

$$\frac{BP_c}{RT_c} = F(T_r; \pi) \qquad \textit{all fluids} \tag{4-91}$$

where π is a third corresponding-states parameter. The dimensionless second virial coefficient BP_c / RT_c depends upon T_r and π only, because the virial coefficient B is a function only of T for a constant-composition fluid.

Pitzer and Curl (1957) developed a correlation for BP_c / RT_c of the form

$$\frac{BP_c}{RT_c} = B^0 + \omega B^1 \tag{4-92}$$

where B^0 and B^1 are dimensionless functions of T_r. As in other Pitzer correlations, B^0 is a simple-fluid term, developed from data for Ar, Kr, and Xe. The term B^1 accounts for departures from simple-fluid behavior. The adequacy of Eq. (4-91) as a correlating scheme is illustrated by Fig. 4-14, where there are plotted reduced data for B for the simple fluids, and also values for B^1 as deduced from data for some nonsimple fluids. Here, B^1 is calculated from the formula

$$B^1 = \frac{1}{\omega}\left(\frac{BP_c}{RT_c} - B^0\right)$$

where values of B^0 are read from a smoothing curve drawn through the simple-fluid data.

Pitzer and Curl present analytical expressions for B^0 and B^1 as functions of T_r, and refinements to these expressions have been developed by Tsonopoulos (1974, 1975, 1978), who also extends the Pitzer-Curl formalism to permit estimation of B for polar and hydrogen-bonding substances. For reduced temperatures between about 0.6 and 2.0, the following formulas provide satisfactory approximations to the data displayed on Fig. 4-14:

$$B^0 = 0.083 - \frac{0.422}{T_r^{1.6}} \tag{4-93a}$$

$$B^1 = 0.139 - \frac{0.172}{T_r^{4.2}} \tag{4-93b}$$

Equations (4-93) should not be used for applications requiring accurate estimates of the temperature *derivatives* of B.

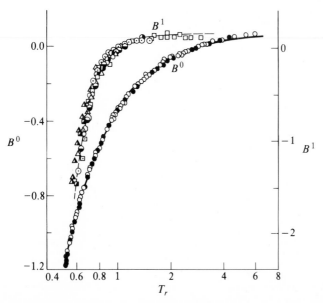

Figure 4-14 Corresponding-states correlation of B for 14 non-polar fluids. Curves are computed from Eqs. (4-93a) and (4-93b). (See Example 4-8.)

4-6 THE VIRIAL EQUATIONS FOR MIXTURES

Application of an equation of state to calculations for mixtures is conventionally done through *mixing rules*, recipes which express the composition dependence of parameters in the equation of state. For the virial equation in density, the parameters are the virial coefficients $\mathscr{B}_n$, and the methods of statistical mechanics provide for these parameters the *exact* mixing rules:

$$B = \sum_i \sum_j y_i y_j B_{ij} \tag{4-94}$$

$$C = \sum_i \sum_j \sum_k y_i y_j y_k C_{ijk} \tag{4-95}$$

etc.

Here, the unsubscripted virial coefficients B, C, etc., refer to the *mixture*, and the y's are mole fractions. (The virial equations apply only to gases, and we adopt in this section the usual convention of representing gas-phase mole fractions by the symbol y.) The subscripted quantities B_{ij}, C_{ijk}, etc., are of two types. If all subscripts are *identical*, then the quantity is a virial coefficient for a pure gas. If the subscripts are *mixed*, then the quantities are called *interaction* virial coefficients, or *cross-coefficients*; the cross-coefficients are composition-independent (but temperature-dependent) parameters characteristic of the mixture.

Consider the case of a binary gas mixture containing species 1 and 2. Carrying out the indicated summations in Eqs. (4-94) and (4-95), we obtain the following expressions for B and C of the mixture:

$$B = y_1^2 B_{11} + y_1 y_2 (B_{12} + B_{21}) + y_2^2 B_{22}$$

and

$$C = y_1^3 C_{111} + y_1^2 y_2 (C_{211} + C_{121} + C_{112})$$
$$+ y_1 y_2^2 (C_{221} + C_{212} + C_{122}) + y_2^3 C_{222}$$

Coefficients B_{11} and C_{111} are virial coefficients for pure gas 1, and B_{22} and C_{222} are virial coefficients for pure gas 2. Quantities B_{12}, B_{21}, C_{211}, C_{121}, C_{112}, C_{221}, C_{212}, and C_{122} are all cross-coefficients for the 12 binary system. Considerable simplification results when we invoke the interpretation of the Nth virial coefficient as representing the effects of N-body molecular interactions, for this implies symmetry relations among the cross-coefficients. Thus, since the composition-independent quantities B_{12} and B_{21} both represent the same interactions between a molecule of type 1 and one of type 2, they are equal:

$$B_{12} = B_{21}$$

Similarly, C_{211}, C_{121}, and C_{112} each represent interactions among two molecules of type 1 and one of type 2, and therefore

$$C_{211} = C_{121} = C_{112}$$

The same reasoning leads us to conclude that

$$C_{221} = C_{212} = C_{122}$$

and thus the expressions for B and C simplify for a binary system to the following equations:

$$B = y_1^2 B_{11} + 2y_1 y_2 B_{12} + y_2^2 B_{22} \tag{4-96}$$

and

$$C = y_1^3 C_{111} + 3y_1^2 y_2 C_{112} + 3y_1 y_2^2 C_{122} + y_2^3 C_{222} \tag{4-97}$$

Similar equations obtain for mixtures containing any number of species. In developing these equations, one makes use of the *general* symmetry relationships

$$B_{ij} = B_{ji} \tag{4-98a}$$

$$C_{ijk} = C_{ikj} = C_{jik} = C_{jki} = C_{kij} = C_{kji} \tag{4-98b}$$

etc.

According to Eq. (4-94), B is a quadratic function of mole fraction. Similarly, C is cubic in mole fraction, and in general the Nth virial coefficient is an Nth-order function of mole fraction. It is frequently convenient, however, to express Eqs. (4-94) and (4-95) in forms containing a leading term *linear* in composition. We illustrate the development of such an expression for B. Equation (4-94) may be written as

$$B = \sum_i y_i B_{ii} + \sum_i \sum_j y_i y_j B_{ij} - \sum_i y_i B_{ii}$$

and the last summation may be decomposed to give

$$\sum_i y_i B_{ii} = \frac{1}{2} \sum_i y_i B_{ii} + \frac{1}{2} \sum_j y_j B_{jj}$$

The two terms on the right-hand side of this equation remain unaltered if we multiply them, respectively, by $\sum_j y_j$ and $\sum_i y_i$, because the mole fractions sum to unity. Thus

$$\frac{1}{2} \sum_i y_i B_{ii} = \frac{1}{2} \left(\sum_j y_j \right) \sum_i y_i B_{ii} = \frac{1}{2} \sum_i \sum_j y_i y_j B_{ii}$$

and

$$\frac{1}{2} \sum_j y_j B_{jj} = \frac{1}{2} \left(\sum_i y_i \right) \sum_j y_j B_{jj} = \frac{1}{2} \sum_i \sum_j y_i y_j B_{jj}$$

Combination of the last four equations gives the result

$$\boxed{B = \sum_i y_i B_{ii} + \frac{1}{2} \sum_i \sum_j y_i y_j \delta_{ij}} \tag{4-99}$$

where

$$\delta_{ij} \equiv 2B_{ij} - B_{ii} - B_{jj}$$ (4-100)

The δ_{ij} have the following useful properties:

$$\delta_{ii} = 0 \quad \text{and} \quad \delta_{ij} = \delta_{ji}$$

which follow immediately from their definition and from Eq. (4-98a). Thus, for a binary system containing species 1 and 2, Eq. (4-99) reduces to

$$B = y_1 B_{11} + y_2 B_{22} + y_1 y_2 \delta_{12}$$ (4-101)

Similarly, for a ternary system containing species 1, 2, and 3, we find

$$B = y_1 B_{11} + y_2 B_{22} + y_3 B_{33} + y_1 y_2 \delta_{12} + y_1 y_3 \delta_{13} + y_2 y_3 \delta_{23}$$ (4-102)

In the last two equations

$$\delta_{12} \equiv 2B_{12} - B_{11} - B_{22}$$

$$\delta_{13} \equiv 2B_{13} - B_{11} - B_{33}$$

$$\delta_{23} \equiv 2B_{23} - B_{22} - B_{33}$$

It is apparent from Eq. (4-101) that parameter δ_{ij} (or, equivalently, B_{ij}) can be determined from data for pure i and j and for the ij binary system. But the same *kinds* of parameters (B_{ii}'s and δ_{ij}'s) appear in expressions for B for systems containing *any* number of species [compare, for example, Eqs. (4-101) and (4-102)]. Thus in general only pure-component and binary data are required for the calculation of a mixture B. To generalize, we observe that the Nth virial coefficient for a mixture containing any number of components depends upon coefficients calculable from measurements on systems containing at most N chemical species.

If $\delta_{ij} = 0$ for all i and j, then Eq. (4-100) yields

$$B_{ij} = \tfrac{1}{2}(B_{ii} + B_{jj})$$ (4-103)

and Eq. (4-99) assumes the simple linear form

$$B = \sum y_i B_{ii}$$ (4-104)

Equation (4-103) is an example of a *combination rule*, a recipe relating an equation-of-state interaction parameter to parameters for the pure components. We show in Chap. 5 that Eq. (4-104), which follows from the special combination rule Eq. (4-103), is one of the features of gas mixtures conforming to *ideal-solution* behavior.

The same line of reasoning that led us from Eq. (4-94) to Eq. (4-99) may also be applied to Eq. (4-95). Thus we obtain for the third virial coefficient of a mixture the expression

$$C = \sum_i y_i C_{iii} + \frac{1}{3}\sum_i \sum_j \sum_k y_i y_j y_k \delta_{ijk}$$ (4-105)

where

$$\delta_{ijk} \equiv 3C_{ijk} - C_{iii} - C_{jjj} - C_{kkk} \qquad (4\text{-}106)$$

The δ_{ijk} have properties similar to those of the δ_{ij}. Thus, by Eqs. (4-106) and (4-98b),

$$\delta_{iii} = 0$$

and

$$\delta_{ijk} = \delta_{ikj} = \delta_{jik} = \delta_{jki} = \delta_{kij} = \delta_{kji}$$

For a binary system, we therefore have, by Eqs. (4-105) and (4-106),

$$C = y_1 C_{111} + y_2 C_{222} + y_1 y_2 (y_1 \delta_{112} + y_2 \delta_{122}) \qquad (4\text{-}107)$$

with

$$\delta_{112} \equiv 3C_{112} - 2C_{111} - C_{222} \qquad (4\text{-}108a)$$

and

$$\delta_{122} \equiv 3C_{122} - C_{111} - 2C_{222} \qquad (4\text{-}108b)$$

One could continue in like fashion with the higher virial coefficients. However, coefficients beyond C are rarely available, and the higher-ordered analogs of Eqs. (4-99) and (4-105) are therefore of little practical value.

Calculation of *mixture* properties from truncated forms of the virial equation is done with the same equations derived for pure fluids in the preceding section: one merely interprets B and C as virial coefficients for the mixture, given in terms of the B_{ij} and C_{ijk} by Eqs. (4-94) and (4-95), or, equivalently, in terms of the B_{ii}, C_{iii}, δ_{ij}, and δ_{ijk} by Eqs. (4-99) and (4-105). Calculation of *partial* properties, on the other hand, requires the evaluation of derivatives with respect to mole numbers or mole fractions. Since the mixture virial coefficients depend upon composition, it is useful to have available expressions for the *partial molar virial coefficients* $\bar{B}_i$ and $\bar{C}_i$, defined as

$$\bar{B}_i \equiv \left[\frac{\partial (nB)}{\partial n_i} \right]_{T, n_j} \qquad (4\text{-}109)$$

and

$$\bar{C}_i \equiv \left[\frac{\partial (nC)}{\partial n_i} \right]_{T, n_j} \qquad (4\text{-}110)$$

Since the virial coefficients are independent of P, these definitions are in accord with Eq. (3-3). We develop in the following paragraphs a set of equivalent expressions for $\bar{B}_i$, and present a set of analogous expressions for $\bar{C}_i$. The results are summarized in Table 4-2 (p. 140).

By Eq. (4-94) we have

$$B = \sum_i \sum_j y_i y_j B_{ij}$$

from which we obtain, on multiplication by n,

$$nB = \frac{1}{n} \sum_k \sum_l n_k n_l B_{kl}$$

Here, we have changed the dummy subscripts of summation from i and j to k and l. Differentiation with respect to n_i in accordance with Eq. (4-109) gives

$$\bar{B}_i = -\frac{1}{n^2} \sum_k \sum_l n_k n_l B_{kl} + \frac{1}{n} \left[\frac{\partial}{\partial n_i} \left(\sum_k \sum_l n_k n_l B_{kl} \right) \right]_{T,\, n_j}$$

$$= -\sum_k \sum_l y_k y_l B_{kl} + \frac{1}{n} \left[\frac{\partial}{\partial n_i} \left(\sum_k \sum_l n_k n_l B_{kl} \right) \right]_{T,\, n_j}$$

But, by Eq. (4-94), the first term on the right is just $-B$. Thus

$$\bar{B}_i = -B + \frac{1}{n} \left[\frac{\partial}{\partial n_i} \left(\sum_k \sum_l n_k n_l B_{kl} \right) \right]_{T,\, n_j} \tag{4-111}$$

Evaluation of the remaining derivative is facilitated if the double summation is first decomposed into sums which explicitly *exclude* the mole number n_i. Thus we write

$$\sum_k \sum_l n_k n_l B_{kl} = \sum_k n_k \sum_l n_l B_{kl} = \sum_k n_k \left({\sum_l}' n_l B_{kl} + n_i B_{ki} \right)$$

where the notation $\sum'$ means that species i is *exluded* from the summation. Proceeding, we find

$$\sum_k \sum_l n_k n_l B_{kl} = {\sum_k}' {\sum_l}' n_k n_l B_{kl} + \sum_k n_k n_i B_{ki}$$

$$= {\sum_l}' n_l \left({\sum_k}' n_k B_{kl} + n_i B_{il} \right) + \sum_k n_k n_i B_{ki}$$

$$= {\sum_k}' {\sum_l}' n_k n_l B_{kl} + {\sum_l}' n_l n_i B_{il} + \sum_k n_k n_i B_{ki}$$

or

$$\sum_k \sum_l n_k n_l B_{kl} = {\sum_k}' {\sum_l}' n_k n_l B_{kl} + 2 n_i {\sum_k}' n_k B_{ki} + n_i^2 B_{ii}$$

Differentiation with respect to n_i then gives

$$\left[\frac{\partial}{\partial n_i} \left(\sum_k \sum_l n_k n_l B_{kl} \right) \right]_{T,\, n_j} = 2 {\sum_k}' n_k B_{ki} + 2 n_i B_{ii} = 2 \sum_k n_k B_{ki}$$

and Eq. (4-111) becomes

$$\boxed{\bar{B}_i = -B + 2 \sum_k y_k B_{ki}} \tag{4-112}$$

Equation (4-112) is the first of our expressions for $\bar{B}_i$. The second is found from it by substitution of Eq. (4-94) for B:

$$\bar{B}_i = -\sum_k \sum_l y_k y_l B_{kl} + 2 \sum_k y_k B_{ki}$$

$$= -\sum_k \sum_l y_k y_l B_{kl} + 2 \sum_k \sum_l y_k y_l B_{ki}$$

from which

$$\boxed{\bar{B}_i = \sum_k \sum_l y_k y_l (2B_{ki} - B_{kl})} \qquad (4\text{-}113)$$

A third equation for $\bar{B}_i$ is based upon Eq. (4-99), which incorporates the δ functions:

$$B = \sum_i y_i B_{ii} + \frac{1}{2} \sum_i \sum_j y_i y_j \delta_{ij}$$

Multiplying by n and changing subscripts i and j to k and l, we get

$$nB = \sum_k n_k B_{kk} + \frac{1}{2n} \sum_k \sum_l n_k n_l \delta_{kl}$$

Differentiation with respect to mole number n_i yields, on simplification

$$\bar{B}_i = B_{ii} + \sum_k y_k \delta_{ki} - \frac{1}{2} \sum_k \sum_l y_k y_l \delta_{kl}$$

$$= B_{ii} + \sum_k \sum_l y_k y_l \delta_{ki} - \frac{1}{2} \sum_k \sum_l y_k y_l \delta_{kl}$$

or

$$\boxed{\bar{B}_i = B_{ii} + \frac{1}{2} \sum_k \sum_l y_k y_l (2\delta_{ki} - \delta_{kl})} \qquad (4\text{-}114)$$

Equations (4-112) through (4-114) are all *equivalent*; however, depending upon the application, one of them may be more convenient than the others. The analogous set of expressions for $\bar{C}_i$ is found by exactly the same procedures illustrated for $\bar{B}_i$. The results are:

$$\bar{C}_i = -2C + 3 \sum_k \sum_l y_k y_l C_{kli} \qquad (4\text{-}115)$$

$$\bar{C}_i = \sum_k \sum_l \sum_m y_k y_l y_m (3C_{kli} - 2C_{klm}) \qquad (4\text{-}116)$$

$$\bar{C}_i = C_{iii} + \frac{1}{3} \sum_k \sum_l \sum_m y_k y_l y_m (3\delta_{kli} - 2\delta_{klm}) \qquad (4\text{-}117)$$

Again, Eqs. (4-115) through (4-117) are all *equivalent*.

Table 4-2 Expressions for the partial molar virial coefficients $\bar{B}_i$ and $\bar{C}_i$

$\bar{B}_i \equiv \left[\dfrac{\partial(nB)}{\partial n_i}\right]_{T,\,n_j}$		where	
$= -B + 2\displaystyle\sum_k y_k B_{ki}$	(4-112)	$B = \displaystyle\sum_k \sum_l y_k y_l B_{kl}$	(4-94)
$= \displaystyle\sum_k \sum_l y_k y_l (2B_{ki} - B_{kl})$	(4-113)	$= \displaystyle\sum_k y_k B_{kk} + \dfrac{1}{2}\displaystyle\sum_k \sum_l y_k y_l \delta_{kl}$	(4-99)
$= B_{ii} + \dfrac{1}{2}\displaystyle\sum_k \sum_l y_k y_l (2\delta_{ki} - \delta_{kl})$	(4-114)	and $\delta_{kl} \equiv 2B_{kl} - B_{kk} - B_{ll}$	(4-100)
$\bar{C}_i \equiv \left[\dfrac{\partial(nC)}{\partial n_i}\right]_{T,\,n_j}$		where	
$= -2C + 3\displaystyle\sum_k \sum_l y_k y_l C_{kli}$	(4-115)	$C = \displaystyle\sum_k \sum_l \sum_m y_k y_l y_m C_{klm}$	(4-95)
$= \displaystyle\sum_k \sum_l \sum_m y_k y_l y_m (3C_{kli} - 2C_{klm})$	(4-116)	$= \displaystyle\sum_k y_k C_{kkk} + \dfrac{1}{3}\displaystyle\sum_k \sum_l \sum_m y_k y_l y_m \delta_{klm}$	(4-105)
$= C_{iii} + \dfrac{1}{3}\displaystyle\sum_k \sum_l \sum_m y_k y_l y_m (3\delta_{kli} - 2\delta_{klm})$	(4-117)	and $\delta_{klm} \equiv 3C_{klm} - C_{kkk} - C_{lll} - C_{mmm}$	(4-106)

Because the virial equation in pressure is a volume-explicit equation of state, calculation of partial properties from its truncations is straightforward. We illustrate the procedure with the derivation of an expression for the fugacity coefficient of a species in a gas mixture described by the two-term virial equation in pressure, Eq. (4-78). Since $\ln \hat{\phi}_i$ is a partial molar property with respect to $\ln \phi$, we have

$$\ln \hat{\phi}_i = \left[\frac{\partial(n \ln \phi)}{\partial n_i}\right]_{T,\,P,\,n_j} \tag{3-77}$$

and operation on Eq. (4-83) gives

$$\ln \hat{\phi}_i = \frac{P}{RT}\left[\frac{\partial(nB)}{\partial n_i}\right]_{T,\,n_j} = \frac{P\bar{B}_i}{RT} \tag{4-118}$$

We have available three equivalent expressions for $\bar{B}_i$. Choosing Eq. (4-114), we then find for $\ln \hat{\phi}_i$ that

$$\ln \hat{\phi}_i = \frac{P}{RT}\left[B_{ii} + \frac{1}{2}\sum_k \sum_l y_k y_l (2\delta_{ki} - \delta_{kl})\right] \tag{4-119}$$

The usefulness of this form of the equation derives from the fact that B_{ii}, the second virial coefficient of pure species i, stands by itself in the result; this leads to certain simplifications in the description of low-pressure vapor/liquid equilibrium problems when the vapor-phase nonidealities are modeled by Eq. (4-78).

Because of the properties of δ_{ij}, the double summation in Eq. (4-119) reduces to relatively compact expressions even for mixtures containing large numbers of components. Thus, for species 1 and 2 in a binary system, Eq. (4-119) yields the pair of equations:

$$\ln \hat{\phi}_1 = \frac{P}{RT}(B_{11} + y_2^2 \delta_{12}) \qquad (4\text{-}120a)$$

$$\ln \hat{\phi}_2 = \frac{P}{RT}(B_{22} + y_1^2 \delta_{12}) \qquad (4\text{-}120b)$$

Similarly, for species 1, 2, and 3 in a ternary gas mixture

$$\ln \hat{\phi}_1 = \frac{P}{RT}[B_{11} + y_2^2 \delta_{12} + y_3^2 \delta_{13} + y_2 y_3(\delta_{12} + \delta_{13} - \delta_{23})] \quad (4\text{-}121a)$$

$$\ln \hat{\phi}_2 = \frac{P}{RT}[B_{22} + y_1^2 \delta_{12} + y_3^2 \delta_{23} + y_1 y_3(\delta_{12} + \delta_{23} - \delta_{13})] \quad (4\text{-}121b)$$

$$\ln \hat{\phi}_3 = \frac{P}{RT}[B_{33} + y_1^2 \delta_{13} + y_2^2 \delta_{23} + y_1 y_2(\delta_{13} + \delta_{23} - \delta_{12})] \quad (4\text{-}121c)$$

Example 4-9 In deriving Eq. (4-119), an expression for $\ln \hat{\phi}_i$, we used the partial property relation of Eq. (3-77) in conjunction with a previously determined expression for $\ln \phi$. An alternative procedure is possible which does not require the prior availability of an expression for $\ln \phi$ of the mixture. By Eq. (3-94)

$$\left(\frac{\partial \ln \hat{\phi}_i}{\partial P}\right)_{T,x} = -\left(\frac{\bar{V}_i' - \bar{V}_i}{RT}\right) = -\frac{1}{RT}\left(\frac{RT}{P} - \bar{V}_i\right)$$

or, since $\bar{V}_i = \bar{Z}_i RT/P$,

$$\left(\frac{\partial \ln \hat{\phi}_i}{\partial P}\right)_{T,x} = \frac{1}{P}(\bar{Z}_i - 1)$$

or

$$d \ln \hat{\phi}_i = (\bar{Z}_i - 1)\frac{dP}{P} \qquad (\text{const } T, x)$$

Integration at constant T and composition from $P = 0$ (where $\hat{\phi}_i = 1$) to arbitrary pressure P gives

$$\boxed{\ln \hat{\phi}_i = \int_0^P (\bar{Z}_i - 1)\frac{dP}{P}} \qquad (\text{const } T, x) \qquad (4\text{-}122)$$

Equation (4-122) is an analog of Eq. (3-70), derived in Example 3-11 for the case of a pure fluid (or constant-composition mixture). It is a perfectly general relationship, valid for the determination of $\ln \hat{\phi}_i$ from *any* volume-explicit equation of state, provided of course that the equation of state is valid over the entire pressure range from $P = 0$ to $P = P$. For the present case

$$Z = 1 + \frac{BP}{RT} \tag{4-78}$$

and

$$nZ = n + \frac{P}{RT}(nB)$$

from which

$$\bar{Z}_i \equiv \left|\frac{\partial(nZ)}{\partial n_i}\right|_{T,P,n_j} = 1 + \frac{P}{RT}\left|\frac{\partial(nB)}{\partial n_i}\right|_{T,n_j} = 1 + \frac{P\bar{B}_i}{RT}$$

Substitution into Eq. (4-122) and integration yield

$$\ln \hat{\phi}_i = \frac{P\bar{B}_i}{RT}$$

which is just Eq. (4-118). The rest of the derivation proceeds as before.

Example 4-10 Given a generalized correlation for the second virial coefficient of pure gases one may, by extension of the corresponding-states concept, devise methods for the estimation of B for mixtures. Knowledge of the mixing rule for B now shifts our point of view somewhat from that of Sec. 4-4, where we treated the calculation of mixture properties from corresponding-states correlations.

According to Eq. (4-94), B for a mixture of given composition is calculable from the B_{ij}. The basis here for estimation of a mixture B by corresponding-states methods is the assumption that Eq. (4-91) of Example 4-8 is applicable to *all* of the B_{ij} for a mixture, not just to those for the pure constituents. Thus, it is assumed that

$$\frac{B_{ij}P_{c_{ij}}}{RT_{c_{ij}}} = F(T_{r_{ij}}; \pi_{ij}) \tag{4-123}$$

where F is the *same function* developed for the correlation of B for pure fluids. Like B_{ij}, quantities $T_{c_{ij}}$, $P_{c_{ij}}$, and π_{ij} are called *interaction parameters* if $i \neq j$; the reduced temperature $T_{r_{ij}}$ is defined by

$$T_{r_{ij}} \equiv \frac{T}{T_{c_{ij}}}$$

The interaction parameters $T_{c_{ij}}$, $P_{c_{ij}}$, and π_{ij} play a role similar to the pseudo-parameters of Sec. 4-4. However, they are necessarily *independent of composition*, because the B_{ij} are independent of composition. Expressions relating the interaction parameters to parameters of the pure fluids are called *combination rules*. Since Eq. (4-123) contains Eq. (4-91) as a special case (i.e., for $j = i$), the combination rules must produce appropriate values for pure i when $j = i$.

Pitzer's correlation for B, Eq. (4-92), has been extended to mixtures by Prausnitz (1969), who proposes the equation

$$\frac{B_{ij}P_{c_{ij}}}{RT_{c_{ij}}} = B^0(T_{r_{ij}}) + \omega_{ij}B^1(T_{r_{ij}}) \tag{4-124}$$

Here, B^0 and B^1 are the same functions developed by Pitzer for pure fluids. Prausnitz recommends the following combination rules:

$$T_{c_{ij}} = (1 - k_{ij})(T_{c_i} T_{c_j})^{1/2} \qquad (4\text{-}125a)$$

$$P_{c_{ij}} = \frac{Z_{c_{ij}} R T_{c_{ij}}}{V_{c_{ij}}} \qquad (4\text{-}125b)$$

and

$$\omega_{ij} = \tfrac{1}{2}(\omega_i + \omega_j) \qquad (4\text{-}125c)$$

where

$$Z_{c_{ij}} = \tfrac{1}{2}(Z_{c_i} + Z_{c_j}) \qquad (4\text{-}125d)$$

and

$$V_{c_{ij}} = \tfrac{1}{8}(V_{c_i}^{1/3} + V_{c_j}^{1/3})^3 \qquad (4\text{-}125e)$$

Here, all quantities with subscript c are critical properties, and quantity k_{ij} is yet another interaction parameter, characteristic of the ij binary. If $i = j$, $k_{ij} = 0$; otherwise it is a small number, positive or negative, which is presumed independent of temperature. For pairs of similar chemical species, k_{ij} is approximately zero.

We illustrate the use of Prausnitz' procedure by a numerical example: the calculation of B for an equimolar gas mixture of methane(1) and n-hexane(2) at 50°C. The calculation is based on Eqs. (4-96) and (4-124) with B^0 and B^1 given by the approximate expressions, Eqs. (4-93) of Example 4-8. Critical properties and acentric factors for the pure fluids are found in App. D. They are:

$$T_{c_1} = 190.6 \text{ K} \qquad\qquad T_{c_2} = 507.4 \text{ K}$$

$$P_{c_1} = 46.0 \text{ bar} \qquad\qquad P_{c_2} = 29.7 \text{ bar}$$

$$V_{c_1} = 99 \text{ cm}^3 \text{ mol}^{-1} \qquad V_{c_2} = 370 \text{ cm}^3 \text{ mol}^{-1}$$

$$Z_{c_1} = 0.288 \qquad\qquad Z_{c_2} = 0.260$$

$$\omega_1 = 0.008 \qquad\qquad \omega_2 = 0.296$$

First we compute B_{11} and B_{22}. For methane(1) at 50°C $(= 323.15 \text{ K})$, $T_{r_1} = T/T_{c_1} = 323.15/190.6 = 1.695$. Then, by Eqs. (4-93),

$$B^0(T_{r_1}) = 0.083 - \frac{0.422}{T_{r_1}^{1.6}} = 0.083 - \frac{0.422}{(1.695)^{1.6}} = -0.098$$

$$B^1(T_{r_1}) = 0.139 - \frac{0.172}{T_{r_1}^{4.2}} = 0.139 - \frac{0.172}{(1.695)^{4.2}} = 0.120$$

and, by Eq. (4-124),

$$B_{11} = \frac{R T_{c_1}}{P_{c_1}}(B^0 + \omega B^1)$$

$$= \frac{(83.14 \text{ bar cm}^3 \text{ mol}^{-1} \text{ K}^{-1})(190.6 \text{ K})}{(46.0 \text{ bar})}[-0.098 + (0.008)(0.120)]$$

or

$$B_{11} = -33 \text{ cm}^3 \text{ mol}^{-1}$$

Similar calculations yield for n-hexane(2) the value

$$B_{22} = -1538 \text{ cm}^3 \text{ mol}^{-1}$$

Estimation of B_{12} requires values for the interaction parameters. These are found from Eqs. (4-125). Since methane and n-hexane are both n-alkanes, they are chemically similar; therefore we set $k_{12} = 0$. Then, by Eq. (4-125a),

$$T_{c_{12}} = (190.6 \times 507.4)^{1/2} = 311.0 \text{ K}$$

Equation (4-125c) gives

$$\omega_{12} = \tfrac{1}{2}(0.008 + 0.296) = 0.152$$

and, by Eqs. (4-125d) and (4-125e),

$$Z_{c_{12}} = \tfrac{1}{2}(0.288 + 0.260) = 0.274$$

$$V_{c_{12}} = \tfrac{1}{8}(99^{1/3} + 370^{1/3})^3 = 206 \text{ cm}^3 \text{ mol}^{-1}$$

from which, by Eq. (4-125b),

$$P_{c_{12}} = \frac{(0.274)(83.14 \text{ bar cm}^3 \text{ mol}^{-1} \text{ K}^{-1})(311.0 \text{ K})}{(206 \text{ cm}^3 \text{ mol}^{-1})} = 34.4 \text{ bar}$$

The reduced temperature $T_{r_{12}}$ is $323.15/311.0 = 1.039$, and, by Eqs. (4-93), we find

$$B^0(T_{r_{12}}) = -0.314 \qquad \text{and} \qquad B^1(T_{r_{12}}) = -0.007$$

Thus, by Eq. (4-124),

$$B_{12} = \frac{RT_{c_{12}}}{P_{c_{12}}}(B^0 + \omega_{12}B^1) = \frac{(83.14)(311.0)}{(34.4)}[-0.314 + (0.152)(-0.007)]$$

or

$$B_{12} = -234 \text{ cm}^3 \text{ mol}^{-1}$$

Finally, we find B for the mixture from Eq. (4-96):

$$B = y_1^2 B_{11} + 2y_1 y_2 B_{12} + y_2^2 B_{22}$$

$$= (0.5)^2(-33) + (2)(0.5)(0.5)(-234) + (0.5)^2(-1538)$$

or

$$B = -510 \text{ cm}^3 \text{ mol}^{-1}$$

This is in excellent agreement with the value of $-517 \text{ cm}^3 \text{ mol}^{-1}$ found from a correlation of experimental virial coefficients for this system.

At moderate densities, the two-term virial equation in pressure may be inadequate; in such cases, calculations of gas-phase properties from a virial equation must be based on the three-term virial equation in density, Eq. (4-79). Because this form of the virial equation is explicit in pressure, expressions for the partial properties cannot be derived by direct application of the definition:

$$\bar{M}_i \equiv \left[\frac{\partial(nM)}{\partial n_i}\right]_{T, P, n_j}$$

An alternative procedure is required; its development follows.

In general, for a differential change of state undergone by a phase, we have from Eq. (3-4) that

$$d(nM) = n\left(\frac{\partial M}{\partial T}\right)_{P, x} dT + n\left(\frac{\partial M}{\partial P}\right)_{T, x} dP + \sum_k \bar{M}_k \, dn_k$$

Division of this equation by dn_i and restriction to constant T, nV, and n_j $(j \neq i)$ give, on rearrangement,

$$\bar{M}_i = \left[\frac{\partial(nM)}{\partial n_i}\right]_{T, nV, n_j} - n\left(\frac{\partial M}{\partial P}\right)_{T, x}\left(\frac{\partial P}{\partial n_i}\right)_{T, nV, n_j} \qquad (4\text{-}126)$$

Equation (4-126) is the basis for the determination of partial properties from *any* pressure-explicit equation of state. Depending upon its intended application, it may be recast into a number of different but equivalent forms. For example, it is often convenient to replace the mole-number derivative of P with the corresponding derivative of the quantity nZ. Since $P = ZRT/V$, then $P = (nZ)RT/(nV)$, and we may write

$$\left(\frac{\partial P}{\partial n_i}\right)_{T, nV, n_j} = \frac{RT}{nV}\left[\frac{\partial(nZ)}{\partial n_i}\right]_{T, nV, n_j} = \frac{P}{nZ}\left[\frac{\partial(nZ)}{\partial n_i}\right]_{T, nV, n_j}$$

Substitution into Eq. (4-126) gives

$$\bar{M}_i = \left[\frac{\partial(nM)}{\partial n_i}\right]_{T, nV, n_j} - \frac{P}{Z}\left(\frac{\partial M}{\partial P}\right)_{T, x}\left[\frac{\partial(nZ)}{\partial n_i}\right]_{T, nV, n_j} \qquad (4\text{-}127)$$

Additionally, it may be convenient to replace the derivative $(\partial M/\partial P)_{T, x}$ by derivatives which may be evaluated directly from a pressure-explicit equation of state. This is easily done through the mathematical relationship

$$\left(\frac{\partial M}{\partial P}\right)_{T, x} = \left(\frac{\partial M}{\partial V}\right)_{T, x}\left(\frac{\partial V}{\partial P}\right)_{T, x} = \left(\frac{\partial M}{\partial V}\right)_{T, x}\left(\frac{\partial P}{\partial V}\right)_{T, x}^{-1}$$

As an application of this material, we consider the derivation of an expression for the fugacity coefficient of a species in a gas mixture described by any pressure-explicit equation of state. We base the derivation of Eq. (4-127), which becomes, with $M \equiv \ln \phi$,

$$\ln \hat{\phi}_i = \left[\frac{\partial(n \ln \phi)}{\partial n_i}\right]_{T, nV, n_j} - \frac{P}{Z}\left(\frac{\partial \ln \phi}{\partial P}\right)_{T, x}\left[\frac{\partial(nZ)}{\partial n_i}\right]_{T, nV, n_j}$$

But, by Eqs. (3-82) and (2-75),

$$\left(\frac{\partial \ln \phi}{\partial P}\right)_{T, x} = -\frac{1}{P}(1 - Z)$$

and thus

$$\ln \hat{\phi}_i = \left[\frac{\partial(n \ln \phi)}{\partial n_i}\right]_{T, nV, n_j} + \left(\frac{1 - Z}{Z}\right)\left[\frac{\partial(nZ)}{\partial n_i}\right]_{T, nV, n_j} \tag{4-128}$$

Equation (4-128) is suitable if an expression is already available for $\ln \phi$ for the mixture. If not, we may develop a more general result by use of Eq. (4-69), which gives

$$n \ln \phi = nZ - n - n \ln (nZ) + n \ln n + \int_V^{\infty} (nZ - n)\frac{dV}{V}$$

Here, we have changed the variable of integration from ρ to V. Differentiation with respect to n_i at constant T, nV, and n_j yields, after simplification,

$$\left[\frac{\partial(n \ln \phi)}{\partial n_i}\right]_{T, nV, n_j} = \int_V^{\infty} \left\{\left[\frac{\partial(nZ)}{\partial n_i}\right]_{T, nV, n_j} - 1\right\}\frac{dV}{V} - \ln Z - \left(\frac{1 - Z}{Z}\right)\left[\frac{\partial(nZ)}{\partial n_i}\right]_{T, nV, n_j}$$

Combination of this equation with Eq. (4-128) gives the required general result:

$$\ln \hat{\phi}_i = \int_V^{\infty} \left\{\left[\frac{\partial(nZ)}{\partial n_i}\right]_{T, nV, n_j} - 1\right\}\frac{dV}{V} - \ln Z \tag{4-129}$$

where integration is carried out at constant temperature and composition. If ρ, rather than V, is the favored volumetric independent variable, then the following equivalent form of Eq. (4-129) is useful:

$$\boxed{\ln \hat{\phi}_i = \int_0^{\rho} \left\{\left[\frac{\partial(nZ)}{\partial n_i}\right]_{T, \rho/n, n_j} - 1\right\}\frac{d\rho}{\rho} - \ln Z} \tag{4-130}$$

Equations (4-129) and (4-130) are valid for *any* pressure-explicit equation of state. We now apply Eq. (4-130) to the three-term virial equation in density, which may be written

$$nZ = n + n(nB)\left(\frac{\rho}{n}\right) + n^2(nC)\left(\frac{\rho}{n}\right)^2$$

Thus

$$\left[\frac{\partial(nZ)}{\partial n_i}\right]_{T, \rho/n, n_j} = 1 + \left\{B + \left[\frac{\partial(nB)}{\partial n_i}\right]_{T, n_j}\right\}\rho + \left\{2C + \left[\frac{\partial(nC)}{\partial n_i}\right]_{T, n_j}\right\}\rho^2$$

or

$$\left[\frac{\partial (nZ)}{\partial n_i}\right]_{T,\,\rho/n,\,n_j} = 1 + (B + \bar{B}_i)\rho + (2C + \bar{C}_i)\rho^2$$

Substitution into Eq. (4-130) and integration give

$$\ln \hat{\phi}_i = (B + \bar{B}_i)\rho + \tfrac{1}{2}(2C + \bar{C}_i)\rho^2 - \ln Z \tag{4-131}$$

Equation (4-131) may be written in many different but equivalent forms, depending on the expressions chosen to represent $\bar{B}_i$ and $\bar{C}_i$. Table 4-2 reveals that the simplest result obtains with Eqs. (4-112) and (4-115), which provide:

$$B + \bar{B}_i = 2 \sum_k y_k B_{ki}$$

and

$$2C + \bar{C}_i = 3 \sum_k \sum_l y_k y_l C_{kli}$$

Equation (4-131) then assumes a form which appears frequently in the literature:

$$\ln \hat{\phi}_i = 2\rho \sum_k y_k B_{ki} + \tfrac{3}{2}\rho^2 \sum_k \sum_l y_k y_l C_{kli} - \ln Z \tag{4-132}$$

Example 4-11 Although Eq. (4-132) is the most concise form of Eq. (4-131), it does not admit the advantages frequently attending the use of the δ notation. We develop in this example an expression for $\ln \hat{\phi}_i$ which incorporates this notation. Noting that

$$Z = 1 + B\rho + C\rho^2$$

we may write Eq. (4-131) as

$$\ln \hat{\phi}_i = Z - 1 - \ln Z + \bar{B}_i \rho + \tfrac{1}{2}\bar{C}_i \rho^2 \tag{4-133}$$

Rrepresenting $\bar{B}_i$ by Eq. (4-114) and $\bar{C}_i$ by Eq. (4-117), we then obtain the required result:

$$\ln \hat{\phi}_i = Z - 1 - \ln Z + \left[B_{ii} + \frac{1}{2} \sum_k \sum_l y_k y_l (2\delta_{ki} - \delta_{kl}) \right]\rho$$
$$+ \frac{1}{2}\left[C_{iii} + \frac{1}{3} \sum_k \sum_l \sum_m y_k y_l y_m (3\delta_{kli} - 2\delta_{klm}) \right]\rho^2 \tag{4-134}$$

The simplest case of interest is a binary gas mixture, for which Eq. (4-134) reduces to the pair of equations

$$\ln \hat{\phi}_1 = Z - 1 - \ln Z + (B_{11} + y_2^2 \delta_{12})\rho$$
$$+ \tfrac{1}{2}[C_{111} + y_2^3 \delta_{122} + y_1 y_2^2 (2\delta_{112} - \delta_{122})]\rho^2 \tag{4-135a}$$

and

$$\ln \hat{\phi}_2 = Z - 1 - \ln Z + (B_{22} + y_1^2 \delta_{12})\rho$$
$$+ \tfrac{1}{2}[C_{222} + y_1^3 \delta_{112} + y_1^2 y_2 (2\delta_{122} - \delta_{112})]\rho^2 \tag{4-135b}$$

4-7 CUBIC EQUATIONS OF STATE:
THE GENERIC REDLICH-KWONG EQUATION

Two methods for representing the PVT behavior of fluids have been treated so far in this chapter: corresponding-states techniques, and the virial equations of state. We consider in this and the next section a third method: the use of empirical equations of state, exemplified by the class of polynomial equations that are *cubic* in molar volume (or, equivalently, in molar density).

Polynomial equations of state are of particular practical importance; for example, truncations of the virial equation in density are polynomials in density. Efficient root-finding techniques are available for the solution of polynomial equations, and moreover the number of roots is always known. The simplest useful polynomial equation of state is cubic, for such an expression is capable of yielding the ideal-gas equation in the limit as $V \to \infty$, *and* of representing both liquid-like and vapor-like molar volumes at low temperatures. This latter feature is necessary for the application of an equation of state to the calculation of vapor/liquid equilibria.

If it is required that a cubic equation be explicit in pressure and that it yield steep (i.e., liquid-like) isotherms for small values of V, then algebraic arguments lead to an expression of the form

$$P = \frac{RT}{V - b} - \frac{\theta(V - \eta)}{(V - b)(V^2 + \delta V + \varepsilon)} \qquad (4\text{-}136)$$

where each of the five parameters b, θ, δ, ε, and η can depend upon temperature and composition.

Equation (4-136) may be considered a generalization of the van der Waals equation, to which it reduces as the simplest nontrivial special case. Thus, for $\eta = b$, $\delta = \varepsilon = 0$, and $\theta = \text{constant} = a$, we obtain

$$P = \frac{RT}{V - b} - \frac{a}{V^2} \qquad (4\text{-}137)$$

which is the van der Waals equation. Numerous other specializations of Eq. (4-136) have been proposed. One of the best known of these is the equation of Redlich and Kwong (1949), hereafter called the "original" Redlich-Kwong equation:

$$P = \frac{RT}{V - b} - \frac{a}{T^{1/2}V(V + b)} \qquad (4\text{-}138)$$

Some other special cases of Eq. (4-136) are listed in Table 4-3, where they are categorized according to the values (or types of functions) assigned to θ, δ, ε, and η.

No single cubic equation of state can provide precise descriptions of real-fluid behavior, except over limited ranges of the state variables. This may seem surprising, in view of the apparent flexibility afforded by the five temperature-dependent parameters of Eq. (4-136). However, a controlling factor is the *volume*

Table 4-3 Classification of some cubic equations of state

Equation†	θ	η	δ	ε
van der Waals (1873)	a	b	0	0
Clausius (1880)	a/T	b	$2c$	c^2
Berthelot (1899)	a/T	b	0	0
Redlich-Kwong (1949)	$a/T^{1/2}$	b	b	0
Wilson‡ (1964a)	$\theta_w(T)$	b	b	0
Lee-Erbar-Edmister (1973)	$\theta_{LEE}(T)$	$\eta(T)$	b	0
Peng-Robinson (1976)	$\theta_{PR}(T)$	b	$2b$	$-b^2$

† Parameters in column headings refer to Eq. (4-136).
‡ Similarly, Barner et al. (1966), Soave (1972), and others, but with different expressions for $\theta(T)$.

(or density) dependence of the equation: with an equation of specified functional form in volume, one can get only so far by adjustment of the temperature-dependent parameters. Thus Eq. (4-136) has inherent limitations which exist solely because it is a *cubic* equation. Nevertheless, because of their simplicity, cubic equations enjoy wide popularity for industrial applications, where repetitive calculations are the rule, and where one typically deals with systems containing large numbers of chemical species.

With Eq. (4-136) as a point of departure, one can present a comprehensive treatment of cubic equations of state. However, so flexible a cubic equation as Eq. (4-136) is rarely used in practice. In an attempt to strike a balance between generality and utility, we consider instead in the following paragraphs a more restricted class of cubic equations, inspired by the original Redlich-Kwong equation, but including also as special cases scores of modifications which have been proposed to it. Thus we define the *generic* Redlich-Kwong equation of state:

$$P = \frac{RT}{V - b} - \frac{\theta}{V(V + b)} \qquad (4\text{-}139)$$

Equation (4-139) is obtained from Eq. (4-136) by the assignments $\delta = \eta = b$ and $\varepsilon = 0$; parameters b and θ are functions of both T and composition. For a pure fluid, the original Redlich-Kwong equation is recovered from Eq. (4-139) by the assignments $b = $ constant and $\theta = a/T^{1/2}$, with $a = $ constant.

Equation (4-139) may be written to display more explicitly its cubic nature. Thus, we obtain on rearrangement the equivalent expression

$$V^3 - \frac{RT}{P} V^2 - \left(b^2 + \frac{bRT}{P} - \frac{\theta}{P}\right)V - \frac{b\theta}{P} = 0 \qquad (4\text{-}140)$$

For constant composition and specified values of T and P, the coefficients of V^n are fixed, and the equation yields three volume roots. Depending upon the values of T and P, the nature of these roots may vary greatly. However, there are only two general possibilities: all three values of V may be *real* (with possibly two or even all three of them equal), or two of them may be *complex* and one real.

When temperature and composition are fixed, Eq. (4-140) provides a relationship between P and V, which defines a curve on a PV diagram. Because of the presence of three zeros in the denominators of Eq. (4-139), at $V = 0$ and at $\pm b$, the isothermal PV curve has four distinct branches. These are shown schematically in Fig. 4-15 for a fixed value of T less than the critical temperature of the fluid; note that this figure is *not* drawn to scale.

Of the four branches shown in Fig. 4-15, only branch I has physical significance. This branch is redrawn *to scale* on Fig. 4-16. It is generated for argon at 120 K from the original Redlich-Kwong equation, Eq. (4-138), with values of parameters a and b given by

$$a = 1.694 \times 10^7 \text{ bar K}^{1/2} \text{ cm}^6 \text{ mol}^{-2}$$

$$b = 22.30 \text{ cm}^3 \text{ mol}^{-1}$$

(The basis for the choices of these values of the parameters will be described later.) Since the critical temperature of argon is 150.8 K, the isotherm corresponds to a reduced temperature of about 0.8.

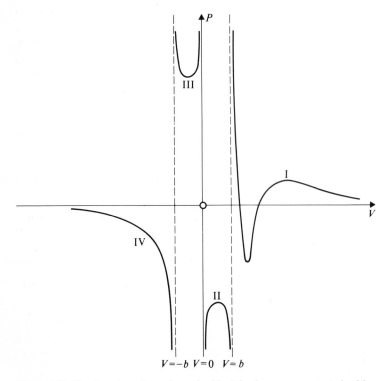

Figure 4-15 The four branches of a subcritical isotherm, as generated with an equation of the Redlich-Kwong type. Branches II, III, and IV are artifacts of the equation of state.

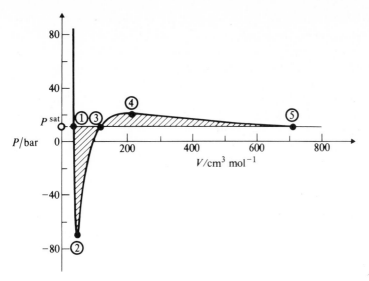

Figure 4-16 Graphical determination of P^{sat} for argon at 120 K from Eq. (4-138).

For small values of V, the isotherm is very steep, with $P \to \infty$ as $V \to b = 22.30$ cm^3 mol^{-1}. As V increases from 22.30 cm^3 mol^{-1}, P decreases very quickly, until the curve reaches a minimum at point 2, with coordinates $P_2 = -71.12$ bar and $V_2 = 45.73$ cm^3 mol^{-1}. Further increase of V is accompanied by an increase of P, until the curve reaches a local maximum at point 4, with $P_4 = 21.50$ bar and $V_4 = 215.0$ cm^3 mol^{-1}. Past point 4, P decreases with increasing V, approaching zero as $V \to \infty$.

It is clear from Fig. 4-16 that at 120 K there is a *range* of pressures (0 bar $< P < 21.50$ bar) for which the equation of state yields three real, positive, finite roots. The smallest of these correspond to liquid-like volumes, and the largest to vapor-like volumes. The middle roots have no physical significance, because they fall on portions of the isotherm for which $(\partial P/\partial V)_T > 0$, and thermodynamic stability criteria require that this derivative be *negative*.

Of the liquid-like and vapor-like roots, only a single pair of them can represent coexisting equilibrium liquid and vapor phases, and the corresponding pressure is the vapor/liquid saturation pressure P^{sat}. For a pure substance, there is only one such pressure at a given temperature; as stated in Sec. 3-6, it is that pressure which yields equal values of the fugacities of the liquid and vapor phases:

$$f^l(T, P^{sat}) = f^v(T, P^{sat}) \tag{3-69}$$

We illustrate later in this section how Eq. (3-69) is used for numerical determination of P^{sat} from the Redlich-Kwong equation. For the meantime we employ an equivalent graphical technique called *Maxwell's equal-area construction*.

With respect to Fig. 4-16, Maxwell's construction requires that the horizontal line representing $P = P^{sat}$ be drawn so that the subtended areas 1-3-2-1 and

3-4-5-3, defined by the intersections of the isobar with the isotherm, be equal in magnitude. Applied to the isotherm of Fig. 4-16, this procedure produces by trial the equal hatched areas, corresponding to an approximate value of $P = P^{sat} = 11.5$ bar. This compares with an experimental value of $P^{sat} = 12.16$ bar for argon at 120 K.

The construction just described defines the states of saturation for liquid and vapor argon at 120 K, as predicted by the original Redlich-Kwong equation with the specified values of a and b. States lying to the left of 1 on the isotherm are for subcooled liquid at 120 K, and those to the right of 5 are for superheated vapor at the same temperature. Referring to the discussion of Sec. 4-1, we are led to interpret the segments 12 and 45 as representing metastable states of super-heated liquid and subcooled vapor. However, the *extents* of these regions as predicted by the equation of state must be interpreted with caution. For example, although it is possible to maintain a liquid in a metastable state of tension (i.e., to have a liquid under " negative pressure "), it would be wrong to infer from the results of Fig. 4-16 that liquid argon at 120 K can in fact support a negative pressure of -71 bar. Although simple cubic equations can provide qualitative description of some of the subtle features of real-fluid behavior, *quantitative* results must often be interpreted with care.

Segment 234 of the isotherm of Fig. 4-16 is an artifact of the equation of state, for $(\partial P/\partial V)_T$ is positive over this range of V; as noted already, $(\partial P/\partial V)_T$ must be negative for a real fluid.

Example 4-12 We develop in this example the basis for Maxwell's equal-area construction, used in the preceding paragraphs for the determination of P^{sat} from an equation of state. Reference is made to Fig. 4-17, a sketch of a subcritical isotherm

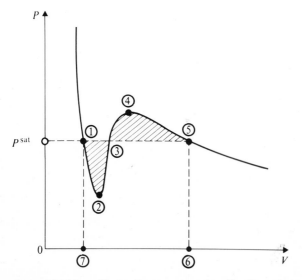

Figure 4-17 Maxwell's equal-area construction. (See Example 4-12.)

similar to that of Fig. 4-16, but changed in detail to aid comprehension of the derivation.

If states 1 and 5 are in phase equilibrium, then according to the discussion of Sec. 4-2, they must have equal values of the Gibbs function:

$$G_1 = G_5$$

or, equivalently,

$$\int_1^5 dG = 0$$

But, by Eq. (2-29), we have for constant T that

$$dG = V \, dP = d(PV) - P \, dV \qquad (\text{const } T)$$

and thus

$$\int_1^5 dG = P_5 V_5 - P_1 V_1 - \int_1^5 P \, dV = 0$$

or, since by assumption $P_1 = P_5 = P^{\text{sat}}$,

$$P^{\text{sat}}(V_5 - V_1) - \int_1^5 P \, dV = 0$$

But, by inspection of Fig. 4-17, we see that

$$P^{\text{sat}}(V_5 - V_1) = \text{area } 1\text{-}3\text{-}5\text{-}6\text{-}7\text{-}1$$

and that

$$\int_1^5 P \, dV = \text{area } 1\text{-}2\text{-}3\text{-}4\text{-}5\text{-}6\text{-}7\text{-}1$$

$$= \text{area } 1\text{-}3\text{-}5\text{-}6\text{-}7\text{-}1 - \text{area } 1\text{-}3\text{-}2\text{-}1 + \text{area } 3\text{-}4\text{-}5\text{-}3$$

Combination of the last three equations gives

$$\text{area } 1\text{-}3\text{-}2\text{-}1 = \text{area } 3\text{-}4\text{-}5\text{-}3$$

which is the desired result. The volumes $V_1 (= V_7)$ and $V_5 (= V_6)$, defined as a result of this construction, are the volumes of saturated liquid and saturated vapor at the temperature of the isotherm.

Expressions for residual functions of constant-composition mixtures may be derived from a cubic equation of state by the same general procedures employed in Sec. 4-5 for the virial equation in density, viz., from Eqs. (4-67) through (4-70). These equations are appropriate because the cubic equations are explicit in *pressure*. We illustrate the procedures for the calculation of $\Delta H'$, $\Delta S'$ and $\ln \phi$ from the generic Redlich-Kwong equation.

First, we write the equation in the form $Z = Z(T, \rho)$. Since

$$P = \frac{RT}{V - b} - \frac{\theta}{V(V + b)} \qquad (4\text{-}139)$$

then we find by the substitutions $P = Z\rho RT$ and $V = \rho^{-1}$ the equivalent expression

$$Z = \frac{1}{1 - b\rho} - \left(\frac{\theta}{bRT}\right)\frac{b\rho}{1 + b\rho} \tag{4-141a}$$

or

$$Z = \frac{1}{1 - h} - \left(\frac{\theta}{bRT}\right)\frac{h}{1 + h} \tag{4-141b}$$

where h is a dimensionless auxiliary volumetric function proportional to the density:

$$h \equiv b\rho \tag{4-142}$$

Equations (4-67) through (4-69) require expressions for $Z - 1$ and for $(\partial Z/\partial T)_\rho$. By Eqs. (4-141) we have

$$Z - 1 = \frac{b\rho}{1 - b\rho} - \left(\frac{\theta}{bRT}\right)\frac{b\rho}{1 + b\rho} \tag{4-143a}$$

or

$$Z - 1 = \frac{h}{1 - h} - \left(\frac{\theta}{bRT}\right)\frac{h}{1 + h} \tag{4-143b}$$

Differentiation of Eq. (4-141a) gives

$$\left(\frac{\partial Z}{\partial T}\right)_\rho = b\rho\left[\frac{1}{(1 - b\rho)^2} - \frac{(\theta/bRT)}{(1 + b\rho)^2}\right]\frac{1}{b}\frac{db}{dT} - \frac{b\rho}{1 + b\rho}\frac{d(\theta/bRT)}{dT} \tag{4-144a}$$

or

$$\left(\frac{\partial Z}{\partial T}\right)_\rho = h\left[\frac{1}{(1 - h)^2} - \frac{(\theta/bRT)}{(1 + h)^2}\right]\frac{1}{b}\frac{db}{dT} - \frac{h}{1 + h}\frac{d(\theta/bRT)}{dT} \tag{4-144b}$$

We are now in a position to determine the expressions for $\Delta H'$ and $\Delta S'$. Transforming the variable of integration from ρ to h, we may write Eqs. (4-67) and (4-68) in the dimensionless forms

$$\frac{\Delta H'}{RT} = T\int_0^h \left(\frac{\partial Z}{\partial T}\right)_\rho \frac{dh}{h} - (Z - 1) \tag{4-145}$$

and

$$\frac{\Delta S'}{R} = T\int_0^h \left(\frac{\partial Z}{\partial T}\right)_\rho \frac{dh}{h} + \int_0^h (Z - 1)\frac{dh}{h} - \ln Z \tag{4-146}$$

Since the integrations are carried out at constant T, we have by Eq. (4-144b) that

$$T \int_0^h \left(\frac{\partial Z}{\partial T}\right)_\rho \frac{dh}{h}$$

$$= \frac{T}{b} \frac{db}{dT} \left[\int_0^h \frac{dh}{(1-h)^2} - \left(\frac{\theta}{bRT}\right) \int_0^h \frac{dh}{(1+h)^2}\right] - T \frac{d(\theta/bRT)}{dT} \int_0^h \frac{dh}{1+h}$$

or

$$T \int_0^h \left(\frac{\partial Z}{\partial T}\right)_\rho \frac{dh}{h} = \frac{T}{b} \frac{db}{dT} \left[\frac{h}{1-h} - \left(\frac{\theta}{bRT}\right)\frac{h}{1+h}\right] - T \frac{d(\theta/bRT)}{dT} \ln (1 + h)$$

Combination of this last equation with Eq. (4-143b) gives the equivalent result

$$T \int_0^h \left(\frac{\partial Z}{\partial T}\right)_\rho \frac{dh}{h} = \frac{T}{b} \frac{db}{dT}(Z-1) - T \frac{d(\theta/bRT)}{dT} \ln (1 + h) \qquad (4\text{-}147)$$

and substitution into Eq. (4-145) yields finally

$$\boxed{\frac{\Delta H'}{RT} = (Z-1)\left(\frac{T}{b}\frac{db}{dT} - 1\right) - T \frac{d(\theta/bRT)}{dT} \ln (1 + h)} \qquad (4\text{-}148)$$

By Eq. (4-143b) we have

$$\int_0^h (Z-1) \frac{dh}{h} = \int_0^h \frac{dh}{1-h} - \frac{\theta}{bRT} \int_0^h \frac{dh}{1+h}$$

or

$$\int_0^h (Z-1) \frac{dh}{h} = -\ln (1 - h) - \left(\frac{\theta}{bRT}\right) \ln (1 + h) \qquad (4\text{-}149)$$

Noting that

$$\frac{\theta}{bRT} + T \frac{d(\theta/bRT)}{dT} = \frac{d(\theta/bR)}{dT}$$

we find by substitution of Eqs. (4-147) and (4-149) into Eq. (4-146) that

$$\boxed{\frac{\Delta S'}{R} = \frac{T}{b}\frac{db}{dT}(Z-1) - \ln (1-h)Z - \frac{d(\theta/bR)}{dT} \ln (1 + h)} \qquad (4\text{-}150)$$

An expression for $\ln \phi$ can be found either by Eq. (4-22), together with Eqs. (4-148) and (4-150), or by Eq. (4-69). Both procedures yield the result

$$\boxed{\ln \phi = (Z-1) - \ln(1-h)Z - \left(\frac{\theta}{bRT}\right) \ln (1 + h)} \qquad (4\text{-}151)$$

Example 4-13 Equations (4-148), (4-150), and (4-151) apply to any of the numerous variants of the Redlich-Kwong equation incorporated in the generic expression, Eq. (4-139). We consider their application to the *original* Redlich-Kwong equation, Eq. (4-138), for which (for a constant-composition fluid),

$$b = \text{constant}$$

$$\theta = a/T^{1/2}$$

$$a = \text{constant}$$

$$\frac{\theta}{bRT} = \frac{a}{bRT^{3/2}}$$

and

$$\frac{\theta}{bR} = \frac{a}{bRT^{1/2}}$$

Thus the equation of state, Eq. (4-141b), becomes

$$Z = \frac{1}{1-h} - \left(\frac{a}{bRT^{3/2}}\right)\frac{h}{1+h} \tag{4-152}$$

Also

$$\frac{db}{dT} = 0$$

$$\frac{d(\theta/bRT)}{dT} = -\frac{3a}{2bRT^{5/2}}$$

and

$$\frac{d(\theta/bR)}{dT} = -\frac{a}{2bRT^{3/2}}$$

Then, by Eqs. (4-148), (4-150), and (4-151),

$$\frac{\Delta H'}{RT} = \frac{3a}{2bRT^{3/2}} \ln (1 + h) - (Z - 1) \tag{4-153}$$

$$\frac{\Delta S'}{R} = \frac{a}{2bRT^{3/2}} \ln (1 + h) - \ln (1 - h)Z \tag{4-154}$$

and

$$\ln \phi = (Z - 1) - \ln (1 - h)Z - \frac{a}{bRT^{3/2}} \ln (1 + h) \tag{4-155}$$

Use of Eqs. (4-153) through (4-155) requires prior evaluation of h and of Z. Since $h \equiv b\rho$ and since $Z = P/\rho RT$, then Z and h are related by

$$Z = \frac{bP}{hRT} \tag{4-156}$$

Substitution of Eq. (4-156) into Eq. (4-152) yields on rearrangement a cubic equation in h, which can be solved explicitly for h when a, b, T, and P are specified. If three real roots are obtained, the smallest value of h is a vapor-like root and the largest is a liquid-like root. Once h is determined, Z is found from Eq. (4-156).

Actually, *explicit* solution of Eq. (4-152) for h is sometimes unnecessary; an efficient but simple iterative procedure may be applicable. By this procedure, one first assumes a value for h, and computes Z from Eq. (4-152). A new estimate of h is obtained from Eq. (4-156), and the process is repeated until successive values of h (or of Z) agree to within some prescribed tolerance. This procedure is useful when one seeks a gas-phase root of Eq. (4-152); it does *not* apply for the determination of liquid-phase roots at subcritical temperatures, and it may yield incorrect values of h when P is sufficiently high so that both branches I and III of Fig. 4-15 offer possible solutions. When the procedure *does* apply, an initial guess of $h = bP/RT$ (corresponding to $Z = 1$) generally leads to convergence to a gas-phase root in a reasonable number of iterations.

As an example, consider the estimation of the molar volume of argon vapor at 120 K and 10 bar. We use Eq. (4-152) with the values of a and b employed earlier for calculation of Fig. 4-16. Thus

$$\frac{a}{bRT^{3/2}} = \frac{1.694 \times 10^7}{(22.30)(83.14)(120)^{1.5}} = 6.951$$

and Eq. (4-152) becomes

$$Z = \frac{1}{1-h} - 6.951\frac{h}{1+h} \tag{A}$$

Equation (4-156) yields, on rearrangement,

$$h = \frac{bP}{RTZ} = \frac{(22.30)(10)}{(83.14)(120)Z}$$

or

$$h = 2.235 \times 10^{-2}/Z \tag{B}$$

Stepwise results of the iterative solution are listed below:

h [from Eq. (B)]	Z [from Eq. (A)]
$= 2.235 \times 10^{-2}$	$= 0.8709$
$= 2.566 \times 10^{-2}$	$= 0.8524$
$= 2.622 \times 10^{-2}$	$= 0.8493$
$= 2.632 \times 10^{-2}$	$= 0.8488$
$= 2.633 \times 10^{-2}$	$= 0.8487$
$= 2.633 \times 10^{-2}$	$= 0.8487$

Thus, for the stated conditions, we find $Z = 0.8487$, from which

$$V = \frac{ZRT}{P} = \frac{(0.8487)(83.14)(120)}{(10)} = 846.7 \text{ cm}^3 \text{ mol}^{-1}$$

Values of $\Delta H'$, $\Delta S'$, and ϕ, if desired, can be estimated from Eqs. (4-153) through (4-155) with the above-determined values of h and Z.

Application of an equation of state to calculations for a specific fluid requires that numerical values first be established for the equation-of-state parameters. This may be done in many ways and, since no cubic equation of state is perfect, different values are obtained depending on the procedure used. One class of methods involves the use of nonlinear regression techniques to determine by analysis of experimental data best values of the parameters for representation of particular properties over limited ranges of temperature and pressure. The equations which result are powerful interpolating tools, which can be quite precise for their intended purpose.

Another, much older, approach is to impose a few selected mathematical or numerical constraints upon the equation of state and to determine values for the parameters by solution of the resulting system of equations. Martin (1967) discusses and applies some of the features of real-fluid behavior which lend themselves to convenient expression as algebraic constraints for equation-of-state studies. The two most often used are the classical derivative conditions on the critical isotherm:

$$(\partial P/\partial V)_{T;\,cr} = 0 \qquad (4\text{-}1a)$$

$$(\partial^2 P/\partial V^2)_{T;\,cr} = 0 \qquad (4\text{-}1b)$$

As explained by Martin and Hou (1955), Eqs. (4-1) when applied to a cubic equation yield the equivalent requirement that the equation give three equal roots for the volume at the critical state, i.e.,

$$(V - V_c)^3 = 0$$

or

$$V^3 - 3V_c V^2 + 3V_c^2 V - V_c^3 = 0 \qquad (4\text{-}157)$$

At the critical state, the generic Redlich-Kwong equation may be written, by Eq. (4-140), as

$$V^3 - \frac{RT_c}{P_c} V^2 - \left(b_c^2 + \frac{b_c R T_c}{P_c} - \frac{\theta_c}{P_c}\right) V - \frac{b_c \theta_c}{P_c} = 0 \qquad (4\text{-}158)$$

Here, T_c and P_c are the usual critical properties; since b and θ may depend upon T, the subscripts on these quantities indicate that they are evaluated at the critical temperature.

Comparison of coefficients of V^n in Eqs. (4-157) and (4-158) yields three equations relating the five quantities P_c, V_c, T_c, b_c, and θ_c:

$$\frac{RT_c}{P_c} = 3V_c \qquad (4\text{-}159a)$$

$$b_c^2 + \frac{b_c R T_c}{P_c} - \frac{\theta_c}{P_c} = -3V_c^2 \qquad (4\text{-}159b)$$

$$\frac{b_c \theta_c}{P_c} = V_c^3 \qquad (4\text{-}159c)$$

By Eq. (4-159a),

$$V_c = \frac{RT_c}{3P_c} \tag{4-160a}$$

and thus, by Eq. (4-159c),

$$\theta_c = \frac{1}{27} \frac{R^3 T_c^3}{b_c P_c^2} \tag{4-160b}$$

Substitution of Eqs. (4-160) into Eq. (4-159b) yields on rearrangement the cubic equation

$$\hat{b}_c^3 + \hat{b}_c^2 + \tfrac{1}{3}\hat{b}_c - \tfrac{1}{27} = 0 \tag{4-161}$$

where $\hat{b}_c$ is a dimensionless value of b_c: $\hat{b}_c \equiv b_c P_c / RT_c$. Equation (4-161) has but one real root, given by

$$\hat{b}_c = \frac{2^{1/3} - 1}{3} = 0.08664$$

and thus

$$b_c = 0.08664 \frac{RT_c}{P_c} \tag{4-162a}$$

Substitution of Eq. (4-162a) into Eq. (4-160b) gives

$$\theta_c = \left(\frac{2^{1/3} + 1}{3}\right)^3 \frac{R^2 T_c^2}{P_c}$$

or

$$\theta_c = 0.42748 \frac{R^2 T_c^2}{P_c} \tag{4-162b}$$

Equations (4-162) are two expressions commonly used for estimation of parameters in Redlich-Kwong equations. Note, however, that they only provide values for b and θ *at the critical temperature*; if b and θ are treated as arbitrary functions of T, the critical constraints of Eqs. (4-1) provide no guidance as to what the temperature dependence might be.

As an application of Eqs. (4-162), we consider the estimation of parameters a and b for argon in the original Redlich-Kwong equation. Since b is a constant, independent of T, then by Eq. (4-162a),

$$b = 0.08664 \frac{RT_c}{P_c} \tag{4-163a}$$

Also, $\theta = a/T^{1/2}$, where a is a constant, and Eq. (4-162b) yields

$$a = 0.42748 \frac{R^2 T_c^{5/2}}{P_c} \tag{4-163b}$$

From App. D, we find for argon that $T_c = 150.8$ K and $P_c = 48.7$ bar. With $R = 83.14$ bar cm^3 mol^{-1} K^{-1}, Eqs. (4-163) give

$$b = 22.30 \text{ cm}^3 \text{ mol}^{-1}$$

$$a = 1.694 \times 10^7 \text{ bar K}^{1/2} \text{ cm}^6 \text{ mol}^{-2}$$

These are the same values used earlier for generation of Fig. 4-16 from Eq. (4-138), and for the numerical calculations of Example 4-13.

The *two* expressions, Eqs. (4-162a) and (4-162b), were obtained as solutions to the *three* equations, Eqs. (4-159a) through (4-159c). Actually, b_c and θ_c are the only *true* unknowns appearing in these equations, because P_c, V_c, and T_c are properties of a substance, having numerical values independent of any equation of state. In solving Eqs. (4-159), we have in fact treated V_c as a third "unknown," and in expressing it in terms of T_c and P_c by Eq. (4-160a), we have incorporated the constraint of Eq. (4-159a) that

$$Z_c \equiv \frac{P_c V_c}{R T_c} = \frac{1}{3}$$

The critical compressibility factor Z_c of real fluids is known from experiment to be generally smaller than 1/3; the entries in App. D show values ranging from about 0.20 to 0.30.

Equation (4-159a) is an inevitable consequence of the classical critical derivative constraints when applied to a Redlich-Kwong equation, and in the above development we have chosen to use it for elimination of V_c from our system of equations, retaining T_c and P_c as the favored critical properties. Obviously, two other options are available. We could eliminate P_c in favor of T_c and V_c, obtaining eventually as analogs of Eqs. (4-162) the pair of expressions:

$$b_c = (2^{1/3} - 1)V_c = 0.25992 V_c \tag{4-164a}$$

$$\theta_c = \frac{(2^{1/3} + 1)^3}{9} R T_c V_c = 1.2824 R T_c V_c \tag{4-164b}$$

Alternatively, we could eliminate T_c in favor of P_c and V_c, obtaining as a consequence the formulas:

$$b_c = (2^{1/3} - 1)V_c = 0.25992 V_c \tag{4-165a}$$

$$\theta_c = \frac{(2^{1/3} + 1)^3}{3} P_c V_c^2 = 3.8473 P_c V_c^2 \tag{4-165b}$$

Clearly, Eqs. (4-162), (4-164), and (4-165) yield different sets of values for b_c and θ_c, except for a (hypothetical) fluid for which $Z_c = 1/3$. Experience shows Eqs. (4-162) to be the preferred set of expressions; an excellent discussion of the thermodynamic implications of rival expressions such as Eqs. (4-162), (4-164), and (4-165) is given by Martin (1967).

The reason for the three conflicting sets of expressions for b_c and θ_c is that comparison of Eqs. (4-157) and (4-158) gives three algebraic equations, whereas the generic Redlich-Kwong equation when applied at the critical point contains but two unknowns. This difficulty can be resolved if one adopts, instead of a two-parameter equation such as Eq. (4-139), a *three*-parameter specialization of the more general cubic equation, Eq. (4-136). One may then treat P_c, V_c, and T_c as independent correlating parameters; that is, one may incorporate experimental values of Z_c into the equation of state, while still satisfying the critical derivative constraints. The advantages here are usually offset by other, more serious, disadvantages, however, as discussed by Martin (1967) and by Abbott (1973, 1979). Therefore Z_c is most often treated as an empirical constant, whatever the nature of the cubic equation.

Example 4-14 The critical derivative constraints are frequently used for fixing the values of b_c and θ_c in the generic Redlich-Kwong equation. As already noted, this yields no information as to the possible temperature dependence of b and θ. In fact, b is often treated as a constant, numerically equal to b_c as given by Eq. (4-162a). Parameter θ, on the other hand, is invariably treated as a function of T, and modern variants of the Redlich-Kwong equation incorporate a temperature dependence different from the original formula $\theta = \text{constant}/T^{1/2}$.

Because of the frequent application of cubic equations to vapor/liquid equilibrium calculations, a reasonable route to the determination of θ is through the analysis of vapor-pressure data for pure substances. By such a procedure, one finds by nonlinear regression analysis an expression for θ which minimizes the differences between experimental and computed values of P^{sat}. This technique was used indirectly by Soave (1972) in his development of a popular Redlich-Kwong variant, and by Peng and Robinson (1976) in their derivation of a cubic equation of different generic form.

It would be inappropriate for us to consider here the mathematical details of the development of such equations of state. Instead, we illustrate by example the converse procedure: the numerical computation of P^{sat}, without the use of the graphical Maxwell construction described earlier in this section. Our basis is the *original* Redlich-Kwong equation of state, applied to the calculation of P^{sat} for argon at 120 K—the same calculation done earlier by graphical construction.

For pure-component vapor/liquid equilibrium, we have by Eq. (3-68) that

$$f^v = f^l$$

or, since P is uniform throughout the two-phase system, that

$$\phi^v = \phi^l$$

or, equivalently, that

$$\ln(\phi^v/\phi^l) = 0 \tag{4-166}$$

An expression for $\ln\phi$ is given by Eq. (4-155) in Example 4-13. Applying this equation separately to the vapor and liquid phases, and subtracting the results, we have

$$\ln(\phi^v/\phi^l) = (Z^v - Z^l) - \ln\left(\frac{1-h^v}{1-h^l}\right)\frac{Z^v}{Z^l} - \left(\frac{a}{bRT^{3/2}}\right)\ln\left(\frac{1+h^v}{1+h^l}\right) \tag{A}$$

The vapor pressure P^{sat} at a specified value of T is that pressure for which the values of Z^v, Z^l, h^v, and h^l satisfy Eq. (4-166) or, more precisely, the pressure for which $\ln (\phi^v/\phi^l)$ differs from zero within some prescribed tolerance. Pressure P is related to Z and to h through Eqs. (4-152) and (4-156), which yield, when applied separately to the two phases,

$$Z^v = \frac{bP}{h^v RT} = \frac{1}{1 - h^v} - \left(\frac{a}{bRT^{3/2}}\right)\frac{h^v}{1 + h^v} \tag{B}$$

and

$$Z^l = \frac{bP}{h^l RT} = \frac{1}{1 - h^l} - \left(\frac{a}{bRT^{3/2}}\right)\frac{h^l}{1 + h^l} \tag{C}$$

For given values of a, b, and T, Eqs. (4-166) and (A) through (C) constitute a system of three equations in three unknowns: h^v, h^l, and $P = P^{\text{sat}}$ (or, equivalently, Z^v, Z^l, and $P = P^{\text{sat}}$). One effects a solution by assuming a value of P, computing the h's and Z's from Eqs. (B) and (C), and then checking to see if $\ln (\phi^v/\phi^l)$, as given by Eq. (A), is zero. If not, a new pressure is assumed, and the procedure is repeated until $\ln (\phi^v/\phi^l) = 0$ to within the prescribed tolerance. The pressure for which this criterion is met is the vapor/liquid saturation pressure P^{sat}.

The solution of Eqs. (B) and (C) was discussed in Example 4-13; for an assumed value of P, values of Z^v and h^v can be determined by the simple iterative scheme illustrated in that example. Values of Z^l and h^l, on the other hand, must be determined by other techniques, e.g., by explicit solution of the cubic equation in h^l, or by bisection methods.

It is unlikely that the first-assumed value of P will yield values of Z's and h's which solve Eq. (4-166). One needs a rational, efficient method of obtaining improved estimates of P from the results of previous, unsuccessful trials. For problems of the present type, *Newton's method*, described in App. E, is appropriate. Equation (E-2) applied to this example yields the recursive formula

$$P_{j+1} = P_j - \frac{\ln (\phi^v/\phi^l)_j}{[\partial \ln (\phi^v/\phi^l)/\partial P]_{T, j}} \tag{D}$$

Here, subscript j identifies the results of the jth iteration, and P_{j+1} is the new estimate of the P ($= P^{\text{sat}}$) which solves Eq. (4-166). Equation (D) can be simplified considerably by use of Eqs. (3-82) and (2-75), from which we obtain

$$\left(\frac{\partial \ln \phi}{\partial P}\right)_T = \frac{Z - 1}{P}$$

and thus

$$\left|\frac{\partial \ln (\phi^v/\phi^l)}{\partial P}\right|_{T, j} = \frac{(Z^v - Z^l)_j}{P_j} \tag{E}$$

Combination of Eqs. (D) and (E) gives, on rearrangement,

$$P_{j+1} = \frac{P_j}{(Z^v - Z^l)_j}[(Z^v - Z^l)_j - \ln (\phi^v/\phi^l)_j] \tag{F}$$

Equation (F) is the basis for our iterative scheme.

For argon, we use values of a and b employed earlier:

$$a = 1.694 \times 10^7 \text{ bar K}^{1/2} \text{ cm}^6 \text{ mol}^{-2}$$

$$b = 22.30 \text{ cm}^3 \text{ mol}^{-1}$$

and, at 120 K, Eqs. (A), (B), and (C) become

$$\ln (\phi^v/\phi^l) = (Z^v - Z^l) - \ln \left(\frac{1 - h^v}{1 - h^l}\right)\frac{Z^v}{Z^l} - 6.951 \ln \left(\frac{1 + h^v}{1 + h^l}\right) \tag{G}$$

$$Z^v = 2.235 \times 10^{-3}\frac{P}{h^v} = \frac{1}{1 - h^v} - 6.951\frac{h^v}{1 + h^v} \tag{H}$$

and

$$Z^l = 2.235 \times 10^{-3}\frac{P}{h^l} = \frac{1}{1 - h^l} - 6.951\frac{h^l}{1 + h^l} \tag{I}$$

In order to ensure four-figure agreement on the values of ϕ^v and ϕ^l resulting from solution to the problem, we approximate Eq. (4-166) by

$$|\ln (\phi^v/\phi^l)| \leq 1 \times 10^{-6} \tag{J}$$

A starting value of pressure P_1 is needed to begin the solution. It follows from our earlier discussion of Fig. 4-16 that

$$0 \text{ bar} < P^{\text{sat}} < 21.5 \text{ bar}$$

and we therefore choose as an initial estimate of P the average of these two values: $P_1 = 10.75$ bar. Deleting superscripts l and v, but introducing numerical subscripts to indicate the number of the iteration, we may write the pair of equations (H) and (I) as the single equation

$$Z_1 = \frac{2.403 \times 10^{-2}}{h_1} = \frac{1}{1 - h_1} - 6.951\frac{h_1}{1 + h_1}$$

where we have incorporated the value $P = P_1 = 10.75$ bar. Solution of this equation yields three values of h, and hence of Z:

$$h_1^v = 2.877045 \times 10^{-2} \qquad Z_1^v = 0.83523203$$

$$h_1^m = 0.1893716 \qquad Z_1^m = 0.12687350$$

$$h_1^l = 0.6345428 \qquad Z_1^l = 3.786384 \times 10^{-2}$$

The smallest and largest values of h are for the vapor and for the liquid phase, respectively. The middle root, denoted by superscript m, has no physical significance. Substitution of Z's and h's into Eq. (G) gives

$$\ln (\phi^v/\phi^l)_1 = -5.545391 \times 10^{-2}$$

which does not satisfy Eq. (J).

A new value of pressure, P_2, is found from Eq. (F)

$$P_2 = \frac{P_1}{(Z^v - Z^l)_1}[(Z^v - Z^l)_1 - \ln (\phi^v/\phi^l)_1]$$

$$= \frac{10.75}{0.79736819}[0.79736819 + 5.545391 \times 10^{-2}]$$

or

$$P_2 = 11.498 \text{ bar}$$

A second series of calculations yields

$$h_2^v = 3.128739 \times 10^{-2} \qquad Z_2^v = 0.82141716$$

$$h_2^l = 0.6350739 \qquad Z_2^l = 4.046484 \times 10^{-2}$$

from which

$$\ln (\phi^v/\phi^l)_2 = -0.34095 \times 10^{-3}$$

and Eq. (J) is still not satisfied.

By Eq. (F) we again find a new value of P:

$$P_3 = 11.532 \text{ bar}$$

A third series of calculations gives

$$h_3^v = 3.139513 \times 10^{-2} \qquad Z_3^v = 0.8208279$$

$$h_3^l = 0.6350979 \qquad Z_3^l = 4.058267 \times 10^{-2}$$

from which

$$\ln (\phi^v/\phi^l)_3 = -1.4 \times 10^{-6}$$

which is close enough to the tolerance implied by Eq. (J). Thus, to four significant figures, we find for argon at 120 K that

$$P^{\text{sat}} = P_3 = 11.53 \text{ bar}$$

$$V^v = 1/\rho_3^v = b/h_3^v = 710.1 \text{ cm}^3 \text{ mol}^{-1}$$

$$V^l = 1/\rho_3^l = b/h_3^l = 35.11 \text{ cm}^3 \text{ mol}^{-1}$$

These may be compared with smoothed experimental values of $P^{\text{sat}} = 12.16$ bar, $V^v = 663.3$ cm^3 mol^{-1}, and $V^l = 34.45$ cm^3 mol^{-1}.

Finally, we may compute separately by Eq. (4-155) the vapor- and liquid-phase fugacity coefficients. We find

$$\phi^v = 0.848145$$

and

$$\phi^l = 0.848146$$

which are in virtual agreement, as they must be.

The relative agreement at saturation conditions between experimental and computed properties illustrated by the preceding example is about as good as one can expect from a two-constant cubic equation of state, with constants determined from the critical derivative constraints. In fact, the original Redlich-Kwong equation performs remarkably well in many respects for the simple fluids Ar, Kr, and Xe. If however the calculations of Example 4-14 were repeated for a more complex fluid, say n-octane, the comparisons would be less satisfactory. A source of this difficulty is that Eq. (4-138), with a and b given by Eqs. (4-163), represents in effect a two-parameter corresponding-states approach to the calculation of fluid properties. That this is the case is easily seen if one combines Eqs. (4-163) and (4-152), obtaining

$$Z = \frac{1}{1-h} - \frac{4.9340}{T_r^{3/2}} \frac{h}{1+h} \qquad (4\text{-}167a)$$

with

$$h \equiv b\rho = b/V = 0.08664 \frac{RT_c}{P_c V}$$

But

$$V = \frac{ZRT}{P} = \frac{RT_c}{P_c} \frac{ZT_r}{P_r}$$

And thus, by the last two equations,

$$h = 0.08664 \frac{P_r}{ZT_r} \qquad (4\text{-}167b)$$

Equations (4-167) thus represent a *particular* corresponding-states correlation, of the form

$$Z = f\left(T_r, \frac{P_r}{ZT_r}\right)$$

or, equivalently, of the form

$$Z = Z(T_r, P_r)$$

The two corresponding-states parameters are, of course, T_c and P_c.

Most modifications of the Redlich-Kwong equation incorporate, in addition to T_c and P_c, a third corresponding-states parameter, usually the acentric factor ω; this improves the performance of the equation for nonsimple fluids. One such modification is that of Soave (1972), who retains the original expression for b,

$$b = 0.08664 \frac{RT_c}{P_c} \qquad (4\text{-}163a)$$

but replaces the original expression for θ by the formula

$$\theta = \theta_c[1 + (0.480 + 1.574\omega - 0.176\omega^2)(1 - T_r^{1/2})]^2 \qquad (4\text{-}168)$$

Here, θ_c is given by Eq. (4-162b); the term in brackets which multiplies it was determined by analysis of data for P^{sat} of pure substances.

Another approach to improving the performance of the original Redlich-Kwong equation is the replacement of Eqs. (4-163) with the similar expressions

$$b = \Omega_b \frac{RT_c}{P_c} \qquad (4\text{-}169a)$$

and

$$a = \Omega_a \frac{R^2 T_c^{5/2}}{P_c}$$
(4-169b)

where Ω_a and Ω_b are pure numbers, determined not from the critical derivative constraints, but instead by fitting of experimental data. By this procedure, values of Ω_a and Ω_b are found which are different for different fluids, and different from the classical values

$$\Omega_b = 0.08664$$

$$\Omega_a = 0.42748$$

implied by Eqs. (4-163). The temperature dependence of the original Redlich-Kwong equation is preserved, but the critical derivative constraints are not satisfied. Such a procedure was used by Chueh and Prausnitz (1967b, c), who determined by analysis of volumetric data at saturation *separate* sets of values for Ω_a amd Ω_b (one set for the liquid phase, and one for the vapor phase) for 19 different fluids.

Any pressure-explicit empirical equation of state which yields $Z = 1$ in the limit as $\rho \to 0$ (or, equivalently, as $V \to \infty$) can be recast into the virial form

$$Z = 1 + \sum_{n=1}^{\infty} \mathscr{B}_n(ES)\rho^n$$
(4-170)

where the $\mathscr{B}_n(ES)$ are density-series virial coefficients *implied by the equation of state*. The results of such an exercise have two uses. First, they provide a convenient basis for testing the predictive capabilities of the equation of state at low densities, for the $\mathscr{B}_n(ES)$, particularly $B(ES)$, can be compared against experimental values of $\mathscr{B}_n$, or against values of $\mathscr{B}_n$ generated from reliable correlations. Second, realistic low-density behavior may be *built into* an empirical equation of state by direct incorporation of expressions for one or more of the virial coefficients.

We illustrate the procedure by deriving the virial equation corresponding to the generic Redlich-Kwong equation. By Eq. (4-141a),

$$Z = \frac{1}{1 - b\rho} - \left(\frac{\theta}{bRT}\right)\frac{b\rho}{1 + b\rho}$$

and by the binomial expansion, for $(b\rho)^2 < 1$,

$$(1 - b\rho)^{-1} = 1 + \sum_{n=1}^{\infty} (b\rho)^n$$

and

$$(1 + b\rho)^{-1} = 1 + \sum_{n=1}^{\infty} (-1)^n (b\rho)^n = \sum_{n=0}^{\infty} (-1)^n (b\rho)^n$$

Combination of the last three equations gives

$$Z = 1 + \sum_{n=1}^{\infty} (b\rho)^n - \left(\frac{\theta}{bRT}\right) \sum_{n=0}^{\infty} (-1)^n (b\rho)^{n+1}$$

$$= 1 + \sum_{n=1}^{\infty} b^n \rho^n - \left(\frac{\theta}{RT}\right) \sum_{n=0}^{\infty} (-1)^n b^n \rho^{n+1}$$

$$= 1 + \sum_{n=1}^{\infty} b^n \rho^n - \left(\frac{\theta}{RT}\right) \sum_{n=1}^{\infty} (-1)^{n-1} b^{n-1} \rho^n$$

or

$$Z = 1 + \sum_{n=1}^{\infty} \left[b^n - \frac{(-b)^{n-1}\theta}{RT} \right] \rho^n \qquad (4\text{-}171)$$

Comparison of Eq. (4-171) with Eq. (4-170) reveals that the virial coefficients $\mathcal{B}_n(\text{GRK})$ implied by the generic Redlich-Kwong (GRK) equation are given by

$$\mathcal{B}_n(\text{GRK}) = b^n - \frac{(-b)^{n-1}\theta}{RT}$$

For example

$$B(\text{GRK}) \equiv \mathcal{B}_1(\text{GRK}) = b - \frac{\theta}{RT} \qquad (4\text{-}172a)$$

$$C(\text{GRK}) \equiv \mathcal{B}_2(\text{GRK}) = b^2 + \frac{b\theta}{RT} \qquad (4\text{-}172b)$$

$$D(\text{GRK}) \equiv \mathcal{B}_3(\text{GRK}) = b^3 - \frac{b^2\theta}{RT} \qquad (4\text{-}172c)$$

etc.

Inspection of Eqs. (4-172) shows that our treatment of b and θ as functions of T and composition only is consistent with the fact that the $\mathcal{B}_n$ also depend only upon T and composition. Moreover, it is clear that *in principle* either b, or θ, or both, may be independent of T, for in either case one still obtains temperature-dependent virial coefficients. However, if b and θ are both independent of T, Eq. (4-172a) yields an expression for the second virial coefficient which is linear in T^{-1}, while Eq. (4-93a) of Example 4-8 suggests that B varies approximately as $T^{-1.6}$. One is led inevitably to the conclusion that either b or θ *must* depend upon T, and that the simplest procedure is to take $b = $ constant and to take θ as approximately proportional to $T^{-0.6}$. This is very nearly the case for the original Redlich-Kwong (ORK) equation, for which Eqs. (4-172) become

$$B(\text{ORK}) = b - \frac{a}{RT^{3/2}} \qquad (4\text{-}173a)$$

$$C(\text{ORK}) = b^2 + \frac{ab}{RT^{3/2}} \qquad (4\text{-}173b)$$

$$D(\text{ORK}) = b^3 - \frac{ab^2}{RT^{3/2}} \qquad (4\text{-}173c)$$

etc.

The first of these equations is of greatest interest, because of the availability of data for B against which to test it. Multiplication of Eq. (4-173a) by P_c/RT_c and introduction of Eqs. (4-163) gives

$$\frac{B(\text{ORK})P_c}{RT_c} = 0.08664 - \frac{0.42748}{T_r^{3/2}} \qquad (4\text{-}174)$$

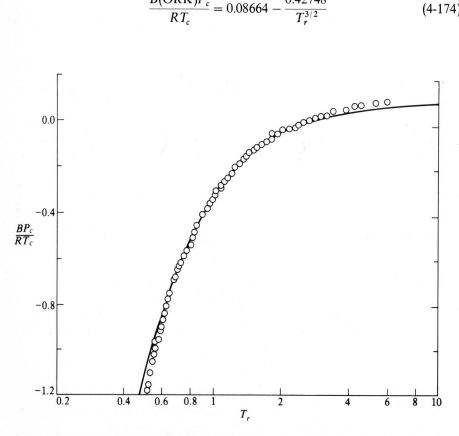

Figure 4-18 The second virial coefficient, as implied by the original Redlich-Kwong equation (solid line). Circles are data for Ar, Kr, and Xe.

Figure 4-18 is a plot of Eq. (4-174) superimposed on data for the *simple fluids*. The agreement is excellent, and guarantees good performance of Eq. (4-138) for simple fluids at low densities. Performance for nonsimple fluids is of course less satisfactory, because there is no contribution to BP_c/RT_c corresponding to the curve for B^1 shown on Fig. 4-14.

4-8 CUBIC EQUATIONS OF STATE FOR MIXTURES: THE GENERIC REDLICH-KWONG EQUATION

As with the virial equation, application of empirical equations of state to mixtures is usually done through mixing rules for the equation-of-state parameters. It should be recognized, however, that whereas the mixing rules for B and C given by Eqs. (4-94) and (4-95) are *exact*, those for parameters in an empirical equation of state are necessarily empirical. Although it is possible in many cases to devise plausible arguments for empirical mixing rules, their ultimate justification is in the performance of the equation of state when applied to the calculation of partial molar properties or of properties of mixtures. In adopting a set of empirical mixing rules, one must make the same compromises made when choosing an equation of state for representation of properties of pure fluids; inevitably, one strikes a balance between generality and utility.

Only a few types of mixing rules have gained general acceptance for use with cubic equations of state; most of them may be considered special cases of the quadratic mixing rule

$$p = \sum_i \sum_j x_i x_j p_{ij} \tag{4-175}$$

Here, the unsubscripted symbol p represents the value of a parameter for a mixture. The doubly subscripted parameters are of two types: if $j = i$, then $p_{ij} = p_{ii} \equiv p_i$, the parameter for pure i; if $j \neq i$, then p_{ij} represents (in some sense) interactions between unlike chemical species, and is called an interaction parameter. By assumption, interaction parameters are independent of composition; they are related to the pure-fluid parameters p_i and p_j by empirical recipes called combination rules. (The jargon appearing in this section is clearly similar to that of Sec. 4-6.)

If we adopt an *arithmetic-mean* combination rule

$$p_{ij} = \tfrac{1}{2}(p_{ii} + p_{jj}) = \tfrac{1}{2}(p_i + p_j) \tag{4-176}$$

then Eq. (4-175) reduces to a *linear* mixing rule:

$$p = \sum_i x_i p_i \tag{4-177}$$

Equation (4-177) is often used for parameter b in the general cubic equation, Eq. (4-136). If, instead, we adopt a *geometric-mean* combination rule

$$p_{ij} = (p_{ii} p_{jj})^{1/2} = (p_i p_j)^{1/2} \tag{4-178}$$

then Eq. (4-175) reduces to the mixing rule

$$p = \left(\sum_i x_i p_i^{1/2} \right)^2 \tag{4-179}$$

Equation (4-179) is sometimes used for parameter θ in Eq. (4-136). Equations (4-177) and (4-179) both have the desirable feature of producing values for mixture parameters from those of the constituent pure species alone. However, they are often inadequate, particularly when one deals with mixtures containing chemically dissimilar species.

The full flexibility of Eq. (4-175) can be retained if one treats the interaction parameters p_{ij} $(j \neq i)$ as empirical parameters, values of which are deduced by analysis of data for the ij binary system. Since the p_{ii} may be functions of temperature, values of p_{ij} determined in this way may be expected also to depend upon T. Various schemes have been proposed for accommodating this complication. A technique which enjoys some popularity is the use of combination rules *based* upon either Eq. (4-176) or Eq. (4-178), but incorporating another interaction parameter, presumably weakly dependent on T, which corrects for the inadequacies of the simpler combination rules. For example, the combination rule Eq. (4-178) is frequently modified by inclusion of an interaction parameter l_{ij}:

$$p_{ij} = (1 - l_{ij})(p_i p_j)^{1/2} \tag{4-180}$$

By definition, $l_{ij} = 0$ if $j = i$; otherwise, it is a (presumably) small quantity, values of which are found by reduction of experimental data with the equation of state. Ideally, l_{ij} is a true constant for a given binary system; in practice, one must sometimes settle for values of l_{ij} which are weak, well-behaved, functions of temperature.

Calculation of mixture properties from a cubic equation of state is straightforward if one has mixing rules and combination rules for all parameters. One merely uses equations such as those derived in the preceding section, interpreting all parameters as parameters for the *mixture*. Calculation of partial properties of course requires the evaluation of derivatives with respect to mole numbers, and we find it convenient here, as we did with the virial equation, to have available expressions for the *partial molar equation-of-state parameters* $\bar{p}_i$, defined as

$$\bar{p}_i \equiv \left[\frac{\partial(np)}{\partial n_i} \right]_{T, n_j} \tag{4-181}$$

The same arguments which led us from the mixing rule for B [Eq. (4-94)] to the first expression for $\bar{B}_i$ [Eq. (4-112)] may be applied to any parameter p depending upon T and x only and given by the quadratic mixing rule, Eq. (4-175). We therefore omit the details of the derivation and merely present the result, analogous to Eq. (4-112):

$$\bar{p}_i = -p + 2 \sum_k x_k p_{ki} \tag{4-182}$$

Equation (4-182) is valid for *any* combination rule for p_{ki}. We consider its application to the two simple special rules given by Eqs. (4-176) and (4-178). If Eq. (4-176) applies, then

$$p_{ki} = \tfrac{1}{2}(p_k + p_i)$$

and thus, by Eq. (4-182),

$$\bar{p}_i = -p + \sum_k x_k p_k + \sum_k x_k p_i$$

With Eq. (4-177), this reduces to

$$\bar{p}_i = -p + p + p_i \sum_k x_k$$

or

$$\bar{p}_i = p_i \tag{4-183}$$

Equation (4-183) of course also follows from direct application of Eq. (4-181) to Eq. (4-177).

If Eq. (4-178) applies, then

$$p_{ki} = p_k^{1/2} p_i^{1/2}$$

and, by Eq. (4-182),

$$\bar{p}_i = -p + 2 \sum_k x_k p_k^{1/2} p_i^{1/2}$$

$$= -p + 2p_i^{1/2} \left(\sum_k x_k p_k^{1/2} \right)$$

With Eq. (4-179), this reduces to

$$\bar{p}_i = -p + 2p_i^{1/2} p^{1/2}$$

or

$$\bar{p}_i = p \left[2 \left(\frac{p_i}{p} \right)^{1/2} - 1 \right] \tag{4-184}$$

No significant simplification of Eq. (4-182) obtains if one applies it to the more flexible combination rule given by Eq. (4-180), and we consider no further applications of Eq. (4-182) to particular combination rules.

Example 4-15 It was noted earlier that plausible arguments may be advanced for the mixing rules of parameters in empirical equations of state. Expressions for the virial coefficients implied by an equation of state are often used for this purpose. Consider the generic Redlich-Kwong equation, for which it was shown in the preceding section that

$$B(\text{GRK}) = b - \frac{\theta}{RT} \tag{4-172a}$$

If we require that the cubic equation be useful at low densities, then the composition dependence of parameters b and θ should be compatible with that of the *true* second virial coefficient B, which is given by Eq. (4-94) as quadratic in the mole fractions. Clearly, either b, or θ, or both, must therefore be quadratic in mole fraction. Common practice is to assume that b is linear:

$$b = \sum_i x_i b_i \qquad (4\text{-}185)$$

and that θ is quadratic:

$$\theta = \sum_i \sum_j x_i x_j \theta_{ij} \qquad (4\text{-}186)$$

If Eq. (4-185) is viewed as a special case of the general quadratic formula, Eq. (4-175), then by Eq. (4-177) the arithmetic-mean combination rule for b_{ij} is implied:

$$b_{ij} = \tfrac{1}{2}(b_i + b_j) \qquad (4\text{-}187)$$

For the original Redlich-Kwong equation, $\theta = a/T^{1/2}$, and the geometric-mean combination rule was proposed:

$$a_{ij} = (a_i a_j)^{1/2} \qquad (4\text{-}188)$$

Thus, for the original Redlich-Kwong equation with the original combination rule for a, we have by Eq. (4-179) that

$$a = \left(\sum_i x_i a_i^{1/2} \right)^2 \qquad (4\text{-}189)$$

In practical applications of cubic equations of state, the two most important partial molar properties are $\bar{V}_i$ and $\ln \hat{\phi}_i$. We derive in the following paragraphs the expressions for these quantities implied by the generic Redlich-Kwong equation.

By Eq. (4-39)

$$\bar{V}_i = \frac{RT}{P}\bar{Z}_i = \frac{\bar{Z}_i}{\rho Z} \qquad (4\text{-}39)$$

and thus we require an expression for $\bar{Z}_i$. Since cubic equations are explicit in pressure, we base our derivation on Eq. (4-127), which becomes, with $M = Z$,

$$\bar{Z}_i = \left[1 - \frac{P}{Z}\left(\frac{\partial Z}{\partial P}\right)_{T,\,x} \right] \left[\frac{\partial(nZ)}{\partial n_i} \right]_{T,\,\rho/n,\,n_j} \qquad (4\text{-}190)$$

In Eq. (4-190) we have replaced the constraint of constant nV on the mole-number derivative of nZ by the equivalent constraint of constant ρ/n. The derivative $(\partial Z/\partial P)_{T,\,x}$ must be written in terms of a derivative evaluable from a pressure-explicit equation of state. In deriving Eq. (4-51a) we showed that

$$\left(\frac{\partial Z}{\partial P}\right)_{T,\,x} = \frac{(\partial Z/\partial \rho)_{T,\,x}}{ZRT + (P/Z)(\partial Z/\partial \rho)_{T,\,x}}$$

which may be written, since $P = Z\rho RT$,

$$\left(\frac{\partial Z}{\partial P}\right)_{T,x} = \frac{Z}{P}\left[\frac{\rho(\partial Z/\partial\rho)_{T,x}}{Z + \rho(\partial Z/\partial\rho)_{T,x}}\right]$$

Substitution of this last equation into Eq. (4-190) gives

$$\bar{Z}_i = \left[\frac{Z}{Z + \rho(\partial Z/\partial\rho)_{T,x}}\right]\left[\frac{\partial(nZ)}{\partial n_i}\right]_{T,\,\rho/n,\,n_j} \qquad (4\text{-}191)$$

Equation (4-191) is a general relationship, valid for the calculation of $\bar{Z}_i$ from *any* pressure-explicit equation of state. To take advantage of the more concise form of the generic Redlich-Kwong equation given by Eq. (4-141*b*), we note that, since $\rho = h/b$ and since b depends upon T and x only

$$\rho(\partial Z/\partial\rho)_{T,x} = h(\partial Z/\partial h)_{T,x}$$

Thus, Eq. (4-191) may be written in the equivalent form, convenient for the present application

$$\bar{Z}_i = \left[\frac{Z}{Z + h(\partial Z/\partial h)_{T,x}}\right]\left[\frac{\partial(nZ)}{\partial n_i}\right]_{T,\,\rho/n,\,n_j} \qquad (4\text{-}192)$$

We now need expressions for the terms appearing in brackets in Eq. (4-192). The first is found by differentiation of Eq. (4-141*b*) and by subsequent algebraic manipulations. The result is:

$$\frac{Z}{Z + h(\partial Z/\partial h)_{T,x}} = \frac{(1-h)(1+h)^2 - (\theta/bRT)h(1+h)(1-h)^2}{(1+h)^2 - (\theta/bRT)h(2+h)(1-h)^2} \qquad (4\text{-}193)$$

Multiplication of Eq. (4-141*b*) by n gives

$$nZ = \frac{n}{1-h} - \frac{n(n\theta)}{(nb)RT}\frac{h}{1+h}$$

and differentiation with respect to n_i at constant T, ρ/n, and n_j yields, on rearrangement,

$$\left[\frac{\partial(nZ)}{\partial n_i}\right]_{T,\,\rho/n,\,n_j} = \frac{1}{1-h} + \frac{\bar{b}_i}{b}\frac{h}{(1-h)^2} + \left(\frac{\theta}{bRT}\right)\left(\frac{\bar{b}_i}{b} - \frac{\bar{\theta}_i}{\theta} - 1\right)\left(\frac{h}{1+h}\right)$$

$$- \left(\frac{\theta}{bRT}\right)\frac{\bar{b}_i}{b}\frac{h}{(1+h)^2} \qquad (4\text{-}194)$$

Here, we have invoked the definitions [see Eq. (4-181)]

$$\bar{b}_i \equiv \left[\frac{\partial(nb)}{\partial n_i}\right]_{T,\,n_j}$$

and

$$\bar{\theta}_i \equiv \left[\frac{\partial(n\theta)}{\partial n_i}\right]_{T,\,n_j}$$

and have made use of the relationship

$$\left(\frac{\partial h}{\partial n_i}\right)_{T,\,\rho/n,\,n_j} = \frac{\rho}{n}\left[\frac{\partial(nb)}{\partial n_i}\right]_{T,\,n_j} = \frac{\rho\bar{b}_i}{n} = \frac{h\bar{b}_i}{nb}$$

Equations (4-39) and (4-191) together provide a *general* expression for $\bar{V}_i$; when combined with Eqs. (4-141*b*), (4-193), and (4-194), Eqs. (4-39) and (4-192) give the expression for $\bar{V}_i$ implied by the generic Redlich-Kwong equation. Note that in deriving Eq. (4-194), we have made *no* assumptions as to the mixing rules for b and θ. If we use the general quadratic mixing rule, Eq. (4-175), for both parameters, we have by Eq. (4-182) that

$$\frac{\bar{b}_i}{b} = \frac{2\sum\limits_{k} x_k b_{ki}}{b} - 1$$

and

$$\frac{\bar{\theta}_i}{\theta} = \frac{2\sum\limits_{k} x_k \theta_{ki}}{\theta} - 1$$

Note that in these last two equations we still have not committed ourselves to combination rules for b_{ki} or θ_{ki}.

Derivation of an expression for $\ln \hat{\phi}_i$ can proceed from either Eq. (4-128) or (4-130), since expressions for both $\ln \phi$ and Z for the generic Redlich-Kwong equation have already been developed. We choose the latter method. By Eq. (4-194),

$$\left\{\left[\frac{\partial(nZ)}{\partial n_i}\right]_{T,\,\rho/n,\,n_j} - 1\right\} = \frac{h}{1-h} + \frac{\bar{b}_i}{b}\frac{h}{(1-h)^2}$$

$$+ \left(\frac{\theta}{bRT}\right)\left(\frac{\bar{b}_i}{b} - \frac{\bar{\theta}_i}{\theta} - 1\right)\left(\frac{h}{1+h}\right) - \left(\frac{\theta}{bRT}\right)\frac{\bar{b}_i}{b}\frac{h}{(1+h)^2}$$

Substitution of this equation into Eq. (4-130) gives, on integration and rearrangement,

$$\ln \hat{\phi}_i = -\ln(1-h)Z + \left(\frac{\theta}{bRT}\right)\left(\frac{\bar{b}_i}{b} - \frac{\bar{\theta}_i}{\theta} - 1\right)\ln(1+h)$$

$$+ \frac{\bar{b}_i}{b}\left(\frac{h}{1-h}\right) - \frac{\theta}{bRT}\frac{\bar{b}_i}{b}\left(\frac{h}{1+h}\right) \quad (4\text{-}195)$$

Note again that in deriving Eq. (4-195) we have made no assumptions as to the mixing rules for b and θ. Equation (4-195) may be written in a more concise form. Adding and subtracting $Z - 1$ on the right-hand side of the equation, we obtain, on rearrangement,

$$\ln \hat{\phi}_i = \left\{ (Z - 1) - \ln (1 - h)Z - \left(\frac{\theta}{bRT}\right) \ln (1 + h) \right\}$$
$$+ \left(\frac{\theta}{bRT}\right)\left(\frac{\bar{b}_i}{b} - \frac{\bar{\theta}_i}{\theta}\right) \ln (1 + h) + \frac{\bar{b}_i}{b}\left[\frac{h}{1 - h} - \left(\frac{\theta}{bRT}\right)\frac{h}{1 + h}\right] - (Z - 1)$$

But by Eq. (4-151) the term in braces $\{\ \}$ is $\ln \phi$ for the mixture, and by Eq. (4-143b) the term in brackets $[\ ]$ is $Z - 1$. Thus we may write, equivalent to Eq. (4-195),

$$\ln \hat{\phi}_i = \ln \phi + \left(\frac{\bar{b}_i}{b} - 1\right)(Z - 1) + \left(\frac{\theta}{bRT}\right)\left(\frac{\bar{b}_i}{b} - \frac{\bar{\theta}_i}{\varrho}\right) \ln (1 + h) \quad (4\text{-}196)$$

For *pure* chemical species i, $\bar{b}_i = b = b_i$, $\bar{\theta}_i = \theta = \theta_i$, and $\phi = \phi_i$. Thus Eq. (4-196) yields in the limit

$$\lim_{x_i \to 1} (\ln \hat{\phi}_i) = \ln \phi_i \tag{A}$$

as it must. Also, multiplication of both sides of Eq. (4-196) by x_i and summation over all i gives

$$\sum_i x_i \ln \hat{\phi}_i = \ln \phi \tag{B}$$

as it must. Here, we have made use of the fact that the $\bar{p}_i$, since they are partial molar quantities, satisfy the equation

$$p = \sum_i x_i \bar{p}_i$$

The two tests represented by Eqs. (A) and (B) for $\ln \hat{\phi}_i$ are examples of the checks one should always make on expressions for partial molar properties derived from equations of state. They are necessary (but of course not sufficient) attributes of correctness.

Example 4-16 We illustrate in this example the calculation of $\ln \hat{\phi}_i$ from the original Redlich-Kwong equation of state. The system is a gas-phase mixture of nitrogen(1) and n-butane(2) at 460.93 K (370°F) and 41.368 bar (600 psia), containing 49.74 mol % nitrogen and 50.26 mol % n-butane. We choose these conditions because of the availability of experimental data against which to compare our results.

With the mixing rules for b and a given by Eqs. (4-185) and (4-189), we have by Eqs. (4-183) and (4-184) that

$$\frac{\bar{b}_i}{b} = \frac{b_i}{b}$$

and

$$\frac{\bar{\theta}_i}{\theta_i} = \frac{\bar{a}_i}{a_i} = 2\left(\frac{a_i}{a}\right)^{1/2} - 1$$

Thus, Eq. (4-196) becomes

$$\ln \hat{\phi}_i = \ln \phi + \left(\frac{b_i}{b} - 1\right)(Z - 1) + \left(\frac{a}{bRT^{3/2}}\right)\left[\frac{b_i}{b} - 2\left(\frac{a_i}{a}\right)^{1/2} + 1\right] \ln (1 + h)$$

(4-197)

In Eq. (4-197), all unadorned symbols refer to the *mixture*. Moreover,

$$\ln \phi = (Z - 1) - \ln (1 - h)Z - \left(\frac{a}{bRT^{3/2}}\right) \ln (1 + h)$$

(4-155)

where, by Eqs. (4-152) and (4-156),

$$Z = \frac{bP}{hRT} = \frac{1}{1 - h} - \left(\frac{a}{bRT^{3/2}}\right)\frac{h}{1 + h}$$

(4-198)

Mixture parameters b and a are functions of the gas-phase mole fractions y_i:

$$b = \sum_i y_i b_i$$

(4-185)

$$a = \left(\sum_i y_i a_i^{1/2}\right)^2$$

(4-189)

The last five equations provide a basis for estimation of $\ln \hat{\phi}_i$ for species i in a mixture of arbitrary temperature, pressure, and composition. For the case at hand, we have but two chemical species, and we estimate values of b_i and a_i $(i = 1, 2)$ from Eqs. (4-163). Critical constants are found from App. D:

$$T_{c_1} = 126.2 \text{ K} \qquad T_{c_2} = 425.2 \text{ K}$$

$$P_{c_1} = 33.9 \text{ bar} \qquad P_{c_2} = 38.0 \text{ bar}$$

With these values, Eqs. (4-163), (4-185), and (4-189) give, for mixtures of arbitrary mole fraction y_1,

$$b = 80.600571 - 53.784934y_1 \text{ cm}^3 \text{ mol}^{-1}$$

$$a = (1.7026198 - 1.3077151y_1)^2 \times 10^8 \text{ bar K}^{1/2} \text{ cm}^6 \text{ mol}^{-2}$$

At the given composition ($y_1 = 0.4974$), these equations yield

$$b = 53.847944 \text{ cm}^3 \text{ mol}^{-1}$$

$$a = 1.1070455 \times 10^8 \text{ bar K}^{1/2} \text{ cm}^6 \text{ mol}^{-2}$$

and thus, for the mixture,

$$\frac{a}{bRT^{3/2}} = 2.4988134$$

Similarly, for pure 1 ($y_1 = 1$) and pure 2 ($y_1 = 0$), we find

$$\left.\begin{array}{l} b_1 = 26.815637 \\ b_2 = 80.600571 \end{array}\right\} \text{cm}^3 \text{ mol}^{-1}$$

$$\left.\begin{array}{l} a_1 = 1.5594972 \times 10^7 \\ a_2 = 2.8989141 \times 10^8 \end{array}\right\} \text{bar K}^{1/2} \text{ cm}^6 \text{ mol}^{-2}$$

We first calculate h, Z, and $\ln \phi$ for the gas mixture. At the stated conditions, Eq. (4-198) becomes

$$Z = \frac{5.8128438 \times 10^{-2}}{h} = \frac{1}{1-h} - 2.4988134 \frac{h}{1+h}$$

and solution for h and Z gives

$$h = 6.3261438 \times 10^{-2}$$

$$Z = 0.91886047$$

Substitution of these values into Eq. (4-155) gives $\ln \phi$ for the mixture:

$$\ln \phi = -8.4447230 \times 10^{-2} \tag{A}$$

Values of $\ln \hat{\phi}_1$ and $\ln \hat{\phi}_2$ may now be computed from Eq. (4-197). For species 1,

$$\ln \hat{\phi}_1 = \ln \phi + \left(\frac{b_1}{b} - 1\right)(Z - 1) + \left(\frac{a}{bRT^{3/2}}\right)\left[\frac{b_1}{b} - 2\left(\frac{a_1}{a}\right)^{1/2} + 1\right] \ln(1 + h)$$

or, numerically

$$\ln \hat{\phi}_1 = -8.4447230 \times 10^{-2} + 4.0733007 \times 10^{-2} + 1.1455124 \times 10^{-1}$$

or

$$\ln \hat{\phi}_1 = 7.0837017 \times 10^{-2} \tag{B}$$

and

$$\hat{\phi}_1 = 1.0734062$$

Similar calculations yield, for species 2,

$$\ln \hat{\phi}_2 = -0.23812487 \tag{C}$$

and

$$\hat{\phi}_2 = 0.78810427$$

We have carried all calculations through with eight significant figures in order to permit a precise numerical check on the internal consistency of the results. Since $\ln \hat{\phi}_i$ is a partial molar property with respect to $\ln \phi$, we must have

$$\sum_i y_i \ln \hat{\phi}_i = \ln \phi$$

By Eqs. (B) and (C), we find that

$$y_1 \ln \hat{\phi}_1 + y_2 \ln \hat{\phi}_2 = (0.4974)(7.0837017 \times 10^{-2}) + (0.5026)(-0.23812487)$$

or

$$\sum_i y_i \ln \hat{\phi}_i = -8.4447227 \times 10^{-2}$$

which is in virtual agreement with $\ln \phi$ as given by Eq. (A), as it must be.

It is instructive to compute values for the pure-component fugacity coefficients ϕ_1 and ϕ_2 at the same conditions. Equations (4-198) and (4-155) are applicable, with $a = a_i$ and $b = b_i$ $(i = 1, 2)$. Results of the calculations are

$$h_1 = 2.8665949 \times 10^{-2}$$

$$Z_1 = 1.0098137$$

$$\ln \phi_1 = 9.1548380 \times 10^{-3} \qquad \text{(D)}$$

$$\phi_1 = 1.0091968$$

and

$$h_2 = 0.13820308$$

$$Z_2 = 0.62956402$$

$$\ln \phi_2 = -0.32487219 \qquad \text{(E)}$$

$$\phi_2 = 0.72261970$$

Significantly, $\hat{\phi}_1$ and $\hat{\phi}_2$ are different from the corresponding values ϕ_1 and ϕ_2 for the pure components.

Data are available against which we may check the results of these calculations. Hilsenrath et al. (1955) give volumetric data for nitrogen(1), and Sage and Lacey (1950) for n-butane(2); Evans and Watson (1956) report results for nitrogen/n-butane mixtures of five compositions, including the one considered here, at 460.93 K (370°F). Reduction of all these data yields eventually the following data for the logarithms of the fugacity coefficients at 460.93 K, 41.368 bar, and $y_1 = 0.4974$:

$$\ln \phi = -0.071$$

$$\ln \hat{\phi}_1 = +0.084$$

$$\ln \hat{\phi}_2 = -0.224$$

$$\ln \phi_1 = +0.016$$

$$\ln \phi_2 = -0.318$$

These results may be compared with Eqs. (A) through (E). Agreement, although not quantitative, is good, considering the inherent limitations of the original Redlich-Kwong equation.

Example 4-17 We have seen that equation-of-state parameters for pure fluids are frequently correlated in terms of the critical properties T_c and P_c. When this is the case, and if mixing rules and combination rules are available for the equation-of-state parameters, it may be possible to develop closed-form expressions for pseudo-critical parameters T_{pc} and P_{pc}, or for interaction parameters $T_{c_{ij}}$ and $P_{c_{ij}}$. Use of these quantities provides alternative routes to the estimation of the equation-of-state parameters for mixtures. We illustrate here the development of formulas for T_{pc}, P_{pc}, $T_{c_{ij}}$, and $P_{c_{ij}}$ appropriate to the original Redlich-Kwong equation.

The following equations apply:

$$b = \Omega_b R \frac{T_c}{P_c} \qquad (4\text{-}163a)$$

$$a = \Omega_a R^2 \frac{T_c^{5/2}}{P_c} \qquad (4\text{-}163b)$$

$$b = \sum_i \sum_j x_i x_j b_{ij} \qquad (A)$$

$$a = \sum_i \sum_j x_i x_j a_{ij} \qquad (B)$$

$$b_{ij} = \tfrac{1}{2}(b_i + b_j) \qquad (4\text{-}187)$$

$$a_{ij} = (a_i a_j)^{1/2} \qquad (4\text{-}188)$$

$$b = \sum_i x_i b_i \qquad (4\text{-}185)$$

$$a = \left(\sum_i x_i a_i^{1/2}\right)^2 \qquad (4\text{-}189)$$

Here, $\Omega_b = 0.08664$ and $\Omega_a = 0.42748$, as determined from the classical derivative constraints, and the particular mixing rules given by Eq. (4-185) and (4-189) are considered special cases of the general quadratic mixing rules, Eqs. (A) and (B).

The pseudocritical parameters T_{pc} and P_{pc} are those values of T_c and P_c which, by definition, make Eqs. (4-163a) and (4-163b) valid for mixtures. Solving Eqs. (4-163) for T_c and P_c, we have

$$T_c = \left(\frac{\Omega_b}{R\Omega_a} \frac{a}{b}\right)^{2/3} \qquad (C)$$

$$P_c = \left(\frac{R\Omega_b^5}{\Omega_a^2} \frac{a^2}{b^5}\right)^{1/3} \qquad (D)$$

Equations (C) and (D) are assumed valid both for pure components and for mixtures. But for a mixture, we have from Eqs. (4-163a), (4-163b), (4-185), and (4-189) that

$$b = \Omega_b R \sum_i x_i (T_{ci}/P_{ci}) \qquad (E)$$

$$a = \Omega_a R^2 \left[\sum_i x_i (T_{ci}^{5/2}/P_{ci})^{1/2}\right]^2 \qquad (F)$$

Substitution of Eqs. (E) and (F) into Eqs. (C) and (D) gives, on identification of T_c with T_{pc} and P_c with P_{pc},

$$T_{pc} = \frac{\left[\sum_i x_i (T_{ci}^{5/2}/P_{ci})^{1/2}\right]^{4/3}}{\left[\sum_i x_i (T_{ci}/P_{ci})\right]^{2/3}} \tag{G}$$

$$P_{pc} = \frac{\left[\sum_i x_i (T_{ci}^{5/2}/P_{ci})^{1/2}\right]^{4/3}}{\left[\sum_i x_i (T_{ci}/P_{ci})\right]^{5/3}} \tag{H}$$

For a "mixture" containing only pure species k ($x_k = 1$), Eqs. (G) and (H) reduce to $T_{pc} = T_{c_k}$ and $P_{pc} = P_{c_k}$, as they must.

The interaction critical parameters $T_{c_{ij}}$ and $P_{c_{ij}}$ are those values of T_c and P_c from which one computes values of a_{ij} and b_{ij} appearing in the *quadratic* mixing rules, Eqs. (A) and (B). By definition, we have from Eq. (4-163a) that

$$b_{ij} = \Omega_b R \frac{T_{c_{ij}}}{P_{c_{ij}}}$$

But, by Eqs. (4-187) and (4-163a),

$$b_{ij} = \frac{\Omega_b R}{2}\left(\frac{T_{c_i}}{P_{c_i}} + \frac{T_{c_j}}{P_{c_j}}\right)$$

Equating the right-hand sides of the last two equations, we find

$$\frac{T_{c_{ij}}}{P_{c_{ij}}} = \frac{T_{c_i} P_{c_j} + T_{c_j} P_{c_i}}{2 P_{c_i} P_{c_j}} \tag{I}$$

Similarly, by Eq. (4-163b),

$$a_{ij} = \Omega_a R^2 \frac{T_{c_{ij}}^{5/2}}{P_{c_{ij}}}$$

and, by Eqs. (4-188) and (4-163b),

$$a_{ij} = \Omega_a R^2 \left(\frac{T_{c_i}^{5/2} T_{c_j}^{5/2}}{P_{c_i} P_{c_j}}\right)^{1/2}$$

from which

$$\frac{T_{c_{ij}}^{5/2}}{P_{c_{ij}}} = \left(\frac{T_{c_i}^{5/2} T_{c_j}^{5/2}}{P_{c_i} P_{c_j}}\right)^{1/2} \tag{J}$$

Equations (I) and (J) may be solved simultaneously for the interaction critical parameters. The results are:

$$T_{c_{ij}} = \left[\frac{4(P_{c_i} P_{c_j})(T_{c_i} T_{c_j})^{5/2}}{(T_{c_i} P_{c_j} + T_{c_j} P_{c_i})^2}\right]^{1/3} \tag{K}$$

$$P_{c_{ij}} = \left[\frac{32(P_{c_i} P_{c_j})^4 (T_{c_i} T_{c_j})^{5/2}}{(T_{c_i} P_{c_j} + T_{c_j} P_{c_i})^5}\right]^{1/3} \tag{L}$$

For $i = j$, Eqs. (K) and (L) reduce to $T_{c_{ij}} = T_{c_i}$ and $P_{c_{ij}} = P_{c_i}$, as they must.

The derivation of expressions for T_{pc}, P_{pc}, $T_{c_{ij}}$, and $P_{c_{ij}}$ is straightforward in this case, because the equation of state contains but two parameters, dependent upon T_c and P_c only. Determination of simple closed-form analogs to Eqs. (G), (H), (K), and (L) is not always possible for more complex equations of state.

4-9 CONCLUDING REMARKS

We have illustrated in Secs. 4-3 through 4-8 how the exact methods of classical thermodynamics are used for calculation of properties of fluids from several kinds of representation of the PVT surface. The types of representation considered in detail—Pitzer correlation, virial equations, and Redlich-Kwong equations—were chosen because of their simplicity, and because of their historical importance. Many other examples could have been treated; however, our intent has been to demonstrate in the simplest useful contexts general *thermodynamic* techniques, not to present critical comparisons of rival equations of state or detailed discussions of property-estimation methods. For these, one must consult the vast and growing literature on the subject; good critical surveys are given in the monographs by Reid et al. [Reid and Sherwood (1966); Reid, Prausnitz, and Sherwood (1977)]. There are also available in tabular or chart form compilations of smoothed values for the thermodynamic properties of many pure fluids. Bett et al. (1975) present a useful bibliography of such compilations for 40 substances, published between 1950 and 1973. More recent examples may be found in the current literature.

In the following paragraphs, we offer a few final comments on material treated in the previous sections, indicating by selected references some modern trends in equation-of-state thermodynamics.

An exposition of the origins and variations of the corresponding states concept is given in a review article by Leland and Chappelear (1968). Pitzer-type correlations are often unsatisfactory for very large nonpolar molecules, and are clearly inappropriate for strongly polar or highly associated substances. Consequently, additional parameters have been proposed for use with extended corresponding-states correlations. These fourth parameters are of various types: some incorporate the dipole moment; some involve a quasi-chemical equilibrium constant; and some are merely additional Pitzer-type parameters, evaluated from the reduced-vapor-pressure curve at a T_r other than 0.7.

A detailed account of the virial equation of state is given by Mason and Spurling (1969), and Dymond and Smith (1980) present an extensive compilation of experimental and recommended values of the virial coefficients of gases. Hayden and O'Connell (1975) and Tarakad and Danner (1977) have developed generalized correlations for the second virial coefficient B; unlike the correlation of Tsonopoulos cited earlier, these correlations do not directly incorporate Pitzer's ω as a corresponding-states parameter. Reliable data for the third virial coefficient are rare, and generalized correlations for C are even rarer. The first such correlation was that of Chueh and Prausnitz (1967a); DeSantis and Grande

(1979) have published an improved version, incorporating a well-defined third corresponding-states parameter.

The literature on cubic equations of state is enormous. A review article by Horvath (1974) cites 112 references on Redlich-Kwong variants alone. Many companies and laboratories have special in-house versions of the cubic equation of state. Of the published specimens, the Soave-Redlich-Kwong equation and the Peng-Robinson equation, or variations on them, are the most widely used. However, there is no real consensus as to what is the best cubic equation for all applications, although Martin (1979) concludes that the Clausius-type equation

$$P = \frac{RT}{V - b} - \frac{\theta(T)}{(V + c)^2}$$

is the best of the simpler cubic equations for representation of volumetric data of pure fluids. Cubic equations are routinely applied to the calculation of vapor/liquid equilibria (VLE), and for systems comprising mixtures of nonpolar or weakly polar substances, the quadratic mixing rules of Sec. 4-8 are normally satisfactory for this application. However, the VLE for systems containing polar or associating species is usually predicted poorly. Vidal (1978) has shown that the use of more complex mixing rules for parameter θ greatly improves the representation of VLE for polar systems by the generic Redlich-Kwong equation.

Although the cubic equations possess the considerable advantage of simplicity, they are necessarily of limited accuracy. Scores of more complex equations have been proposed, many of them inspired by the eight-constant Benedict-Webb-Rubin (BWR) equation [Benedict et al., 1940, 1942]:

$$P = RT\rho + (B_0 RT - A_0 - C_0/T^2)\rho^2 + (bRT - a)\rho^3 + a\alpha\rho^6$$

$$+ \frac{c\rho^3}{T^2}(1 + \gamma\rho^2)\exp(-\gamma\rho^2) \quad (4\text{-}199)$$

The complicated density dependence of the BWR equation makes its use expensive when large numbers of iterative calculations are required, as in the computation of multicomponent VLE; moreover, it is not so readily generalizable as are the cubic equations. Nevertheless, it is widely used in the petroleum industry. Starling and Powers (1970) improved the accuracy of the BWR equation by treating parameters C_0 and a as functions of temperature; this increased the number of adjustable constants to eleven. Bender (1973) further modified the BWR equation by adding to it terms proportional to ρ^4 and ρ^5; Bender's equation contains twenty adjustable constants.

Roughly speaking, the pressure of a fluid may be written as the difference of two terms, one (P_{HC}) representing the effects of hard-core intermolecular repulsions, and the other (P_A) representing contributions of intermolecular attractions:

$$P = P_{HC} - P_A$$

In most cubic equations of state, P_{HC} is represented by

$$P_{HC} = \frac{RT}{V - b}$$

which approximates the repulsive pressure of hard spheres. However, exact results are available for the hard-sphere pressure, and they are well represented by the analytical expression of Carnahan and Starling (1969):

$$P_{HC} = \frac{RT(64V^3 + 16bV^2 + 4b^2V - b^3)}{V(4V - b)^3}$$

Empirical higher-order polynomial equations of state may therefore be constructed by replacing the approximate P_{HC} term in a cubic equation by the formula of Carnahan and Starling. This was done by Carnahan and Starling (1972), who thus obtained improved versions of the van der Waals and Redlich-Kwong equations. Semitheoretical extensions of this technique to fluids comprising nonspherical molecules have been made by Beret and Prausnitz (1975) and Donohue and Prausnitz (1978), and to polar substances by Gmehling et al. (1979).

Except for the virial equations of state, the methods treated in Secs. 4-3 through 4-8 can in principle be used for estimation of liquid volumes. However, accuracy is often very poor. Some of the more comprehensive equations of state, for example the BWR equation and its modifications, are suitable for quantitative work, but values for the many required constants are available for only a few substances (mainly hydrocarbons and cryogenic fluids). Hence, many generalized equations and correlations have been developed specifically for estimation of liquid volumes or densities, particularly at saturation conditions. These have been critically evaluated by Spencer and coworkers [Spencer and Danner (1972); Rea, Spencer, and Danner (1973); Spencer and Adler (1978)].

FIVE

PROPERTY CHANGES OF MIXING

The thermodynamic properties of mixtures, particularly liquid mixtures, are usefully expressed in relation to the properties of the pure constituent chemical species. These relations require the definition of a new class of thermodynamic functions—the property changes of mixing. The further definition of partial property changes of mixing naturally follows. In addition, there arises the concept of an *ideal* solution, for which the property changes of mixing are given by particularly simple expressions. This in turn leads to the definition of still another class of thermodynamic functions—the *excess* properties and their corresponding partial properties—which relate mixture properties to the properties of ideal solutions. Thus, we are confronted with what appears at first a bewildering array of interrelated thermodynamic functions for mixtures. In this chapter we display the structure of "solution thermodynamics," stressing the unity which in reality characterizes the multitude of new functions and equations; we present the definitions of the functions, develop their interrelationships, discuss their connection with experimental measurement, and lay the foundation for their application to problems of phase equilibrium.

5-1 EXPERIMENTAL BASIS AND DEFINITION

Solutions are homogeneous mixtures of chemical species, formed in many different ways in both natural and industrial processes. Specific amounts of nonreactive species may of course be mixed directly to produce solutions of known composition. Each such mixing process results in a particular change of state, depending on initial and final conditions of temperature and pressure. For study of the properties of solutions, we must as a practical matter focus on some *standard* mixing process, and experimental feasibility dictates that this process be mixing at constant T and P. Thus, one mixes appropriate amounts of pure chemical species, all at T and P, to form a solution of desired composition, also at T and P. The pure species at T and P are said to be in their *standard states* with respect to this process, and their properties in this state are the pure-species properties V_i, H_i, S_i, G_i, $\ln f_i$, etc.

The standard mixing process is represented schematically in Fig. 5-1 for mixing of two pure species 1 and 2. Initially, the system is divided by a partition into two parts, with n_1 moles of pure species 1 on the left and n_2 moles of pure species 2 on the right, both at T and P. Withdrawal of the partition initiates mixing, and in time the system becomes a homogeneous solution of composition, $x_1 = n_1/(n_1 + n_2)$. The observable phenomena accompanying the mixing process are expansion (or contraction) of the fluid and heat transfer to (or from) the system. Expansion is accommodated by movement of the piston, and this maintains the pressure at P. Heat transfer is controlled so as to hold the temperature at T.

When mixing is complete, the piston has moved a distance d from its initial position, and from this measured displacement one calculates the total volume change ΔV^t resulting from mixing. Since this volume change is the difference between final and initial total volumes, we may write

$$\Delta V^t = V^t - V_1^t - V_2^t$$

or

$$\Delta V^t = (n_1 + n_2)V - n_1 V_1 - n_2 V_2$$

Division by $n_1 + n_2$ gives

$$\Delta V = V - x_1 V_1 - x_2 V_2 \tag{A}$$

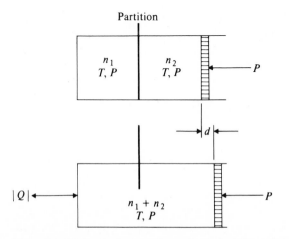

Figure 5-1 Schematic diagram of experimental mixing process.

where ΔV is the volume change per mole of solution, and is known as the *volume change of mixing*.

Heat transferred to the system during mixing can also be measured, and we now show that this quantity is equal to the enthalpy change of the system. We need only justify application of the results of Example 2-2 to the constant-pressure mixing process. This example shows that for a *reversible*, constant-pressure process the heat transferred equals the enthalpy change. However, only *external mechanical* reversibility is, in fact, required. The mixing process described here is certainly not *internally* reversible; however, if the process proceeds slowly and if the piston moves with negligible friction, external reversibility is for practical purposes achieved. We can then identify the total heat transfer with the total enthalpy change ΔH^t resulting from mixing. On a molar basis, we have a result analogous to Eq. (A):

$$\Delta H = H - x_1 H_1 - x_2 H_2 \qquad \text{(B)}$$

Because of its experimental association with heat, ΔH is often called the *heat of mixing* as well as the enthalpy change of mixing.

Equations (A) and (B) may be combined into a single equation and generalized to apply for the mixing of any number of species:

$$\boxed{\Delta M \equiv M - \sum x_i M_i} \qquad \text{(5-1)}$$

Although experimentally justified only for M as V and H, this equation can also be written for any other intensive solution property, and M can represent, for example, U, C_P, S, G, Z, ρ, and $\ln f$. Thus, Eq. (5-1) emerges as the *defining* expression for a large class of thermodynamic functions, known as *property changes of mixing*. They are functions of temperature, pressure, and composition.

In ΔM we have a solution property measured not from a base of zero (as with M), but from a reference defined as a simple linear combination of pure-species properties. This is illustrated in Fig. 5-2 where a plot of M versus x_1 is shown for a binary solution of species 1 and 2. Clearly, ΔM itself can also be expressed as a function of x_1, and a plot of ΔM versus x_1 allows a considerable magnification of scale, because the function is zero at the two composition limits. As an example, Fig. 5-3 shows the heat of mixing for sulfuric acid/water at 25°C. In this case $x_{H_2SO_4}$ is the *mass* fraction of sulfuric acid, and ΔH is on a *unit-mass* basis. The heat of mixing is everywhere negative; the system is characterized as *exothermic*, with heat given off during isothermal mixing. In Fig. 5-4 we show data for ethanol/*n*-heptane at 30°C, for which all values of ΔH are positive; the system is *endothermic*, with heat absorbed during isothermal mixing. Figure 5-5 is for ethanol/chloroform at 30°C, and shows regions of both exothermic and endothermic behavior. In these last two figures the molar heat of mixing is divided by RT to provide dimensionless values, which are plotted versus mole fraction. In all cases the data are for atmospheric pressure.

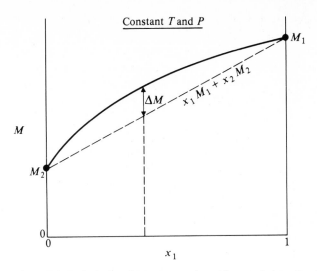

Figure 5-2 Typical plot of M versus x_1 for a binary solution, showing the relation of ΔM to M.

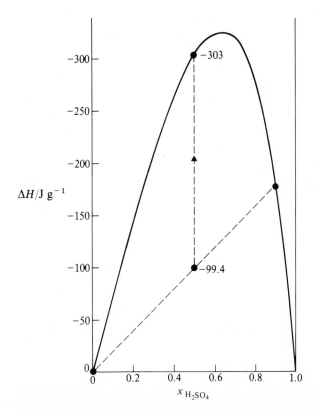

Figure 5-3 Heat of mixing for sulfuric acid/water at 25°C. The straight-line constructions refer to Example 5-1.

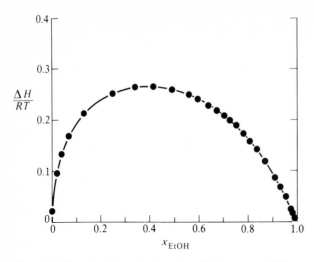

Figure 5-4 Heat of mixing data for ethanol/n-heptane at 30°C.

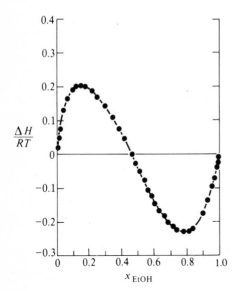

Figure 5-5 Heat of mixing data for ethanol/chloroform at 30°C.

Example 5-1 A plot of ΔH versus x_i such as Fig. 5-3 for sulfuric acid/water is just an enthalpy-concentration diagram with a single isotherm. By Eq. (5-1)

$$H = \Delta H + x_1 H_1 + x_2 H_2$$

If the reference enthalpies H_1 and H_2 are arbitrarily taken as zero, then $H = \Delta H$ for the isotherm of the diagram. It is well known that *adiabatic* mixing is represented by a straight line on an H-x diagram. *Isothermal* mixing is represented by two steps: first, adiabatic mixing; second, a heating or cooling process at constant composition to restore the temperature to its initial value.

Consider the mixing of pure water with a 90% (by mass) aqueous solution of sulfuric acid to dilute it to 50%. How much heat must be removed during the process if initial and final temperatures are 25°C? The process is represented by two straight lines on Fig. 5-3. First, the line connecting the point on the ΔH curve for pure water with the point for 90% acid represents adiabatic mixing. The enthalpy of the 50% acid formed lies on this line at $x_{H_2SO_4} = 0.5$, and we read a value of -99.4 J g^{-1}. This point does not of course lie on the ΔH curve, because its temperature is well above 25°C. The process of cooling this solution to 25°C is represented by the straight vertical line connecting this point with the ΔH curve, where the enthalpy is -303 J g^{-1}. Thus the enthalpy change of cooling, which is also Q for this constant-pressure process, is

$$Q = -303 - (-99.4) = -203.6 \text{ J g}^{-1}$$

Since the initial step is adiabatic, this is the total heat transferred. The answer, with its minus sign, indicates that 203.6 J are removed from the system for each gram of 50% acid formed.

5-2 PARTIAL MOLAR PROPERTY CHANGE OF MIXING

A general expression for M is provided by Eq. (3-6):

$$M = \sum x_i \bar{M}_i$$

Substitution for M in Eq. (5-1) gives

$$\Delta M = \sum x_i (\bar{M}_i - M_i)$$

or

$$\boxed{\Delta M = \sum x_i \, \overline{\Delta M}_i} \tag{5-2}$$

where by definition

$$\boxed{\overline{\Delta M}_i \equiv \bar{M}_i - M_i} \tag{5-3}$$

This quantity is the property change experienced by a mole of pure species i when it becomes a constituent in solution at constant T and P. We now show that it stands in relation to ΔM as a partial molar property.

Multiplication of Eq. (5-1) by n gives

$$n \, \Delta M = nM - \sum n_i M_i$$

Letting subscript k denote a *particular* species included in the set of species i, we differentiate with respect to n_k at constant T, P, and n_j $(j \neq k)$:

$$\left[\frac{\partial (n \, \Delta M)}{\partial n_k} \right]_{T, P, n_j} = \left[\frac{\partial (nM)}{\partial n_k} \right]_{T, P, n_j} - \sum M_i \left(\frac{\partial n_i}{\partial n_k} \right)_{T, P, n_j}$$

Since the n_i are independent, $(\partial n_i/\partial n_k)$ is zero for all terms of the sum except for $i = k$, in which case it is unity. Moreover, the first term on the right is clearly $\bar{M}_k$, and this equation becomes

$$\left[\frac{\partial(n\,\Delta M)}{\partial n_k}\right]_{T,\,P,\,n_j} = \bar{M}_k - M_k$$

Species k can of course be any of the species i, and we may therefore write

$$\left[\frac{\partial(n\,\Delta M)}{\partial n_i}\right]_{T,\,P,\,n_j} = \bar{M}_i - M_i$$

Comparison with Eq. (5-3) shows that

$$\boxed{\overline{\Delta M}_i = \left[\frac{\partial(n\,\Delta M)}{\partial n_i}\right]_{T,\,P,\,n_j}} \qquad (5\text{-}4)$$

Since this result conforms to the definition of a partial molar property as given by Eq. (3-3), it demonstrates that $\overline{\Delta M}_i$ is indeed related to ΔM as a partial molar property, and it is called a *partial molar property change of mixing*.

Equation (5-2) is therefore completely analogous to Eq. (3-6); moreover, we can write very general equations for ΔM analogous to Eqs. (3-4) and (3-15):

$$\boxed{d(n\,\Delta M) = n\left(\frac{\partial\Delta M}{\partial T}\right)_{P,\,x} dT + n\left(\frac{\partial\Delta M}{\partial P}\right)_{T,\,x} dP + \sum \overline{\Delta M}_i\,dn_i} \qquad (5\text{-}5)$$

and

$$\boxed{\left(\frac{\partial\Delta M}{\partial T}\right)_{P,\,x} dT + \left(\frac{\partial\Delta M}{\partial P}\right)_{T,\,x} dP - \sum x_i\,d\overline{\Delta M}_i = 0} \qquad (5\text{-}6)$$

Equation (5-6), a form of the Gibbs-Duhem equation, yields Eq. (3-20) directly. The discussion of binary systems following Eq. (3-20) relates, in fact, to partial property changes of mixing, and Fig. 3-3 is a plot of $\overline{\Delta M}_1$ and $\overline{\Delta M}_2$ versus x_1.

Equations relating the partial properties $\overline{\Delta M}_i$ to ΔM and the mole fractions are completely analogous to those relating $\bar{M}_i$ to M and the mole fractions. Thus Eqs. (3-9) through (3-12) can be written with $\bar{M}_i$ replaced by $\overline{\Delta M}_i$ and M replaced by ΔM. For example, Eqs. (3-12) for a binary system become

$$\boxed{\overline{\Delta M}_1 = \Delta M + x_2\frac{d\Delta M}{dx_1}} \qquad (5\text{-}7a)$$

and

$$\boxed{\overline{\Delta M}_2 = \Delta M - x_1\frac{d\Delta M}{dx_1}} \qquad (5\text{-}7b)$$

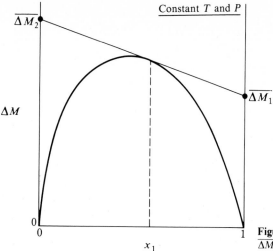

Figure 5-6 Graphical construction yielding $\overline{\Delta M}_1$ and $\overline{\Delta M}_2$ for a binary solution.

These equations are the basis for a graphical construction analogous to that of Fig. 3-1. Here, one plots ΔM versus x_1, and the tangent intercepts are $\overline{\Delta M}_1$ and $\overline{\Delta M}_2$, as illustrated in Fig. 5-6. In the limit at $x_i = 1$, $\overline{\Delta M}_i = 0$, and in the limit at $x_i = 0$, $\overline{\Delta M}_i = \overline{\Delta M}_i^\infty$, the infinite-dilution value.

Example 5-2 Equations (5-7) may be applied to the heat-of-mixing data of Fig. 5-3 for the sulfuric acid/water system, yielding values for partial heats of mixing $\overline{\Delta H}_{H_2SO_4}$ and $\overline{\Delta H}_{H_2O}$ at various compositions. A plot of the results is shown in Fig. 5-7, where all values are on a unit-mass rather than a mole basis. The two curves are far from

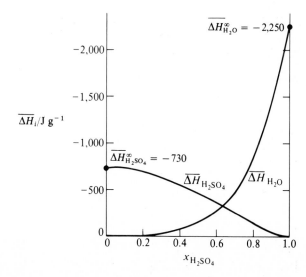

Figure 5-7 Partial heats of mixing for sulfuric acid/water at 25°C.

symmetric, a consequence of the skewed nature of the ΔH curve. At high concentrations of H_2SO_4, $\overline{\Delta H}_{H_2O}$ reaches very high values; in fact, $\overline{\Delta H}^{\infty}_{H_2O}$ approaches the latent heat of water. Thus when water is added to pure sulfuric acid, a very high rate of heat removal is required for isothermal mixing. Under usual circumstances the heat-transfer rate is far from adequate, and the resulting temperature rise causes local boiling or sputtering. This problem does not arise when acid is added to water, because $\overline{\Delta H}^{\infty}_{H_2SO_4}$ is less than a third the infinite-dilution value of water.

Example 5-3 We present a graphical construction which shows the parent function M and its partial properties $\overline{M}_i$ in relation to ΔM and its partial properties $\overline{\Delta M}_i$. This is practical only for a system of two species, which we identify as 1 and 2. The M versus x_1 relation is shown in Fig. 5-8 as the heavy curve terminating at M_1 and M_2, the pure-species values. The curve drawn is characteristic of the behavior of M when it represents such properties as V, U, C_V, H, C_P, Z, and $\ln f$. For reasons which are presented later, M as shown does not properly represent S, A, or G.

A tangent to the M versus x_1 curve drawn at a particular value of x_1 produces intercepts which are values of $\overline{M}_1$ and $\overline{M}_2$ for this x_1. Similar constructions over the

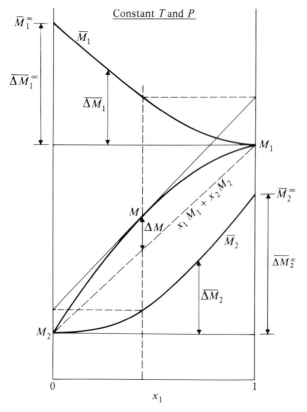

Figure 5-8 The general property M ($M \neq G$, A, or S) and related properties as functions of x_1 for a binary system.

full composition range yield values for $\bar{M}_1$ and $\bar{M}_2$ as functions of x_1, as shown in Fig. 5-8. The line segments shown as representing ΔM, $\overline{\Delta M}_1$, and $\overline{\Delta M}_2$ conform to the definitions of these functions as given by Eqs. (5-1) and (5-3).

The diagram which results when $M = \ln f$ is of particular interest, owing to the importance of fugacity in phase-equilibrium studies. For this case, Eq. (5-1) becomes

$$\boxed{\Delta \ln f = \ln f - \sum x_i \ln f_i} \tag{A}$$

Since $\bar{M}_i = \ln (\hat{f}_i / x_i)$, Eq. (5-3) may be written

$$\overline{\Delta \ln f_i} = \ln \frac{\hat{f}_i}{x_i} - \ln f_i = \ln \frac{\hat{f}_i}{x_i f_i}$$

The group $\hat{f}_i / x_i f_i$ has traditionally been called the *activity coefficient* of species i and given the symbol γ_i. This allows us to replace the cumbersome notation of $\overline{\Delta \ln f_i}$ through the identity

$$\overline{\Delta \ln f_i} \equiv \ln \gamma_i$$

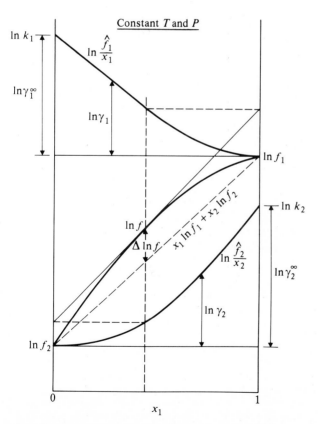

Figure 5-9 Composition dependence of $\ln f$ and related properties for a binary system.

Equation (5-3) is then written

$$\ln \gamma_i = \ln \frac{\hat{f}_i}{x_i} - \ln f_i$$

and Eq. (5-2) becomes

$$\Delta \ln f = \sum x_i \ln \gamma_i$$

The function $\ln \gamma_i$ of course retains its relationship to $\Delta \ln f$ as a partial molar property.

We show in Fig. 5-9 a reproduction of Fig. 5-8, but labeled as appropriate for the particular case of $M = \ln f$. In accord with Eq. (3-95), we have represented the infinite-dilution value of $\ln (\hat{f}_i/x_i)$ by $\ln k_i$, where k_i is Henry's constant.

5-3 THE IDEAL SOLUTION

The calculation and correlation of fluid properties are often facilitated when one adopts some model of *ideal* behavior as a basis from which to work. Such a model should be simple, yet sufficiently realistic to approximate real-fluid behavior over some useful range of conditions. Thus the ideal gas serves as a model for the behavior of gases, and does approximate the actual behavior of gases at low pressures. The *ideal solution*, a useful model appropriate to nonelectrolyte solutions, is an idealization in the same sense as is the ideal gas, and plays the same kind of role.

The ideal solution provides a model for the composition dependence of the fugacity of species in solution. Actually, more than one reasonable model can be proposed, but for the moment we consider only the model represented by the Lewis-Randall rule. Equation (3-99) gives mathematical expression to this rule, here rewritten as

$$\boxed{\hat{f}_i^{id} = f_i(T, P)x_i} \tag{5-8}$$

where the superscript id identifies the fugacity as a value calculated by the model equation. By definition, an ideal solution (in the sense of the Lewis-Randall rule) is a model fluid for which the fugacity of each component species is given by Eq. (5-8) for the entire composition range at all conditions of temperature and pressure. Equation (5-8) expresses a direct proportionality between $\hat{f}_i^{id}$ and x_i, with f_i, the fugacity of pure species i at T and P, as the proportionality factor. Thus the T and P dependence of $\hat{f}_i^{id}$ come entirely from the T and P dependence of f_i.

We now develop the property relationships which thermodynamics imposes on the ideal solution as a result of Eq. (5-8). For what follows, we need *general* equations for the properties of an ideal solution. Equation (5-3) written for an ideal solution becomes

$$\overline{\Delta M_i^{id}} \equiv \overline{M_i^{id}} - M_i \tag{5-9}$$

and by Eq. (5-2)

$$\Delta M^{id} = \sum x_i \, \overline{\Delta M_i^{id}} \tag{5-10}$$

Finally, an expression for the molar property of the ideal solution is provided by Eq. (5-1):

$$M^{id} = \Delta M^{id} + \sum x_i M_i \tag{5-11}$$

Equation (5-8) for given T and P may be written

$$\ln \frac{\hat{f}_i^{id}}{x_i} = \ln f_i \tag{5-12}$$

Differentiation with respect to pressure gives

$$\left[\frac{\partial \ln (\hat{f}_i^{id}/x_i)}{\partial P} \right]_{T,x} = \left(\frac{\partial \ln f_i}{\partial P} \right)_T$$

Both of these derivatives are evaluated as special cases of Eq. (3-92), the one on the left for a species in an ideal solution and the one on the right for the pure species. Thus we have

$$\frac{\overline{V}_i^{id}}{RT} = \frac{V_i}{RT}$$

or simply

$$\overline{V}_i^{id} = V_i \tag{5-13}$$

Similarly, differentiation of Eq. (5-12) with respect to temperature yields

$$\left[\frac{\partial \ln (\hat{f}_i^{id}/x_i)}{\partial T} \right]_{P,x} = \left(\frac{\partial \ln f_i}{\partial T} \right)_P$$

These derivatives are given as special cases of Eq. (3-91); thus

$$\frac{H_i' - \overline{H}_i^{id}}{RT^2} = \frac{H_i' - H_i}{RT^2}$$

or

$$\overline{H}_i^{id} = H_i \tag{5-14}$$

Differentiating Eq. (5-14) with respect to T at constant pressure and composition, we have

$$\left(\frac{\partial \overline{H}_i^{id}}{\partial T} \right)_{P,x} = \left(\frac{\partial H_i}{\partial T} \right)_P$$

In view of Eqs. (2-40) and (3-38) this becomes

$$\overline{C}_{P_i}^{id} = C_{P_i} \tag{5-15}$$

By Eqs. (3-35) and (2-12), we have

$$\bar{U}_i^{id} = \bar{H}_i^{id} - P\bar{V}_i^{id}$$

and

$$U_i = H_i - PV_i$$

By difference, we get

$$\bar{U}_i^{id} - U_i = (\bar{H}_i^{id} - H_i) - P(\bar{V}_i^{id} - V_i)$$

According to Eqs. (5-13) and (5-14), both terms on the right are zero; we therefore have

$$\bar{U}_i^{id} = U_i \qquad (5\text{-}16)$$

This equation may be differentiated with respect to T at constant volume and composition:

$$\left(\frac{\partial \bar{U}_i^{id}}{\partial T}\right)_{V,x} = \left(\frac{\partial U_i}{\partial T}\right)_V$$

In view of Eqs. (2-49) and (3-39), this reduces to

$$\bar{C}_{V_i}^{id} = C_{V_i} \qquad (5\text{-}17)$$

Equations (5-12) through (5-17) are all particular expressions of the general relation

$$\bar{M}_i^{id} = M_i$$

When this result is obtained, as it is when M represents $\ln f$, V, H, C_P, U, or C_V, then Eqs. (5-9) through (5-11) become

$$\overline{\Delta M_i^{id}} = 0 \qquad (5\text{-}18)$$

$$\Delta M^{id} = 0 \qquad (5\text{-}19)$$

and

$$M^{id} = \sum x_i M_i \qquad (5\text{-}20)$$

When these equations apply, M^{id} is represented by the base line (shown dashed) in Fig. 5-8 from which ΔM is measured. These equations do not apply, however, to the Gibbs function, the Helmholtz function, or the entropy.

The fugacity of a species in solution is related to the Gibbs function by Eq. (3-56):

$$d\bar{G}_i = RT \, d \ln \hat{f}_i \qquad (\text{const } T)$$

We integrate this equation for the change of state from that of pure species i at T and P to that of species i in solution at T and P:

$$\bar{G}_i - G_i = RT \ln \frac{\hat{f}_i}{f_i} \qquad (5\text{-}21)$$

This general equation may be applied to an ideal solution:

$$\bar{G}_i^{id} = G_i + RT \ln \frac{\hat{f}_i^{id}}{f_i}$$

In view of Eq. (5-8), this simplifies to

$$\bar{G}_i^{id} = G_i + RT \ln x_i \qquad (5\text{-}22)$$

and Eqs. (5-9) through (5-11) become

$$\overline{\Delta G}_i^{id} = RT \ln x_i \qquad (5\text{-}23)$$

$$\Delta G^{id} = RT \sum x_i \ln x_i \qquad (5\text{-}24)$$

and

$$G^{id} = \sum x_i G_i + RT \sum x_i \ln x_i \qquad (5\text{-}25)$$

Since $A = G - PV$ (see rows 3 and 4 of Table 2-1), we have

$$\overline{\Delta A}_i^{id} = \overline{\Delta G}_i^{id} - P \overline{\Delta V}_i^{id}$$

However, $\overline{\Delta V}_i^{id} = 0$, giving

$$\overline{\Delta A}_i^{id} = \overline{\Delta G}_i^{id}$$

Therefore the ideal-solution equations for the Helmholtz function are analogous to those for G, and are included in the summary of results provided by Table 5-1.

The entropy is related to the Gibbs function through the defining equation

$$G = H - TS$$

Thus we can write

$$\bar{G}_i^{id} - G_i = (\bar{H}_i^{id} - H_i) - T(\bar{S}_i^{id} - S_i)$$

Since the first term on the right is zero, this can be written

$$\bar{S}_i^{id} = S_i - \frac{\bar{G}_i^{id} - G_i}{T} = S_i - \frac{\overline{\Delta G}_i^{id}}{T}$$

With Eq. (5-23), this becomes

$$\bar{S}_i^{id} = S_i - R \ln x_i \qquad (5\text{-}26)$$

Table 5-1 Property relations for ideal solutions

For $M \equiv \ln f,\ V,\ Z,\ H,\ C_P,\ U,$ and C_V:

$\bar{M}_i^{id} = M_i$	$\overline{\Delta M}_i^{id} = 0$	$\Delta M^{id} = 0$	$M^{id} = \sum x_i M_i$
$\bar{S}_i^{id} = S_i - R \ln x_i$	$\overline{\Delta S}_i^{id} = -R \ln x_i$	$\Delta S^{id} = -R \sum x_i \ln x_i$	$S^{id} = \sum x_i S_i - R \sum x_i \ln x_i$
$\bar{A}_i^{id} = A_i + RT \ln x_i$	$\overline{\Delta A}_i^{id} = RT \ln x_i$	$\Delta A^{id} = RT \sum x_i \ln x_i$	$A^{id} = \sum x_i A_i + RT \sum x_i \ln x_i$
$\bar{G}_i^{id} = G_i + RT \ln x_i$	$\overline{\Delta G}_i^{id} = RT \ln x_i$	$\Delta G^{id} = RT \sum x_i \ln x_i$	$G^{id} = \sum x_i G_i + RT \sum x_i \ln x_i$

and from Eqs. (5-9) through (5-11) we obtain

$$\overline{\Delta S_i^{id}} = -R \ln x_i \tag{5-27}$$

$$\Delta S^{id} = -R \sum x_i \ln x_i \tag{5-28}$$

and

$$S^{id} = \sum x_i S_i - R \sum x_i \ln x_i \tag{5-29}$$

The ideal-solution equations which follow from the Lewis-Randall rule are collected in Table 5-1 for ready reference.

The fugacity of a species in a mixture of ideal gases is given by

$$\hat{f}_i = x_i P$$

For the pure ideal gas at the same temperature and pressure,

$$f_i = P$$

Elimination of P between these two equations gives

$$\hat{f}_i = x_i f_i$$

which is Eq. (5-8). Thus, an ideal-gas mixture is just a special case of an ideal solution, and therefore the equations developed in Example 3-10 for ideal gases are consistent with those derived here.

Example 5-4 A fog consists of spherical water droplets with a radius of about 10^{-6} m. Because of surface tension the internal pressure in the water droplet is greater than the external pressure by

$$\delta P = \frac{2\sigma}{r}$$

where σ is surface tension and r is radius. At 25°C, the surface tension is 0.0694 N m^{-1}, and we have

$$\delta P = \frac{(2)(0.0694)}{10^{-6}} = 0.1388 \times 10^6 \text{ Pa}$$

or

$$\delta P = 1.388 \text{ bar}$$

This pressure increase in the droplet with respect to water with a flat surface results in a corresponding fugacity increase for the water, given by Eq. (3-47):

$$d \ln f_i = \frac{V_i}{RT} dP$$

Since the molar volume of water is virtually unaffected by the pressure change considered, integration gives

$$\delta \ln f_{H_2O} = \frac{V_{H_2O}}{RT} \delta P$$

Taking the molar volume of water as 18 cm^3 mol^{-1}, we get

$$\delta \ln f_{H_2O} = \frac{(18 \text{ cm}^3 \text{ mol}^{-1})(1.388 \text{ bar})}{(83.14 \text{ cm}^3 \text{ bar mol}^{-1} \text{ K}^{-1})(298 \text{ K})} = 0.00101$$

Thus the fugacity of water in fog droplets is greater by this amount than the fugacity of surface water at the same temperature. Thus, the fog is not stable with respect to surface water at the same temperature, and dissipates by evaporation. However a temperature difference between the surface water and the fog serves to make the fog stable. The temperature difference required to counteract the fugacity difference resulting from surface tension is given by Eq. (3-79):

$$\left(\frac{\partial \ln f}{\partial T}\right)_{P,x} = \frac{\Delta H'}{RT^2}$$

We apply this equation here to pure water at 25°C, observing that $\Delta H'$ is very nearly the latent heat of water ΔH^{lv} at this temperature, 2,442.3 J g^{-1}:

$$\left(\frac{\partial \ln f_{H_2O}}{\partial T}\right)_P = \frac{2{,}442.3 \times 18 \text{ J mol}^{-1}}{(8.314 \text{ J mol}^{-1} \text{ K}^{-1})(298 \text{ K})^2} = 0.0595 \text{ K}^{-1}$$

For a small temperature change, we have

$$\delta \ln f_{H_2O} \simeq (0.0595) \, \delta T$$

To calculate δT, we set this equal to the *negative* of the fugacity difference calculated earlier, because we want the δT that counteracts the effect of surface tension. Thus

$$(0.0595) \, \delta T = -0.00101$$

and

$$\delta T = -0.017 \text{ K}$$

This is the minimum temperature difference between the fog and surface water that stabilizes the fog.

The fugacity of water in the fog droplets is also lowered by dissolution of impurities, such as atmospheric pollutants. The droplets then become solutions with water as the primary constituent, and its fugacity is $\hat{f}_{H_2O}$. Since the mole fraction of water is near unity, the Lewis-Randall rule provides an excellent approximation:

$$\hat{f}_{H_2O} = f_{H_2O} x_{H_2O}$$

The fugacity change of the water resulting from dissolution of impurities is then

$$\hat{f}_{H_2O} - f_{H_2O} = f_{H_2O} x_{H_2O} - f_{H_2O} = f_{H_2O}(x_{H_2O} - 1) = -f_{H_2O} x_{impurity}$$

or

$$x_{impurity} = \frac{-\delta f_{H_2O}}{f_{H_2O}} \simeq -\delta \ln f_{H_2O}$$

This $\delta \ln f_{H_2O}$ is again the negative of the increase caused by surface tension. Thus,

$$x_{impurity} = 0.00101$$

and an impurity of only 0.1 percent stabilizes the fog.

5-4 EXCESS THERMODYNAMIC FUNCTIONS

Equation (5-21) is a general expression relating the properties $\bar{G}_i$ and $\hat{f}_i$ for species i in solution to the properties G_i and f_i of pure species i at the temperature and pressure of the solution:

$$\bar{G}_i - G_i = RT \ln \frac{\hat{f}_i}{f_i}$$

Addition and subtraction of $RT \ln x_i$ on the right-hand side gives

$$\bar{G}_i - G_i = RT \ln \frac{\hat{f}_i}{x_i f_i} + RT \ln x_i$$

where x_i is the mole fraction of species i in solution. As a matter of convenience, we introduce the *activity coefficient*, already mentioned in Example 5-3, and defined as

$$\gamma_i \equiv \frac{\hat{f}_i}{x_i f_i} \tag{5-30}$$

Substituting this auxiliary function into the preceding equation, we get

$$\bar{G}_i - G_i = RT \ln \gamma_i + RT \ln x_i \tag{5-31}$$

When species i becomes infinitely dilute, $x_i = 0$, and Eq. (5-31) becomes

$$\bar{G}_i^{\infty} - G_i = RT \ln \gamma_i^{\infty} - \infty$$

Experimental data (from vapor/liquid equilibrium measurements) show γ_i^{∞} to be finite for nonelectrolyte solutions; in this event, and given a finite value for the pure-species property G_i, we conclude that $\bar{G}_i^{\infty} = -\infty$.

The same result is obtained for the Helmholtz function. Since

$$A = G - PV$$

we can also write

$$\bar{A}_i^{\infty} = \bar{G}_i^{\infty} - P\bar{V}_i^{\infty}$$

Again, experiment shows that $\bar{V}_i^{\infty}$ is finite for nonelectrolyte solutions. Thus if $\bar{G}_i^{\infty}$ is negative infinite, so too is $\bar{A}_i^{\infty}$. The entropy is related to the Gibbs function by the definition

$$G = H - TS$$

and this allows us to write

$$\bar{S}_i^{\infty} = \frac{\bar{H}_i^{\infty} - \bar{G}_i^{\infty}}{T}$$

By experiment we find that $\bar{H}_i^\infty$ too is finite (see Fig. 5-7 for an example). Thus, when $\bar{G}_i^\infty$ is negative infinite, $\bar{S}_i^\infty$ is positive infinite. In summary, when M represents G, A, or S, the partial property $\bar{M}_i^\infty$ of a species at infinite dilution is infinite.

This is true as well for the corresponding partial property changes of mixing. For infinite dilution, Eq. (5-3) becomes

$$\overline{\Delta M_i^\infty} = \bar{M}_i^\infty - M_i$$

Given a finite value for M_i, $\overline{\Delta M_i^\infty}$ becomes infinite along with $\bar{M}_i^\infty$. In addition, Eqs. (3-12) and (5-7) for a binary solution show that both dM/dx_i and $d\Delta M/dx_i$ become infinite when $\bar{M}_i$ and $\overline{\Delta M_i}$ for either component become infinite. Thus, when M represents G, A, or S, plots of M or ΔM versus x_i terminate at both $x_i = 0$ and $x_i = 1$ with infinite slopes. That is, the vertical axes represent tangents to these curves at each end.

Since Fig. 5-8 is not drawn to reflect these special characteristics, it does not properly describe solution behavior when M represents G, A, or S.

By Eq. (5-22) for an ideal solution

$$\bar{G}_i^{id} = G_i + RT \ln x_i$$

Here too, for infinite dilution of species i, $(\bar{G}_i^{id})^\infty = -\infty$. However, we may subtract this equation from Eq. (5-31), thus eliminating the $RT \ln x_i$ term:

$$\bar{G}_i - \bar{G}_i^{id} = RT \ln \gamma_i \tag{5-32}$$

This new function is known from experiment to be finite for nonelectrolyte solutions at all compositions. Moreover, we may multiply Eq. (5-32) by x_i and sum over all i:

$$\sum x_i \bar{G}_i - \sum x_i \bar{G}_i^{id} = RT \sum x_i \ln \gamma_i$$

In view of Eq. (3-6), this becomes

$$G - G^{id} = RT \sum x_i \ln \gamma_i \tag{5-33}$$

These observations suggest the creation of a new class of thermodynamic functions known as *excess properties*, defined as the difference between an actual property value and the value calculated for an ideal solution at the same T, P, and x. There are two such properties, exemplified by Eqs. (5-32) and (5-33), one for species in solution and one for the solution itself; both are designated by the superscript E:

$$\boxed{\bar{M}_i^E \equiv \bar{M}_i - \bar{M}_i^{id}} \tag{5-34}$$

and

$$\boxed{M^E \equiv M - M^{id}} \tag{5-35}$$

The first is a partial property with respect to the second, as we now show. Multiplication of Eq. (5-35) by n and differentiation with respect to n_i at constant T, P, and n_j gives:

$$\left[\frac{\partial(nM^E)}{\partial n_i}\right]_{T,P,n_j} = \left[\frac{\partial(nM)}{\partial n_i}\right]_{T,P,n_j} - \left[\frac{\partial(nM^{id})}{\partial n_i}\right]_{T,P,n_j}$$

The two terms on the right are definitions of the two partial properties $\bar{M}_i$ and $\bar{M}_i^{id}$. Therefore

$$\left[\frac{\partial(nM^E)}{\partial n_i}\right]_{T,P,n_j} = \bar{M}_i - \bar{M}_i^{id}$$

Comparison of this result with Eq. (5-34) shows that

$$\boxed{\bar{M}_i^E = \left[\frac{\partial(nM^E)}{\partial n_i}\right]_{T,P,n_j}} \tag{5-36}$$

which is the expression defining $\bar{M}_i^E$ as a partial property with respect to M^E. As a result of this relationship, Eq. (3-6) may be extended to excess properties, and we have

$$\boxed{M^E = \sum x_i \bar{M}_i^E} \tag{5-37}$$

In addition, Eqs. (3-9) and (3-11), relating partial properties to the solution property and the mole fractions, also extend to excess properties. Equations (3-12) for binary solutions become

$$\boxed{\bar{M}_1^E = M^E + x_2 \frac{dM^E}{dx_1}} \tag{5-38a}$$

and

$$\boxed{\bar{M}_2^E = M^E - x_1 \frac{dM^E}{dx_1}} \tag{5-38b}$$

Thus the method of tangent intercepts allows graphical determination for $\bar{M}_1^E$ and $\bar{M}_2^E$ from a plot of M^E versus x_1.

In complete analogy with the definitions of the excess properties themselves, we can also define *excess property changes of mixing*:

$$\overline{\Delta M_i^E} \equiv \overline{\Delta M_i} - \overline{\Delta M_i^{id}}$$

and

$$\Delta M^E \equiv \Delta M - \Delta M^{id}$$

However, these functions are identical with $\overline{M}_i^E$ and M^E, as we now show. The terms on the right in these equations are replaced by their defining expressions as given by Eqs. (5-1) and (5-3):

$$\overline{\Delta M_i^E} = \overline{M}_i - M_i - (\overline{M}_i^{id} - M_i) = \overline{M}_i - \overline{M}_i^{id} \equiv \overline{M}_i^E$$

and

$$\Delta M^E = M - \sum x_i M_i - (M^{id} - \sum x_i M_i) = M - M^{id} \equiv M^E$$

Thus, we have

$$\overline{M}_i^E = \overline{\Delta M_i^E} \equiv \overline{\Delta M}_i - \overline{\Delta M_i^{id}} \tag{5-39}$$

and

$$M^E = \Delta M^E \equiv \Delta M - \Delta M^{id} \tag{5-40}$$

The equality of an excess property with the corresponding excess property change of mixing allows their interchangeable use. If one thinks in terms of solution properties, then $\overline{M}_i^E$ and M^E naturally come to mind. On the other hand, if one thinks in terms of a mixing operation, then $\overline{\Delta M_i^E}$ and ΔM^E may seem more appropriate. Both notations are found in the literature, but the simpler one is now more common, and we shall prefer it. Nevertheless, the equalities in Eqs. (5-39) and (5-40) are often useful alternatives to the definitions of Eqs. (5-34) and (5-35).

When M represents V, Z, U, C_V, H, C_P and $\ln f$, we have by Eqs. (5-1) and (5-20) that

$$M = \sum x_i M_i + \Delta M$$

and

$$M^{id} = \sum x_i M_i$$

Substitution of these expressions into Eq. (5-35) reduces it to

$$M^E = \Delta M$$

Similarly, for these functions,

$$\overline{M}_i^E = \overline{\Delta M}_i$$

Thus, for the common thermodynamic functions other than G, A, and S, the excess properties are not new thermodynamic functions. Thus, for example, $\Delta H \equiv H^E$, and one can regard Figs. 5-3 through 5-5 as representing H^E rather than ΔH. This is, in fact, a common notation.

We now examine those excess functions which *do* represent new properties: G^E, A^E, and S^E. By definition, we have

$$G^E = G - G^{id}$$

Substitution for G^{id} by Eq. (5-25) gives

$$G^E = G - \sum x_i G_i - RT \sum x_i \ln x_i \tag{5-41}$$

which, with Eq. (5-1), becomes

$$G^E = \Delta G - RT \sum x_i \ln x_i \tag{5-42}$$

Similarly, for the partial property,

$$\bar{G}_i^E = \bar{G}_i - \bar{G}_i^{\text{id}}$$

Elimination of $\bar{G}_i^{\text{id}}$ by Eq. (5-22) gives

$$\bar{G}_i^E = \bar{G}_i - G_i - RT \ln x_i$$

In view of Eq. (5-3), this reduces to

$$\overline{G}_i^E = \overline{\Delta G}_i - RT \ln x_i \tag{5-43}$$

The excess Gibbs function is directly related to the activity coefficient by Eq. (5-32), which may be written

$$\bar{G}_i^E = RT \ln \gamma_i \tag{5-44}$$

or

$$\boxed{\ln \gamma_i = \frac{\bar{G}_i^E}{RT}} \tag{5-45}$$

Multiplication of Eq. (5-44) by x_i and summation over all i gives

$$\sum x_i \bar{G}_i^E = RT \sum x_i \ln \gamma_i$$

which, in view of Eq. (5-37), becomes

$$\frac{G^E}{RT} = \sum x_i \ln \gamma_i \tag{5-46}$$

Another form of this equation results when we substitute for γ_i by Eq. (5-30):

$$\frac{G^E}{RT} = \sum x_i \ln \frac{\hat{f}_i}{x_i} - \sum x_i \ln f_i$$

However, Eq. (3-76) shows the first sum to be $\ln f$. Therefore

$$\frac{G^E}{RT} = \ln f - \sum x_i \ln f_i$$

or

$$\frac{G^E}{RT} = \Delta \ln f$$

Combining this result with Eq. (5-46), we have

$$\boxed{\frac{G^E}{RT} = \Delta \ln f = \sum x_i \ln \gamma_i} \tag{5-47}$$

Equation (5-45) shows that $\ln \gamma_i$ is related to G^E/RT and therefore to $\Delta \ln f$ as a partial molar property. The relation of $\ln \gamma_i$ to $\Delta \ln f$ was introduced in Example 5-3.

Equations (5-42) and (5-43) have their counterparts for the excess Helmholtz function. One simply replaces G by A. For the entropy

$$S^E = S - S^{\mathrm{id}}$$

Substitution for S^{id} by Eq. (5-29) leads to

$$S^E = \Delta S + R \sum x_i \ln x_i \tag{5-48}$$

For the partial excess entropy

$$\bar{S}_i^E = \bar{S}_i - \bar{S}_i^{\mathrm{id}}$$

An expression for $\bar{S}_i^{\mathrm{id}}$ comes from Eq. (5-26), and leads to

$$\bar{S}_i^E = \overline{\Delta S}_i + R \ln x_i \tag{5-49}$$

Example 5-5 We illustrate here the behavior of the Gibbs function and related properties with respect to composition for a binary solution at constant T and P. Actually, for convenience, we treat the dimensionless properties G/RT, G^E/RT, etc., and consider an arbitrary and simple, yet representative, specific case. The following are specified as the pure-species properties:

$$\frac{G_1}{RT} = 1.5 \quad \text{and} \quad \frac{G_2}{RT} = 2.0$$

Further, the composition dependence of the excess Gibbs function is taken as

$$\frac{G^E}{RT} = -1.5 x_1 x_2$$

Such an equation would, in practice, come from a fit to experimental data originating with vapor/liquid equilibrium measurements, as discussed in Chap. 6.

We solve Eq. (5-41) for G, and divide through by RT; the result is a general expression for G/RT:

$$\frac{G}{RT} = \sum x_i \frac{G_i}{RT} + \sum x_i \ln x_i + \frac{G^E}{RT} \tag{A}$$

By the definition of $\Delta G/RT$, we can also write

$$\frac{\Delta G}{RT} = \frac{G}{RT} - \sum x_i \frac{G_i}{RT} = \sum x_i \ln x_i + \frac{G^E}{RT} \tag{B}$$

The term $\sum x_i(G_i/RT)$ is just a linear combination of the pure-species values, here represented by

$$1.5 x_1 + 2.0 x_2$$

and shown in Fig. 5-10 as the straight dashed line connecting G_1/RT and G_2/RT.

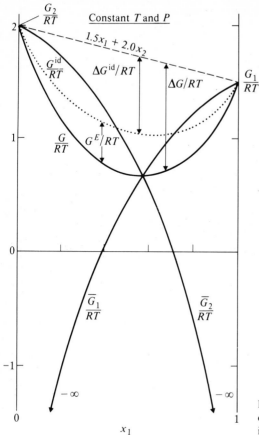

Figure 5-10 Graphical representation of G/RT and related properties as given in Example 5-5.

The first two terms on the right-hand side of Eq. (A) together represent G^{id}/RT; this result follows from Eq. (5-25):

$$\frac{G^{id}}{RT} = \sum x_i \frac{G_i}{RT} + \sum x_i \ln x_i \qquad (C)$$

Again, by definition

$$\frac{\Delta G^{id}}{RT} = \frac{G^{id}}{RT} - \sum x_i \frac{G_i}{RT} = \sum x_i \ln x_i \qquad (D)$$

Thus $\Delta G^{id}/RT$ is always the same regardless of species, temperature, or pressure.

The excess property G^E/RT is clearly given either as the difference of Eqs. (A) and (C):

$$\frac{G^E}{RT} = \frac{G}{RT} - \frac{G^{id}}{RT} \qquad (E)$$

or as the difference between Eqs. (B) and (D)

$$\frac{G^E}{RT} = \frac{\Delta G}{RT} - \frac{\Delta G^{id}}{RT} \tag{F}$$

For the particular case represented here, Eqs. (A) and (C) become

$$\frac{G}{RT} = 1.5x_1 + 2.0x_2 + x_1 \ln x_1 + x_2 \ln x_2 - 1.5x_1x_2 \tag{G}$$

and

$$\frac{G^{id}}{RT} = 1.5x_1 + 2.0x_2 + x_1 \ln x_1 + x_2 \ln x_2 \tag{H}$$

Both equations are represented by curves on Fig. 5-10 connecting G_1/RT and G_2/RT, the first by the solid line, the second by the dotted line. The vertical line segments shown clearly conform to the definitions of Eqs. (B), (D), (E), and (F).

Differentiating Eq. (G) with respect to x_1 and taking into account the constraint $dx_2 = -dx_1$, we get

$$\frac{d(G/RT)}{dx_1} = -0.5 + \ln x_1 - \ln x_2 - 1.5(x_2 - x_1) \tag{I}$$

Similar differentiation of Eq. (H) gives the same result with deletion of the final term:

$$\frac{d(G^{id}/RT)}{dx_1} = -0.5 + \ln x_1 - \ln x_2 \tag{J}$$

For both of these derivatives the limiting values at $x_1 = 0$ and at $x_1 = 1$ are infinite:

$$\left[\frac{d(G/RT)}{dx_1}\right]_{x_1=0} = \left[\frac{d(G^{id}/RT)}{dx_1}\right]_{x_1=0} = -\infty$$

$$\left[\frac{d(G/RT)}{dx_1}\right]_{x_1=1} = \left[\frac{d(G^{id}/RT)}{dx_1}\right]_{x_1=1} = +\infty$$

Surprisingly, neither of these results is evident from Fig. 5-10, which is drawn to scale. The change in slope of the two curves that makes them tangent to the vertical axes at the composition limits occurs very rapidly as these limits are approached. In fact, the second derivatives are both given by

$$\frac{d^2(G/RT)}{dx_1^2} = \frac{d^2(G^{id}/RT)}{dx_1^2} = \frac{1}{x_1} + \frac{1}{x_2} + C$$

where $C = 3$ in the first instance and is zero in the second. In either case, the second derivative also becomes infinite for $x_1 = 0$ and for $x_2 = 0$.

We note with respect to Fig. 5-10 that $\Delta G/RT$ is everywhere negative. This is a requirement imposed by the second law of thermodynamics, as discussed in Chap. 6. It is clear also that a plot of G/RT versus x_1 must always exhibit a minimum, because of the infinite values of the limiting slopes. However, the *excess* function G^E/RT, also shown in this example as everywhere negative, could well be positive, in which case the G/RT curve would lie above the G^{id}/RT curve. There are also examples for which G^E/RT is positive over part of the composition range and negative over the rest of the range; in this event the G/RT and G^{id}/RT curves cross.

The partial properties $\bar{G}_1/RT$ and $\bar{G}_2/RT$ are given by Eqs. (3-12), here written

$$\frac{\bar{G}_1}{RT} = \frac{G}{RT} + x_2 \frac{d(G/RT)}{dx_1}$$

and

$$\frac{\bar{G}_2}{RT} = \frac{G}{RT} - x_1 \frac{d(G/RT)}{dx_1}$$

These, with Eqs. (G) and (I), lead to the following expressions for the partial properties:

$$\frac{\bar{G}_1}{RT} = 1.5 + \ln x_1 - 1.5x_2^2 \tag{K}$$

and

$$\frac{\bar{G}_2}{RT} = 2.0 + \ln x_2 - 1.5x_1^2 \tag{L}$$

We see by Eqs. (K) and (L) that $\bar{G}_1/RT = -\infty$ at $x_1 = 0$, and $\bar{G}_2/RT = -\infty$ for $x_2 = 0$. This result also follows from consideration of the partial properties as tangent intercepts, because of the infinite slopes of the G/RT curve at $x_1 = 0$ and $x_2 = 0$. Differentiation of Eqs. (K) and (L) with respect to x_1 gives

$$\frac{d(\bar{G}_1/RT)}{dx_1} = \frac{1}{x_1} + 3.0x_2 \tag{M}$$

and

$$\frac{d(\bar{G}_2/RT)}{dx_1} = -\frac{1}{x_2} - 3.0x_1 \tag{N}$$

The limiting values of these derivatives are therefore

$$\left[\frac{d(\bar{G}_1/RT)}{dx_1}\right]_{x_1=0} = \infty \qquad \left[\frac{d(\bar{G}_1/RT)}{dx_1}\right]_{x_1=1} = 1$$

and

$$\left[\frac{d(\bar{G}_2/RT)}{dx_1}\right]_{x_1=0} = -1 \qquad \left[\frac{d(\bar{G}_2/RT)}{dx_1}\right]_{x_1=1} = -\infty$$

Thus, as shown in Fig. 5-10, the curve representing $\bar{G}_1/RT$ versus x_1 originates at $x_1 = 0$ with a value of $-\infty$ and with infinite slope, rising to the pure-species value G_1/RT at $x_1 = 1$, where its slope is unity. The curve for $\bar{G}_2/RT$ versus x_1 behaves in the same way, but with the description reversed. We note also that the curves for $\bar{G}_1/RT$, $\bar{G}_2/RT$, and G/RT intersect at a common point, namely, the minimum point of the G/RT curve. At this point, the tangent to the G/RT curve is horizontal, yielding tangent intercepts that both have the value of G/RT.

The Gibbs-Duhem equation for a binary system at constant T and P, given by Eq. (3-19), may be written:

$$\frac{d\bar{M}_1}{dx_1} = -\frac{x_2}{x_1}\frac{d\bar{M}_2}{dx_1}$$

with $x_2 = 0$, this becomes

$$\left(\frac{d\bar{M}_1}{dx_1}\right)_{x_1=1} = -(0)\left(\frac{d\bar{M}_2}{dx_1}\right)^{\infty}$$

When the infinite-dilution derivative $(d\bar{M}_2/dx_1)^{\infty}$ is finite, as it is for all of the properties M considered in Example 5-3 and represented by Fig. 5-8, $(d\bar{M}_1/dx_1)_{x_1=1}$ is zero, and the $\bar{M}_1$-versus-x_1 curve becomes horizontal at $x_1 = 1$. When M is G, A, or S (or their dimensionless forms), the infinite-dilution derivative $(d\bar{M}_2/dx_1)^{\infty}$ is $-\infty$, and we find that $(d\bar{M}_1/dx_1)_{x_1=1}$ is not zero. In fact, for $\bar{M}_1 = \bar{G}_1/RT$ it is unity in the example presented here. Similar considerations apply to component 2.

Thus Fig. 5-10 differs from Fig. 5-8 in significant ways. The same is true for the Helmholtz function and the entropy. The corresponding plot for the Helmholtz function looks very like Fig. 5-10. One for the entropy is similar in principle, but ΔS^{id} is everywhere positive rather than negative, and the infinite-dilution values $\bar{S}_1^{\infty}$ and $\bar{S}_2^{\infty}$ are positive infinite.

When M represents G, A, or S, it is far better to work directly with M^E. For the present example

$$\frac{G^E}{RT} = -1.5x_1 x_2$$

and a plot of this function versus x_1 is shown by Fig. 5-11. There are no complications. The derivative

$$\frac{d(G^E/RT)}{dx_1} = -1.5(x_2 - x_1)$$

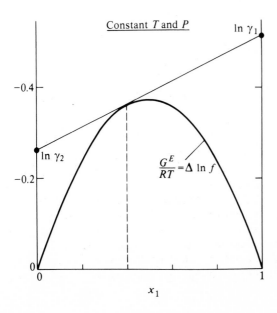

Figure 5-11 Graphical determination of activity coefficients from $G^E/RT \equiv \Delta \ln f$ as given in Example 5-5.

is finite for all values of x_1. The partial properties, shown by Eq. (5-45) to be $\ln \gamma_i$ values and given by the tangent intercepts, are everywhere finite. They are, in fact, related to composition by the equations:

$$\ln \gamma_1 = -1.5x_2^2$$

and

$$\ln \gamma_2 = -1.5x_1^2$$

We note also, as shown by Eq. (5-47), that G^E/RT is identical with $\Delta \ln f$, a function represented by Fig. 5-8 and given particular expression by Fig. 5-9.

The correlation of solution properties is unified through the excess functions, because the general nature of M^E is the same for *all* the properties we have considered. The transition from M^E to ΔM is governed by Eq. (5-40) for all of these properties:

$$\Delta M = M^E + \Delta M^{\text{id}}$$

The difference comes in ΔM^{id}, which is zero except for the properties G, A, and S.

An extensive array of thermodynamic functions has now been developed. Instant comprehension of the whole can hardly be expected. Table 5-2 is presented as an aid to understanding, both as a summary and as a convenient point of reference. In the first column we list the various functions in their generic form, symbolized by the letter M. Each function is given its simplest expression in terms of previous entries; substitutions then yield additional expressions. The remaining columns show examples of specific properties that M may represent, along with the ultimate reductions of the functions. Column 2 for the enthalpy H is typical of a class of properties that also includes V, U, C_V, C_P, Z, and $\ln f$. However, when $M = \ln f$, a special notation intrudes, and column 3 is therefore given over to this property. In column 4, we let $M = G$, a property, along with A and S, for which the expressions typical of H are not appropriate.

5-5 GENERAL EQUATIONS FOR THE GIBBS FUNCTION

We first apply the general expressions given by Eqs. (5-5) and (5-6) to the particular case for which ΔM represents the dimensionless function $\Delta G/RT$. The corresponding partial property $\overline{\Delta G_i}/RT$ is related to the activity coefficient. By Eq. (5-39)

$$\frac{\overline{\Delta G_i}}{RT} = \frac{\overline{G_i^E}}{RT} + \frac{\overline{\Delta G_i^{\text{id}}}}{RT}$$

The two terms on the right are given by Eqs. (5-45) and (5-23):

$$\frac{\overline{\Delta G_i}}{RT} = \ln \gamma_i + \ln x_i = \ln \gamma_i x_i$$

Table 5-2 Summary of thermodynamic functions for solutions

M_i	H_i	$\ln f_i$	G_i
$\bar{M}_i$	$\bar{H}_i$	$\ln (\hat{f}_i/x_i)$	$\bar{G}_i \equiv \mu_i$
$M = \sum x_i \bar{M}_i$	$H = \sum x_i \bar{H}_i$	$\ln f = \sum x_i \ln (\hat{f}_i/x_i)$	$G = \sum x_i \bar{G}_i \equiv \sum x_i \mu_i$
$\bar{M}_i^{id} = M_i + m(x_i)^\dagger$	$\bar{H}_i^{id} = H_i$	$\ln (\hat{f}_i^{id}/x_i) = \ln f_i$	$\bar{G}_i^{id} = G_i + RT \ln x_i$
$M^{id} = \sum x_i \bar{M}_i^{id}$	$H^{id} = \sum x_i H_i$	$\ln f^{id} = \sum x_i \ln f_i$	$G^{id} = \sum x_i G_i + RT \sum x_i \ln x_i$
$\overline{\Delta M}_i = \bar{M}_i - M_i$	$\overline{\Delta H}_i = \bar{H}_i - H_i$	$\overline{\Delta \ln f_i} = \ln (\hat{f}_i/x_i) - \ln f_i \equiv \ln \gamma_i$	$\overline{\Delta G}_i = \bar{G}_i - G_i \equiv RT \ln \hat{a}_i$
$\Delta M = \sum x_i \overline{\Delta M}_i$	$\Delta H = \sum x_i \overline{\Delta H}_i = H - H^{id}$	$\Delta \ln f = \sum x_i \ln \gamma_i$	$\Delta G = \sum x_i \overline{\Delta G}_i = RT \sum x_i \ln \hat{a}_i$
$\overline{\Delta M}_i^{id} = \bar{M}_i^{id} - M_i$	$\overline{\Delta H}_i^{id} = 0$	$\overline{\Delta \ln f_i^{id}} = \ln \gamma_i^{id} = 0$	$\overline{\Delta G}_i^{id} = RT \ln x_i$
$\Delta M^{id} = \sum x_i \overline{\Delta M}_i^{id}$	$\Delta H^{id} = 0$	$\Delta \ln f^{id} = 0$	$\overline{\Delta G}_i^{id} = RT \sum x_i \ln x_i$
$\bar{M}_i^E = \bar{M}_i - \bar{M}_i^{id}$	$\bar{H}_i^E = \bar{H}_i - H_i = \overline{\Delta H}_i$	$[\ln (\hat{f}_i/x_i)]^E = \ln (\hat{f}_i/x_i) - \ln f_i \equiv \ln \gamma_i$	$\bar{G}_i^E = RT \ln \gamma_i$
$M^E = \sum x_i \bar{M}_i^E$	$H^E = \sum x_i \bar{H}_i^E = \Delta H$	$(\ln f)^E = \Delta \ln f = \sum x_i \ln \gamma_i$	$G^E = RT \sum x_i \ln \gamma_i$

† The notation $m(x_i)$ represents a function of composition which is zero for all M except $M = G$, A, and S.

The product $\gamma_i x_i$ may be given an alternative expression if we substitute for γ_i by its definition, Eq. (5-30):

$$\gamma_i x_i = \left(\frac{\hat{f}_i}{x_i f_i}\right) x_i = \frac{\hat{f}_i}{f_i}$$

This ratio of fugacities is yet another common auxiliary function, called the *activity* $\hat{a}_i$ of species i in solution. Thus, by definition,

$$\boxed{\hat{a}_i \equiv \frac{\hat{f}_i}{f_i} = \gamma_i x_i}$$

and therefore

$$\overline{\Delta G}_i / RT = \ln \hat{a}_i$$

Equations (5-5) and (5-6) for this case may now be written

$$d\left(\frac{n\,\Delta G}{RT}\right) = n\left[\frac{\partial(\Delta G/RT)}{\partial T}\right]_{P,\,x} dT + n\left[\frac{\partial(\Delta G/RT)}{\partial P}\right]_{T,\,x} dP + \sum \ln \hat{a}_i \, dn_i$$

and

$$\left[\frac{\partial(\Delta G/RT)}{\partial T}\right]_{P,\,x} dT + \left[\frac{\partial(\Delta G/RT)}{\partial P}\right]_{T,\,x} dP - \sum x_i \, d \ln \hat{a}_i = 0$$

Evaluation of the partial derivatives follows from Eqs. (3-30) and (3-31), which may be directly converted to

$$\left[\frac{\partial(\Delta G/RT)}{\partial T}\right]_{P,\,x} = -\frac{\Delta H}{RT^2} = -\frac{H^E}{RT^2}$$

and

$$\left[\frac{\partial(\Delta G/RT)}{\partial P}\right]_{T,\,x} = \frac{\Delta V}{RT} = \frac{V^E}{RT}$$

As the final result, we have

$$\boxed{d\left(\frac{n\,\Delta G}{RT}\right) = -\frac{nH^E}{RT^2} dT + \frac{nV^E}{RT} dP + \sum \ln \hat{a}_i \, dn_i} \qquad (5\text{-}50)$$

and

$$\boxed{\frac{-H^E}{RT^2} dT + \frac{V^E}{RT} dP - \sum x_i \, d \ln \hat{a}_i = 0} \qquad (5\text{-}51)$$

Equations (5-5) and (5-6) may also be applied to the function $\Delta \ln f$, for which the corresponding partial property is $\ln \gamma_i$. In this case, we have for Eq. (5-5)

$$d\,(n\,\Delta \ln f) = n\left(\frac{\partial \Delta \ln f}{\partial T}\right)_{P,\,x} dT + n\left(\frac{\partial \Delta \ln f}{\partial P}\right)_{T,\,x} dP + \sum \ln \gamma_i \, dn_i$$

In view of Eq. (5-47), this may also be written

$$d\left(\frac{nG^E}{RT}\right) = n\left(\frac{\partial \Delta \ln f}{\partial T}\right)_{P,\,x} dT + n\left(\frac{\partial \Delta \ln f}{\partial P}\right)_{T,\,x} dP + \sum \ln \gamma_i \, dn_i \quad (5\text{-}52)$$

The corresponding expression of Eq. (5-6) is

$$\left(\frac{\partial \Delta \ln f}{\partial T}\right)_{P,\,x} dT + \left(\frac{\partial \Delta \ln f}{\partial P}\right)_{T,\,x} dP - \sum x_i \, d \ln \gamma_i = 0 \quad (5\text{-}53)$$

Expressions for the partial derivatives in these two equations follow from Eqs. (3-79) and (3-81). The former may be directly converted to

$$\left(\frac{\partial \Delta \ln f}{\partial T}\right)_{P,\,x} = \frac{\Delta H' - \sum x_i \,\Delta H_i'}{RT^2} = \frac{H' - H - \sum x_i H_i' + \sum x_i H_i}{RT^2}$$

By Eq. (G) of Example 3-10

$$H' - \sum x_i H_i' = 0$$

and by Eq. (5-1)

$$-(H - \sum x_i H_i) = -\Delta H = -H^E$$

Therefore

$$\left(\frac{\partial \Delta \ln f}{\partial T}\right)_{P,\,x} = \frac{-H^E}{RT^2}$$

Equation (3-81) converts directly to

$$\left(\frac{\partial \Delta \ln f}{\partial P}\right)_{T,\,x} = \frac{\Delta V}{RT} = \frac{V^E}{RT}$$

Replacing the partial derivatives in Eqs. (5-52) and (5-53) by their values from these equations, we get

$$d\left(\frac{nG^E}{RT}\right) = -\frac{nH^E}{RT^2} dT + \frac{nV^E}{RT} dP + \sum \ln \gamma_i \, dn_i \quad (5\text{-}54)$$

and

$$-\frac{H^E}{RT^2} dT + \frac{V^E}{RT} dP - \sum x_i \, d \ln \gamma_i = 0 \quad (5\text{-}55)$$

If we apply Eq. (5-54) to the special case of one mole of a constant-composition solution, it reduces to

$$d\left(\frac{G^E}{RT}\right) = -\frac{H^E}{RT^2}\,dT + \frac{V^E}{RT}\,dP \tag{5-56}$$

The analog to this equation for partial properties in a constant-composition solution is

$$d\left(\frac{\bar{G}_i^E}{RT}\right) = d\ln\gamma_i = -\frac{\bar{H}_i^E}{RT^2}\,dT + \frac{\bar{V}_i^E}{RT}\,dP \tag{5-57}$$

We have by inspection from Eq. (5-57) that

$$\left(\frac{\partial\ln\gamma_i}{\partial T}\right)_{P,\,x} = -\frac{\bar{H}_i^E}{RT^2} \tag{5-58}$$

and

$$\left(\frac{\partial\ln\gamma_i}{\partial P}\right)_{T,\,x} = \frac{\bar{V}_i^E}{RT} \tag{5-59}$$

One should keep in mind with respect to all of these equations the interchange-ability of H^E with ΔH, $\bar{H}_i^E$ with $\overline{\Delta H}_i$, V^E with ΔV, and $\bar{V}_i^E$ with $\overline{\Delta V}_i$.

The major equations of this section and those for related functions, developed earlier, are collected in Table F-1 of App. F.

5-6 EXCESS PROPERTIES FROM EXPERIMENT

Thermodynamics provides equations which relate the excess properties G^E, H^E, and S^E to V^E. When written for constant temperature, Eq. (5-56), applicable to one mole of a constant-composition mixture, becomes

$$dG^E = V^E\,dP \qquad (\text{const } T,\, x)$$

Integration from the zero-pressure state to a state at finite pressure gives

$$G^E - G^E(P=0) = \int_0^P V^E\,dP$$

As a result of Eq. (5-47), we can write

$$\frac{G^E}{RT} = \Delta\ln f \equiv \ln f - \sum x_i\ln f_i$$

Since the definition of fugacity requires that $f = f_i = P$ in the zero-pressure state, $G^E(P=0) = 0$; therefore

$$G^E = \int_0^P V^E\,dP \qquad (\text{const } T,\, x) \tag{5-60}$$

At zero pressure the volume of a fluid becomes infinite, and $V^E \ (= \Delta V)$ becomes a difference between infinite quantities, known from experiment to be finite and in general nonzero.

When restricted to constant pressure, Eq. (5-56) becomes

$$\left[\frac{\partial (G^E / RT)}{\partial T} \right]_{P,\,x} = -\frac{H^E}{RT^2} \tag{5-61}$$

This expression is another example of a Gibbs-Helmholtz equation [see Eq. (3-30)]. Expansion of the derivative and rearrangement lead to

$$\left(\frac{\partial G^E}{\partial T} \right)_{P,\,x} = \frac{G^E - H^E}{T}$$

Since by definition $G^E = H^E - TS^E$, this reduces to

$$S^E = -\left(\frac{\partial G^E}{\partial T} \right)_{P,\,x} \tag{5-62}$$

With G^E and S^E given by Eqs. (5-60) and (5-62), we can evaluate H^E from

$$H^E = G^E + TS^E \tag{5-63}$$

These general relations allow calculation of the other excess properties when V^E is known as a function of temperature, pressure, and composition.

If Eq. (5-60) is applied to the calculation of G^E for a liquid solution, then integration must be from zero pressure through the vapor/liquid phase transition. Because of the difficulty of this operation, the calculation of excess properties from $P - V^E - T - x$ data is not common for liquids. For gases, the $P - V^E - T - x$ data are most conveniently represented through use of an equation of state, for this allows the mathematical operations to be done analytically. As an example, we develop the equations which result from application of the virial equation truncated to two terms:

$$\frac{PV}{RT} = 1 + \frac{BP}{RT} \tag{4-78}$$

or

$$V = \frac{RT}{P} + B$$

This equation applies to the mixture, and an analogous equation can be written for each pure species i:

$$V_i = \frac{RT}{P} + B_{ii}$$

The excess volume is given by

$$V^E = \Delta V \equiv V - \sum y_i V_i$$

Elimination of V and the V_i by the virial equations yields

$$V^E = B - \sum y_i B_{ii}$$

which by Eq. (4-99) becomes

$$V^E = \frac{1}{2} \sum_i \sum_j y_i y_j \delta_{ij} \tag{5-64}$$

Since the δ_{ij} are independent of pressure, V^E as given by this equation does not depend on pressure. Substitution into Eq. (5-60) and integration therefore give

$$G^E = \frac{P}{2} \sum_i \sum_j y_i y_j \delta_{ij} \tag{5-65}$$

Differentiation in accord with Eq. (5-62) provides an expression for S^E:

$$S^E = -\frac{P}{2} \sum_i \sum_j y_i y_j \frac{d\delta_{ij}}{dT} \tag{5-66}$$

Finally, Eq. (5-63) yields

$$H^E = \frac{P}{2} \sum_i \sum_j y_i y_j \left(\delta_{ij} - T\frac{d\delta_{ij}}{dT} \right) \tag{5-67}$$

Thus, when the simplest form of the virial equation is valid, G^E, S^E, and H^E are all directly proportional to pressure for fixed temperature and composition.

For an ideal solution, all excess properties are zero, a result obtained from Eqs. (5-64) through (5-67) when all of the δ_{ij} are zero. Since

$$\delta_{ij} \equiv 2B_{ij} - B_{ii} - B_{jj} \tag{4-100}$$

this can be true only when

$$B_{ij} = \tfrac{1}{2}(B_{ii} + B_{jj})$$

Equations of state explicit in pressure can also be applied to the calculation of excess properties, though the results cannot be given as compact expressions. Equations already developed for $\Delta H'$, $\Delta S'$, and $\ln \phi$ in Chap. 4 provide the most convenient point of departure. The excess enthalpy for a mixture is defined as

$$H^E = H - H^{\mathrm{id}}$$

and the residual enthalpy of the mixture is

$$\Delta H' = H' - H$$

Eliminating H between these equations gives

$$H^E = -\Delta H' + H' - H^{\mathrm{id}}$$

Equation (G) of Example 3-10 and Eq. (5-20) provide the relations

$$H' = \sum x_i H'_i$$

and

$$H^{\mathrm{id}} = \sum x_i H_i$$

Combination of the last three equations yields

$$H^E = -\Delta H' + \sum x_i(H'_i - H_i)$$

or

$$H^E = \sum x_i \,\Delta H'_i - \Delta H' \tag{5-68}$$

Similarly

$$S^E = \sum x_i \,\Delta S'_i - \Delta S' \tag{5-69}$$

The excess Gibbs function can, of course, be evaluated from H^E and S^E through its definition, or it can be found from $\Delta \ln \phi$. By definition

$$\Delta \ln \phi \equiv \ln \phi - \sum x_i \ln \phi_i = \ln \frac{f}{P} - \sum x_i \ln \frac{f_i}{P}$$

or

$$\Delta \ln \phi = \ln f - \sum x_i \ln f_i \equiv \Delta \ln f$$

In view of Eq. (5-47), we have

$$\boxed{\frac{G^E}{RT} = \Delta \ln \phi \equiv \ln \phi - \sum x_i \ln \phi_i} \tag{5-70}$$

Thus, equations such as Eqs. (4-148), (4-150), and (4-151), which are based on the generic form of the Redlich-Kwong equation, may be applied to the mixture and to its constituent species at the same T and P to yield values required in Eqs. (5-68) through (5-70).

Example 5-6 In Example 4-16 we calculated fugacity coefficients for a nitrogen/n-butane gas mixture through application of the original Redlich-Kwong equation; here, we calculate H^E, S^E, and G^E for exactly the same mixture by application of Eqs. (5-68) through (5-70). As in the earlier example, we base our calculations on the original Redlich-Kwong equation, and therefore compute values of $\Delta H'$ and $\Delta S'$ by Eqs. (4-153) and (4-154):

$$\frac{\Delta H'}{RT} = 1.5A \ln (1 + h) - (Z - 1)$$

and

$$\frac{\Delta S'}{R} = \frac{A}{2} \ln (1 + h) - \ln (1 - h)Z$$

where

$$A \equiv \frac{a}{bRT^{3/2}}$$

We apply these equations both to the mixture and to the pure species, drawing on the results of Example 4-16 for values of A, h, and Z. Rounded to four decimal places, the appropriate values are:

	A	h	Z
Nitrogen(1)	0.7069	0.0287	1.0098
n-butane(2)	4.3715	0.1382	0.6296
Mixture	2.4988	0.0633	0.9189

Thus, for pure nitrogen

$$\frac{\Delta H'_1}{RT} = 1.5A_1 \ln (1 + h_1) - (Z_1 - 1)$$

$$= (1.5)(0.7069) \ln 1.0287 - 0.0098$$

$$= 0.0202$$

Similarly, for pure n-butane:

$$\frac{\Delta H'_2}{RT} = 1.2192$$

and for the mixture:

$$\frac{\Delta H'}{RT} = 0.3112$$

By Eq. (5-68)

$$\frac{H^E}{RT} = x_1 \frac{\Delta H'_1}{RT} + x_2 \frac{\Delta H'_2}{RT} - \frac{\Delta H'}{RT}$$

$$= (0.4974)(0.0202) + (0.5026)(1.2192) - 0.3112$$

$$= 0.3116$$

Calculations for $\Delta S'$ yield

$$\frac{\Delta S'_1}{R} = 0.0294$$

$$\frac{\Delta S'_2}{R} = 0.8943$$

$$\frac{\Delta S'}{R} = 0.2267$$

and by Eq. (5-69)

$$\frac{S^E}{R} = x_1 \frac{\Delta S'_1}{R} + x_2 \frac{\Delta S'_2}{R} - \frac{\Delta S'}{R}$$

$$= (0.4974)(0.0294) + (0.5026)(0.8943) - 0.2267$$

$$= 0.2374$$

A value for G^E/RT is given by

$$\frac{G^E}{RT} = \frac{H^E}{RT} - \frac{S^E}{R}$$

$$= 0.3116 - 0.2374$$

$$= 0.0742$$

Alternatively, we can calculate G^E/RT by Eq. (5-70),

$$\frac{G^E}{RT} = \Delta \ln \phi \equiv \ln \phi - \sum x_i \ln \phi_i$$

Taking rounded values from the results of Example 4-16, we get

$$\frac{G^E}{RT} = -0.0844 - (0.4974)(0.0092) - (0.5026)(-0.3249)$$

$$= 0.0743$$

These two results agree within the rounding error, as they should.

The calculations illustrated in this example and in Example 4-16 are based on the original Redlich-Kwong equation, and their validity depends on the accuracy of this equation in representing the volumetric behavior of the nitrogen/n-butane system. Some other equation of state may well be more appropriate and yield better results.

For liquid mixtures one takes advantage of the fact that both V^E $(= \Delta V)$ and H^E $(= \Delta H)$ are readily measured directly. Such data for the liquid phase alone do not allow calculation of S^E or G^E. For these, additional data are required, and are usually provided by vapor/liquid equilibrium measurements, as discussed in Chap. 6.

Except in the critical region, the thermodynamic properties of liquids, including the excess properties, are only weakly dependent on pressure. The usual practice therefore is to take data at normal pressures to provide the composition and perhaps the temperature dependence of the excess properties. The influence of pressure on G^E and H^E is readily found from Eq. (5-56). By inspection, we see that

$$\boxed{\left[\frac{\partial(G^E/RT)}{\partial P}\right]_{T,x} = \frac{V^E}{RT}} \tag{5-71}$$

and from the reciprocity relation we get

$$\left[\frac{\partial(H^E/RT)}{\partial P}\right]_{T,x} = -T\left[\frac{\partial(V^E/RT)}{\partial T}\right]_{P,x} \tag{5-72}$$

Example 5-7 Outside the critical region, the quantities on the right of Eqs. (5-71) and (5-72) change only slowly with pressure. Therefore, integration with these quantities held constant usually yields results valid to a good approximation. Thus, for a change in pressure from P_1 to P_2 at constant T and x, we have

$$\left(\frac{G^E}{RT}\right)_{P_2} \simeq \left(\frac{G^E}{RT}\right)_{P_1} + \frac{V^E}{RT}(P_2 - P_1)$$

and

$$\left(\frac{H^E}{RT}\right)_{P_2} \simeq \left(\frac{H^E}{RT}\right)_{P_1} - T\left[\frac{\partial(V^E/RT)}{\partial T}\right]_{P,x}(P_2 - P_1)$$

where the integrands are usually evaluated at the initial pressure P_1.

For an equimolar mixture of ethanol and water at 25°C and 1 bar, we have the following values:

$$\frac{V^E}{RT} = -4.3 \times 10^{-5} \text{ bar}^{-1}$$

$$\left[\frac{\partial(V^E/RT)}{\partial T}\right]_{P,x} = 3.7 \times 10^{-7} \text{ bar}^{-1} \text{ K}^{-1}$$

$$\frac{G^E}{RT} = 0.296$$

$$\frac{H^E}{RT} = -0.168$$

If $P_1 = 1$ bar and $P_2 = 100$ bar, then we have

$$\left(\frac{G^E}{RT}\right)_{P_2} \simeq 0.296 - (4.3 \times 10^{-5})(99) = 0.292$$

$$\left(\frac{H^E}{RT}\right)_{P_2} \simeq -0.168 - (298.15)(3.7 \times 10^{-7})(99) = -0.179$$

Thus, a pressure change of almost 100 bar causes only small changes in G^E and H^E for this system at 25°C.

5-7 COMPOSITION DEPENDENCE OF THE EXCESS FUNCTIONS

No general theory exists that adequately describes the composition dependence of liquid-solution properties. This functional dependence for the excess properties is therefore commonly represented by empirical equations. We consider here those equations of general applicability, leaving aside for the moment equations developed for special purposes.

The treatment of binary solutions is facilitated by definition of the function

$$\mathscr{M} \equiv \frac{M^E}{x_1 x_2} \tag{5-73}$$

Thus,

$$M^E = x_1 x_2 \mathscr{M} \tag{5-74}$$

and at constant T and P

$$\frac{dM^E}{dx_1} = x_1 x_2 \frac{d\mathscr{M}}{dx_1} + \mathscr{M}(x_2 - x_1) \tag{5-75}$$

Substitution of Eqs. (5-74) and (5-75) into Eqs. (5-38) yields

$$\bar{M}_1^E = x_2^2 \left(\mathscr{M} + x_1 \frac{d\mathscr{M}}{dx_1} \right) \tag{5-76a}$$

and

$$\bar{M}_2^E = x_1^2 \left(\mathscr{M} - x_2 \frac{d\mathscr{M}}{dx_1} \right) \tag{5-76b}$$

When $x_1 = 0$, Eq. (5-76a) yields the infinite-dilution value of $\bar{M}_1^E$:

$$(\bar{M}_1^E)^\infty = \mathscr{M}(x_1 = 0) \tag{5-77}$$

Similarly, when $x_1 = 1$, Eq. (5-76b) yields the infinite-dilution value of $\bar{M}_2^E$:

$$(\bar{M}_2^E)^\infty = \mathscr{M}(x_1 = 1) \tag{5-78}$$

Thus, the intercepts at $x_1 = 0$ and $x_1 = 1$ on a plot of $\mathscr{M}$ versus x_1 yield directly the infinite-dilution values of the partial molar excess properties, and extrapolation to these limits provides the most convenient graphical method for determination of these quantities. Partial properties at intermediate compositions are found from the tangent intercepts according to the equations

$$\bar{M}_1^E = x_2^2 (2\mathscr{M} - I_1) \tag{5-79}$$

and

$$\bar{M}_2^E = x_1^2 (2\mathscr{M} - I_2) \tag{5-80}$$

where I_1 and I_2 are the tangent intercepts as shown by Fig. 5-12. In Fig. 5-13 we show as a specific example the heat-of-mixing data for sulfuric acid/water at 25°C, where $\mathscr{H} \equiv H^E / x_1 x_2$ is plotted versus x_1. Again, the data for this system are on a unit-mass basis, and x_1 and x_2 are mass fractions. The partial-property values of Fig. 5-7 are also shown on Fig. 5-13.

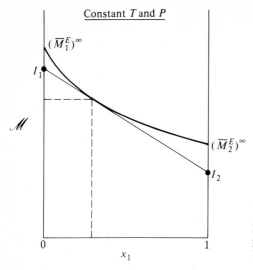

Figure 5-12 Graphical construction for partial properties from $\mathscr{M} \equiv M^E/x_1 x_2$. [Van Ness and Mrazek (1959)].

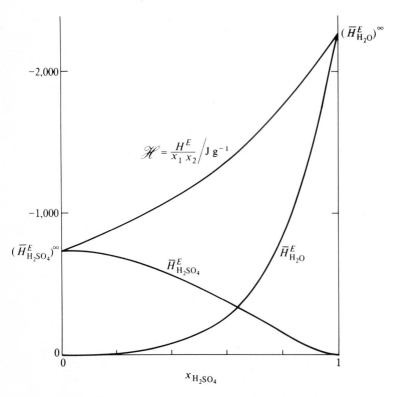

Figure 5-13 Partial excess enthalpies and $\mathscr{H}$ versus mass fraction of H_2SO_4 for sulfuric acid/water at 25°C.

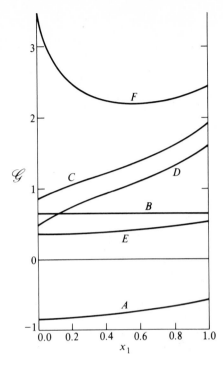

Figure 5-14 Correlations of $\mathscr{G} \equiv G^E/x_1 x_2 RT$ as functions of mole fraction for (A) acetone/chloroform, (B) actone/methanol, (C) chloroform/methanol, (D) chloroform/ethanol, (E) chloroform/n-heptane, (F) ethanol/n-heptane. First-named species is component 1.

A wide diversity of shapes is obtained for plots of $\mathscr{M}$ versus x_1 for different properties and different systems. This is illustrated in Fig. 5-14, where the function $\mathscr{G} \equiv G^E/x_1 x_2 RT$ is plotted for several binary solutions. The flexibility required in an equation for fitting the diverse curves obtained by experimental measurement of the excess properties is provided by *rational functions*, i.e., by ratios of polynomials expressed as

$$\mathscr{M} = \frac{A_0 + \sum\limits_{n=1}^{a} A_n z^n}{1 + \sum\limits_{m=1}^{b} B_m z^m} \tag{5-81}$$

where

$$z \equiv x_1 - x_2 = 1 - 2x_2 = 2x_1 - 1$$

This general empirical treatment of excess properties was first proposed by Malanowski (1974) and further elaborated by Marsh (1977). It incorporates as special cases most of the equations found in general use for analytical expression of the composition dependence of the excess properties of binary liquid solutions.

Consider first the special case for which A_n $(n \geq 1) = 0$. For this specializa-tion Eq. (5-81) can be written

$$\frac{1}{\mathscr{M}} = \frac{1 + \sum\limits_{m=1}^{b} B_m z^m}{A_0} \tag{5-82}$$

This equation has not proved useful when more than two terms are retained in the sum. Truncation to $b = 2$ yields

$$\frac{1}{\mathscr{M}} = \frac{1 + B_1 z + B_2 z^2}{A_0} \tag{5-83}$$

Since $x_1 - x_2 \equiv z$ and $x_1 + x_2 = 1$, we have

$$x_1 = \frac{1+z}{2} \quad \text{and} \quad x_2 = \frac{1-z}{2}$$

from which

$$x_1 x_2 = \frac{1 - z^2}{4}$$

or

$$z^2 = 1 - 4x_1 x_2 \tag{5-84}$$

Substitution for z and z^2 in Eq. (5-83) yields

$$\frac{1}{\mathscr{M}} = \frac{1 + B_1(x_1 - x_2) + B_2(1 - 4x_1 x_2)}{A_0}$$

Since $x_1 + x_2 = 1$, this may be rewritten as

$$\frac{1}{\mathscr{M}} = \frac{(1 + B_2)(x_1 + x_2) + B_1(x_1 - x_2) - 4B_2 x_1 x_2}{A_0}$$

or

$$\frac{1}{\mathscr{M}} = \frac{x_1}{A'_{21}} + \frac{x_2}{A'_{12}} - \eta x_1 x_2 \tag{5-85}$$

where

$$A'_{21} = \frac{A_0}{1 + B_1 + B_2}$$

$$A'_{12} = \frac{A_0}{1 - B_1 + B_2}$$

and

$$\eta = \frac{4B_2}{A_0}$$

When inverted, Eq. (5-85) becomes

$$\mathcal{M} = \frac{A'_{12} A'_{21}}{A'_{12} x_1 + A'_{21} x_2 - A'_{12} A'_{21} \eta x_1 x_2} \tag{5-86}$$

If $B_2 = 0$, then this equation reduces to the *van Laar equation*:

$$\boxed{\mathcal{M} = \frac{A'_{12} A'_{21}}{A'_{12} x_1 + A'_{21} x_2}} \tag{5-87}$$

where

$$A'_{12} = \frac{A_0}{1 - B_1}$$

and

$$A'_{21} = \frac{A_0}{1 + B_1}$$

This equation holds whenever a plot of $1/\mathcal{M}$ versus x_1 is linear.

A special case of Eq. (5-81) that finds widespread use results when $B_m = 0$ for all m. Then

$$\mathcal{M} = A_0 + \sum_{n=1}^{a} A_n z^n \tag{5-88}$$

an equation popularized by Redlich and Kister (1948). Its simplest expression results when $A_n \, (n \geq 1) = 0$, in which case $\mathcal{M} = A_0$, and

$$M^E = A_0 x_1 x_2 \tag{5-89}$$

Other truncations of Eq. (5-88) with $a \leq 5$ are frequent in the literature. When a still higher order is indicated, an equation of different form is probably more appropriate.

The Redlich-Kister equation, Eq. (5-88), may be transformed into an alternative and equivalent polynomial known as the *Margules equation*. For truncation to six terms Eq. (5-88) can be written

$$\mathcal{M} = A_0 + A_1 z + (A_2 + A_3 z) z^2 + (A_4 + A_5 z) z^4$$

Equation (5-84) provides an expression for z^2:

$$z^2 = 1 - 4x_1 x_2$$

Therefore

$$z^4 = 1 - 8x_1 x_2 + 16 x_1^2 x_2^2$$

Combining the last three equations, we get

$$\mathcal{M} = (A_0 + A_2 + A_4) + (A_1 + A_3 + A_5) z$$
$$- [(4A_2 + 8A_4) + (4A_3 + 8A_5) z] x_1 x_2 + 16(A_4 + A_5 z) x_1^2 x_2^2$$

However, we have the general relation:

$$N + Qz = N(x_1 + x_2) + Q(x_1 - x_2) = (N + Q)x_1 + (N - Q)x_2$$

Algebraic rearrangement of the equation for $\mathcal{M}$ in accord with this result yields the Margules equation:

$$\boxed{\mathcal{M} = A_{21}x_1 + A_{12}x_2 - (C_{21}x_1 + C_{12}x_2)x_1 x_2 + (D_{21}x_1 + D_{12}x_2)x_1^2 x_2^2}$$

$$(5\text{-}90)$$

where

$$A_{21} = A_0 + A_1 + A_2 + A_3 + A_4 + A_5$$
$$A_{12} = A_0 - A_1 + A_2 - A_3 + A_4 - A_5$$
$$C_{21} = 4(A_2 + A_3) + 8(A_4 + A_5)$$
$$C_{12} = 4(A_2 - A_3) + 8(A_4 - A_5)$$
$$D_{21} = 16(A_4 + A_5)$$
$$D_{12} = 16(A_4 - A_5)$$

The inverse relations among the coefficients are also useful:

$$A_5 = \frac{D_{21} - D_{12}}{32}$$

$$A_4 = \frac{D_{21} + D_{12}}{32}$$

$$A_3 = \frac{C_{21} - C_{12}}{8} - 2A_5$$

$$A_2 = \frac{C_{21} + C_{12}}{8} - 2A_4$$

$$A_1 = \frac{A_{21} - A_{12}}{2} - A_3 - A_5$$

$$A_0 = \frac{A_{21} + A_{12}}{2} - A_2 - A_4$$

The various truncations of the Margules equation correspond to those of the Redlich-Kister equation. For example, if

$$A_3 = A_4 = A_5 = 0$$

then

$$D_{21} = D_{12} = 0 \quad \text{and} \quad C_{21} = C_{12} = C = 4A_2$$

Equation (5-90) in this case becomes

$$\mathcal{M} = A_{21}x_1 + A_{12}x_2 - Cx_1x_2 \tag{5-91}$$

If further, $A_2 = 0$, then $C_{21} = C_{12} = C = 0$, and

$$\mathcal{M} = A_{21}x_1 + A_{12}x_2 \tag{5-92}$$

This equation holds whenever a plot of $\mathcal{M}$ versus x_1 is linear.

Equation (5-81) truncated to yield

$$\mathcal{M} = \frac{A_0 + A_1 z + A_2 z^2 + A_3 z^3}{1 + B_1 z + B_2 z^2} \tag{5-93}$$

is probably the most complex rational function of practical use. By involved algebraic manipulations, this six-parameter equation may be put into an alternative form:

$$\mathcal{M} = A_{21}x_1 + A_{12}x_2 - \frac{(\psi + \Omega z)x_1 x_2}{1 + B_1 z + B_2 z^2} \tag{5-94}$$

where in addition to B_1 and B_2 the parameters are

$$A_{21} = \frac{A_0 + A_1 + A_2 + A_3}{1 + B_1 + B_2}$$

$$A_{12} = \frac{A_0 - A_1 + A_2 - A_3}{1 - B_1 + B_2}$$

$$\psi = 4\left\{ \frac{A_0[B_1^2 - B_2(1 + B_2)] + A_2(1 + B_2) - (A_1 + A_3)B_1}{(1 + B_2)^2 - B_1^2} \right\}$$

and

$$\Omega = 4\left\{ \frac{B_2[(A_0 + A_2)B_1 - A_1(1 + B_2)] + A_3(1 + B_2 - B_1^2)}{(1 + B_2)^2 - B_1^2} \right\}$$

If $B_2 = 0$, the resulting five-parameter equation can be written:

$$\mathcal{M} = A_{21}x_1 + A_{12}x_2 - \left[\Gamma + \frac{\alpha_{12}\alpha_{21}}{\alpha_{12}x_1 + \alpha_{21}x_2} \right]x_1 x_2 \tag{5-95}$$

where

$$A_{21} = \frac{A_0 + A_1 + A_2 + A_3}{1 + B_1}$$

$$A_{12} = \frac{A_0 - A_1 + A_2 - A_3}{1 - B_1}$$

$$\Gamma = \frac{4A_3}{B_1}$$

$$\alpha_{12} = \frac{4[B_1^2(A_0 B_1 - A_1) + A_2 B_1 - A_3]}{B_1(1 - B_1^2)(1 - B_1)}$$

and

$$\alpha_{21} = \frac{4[B_1^2(A_0 B_1 - A_1) + A_2 B_1 - A_3]}{B_1(1 - B_1^2)(1 + B_1)}$$

If in Eq. (5-95) $A_3 = 0$, we get the four-parameter equation

$$\mathscr{M} = A_{21} x_1 + A_{12} x_2 - \frac{\alpha_{12}\alpha_{21} x_1 x_2}{\alpha_{12} x_1 + \alpha_{21} x_2} \qquad (5\text{-}96)$$

where

$$A_{21} = \frac{A_0 + A_1 + A_2}{1 + B_1}$$

$$A_{12} = \frac{A_0 - A_1 + A_2}{1 - B_1}$$

$$\alpha_{12} = \frac{4(A_0 B_1^2 - A_1 B_1 + A_2)}{(1 - B_1^2)(1 - B_1)}$$

and

$$\alpha_{21} = \frac{4(A_0 B_1^2 - A_1 B_1 + A_2)}{(1 - B_1^2)(1 + B_1)}$$

This equation was introduced by Abbott and Van Ness (1975) as the modified Margules equation. Indeed, when $\alpha_{12} = \alpha_{21}$, we must have

$$B_1 = -B_1 = 0$$

and

$$\alpha_{12} = \alpha_{21} = 4A_2$$

The modified Margules equation then becomes

$$\mathscr{M} = A_{21} x_1 + A_{12} x_2 - 4A_2 x_1 x_2$$

which is Eq. (5-91), the three-parameter Margules equation.

Additional terms may be appended to the denominator of Eq. (5-96), giving in the simplest case

$$\boxed{\mathscr{M} = A_{21} x_1 + A_{12} x_2 - \frac{\alpha_{12}\alpha_{21} x_1 x_2}{\alpha_{12} x_1 + \alpha_{21} x_2 + \eta x_1 x_2}} \qquad (5\text{-}97)$$

This equation is not, however, equivalent to a particular truncation of Eq. (5-81), although it does result as a special case of Eq. (5-93) when the coefficients are constrained by the relation

$$A_3 = \frac{B_2[A_1(1 + B_2) - B_1(A_0 + A_2)]}{1 + B_2 - B_1^2}$$

When $A_2 = A_3 = 0$, Eq. (5-94) is not useful as an alternative form of Eq. (5-93), which becomes

$$\mathcal{M} = \frac{A_0 + A_1 z}{1 + B_1 z + B_2 z^2} \tag{5-98}$$

An equivalent form of this equation may be written

$$\mathcal{M} = \frac{G_{12}\tau_{12}}{x_2 + x_1 G_{12}} + \frac{G_{21}\tau_{21}}{x_1 + x_2 G_{21}} \tag{5-99}$$

The relations between coefficients are given by

$$A_0 = \frac{G_{12}\tau_{12}(1 + G_{21}) + G_{21}\tau_{21}(1 + G_{12})}{1 + G_{12}G_{21}}$$

$$A_1 = \frac{G_{12}\tau_{12}(1 - G_{21}) + G_{21}\tau_{21}(1 - G_{12})}{1 + G_{12}G_{21}}$$

$$B_1 = \frac{G_{12} - G_{21}}{1 + G_{12}G_{21}}$$

and

$$B_2 = \frac{(1 - G_{12})(G_{21} - 1)}{2(1 + G_{12}G_{21})}$$

Finally, when $B_2 = 0$, Eq. (5-98) becomes

$$\mathcal{M} = \frac{A_0 + A_1 z}{1 + B_1 z} = \frac{1}{B_1}\left(A_1 + \frac{A_0 B_1 - A_1}{1 + B_1 z}\right)$$

or

$$\mathcal{M} = \frac{A_1}{B_1} + \frac{\alpha_{12}\alpha_{21}}{\alpha_{12}x_1 + \alpha_{21}x_2} \tag{5-100}$$

where

$$\alpha_{12} = \frac{A_0 B_1 - A_1}{B_1(1 - B_1)}$$

and

$$\alpha_{21} = \frac{A_0 B_1 - A_1}{B_1(1 + B_1)}$$

When $A_1 = 0$, we recover the van Laar equation.

The denominator of the rational functions must never become zero, for this would make $\mathcal{M}$ infinite. Thus, the denominator cannot change sign in the range of x_1 from zero to unity or in the range of z from -1 to $+1$. Since z passes through zero at $x_1 = x_2 = 0.5$, the denominator must be positive. When the denominator is given by $1 + B_1 z + B_2 z^2$, we therefore have the following constraints:

$$B_1 + B_2 > -1 \quad \text{and} \quad B_1 - B_2 < 1$$

When $B_2 = 0$, these combine, and require that

$$1 > B_1 > -1$$

General expressions for the partial molar excess properties $\bar{M}_1^E$ and $\bar{M}_2^E$ implied by the rational functions of Eq. (5-81) are readily derived. Following Marsh (1977), we let

$$A \equiv A_0 + \sum_{n=1}^{a} A_n z^n \tag{5-101}$$

and

$$B \equiv 1 + \sum_{m=1}^{b} B_m z^m \tag{5-102}$$

Then

$$\mathscr{M} = \frac{A}{B} \tag{5-103}$$

and

$$\frac{d\mathscr{M}}{dz} = \frac{A'}{B} - \frac{AB'}{B^2} \tag{5-104}$$

where

$$A' \equiv \frac{dA}{dz} = \sum_{n=1}^{a} nA_n z^{n-1} \tag{5-105}$$

and

$$B' \equiv \frac{dB}{dz} = \sum_{m=1}^{b} mB_m z^{m-1} \tag{5-106}$$

Since

$$z \equiv x_1 - x_2$$
$$dz = dx_1 - dx_2 = 2 \, dx_1$$

Therefore

$$\frac{d\mathscr{M}}{dx_1} = 2\frac{d\mathscr{M}}{dz} = \frac{2}{B}\left(A' - \frac{AB'}{B}\right) \tag{5-107}$$

Combination of Eqs. (5-103) and (5-107) with Eqs. (5-76) gives

$$\bar{M}_1^E = \frac{x_2^2}{B}\left[A + 2x_1\left(A' - \frac{AB'}{B}\right)\right] \qquad (5\text{-}108a)$$

and

$$\bar{M}_2^E = \frac{x_1^2}{B}\left[A - 2x_2\left(A' - \frac{AB'}{B}\right)\right] \qquad (5\text{-}108b)$$

For the Redlich-Kister equation, $B_m = 0$ for all m, and therefore $B = 1$, $A = \mathcal{M}$, and $B' = 0$.

Because of the relative scarcity of accurate data for multicomponent systems, comparatively little attention has been given to the development of empirical expressions to represent the composition dependence of their excess properties. One procedure that has met with some success for ternary systems is represented by the equation

$$M_{123}^E = M_{12}^E + M_{13}^E + M_{23}^E + x_1 x_2 x_3 F(x) \qquad (5\text{-}109)$$

Thus, the excess property of the ternary system is given as the sum of the expressions for the composition dependence of the constituent binaries plus a "ternary term" that incorporates a function of composition selected so as to fit the data in any particular instance. A simple expression of this kind is given by Eq. (A) of Example 3-4 with M replaced by M^E. The expressions for the M_{ij}^E can be any of those resulting from truncation of Eq. (5-81), and different forms can be used for the individual binaries, as necessity requires. Unfortunately, the expressions required for the binaries offer no reliable guide as to the nature of $F(x)$. This requires an additional and unrelated empirical step. Moreover, extension to higher-ordered systems results in ever more cumbersome equations. The hope is that a realistic theory of solutions will ultimately be developed that makes equations for binary systems implicitly generalizable to multicomponent systems.

5-8 ALTERNATIVE IDEAL-SOLUTION MODELS FOR LIQUIDS

In Sec. 5-3 we presented a model of ideal-solution behavior derived from the Lewis-Randall rule. This model is entirely appropriate for liquid solutions when all constituent species are stable as pure liquids at the temperature and pressure of the solution. However, one must sometimes deal with solutions for which one or more of the constituents does not exist pure as a stable liquid. Obvious examples are liquid solutions formed by dissolution of solids or gases in a liquid solvent. Since the solute species do not exist in the pure state as liquids at the T and P of the solution, one cannot measure their properties in this state. Moreover, the solubility of such species is limited at a given T and P, and therefore experimental data can provide property values for the solution over no more than a portion of the composition range.

For a binary system of species 1 and 2, where species 1 is such a solute and species 2 is the solvent, this means with respect to Fig. 3-8 that some portion of the right-hand side of the diagram is missing, as shown in Fig. 5-15. Since the value of f_2, the fugacity of pure species 2 as a liquid, is known, the line representing the Lewis-Randall rule for the solvent is readily constructed; thus, for species 2 the ideal-solution fugacity can be given by

$$\hat{f}_2^{\,\mathrm{id}} = f_2 x_2 \tag{5-110}$$

There are, however, no data for species 2 at high dilution, and we cannot construct the line representing Henry's law. For solute species 1, on the other hand, the tangent at $x_1 = 0$ is readily drawn, giving the Henry's-law line, but we have no experimental value for f_1, the fugacity of pure species 1 as a liquid, from which to establish the line for the Lewis-Randall rule. Thus, the Lewis-Randall rule does not appear to be a suitable representation of ideal-solution behavior

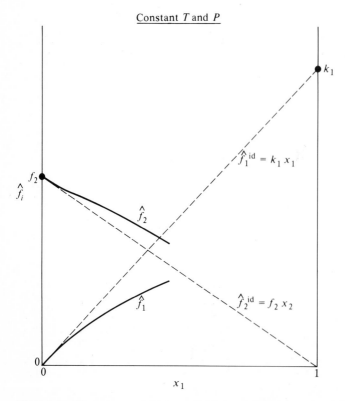

Figure 5-15 When solute species 1 is of limited solubility in solvent species 2, the composition dependence of $\hat{f}_1$ and $\hat{f}_2$ is known from experiment for only part of the composition range.

for the solute, and we therefore define an alternative model of ideal-solution behavior for this species based on Henry's law:

$$\hat{f}_1^{id} = k_1 x_1 \tag{5-111}$$

where k_1 is Henry's constant. The lines representing Eqs. (5-110) and (5-111) are shown on Fig. 5-15.

When Eq. (5-111) defines ideal-solution behavior for the solute, Henry's constant takes over the role that would be played by the pure-species fugacity f_1 in the Lewis-Randall model of ideality. Indeed, k_1 is best regarded as the fugacity of pure species 1 in a *fictitious or hypothetical liquid state*. As seen from Fig. 5-15, k_1 is a value at $x_1 = 1$, and is the fugacity that pure liquid species 1 would have were Henry's law actually valid for this species over the entire composition range from $x_1 = 0$ to $x_1 = 1$.

Both the Lewis-Randall rule and Henry's law are models of behavior which make $\hat{f}_i^{id}$ directly proportional to x_i for given T and P, and both can be represented by the equation

$$\boxed{\hat{f}_i^{id} = f_i^{\circ}(T, P)x_i} \tag{5-112}$$

where f_i° is the fugacity of species i in a specified *standard state*. For ideality in the sense of the Lewis-Randall rule, the standard state of species i is the state of pure liquid i at the T and P of the solution; for this standard state, $f_i^{\circ} = f_i$, and we recover Eq. (5-8) as a special case. For ideality in the sense of Henry's law, the standard state of species i is the hypothetical state of pure liquid i for which $f_i^{\circ} = k_i$. In this case Eq. (5-112) becomes

$$\hat{f}_i^{id} = k_i(T, P)x_i \tag{5-113}$$

A standard state of species i is no more than a particular state, either real or hypothetical, of the species at specified temperature, pressure, and composition. It serves as a reference state, and may in principle be selected arbitrarily, provided only that it *always* be at the temperature of the system. This restriction is ultimately seen as a consequence of the restriction of Eq. (3-59) to constant T. In any particular application, the standard state of species i must be its state in a solution of fixed, though arbitrary, composition. For applications to phase equilibrium, this composition is almost always $x_i = 1$, and the standard state is then a state (real or hypothetical) of pure i. The standard-state pressure is often the solution pressure, but it may also be set equal to a selected vapor pressure or to a fixed reference value, such as atmospheric pressure or even a pressure approaching zero. By Eq. (5-112), we limit consideration here to standard states taken at the temperature and pressure of the solution; thus, the standard-state temperature and pressure vary with the T and P of the solution.

An expression for f^{id}, the fugacity of an ideal solution, comes from Eq. (3-76):

$$\ln f^{id} = \sum x_i \ln \frac{\hat{f}_i^{id}}{x_i} \tag{5-114}$$

Substitution for $\hat{f}_i^{id}$ by Eq. (5-112) gives

$$\ln f^{id} = \sum x_i \ln f_i^{\circ} \tag{5-115}$$

The function $\Delta \ln f$ may now be redefined to give it a broader range of applicability [see Eq. (A) of Example 5-3]:

$$\boxed{\Delta \ln f \equiv \ln f - \sum x_i \ln f_i^{\circ}} \tag{5-116}$$

When ideality is defined in the sense of the Lewis-Randall rule for *all* species, then the standard state for each is the pure-liquid state at the T and P of the solution, and Eq. (5-115) becomes

$$\ln f^{id} = \sum x_i \ln f_i$$

This is a special case of Eq. (5-20), and is an equation appearing in the third column of Table 5-2; it is also represented for a binary solution by the straight dashed line of Fig. 5-9. This treatment is based on what is known as the *symmetric convention* for the standard states, because all are related to the Lewis-Randall rule. It is universally adopted when the required fugacities of all pure liquid species are experimentally accessible, because it leads to straightforward and unambiguous analysis of phase-equilibrium problems.

We return now to the situation represented by Fig. 5-15, where the system consists of solute species 1 dissolved in solvent species 2. Here we define ideality for species 1 by Eq. (5-111) and for species 2 by Eq. (5-110). In this case Eqs. (5-115) and (5-116) become

$$\ln f^{id} = x_1 \ln k_1 + x_2 \ln f_2 \tag{5-117}$$

and

$$\Delta \ln f^* = \ln f - x_1 \ln k_1 - x_2 \ln f_2 \tag{5-118}$$

where we use the asterisk to identify $\Delta \ln f^*$ as a quantity based on standard states taken differently for the solute and solvent. This choice of standard states is known as the *unsymmetric convention*.

The activity coefficient defined in Example 5-3 and in Sec. 5-4 is given by

$$\gamma_i \equiv \frac{\hat{f}_i}{x_i f_i} \tag{5-30}$$

The denominator is just $\hat{f}_i^{id} = x_i f_i$, the fugacity of a species as given by the Lewis-Randall rule. Thus, we may equally well write the defining equation for the activity coefficient as

$$\gamma_i \equiv \frac{\hat{f}_i}{\hat{f}_i^{id}} \tag{5-119}$$

In this form, the definition accommodates other models of ideality than the Lewis-Randall rule, and substitution of the general expression for $\hat{f}_i^{id}$, as given by Eq. (5-112), into Eq. (5-119) gives

$$\gamma_i \equiv \frac{\hat{f}_i}{x_i f_i^{\circ}} \equiv \frac{(\hat{f}_i/x_i)}{f_i^{\circ}} \tag{5-120}$$

This *general* definition of the activity coefficient shows explicitly its relation to the standard-state fugacity.

For a standard state based on the Lewis-Randall rule, $f_i^{\circ} = f_i$, and we recover Eq. (5-30). When $x_i = 1$, $\hat{f}_i = f_i$, and $\gamma_i = 1$. Thus, the standard-state fugacity may be regarded as a normalizing factor which in this case makes $\gamma_i = 1$ in the limit as species i becomes pure. When the activity coefficients for all species of a solution are so defined, the normalization is said to be symmetric.

When ideal-solution behavior for species i is defined by Henry's law, the standard-state fugacity is $f_i^{\circ} = k_i$, and Eq. (5-120) becomes

$$\gamma_i^* \equiv \frac{\hat{f}_i}{x_i k_i} \equiv \frac{(\hat{f}_i/x_i)}{k_i} \tag{5-121}$$

where the asterisk is an identifying mark for this definition of an activity coefficient. When $x_i = 0$, $\gamma_i^* = 1$, a result that follows from Eq. (3-95). Thus, Henry's constant is a normalizing factor that makes $\gamma_i^* = 1$ in the limit as species i becomes infinitely dilute. When activity coefficients for different species of a solution are defined differently, normalization is said to be unsymmetric.

We may combine the component fugacities $\hat{f}_1$ and $\hat{f}_2$ as represented in Fig. 5-15 in accord with Eq. (3-76):

$$\ln f = x_1 \ln \frac{\hat{f}_1}{x_1} + x_2 \ln \frac{\hat{f}_2}{x_2} \tag{5-122}$$

A plot of $\ln f$ versus x_1 may now be constructed for the concentration range over which data are available. The resulting curve appears in Fig. 5-16 along with the ideal-solution line as given by Eq. (5-117). This straight line is tangent to the $\ln f$ curve at $x_1 = 0$, because by definition $\ln k_1$ is the limiting value of the partial property $\ln (\hat{f}_1/x_1)$ at $x_1 = 0$. (See Example 5-3 and Fig. 5-9.) The difference between these two lines is $\Delta \ln f^*$ as given by Eq. (5-118). Combining Eqs. (5-118) and (5-122), we get

$$\Delta \ln f^* = x_1 \ln \frac{\hat{f}_1}{x_1 k_1} + x_2 \ln \frac{\hat{f}_2}{x_2 f_2}$$

which with Eqs. (5-121) and (5-30) becomes

$$\Delta \ln f^* = x_1 \ln \gamma_1^* + x_2 \ln \gamma_2 \tag{5-123}$$

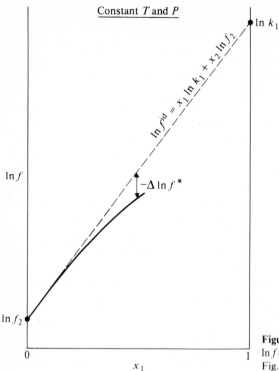

Figure 5-16 Composition dependence of $\ln f$ corresponding to the curves shown in Fig. 5-15.

Derivation of the relation between an activity coefficient and the Gibbs function starts with Eq. (3-56):

$$d\bar{G}_i = RT\, d\ln \hat{f}_i \qquad (\text{const } T)$$

Integration from any standard state of species i at the solution temperature to the state of i in solution at T and P gives

$$\bar{G}_i - G_i^\circ = RT \ln \frac{\hat{f}_i}{f_i^\circ}$$

By addition and subtraction of $RT \ln x_i$ on the right, we get

$$\bar{G}_i - G_i^\circ = RT \ln \frac{\hat{f}_i}{x_i f_i^\circ} + RT \ln x_i$$

With Eq. (5-120), the general definition of an activity coefficient, this becomes

$$\bar{G}_i - G_i^\circ = RT \ln \gamma_i + RT \ln x_i \qquad (5\text{-}124)$$

For an ideal solution, $\hat{f}_i = x_i f_i^\circ$, and $\gamma_i = 1$. Thus

$$\bar{G}_i^{\mathrm{id}} - G_i^\circ = RT \ln x_i$$

The difference between the last two equations is

$$\bar{G}_i - \bar{G}_i^{\text{id}} = RT \ln \gamma_i$$

This result is the same as Eq. (5-32), derived for the special case of solution ideality based on the Lewis-Randall rule. It applies regardless of what standard state is chosen, but both $\bar{G}_i^{\text{id}}$ and γ_i depend upon the choice. By the definition of the partial molar excess Gibbs function, we have

$$\bar{G}_i^E \equiv \bar{G}_i - \bar{G}_i^{\text{id}} = RT \ln \gamma_i$$

Moreover,

$$G^E = \sum x_i \bar{G}_i^E = RT \sum x_i \ln \gamma_i$$

These are Eqs. (5-44) and (5-46), but they are here seen to hold for the *general* standard state.

We now apply the last equation to the binary solution for which the activity coefficients are unsymmetrically normalized. In this case it becomes

$$\left(\frac{G^E}{RT}\right)^* = x_1 \ln \gamma_1^* + x_2 \ln \gamma_2$$

Combining this result with Eq. (5-123), we get

$$\left(\frac{G^E}{RT}\right)^* \equiv \Delta \ln f^* = x_1 \ln \gamma_1^* + x_2 \ln \gamma_2 \qquad (5\text{-}125)$$

where the asterisk signals a choice of standard states according to the unsymmetric convention. Equation (5-125) is a special case of the general expression

$$\boxed{\frac{G^E}{RT} \equiv \Delta \ln f = \sum x_i \ln \gamma_i} \qquad (5\text{-}126)$$

which applies for any set of standard states consistent with the definitions of Eqs. (5-116) and (5-120). This equation is identical with Eq. (5-47), which was presented for the special case of Lewis-Randall standard states.

The treatment we have described for a solute/solvent system through application of the unsymmetric convention for standard states is not the only way to proceed. As an alternative, we may extrapolate the $\ln f$ curve of Fig. 5-16 across the diagram to $x_1 = 1$, as shown in Fig. 5-17. This yields a value for $\ln f_1$, and thus a value of f_1 to serve as the standard-state fugacity for the solute. The location of the extrapolated curve is, of course, arbitrary, and different extrapolations produce different values of f_1. Nevertheless, once the extrapolation is established, f_1 is fixed, and we have a value for the fugacity of the pure solute in a fictitious or hypothetical liquid state. If we adopt this value as a standard-state fugacity, then we can apply the Lewis-Randall rule to the *solute* and the symmetric convention of standard states to the solution.

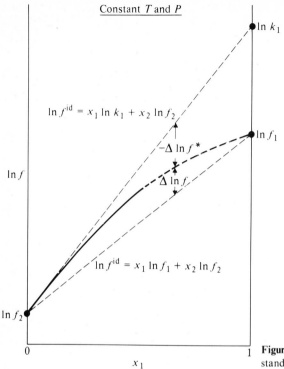

Figure 5-17 Comparison of choices of the standard states for solute species 1.

The significance of the choice of convention for the standard states is illustrated by Fig. 5-17. The upper straight line (unsymmetric convention) represents ideal-solution behavior in the sense of Eq. (5-117), whereas the lower straight line (symmetric convention) represents ideal-solution behavior in the sense of Eq. (5-20), which here becomes

$$\ln f^{id} = x_1 \ln f_1 + x_2 \ln f_2$$

The two treatments are, of course, related. From the geometry of Fig. 5-17, we can, for example, write

$$\Delta \ln f - \Delta \ln f^* = x_1 (\ln k_1 - \ln f_1)$$

or

$$\Delta \ln f = \Delta \ln f^* + x_1 \ln \frac{k_1}{f_1} \qquad (5\text{-}127)$$

Thus, if we have values for k_1 and f_1, we can calculate $\Delta \ln f$ from $\Delta \ln f^*$ and vice versa.

Further relationships become evident when we plot the partial properties $\ln (\hat{f}_i/x_i)$ versus x_1 as shown in Fig. 5-18. This figure is much the same as

Fig. 5-9, but shows additional quantities for solute species 1. It is evident from Fig. 5-18 that the following equations hold:

$$\ln k_1 = \ln f_1 + \ln \gamma_1^\infty \tag{5-128}$$

and

$$\ln \gamma_1^* = \ln \gamma_1 - \ln \gamma_1^\infty \tag{5-129}$$

where

$$\ln \gamma_1^\infty = \lim_{x_1 \to 0} \ln \gamma_1 = - \lim_{x_1 \to 1} \ln \gamma_1^* \tag{5-130}$$

These equations allow complete interconvertibility between unsymmetrically and symmetrically normalized activity coefficients. Thus, there is no inherent advantage to the use of one standard-state convention or the other for a solute/solvent system.

For the solute, both k_1 and f_1 are fugacities of the pure liquid solute in a hypothetical state. Henry's constant k_1 is defined unambiguously by Eq. (3-95); mathematically, there is nothing arbitrary about it. However, as a practical matter, there is often considerable uncertainty attached to the evaluation of a slope at the end point of a curve. Furthermore, the value of Henry's constant depends on the solvent; for a given solute, Henry's constant (and its T and P

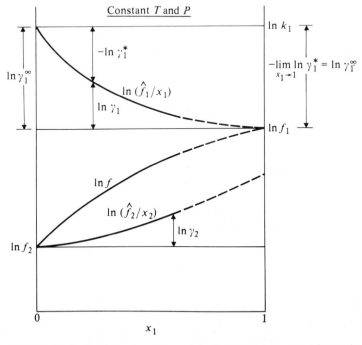

Figure 5-18 Composition dependence of $\ln f$ and related properties for a solute(1)/solvent(2) system.

dependence) must be determined anew for each solvent. The value of f_1, determined by arbitrary extrapolation, is mathematically undefined, and there is no "correct" value. Conversely, there is no incorrect value. Each choice of f_1 is accompanied by its own set of activity coefficients. If pure liquid 1 actually existed, f_1 could be measured, and it would be the same for a given temperature and pressure, regardless of solvent species 2. However, when f_1 is determined by independent extrapolation of two sets of data for two separate solvents, two different values of f_1 most likely result.

Example 5-8 Consider a binary solute(1)/solvent(2) system at constant T and P for which we have a set of data points for $\ln f$ as a function of x_1 up to the limit of solubility of the solute. The data points are shown by the circles of Fig. 5-19. We wish now to find an equation which correlates these values and expresses $\ln f$ as a function of composition. Since the data do not exhibit marked departure from linearity, we attempt to fit them with a quadratic equation of the form

$$\ln f = x_1 \ln f_1 + x_2 \ln f_2 + x_1 x_2 A \tag{A}$$

where A is a constant.

When $x_1 = 0$, this equation reduces to

$$\ln f (x_1 = 0) = \ln f_2$$

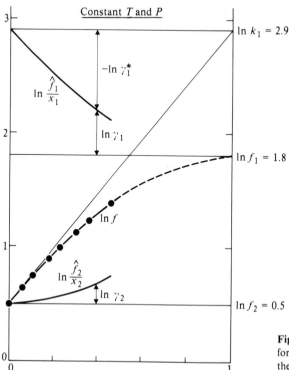

Figure 5-19 Experimental points for $\ln f$ and derived properties for the solute/solvent system of Example 5-8.

This result is, of course, necessary. Since we have the experimental value, $\ln f_2 = 0.5$, we can write

$$\ln f = x_1 \ln f_1 + 0.5x_2 + x_1 x_2 A \qquad \text{(B)}$$

When $x_2 = 0$, this becomes

$$\ln f(x_2 = 0) = \ln f_1$$

However, we do not have an experimental value for $\ln f_1$; it is the value $\ln f$ would have at $x_1 = 1$ were the equation valid for the liquid solution over the entire concentration range. If we find values of $\ln f_1$ and A such that the data points are properly correlated by Eq. (B), then this equation provides a suitable means for extrapolation of the data beyond the solubility limit, and $\ln f_1$ is the value for a hypothetical liquid state of the pure solute. The corresponding value of f_1 is therefore an appropriate standard-state fugacity of the solute.

We find, in fact, that Eq. (B) does correlate the given data when

$$\ln f_1 = 1.8$$

and

$$A = 1.1$$

Equation (B) then becomes

$$\ln f = 1.8x_1 + 0.5x_2 + 1.1x_1 x_2 \qquad \text{(C)}$$

Had we not been able to fit the data by an equation of this form, we would have tried equations of different form until a fit was obtained. Regardless of form, any equation found suitable yields a value for $\ln f_1$.

The partial properties $\ln(\hat{f}_1/x_1)$ and $\ln(\hat{f}_2/x_2)$ are given by Eqs. (3-12) with $M \equiv \ln f$:

$$\ln \frac{\hat{f}_1}{x_1} = \ln f + x_2 \frac{d \ln f}{dx_1} \qquad \text{(D)}$$

and

$$\ln \frac{\hat{f}_2}{x_2} = \ln f - x_1 \frac{d \ln f}{dx_1} \qquad \text{(E)}$$

By differentiation of Eq. (C), we get

$$\frac{d \ln f}{dx_1} = 1.8 - 0.5 + 1.1(x_2 - x_1) = 1.3 + 1.1(x_2 - x_1) \qquad \text{(F)}$$

Substitution of Eqs. (C) and (F) in Eqs. (D) and (E) yields

$$\ln \frac{\hat{f}_1}{x_1} = 1.8 + 1.1x_2^2$$

and

$$\ln \frac{\hat{f}_2}{x_2} = 0.5 + 1.1x_1^2$$

The lines representing these relations are shown on Fig. 5-19 up to the solubility limit. We note that

$$\ln k_1 = \lim_{x_1 \to 0} \ln \frac{\hat{f}_1}{x_1} = 1.8 + 1.1 = 2.9$$

This value is also the intercept at $x_1 = 1$ of the tangent drawn to the $\ln f$ curve at $x_1 = 0$, as indicated on Fig. 5-19. We can also find expressions for $\ln \gamma_1^*$ and $\ln \gamma_2$:

$$\ln \gamma_1^* \equiv \ln \frac{\hat{f}_1}{x_1 k_1} = \ln \frac{\hat{f}_1}{x_1} - \ln k_1$$

and

$$\ln \gamma_2 \equiv \ln \frac{\hat{f}_2}{x_2 f_2} = \ln \frac{\hat{f}_2}{x_2} - \ln f_2$$

The graphical interpretation of these quantities is represented by vertical line segments on Fig. 5-19. Numerically, we have

$$\ln \gamma_1^* = 1.8 + 1.1x_2^2 - 2.9 = 1.1(x_2^2 - 1)$$

and

$$\ln \gamma_2 = 0.5 + 1.1x_1^2 - 0.5 = 1.1x_1^2$$

In addition, by Eq. (5-125)

$$\left(\frac{G^E}{RT}\right)^* \equiv \Delta \ln f^* = x_1 \ln \gamma_1^* + x_2 \ln \gamma_2$$

$$= 1.1x_1(x_2^2 - 1) + 1.1x_1^2 x_2 = -1.1x_1^2$$

The function $(G^E/RT)^*$ is based on the unsymmetric normalization of activity coefficients, and depends in no way on the value of $\ln f_1$.

For a treatment based on symmetrically normalized activity coefficients, we must have an expression for $\ln \gamma_1$, and this requires the value for $\ln f_1$:

$$\ln \gamma_1 \equiv \ln \frac{\hat{f}_1}{x_1 f_1} = \ln \frac{\hat{f}_1}{x_1} - \ln f_1$$

Again, the graphical interpretation of this quantity is clear from Fig. 5-19. Numerically,

$$\ln \gamma_1 = 1.8 + 1.1x_2^2 - 1.8 = 1.1x_2^2$$

By Eq. (5-126), we have

$$\frac{G^E}{RT} \equiv \Delta \ln f = x_1 \ln \gamma_1 + x_2 \ln \gamma_2$$

$$= 1.1x_2^2 x_1 + 1.1x_1^2 x_2 = 1.1x_1 x_2$$

In Fig. 5-20 we show plots of all results for both the symmetric and unsymmetric normalizations of activity coefficients. Note that the curves for $\ln \gamma_1$ and $\ln \gamma_1^*$ are displaced by a constant amount, in accord with Eq. (5-129):

$$\ln \gamma_1 - \ln \gamma_1^* = \ln \gamma_1^\infty = 1.1$$

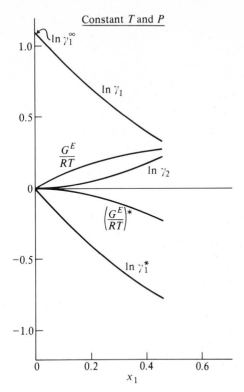

Figure 5-20 Calculated results of Example 5-8.

The curves for G^E/RT and $(G^E/RT)^*$ are displaced from each other in accord with Eq. (5-127), which may be written:

$$\frac{G^E}{RT} - \left(\frac{G^E}{RT}\right)^* = x_1 \ln \frac{k_1}{f_1}$$

Any state of species i has associated with it a full complement of properties; a standard state is in this respect no different from any other. The only standard-state property so far discussed is the fugacity f_i°; it is, as indicated in Eq. (5-112), a function of T and P. Since fugacity is defined in direct relation to the Gibbs function G, it has, like G, the temperature and pressure as its canonical variables (App. A-3). Thus, given f_i° as a function of T and P, one can calculate standard-state values for V_i°, H_i°, S_i°, etc. When the standard state can be chosen as a stable pure liquid with fugacity f_i, then the standard-state properties are those of the real liquid, V_i, H_i, S_i, etc. When the standard state is chosen as the hypothetical pure liquid with fugacity equal to Henry's constant k_i, the other properties for this standard state are found less directly.

In view of Eq. (5-112), Eq. (5-12) can be written more generally as

$$\ln \frac{\hat{f}_i^{id}}{x_i} = \ln f_i^\circ \tag{5-131}$$

This equation, along with the more general forms of Eqs. (5-13) through (5-17) which follow from it, then become particular expressions of the generic equation

$$\bar{M}_i^{id} = M_i^{\circ} \qquad (5\text{-}132)$$

where M may represent $\ln f$, V, Z, H, C_P, U, and C_V. For these properties (but not for G, A, and S) ideality in the sense of the Lewis-Randall (LR) rule implies that M_i° is simply M_i, the property of pure species i at the temperature and pressure of the solution and in the same physical state. Equation (5-132) then becomes

$$M_i^{\circ}(\text{LR}) = M_i = \bar{M}_i^{id}(\text{LR}) \qquad (M \neq G, A, S) \qquad (5\text{-}132a)$$

On the other hand, for ideality in the sense of Henry's law (HL), $f_i^{\circ}(\text{HL}) = k_i$, and Eq. (5-131) becomes

$$\ln \frac{\hat{f}_i^{id}(\text{HL})}{x_i} = \ln k_i$$

Since Henry's law is in fact valid for species i in any real solution of non-electrolytes as i becomes infinitely dilute, we may write (see Fig. 5-9):

$$\left(\ln \frac{\hat{f}_i}{x_i} \right)^{\infty} = \ln k_i$$

From these last two equations, we see that

$$\ln k_i = \left(\ln \frac{\hat{f}_i}{x_i} \right)^{\infty} = \ln \frac{\hat{f}_i^{id}(\text{HL})}{x_i}$$

The same reasoning applied to the generic property M (see Fig. 5-8) allows us to write Eq. (5-132) as

$$M_i^{\circ}(\text{HL}) = \bar{M}_i^{\infty} = \bar{M}_i^{id}(\text{HL}) \qquad (M \neq G, A, S) \qquad (5\text{-}132b)$$

Thus, for example, we have

$$V_i^{\circ}(\text{HL}) = \bar{V}_i^{\infty}$$

and

$$H_i^{\circ}(\text{HL}) = \bar{H}_i^{\infty}$$

We see from Eqs. (5-132a) and (5-132b) that in either case $\bar{M}_i^{id}$ is independent of composition, and for a binary solution

$$M^{id} = x_1 \bar{M}_1^{id} + x_2 \bar{M}_2^{id}$$

must be represented by a straight line on a diagram of M versus x_1, for only then are the tangent intercepts (which represent $\bar{M}_1^{id}$ and $\bar{M}_2^{id}$) independent of composition. When standard states based on the Lewis-Randall rule are chosen for both constituents, then

$$M^{id} = x_1 M_1 + x_2 M_2 \qquad (M \neq G, A, S)$$

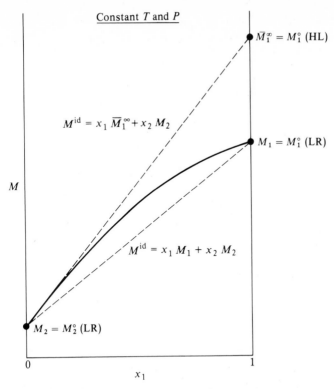

Figure 5-21 Two expressions of ideal-solution behavior for a binary solution in relation to the experimental M versus x_1 curve ($M \neq G$, A, or S).

When the standard state for species 1 is based on Henry's law and that for species 2 on the Lewis-Randall rule, then

$$M^{id} = x_1 \bar{M}_1^{\infty} + x_2 M_2 \qquad (M \neq G, A, S)$$

These equations for ideal behavior are shown in relation to an experimental M-versus-x_1 curve in Fig. 5-21. The special case for which $M = \ln f$ is represented by Fig. 5-17.

One must not conclude from these results that for species i the standard state based on Henry's law is in fact the state of species i at infinite dilution or that all properties for the two states are the same. Were this true, we would have equality of $G_i^{\circ}(\text{HL})$ with $\bar{G}_i^{\infty}$ and of $S_i^{\circ}(\text{HL})$ with $\bar{S}_i^{\infty}$. However, if we base Eq. (5-124) on Henry's-law standard state, it becomes

$$\bar{G}_i - G_i^{\circ}(\text{HL}) = RT \ln \gamma_i^* + RT \ln x_i$$

In the limit as $x_i \to 0$, we have $\bar{G}_i \to \bar{G}_i^{\infty}$ and $\gamma_i^* \to 1$; therefore,

$$\bar{G}_i^{\infty} - G_i^{\circ}(\text{HL}) = RT \ln 0 = -\infty$$

In addition

$$\bar{S}_i^\infty - S_i^\circ(\text{HL}) = \frac{\bar{H}_i^\infty - \bar{G}_i^\infty}{T} - \frac{H_i^\circ(\text{HL}) - G_i^\circ(\text{HL})}{T}$$

Since $\bar{H}_i^\infty = H_i^\circ(\text{HL})$, this becomes

$$\bar{S}_i^\infty - S_i^\circ(\text{HL}) = \frac{-[\bar{G}_i^\infty - G_i^\circ(\text{HL})]}{T} = \infty$$

Not only do we have $G_i^\circ(\text{HL}) \neq \bar{G}_i^\infty$ and $S_i^\circ(\text{HL}) \neq \bar{S}_i^\infty$, but in each case we see that the values for the two states differ by infinity.

Since the standard states based on Henry's law and on the Lewis-Randall rule are states of a pure species, we may integrate Eq. (3-46) between the two standard states; this gives

$$G_i^\circ(\text{HL}) - G_i^\circ(\text{LR}) = RT \ln \frac{f_i^\circ(\text{HL})}{f_i^\circ(\text{LR})}$$

or

$$G_i^\circ(\text{HL}) = G_i + RT \ln \frac{k_i}{f_i}$$

Since $S = (H - G)/T$, we can also write

$$S_i^\circ(\text{HL}) - S_i = \frac{H_i^\circ(\text{HL}) - H_i - [G_i^\circ(\text{HL}) - G_i]}{T}$$

which reduces to

$$S_i^\circ(\text{HL}) = S_i + \frac{\overline{\Delta H_i^\infty}}{T} - R \ln \frac{k_i}{f_i}$$

These equations contrast with those from Eq. (5-132b)

$$M_i^\circ(\text{HL}) - M_i = \bar{M}_i^\infty - M_i$$

or

$$M_i^\circ(\text{HL}) = M_i + \overline{\Delta M_i^\infty} \qquad (M \neq G, A, S)$$

For pure i Eq. (3-87) may be written

$$d \ln f_i = \frac{H_i' - H_i}{RT^2} dT + \frac{V_i}{RT} dP$$

If the standard state of species i is a state of pure i (real or hypothetical) at the T and P of the solution, then application of this equation to the standard state yields

$$d \ln f_i^\circ = \frac{H_i' - H_i^\circ}{RT^2} dT + \frac{V_i^\circ}{RT} dP$$

Thus, the temperature and pressure dependence of the standard-state fugacity are given by

$$\left(\frac{\partial \ln f_i^{\circ}}{\partial T}\right)_P = \frac{H_i' - H_i^{\circ}}{RT^2} \qquad (5\text{-}133)$$

and

$$\left(\frac{\partial \ln f_i^{\circ}}{\partial P}\right)_T = \frac{V_i^{\circ}}{RT} \qquad (5\text{-}134)$$

When $f_i^{\circ} = k_i$, these become

$$\left(\frac{\partial \ln k_i}{\partial T}\right)_P = \frac{H_i' - \bar{H}_i^{\infty}}{RT^2} \qquad (5\text{-}135)$$

and

$$\left(\frac{\partial \ln k_i}{\partial P}\right)_T = \frac{\bar{V}_i^{\infty}}{RT} \qquad (5\text{-}136)$$

When pure i exists as a stable liquid at the T and P of the solution, then $f_i^{\circ} = f_i$, $H_i^{\circ} = H_i$, and $V_i^{\circ} = V_i$, and each of these quantities can be measured by experiment; there is no difficulty beyond that of accurate measurement. On the other hand, if $f_i^{\circ} = f_i$ represents an extrapolated value, as shown for species 1 in Figs. 5-17 through 5-19, then pure species i does not exist as a liquid, and experimental values of $H_i^{\circ} = H_i$ and $V_i^{\circ} = V_i$ cannot be obtained. This problem is inherent in the use of standard-state fugacities obtained by arbitrary extrapolation.

Example 5-9 We presented in Secs 5-1 through 5-6 a large number of definitions and equations for property changes of mixing, excess functions, and their differentials and derivatives. However, all of these expressions presumed the use of Lewis-Randall standard states. In this section, we have seen how the more general definitions of ideal-solution behavior and of the activity coefficient [Eqs. (5-112) and (5-120)] lead to a correspondingly general expression relating G^E and the $\ln \gamma_i$:

$$\frac{G^E}{RT} = \sum x_i \ln \gamma_i \qquad (5\text{-}47), (5\text{-}126)$$

Although Eqs. (5-47) and (5-126) are formally identical, one must remember that numerical values of the terms depend on the choice of standard states. We illustrate in this example that similar formal identities also obtain between other equations for the special and general cases.

The *general* property change of mixing ΔM is defined by the expression

$$\boxed{\Delta M \equiv M - \sum x_i M_i^{\circ}} \qquad (A)$$

Equation (A) is merely an extension of Eq. (5-1), and it includes as a special case Eq. (5-116), obtained by the assignment $M \equiv \ln f$. Note, however, that the association of ΔM with an actual property change resulting from the standard mixing process (see Sec. 5-1) must be abandoned if Lewis-Randall standard states are not adopted for all species.

It has already been remarked that the general definition of ideal-solution behavior leads to the generic relation

$$\boxed{\bar{M}_i^{id} = M_i^\circ} \qquad (M \neq G, A, S) \tag{5-132}$$

If $M \neq G, A, S$ we thus find for arbitrary standard states that

$$\Delta M^{id} \equiv M^{id} - \sum x_i M_i^\circ$$
$$= \sum x_i \bar{M}_i^{id} - \sum x_i M_i^\circ$$
$$= \sum x_i M_i^\circ - \sum x_i M_i^\circ$$

or

$$\boxed{\Delta M^{id} = 0} \qquad (M \neq G, A, S) \tag{B}$$

Equation (B) is identical with Eq. (5-19). We have shown that [see Eq. (5-124) et seq.]

$$\bar{G}_i^{id} - G_i^\circ = RT \ln x_i$$

Thus, since $\Delta G^{id} \equiv G^{id} - \sum x_i G_i^\circ = \sum x_i(\bar{G}_i^{id} - G_i^\circ)$, it follows that

$$\boxed{\Delta G^{id} = RT \sum x_i \ln x_i} \tag{C}$$

It is also readily demonstrated that $\Delta A^{id} = \Delta G^{id}$, and that

$$\boxed{\Delta S^{id} = -R \sum x_i \ln x_i} \tag{D}$$

Equations (C) and (D) are identical with Eqs. (5-24) and (5-28), derived previously for the special case of Lewis-Randall standard states.

The excess functions are defined as before. Thus

$$\boxed{M^E \equiv M - M^{id}} \tag{5-35}$$

from which we obtain

$$M^E = (M - \sum x_i M_i^\circ) - (M^{id} - \sum x_i M_i^\circ)$$

or, by Eq. (A),

$$\boxed{M^E = \Delta M^E \equiv \Delta M - \Delta M^{id}} \tag{E}$$

Equation (E) is formally identical with Eq. (5-40). Thus, by Eq. (B) we find again that

$$\boxed{M^E = \Delta M} \qquad (M \neq G, A, S) \tag{F}$$

and also that

$$G^E = \Delta G - RT \sum x_i \ln x_i \qquad \text{(G)}$$

$$A^E = \Delta A - RT \sum x_i \ln x_i \qquad \text{(H)}$$

$$S^E = \Delta S + R \sum x_i \ln x_i \qquad \text{(I)}$$

For arbitrary standard states, the differential equations (5-54) and (5-55) still hold. Moreover, if we define the activity $\hat{a}_i$ as

$$\hat{a}_i \equiv \hat{f}_i / f_i^\circ = \gamma_i x_i \qquad \text{(J)}$$

then the differential equations (5-50) and (5-51) also still hold. Finally, for arbitrary standard states, the following relations among the excess functions remain valid:

$$H^E = G^E + TS^E \qquad \text{(K)}$$

$$H^E = -RT^2 \left[\frac{\partial(G^E/RT)}{\partial T} \right]_{P,\,x} \qquad \text{(L)}$$

$$S^E = -(\partial G^E/\partial T)_{P,\,x} \qquad \text{(M)}$$

$$V^E = (\partial G^E/\partial P)_{T,\,x} \qquad \text{(N)}$$

Equations (K) through (N) are formal extensions of Eqs. (5-63), (5-61), (5-62), and (5-71). Again, numerical values depend on the choice of standard states.

We have considered thus far only the case of a single-solute/single-solvent system. However, one often encounters in practice multisolute/multisolvent systems, and extension to these systems of the methods applicable to the binary case introduces additional problems. Consider the least complex situation: a ternary solution in which species 1 and 2 are miscible liquid solvents and species 3 is a solute of limited solubility in the mixed solvent. For this case, Fig. 5-22 depicts a representative $\ln f$ surface at fixed T and P plotted above a mole-fraction grid. The surface is incomplete, because no experimental values exist in the neighborhood of the pure solute.

Tangents drawn at $x_3 = 0$ to the lines representing the 1-3 and 2-3 binary solutions yield intercepts on the $x_3 = 1$ axis equal to $\ln k_{3,\,1}$ and $\ln k_{3,\,2}$. These are the logarithms of Henry's constant for solute 3 in each pure solvent. The values differ, because Henry's constant depends on the nature of the solvent. Thus, for the mixed solvent Henry's constant k_3 is a function of solvent composition and has the limiting values $k_{3,\,1}$ and $k_{3,\,2}$. A general expression for Henry's constant in the mixed solvent is found from Eq. (J) of Example 3-4: Setting $M \equiv \ln f$ in this equation, we get

$$\ln \frac{\hat{f}_3}{x_3} = \ln f + (1 - x_3) \left(\frac{\partial \ln f}{\partial x_3} \right)_{T,\,P,\,x_1/x_2}$$

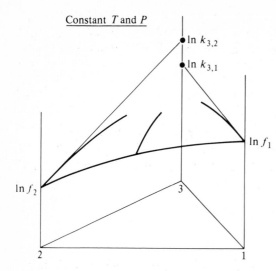

Figure 5-22 A representative $\ln f$ surface for a ternary system in which species 3 is a solute of limited solubility.

In the limit as $x_3 \to 0$, this becomes

$$\ln k_3 \equiv \lim_{x_3 \to 0} \ln \frac{\hat{f}_3}{x_3} = \ln f_{12} + \left(\frac{\partial \ln f}{\partial x_3}\right)^{\infty}_{T, P, x_1/x_2} \tag{5-137}$$

where $\ln f_{12}$ is a value for the mixed solvent and the derivative is at infinite dilution of species 3. Thus, both quantities are evaluated along the curve representing the 1-2 binary solution, and both depend on solvent composition.

The graphical interpretation of Eq. (5-137) is indicated by Fig. 5-23. A vertical plane containing the $x_3 = 1$ axis also contains a set of points for which x_1/x_2 has a unique value. In particular, when $x_3 \to 0$, x_1 and x_2 are the mole fractions

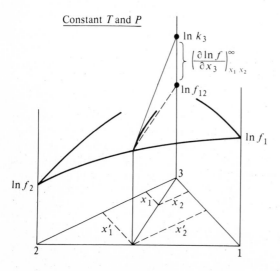

Figure 5-23 Graphical interpretation of Eq. (5-137) for Henry's constant k_3 of the solute in a ternary system.

of the mixed solvent in which the solute is infinitely dilute. One vertical plane and its line of intersection with the $\ln f$ surface are shown in Fig. 5-23. The tangent to the $\ln f$ surface drawn in this plane at $x_3 = 0$ has a slope equal to the value of the derivative in Eq. (5-137). Since the horizontal distance from the point of tangency at $x_3 = 0$ to the $x_3 = 1$ axis is unity, the vertical distance indicated along the $x_3 = 1$ axis also represents the value of this derivative. In view of Eq. (5-137), we see from the construction shown that the intercept of the tangent on the $x_3 = 1$ axis is $\ln k_3$. This value clearly depends on the mixed-solvent composition, and takes on the limiting values $\ln k_{3,2}$ at $x_1 = 0$ and $\ln k_{3,1}$ at $x_1 = 1$, as shown in Fig. 5-22.

If Henry's constant k_3 is to serve as a standard-state fugacity for species 3, we must either select a *particular* value of k_3 or let the standard-state fugacity vary with solvent composition. If for given T and P a *particular* value of Henry's constant $k_3^\dagger$ is defined as the standard-state fugacity of species 3, then

$$\gamma_3^* \equiv \frac{\hat{f}_3}{x_3 k_3^\dagger}$$

and

$$\lim_{x_3 \to 0} \gamma_3^* = \frac{\lim\limits_{x_3 \to 0} (\hat{f}_3/x_3)}{k_3^\dagger} = \frac{k_3}{k_3^\dagger}$$

The general limit of γ_3^* at infinite dilution is therefore not unity for this choice of standard state; only at the particular solvent composition for which $k_3 \equiv k_3^\dagger$ does $\lim_{x_3 \to 0} \gamma_3^* = 1$.

If we abandon the concept of a standard state for species 3 as a *particular* state of this species for given T and P, then we may choose the standard-state fugacity as k_3, and accept the fact of its dependence on solvent composition. Van Ness and Abbott (1979) discuss the complications which ensue as a result of this choice. The best one can say is that it preserves the normalization property which makes

$$\lim_{x_3 \to 0} \gamma_3^* = \lim_{x_3 \to 0} \frac{\hat{f}_3}{x_3 k_3} = 1$$

for all solvent compositions.

Although use of Henry's constant as a standard-state fugacity for the solute in mixed solvents has not proved generally attractive, Henry's law itself is of unquestioned value. For solutions dilute in solute species i, Henry's law provides the approximate relation

$$\hat{f}_i = k_i x_i \tag{5-138}$$

where Henry's constant k_i is a function of temperature, pressure, and solvent composition. Because of the considerable experimental effort required for measurement of Henry's constants, the relation of k_i for solute i in a mixed solvent to the $k_{i,j}$ for solute i in the individual solvent species j is of potential value. The derivation of several such relationships follows.

Consider an experiment wherein we start with a quantity of solute-free solvent and make successive additions to it of the solute species i. During this process the quantity of solvent remains constant, as does the *solute-free* composition of the solution. With solvent species identified by subscript j and solute-free mole fractions denoted by x'_j, we have

$$x'_j \equiv \frac{n_j}{\sum\limits_{j \neq i} n_j} = \frac{n_j/n}{\sum\limits_{j \neq i} (n_j/n)} = \frac{x_j}{\sum\limits_{j \neq i} x_j}$$

Clearly

$$\sum\limits_{j \neq i} x'_j = 1$$

For *all* species, including solute i,

$$x_i + \sum\limits_{j \neq i} x_j = 1$$

or

$$\sum\limits_{j \neq i} x_j = 1 - x_i$$

Therefore

$$x'_j = \frac{x_j}{1 - x_i}$$

or

$$x_j = (1 - x_i)x'_j \tag{5-139}$$

and

$$\left(\frac{\partial x_j}{\partial x_i}\right)_{x'_j} = -x'_j = \frac{-x_j}{1 - x_i} \tag{5-140}$$

If the process considered occurs at constant T and P, then Eq. (3-4) for a total property change can be written

$$d(nM) = \sum \bar{M}_k \, dn_k \qquad \text{(const } T \text{ and } P)$$

where subscript k denotes the general species. For $n = 1$, $n_k = x_k$, and this equation becomes

$$dM = \sum \bar{M}_k \, dx_k \qquad \text{(const } T \text{ and } P)$$

Distinguishing now between solute species i and the solvent species j, we have

$$dM = \bar{M}_i \, dx_i + \sum\limits_{j \neq i} \bar{M}_j \, dx_j \qquad \text{(const } T \text{ and } P)$$

Division of this equation by dx_i and restriction to constant solute-free composition give

$$\left(\frac{\partial M}{\partial x_i}\right)_{x'_j} = \bar{M}_i + \sum_{j \neq i} \bar{M}_j \left(\frac{\partial x_j}{\partial x_i}\right)_{x'_j}$$

with the implicit understanding that the derivatives are at constant T and P. Substitution for the partial derivatives on the right by Eq. (5-140) yields

$$\left(\frac{\partial M}{\partial x_i}\right)_{x'_j} = \bar{M}_i - \frac{1}{1 - x_i} \sum_{j \neq i} x_j \bar{M}_j \qquad (5\text{-}141)$$

By Eq. (3-6), we have

$$M = \sum x_k \bar{M}_k = x_i \bar{M}_i + \sum_{j \neq i} x_j \bar{M}_j$$

or

$$\sum_{j \neq i} x_j \bar{M}_j = M - x_i \bar{M}_i$$

Substitution for this quantity in Eq. (5-141) gives

$$\left(\frac{\partial M}{\partial x_i}\right)_{x'_j} = \bar{M}_i - \frac{M - x_i \bar{M}_i}{1 - x_i}$$

from which we get

$$\boxed{\bar{M}_i = M + (1 - x_i)\left(\frac{\partial M}{\partial x_i}\right)_{x'_j, T, P}} \qquad (5\text{-}142)$$

This result is a generalization of Eq. (J) of Example 3-4, and is valid for solute i dissolved in a solvent mixture of any number of species j.

If we apply Eq. (5-142) to the property $M \equiv \ln f$, it becomes (again with constancy of T and P for the derivative understood):

$$\ln \frac{\hat{f}_i}{x_i} = \ln f + (1 - x_i)\left(\frac{\partial \ln f}{\partial x_i}\right)_{x'_j} \qquad (5\text{-}143)$$

In the limit when the solute i becomes infinitely dilute, we have $x_i = 0$ and $\hat{f}_i/x_i \equiv k_i$; Eq. (5-143) then becomes

$$\ln k_i = \ln f' + \left(\frac{\partial \ln f}{\partial x_i}\right)_{x'_j}^{\infty} \qquad (5\text{-}144)$$

where f' is the fugacity of the solute-free mixture and the superscript ∞ indicates a value of the derivative at infinite dilution of solute species i. Both $\ln f'$ and the derivative are functions of the solvent (solute-free) composition at constant T and P. Equation (5-137) is an example of a particular application of this relation. Equation (5-144) is a general expression for Henry's constant for solute species i dissolved in any solvent mixture. In the special case where the solvent is pure species j, it becomes

$$\ln k_{i,j} = \ln f_j + \left(\frac{\partial \ln f_{ij}}{\partial x_i}\right)^{\infty} \tag{5-145}$$

where f_j is the fugacity of pure solvent species j and f_{ij} represents the fugacity of the i-j binary mixture. Multiplication of this equation by x'_j and summation over all solvent species j gives

$$\sum x'_j \ln k_{i,j} = \sum x'_j \ln f_j + \sum x'_j \left(\frac{\partial \ln f_{ij}}{\partial x_i}\right)^{\infty} \quad (j \neq i)$$

Subtracting this expression from Eq. (5-144), we get

$$\ln k_i - \sum x'_j \ln k_{i,j} = \ln f' - \sum x'_j \ln f_j + \left(\frac{\partial \ln f}{\partial x_i}\right)^{\infty}_{x'_j}$$

$$- \sum x'_j \left(\frac{\partial \ln f_{ij}}{\partial x_i}\right)^{\infty} \quad (j \neq i)$$

The first two terms on the right represent $\Delta \ln f' \equiv (G^E/RT)'$, the dimensionless excess Gibbs function for the solute-free mixture. Thus, we may rewrite this equation as

$$\ln k_i = \sum_{j \neq i} x'_j \ln k_{i,j} + \left(\frac{G^E}{RT}\right)' + \mathscr{D}^{\infty} \tag{5-146a}$$

where

$$\mathscr{D}^{\infty} \equiv \left(\frac{\partial \ln f}{\partial x_i}\right)^{\infty}_{x'_j} - \sum_{j \neq i} x'_j \left(\frac{\partial \ln f_{ij}}{\partial x_i}\right)^{\infty} \tag{5-146b}$$

For a ternary mixture in which species 3 is the solute, Eqs. (5-146) become

$$\ln k_3 = x'_1 \ln k_{3,1} + x'_2 \ln k_{3,2} + \frac{G^E_{12}}{RT} + \mathscr{D}^{\infty} \tag{5-147}$$

with

$$\mathscr{D}^{\infty} \equiv \left(\frac{\partial \ln f}{\partial x_3}\right)^{\infty}_{x'_1, x'_2} - x'_1 \left(\frac{\partial \ln f_{31}}{\partial x_3}\right)^{\infty} - x'_2 \left(\frac{\partial \ln f_{32}}{\partial x_3}\right)^{\infty}$$

The various quantities appearing in this equation are shown in Fig. 5-24, which is a composite of Fig. 5-22 and 5-23. The slopes of the tangents drawn to the $\ln f$ surface at $x_3 = 0$ are equal to the values of the derivatives in the expression for $\mathscr{D}^{\infty}$.

The three truncated curves of Fig. 5-24, lying in the $\ln f$ surface, can be extrapolated to the $x_3 = 1$ axis. Independent extrapolations likely produce three

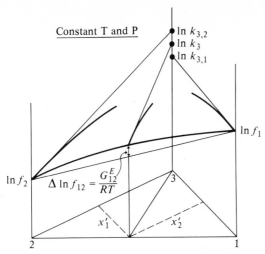

Figure 5-24 Graphical representation of the quantities in Eq. (5-147).

different intercepts, as indicated by Fig. 5-25. All represent $\ln f_3$ values for the pure solute in hypothetical states. If f_3 is to serve as a standard-state fugacity, we prefer a single value; otherwise we encounter the same problems that attend the use of Henry's constants as standard-state fugacities. To realize this objective, we can extrapolate the $\ln f$ *surface* to intercept the $x_3 = 1$ axis at a point, as shown in Fig. 5-26. Such extrapolation is, of course, arbitrary, and the value of f_3 obtained depends on the details of extrapolation. However, once a particular value of f_3 is established for a given system, lack of uniqueness does not hinder its use as a standard-state fugacity for that system within the framework of the symmetric convention for standard states.

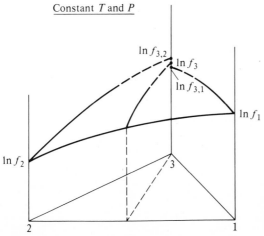

Figure 5-25 Independent extrapolations of $\ln f$ curves at constant x_1' and x_2' to $x_3 = 1$.

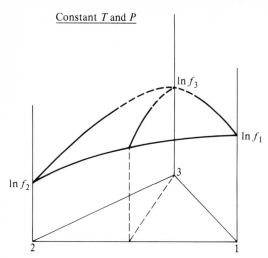

Constant T and P

Figure 5-26 Extrapolation of the $\ln f$ surface to $x_3 = 1$.

Given such a standard-state value for the solute, we may develop alternative expressions for $\mathcal{D}^\infty$ in Eq. (5-146b). By definition

$$\Delta \ln f \equiv \ln f - \sum x_k \ln f_k$$

where subscript k is the general index identifying a species. Taking species i as the solute and species j as solvents, we rewrite this equation as

$$\Delta \ln f = \ln f - \sum_{j \neq i} x_j \ln f_j - x_i \ln f_i$$

or

$$\ln f = \Delta \ln f + \sum_{j \neq i} x_j \ln f_j + x_i \ln f_i$$

With Eq. (5-139), this becomes

$$\ln f = \Delta \ln f + (1 - x_i) \sum_{j \neq i} x_j' \ln f_j + x_i \ln f_i$$

Differentiation at constant solute-free composition (and at constant T and P) yields

$$\left(\frac{\partial \ln f}{\partial x_i} \right)_{x_j'} = \left(\frac{\partial \Delta \ln f}{\partial x_i} \right)_{x_j'} - \sum_{j \neq i} x_j' \ln f_j + \ln f_i$$

In the limit as $x_i \to 0$, this becomes

$$\left(\frac{\partial \ln f}{\partial x_i} \right)_{x_j'}^\infty = \left(\frac{\partial \Delta \ln f}{\partial x_i} \right)_{x_j'}^\infty - \sum_{j \neq i} x_j' \ln f_j + \ln f_i \qquad (5\text{-}148)$$

Application of Eq. (5-148) to the special case where the solvent is a single species j gives

$$\left(\frac{\partial \ln f_{ij}}{\partial x_i}\right)^{\infty} = \left(\frac{\partial \Delta \ln f_{ij}}{\partial x_i}\right)^{\infty} - \ln f_j + \ln f_i \qquad (j \neq i)$$

where the subscript ij refers to the i-j binary mixture. Multiplication of this equation by x'_j and summation over all $j \neq i$ yield

$$\sum_{j \neq i} x'_j \left(\frac{\partial \ln f_{ij}}{\partial x_i}\right)^{\infty} = \sum_{j \neq i} x'_j \left(\frac{\partial \Delta \ln f_{ij}}{\partial x_i}\right)^{\infty} - \sum_{j \neq i} x'_j \ln f_j + \ln f_i \qquad (5\text{-}149)$$

The difference between Eq. (5-148) and Eq. (5-149) is $\mathscr{D}^{\infty}$ as given by Eq. (5-146b). Thus

$$\mathscr{D}^{\infty} = \left(\frac{\partial \Delta \ln f}{\partial x_i}\right)^{\infty}_{x'_j} - \sum_{j \neq i} x'_j \left(\frac{\partial \Delta \ln f_{ij}}{\partial x_i}\right)^{\infty} \qquad (5\text{-}150)$$

However, by Eq. (5-126) we have in general that

$$\Delta \ln f \equiv \frac{G^E}{RT} \equiv g$$

where we introduce the symbol g to simplify notation. Equation (5-150) may now be written

$$\boxed{\mathscr{D}^{\infty} = \left(\frac{\partial g}{\partial x_i}\right)^{\infty}_{x'_j} - \sum_{j \neq i} x'_j \left(\frac{\partial g_{ij}}{\partial x_i}\right)^{\infty}} \qquad (5\text{-}151)$$

For a ternary mixture of solute species 3 and solvent species 1 and 2, this becomes

$$\mathscr{D}^{\infty} = \left(\frac{\partial g}{\partial x_3}\right)^{\infty}_{x'_1, x'_2} - x'_1 \left(\frac{\partial g_{31}}{\partial x_3}\right)^{\infty} - x'_2 \left(\frac{\partial g_{32}}{\partial x_3}\right)^{\infty} \qquad (5\text{-}152)$$

All derivatives in Eqs. (5-150) through (5-152) are understood to be at constant T and P.

The derivation of these general equations for $\mathscr{D}^{\infty}$ is based on the symmetrical convention for standard states, and presumes a single standard-state value for each species at the T and P of the system. For a solvent species, f_j is the fugacity of pure j in its real state as a liquid; for the solute, f_i is the fugacity of species i as a *hypothetical* pure liquid. In the subtraction that yields Eq. (5-150), both the $\ln f_j$ terms and $\ln f_i$ disappear; in the resulting equations, the dependence of $\mathscr{D}^{\infty}$ on the standard states is implicit. Consider, for example, a ternary mixture for which

$$\Delta \ln f \equiv g = \ln f - (x_1 \ln f_1 + x_2 \ln f_2 + x_3 \ln f_3)$$

The $\ln f$ surface shown in Fig. 5-26 passes through the terminal points $\ln f_1$, $\ln f_2$, and $\ln f_3$, and the expression in parentheses is the equation of a plane surface passing through these same points. Thus, $\Delta \ln f$ is measured from this plane, and clearly depends upon the arbitrary extrapolation of the $\ln f$ surface that establishes the $\ln f_3$ value. Any empirical expression for $\Delta \ln f \equiv g$ based on the symmetrical convention for standard states implies a fit of the $\ln f$ data consistent with an extrapolation of the $\ln f$ surface to a particular value of $\ln f_3$, whether or not the value is stated or known.

Example 5-10 Suppose that the excess Gibbs function for a ternary mixture in which species 3 is the solute can be expressed as

$$g \equiv \frac{G^E}{RT} \equiv \Delta \ln f = x_1 x_2 A_{12} + x_1 x_3 A_{13} + x_2 x_3 A_{23} \tag{A}$$

where A_{12}, A_{13}, and A_{23} are constants for a given T and P. With Eq. (5-139), Eq. (A) becomes

$$g = A_{12} x_1' x_2' (1 - x_3)^2 + A_{13} x_1' (1 - x_3) x_3 + A_{23} x_2' (1 - x_3) x_3$$

Differentiation gives

$$\left(\frac{\partial g}{\partial x_3} \right)_{x_1', x_2'} = -2 A_{12} x_1' x_2' (1 - x_3) + A_{13} x_1' (1 - 2x_3) + A_{23} x_2' (1 - 2x_3)$$

which, for $x_3 = 0$, reduces to

$$\left(\frac{\partial g}{\partial x_3} \right)_{x_1', x_2'}^\infty = -2 A_{12} x_1' x_2' + A_{13} x_1' + A_{23} x_2' \tag{B}$$

When $x_2' = 0$, $x_1' = 1$, and Eq. (B) becomes

$$\left(\frac{\partial g_{31}}{\partial x_3} \right)^\infty = A_{13} \tag{C}$$

Similarly, when $x_1' = 0$, $x_2' = 1$, and

$$\left(\frac{\partial g_{32}}{\partial x_3} \right)^\infty = A_{23} \tag{D}$$

Substitution of Eqs. (B), (C), and (D) into Eq. (5-152) gives

$$\mathscr{D}^\infty = -2 A_{12} x_1' x_2' \tag{E}$$

In Eq. (5-147), the term G_{12}^E / RT becomes

$$g_{12} = A_{12} x_1' x_2'$$

and this equation reduces to

$$\ln k_3 = x_1' \ln k_{3,1} + x_2' \ln k_{3,2} - A_{12} x_1' x_2' \tag{F}$$

The result expressed by Eq. (F) is, of course, dependent on the validity of Eq. (A), which for the 3-1 and 3-2 binary systems implies the equations:

$$g_{31} \equiv \Delta \ln f_{31} = x_1 x_3 A_{13} \tag{G}$$

and

$$g_{32} \equiv \Delta \ln f_{32} = x_2 x_3 A_{23} \tag{H}$$

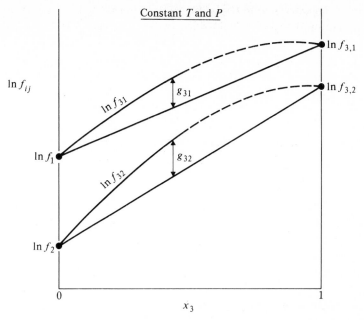

Figure 5-27 Correlations of $\ln f_{31}$ and $\ln f_{32}$ which do not yield a common value of $\ln f_3$ and which therefore do not satisfy the requirements for application of Eq. (F) of Example 5-10.

Making use of the definition of $\Delta \ln f$, we may rewrite these equations as

$$\ln f_{31} = x_1 x_3 A_{13} + x_1 \ln f_1 + x_3 \ln f_3 \tag{I}$$

and

$$\ln f_{32} = x_2 x_3 A_{23} + x_2 \ln f_2 + x_3 \ln f_3 \tag{J}$$

A fundamental requirement for application of Eq. (5-152), from which Eq. (F) is derived, is that Eqs. (I) and (J) be capable of fitting the 3-1 and 3-2 binary data with the same value of $\ln f_3$. The correlations represented in Fig. 5-27, with g_{31} and g_{32} given by Eqs. (G) and (H) are *not* adequate for the validity of Eq. (F). The general requirement is evident when we eliminate $\Delta \ln f$ in Eq. (A) by its definition, and write:

$$\ln f = x_1 x_2 A_{12} + x_1 x_3 A_{13} + x_2 x_3 A_{23} + x_1 \ln f_1 + x_2 \ln f_2 + x_3 \ln f_3$$

All data for the ternary mixture must be capable of correlation by this equation with a single value of $\ln f_3$. If this is possible, then Eq. (F) is a valid result.

Equation (5-146a), a general expression for $\ln k_i$, may be combined with the expression for $\mathscr{L}^\infty$ given by Eq. (5-151):

$$\ln k_i = \sum_{j \neq i} x_j' \ln k_{i,j} + g' + \left(\frac{\partial g}{\partial x_i}\right)_{x_j'}^\infty - \sum_{j \neq i} x_j' \left(\frac{\partial g_{ij}}{\partial x_i}\right)^\infty \tag{5-153}$$

where we have replaced $(G^E/RT)'$ by g'. Equation (5-142) in the limit of infinite dilution of species i becomes

$$\bar{M}_i^\infty = M' + \left(\frac{\partial M}{\partial x_i}\right)_{x'_j}^\infty$$

If we let $M \equiv G^E/RT \equiv g$, then $M' \equiv g'$ and $\bar{M}_i^\infty \equiv (\bar{G}_i^E/RT)^\infty = \ln \gamma_i^\infty$. We may therefore write

$$\ln \gamma_i^\infty = g' + \left(\frac{\partial g}{\partial x_i}\right)_{x'_j}^\infty$$

and Eq. (5-153) becomes

$$\ln k_i = \sum_{j \neq i} x'_j \ln k_{i,j} + \ln \gamma_i^\infty - \sum_{j \neq i} x'_j \left(\frac{\partial g_{ij}}{\partial x_i}\right)^\infty \qquad (5\text{-}154)$$

For an i-j binary mixture, Eq. (5-38a) may be written

$$\bar{M}_{i,j}^E = M_{ij}^E + x_j \left(\frac{\partial M_{ij}^E}{\partial x_i}\right)$$

In the limit as $x_i \to 0$, $x_j \to 1$, and $M_{ij}^E \to 0$; thus

$$(\bar{M}_{i,j}^E)^\infty = \left(\frac{\partial M_{ij}^E}{\partial x_i}\right)^\infty$$

For $M_{ij}^E \equiv G_{ij}^E/RT \equiv g_{ij}$, this becomes

$$\ln \gamma_{i,j}^\infty = \left(\frac{\partial g_{ij}}{\partial x_i}\right)^\infty$$

Equation (5-154) may now be written

$$\boxed{\ln k_i = \sum_{j \neq i} x'_j \ln k_{i,j} + \ln \gamma_i^\infty - \sum_{j \neq i} x'_j \ln \gamma_{i,j}^\infty} \qquad (5\text{-}155)$$

All activity coefficients in this equation are, of course, based on the same standard-state fugacity f_i.

Equation (5-155) can, in fact, be derived much more directly. By definition

$$k_i \equiv \lim_{x_i \to 0} (\hat{f}_i/x_i) \qquad (3\text{-}95)$$

and

$$\gamma_i \equiv \frac{(\hat{f}_i/x_i)}{f_i} \qquad (5\text{-}30)$$

In the limit as $x_i \to 0$, this last equation becomes

$$\gamma_i^\infty = \frac{\lim\limits_{x_i \to 0} (\hat{f}_i/x_i)}{f_i}$$

With Eq. (3-95), this reduces to

$$\gamma_i^{\infty} = \frac{k_i}{f_i} \tag{5-156}$$

or, in logarithmic form,

$$\ln k_i = \ln f_i + \ln \gamma_i^{\infty} \tag{5-157}$$

This general equation may be applied to the special case of an i-j binary mixture:

$$\ln k_{i,j} = \ln f_i + \ln \gamma_{i,j}^{\infty}$$

Multiplication by x_j' and summation over all $j \neq i$ gives

$$\sum_{j \neq i} x_j' \ln k_{i,j} = \ln f_i + \sum_{j \neq i} x_j' \ln \gamma_{i,j}^{\infty}$$

where we have made use of the fact that $\sum_{j \neq i} x_j' = 1$. Subtraction of this expression from Eq. (5-157) yields

$$\ln k_i - \sum_{j \neq i} x_j' \ln k_{i,j} = \ln \gamma_i^{\infty} - \sum_{j \neq i} x_j' \ln \gamma_{i,j}^{\infty}$$

which is Eq. (5-155).

For an ideal solution in the sense of the Lewis-Randall rule, all of the $\ln \gamma^{\infty}$ values are zero, and Eq. (5-155) reduces to

$$\ln k_i = \sum_{j \neq i} x_j' \ln k_{i,j}$$

This is, however, a trivial case, because, in addition,

$$\ln k_i = \ln k_{i,j} = \ln f_i$$

An alternative form of Henry's law results from combination of Eqs. (5-138) and (5-156):

$$\hat{f}_i = f_i x_i \gamma_i^{\infty} \tag{5-158}$$

Since the exact expression is

$$\hat{f}_i = f_i x_i \gamma_i$$

Henry's law is inexact to the extent that γ_i differs from γ_i^{∞}.

SIX

APPLICATIONS TO PHASE EQUILIBRIA

For a multiphase PVT system in thermal and mechanical equilibrium, *phase equilibrium* is established when there is no driving force for the transport of any chemical species from one phase to another. According to Eq. (2-9), one set of criteria for the existence of such an equilibrium state is that the chemical potentials of all species be uniform throughout the system. An alternative set of criteria, provided by Eq. (3-67), is that the fugacities exhibit a like uniformity. Our purpose here is to show how such thermodynamic criteria relate to the phenomenological description of equilibrium states as characterized by temperature, pressure, and the phase compositions.

6-1 THE PHASE RULE; DUHEM'S THEOREM

The *intensive* state of a PVT system containing N chemical species and comprising π phases in equilibrium is fully described by values for

(a) the temperature T and pressure P, and
(b) the $N - 1$ independent mole fractions for each of the π phases.

These are the intensive thermodynamic coordinates of the equilibrium state, and their number is

$$2 + \pi(N - 1)$$

The equations of equilibrium are given by

$$\boxed{\mu_i^\alpha = \mu_i^\beta = \cdots = \mu_i^\pi} \qquad (i = 1, 2, \ldots, N) \qquad (2\text{-}9)$$

or by

$$\boxed{\hat{f}_i^\alpha = \hat{f}_i^\beta = \cdots = \hat{f}_i^\pi} \qquad (i = 1, 2, \ldots, N) \qquad (3\text{-}67)$$

In either case there are $\pi - 1$ independent equations for each species, and for N species the total is

$$N(\pi - 1)$$

Since each chemical potential and each fugacity is a function of temperature, pressure, and the composition of a phase, these equations implicitly relate the intensive thermodynamic coordinates of the equilibrium state. Thus the number of these coordinates which must be specified to make this set of equations determinate is the difference

$$F = 2 + \pi(N - 1) - N(\pi - 1)$$

or

$$F = 2 - \pi + N \qquad (6\text{-}1)$$

where F is known as the number of *degrees of freedom* of the system. Equation (6-1) is the *phase rule* applicable when no equations other than the phase-equilibrium criteria constrain the behavior of the system. If the system is subject in addition to *special constraints*, then additional equations may apply. Thus, if one can write s special constraining equations relating the intensive thermodynamic coordinates, then F in Eq. (6-1) must be reduced by this number, and the phase rule for nonreacting systems is given its ultimate expression by

$$\boxed{F = 2 - \pi + N - s} \qquad (6\text{-}2)$$

In applications to vapor/liquid equilibrium, $\pi = 2$, and Eq. (6-2) becomes

$$F = N - s$$

When $s = 0$, as is most often the case, then the number of degrees of freedom of the system equals the number of chemical species present, and this number of intensive thermodynamic coordinates must be specified to fix the intensive state of the system. No further assignment of intensive coordinates is possible; all others are provided by nature, and are subject, in principle, to calculation.

If we require the vapor/liquid equilibrium state to be an azeotrope, then we impose special constraining equations which relate the $N - 1$ independent vapor-phase mole fractions y_i to the $N - 1$ independent liquid-phase mole fractions x_i:

$$y_i = x_i \qquad (i = 1, 2, \ldots, N - 1)$$

Thus

$$s = N - 1$$

and

$$F = 1$$

This result shows that the azeotropic state has but one degree of freedom, and for such a state one may specify but a single intensive coordinate. For example, when an azeotrope exists at a specified temperature, it exhibits a preordained pressure and composition.

The typical phase-equilibrium problem is to calculate from the equilibrium equations those intensive coordinates unspecified in the formulation of the problem. The essential information of the phase rule is the number of such coordinates that must be assigned values in the statement of the problem to make its solution possible. The assigned values must of course be such that the supposed equilibrium condition is physically attainable.

Example 6-1 The mathematical content of the phase rule follows from the definition of F as the difference between the minimum number of variables required to describe the intensive state of a system and the number of independent equations relating these variables at equilibrium. A positive value for F merely means that the variables outnumber the equations; numerical values must then be specified for F of the variables. A *negative* value of F would imply more equations than variables. For independent equations, this is a mathematically untenable situation, for there cannot even in principle exist values for the variables which satisfy all of the equations. Thus, proposed equilibrium states implying negative values of F are impossible.

If F is *zero*, then the number of variables and the number of equations are equal; specification of variables is neither necessary nor permissible for solution of the equations. Writing Eq. (6-2) as

$$\pi = 2 - F + N - s$$

we see that the *maximum* number of phases compatible with a given value of N obtains when $F = s = 0$. The simplest case is that of a pure substance ($N = 1$) subject to no special constraints ($s = 0$), for which,

$$\pi \, (\text{max}) = 3$$

The maximum number of coexisting equilibrium phases for a pure chemical species is thus *three*. The solid/liquid/vapor triple point is an example of such an equilibrium state; it is not, however, the only possible one, for the phase rule says nothing about the *number* of such states that may exist for a given system. For example, Fig. 6-1a depicts a portion of a PT diagram for a pure substance for which there are observed four triple points; this is entirely compatible with the phase rule. On the other hand, the pure-component quadruple point shown on Fig. 6-1b is impossible, for, by Eq. (6-2), $F = -1$, even with $s = 0$.

Special constraints on the equilibrium state most commonly apply to *mixtures* ($N > 1$), and normally involve the mole fractions. However, constraining equations

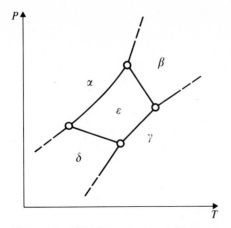

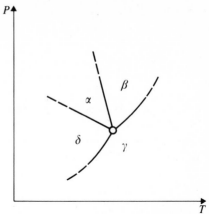

Figure 6-1a Multiple triple-point behavior of a pure substance. Symbols α, β, γ, δ, and ε denote distinct phases.

Figure 6-1b A quadruple point for a pure substance. Such behavior is forbidden by the phase rule.

may also enter into the description of pure substances. Consider the liquid-vapor critical point. Treated as a limiting case of pure-component ($N = 1$), single-phase ($\pi = 1$) behavior, it may be defined as a special state for which the isotherm exhibits a horizontal inflection:

$$\left(\frac{\partial P}{\partial V}\right)_{T;\,\mathrm{cr}} = 0 \tag{4-1a}$$

and

$$\left(\frac{\partial^2 P}{\partial V^2}\right)_{T;\,\mathrm{cr}} = 0 \tag{4-1b}$$

Equations (4-1) are not merely empirical observations; they follow from thermodynamic stability theory as mathematical conditions for the stability of states arbitrarily near to the critical point. Thus, $s = 2$, and, by Eq. (6-2)

$$F = 2 - 1 + 1 - 2 = 0$$

This is in accord with the observation that the liquid/vapor critical state is invariant. Experiment shows that there is but *one* such state; however, this is not a consequence of the phase rule.

When the intensive state of a system is determined, all of its intensive thermodynamic properties are fixed, including the molar or specific properties of the phases and the partial properties of all species in each phase. However, nothing is implied about the amounts or relative amounts of the phases. Thus, the phase rule, which takes account of intensive coordinates only, is applicable to both open and closed systems.

If the masses or numbers of moles of the phases are established along with the intensive state of the system, then the *extensive* as well as the intensive state is fixed, and the state of the system is said to be *completely determined*. Such states are characterized not only by the $2 + \pi(N - 1)$ intensive coordinates of the system but also by the π extensive coordinates represented by the masses (or mole numbers) of the phases. The total number of coordinates is

$$2 + \pi(N - 1) + \pi = 2 + \pi N$$

If the system is closed and formed from specified amounts of the chemical species present, then, in addition to the $N(\pi - 1)$ equilibrium equations, we can write a material-balance equation for each of the N chemical species; the total number of independent equations in this case is therefore

$$N(\pi - 1) + N = N\pi$$

The difference between the total number of coordinates and the number of independent equations relating them is

$$2 + \pi N - N\pi = 2$$

This remarkable result is the basis for *Duhem's theorem*:

> For any closed system formed initially from given masses of prescribed chemical species, the equilibrium state is completely determined by any two coordinates of the system, provided only that these two coordinates are independently variable at the equilibrium state.

Application of Duhem's theorem can be illustrated by simple examples. Let a system be formed by placing a *given mass* of steam in a piston-and-cylinder assembly at subatmospheric pressure. We now hold the temperature constant at 100°C and adjust the pressure by pushing the piston in. Thus we take T and P as our variables, and fixing these variables establishes both the intensive and extensive states of the system so long as the saturation pressure is not reached. However, once we reach the saturation pressure the state of the system is no longer completely determined by T and P, for they are no longer *independently variable* for an equilibrium state consisting of liquid and vapor H_2O. On the other hand, T and V^t, or T and S^t, or T and H^t *are* independently variable, and fixing one such pair does fix the state of the system. Once condensation is complete, T and P again become appropriate variables.

A similar system made up of a vapor mixture of ethanol and water behaves differently: T and P remain independently variable in the two-phase region and are thus suitable variables, with one exception. If the initial composition happens to be the azeotropic composition for the temperature considered, then condensation occurs just as with a pure material, and in this region T and P are not independently variable.

In the first case, H_2O as a superheated vapor or as a subcooled liquid is a single-phase system for which the phase rule yields $F = 2$. Thus, fixing T and P establishes the intensive state of the system; since the mass of the phase is the initial mass, its extensive state is also established. When the steam is only partially condensed, both liquid and vapor phases are present; by the phase rule, we now have $F = 1$. Thus, only a single *intensive* coordinate can be arbitrarily fixed or independently varied, and at 100°C all intensive coordinates have unique values. The second coordinate of Duhem's theorem must here be extensive. It may be the mass of either phase; the total volume, internal energy, enthalpy, etc., of either phase; or a total system property, such as V^t, S^t, H^t, etc.

For the ethanol/water mixture as a superheated vapor or as a subcooled liquid, the phase rule yields $F = 3$; when liquid and vapor phases exist in equilibrium, $F = 2$. Thus, T and P remain independently variable throughout the entire compression process and are suitable coordinates with respect to Duhem's theorem. However, if the initial mixture has the azeotrope compositon for the temperature of the process, then this special constraint makes $F = 1$ for the two-phase region, and the second coordinate of Duhem's theorem must be extensive.

In the enumeration of equations that led to the statement of Duhem's theorem, no account was taken of special constraining equations. One might suppose, where such equations apply, that the number of coordinates required to completely determine the state of the system would be less than two, the number given by Duhem's theorem. All experimental evidence, however, supports Duhem's theorem. The reason is that the equations of special constraint inevitably interact with the material-balance equations, reducing the number of such equations with meaningful content by exactly the number of special constraining equations, thus preserving the generality of Duhem's theorem.

In the case where the composition of the ethanol/water system is that of the azeotrope, the two phases existing during condensation have the same composition, exactly that of the initial mixture. This reduces the material-balance equation to a trivial identity with respect to a two-phase system.

The general limitations on choice of the two coordinates of Duhem's theorem are summarized as follows. When the phase rule yields $F \geq 2$, the state of the system is completely determined by specification of any two coordinates, intensive or extensive. When $F = 1$, only one of the two coordinates may be intensive; both may be extensive. When $F = 0$, both must be extensive. This last case is illustrated by the triple point of a pure substance, for which no intensive coordinate may be varied. The provision in Duhem's theorem that the coordinates chosen be independently variable implies all of these limitations.

Example 6-2 The mathematical substance of Duhem's theorem can be illustrated with a simple example. Consider the vapor/liquid equilibrium of a pure fluid. Since $\mu_i = G_i$ for a pure substance, the equilibrium criterion of Eq. (2-9) can be written

$$G^l(T, P) = G^v(T, P) \qquad \text{(A)}$$

Here, we delete subscript i and indicate explicitly the dependence of G on T and P. According to Eq. (A), T and P are not independent; fixing one of them in principle determines the other, in conformance with the phase rule.

Application of Duhem's theorem requires that the total number of moles in the system be known; call this number n^t. Then, by material balance,

$$n^l + n^v = n^t \tag{B}$$

where n^l and n^v are the numbers of moles of liquid and vapor present at equilibrium. Suppose now that n^l is also given. Then by Eq. (B) n^v is known. If in addition T is specified, then P is determined by Eq. (A), and, by Postulate 1.5, all of the intensive properties M^l and M^v of the two equilibrium phases are determined. Hence, so are the *total* properties of each phase and of the entire two-phase system, for

$$(M^t)^l = n^l M^l$$

$$(M^t)^v = n^v M^v$$

and

$$M^t = (M^t)^l + (M^t)^v = n^l M^l + n^v M^v$$

Thus, as required by Duhem's theorem, specification of the two coordinates n^l and T (one extensive, and one intensive) *completely* determines the equilibrium state, provided that n^t is known.

Extensive quantities other than n^l or n^v may serve as coordinates for Duhem's theorem. Suppose that the value of some total property M^t is known for the entire two-phase system. Then

$$n^l M^l + n^v M^v = M^t \tag{C}$$

The mole numbers n^v and n^l are found by solution of Eqs. (B) and (C):

$$\left. \begin{aligned} n^l &= \frac{n^t M^v - M^t}{M^v - M^l} \\[2mm] n^v &= \frac{M^t - n^t M^l}{M^v - M^l} \end{aligned} \right\} \tag{D}$$

If, as before, T is specified, then again the molar properties M^l and M^v are known, and the equilibrium state of the two-phase system is thus completely determined. Note that M^t *cannot* be identified with G^t because, by Eq. (A), G is uniform throughout the system, and Eq. (C) does not in this case represent an independent constraint on the equilibrium state. This is also seen from Eqs. (D), which yield indeterminate values for n^l and n^v if $M = G$.

6-2 FUNDAMENTAL EQUATIONS OF EQUILIBRIUM

Our object here is to develop expressions for the property changes which occur in closed systems as they proceed *from* initial nonequilibrium states *toward* a final state of phase equilibrium. We consider a closed multicomponent system comprising an arbitrary number of phases in which the temperature and pressure are uniform (but not necessarily constant). Although the initial state is one of nonequilibrium with respect to mass transfer between phases, we assume thermal and mechanical equilibrium of the system with its surroundings. The irreversible changes occurring within the system result from mass transfer, and take the system ever closer to a state of phase equilibrium.

The first law as applied to any increment of this process may be written

$$dU^t = dQ + dW$$

However, under conditions of mechanical equilibrium (or mechanical reversibility), we have

$$dW = -P\ dV^t$$

Combination of these two equations yields

$$dU^t = dQ - P\ dV^t \qquad (6\text{-}3)$$

The entropy change of the system may be considered to consist of two parts— that resulting from heat transfer to the system under the assumed conditions of thermal equilibrium, and that resulting from irreversible mass transfer within the system. The total entropy change of the system can therefore be written:

$$dS^t = \frac{dQ}{T} + dS_{irr}$$

from which we have

$$dQ = T\ dS^t - T\ dS_{irr} \qquad (6\text{-}4)$$

Substitution in Eq. (6-3) gives

$$dU^t = T\ dS^t - P\ dV^t - T\ dS_{irr} \qquad (6\text{-}5)$$

This equation describes the irreversible processes we are considering as they actually occur. It may be compared with the general relation describing reversible processes, for which $dS_{irr} = 0$:

$$dU^t = T\ dS^t - P\ dV^t \qquad (2\text{-}1)$$

Of course, when integrated, this latter equation connects any two *equilibrium* states of the system regardless of how the change actually occurs—reversibly or irreversibly; but as a differential equation it can only describe *reversible* processes as they actually occur. This is the reason for the requirement that the two states between which it is integrated be equilibrium states and hence *possible* of connection by a reversible process.

Values of dS_{irr} are usually unknown. However, a general requirement as a result of the second law is that dS_{irr} must be positive, approaching zero in the limit as the process approaches reversibility. Thus

$$dS_{irr} \geq 0 \qquad (6\text{-}6)$$

The best we can do with Eq. (6-5) is to insert this inequality, and write:

$$dU^t \leq T\ dS^t - P\ dV^t \qquad (6\text{-}7)$$

If a process occurs at constant entropy and volume, then Eq. (6-7) becomes

$$\boxed{dU^t_{S^t, V^t} \leq 0} \tag{6-8}$$

What this means is that in any change toward equilibrium of a closed system *constrained to constant entropy and volume* the total internal energy of the system must decrease. No change whatsoever in the opposite direction (away from equilibrium) is possible. It is not sufficient that $\Delta U^t_{S^t, V^t} < 0$ for a finite change of state. *Every increment* of the change must result in a decrease in the internal energy of the system. Hence the equilibrium state, if reached along a path of constant S^t and V^t, must be one of minimum total internal energy. It follows that any closed system not initially in phase equilibrium and constrained to changes at constant S^t and V^t will adjust itself to a state of minimum total internal energy insofar as it is able and must always tend in this direction.

If the equilibrium state at a given S^t and V^t is one of minimum internal energy with respect to all possible changes, then at equilibrium

$$\boxed{dU^t_{S^t, V^t} = 0} \tag{6-9}$$

This is a general criterion of equilibrium, but it is by no means the only possible one.

By definition

$$G^t = U^t + PV^t - TS^t$$

Thus

$$dG^t = dU^t + P\,dV^t + V^t\,dP - T\,dS^t - S^t\,dT$$

Substitution for dU^t by Eq. (6-5) gives

$$dG^t = V^t\,dP - S^t\,dT - T\,dS_{irr}$$

The same remarks apply to this equation as to Eq. (6-5). Also, since

$$dS_{irr} \geq 0$$

$$dG^t \leq V^t\,dP - S^t\,dT$$

and

$$\boxed{dG^t_{T, P} \leq 0} \tag{6-10}$$

Equation (6-10) is entirely analogous to Eq. (6-8). It shows that a closed system not initially in phase equilibrium and constrained to changes at constant T and P will always change toward a state representing a minimum value of the Gibbs function, which state is the equilibrium state for that T and P. Hence the equation

$$\boxed{dG^t_{T, P} = 0} \tag{6-11}$$

is another criterion of equilibrium. Other criteria of equilibrium are also possible and are found by analogous methods to be

$$dH^t_{S^t, P} = 0 \quad \text{and} \quad dA^t_{T, V^t} = 0$$

Since Duhem's theorem requires the two variables considered to establish the state of a closed system to be independently variable at the equilibrium state, it might be thought that when the several criteria of equilibrium are applied, the variables considered must be independent. That is, for $dU^t_{S^t, V^t} = 0$ to apply, S^t and V^t should be independently variable, and for $dG^t_{T, P} = 0$ to apply, T and P should be independently variable, etc. This is *not* true, for the pair of variables used in each criterion is special. It was shown in Chap. 2 that $U^t = U^t(S^t, V^t)$, $G^t = G^t(T, P)$, etc., for closed systems in equilibrium states *without exception*. Thus T and P determine G^t even when T and P are not independently variable and S^t and V^t determine U^t even when S^t and V^t are not independently variable. However, this is no violation of Duhem's theorem, for while G^t is always a function of its special variables T and P in closed systems at equilibrium, the other thermodynamic properties are not, unless T and P are independently variable. Thus when T and P are not independent, fixing them determines G^t only and not the remaining thermodynamic properties, and hence does not completely determine the state of the system. The same may be said for the other functions and their special variables.

The four criteria for equilibrium are equivalent, and any one could be applied to any problem. However, convenience usually dictates the choice of the Gibbs function criterion, for in practice we invariably establish or know the temperature and pressure at which our systems are to reach equilibrium. When equilibrium is established between phase α and phase β, this criterion requires that the transfer of dn_i moles of component i from one phase to the other must satisfy Eq. (6-11). In general for this transfer

$$dG^t_{T, P} = (\bar{G}^\alpha_i - \bar{G}^\beta_i)\, dn_i$$

If $dG^t_{T, P}$ is to be zero, then $\bar{G}^\alpha_i = \bar{G}^\beta_i$, or

$$\mu^\alpha_i = \mu^\beta_i$$

which result conforms to the general requirement of phase equilibrium expressed by Eq. (2-9). Thus, equilibrium is established between contacting phases when

(a) The temperature is uniform throughout the system.
(b) The pressure is uniform throughout the system.
(c) The chemical potential (and fugacity) for each constituent is uniform throughout the system.

For a completely rigorous proof of the necessity and sufficiency of these criteria, reference may be made to the original works of J. Willard Gibbs (1961).

6-3 VAPOR/LIQUID EQUILIBRIUM (VLE): THE GENERAL PROBLEM

The thermodynamic basis for the solution of VLE problems is provided by any of the equivalent equilibrium criteria represented by Eqs. (2-9), (3-67), (6-9), and (6-11). The commonly used working equations are most conveniently derived from Eq. (3-67), which for VLE in a multicomponent system becomes:

$$\hat{f}_i^v = \hat{f}_i^l \qquad (i = 1, 2, \ldots, N) \tag{6-12}$$

Each $\hat{f}_i^v$ is a function of temperature T, pressure P, and $N-1$ independent vapor-phase mole fractions y_i. Similarly, each $\hat{f}_i^l$ is a function of T, P, and $N-1$ independent liquid-phase mole fractions x_i. Thus, the $2N$ variables are related by the N equations represented by Eq. (6-12). One must therefore specify N variables in the formulation of a VLE problem in order to allow calculation of the remaining N variables by simultaneous solution of the N equilibrium relations of Eq. (6-12). This conclusion also follows from the phase rule, which for this case yields $F = N$.

Usually, one specifies the N variables by fixing either T or P *and* either the liquid-phase or the vapor-phase composition. Thus, many VLE problems fall into one of the four following categories:

1. Calculate T and the y_i at specified P and the x_i.
2. Calculate P and the y_i at specified T and the x_i.
3. Calculate T and the x_i at specified P and the y_i.
4. Calculate P and the x_i at specified T and the y_i.

The first two are known as bubble-point and the last two as dew-point calculations. Although the details of the calculational procedure differ for the four cases, all start from the same mathematical formulation of the problem.

One formal procedure replaces the fugacities in Eq. (6-12) in favor of fugacity coefficients, defined by Eq. (3-58):

$$\hat{\phi}_i = \hat{f}_i / x_i P$$

Thus, letting y_i represent a vapor-phase mole fraction, we can write

$$\hat{f}_i^v = \hat{\phi}_i^v y_i P$$

Similarly, representing a liquid-phase mole fraction by x_i, we have

$$\hat{f}_i^l = \hat{\phi}_i^l x_i P$$

With these substitutions, Eq. (6-12) becomes

$$\boxed{y_i \hat{\phi}_i^v = x_i \hat{\phi}_i^l} \qquad (i = 1, 2, \ldots, N) \tag{6-13}$$

Since $\hat{\phi}_i^l$ is a function of T, P, and the liquid-phase composition and $\hat{\phi}_i^v$ is similarly a function of T, P, and the vapor-phase composition, Eq. (6-13) actually represents N highly complex expressions relating T, P, the x_i, and the y_i.

Solution for the N unknowns is most conveniently carried out by an iterative procedure with the aid of a computer. The fugacity coefficients are expressed as functions of T, P, and composition by means of an equation of state. Equations (4-128), (4-129), and (4-130) are generally applicable for this purpose.

This computational procedure is usually reserved for systems at pressures high enough that the vapor phase deviates significantly from ideal-gas behavior. Moreover, it is most commonly applied to systems made up of nonpolar and nonassociating species, such as light hydrocarbons and cryogenic gases, for which mixing rules and conbination rules for equation-of-state parameters are firmly based on experimental data. Detailed treatment and examples are given in the next section.

An alternative calculational procedure results when the liquid-phase fugacities in Eq. (6-12) are eliminated in favor of activity coefficients, as defined by Eq. (5-120):

$$\gamma_i \equiv \frac{\hat{f}_i}{x_i f_i^\circ}$$

Thus, we can write

$$\hat{f}_i^l = \gamma_i x_i f_i^\circ$$

For the vapor phase, we have, as before:

$$\hat{f}_i^v = \hat{\phi}_i y_i P$$

Equation (6-12) now becomes

$$\boxed{y_i \hat{\phi}_i P = x_i \gamma_i f_i^\circ} \qquad (i = 1, 2, \dots, N) \qquad (6\text{-}14)$$

where we have omitted phase-identifying superscripts. The understanding is that $\hat{\phi}_i$ applies to the vapor phase, whereas γ_i and f_i° apply to the liquid phase. When all quantities are correctly evaluated at the equilibrium T and P, this equation is exact and entirely equivalent to Eq. (6-12).

Application of Eq. (6-14) is most commonly made to VLE at relatively low pressures; the standard-state fugacity f_i° is then taken as f_i, the fugacity of pure liquid i at the T and P of the system. For convenience, we recast Eq. (6-14) as

$$y_i \Phi_i P = x_i \gamma_i P_i^{\text{sat}} \qquad (i = 1, 2, \dots, N) \qquad (6\text{-}15)$$

where

$$\Phi_i \equiv \hat{\phi}_i \frac{P_i^{\text{sat}}}{f_i}$$

and P_i^{sat} is the vapor pressure of pure i at the equilibrium temperature. At low pressures, Φ_i is usually of order unity, and is identically unity under the assumptions that:

(a) The vapor phase is an ideal gas.
(b) The fugacities of liquids are independent of pressure.

Equation (6-15) then becomes

$$\boxed{y_i P = x_i \gamma_i P_i^{\text{sat}}} \qquad (i = 1, 2, \ldots, N) \qquad (6\text{-}16)$$

where γ_i is a function of liquid-phase composition and temperature, but not of pressure. This equation is widely used for low-pressure VLE, and provides an adequate approximation for many practical purposes. A full treatment of the "gamma/phi" approach to VLE is given in Sec. 6-5.

The activity coefficients γ_i in Eq. (6-16) account for deviations from ideal-solution behavior in the liquid phase; for an ideal solution, they become unity, and Eq. (6-16) reduces to an expression of *Raoult's law*:

$$\boxed{y_i P = x_i P_i^{\text{sat}}} \qquad (i = 1, 2, \ldots, N) \qquad (6\text{-}17)$$

Thus, Raoult's law correctly expresses the VLE relationship when the vapor phase is an ideal gas, the liquid phase is an ideal solution, and the liquid-phase fugacities are independent of pressure. Applications of Raoult's law require nothing more than vapor-pressure data for the pure species.

Example 6-3 Experimental data show that the VLE relationship for acetone(1)/acetonitrile(2) is well represented by Raoult's law. We illustrate for this simplest kind of behavior all of the possible phase-equilibrium calculations. Since there are two chemical species and two phases, there are two degrees of freedom. Thus, specification of any two of the phase-rule variables—T, P, x_1, and y_1—allows calculation of the other two. Vapor pressures are represented as a function of temperature by Antoine equations:

$$\ln P_i^{\text{sat}} = A_i - \frac{B_i}{t + C_i} \qquad (A)$$

or

$$t = \frac{B_i}{A_i - \ln P_i^{\text{sat}}} - C_i \qquad (B)$$

For P_i^{sat} in kPa and t in °C, suitable values for the parameters in these equations are:

	A_i	B_i	C_i
Acetone(1)	14.37284	2787.498	229.664
Acetonitrile(2)	14.88567	3413.099	250.523

Equation (6-17) applies to each of the two species; thus

$$y_1 P = x_1 P_1^{\text{sat}} \qquad (C)$$

and

$$y_2 P = x_2 P_2^{\text{sat}} \qquad (D)$$

By division and rearrangement, we get

$$\frac{y_1/x_1}{y_2/x_2} = \frac{P_1^{\text{sat}}}{P_2^{\text{sat}}}$$

The quantity on the left is regarded as the volatility of species 1 relative to the volatility of species 2. Thus, by definition we have the *relative volatility*:

$$\alpha_{12} \equiv \frac{y_1/x_1}{y_2/x_2} \tag{E}$$

When Raoult's law applies, this quantity is given by

$$\alpha_{12} = P_1^{\text{sat}}/P_2^{\text{sat}} \tag{F}$$

Although P_1^{sat} and P_2^{sat} increase rapidly as t increases, α_{12} changes only slowly with t; this is evident from the values calculated for acetone(1)/acetonitrile(2) and listed in Table 6-1. Moreover, α_{12} is for practical purposes linear in t, with

$$\frac{d\alpha_{12}}{dt} = -0.0052°\text{C}^{-1} \tag{G}$$

(a) Given $t = 50°\text{C}$, $P = 64$ kPa, find x_1, y_1. Addition of Eqs. (C) and (D) yields, since $y_1 + y_2 = 1$:

$$P = x_1 P_1^{\text{sat}} + x_2 P_2^{\text{sat}} \tag{H}$$

Substitution of $x_2 = 1 - x_1$ and solution for x_1 leads to:

$$x_1 = \frac{P - P_2^{\text{sat}}}{P_1^{\text{sat}} - P_2^{\text{sat}}} \tag{I}$$

Taking values for P_1^{sat} and P_2^{sat} from Table 6-1, we get

$$x_1 = \frac{64 - 34.07}{81.90 - 34.07} = 0.626$$

Table 6-1 Vapor pressures for acetone(1)/acetonitrile(2)

$t/°\text{C}$	$P_1^{\text{sat}}/\text{kPa}$	$P_2^{\text{sat}}/\text{kPa}$	$\alpha_{12} = P_1^{\text{sat}}/P_2^{\text{sat}}$
40	56.59	23.05	2.456
42	61.07	24.98	2.445
44	65.82	27.03	2.435
46	70.87	29.23	2.425
48	76.23	31.58	2.414
50	81.90	34.07	2.404
52	87.91	36.73	2.394
54	94.26	39.55	2.383

By Eq. (C)

$$y_1 = \frac{x_1 P_1^{sat}}{P} = \frac{(0.626)(81.90)}{64} = 0.801$$

(b) Given $x_1 = 0.400$, $y_1 = 0.620$, find t, P. By Eq. (E)

$$\alpha_{12} = \frac{y_1 x_2}{y_2 x_1} = \frac{(0.620)(0.600)}{(0.380)(0.400)} = 2.447$$

Interpolation in Table 6-1 gives

$$t = 41.6°C$$

and by Eq. (A) we find

$$P_1^{sat} = 60.15 \text{ kPa}$$

Equation (C) then yields

$$P = \frac{x_1 P_1^{sat}}{y_1} = \frac{(0.400)(60.15)}{0.620} = 38.81 \text{ kPa}$$

(c) Given $P = 64$ kPa, $x_1 = 0.600$, find t, y_1. Application of Eq. (H) provides

$$64 = 0.6 P_1^{sat} + 0.4 P_2^{sat}$$

or

$$64 = P_2^{sat}\left(\frac{0.6 P_1^{sat}}{P_2^{sat}} + 0.4\right) = P_2^{sat}(0.6\alpha_{12} + 0.4)$$

Thus

$$P_2^{sat} = \frac{64}{0.6\alpha_{12} + 0.4}$$

One picks a value for α_{12}, say 2.4, and solves for P_2^{sat}:

$$P_2^{sat} = \frac{64}{(0.6)(2.4) + 0.4} = 34.78 \text{ kPa}$$

From this one calculates $t = 50.55°C$ by Eq. (B). Interpolation in Table 6-1 gives a new value of $\alpha_{12} = 2.401$. The process is repeated, yielding

$$P_2^{sat} = 34.77 \text{ kPa}$$

and

$$t = 50.54°C$$

Further iteration is unnecessary; y_2 is found from Eq. (D):

$$y_2 = \frac{x_2 P_2^{sat}}{P} = \frac{(0.400)(34.77)}{64} = 0.217$$

and

$$y_1 = 0.783$$

(d) Given $t = 50°C$, $x_1 = 0.600$, find P, y_1. By Eq. (H)

$$P = (0.600)(81.90) + (0.400)(34.07) = 62.77 \text{ kPa}$$

and by Eq. (C):

$$y_1 = \frac{x_1 P_1^{\text{sat}}}{P} = \frac{(0.600)(81.90)}{62.77} = 0.783$$

(e) Given $P = 64 \text{ kPa}$, $y_1 = 0.700$, find t, x_1. Solving Eqs. (C) and (D) for x_1 and x_2 and adding, we get

$$x_1 + x_2 = 1 = \frac{y_1 P}{P_1^{\text{sat}}} + \frac{y_2 P}{P_2^{\text{sat}}}$$

or

$$\left(\frac{y_1}{P_1^{\text{sat}}} + \frac{y_2}{P_2^{\text{sat}}} \right) P = 1 \tag{J}$$

Multiplication by P_1^{sat} yields

$$(y_1 + y_2 \alpha_{12}) P = P_1^{\text{sat}}$$

or

$$P_1^{\text{sat}} = (0.7 + 0.3\alpha_{12})(64)$$

Choosing a value for α_{12}, say 2.4, we calculate

$$P_1^{\text{sat}} = 90.88 \text{ kPa}$$

and by Eq. (B),

$$t = 52.95°C$$

Interpolation in Table 6-1 yields the new value, $\alpha_{12} = 2.389$. Repeating the process, we find

$$P_1^{\text{sat}} = 90.67 \text{ kPa}$$

and

$$t = 52.88°C$$

Since the value of α_{12} for this temperature is essentially unchanged from the preceding value, no further iteration is necessary. By Eq. (C),

$$x_1 = \frac{y_1 P}{P_1^{\text{sat}}} = \frac{(0.700)(64)}{90.67} = 0.494$$

(f) Given $t = 50°C$, $y_1 = 0.600$, find P, x_1. By Eq. (J)

$$P = \frac{1}{y_1/P_1^{\text{sat}} + y_2/P_2^{\text{sat}}} = \frac{1}{0.600/81.90 + 0.400/34.07} = 52.45 \text{ kPa}$$

and

$$x_1 = \frac{y_1 P}{P_1^{\text{sat}}} = \frac{(0.600)(52.45)}{81.90} = 0.384$$

Another common computation requiring knowledge of VLE is the *flash calculation*. The name derives from the process wherein a liquid passing through a valve undergoes a pressure drop sufficient to cause "flashing" or partial vaporization, producing a two-phase stream of liquid and vapor in equilibrium. However, the term now refers to any calculation which for given T and P determines the physical state of a fluid mixture of known *overall* composition. In particular, when T and P are such that liquid and vapor coexist in equilibrium, one calculates the amounts and compositions of the phases. The feasibility of complete determination of the state of the system rests on Duhem's theorem.

For a system containing a total of 1 mole of chemical species, let the *overall* composition be represented by the mole fractions $z_1, z_2, ..., z_N$. Depending on T and P, the system may be entirely liquid or entirely vapor. However, our interest centers on states for which the system consists of liquid and vapor in equilibrium. Let L represent the number of moles of liquid, with mole fractions $x_1, x_2, ..., x_N$, and let V be the moles of vapor, with mole fractions $y_1, y_2, ..., y_N$. The following material-balance equations must be satisfied:

$$L + V = 1$$

$$z_i = x_i L + y_i V \qquad (i = 1, 2, ..., N)$$

Either V or L may be eliminated from the set of equations for z_i, giving

$$z_i = x_i L + y_i(1 - L) \qquad (i = 1, 2, ..., N) \tag{6-18}$$

or

$$z_i = x_i(1 - V) + y_i V \qquad (i = 1, 2, ..., N) \tag{6-19}$$

The VLE relationships in flash calculations are invariably represented by

$$y_i = K_i x_i \qquad (i = 1, 2, ..., N) \tag{6-20}$$

where the K_i are called equilibrium K-values. They are in general functions of T, P, liquid composition, and vapor composition. Use of Eq. (6-20) presumes knowledge of the K-values, but separates their calculation from the flash calculation as a matter of convenience. They have no intrinsic thermodynamic content, and must be evaluated from fundamental VLE relationships. Where Raoult's law, Eq. (6-17), applies, we have

$$K_i = \frac{y_i}{x_i} = \frac{P_i^{\text{sat}}}{P} \tag{6-21}$$

In this simplest of cases, K_i increases as temperature increases, decreases with increasing pressure, and is independent of the phase compositions. In view of the definition of *relative* volatility, we may write

$$\alpha_{12} = \frac{y_1/x_1}{y_2/x_2} = \frac{K_1}{K_2}$$

Thus, K_i can be regarded as a measure of the volatility of a species in a particular equilibrium situation.

Example 6-4 For the acetone(1)/acetonitrile(2) system considered in Example 6-3, we wish to find V, L, and the phase compositions when $t = 50°C$, $P = 64$ kPa, and $z_1 = 0.700$. Application of the phase rule to this binary system in VLE gives $F = 2$. Thus, specification of t and P fixes the intensive state of the system, and as shown in Example 6-3a,

$$x_1 = 0.626 \quad \text{and} \quad y_1 = 0.801$$

These results are independent of z_1 within the range of values for which two equilibrium phases are possible.

Solving Eq. (6-19) for V, we get

$$V = \frac{z_i - x_i}{y_i - x_i} \quad (i = 1, 2)$$

For $i = 1$ and $z_1 = 0.700$

$$V = \frac{0.700 - 0.626}{0.801 - 0.626} = 0.423$$

and

$$L = 1 - V = 0.577$$

Different values for z_1 merely produce different values of L and V, all for the same phase compositions. However, there are limits to the values of z_1 if two phases are to exist. Thus, when $z_1 = 0.801$, $V = 1$, and $L = 0$; the system is entirely saturated vapor. When $z_1 = 0.626$, $V = 0$, and $L = 1$; the system is entirely saturated liquid. Values of z_1 between these limits yield the full range of values for V from unity to zero.

One can, of course, use K-values in the solution of this problem. By Eq. (6-20), we have

$$y_1 = K_1 x_1 \quad \text{and} \quad y_2 = K_2 x_2$$

Addition gives

$$y_1 + y_2 = K_1 x_1 + K_2 x_2$$

Since $y_1 + y_2 = 1$ and $x_2 = 1 - x_1$, we have

$$x_1 = \frac{1 - K_2}{K_1 - K_2}$$

The K-values are here given by Eq. (6-21), with values of P_i^{sat} from Table 6-1 at 50°C:

$$K_1 = \frac{81.90}{64} = 1.280$$

and

$$K_2 = \frac{34.07}{64} = 0.532$$

Then

$$x_1 = \frac{1 - 0.532}{1.280 - 0.532} = 0.626$$

and

$$y_1 = K_1 x_1 = (1.280)(0.626) = 0.801$$

These are the values obtained in Example 6-3a, and used in the flash calculation.

We may use Eq. (6-20) to eliminate either y_i or x_i from either Eq. (6-18) or Eq. (6-19); the four alternative expressions which result are given in App. G. For example, substituting $x_i = y_i/K_i$ in Eq. (6-19) yields:

$$y_i = \frac{z_i K_i}{1 + V(K_i - 1)} \qquad (i = 1, 2, \ldots, N) \qquad (6\text{-}22)$$

For VLE in systems containing three or more species, the phase rule shows that

$$F = N > 2$$

and specification of t and P does not fix the intensive state of the system independent of material-balance equations. Since $\sum y_i = 1$, the sum of Eqs. (6-22) gives

$$\sum \frac{z_i K_i}{1 + V(K_i - 1)} = 1 \qquad (6\text{-}23)$$

Again, as shown in App. G, this is but one of the four alternative expressions that can be written. In any case, solution is by a trial or iterative procedure.

Example 6-5 A system containing benzene(1)/toluene(2)/ethylbenzene(3) at 100°C and 0.9521 bar has an overall composition given by $z_1 = 0.45$, $z_2 = 0.35$, $z_3 = 0.20$. The vapor pressures of the three species at 100°C are:

$$P_1^{sat} = 1.8005 \text{ bar} \qquad P_2^{sat} = 0.7417 \text{ bar} \qquad P_3^{sat} = 0.3426 \text{ bar}$$

We assume Raoult's law, and calculate V, L, and the phase compositions. The K-values as given by Eq. (6-21) are:

$$K_1 = 1.8911 \qquad K_2 = 0.7790 \qquad K_3 = 0.3598$$

Thus, Eq. (6-23) becomes

$$\frac{(0.45)(1.8911)}{1 + 0.8911V} + \frac{(0.35)(0.7790)}{1 - 0.2210V} + \frac{(0.20)(0.3598)}{1 - 0.6402V} = 1$$

The value of V, found by trial, which satisfies this equation is

$$V = 0.505$$

With this value of V, each term of the above equation becomes a y_i. Thus,

$$y_1 = 0.587 \qquad y_2 = 0.307 \qquad y_3 = 0.106$$

The liquid-phase compositions now come from $x_i = y_i/K_i$:

$$x_1 = 0.310 \qquad x_2 = 0.394 \qquad x_3 = 0.296$$

When flash calculations are done by computer, one must have a systematic iterative procedure for rapid convergence to the correct answer. A function particularly suited to this purpose is developed in App. G.

In many cases, experimental VLE data show a marked departure from Raoult's law. For data at relatively low pressures, this is the result of liquid-phase nonidealities, which make the activity coefficients greater than or less than unity. For a binary solution, we write Eq. (6-16) for $i = 1$ and $i = 2$:

$$y_1 P = x_1 \gamma_1 P_1^{\text{sat}}$$

$$y_2 P = x_2 \gamma_2 P_2^{\text{sat}}$$

The quantities on the left are the partial pressures of species 1 and 2 in the vapor phase. Addition yields the total pressure:

$$P = x_1 \gamma_1 P_1^{\text{sat}} + x_2 \gamma_2 P_2^{\text{sat}} \qquad P = x_i P_i^{\text{sat}}$$

When γ_1 and γ_2 are unity, we recover the linear equations that characterize Raoult's law. Activity coefficients greater than unity represent positive deviations from ideality, and result in pressures greater than predicted by Raoult's law. Systems showing this behavior are said to exhibit positive deviations from Raoult's law. Typical curves of pressure versus liquid composition at constant temperature appear in Fig. 6-2a, where for comparison the linear relations based

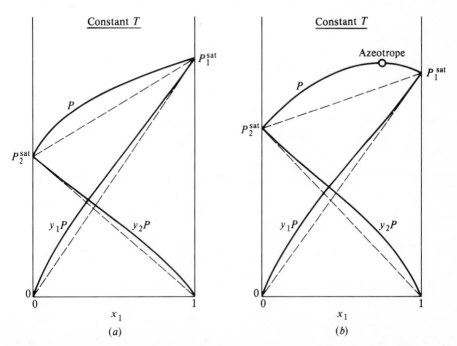

Figure 6-2 Plots showing P, $y_1 P$, and $y_2 P$ versus x_1 for positive deviations from Raoult's law, which is represented by the dashed lines.

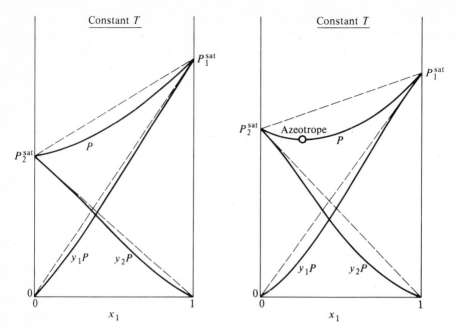

Figure 6-3 Plots showing P, y_1P, and y_2P versus x_1 for negative deviations from Raoult's law, which is represented by the dashed lines.

on Raoult's law are also shown. When positive deviations are sufficiently large, the P-x curve exhibits a maximum, as shown by Fig. 6-2b; this maximum-pressure state is called an *azeotrope*.

Liquid solutions with activity coefficients less than unity show negative deviations from ideality and negative deviations from Raoult's law, as illustrated by Fig. 6-3. As shown by Fig. 6-3b, sufficiently large deviations result in a minimum in the P-x curve. The minimum-pressure state, like the maximum-pressure state, is an azeotrope.

It is clear that deviations from Raoult's law are necessary for the occurrence of azeotropes. However, the magnitude of the deviation required depends on the system considered. Thus, if the vapor pressures of the two species forming a binary system are almost the same, only slight deviations result in a maximum or minimum in the P-x_1 curve. When the vapor pressures of the pure species are quite different, large deviations are required.

Example 6-6 In Figs. 6-2 and 6-3 the partial-pressure (y_iP) curves are all drawn tangent to the Raoult's-law line at $x_i = 1$. We wish to show why. We differentiate Eq. (6-16) with respect to x_i at constant temperature:

$$\frac{d(y_iP)}{dx_i} = P_i^{\text{sat}}\left(\gamma_i + \frac{d\gamma_i}{dx_i}\right) \tag{A}$$

For Raoult's law, γ_i is everywhere unity; therefore

$$\left[\frac{d(y_iP)}{dx_i}\right]_{RL} = P_i^{sat} \tag{B}$$

Equation (5-55) is a form of the Gibbs-Duhem equation, and for a binary system it may be written

$$\frac{d\ln\gamma_1}{dx_1} = -\frac{x_2}{x_1}\frac{d\ln\gamma_2}{dx_1} \qquad (\text{const } T, P)$$

The pressure is not in fact constant, but for low-pressure data its effect on the activity coefficients is negligible. For nonelectrolyte solutions, infinite-dilution activity coefficients are finite; therefore, when $x_1 = 1$ $(x_2 = 0)$, we get

$$\left(\frac{d\ln\gamma_1}{dx_1}\right)_{x_1=1} = 0$$

An analogous result holds for species 2; thus we have

$$\left(\frac{d\ln\gamma_i}{dx_i}\right)_{x_i=1} = 0$$

Moreover, $(\gamma_i)_{x_i=1} = 1$, and therefore

$$\left(\frac{d\gamma_i}{dx_i}\right)_{x_i=1} = 0$$

Thus, when $x_i = 1$, Eq. (A) reduces to

$$\left[\frac{d(y_iP)}{dx_i}\right]_{x_i=1} = P_i^{sat}$$

the same value given by Eq. (B) for Raoult's law.

6-4 VLE FROM EQUATIONS OF STATE

Calculation of VLE from an equation of state is based on the equilibrium equations

$$y_i\hat{\phi}_i^v = x_i\hat{\phi}_i^l \qquad (i = 1, 2, \dots, N) \tag{6-13}$$

Application of Eq. (6-13) requires the availability of a single PVT equation of state suitable for both liquid and vapor mixtures. Experience shows that such an equation is invariably explicit in pressure, and thus expressions for the $\hat{\phi}_i$ are computed from Eq. (4-130) or one of its equivalents:

$$\ln\hat{\phi}_i = \int_0^\rho \left\{\left[\frac{\partial(nZ)}{\partial n_i}\right]_{T,\,\rho/n,\,n_j} - 1\right\}\frac{d\rho}{\rho} - \ln Z \tag{4-130}$$

The resulting expressions for the $\hat{\phi}_i$ are generally complicated, and the calculations involve considerable iteration. They are therefore done with a computer.

We noted in Sec. 6-3 that many VLE calculations fall into one of four categories, in which either T or P *and* either the x_i or the y_i are specified. In this section we treat only the calculation of P and the y_i for specified values of T and the x_i. For this case the liquid of known composition is at its *bubble point*, and pressure is one of the quantities sought; we borrow the nomenclature of Prausnitz et al. (1967) and designate it a "BUBL P" calculation. A schematic block diagram for a BUBL P calculation is shown in Fig. 6-4.

One starts with given values of T and the x_i, and with the physical properties necessary for evaluation of all parameters appearing in the equation of state. The pressure and the vapor compositions are unknowns and are to be calculated. However, the $\hat{\phi}_i^l$ depend on P, and the $\hat{\phi}_i^v$ depend on P and the y_i. We therefore include as input initial estimates for P and for the y_i.

The first step in the solution is a calculation of the $\hat{\phi}_i^l$ and $\hat{\phi}_i^v$ from Eq. (4-130); this is done with appropriate subroutines. Given these initial estimates of the $\hat{\phi}_i$, one can compute a set of equilibrium K-values:

$$K_i = \hat{\phi}_i^l/\hat{\phi}_i^v \qquad (i = 1, 2, \ldots, N) \qquad (6\text{-}24)$$

Equation (6-24) is merely a rearrangement of Eq. (6-13), incorporating the definition $K_i \equiv y_i/x_i$. New estimates of the y_i then follow immediately from Eq. (6-20):

$$y_i = K_i x_i \qquad (i = 1, 2, \ldots, N) \qquad (6\text{-}20)$$

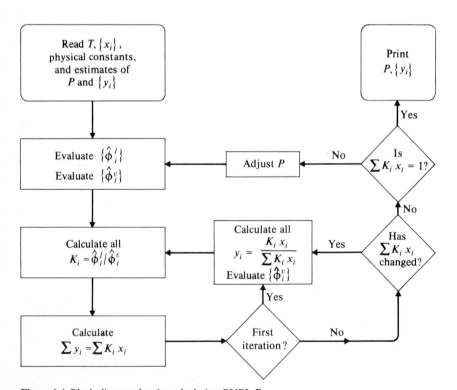

Figure 6-4 Block diagram for the calculation BUBL P.

Each y_i is determined from Eq. (6-20) by an independent calculation; the condition $\sum y_i = 1$ has nowhere been imposed. Ultimately the results must satisfy this condition, but it is unlikely that first estimates of the y_i from Eq. (6-20) will conform to it. In any event $\sum y_i$ is a key quantity in this scheme, and our next step is to sum the calculated y_i's.

A set of y_i's is now available from which we can recalculate the $\hat{\phi}_i^v$ by Eq. (4-130). For the first iteration we make this calculation immediately. However, the calculated y_i's are first normalized, each value being divided by $\sum y_i (= \sum K_i x_i)$. This ensures that the set of y_i's used for the calculation of the $\hat{\phi}_i^v$ do sum to unity. Once the $\hat{\phi}_i^v$ are determined, the inner loop of the block diagram is completed by a recalculation of the y_i's; since T, P, and the x_i are the same as for the preceding calculation, the $\hat{\phi}_i^l$ remain unchanged.

Again we calculate $\sum y_i$; since this is a second iteration, the new $\sum y_i$ is compared with the sum found in the first iteration. If it has changed, the $\hat{\phi}_i^v$ are recomputed and another iteration starts. This process is repeated until the change in $\sum y_i$ from one iteration to the next is less than some preset tolerance. When this conditon is realized, the next step is to ask whether $\sum y_i$ is unity. If it is, the calculations are complete; the computed values of the y_i are those of the equilibrium vapor phase, and the pressure assumed initially is the equilibrium pressure.

If $\sum y_i \neq 1$, then the assumed value of P must be adjusted according to some reasonable scheme. If $\sum y_i > 1$, the assumed pressure is too low; if $\sum y_i < 1$, it is too high. The entire iterative procedure is reinitiated with a new pressure. In the first iteration, normalized values of the last-calculated set of y_i's may be used for computation of an initial set of the $\hat{\phi}_i^v$.

The scheme just outlined, although rational and straightforward in principle, can be difficult to implement in practice. Depending upon the system, the conditions, and the equation of state, convergence problems may be encountered, and it is sometimes essential to have available at the outset very sharp estimates of the equilibrium P and y_i's. Discussions of problems in the calculation of VLE from equations of state and algorithms for circumventing some of the computational difficulties are given by Asselineau et al. (1979) and by Michelsen (1980).

We present as examples the results of some VLE calculations done with Soave's 1972 modification of the Redlich-Kwong equation of state. The Soave-Redlich-Kwong (SRK) equation is a special case of the generic Redlich-Kwong equation

$$Z = \frac{1}{1-h} - \left(\frac{\theta}{bRT}\right)\frac{h}{1+h} \qquad (4\text{-}141b)$$

where

$$h \equiv b\rho \qquad (4\text{-}142)$$

and ρ is the molar density. For pure species i, parameters b and θ are given by the recipes

$$b_i = 0.08664 \frac{RT_{c_i}}{P_{c_i}} \qquad (6\text{-}25)$$

and

$$\theta_i = \theta_{c_i}[1 + (0.480 + 1.574\omega_i - 0.176\omega_i^2)(1 - T_{r_i}^{1/2})]^2 \tag{6-26}$$

where

$$\theta_{c_i} = 0.42748 \frac{R^2 T_{c_i}^2}{P_{c_i}} \tag{6-27}$$

The following mixing rules are used:

$$b = \sum x_j b_j \tag{6-28}$$

and

$$\theta = \sum \sum x_j x_k \theta_{jk} \tag{6-29}$$

where

$$\theta_{jk} = (1 - l_{jk})(\theta_j \theta_k)^{1/2} \tag{6-30}$$

Here, l_{jk} is an empirical interaction parameter, presumed characteristic of inter-actions between j-k molecular pairs. (See the discussion of combination rules in Sec. 4-8.)

An expression for $\ln \hat{\phi}_i$ for the generic Redlich-Kwong equation, based on Eqs. (4-130) and (4-141b), is derived in Sec. 4-8 and given as Eq. (4-195). Applied to the present case, it becomes

$$\ln \hat{\phi}_i = -\ln (1 - h)Z + \left(\frac{\theta}{bRT}\right)\left(\frac{b_i}{b} - 2\frac{\sum x_k \theta_{ki}}{\theta}\right) \ln (1 + h)$$

$$+ \frac{b_i}{b}\left(\frac{h}{1 - h}\right) - \frac{\theta}{bRT}\frac{b_i}{b}\left(\frac{h}{1 + h}\right) \tag{6-31}$$

Although we have used the symbol x for mole fraction, Eqs. (6-28), (6-29), and (6-31) apply to either the liquid or the vapor phase. All unsubscripted quantities in these equations refer to an entire phase, and thus are properties of homogen-eous liquid or vapor solutions, evaluated from the mixing rules or from the equation of state.

As a first example, we treat the calculation of isothermal VLE for the ethane/propylene system at 277.59 K (40°F), for which experimental data are reported by Sage and Lacey (1955). The solid lines on Fig. 6-5 are computed from the SRK equation with a BUBL P program similar to that illustrated by Fig. 6-4. The upper line is the calculated P-x (bubble-point) curve; the lower line is the corresponding P-y (dew-point) curve. Equation-of-state parameters are determined from Eqs. (6-25) through (6-30), with values of T_c, P_c, and ω given in App. D. Since both species are light hydrocarbons, the value of the interaction parameter l_{12} is taken to be zero. At 277.59 K, pure ethane and pure propylene are both below their critical temperatures. Thus states of VLE are possible for

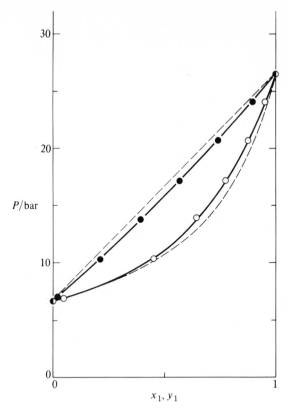

Figure 6-5 VLE for the ethane(1)/ propylene(2) system at 277.59 K (40°F). Circles are data of Sage and Lacey (1955): ● ≡ bubble points, ○ ≡ dew points, and ◐ ≡ P_i^{sat} for pure i. Dashed lines are computed from Raoult's law. Solid lines are computed from the SRK equation with $l_{12} = 0$.

the full range of liquid and vapor compositions, and Raoult's law, Eq. (6-17), provides a standard of comparison. The dashed curves on Fig. 6-5 are computed from Raoult's law, and the circles are data of Sage and Lacey. The system exhibits negative deviations from Raoult's law, and the SRK equation of state provides good predictions of the VLE.

Figure 6-6 shows experimental and calculated VLE for the ethane/hydrogen sulfide system at 283.15 K (50°F); the data are those of Kalra et al. (1977). This system exhibits strong positive deviations from Raoult's law, enough to produce a maximum-pressure azeotrope. However, ethane and hydrogen sulfide are chemically dissimilar, and curves computed from the SRK equation with $l_{12} = 0$ (the dashed lines) deviate significantly from the experimental results. In this case, a nonzero interaction parameter is required; the solid curves, which provide a compromise representation of the data, are calculated from the SRK equation with $l_{12} = 0.09$.

As a final example, we consider the methane/n-decane system at 477.59 K (400°F). Methane cannot exist as a pure liquid at this temperature (its critical temperature is only 190.6 K) so VLE does not obtain for the full range of liquid and vapor compositions. Figure 6-7 shows experimental data from Sage and

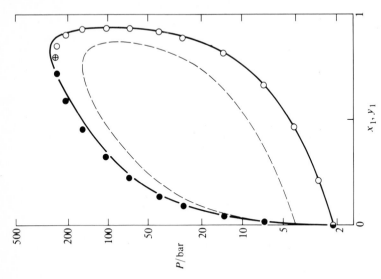

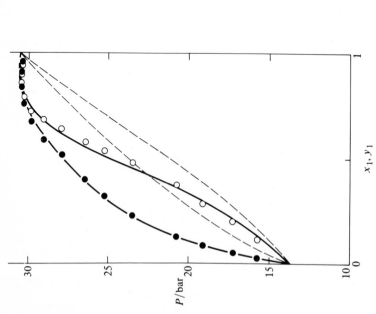

Figure 6-7 VLE for the methane(1)/n-decane(2) system at 477.59 K (400°F). Circles are data of Sage and Lacey (1950): ● = bubble points, ○ = dew points, ◖ = P_2^{sat}, and ⊕ = mixture critical point. Dashed lines are computed from the ORK equation. Solid lines are from the SRK equation with $l_{12} = 0$.

Figure 6-6 VLE for the ethane(1)/hydrogen sulfide(2) system at 283.15 K (50°F). Circles are data of Kalra et al. (1977): ● = bubble points, and ○ = dew points. Dashed lines are computed from the SRK equation with $l_{12} = 0$. Solid lines are from the SRK equation with $l_{12} = 0.09$.

Lacey (1950), and curves computed with the original Redlich-Kwong (ORK) equation (dashed lines) and with the SRK equation (solid lines); in each case, we take $l_{12} = 0$. Significantly, both equations of state are able to produce qualitative descriptions of VLE of this kind. However, the SRK equation is clearly superior.

Because the results are most easily displayed, we have treated only binary systems in our examples. However, the equation-of-state approach is applicable to systems containing any number of components. For the SRK equation, all that is required are corresponding-states parameters (T_c, P_c, and ω) for each component and values of l_{ij} for each unlike ($i \neq j$) binary pair. The relative agreement with experiment illustrated by the examples is representative of what one can expect in applications of the SRK equation to systems comprising hydrocarbons and nonpolar or weakly polar fluids. Some other cubic equations of state, e.g., the Peng-Robinson equation (1976), perform comparably. However, VLE for systems containing polar or associating species is often predicted poorly. Vidal (1978) and Huron and Vidal (1979) have shown that the use of more flexible mixing rules greatly improves the representation of VLE for such systems by cubic equations of state.

6-5 THE "GAMMA/PHI" APPROACH TO VLE: FUNDAMENTALS

The equation-of-state approach of Sec. 6-4 to determination of VLE relationships has great intellectual appeal. However, practical application requires an equation of state that accurately represents the volumetric properties of both liquid-phase and vapor-phase solutions as functions of temperature, pressure, and composition. Although much has been accomplished in the development of PVT equations of state, we are not yet able to treat all systems successfully by this approach. For systems at low to moderate pressure (well below the critical pressure), the difficulty lies in description of the liquid-phase properties, particularly when there is appreciable departure from ideal-solution behavior. Here, one can still calculate vapor-phase properties from a suitable PVT equation of state.

For the liquid phase, one could instead use an equation relating the Gibbs function G to its canonical variables—T, P, and the n_i. (See Sec. 2-4 and App. A-3.) This *canonical* equation of state provides by differentiation all pertinent thermodynamic functions, including the fugacities of the species as functions of temperature, pressure, and composition. Unfortunately, we do not have available any such complete thermodynamic description of nonideal liquid solutions. We can, however, usually write an adequate expression relating the excess Gibbs function G^E to composition at constant T and P, partially fulfilling the function of a canonical equation of state, and allowing calculation at constant T and P of the activity coefficients γ_i of the species. This is the basis for the "gamma/phi" approach to VLE, an effective and highly refined alternative to the equation-of-state approach for systems at low to moderate pressures.

Given the composition dependence of G^E for the liquid phase at constant temperature and pressure, the activity coefficients follow from the equations:

$$\ln \gamma_i = \frac{\bar{G}_i^E}{RT} \tag{5-45}$$

and

$$\bar{M}_i^E = \left[\frac{\partial(nM^E)}{\partial n_i}\right]_{T, P, n_j} \tag{5-36}$$

With $M^E \equiv G^E/RT$, Eq. (5-36) becomes

$$\frac{\bar{G}_i^E}{RT} = \left[\frac{\partial(nG^E/RT)}{\partial n_i}\right]_{T, P, n_j} \tag{6-32}$$

which, with Eq. (5-45), yields

$$\boxed{\ln \gamma_i = \left[\frac{\partial(nG^E/RT)}{\partial n_i}\right]_{T, P, n_j}} \tag{6-33}$$

If we choose a particular reference temperature T^+ and a particular reference pressure P^+ for which to express the composition dependence of G^E/RT, then Eq. (6-33) becomes

$$\ln \gamma_i^+ = \left[\frac{\partial(nG^E/RT)^+}{\partial n_i}\right]_{T^+, P^+, n_j} \tag{6-34}$$

where the superscript $+$ designates values at the reference conditions. The relation of these γ_i^+ values to fugacity is given by Eq. (5-120), written as

$$\gamma_i^+ \equiv \frac{\hat{f}_i^+}{x_i f_i^+} \tag{6-35}$$

where the standard-state fugacity f_i° has been set equal to f_i^+, the fugacity of pure species i as a liquid at T^+ and P^+. Thus, the standard states are here based on the Lewis-Randall rule.

The phase-equilibrium relationships as given by

$$\hat{f}_i^v = \hat{f}_i^l \qquad (i = 1, 2, \ldots, N) \tag{6-12}$$

relate fugacities at the equilibrium conditions T and P, not at T^+ and P^+. This presents no difficulty with respect to the vapor phase, for which we assume the availability of a suitable PVT equation of state from which to evaluate the fugacity coefficients $\hat{\phi}_i^v$. These are related to fugacity by the definition of Eq. (3-58):

$$\hat{\phi}_i^v \equiv \frac{\hat{f}_i^v}{y_i P}$$

where y_i represents the mole fraction of species i in the vapor phase. Thus, for the vapor phase, we have the simple expression

$$\hat{f}_i^v = y_i P \hat{\phi}_i^v$$

Equation (6-12) now becomes

$$y_i P \hat{\phi}_i^v = \hat{f}_i^l \qquad (i = 1, 2, \ldots, N)$$

For simplicity, we drop the superscripts v and l, and write

$$y_i P \hat{\phi}_i = \hat{f}_i \qquad (i = 1, 2, \ldots, N) \qquad (6\text{-}36)$$

with the implicit understanding that $\hat{\phi}_i$ is for the vapor phase and that $\hat{f}_i$ is a liquid-phase fugacity. To relate $\hat{f}_i$ at the equilibrium T and P to $\hat{f}_i^+$ at the reference conditions T^+ and P^+, we write the identity:

$$\hat{f}_i \equiv \hat{f}_i^+ \left(\frac{\hat{f}_i}{\hat{f}_i^+} \right)$$

Since Eq. (6-35) gives $\hat{f}_i^+ = x_i \gamma_i^+ f_i^+$, this is written

$$\hat{f}_i = x_i \gamma_i^+ f_i^+ \left(\frac{\hat{f}_i}{\hat{f}_i^+} \right) \qquad (i = 1, 2, \ldots, N) \qquad (6\text{-}37)$$

The standard-state fugacity f_i^+, evaluated at T^+ and P^+, is related to the vapor pressure P_i^{sat} of pure liquid i by another identity:

$$f_i^+ \equiv P_i^{\text{sat}} \left(\frac{f_i^{\text{sat}}}{P_i^{\text{sat}}} \right) \left(\frac{f^+}{f_i^{\text{sat}}} \right)$$

where P_i^{sat} is evaluated at the equilibrium temperature T, and f_i^{sat} is the fugacity of pure saturated liquid i at T and P_i^{sat}. Since f_i^{sat} is the same for saturated vapor as for saturated liquid, the ratio $f_i^{\text{sat}}/P_i^{\text{sat}}$ is written as ϕ_i^{sat}, the fugacity coefficient of pure saturated vapor at T and P_i^{sat}. It may therefore be evaluated by the PVT equation of state assumed for the vapor phase. Thus

$$f_i^+ = P_i^{\text{sat}} \phi_i^{\text{sat}} \left(\frac{f_i^+}{f_i^{\text{sat}}} \right)$$

Combination of this equation with Eqs. (6-37) and (6-36) gives

$$y_i P \hat{\phi}_i = x_i \gamma_i^+ P_i^{\text{sat}} \phi_i^{\text{sat}} \left(\frac{f_i^+}{f_i^{\text{sat}}} \right) \left(\frac{\hat{f}_i}{\hat{f}_i^+} \right)$$

or

$$\boxed{y_i P \Phi_i = x_i \gamma_i^+ P_i^{\text{sat}}} \qquad (i = 1, 2, \ldots, N) \qquad (6\text{-}38)$$

where

$$\Phi_i \equiv \left(\frac{\hat{\phi}_i}{\phi_i^{\text{sat}}} \right) \left(\frac{\hat{f}_i^+ / \hat{f}_i}{f_i^+ / f_i^{\text{sat}}} \right) \qquad (6\text{-}39)$$

The fugacity coefficients of the first ratio on the right of Eq. (6-39) are evaluated through use of the equation of state for the vapor phase. The other two ratios are given by integration of Eqs. (3-87) and (3-89). For pure species i, we write Eq. (3-87) as

$$d \ln f_i = \frac{\Delta H_i'}{RT^2} dT + \frac{V_i}{RT} dP$$

Integration for the change of state from $\ln f_i^{\text{sat}}$ at T and P_i^{sat} to $\ln f_i^+$ at T^+ and P^+ gives

$$\ln \frac{f_i^+}{f_i^{\text{sat}}} = \int_T^{T^+} \frac{\Delta H_i'}{RT^2} dT + \int_{P_i^{\text{sat}}}^{P^+} \frac{V_i}{RT} dP \tag{6-40}$$

Since this integration gives the change in a state function, the path of integration is arbitrary. The preferred path here is the one for which $\Delta H_i'$ is evaluated at P^+ and V_i at T.

For species i in solution at fixed composition, we have by Eq. (3-89) that

$$d \ln \hat{f}_i = \frac{H_i' - \bar{H}_i}{RT^2} dT + \frac{\bar{V}_i}{RT} dP$$

Integration for the change of state from $\ln \hat{f}_i$ at T and P to $\ln \hat{f}_i^+$ at T^+ and P^+ yields

$$\ln \frac{\hat{f}_i^+}{\hat{f}_i} = \int_T^{T^+} \frac{H_i' - \bar{H}_i}{RT^2} dT + \int_P^{P^+} \frac{\bar{V}_i}{RT} dP \tag{6-41}$$

Again the preferred path of integration is that for which $(H_i' - \bar{H}_i)$ is evaluated at P^+ and $\bar{V}_i$ at T.

Substitution of Eqs. (6-40) and (6-41) into Eq. (6-39) gives, after reduction and rearrangement,

$$\Phi_i = \left(\frac{\hat{\phi}_i}{\phi_i^{\text{sat}}} \right) \exp \left[-\int_T^{T^+} \frac{\bar{H}_i^E}{RT^2} dT + \int_P^{P^+} \frac{\bar{V}_i^E}{RT} dP - \int_{P_i^{\text{sat}}}^P \frac{V_i}{RT} dP \right] \tag{6-42}$$

The first integrand is evaluated at the reference pressure P^+ and the other two are evaluated at the equilibrium temperature T.

The foregoing treatment has presumed use of standard states based on the Lewis-Randall rule. If the standard state of species i is based on Henry's law, then by Eq. (5-121)

$$\hat{f}_i^+ = x_i (\gamma_i^*)^+ k_i^+$$

and in place of Eq. (6-37) we have

$$\hat{f}_i = x_i (\gamma_i^*)^+ k_i^+ \left(\frac{\hat{f}_i}{\hat{f}_i^+} \right) \tag{6-43}$$

where k_i^+ is Henry's constant for species i at the reference conditions T^+ and P^+. Equations (6-38) and (6-39) are therefore replaced by

$$\boxed{y_i P \Phi_i^* = x_i (\gamma_i^*)^+ k_i^+}$$

(6-44)

and

$$\Phi_i^* \equiv \hat{\phi}_i \left(\frac{\hat{f}_i^+}{\hat{f}_i} \right)$$

(6-45)

Since Eq. (6-41) still applies, this last equation becomes

$$\Phi_i^* = \hat{\phi}_i \exp \left[\int_T^{T^+} \frac{H_i' - \bar{H}_i}{RT^2} \, dT + \int_P^{P^+} \frac{\bar{V}_i}{RT} \, dP \right]$$

(6-46)

Equation (6-38), with Φ_i evaluated by Eq. (6-42), represents a general and thermodynamically rigorous treatment of VLE when G^E/RT can be expressed as a function of liquid-phase composition at fixed T^+ and P^+. It may be applied both in the reduction of VLE data to find the G^E/RT-versus-x relation and in the determination of VLE states once the G^E/RT-versus-x relation is known. In data reduction, one almost always deals with data sets either at fixed temperature or at fixed pressure. In each case, some simplification of Eq. (6-42) is possible.

For VLE at fixed temperature, the variables are pressure and the phase compositions. Since the value of T^+ may be chosen arbitrarily, it is in this case advantageously set equal to T, the fixed equilibrium temperature. This choice reduces Eq. (6-42) to

$$\Phi_i = \left(\frac{\hat{\phi}_i}{\phi_i^{\text{sat}}} \right) \exp \left[\int_P^{P^+} \frac{\bar{V}_i^E}{RT} \, dP - \int_{P_i^{\text{sat}}}^{P} \frac{V_i}{RT} \, dP \right]$$

(6-47)

Although rigor requires P^+ to be a fixed (but arbitrary) value, Eq. (6-47) is further simplified when P^+ is set equal to the equilibrium pressure P. Since this pressure varies with liquid-phase composition, the activity coefficients calculated from the resulting equation are not values of $\gamma_i^+(T, P^+)$, but are values of $\gamma_i(T, P)$ at the equilibrium temperature and pressure. Since P is a variable, these values are to some degree inconsistent with those given by Eq. (6-34), which yields values at *fixed* temperature and pressure. However, for data at pressures up to a few bars, this inconsistency is of no significance.

For isothermal VLE, when we take $P^+ = P$, Eq. (6-47) reduces to

$$\boxed{\Phi_i = \left(\frac{\hat{\phi}_i}{\phi_i^{\text{sat}}} \right) \exp \left[- \int_{P_i^{\text{sat}}}^{P} \frac{V_i}{RT} \, dP \right]}$$

(6-48)

The relative error associated with use of this equation is obtained by subtraction of Eq. (6-47) from Eq. (6-48) and division by Eq. (6-47):

$$\frac{\delta \Phi_i}{\Phi_i} = \exp \left[- \int_P^{P^+} \frac{\bar{V}_i^E}{RT} \, dP \right] - 1$$

(6-49)

Since values of $\bar{V}_i^E/RT$ are very small for liquid solutions at temperatures well below the critical and since the integration limits cannot be widely separated for low-pressure application, this equation shows that for these conditions the error implicit in use of Eq. (6-48) is quite negligible.

Example 6-7 For ethanol(1)/water(2) at 50°C, the VLE data of Larkin and Pemberton (1976) and the V^E data of Winnick and Kong (1974) are available. We use these data with Eq. (6-49) to illustrate how $\gamma_i(T, P)$ and $\gamma_i^+(T, P^+)$ differ for several arbitrary values of P^+. Values of $\bar{V}_i^E$ are so insensitive to pressure that the integral of Eq. (6-49) is accurately evaluated as

$$\int_P^{P^+} \frac{\bar{V}_i^E}{RT}\, dP = \frac{\bar{V}_i^E(P^+ - P)}{RT}$$

with $\bar{V}_i^E$ calculated from the atmospheric-pressure values of V^E given by Winnick and Kong. Equation (6-49) is therefore written

$$\frac{\delta\Phi_i}{\Phi_i} = \exp\left[\frac{\bar{V}_i^E(P - P^+)}{RT}\right] - 1$$

With $\bar{V}_i^E$ in cm^3 mol^{-1}, P in kPa, and $T = 323.15$ K, this becomes

$$\frac{\delta\Phi_i}{\Phi_i} = \exp\left[\frac{\bar{V}_i^E(P - P^+)}{(8314)(323.15)}\right] - 1$$

For various x_1 values, Table 6-2 lists the experimental phase-equilibrium pressures P and the corresponding values of $\bar{V}_1^E$ and $\bar{V}_2^E$. Calculated values of $\delta\Phi_i/\Phi_i$ for three different values of P^+ complete the table. The value $P^+ = 21$ kPa is an intermediate pressure, approximately the average of P_1^{sat} and P_2^{sat}. Such a value of P^+ results in a minimal overall effect of pressure. The value $P^+ = 0$ represents a reasonable standard reference pressure which might be used in general. The liquid state at zero pressure is of course hypothetical, but its assumption presents no problem. The value $P^+ = 100$ kPa = 1 bar is another possible standard reference pressure.

The results of Table 6-2 are typical. They mean that if Φ_i values calculated by Eq. (6-48) are regarded as values for the fixed pressure P^+, then they are in error by the amount shown. The same relative errors apply to γ_i, since they propagate directly by Eq. (6-38). These errors are clearly very small for any of the P^+ values considered,

Table 6-2 Values of $\delta\Phi_i/\Phi_i$ [Eq. (6-49)] for ethanol(1)/water(2) at 50°C

		$\bar{V}_i^E/\text{cm}^3\text{ mol}^{-1}$		$\dfrac{\delta\Phi_i}{\Phi_i} \times 10^5: P^+ = 21$ kPa		$\dfrac{\delta\Phi_i}{\Phi_i} \times 10^5: P^+ = 0$		$\dfrac{\delta\Phi_i}{\Phi_i} \times 10^5: P^+ = 100$ kPa	
x_1	P/kPa	$i = 1$	$i = 2$	$i = 1$	$i = 2$	$i = 1$	$i = 2$	$i = 1$	$i = 2$
0.0	12.34	−6.16	0.00	2.0	0.0	−2.8	0.0	20.1	0.0
0.2	24.21	−2.52	−0.36	−0.3	0.0	−2.3	−0.3	7.1	1.0
0.4	26.66	−1.04	−0.93	−0.2	−0.2	−1.0	−0.9	2.8	2.5
0.6	28.27	−0.46	−1.56	−0.1	−0.4	−0.5	−1.6	1.2	4.2
0.8	29.33	−0.13	−2.33	0.0	−0.7	−0.1	−2.5	0.3	6.1
1.0	29.51	0.00	−3.64	0.0	−1.2	0.0	−4.0	0.0	9.6

but they are smallest for $P^+ = 21$ kPa, a pressure in midrange of the data. Here, the maximum relative error is 2×10^{-5}; since Φ_i is of order 1.0, this represents an error of two parts in 10^5. Data of this accuracy do not exist. Thus for VLE calculations at low pressure and fixed temperature, evaluation of Φ_i by Eq. (6-48) yields activity coefficients that are for practical purposes constant-temperature, constant-pressure values.

For VLE at fixed pressure, Eq. (6-42) again applies, and in this case we may set $P^+ = P$. In this event, Eq. (6-42) reduces to

$$\Phi_i = \left(\frac{\hat{\phi}_i}{\phi_i^{\text{sat}}}\right) \exp\left[-\int_T^{T^+} \frac{\bar{H}_i^E}{RT^2} dT - \int_{P_i^{\text{sat}}}^P \frac{V_i}{RT} dP\right] \tag{6-50}$$

The question now is whether we can justify an approximation like that found adequate in the fixed-temperature case. That is, does setting $T^+ = T$ and letting it vary introduce appreciable error? The expression for relative error is here given by

$$\frac{\delta\Phi_i}{\Phi_i} = \exp\left[\int_T^{T^+} \frac{\bar{H}_i^E}{RT^2} dT\right] - 1$$

The magnitude of this error can readily be estimated. For a binary system at atmospheric pressure, the temperature is often about 300 K, and the temperature range is typically 20 K. For T^+ set at an intermediate value, the maximum integration interval is about 10 K, and occurs when one species or the other is at infinite dilution. The value of $\bar{H}_i^E$ is also usually at its maximum when species i is infinitely dilute, and is typically 3000 J mol^{-1}. The integrand of the last equation of course varies with temperature, but over a 10-K interval the variation is relatively small. Thus, for a reasonable estimate we can write:

$$\frac{\delta\Phi_i}{\Phi_i} \simeq \exp\left[\frac{\bar{H}_i^E(T^+ - T)}{RT^2}\right] - 1$$

With the values cited, this gives

$$\frac{\delta\Phi_i}{\Phi_i} \simeq \exp\left[\frac{(3,000)(10)}{(8.314)(300)^2}\right] - 1 = 0.041$$

This calculation shows that errors of up to four percent can typically be expected from the approximation considered. They may of course be more or less, depending on the particular system considered, but this result is enough to show that no general simplification of Eq. (6-50) is appropriate for the case of VLE data at fixed pressure. Proper application of Eq. (6-50) requires H^E data as a function of both composition and temperature. If one has such data, then an alternative procedure is to base calculations on an expression for G^E that incorporates both its temperature and composition dependence. This procedure makes $T^+ = T$, and Eq. (6-50) correctly reduces to Eq. (6-48). Moreover, γ_i^+ in Eq. (6-38) becomes γ_i, the activity coefficient of species i at the equilibrium temperature and pressure. Thus, for applications where the effect of pressure is insignificant, use of an expression for G^E as a function of both x and T provides a treatment of general applicability, for which the appropriate equilibrium relation is

$$\boxed{y_i P \Phi_i = x_i \gamma_i P_i^{sat}} \qquad (i = 1, 2, \ldots, N) \qquad (6\text{-}51)$$

This is the equation in common use, and for either constant-pressure or constant-temperature data Φ_i is evaluated by Eq. (6-48).

The derivatives with respect to temperature of the excess functions are interrelated by exact thermodynamic equations. For liquids of constant composition, it follows directly from Eqs. (2-40) and (2-41) that

$$\left(\frac{\partial H^E}{\partial T} \right)_P = T \left(\frac{\partial S^E}{\partial T} \right)_P = C_P^E \qquad (6\text{-}52)$$

Where the influence of pressure on liquid properties may be disregarded, we may write

$$\frac{dH^E}{dT} = C_P^E \qquad (\text{const } x) \qquad (6\text{-}53)$$

and

$$\frac{dS^E}{dT} = \frac{C_P^E}{T} \qquad (\text{const } x) \qquad (6\text{-}54)$$

Similarly, Eqs. (5-61) and (5-62) become

$$\frac{d(G^E/T)}{dT} = \frac{-H^E}{T^2} \qquad (\text{const } x) \qquad (6\text{-}55)$$

and

$$\frac{dG^E}{dT} = -S^E \qquad (\text{const } x) \qquad (6\text{-}56)$$

For pure liquids and their mixtures, the temperature dependence of C_P is usually not far from linear. Thus, C_P^E is usually well represented over a considerable temperature range by a quadratic expression:

$$C_P^E = c_2 + c_3 T + c_4 T^2 \qquad (\text{const } x)$$

Substitution in Eq. (6-53) and integration give

$$H^E = c_0 + c_2 T + \frac{c_3}{2} T^2 + \frac{c_4}{3} T^3 \qquad (\text{const } x) \qquad (6\text{-}57)$$

where c_0 is a constant of integration. Substitution of this expression in Eq. (6-55) and integration yield

$$\frac{G^E}{T} = \frac{c_0}{T} + c_1 - c_2 \ln T - \frac{c_3}{2} T - \frac{c_4}{6} T^2 \qquad (\text{const } x) \qquad (6\text{-}58)$$

where c_1 is another integration constant. Finally, differentiation in accord with Eq. (6-56) provides

$$S^E = c_2 - c_1 + c_2 \ln T + c_3 T + \frac{c_4}{2} T^2 \qquad \text{(const } x) \qquad \text{(6-59)}$$

Ideally, the parameters c_2, c_3, and c_4 are found for a given composition from data for C_P^E as a function of temperature; single experimental values for H^E and G^E then determine c_0 and c_1. Unfortunately, C_P^E data are rare, available for only a few binary systems, usually at 25°C, a temperature well below the range likely to be of practical interest.

Simplifications of Eqs. (6-57) through (6-59) result immediately when C_P^E is assumed linear in T or independent of T. In the latter case, $c_3 = c_4 = 0$, and we get

$$H^E = c_0 + c_2 T \qquad \qquad \text{(6-60)}$$

$$\left. \frac{G^E}{T} = \frac{c_0}{T} + c_1 - c_2 \ln T \right\} \qquad \text{(const } x) \qquad \text{(6-61)}$$

and

$$S^E = c_2 - c_1 + c_2 \ln T \qquad \qquad \text{(6-62)}$$

For a relatively narrow temperature range, the assumption that C_P^E is independent of T is an excellent approximation, and is equivalent to the assumption that H^E is linear in T. Parameter values can be determined from appropriate H^E and G^E data. Fortunately, modern experimental methods allow rapid accumulation of accurate data for these functions, and the required data are therefore increasingly available.

For convenience, one combines the temperature dependence of H^E and G^E as given by Eqs. (6-60) and (6-61) with appropriate expressions for the composition dependence of these functions. Assume, for example, that for a binary system G^E at a particular temperature is given by the four-parameter Margules equation [see Eq. (5-90)]:

$$\frac{G^E}{x_1 x_2 RT} = A_{21} x_1 + A_{12} x_2 - (C_{21} x_1 + C_{12} x_2) x_1 x_2 \qquad \text{(6-63)}$$

A direct procedure is to express each parameter as a function of T in accord with Eq. (6-61)

$$A_{21} = \frac{A_{210}}{T} + A_{211} - A_{212} \ln T \qquad \text{(6-64a)}$$

$$A_{12} = \frac{A_{120}}{T} + A_{121} - A_{122} \ln T \qquad \text{(6-64b)}$$

$$C_{21} = \frac{C_{210}}{T} + C_{211} - C_{212} \ln T \qquad \text{(6-64c)}$$

$$C_{12} = \frac{C_{120}}{T} + C_{121} - C_{122} \ln T \qquad \text{(6-64d)}$$

These expressions, in which A_{210}, A_{211}, A_{212}, etc. are constants, provide realistic approximations for the temperature dependence of the parameters in Eq. (6-63) for applications within a modest temperature range.

Equation (6-55) may be written as

$$\frac{H^E}{x_1 x_2 RT} = -T \frac{d(G^E/x_1 x_2 RT)}{dT} \qquad (\text{const } x)$$

Combining this with the derivative of Eq. (6-63) gives

$$\frac{H^E}{x_1 x_2 RT} = \left(-T \frac{dA_{21}}{dT}\right) x_1 + \left(-T \frac{dA_{12}}{dT}\right) x_2$$

$$- \left[\left(-T \frac{dC_{21}}{dT}\right) x_1 + \left(-T \frac{dC_{12}}{dT}\right) x_2\right] x_1 x_2$$

This may also be written

$$\frac{H^E}{x_1 x_2 RT} = A'_{21} x_1 + A'_{12} x_2 - (C'_{21} x_1 + C'_{12} x_2) x_1 x_2 \qquad (6\text{-}65)$$

where

$$A'_{21} = -T \frac{dA_{21}}{dT} \qquad A'_{12} = -T \frac{dA_{12}}{dT} \qquad \text{etc.} \qquad (6\text{-}66a)$$

Alternatively

$$\frac{dA_{21}}{dT} = -\frac{A'_{21}}{T} \qquad \frac{dA_{12}}{dT} = -\frac{A'_{12}}{T} \qquad \text{etc.} \qquad (6\text{-}66b)$$

Equations (6-63) and (6-65) are of identical form. Furthermore, both parameter sets, as determined from experimental data at a given T, are usually found to be of the same order of magnitude. Because T, with values usually greater than 300 K, appears as a divisor in Eqs. (6-66b), one finds that the derivatives dA_{21}/dT, etc., are relatively small. As a result, G^E/T is generally a weak function of temperature, and interpolations or extrapolations of G^E data within a modest temperature range can be based on minimal data.

Substitution of the derivatives of Eqs. (6-64) into Eqs. (6-66a) gives the following expressions for the temperature dependence of the parameters of Eq. (6-65):

$$A'_{21} = \frac{A_{210}}{T} + A_{212} \qquad (6\text{-}67a)$$

$$A'_{12} = \frac{A_{120}}{T} + A_{122} \qquad (6\text{-}67b)$$

$$C'_{21} = \frac{C_{210}}{T} + C_{212} \qquad (6\text{-}67c)$$

$$C'_{12} = \frac{C_{120}}{T} + C_{122} \qquad (6\text{-}67d)$$

Given data sets for H^E as a function of x at two temperatures, both fit by a Margules equation of up to four parameters, one can solve directly for all constants in Eqs. (6-67). These constants apply as well to Eqs. (6-64), in which the additional constants A_{211}, A_{121}, C_{211}, and C_{121} must be found from a data set for G^E at a single temperature, fit by Eq. (6-63).

The constants of Eqs. (6-64) and (6-67) can, in fact, be determined from any combination of three data sets that includes one set of data for G^E. When only two data sets are available, one for H^E and one for G^E, or two for G^E, then one must assume that H^E is independent of T. This eliminates the terms in A_{212}, A_{122}, C_{212}, and C_{122} from Eqs. (6-64) and (6-67). This assumption is of course more restrictive, but it does allow reasonable approximations for temperature dependence over a short temperature interval. When data sets for both H^E and G^E are used, they should be for the same temperature, or at least for temperatures close to one another.

Example 6-8 The heat-of-mixing data of Nicolaides and Eckert (1978) for the acetone(1)/ethanol(2) system at 25 and 50°C are well represented by Margules equations with four parameters:

For $T = 298.15$ K (25°C)

$$\frac{H^E}{x_1 x_2 RT} = 2.0766x_1 + 1.8797x_2 - (0.8147x_1 + 0.6367x_2)x_1 x_2$$

For $T = 323.15$ K (50°C)

$$\frac{H^E}{x_1 x_2 RT} = 1.9694x_1 + 1.9785x_2 - (0.3430x_1 + 0.7377x_2)x_1 x_2$$

The numerical parameters in these equations are values of A'_{21}, A'_{12}, C'_{21}, and C'_{12} in Eq. (6-65). Substitution of these values and T in Eqs. (6-67) allows solution for the constants:

$$A_{210} = 413.14 \qquad C_{210} = 1{,}817.88$$
$$A_{212} = 0.6902 \qquad C_{212} = -5.2825$$
$$A_{120} = -380.76 \qquad C_{120} = -389.24$$
$$A_{122} = 3.1568 \qquad C_{122} = 1.9422$$

An expression for $G^E/x_1 x_2 RT$ for the same system at 50°C is given by Chaudhry et al. (1980):

For $T = 323.15$ K

$$\frac{G^E}{x_1 x_2 RT} = 0.6784x_1 + 0.7815x_2 - (0.0531x_1 + 0.1578x_2)x_1 x_2$$

The numerical parameters here are values of A_{21}, A_{12}, C_{21}, and C_{12} in Eq. (6-63). Substitution of these values, T, and the constants already determined into Eqs. (6-64) provides values for the remaining constants:

$$A_{211} = 3.3880 \qquad C_{211} = -36.0953$$
$$A_{121} = 20.2001 \qquad C_{121} = 12.5846$$

These values, together with Eqs. (6-64) and (6-63) provide an expression giving the composition and temperature dependence of G^E for the acetone/ethanol system. It faithfully represents the data at 50°C, of course, and should provide a good approximation at temperatures at least 30° above and below that value.

For the acetone(1)/methanol(2) system, data are available for both H^E and G^E at $T = 323.15$ K (50°C). The data of Morris et al. (1975) for H^E are well represented by

$$\frac{H^E}{x_1 x_2 RT} = 1.3779x_1 + 1.0309x_2 - (0.0438x_1 + 0.2739x_2)x_1 x_2$$

and those reported by Van Ness and Abbott (1978c) for VLE are correlated by

$$\frac{G^E}{x_1 x_2 RT} = 0.6369x_1 + 0.6523x_2$$

Here, the *two*-parameter Margules equation gives a good fit of the data for G^E, and within the precision of the data C_{21} and C_{12} are zero at 50°C. However, their derivatives are not zero, since the C'_{21} and C'_{12} values in the equation for H^E are nonzero. Thus, we must presume nonzero values for C_{21} and C_{12} at temperatures other than 50°C. With just one set of data for H^E and one for G^E, we can evaluate but two constants for each parameter. Thus, with $A_{212} = 0$, etc., Eqs. (6-67) become

$$A'_{21} = \frac{A_{210}}{T} \qquad \text{etc.}$$

and Eqs. (6-64) become

$$A_{21} = \frac{A_{210}}{T} + A_{211} \qquad \text{etc.}$$

From these equations, we determine the following constants:

$$A_{210} = 445.27 \qquad A_{211} = -0.7410$$

$$A_{120} = 333.14 \qquad A_{121} = -0.3786$$

$$C_{210} = 14.15 \qquad C_{211} = -0.0438$$

$$C_{120} = 88.51 \qquad C_{121} = -0.2739$$

The general expression for $G^E/x_1 x_2 RT$ is therefore

$$\frac{G^E}{x_1 x_2 RT} = \left(\frac{445.27}{T} - 0.7410\right)x_1 + \left(\frac{333.14}{T} - 0.3786\right)x_2$$
$$- \left[\left(\frac{14.15}{T} - 0.0438\right)x_1 + \left(\frac{88.51}{T} - 0.2739\right)x_2\right]x_1 x_2$$

This equation should yield excellent results over at least the range from 30 to 70°C. At $T = 343.15$ K (70°C), for example, it becomes

$$\frac{G^E}{x_1 x_2 RT} = 0.5566x_1 + 0.5922x_2 + (0.0026x_1 + 0.0160x_2)x_1 x_2$$

Although the values of C_{21} and C_{12} are small, consistency requires that they be included.

We have discussed the Margules equation with up to four parameters as an example. Other equations may be treated in similar fashion, and additional examples appear in Sec. 6-8.

6-6 THE COEXISTENCE EQUATION FOR TWO-PHASE EQUILIBRIA

We showed in Sec. 3-7 that $\ln{(\hat{f}_i/x_i)}$ is a partial molar property. Therefore, the $\hat{f}_i$ for the various species in a phase are not independent, but are related to each other through the Gibbs-Duhem equation. Up to now, we have not explicitly incorporated this fact into our phase-equilibrium expressions; we do so in this section in the development of the *coexistence equation for two-phase equilibria*.

For multicomponent equilibrium between two phases α and β, we have

$$\hat{f}_i^\alpha = \hat{f}_i^\beta \equiv \hat{f}_i \qquad (i = 1, 2, \ldots, N)$$

or, equivalently,

$$\ln \hat{f}_i^\alpha = \ln \hat{f}_i^\beta \equiv \ln \hat{f}_i \qquad (i = 1, 2, \ldots, N)$$

For differential *changes* in the equilibrium state, the last equation yields

$$d \ln \hat{f}_i^\alpha = d \ln \hat{f}_i^\beta \equiv d \ln \hat{f}_i \qquad (6\text{-}68)$$

An appropriate form of the Gibbs-Duhem equation is given by Eq. (3-85b). Separate application of this expression to phases α and β gives

$$\sum x_i^\alpha \, d \ln \hat{f}_i^\alpha = \frac{(\Delta H')^\alpha}{RT^2} dT + \frac{V^\alpha}{RT} dP \qquad (6\text{-}69a)$$

and

$$\sum x_i^\beta \, d \ln \hat{f}_i^\beta = \frac{(\Delta H')^\beta}{RT^2} dT + \frac{V^\beta}{RT} dP \qquad (6\text{-}69b)$$

For differential changes in the equilibrium state, dT and dP are the same for both phases, because T and P must at all times be uniform throughout the system. Thus Eqs. (6-68) and (6-69) apply simultaneously; when combined, they give

$$\frac{(\Delta H')^\beta - (\Delta H')^\alpha}{RT^2} dT + \frac{(V^\beta - V^\alpha)}{RT} dP = \sum (x_i^\beta - x_i^\alpha) \, d \ln \hat{f}_i \qquad (6\text{-}70)$$

By definition, the residual enthalpy $\Delta H'$ of a phase is

$$\Delta H' = H' - H$$

where in this case H' is the enthalpy of an ideal-gas *mixture* having the same T, P, and *composition* as the real phase. But ideal-gas mixtures are ideal solutions and therefore [see Eq. (G) of Example 3-10]

$$H' = \sum x_i H_i'$$

where H'_i is the enthalpy of pure i in the ideal-gas state. Thus,

$$(\Delta H')^\alpha = \sum x_i^\alpha H'_i - H^\alpha \qquad \text{and} \qquad (\Delta H')^\beta = \sum x_i^\beta H'_i - H^\beta$$

and substitution of these expressions into Eq. (6-70) yields

$$\frac{\sum (x_i^\beta - x_i^\alpha)H'_i - (H^\beta - H^\alpha)}{RT^2} dT + \frac{(V^\beta - V^\alpha)}{RT} dP = \sum (x_i^\beta - x_i^\alpha) \, d \ln \hat{f}_i \quad (6\text{-}71)$$

Equation (6-71) is the primitive form of the coexistence equation for two-phase equilibria, and as such it is not particularly useful for applications to multi-component systems. However, as illustrated in the following examples, it yields important results for two special cases.

Example 6-9 We consider the case of vapor/liquid equilibrium, making the identifications $\alpha \equiv l$ and $\beta \equiv v$. Then $x_i^\alpha \equiv x_i$ and $x_i^\beta \equiv y_i$, and Eq. (6-71) becomes

$$\frac{\sum (y_i - x_i)H'_i - (H^v - H^l)}{RT^2} dT + \frac{(V^v - V^l)}{RT} dP = \sum (y_i - x_i) \, d \ln \hat{f}_i \quad (6\text{-}72)$$

For a *pure material*, there is but one chemical species i, and $x_i = y_i = 1$. Moreover, $H^v - H^l$ and $V^v - V^l$ are identified with the property changes of vaporization ΔH_i^{lv} and ΔV_i^{lv}. Thus, Eq. (6-72) simplifies to an expression developed in Example 4-1 and presented there as Eq. (4-11):

$$-\frac{\Delta H_i^{lv}}{RT^2} dT + \frac{\Delta V_i^{lv}}{RT} dP = 0 \tag{4-11}$$

As shown in Example 4-1, Eq. (4-11) is a basis for the derivation of the Clapeyron equation of a pure fluid.

Example 6-10 General changes in the equilibrium state of a multicomponent vapor/liquid system are accompanied by changes in the liquid and vapor compositions; for differential changes in state, the liquid and vapor mole fractions of a species k change by the amounts dx_k and dy_k. Formally dividing Eq. (6-72) by dx_k, we obtain an equivalent expression relating derivatives with respect to x_k:

$$\frac{\sum (y_i - x_i)H'_i - (H^v - H^l)}{RT^2} \frac{dT}{dx_k} + \frac{(V^v - V^l)}{RT} \frac{dP}{dx_k} = \sum (y_i - x_i) \frac{d \ln \hat{f}_i}{dx_k} \tag{A}$$

Alternatively, we can write on division by dy_k an expression relating derivatives with respect to y_k:

$$\frac{\sum (y_i - x_i)H'_i - (H^v - H^l)}{RT^2} \frac{dT}{dy_k} + \frac{(V^v - V^l)}{RT} \frac{dP}{dy_k} = \sum (y_i - x_i) \frac{d \ln \hat{f}_i}{dy_k} \tag{B}$$

At a vapor/liquid azeotrope, $x_i = y_i$ for all i, and Eqs. (A) and (B) reduce to

$$-\frac{(H^v - H^l)}{RT^2} \frac{dT}{dx_k} + \frac{(V^v - V^l)}{RT} \frac{dP}{dx_k} = 0 \qquad \text{(azeotrope)} \tag{C}$$

and

$$-\frac{(H^v - H^l)}{RT^2} \frac{dT}{dy_k} + \frac{(V^v - V^l)}{RT} \frac{dP}{dy_k} = 0 \qquad \text{(azeotrope)} \tag{D}$$

For conditions of constant pressure, $dP/dx_k = dP/dy_k = 0$; since $H^v \neq H^l$ except at a mixture critical state, it follows from Eqs. (C) and (D) that

$$\frac{dT}{dx_k} = \frac{dT}{dy_k} = 0 \qquad \text{(azeotrope, const } P) \qquad (6\text{-}73a)$$

Similarly, $dT/dx_k = dT/dy_k = 0$ for isothermal conditions, and we obtain from Eqs. (C) and (D) the analogous result

$$\frac{dP}{dx_k} = \frac{dP}{dy_k} = 0 \qquad \text{(azeotrope, const } T) \qquad (6\text{-}73b)$$

Equations (6-73) reflect the well-known attributes of the azeotropic state as representing an *extremum* in T (or P) at conditions of constant P (or T). These features were illustrated earlier on Figs. 6-2b and 6-3b for a binary system.

Identification of P with P^{az} and rearrangement of either Eq. (C) or Eq. (D) yields an expression for the temperature dependence of the azeotropic pressure:

$$\frac{dP^{az}}{dT} = \frac{H^v - H^l}{T(V^v - V^l)} \qquad (6\text{-}74)$$

Equation (6-74) is an analog of Eq. (4-6), the Clapeyron equation. However, the property changes of vaporization $H^v - H^l$ and $V^v - V^l$ are for a *mixture* and thus depend implicitly on the (variable) composition of the azeotropic state.

For most applications, Eq. (6-71) is advantageously recast through the definition of the activity coefficient, Eq. (5-120), rewritten here as

$$\hat{f}_i = x_i \gamma_i f_i^\circ$$

Application of this expression requires that x_i, and hence $\hat{f}_i$, γ_i, and f_i°, refer to a *particular* phase. Arbitrarily selecting the β phase for this purpose, we have

$$\hat{f}_i = \hat{f}_i^\beta = x_i^\beta \gamma_i^\beta (f_i^\circ)^\beta$$

We thus find the following alternative expression for the right-hand side of Eq. (6-71):

$$\sum (x_i^\beta - x_i^\alpha)\, d \ln \hat{f}_i = \sum (x_i^\beta - x_i^\alpha)\, d \ln x_i^\beta$$
$$+ \sum (x_i^\beta - x_i^\alpha)\, d \ln \gamma_i^\beta + \sum (x_i^\beta - x_i^\alpha)\, d \ln (f_i^\circ)^\beta \qquad (6\text{-}75)$$

But we also have by Eqs. (5-133) and (5-134) that

$$d \ln (f_i^\circ)^\beta = \frac{H_i' - (H_i^\circ)^\beta}{RT^2}\, dT + \frac{(V_i^\circ)^\beta}{RT}\, dP \qquad (6\text{-}76)$$

Combination of Eqs. (6-71), (6-75), and (6-76) gives on rearrangement the following form of the coexistence equation:

$$\frac{(V^E)^\beta + \sum x_i^\alpha (V_i^\circ)^\beta - V^\alpha}{RT}\, dP - \frac{(H^E)^\beta + \sum x_i^\alpha (H_i^\circ)^\beta - H^\alpha}{RT^2}\, dT$$
$$= \sum (x_i^\beta - x_i^\alpha)\, d \ln \gamma_i^\beta + \sum (x_i^\beta - x_i^\alpha)\, d \ln x_i^\beta \qquad (6\text{-}77)$$

Here, we have invoked the general definitions of the excess volume and the excess enthalpy for the β phase (see Example 5-9)

$$(V^E)^\beta = \Delta V^\beta \equiv V^\beta - \sum x_i^\beta (V_i^\circ)^\beta$$

$$(H^E)^\beta = \Delta H^\beta \equiv H^\beta - \sum x_i^\beta (H_i^\circ)^\beta$$

Since the mole fractions for a phase must sum to unity, the $d \ln x_i^\beta$ terms on the right-hand side of Eq. (6-77) are not mathematically independent. We therefore eliminate from the summations on the right-hand side of Eq. (6-77) the term for a particular species j. Designating by the symbol $\sum'$ a summation in which species j is excluded, and letting Y_k stand for any subscripted quantity appearing in a summand, we can write:

$$\sum (x_i^\beta - x_i^\alpha) Y_i = \sum' (x_i^\beta - x_i^\alpha) Y_i + (x_j^\beta - x_j^\alpha) Y_j$$

Since

$$x_j^\alpha = 1 - \sum' x_i^\alpha \quad \text{and} \quad x_j^\beta = 1 - \sum' x_i^\beta$$

this becomes

$$\sum (x_i^\beta - x_i^\alpha) Y_i = \sum' (x_i^\beta - x_i^\alpha)(Y_i - Y_j)$$

If we first let $Y_k \equiv d \ln \gamma_k^\beta$, and second let $Y_k \equiv d \ln x_k^\beta$, we get

$$\sum (x_i^\beta - x_i^\alpha) d \ln \gamma_i^\beta = \sum' (x_i^\beta - x_i^\alpha) d \ln (\gamma_i/\gamma_j)^\beta$$

and

$$\sum (x_i^\beta - x_i^\alpha) d \ln x_i^\beta = \sum' (x_i^\beta - x_i^\alpha) d \ln (x_i/x_j)^\beta$$

Substituting these two equations into Eq. (6-77), we obtain a particularly convenient form of the *general coexistence equation for two-phase* equilibrium:

$$\boxed{\psi \, dP - \Omega \, dT = \sum' (x_i^\beta - x_i^\alpha) d \ln (\gamma_i/\gamma_j)^\beta + \sum' (x_i^\beta - x_i^\alpha) d \ln (x_i/x_j)^\beta} \quad (6\text{-}78)$$

Here

$$\psi \equiv \frac{(V^E)^\beta + \sum x_i^\alpha (V_i^\circ)^\beta - V^\alpha}{RT} \quad (6\text{-}79a)$$

and

$$\Omega \equiv \frac{(H^E)^\beta + \sum x_i^\alpha (H_i^\circ)^\beta - H^\alpha}{RT^2} \quad (6\text{-}80a)$$

The definitions of coefficients ψ and Ω may be cast in different but equivalent forms. Three such sets of expressions are the following:

$$\psi \equiv \frac{(V^E)^\beta - (V^E)^\alpha + \sum x_i^\alpha[(V_i^\circ)^\beta - (V_i^\circ)^\alpha]}{RT} \qquad (6\text{-}79b)$$

$$\Omega \equiv \frac{(H^E)^\beta - (H^E)^\alpha + \sum x_i^\alpha[(H_i^\circ)^\beta - (H_i^\circ)^\alpha]}{RT^2} \qquad (6\text{-}80b)$$

$$\psi \equiv \frac{(V^\beta - V^\alpha) - \sum (x_i^\beta - x_i^\alpha)(V_i^\circ)^\beta}{RT} \qquad (6\text{-}79c)$$

$$\Omega \equiv \frac{(H^\beta - H^\alpha) - \sum (x_i^\beta - x_i^\alpha)(H_i^\circ)^\beta}{RT^2} \qquad (6\text{-}80c)$$

$$\psi \equiv \frac{\sum x_i^\alpha(\bar{V}_i^\beta - \bar{V}_i^\alpha) + \sum (x_i^\beta - x_i^\alpha)[\bar{V}_i^\beta - (V_i^\circ)^\beta]}{RT} \qquad (6\text{-}79d)$$

$$\Omega \equiv \frac{\sum x_i^\alpha(\bar{H}_i^\beta - \bar{H}_i^\alpha) + \sum (x_i^\beta - x_i^\alpha)[\bar{H}_i^\beta - (H_i^\circ)^\beta]}{RT^2} \qquad (6\text{-}80d)$$

Equations (6-79b) and (6-80b) incorporate excess functions for *both* phases, while the other two sets of definitions display respectively the integral and component property changes $M^\beta - M^\alpha$ and $\bar{M}_i^\beta - \bar{M}_i^\alpha$ accompanying the $\alpha\beta$ phase transition.

As they stand, Eqs. (6-78) through (6-80) apply to any kind of multicomponent, two-phase equilibrium. Moreover, any standard-state convention may be chosen for any of the species in either phase; the only restrictions are that the standard state T and P be those of the actual two-phase system. Our applications of these expressions are to vapor/liquid equilibrium, and for this case it is conventional to make the identifications $\alpha \equiv l$ and $\beta \equiv v$, and to use Lewis-Randall standard states for species in the vapor phase. Thus $x_i^\alpha \equiv x_i$, $x_i^\beta \equiv y_i$, $(V_i^\circ)^\beta \equiv V_i^v$, and $(H_i^\circ)^\beta \equiv H_i^v$. Equations (6-78), (6-79a), and (6-80a) then yield, for multicomponent VLE,

$$\frac{(V^E)^v + \sum x_i V_i^v - V^l}{RT} dP - \frac{(H^E)^v + \sum x_i H_i^v - H^l}{RT^2} dT$$

$$= \sum{}' (y_i - x_i) \, d \ln (\gamma_i/\gamma_j)^v + \sum{}' (y_i - x_i) \, d \ln (y_i/y_j) \qquad (6\text{-}81)$$

Equation (6-81) is entirely equivalent to Eq. (6-72) of Example 6-9; however, elimination of the fugacities in favor of vapor-phase mole fractions and activity coefficients makes it more convenient for application.

Example 6-11 As an application of Eq. (6-81), we consider the special case of binary VLE. In this case there are but two species ($i = 1, 2$), and we may exclude either *one* of them from the sums on the right-hand side of Eq. (6-81). Choosing $j = 2$, we obtain

$$\sum{}' (y_i - x_i) \, d \ln (\gamma_i/\gamma_j)^v = (y_1 - x_1) \, d \ln (\gamma_1/\gamma_2)^v \qquad (A)$$

and

$$\sum{}' (y_i - x_i)\, d\ln (y_i/y_j) = (y_1 - x_1)\, d\ln (y_1/y_2) \tag{B}$$

But

$$d\ln (y_1/y_2) = \frac{d(y_1/y_2)}{(y_1/y_2)} = \frac{y_2}{y_1}\left(\frac{1}{y_2}\, dy_1 - \frac{y_1}{y_2^2}\, dy_2\right)$$

Also

$$y_1 + y_2 = 1$$

and thus

$$dy_2 = -dy_1$$

Hence

$$d\ln (y_1/y_2) = \frac{1}{y_1 y_2}\, dy_1 = \frac{1}{y_1(1 - y_1)}\, dy_1$$

and Eq. (B) becomes

$$\sum{}' (y_i - x_i)\, d\ln (y_i/y_j) = \frac{y_1 - x_1}{y_1(1 - y_1)}\, dy_1 \tag{C}$$

Combination of Eqs. (A) and (C) with Eq. (6-81) then yields the *coexistence equation for binary VLE*:

$$
\begin{aligned}
\frac{(V^E)^v + x_1 V_1^v + x_2 V_2^v - V^l}{RT}\, dP &- \frac{(H^E)^v + x_1 H_1^v + x_2 H_2^v - H^l}{RT^2} \\
&= (y_1 - x_1)\, d\ln (\gamma_1/\gamma_2)^v + \frac{y_1 - x_1}{y_1(1 - y_1)}\, dy_1
\end{aligned}
\tag{6-82}
$$

Other expressions of the coefficients of dP and dT are possible, corresponding to the alternative definitions of ψ and Ω given by Eqs. (6-79b,c,d) and (6-80b,c,d).

6-7 REDUCTION OF LOW-PRESSURE VLE DATA

The primary thermodynamic value of VLE data taken at relatively low pressure is that from them one can calculate values for the excess Gibbs function. This is the process of *data reduction*, and its usual product is an expression, such as the Margules or Redlich-Kister equation, for the composition dependence of G^E.

The two common types of equipment for measurement of VLE data differ fundamentally in the way that equilibrium between the phases is established. In the *equilibrium still*, heat is applied in a still pot to induce continuous boiling of the liquid phase. The still is designed to promote intimate contact between the boiling liquid and the effluent vapor. Most often, the boiling liquid is directed into a vertical tube, where it surges upward, carrying slugs of vapor into a disengaging chamber. The phases are here assumed to be in equilibrium, and this is where the pressure is controlled and the temperature is measured. Here also, the liquid and vapor phases separate, the vapor flowing upward into a condenser. Both the liquid and condensed vapor recirculate to the still pot, where they mix prior to reboiling. Each returning stream passes through a small reservoir from which liquid samples may be withdrawn for analysis. Operation of the still continues until a steady state is reached, after which the compositions no longer change with time. These compositions are presumed those of the phases in equilibrium at the temperature and pressure of the disengaging chamber. Each experiment provides one data point, consisting for a binary system of measured values of x_1, y_1, T, and P. Data taken over the full composition range at either constant T or constant P constitute a data *set*, subject to reduction.

This type of equipment achieves at best a state of *dynamic* equilibrium, which one hopes is close to true thermodynamic equilibrium. Problems such as superheating of the boiling liquid, partial condensation of the vapor in the disengaging section, entrainment of liquid into the condenser, and evaporation of samples prior to analysis all present obstacles to the collection of accurate data. The many published designs of equilibrium stills attest to the difficulty of overcoming these and other problems. Hála et al. (1967) present a comprehensive review of equilibrium stills and a detailed discussion of their operation.

The other basic type of equipment is the *equilibrium cell*, in which *static* equilibrium between phases is attained. In principle, all one need do after loading the cell is to place it in a constant-temperature bath, agitate to assure equilibrium, measure the pressure in the cell, and sample the phases for analysis. There are, however, two impediments, which long prevented exploitation of this simple procedure. First, not only must the cell be thoroughly evacuated before introduction of the sample, but the sample itself must be degassed, i.e., freed of all noncondensable gases. Although degassing by distillation is now known to be effective (Van Ness and Abbott, 1978a), earlier methods were tedious and uncertain. Second, direct sampling, particularly of the vapor phase, upsets the equilibrium. The mass of vapor in the cell is very small; yet an appreciable mass must be withdrawn to yield an amount of *condensate* suitable for accurate analysis. Thus, the static equilibrium method was long out of favor in deference to the equilibrium still, a device designed to provide adequate samples of both phases.

However, as a consequence of Duhem's theorem, sampling of the phases is not, in fact, necessary. Given a set of equilibrium x, P data at constant T, thermodynamics allows calculation of the y-values. Thus, the equilibrium vapor need not be sampled for analysis. If an equilibrium cell is charged initially with known masses of the species, then the liquid-phase compositions are given by material-balance equations. Again, no sampling is required. Properly done, the calculations are complex and iterative, suited only to machine computation. Thus, it is hardly surprising that wide application of the static method awaited the development of the electronic computer. It has now largely superseded the dynamic equilibrium methods, particularly for isothermal VLE data. The only measurements required are of pressure and mass, both of which can be made with high accuracy. Descriptions of suitable equipment include those of Gibbs and Van Ness (1972), Tomlins and Marsh (1976), Steele et al. (1976), Pemberton and Mash (1978), and Maher and Smith (1979). In a general review of experimental VLE measurements, Marsh (1978) includes not only the static and dynamic methods but also several of secondary importance.

Given an experimental data point (P, T, x, y), the corresponding activity coefficients follow from Eq. (6-51):

$$\gamma_i = \frac{y_i P \Phi_i}{x_i P_i^{\text{sat}}} \tag{6-83}$$

Evaluation of Φ_i by Eq. (6-48) requires information outside the scope of the VLE data. For low to moderate pressures and for temperatures well below critical, the integral of Eq. (6-48) is accurately evaluated when V_i is taken to be constant. Then

$$\Phi_i = \frac{\hat{\phi}_i}{\phi_i^{\text{sat}}} \exp \left[-\frac{V_i(P - P_i^{\text{sat}})}{RT} \right]$$

Under the same conditions, good approximations for $\hat{\phi}_i$ and ϕ_i^{sat} result when the PVT behavior of the vapor is represented by the two-term virial equation in pressure. Thus, by Eq. (4-118), we have

$$\hat{\phi}_i = \exp \frac{P \bar{B}_i}{RT}$$

where $\bar{B}_i$ is evaluated by Eq. (4-112), (4-113), or (4-114). For pure species i at its vapor pressure, this becomes

$$\phi_i^{\text{sat}} = \exp \frac{P_i^{\text{sat}} B_{ii}}{RT}$$

Combining these last three equations gives

$$\Phi_i = \exp \left[\frac{P \bar{B}_i - P_i^{\text{sat}} B_{ii} - V_i(P - P_i^{\text{sat}})}{RT} \right] \tag{6-84}$$

For an i-j binary system, with $\bar{B}_i$ given by Eq. (4-114), Eq. (6-84) reduces to

$$\Phi_i = \exp \left[\frac{(B_{ii} - V_i)(P - P_i^{\text{sat}}) + P y_j^2 \delta_{ij}}{RT} \right] \tag{6-85}$$

where δ_{ij} is defined by Eq. (4-100).

The classical (precomputer) data-reduction procedure is necessarily direct. By Eq. (5-47), we have

$$g = \sum x_i \ln \gamma_i \tag{6-86}$$

where, by definition,

$$g \equiv \frac{G^E}{RT} \tag{6-87}$$

Activity coefficients calculated by Eq. (6-83) and substituted into Eq. (6-86) yield values of g, which are then fit to an appropriate analytical expression giving the composition dependence of g. For isothermal VLE data, there is no complication, but for isobaric data, the equation should include the predetermined temperature dependence of g, as indicated in Example 6-8. If this is not done, then the temperature dependence of g cannot be separated from its composition dependence, and application of Eq. (6-33) yields activity coefficients which are not in complete accord with the experimental values.

The general practicality of other methods for reduction of VLE data depends largely on the computer. In the formal development that follows, simplicity requires emphasis on the treatment of isothermal data for binary systems. Applications to other cases are presented later.

Writing Eq. (6-86) for a binary system containing species 1 and 2 and differentiating with respect to x_1, we get

$$\frac{dg}{dx_1} = x_1 \frac{d \ln \gamma_1}{dx_1} + \ln \gamma_1 + x_2 \frac{d \ln \gamma_2}{dx_1} - \ln \gamma_2$$

Equation (5-55), a Gibbs-Duhem equation, when written for a binary system at constant T and P, becomes

$$x_1 \, d \ln \gamma_1 + x_2 \, d \ln \gamma_2 = 0$$

Although pressure is not constant for isothermal VLE data, we have shown that its influence on the activity coefficients is negligible. Division of this equation by dx_1 gives

$$x_1 \frac{d \ln \gamma_1}{dx_1} + x_2 \frac{d \ln \gamma_2}{dx_1} = 0 \tag{6-88}$$

which reduces the expression for dg/dx_1 to

$$\frac{dg}{dx_1} = \ln \frac{\gamma_1}{\gamma_2} \tag{6-89}$$

Thus, we may fit values of $\ln (\gamma_1/\gamma_2)$, calculated from the data, directly to an analytical expression obtained by differentiation of a suitable equation for the composition dependence of g.

The most interesting aspect of this procedure is that pressure cancels when one forms the ratio of activity coefficients:

$$\frac{\gamma_1}{\gamma_2} = \frac{y_1 \Phi_1 x_2 P_2^{\text{sat}}}{y_2 \Phi_2 x_1 P_1^{\text{sat}}} \tag{6-90}$$

Although pressure does appear in the equations for the secondary functions Φ_1 and Φ_2, experimental values are not needed. Calculated values result by simple iteration. For an initial fit, the Φ_i values are set equal to unity. The expression for $g \equiv G^E/RT$ so obtained, together with Eq. (6-33), yield initial values for the activity coefficients. Writing Eq. (6-51) for each species as

$$y_1 P = \frac{x_1 \gamma_1 P_1^{\text{sat}}}{\Phi_1}$$

and

$$y_2 P = \frac{x_2 \gamma_2 P_2^{\text{sat}}}{\Phi_2}$$

we get by addition an expression for P:

$$P = \frac{x_1 \gamma_1 P_1^{\text{sat}}}{\Phi_1} + \frac{x_2 \gamma_2 P_2^{\text{sat}}}{\Phi_2} \qquad (6\text{-}91)$$

Initial values for P calculated by this equation (with $\Phi_i = 1$) are used for the evaluation of Φ_1 and Φ_2. The process is repeated until there is no significant change in the calculated pressures. Thus, we see that the equilibrium pressures can be calculated from a subset of x_1, y_1 data at constant temperature.

In fact, one can also calculate x_1 values from the y_1, P data subset and y_1 values from the x_1, P subset. To illustrate conceptually how this is possible, we make use of a simplified form of the binary coexistence equation. For isothermal VLE data, Eq. (6-82) becomes

$$\frac{(V^E)^v + x_1 V_1^v + x_2 V_2^v - V^l}{RT} \, dP = (y_1 - x_1) \, d \ln (\gamma_1/\gamma_2)^v + \frac{y_1 - x_1}{y_1(1 - y_1)} \, dy_1$$

This equation is greatly simplified when the vapor is assumed an ideal gas and the liquid volume is taken as negligible compared with the vapor volume. Then

$$(V^E)^v = 0 \qquad V_1^v = \bar{V}_2^v = \frac{RT}{P} \qquad V^l = 0$$

and the term on the left reduces to dP/P. Moreover, $(\gamma_1/\gamma_2)^v = 1$, eliminating the first term on the right. As a result, we have

$$\frac{dP}{P} = \frac{y_1 - x_1}{y_1(1 - y_1)} \, dy_1 \qquad (6\text{-}92)$$

Solution for x_1 gives

$$x_1 = y_1 \left[1 - \frac{(1 - y_1)}{P} \frac{dP}{dy_1} \right]$$

Clearly, values of x_1 can be directly calculated from the subset of y_1, P data, provided they are sufficiently precise for evaluation of derivatives dP/dy_1.

Equation (6-92) may also be written

$$\frac{dy_1}{dP} = \frac{y_1(1 - y_1)}{P(y_1 - x_1)}$$

In this form the equation is suitable for numerical integration to yield values of y_1 from a subset of x_1, P data. The procedure is discussed by Van Ness (1970). The same calculations can of course be made with the unsimplified coexistence equation; however, alternative procedures have proved to be more efficient.

The calculation of y_1 values from a subset of x_1, P data is of far greater interest than the calculation of x_1 values from a subset of y_1, P data, because x_1 is not only more easily measured but is the independent variable in the ultimate correlation of G^E as a function of composition. A general calculation procedure follows from Eq. (6-91) when γ_1 and γ_2 are eliminated in favor of $g \equiv G^E/RT$ and its derivatives. The required expressions follow from Eqs. (5-38) when written for

$$M^E \equiv G^E/RT \equiv g \qquad \text{and} \qquad \bar{M}_i^E \equiv \bar{G}_i^E/RT = \ln \gamma_i$$

In exponential form, these equations are

$$\gamma_1 = \exp \left[g + x_2 \frac{dg}{dx_1} \right] \tag{6-93a}$$

and

$$\gamma_2 = \exp \left[g - x_1 \frac{dg}{dx_1} \right] \tag{6-93b}$$

Substitution into Eq. (6-91) yields

$$P = \frac{x_1 P_1^{\text{sat}}}{\Phi_1} \exp \left[g + x_2 \frac{dg}{dx_1} \right] + \frac{x_2 P_2^{\text{sat}}}{\Phi_2} \exp \left[g - x_1 \frac{dg}{dx_1} \right] \tag{6-94}$$

The vapor compositions y_1 and y_2 appear only in the secondary functions Φ_1 and Φ_2, and need not be known initially. They are in fact to be determined, and the process is iterative, starting with $\Phi_1 = \Phi_2 = 1$. Thus, Eq. (6-94) in essence relates P to x_1 and to g, which is also a function of x_1. All that is needed is some technique, an algorithm, to search for the g-versus-x_1 relation which yields values of P calculated by Eq. (6-94) in agreement with experimental values. Vapor compositions are calculated by Eq. (6-51), written as

$$\boxed{y_i = \frac{x_i \gamma_i P_i^{\text{sat}}}{\Phi_i P}} \tag{6-95}$$

with the γ_i values from Eqs. (6-93). Each iteration produces a set of y_i values, allowing continual refinement of the Φ_i values by Eq. (6-85).

Equation (6-94) is readily generalized for application to multicomponent systems. In this case, Eq. (6-91) becomes

$$P = \sum_i \frac{x_i \gamma_i P_i^{\text{sat}}}{\Phi_i}$$

Expressions for the activity coefficients follow from Eq. (3-11) when we make the identifications $M \equiv g$ and $\bar{M}_i \equiv \ln \gamma_i$:

$$\ln \gamma_i = g - \sum_{k \neq i} x_k \left(\frac{\partial g}{\partial x_k} \right)_{x_{j \neq i, k}}$$

Thus

$$P = \sum_i \frac{x_i P_i^{\text{sat}}}{\Phi_i} \exp \left[g - \sum_{k \neq i} x_k \left(\frac{\partial g}{\partial x_k} \right)_{x_{j \neq i, k}} \right] \tag{6-96}$$

where Φ_i is evaluated by Eq. (6-84).

For either the binary or the multicomponent case, there are two general methods by which the reduction of an x, P subset of isothermal VLE data is accomplished. One of these requires an initial choice of the form taken by an analytical expression of G^E as a function of the x_i. Presume, for example, that data for a binary system can be fit by an expression of the form

$$g \equiv \frac{G^E}{RT} = A x_1 x_2$$

where A is a parameter independent of composition. Then

$$\gamma_1 = \exp A x_2^2 \qquad \gamma_2 = \exp A x_1^2$$

and Eq. (6-94) becomes

$$P = \frac{x_1 P_1^{\text{sat}}}{\Phi_1} \exp A x_2^2 + \frac{\dot{x}_2 P_2^{\text{sat}}}{\Phi_2} \exp A x_1^2$$

We have only to find a value for A that provides the closest correspondence between experimental and calculated values of P. In this simple case, trial calculations done by hand can lead quite easily to a suitable value for A. In general, however, parameter evaluation is done by computer. One may well find with a single parameter that there is no value of the parameter which eliminates systematic differences between experimental and calculated pressure. In this event, a new form of expression for g is chosen, perhaps

$$\frac{g}{x_1 x_2} = A_{21} x_1 + A_{12} x_2$$

One continues the process until an expression is found that eliminates systematic discrepancies between the pressures. This method was proposed by Barker (1953), and is known as Barker's method.

The other general method for data reduction based on Eq. (6-94) or (6-96) solves the problem through a numerical algorithm based on an initial fit of the P-versus-x data by an empirical expression or set of expressions that allows interpolation between experimental points. No assumption is made with respect to an expression for g. The method results in a set of numerical values for g as a function of x, which may be directly fit by a suitable analytical expression. The method was first proposed by Mixon et al. (1965). An equivalent method, based on the relative volatility rather than on g, is described by Martinez-Ortiz and Manley (1977). A detailed discussion of "model-free" methods of data reduction for binary systems is given by Sayegh and Vera (1980).

Given a full set of VLE data (x_1, y_1, P) for a binary system at constant temperature, one clearly has some choice as to a data-reduction method. We can get a much better understanding of the nature of this choice by a systematic examination of the possibilities. The key to this is the definition of a *residual*:

$$\boxed{\delta Y \equiv \text{predicted value of } Y - \text{experimental value of } Y}$$

According to the phase rule, a binary system in vapor/liquid equilibrium has two degrees of freedom. Thus, of the experimental variables (T, P, x_1, y_1) only two can be regarded as independent. These are chosen as T and x_1, because these are the variables pertinent to the liquid phase, to which the ultimate correlation applies. With this understanding, we regard the values of T and x_1 as fixed by the data set. On the other hand, the dependent variables P and y_1, though measured, are in addition subject to calculation or prediction. Thus, we can determine the residuals δP and δy_1. Since they compare a predicted value with a direct experimental measurement, they are the *primary* residuals. Experimental values of γ_1 and γ_2 are calculated from the VLE data by Eq. (6-83); the experimental value of g is then given by Eq. (6-86). As a result, we have available experimental values for P, y_1, γ_1, γ_2, and g. Note that P_1^{sat} and P_2^{sat} are functions of temperature only, presumed part of the data set, and fixed for a given value of the independent variable T.

Predicted values of pressure, vapor composition, and the thermodynamic functions come from a correlating expression for g, and are identified by the superscript †. Thus, when we know

$$g^{\dagger} = g(x_1; \alpha, \beta, \ldots) \quad \text{(const } T) \tag{6-97}$$

where $\alpha, \beta, \ldots$ are the correlating parameters, values of $\gamma_1^{\dagger}$ and $\gamma_2^{\dagger}$ are provided by Eqs. (6-93). Predicted values of $P^{\dagger}$ and $y_1^{\dagger}$ come from Eqs. (6-91) and (6-95), written as

$$P^{\dagger} = \frac{x_1 \gamma_1^{\dagger} P_1^{\text{sat}}}{\Phi_1} + \frac{x_2 \gamma_2^{\dagger} P_2^{\text{sat}}}{\Phi_2} \tag{6-98}$$

and

$$y_1^{\dagger} = \frac{x_1 \gamma_1^{\dagger} P_1^{\text{sat}}}{P^{\dagger} \Phi_1} \tag{6-99}$$

From these equations we therefore have the predicted values $P^\dagger$, $y_1^\dagger$, $\gamma_1^\dagger$, $\gamma_2^\dagger$, and $g^\dagger$. In Eqs. (6-98) and (6-99), we have written the secondary functions as Φ_1 and Φ_2, rather than as $\Phi_1^\dagger$ and $\Phi_2^\dagger$. Since these quantities are of relatively minor influence, it is, for practical purposes, immaterial whether they are evaluated at measured or predicted values of P and y_1.

The residuals of immediate interest are defined as

$$\delta P \equiv P^\dagger - P$$

$$\delta y_1 \equiv y_1^\dagger - y_1$$

$$\delta \gamma_1^\dagger \equiv \gamma_1^\dagger - \gamma_1$$

$$\delta \gamma_2^\dagger \equiv \gamma_2^\dagger - \gamma_2$$

and

$$\delta g \equiv g^\dagger - g$$

Other residuals are, of course, possible; given values for γ_1, γ_2, $\gamma_1^\dagger$, and $\gamma_2^\dagger$, we can, for example, calculate values of the residual

$$\delta \ln \frac{\gamma_1}{\gamma_2} \equiv \ln \frac{\gamma_1^\dagger}{\gamma_2^\dagger} - \ln \frac{\gamma_1}{\gamma_2}$$

and will return to this quantity later. Additional residuals can equally well be defined for other thermodynamic functions. For example, the relative volatility is

$$\alpha_{12} \equiv \frac{y_1/x_1}{y_2/x_2} = \frac{\gamma_1 P_1^{\text{sat}} \Phi_2}{\gamma_2 P_2^{\text{sat}} \Phi_1}$$

However, one quickly finds that

$$\delta \ln \alpha_{12} \equiv \ln \alpha_{12}^\dagger - \ln \alpha_{12} = \delta \ln \frac{\gamma_1}{\gamma_2}$$

Given a suitable expression of Eq. (6-97), the data-reduction procedure is designed to adjust the correlating parameters α, β, ... until values are found that make a selected set of residuals very small. The usual criterion is that the sum of squares of the residuals be minimized. This sum

$$\boxed{S \equiv \sum (\delta Y)^2}$$

is known as an *objective function*.

A particular objective function implies a particular data-reduction procedure; with a variety of objective functions, we have a variety of procedures from which to choose. Since we wish to represent experimental values of P and y_1, an objective function formed from the δP or δy_1 values is indicated. There is, however, no evident reason to choose one or the other. Thus, common practice has been to base data reduction on an objective function formed from a thermodynamic function related to *both* of the primary residuals. The nature of these relationships follows from Eq. (6-83), which we write as

$$\gamma_i \simeq \frac{y_i P}{x_i P_i^{\text{sat}}} \tag{6-100}$$

The approximation results because we have omitted the secondary function Φ_i, which is of order unity and of little importance to our present purpose. For fixed values of the independent variables, x_i, T, and P_i^{sat} are fixed. Differentiation therefore gives

$$d\gamma_i \simeq \frac{y_i}{x_i P_i^{\text{sat}}} dP + \frac{P}{x_i P_i^{\text{sat}}} dy_i$$

With Eq. (6-100), this becomes

$$d\gamma_i \simeq \frac{\gamma_i}{P} dP + \frac{\gamma_i}{y_i} dy_i$$

Making a further approximation, we replace the differentials by differences, which are the residuals of interest:

$$\delta\gamma_i \simeq \gamma_i \left(\frac{\delta P}{P} + \frac{\delta y_i}{y_i} \right)$$

For the two species in a binary system, this becomes

$$\delta\gamma_1 \simeq \gamma_1 \left(\frac{\delta P}{P} + \frac{\delta y_1}{y_1} \right) \tag{6-101a}$$

and

$$\delta\gamma_2 \simeq \gamma_2 \left(\frac{\delta P}{P} - \frac{\delta y_1}{y_2} \right) \tag{6-101b}$$

Since the function g is related to the activity coefficients by

$$g = x_1 \ln \gamma_1 + x_2 \ln \gamma_2$$

we have, for given values of x_1 and x_2,

$$dg = x_1 \, d \ln \gamma_1 + x_2 \, d \ln \gamma_2$$

Thus

$$\delta g \simeq x_1 \frac{\delta\gamma_1}{\gamma_1} + x_2 \frac{\delta\gamma_2}{\gamma_2}$$

With Eqs. (6-101), this becomes, upon simplification,

$$\delta g \simeq \frac{\delta P}{P} + (x_1 - y_1) \frac{\delta y_1}{y_1 y_2} \tag{6-102}$$

Clearly, each of the residuals $\delta\gamma_1$, $\delta\gamma_2$, and δg is uniquely related to the primary residuals δP and δy_1. Because empirical fitting equations may not precisely mirror physical behavior and because experimental data incorporate, at the very least, random measurement errors, a perfect fit of data is not possible. The best one can expect is a correlating equation which yields values of the primary residuals δP and δy_1 that scatter around zero. However, data-reduction procedures based on an objective function formed from $\delta\gamma_1$, $\delta\gamma_2$, or δg often *promote* bias in the δP and δy_1 residuals. Since the objective function in each case is a combination of these residuals, as indicated by Eqs. (6-101) and (6-102), a fit is obtained at the expense of exaggerated but compensatory values of δP and δy_1. In Eq. (6-101a) for $\delta\gamma_1$, these residuals combine by addition; thus, one finds a trend to opposite signs in the values of δP and δy_1. Since the residual $\delta\gamma_2$, as given by Eq. (6-101b), equals a difference between quantities that include δP and δy_1, a trend to like signs is found in these values. Similar qualitative observations apply to Eq. (6-102) for δg in any specific application; however, the sign of $(x_1 - y_1)$ depends on the application, and, moreover, changes at an azeotrope.

Example 6-12 The VLE data of Scatchard and Raymond (1938) for chloroform(1)/ethanol(2) have long been regarded as exemplary. The data are shown by P-x_1 and P-y_1 curves in Fig. 6-8. These data and more recent data for this system (Van Ness and Abbott, 1978b) are well fit by the four-parameter Margules equation, Eq. (6-63). We reduce Scatchard and Raymond's data for this system at 45°C by the classical procedure, minimizing the objective function $\sum (\delta g)^2$, with $g^\dagger$ given by the four-parameter Margules equation.

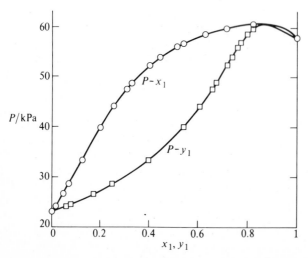

Figure 6-8 Plots of P versus x_1 and P versus y_1 for chloroform(1)/ethanol(2) at 45°C. Data of Scatchard and Raymond (1938). For clarity, data points are omitted to the right of the azeotrope.

Table 6-3 Results of VLE data reduction for chloroform(1)/ethanol(2) at 45°C

Objective function	$\sum (\delta g)^2$ Example 6-12	$\sum [\delta \ln (\gamma_1/\gamma_2)]^2$ Example 6-13	$\sum (\delta P)^2$ Example 6-14	$\sum (\delta y_1)^2$ Example 6-14	Eq. (6-111)
Parameter, Eq. (6-63)					
A_{21}	1.6950	1.7012	1.7091	1.6578	1.6915
A_{12}	0.4909	0.4355	0.4592	0.4252	0.4395
C_{21}	0.5422	0.8543	0.6915	0.7150	0.7248
C_{12}	−0.3620	−0.5683	−0.4069	−0.5900	−0.5164
RMS δP/kPa	0.22	0.23	0.07	0.33	0.15
RMS δy_1	0.0043	0.0020	0.0030	0.0017	0.0022

Ancillary data, cm^3 mol^{-1}

$B_{11} = -1,000 \qquad V_1 = 80$
$B_{22} = -1,520 \qquad V_2 = 60$
$B_{12} = -690$

Since

$$g^\dagger = x_1 \ln \gamma_1^\dagger + x_2 \ln \gamma_2^\dagger$$

and

$$g = x_1 \ln \gamma_1 + x_2 \ln \gamma_2$$

we have

$$\delta g = x_1 \ln \frac{\gamma_1^\dagger}{\gamma_1} + x_2 \ln \frac{\gamma_2^\dagger}{\gamma_2}$$

Substitution for γ_1 and γ_2 by Eq. (6-83) gives

$$\delta g = x_1 \ln \frac{x_1 P_1^{sat} \gamma_1^\dagger}{y_1 P \Phi_1} + x_2 \ln \frac{x_2 P_2^{sat} \gamma_2^\dagger}{y_2 P \Phi_2} \qquad (6\text{-}103)$$

Values of x_1, y_1, P, P_1^{sat}, and P_2^{sat} are provided by the data set. The factors Φ_1 and Φ_2 come from Eq. (6-85) with values of the virial coefficients calculated from the correlation of Hayden and O'Connell (1975). Values of $\gamma_1^\dagger$ and $\gamma_2^\dagger$ result from Eqs. (6-93) applied to the four-parameter Margules equation for $g^\dagger$. The parameters which minimize $\sum (\delta g)^2$ are given in Table 6-3 along with ancillary data. The final values of δg scatter around zero on a plot of δg versus x_1.

This is not the case, however, for the resulting values of δP and δy_1, which are shown by Fig. 6-9. The quantity $(x_1 - y_1)$ in Eq. (6-102) is negative for all values of x_1 up to the azeotrope mole fraction of about 0.88. At higher values of x_1, this difference is positive. However, for x_1 values above 0.8 it is very small, and the second term of Eq. (6-102) is negligible. The fitting procedure then minimizes just the δP residuals, which are seen at the right-hand end of Fig. 6-9 to scatter closely around zero. At lower values of x_1, we find appreciable positive values for both δP and δy_1. According to Eq. (6-102), with $(x_1 - y_1)$ negative, they combine by difference, thus producing a distribution of δg values around zero. Although g is well fit by the correlation, the measured variables P and y_1 are less well represented.

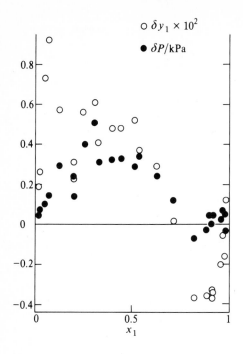

Figure 6-9 Residuals δy_1 and δP resulting from a fit of the four-parameter Margules equation to VLE data for chloroform(1)/ethanol(2) at 45°C. Fit based on minimization of $\sum (\delta g)^2$, where $g \equiv G^E/RT$. See Example 6-12.

As mentioned earlier, we can define a residual for yet another thermo-dynamic function:

$$\delta \ln \frac{\gamma_1}{\gamma_2} \equiv \ln \frac{\gamma_1^\dagger}{\gamma_2^\dagger} - \ln \frac{\gamma_1}{\gamma_2} \qquad (6\text{-}104)$$

The ratio of experimental values γ_1/γ_2 is given by Eq. (6-90):

$$\frac{\gamma_1}{\gamma_2} = \frac{y_1 \Phi_1 x_2 P_2^{\text{sat}}}{y_2 \Phi_2 x_1 P_1^{\text{sat}}}$$

For the ratio of predicted values $\gamma_1^\dagger/\gamma_2^\dagger$ at the same T and x, we have

$$\frac{\gamma_1^\dagger}{\gamma_2^\dagger} = \frac{y_1^\dagger \Phi_1^\dagger x_2 P_2^{\text{sat}}}{y_2^\dagger \Phi_2^\dagger x_1 P_1^{\text{sat}}}$$

Dividing the second of these equations by the first gives

$$\frac{\gamma_1^\dagger/\gamma_2^\dagger}{\gamma_1/\gamma_2} = \left(\frac{y_1^\dagger/y_2^\dagger}{y_1/y_2}\right)\left(\frac{\Phi_1^\dagger/\Phi_2^\dagger}{\Phi_1/\Phi_2}\right)$$

In logarithmic form, this becomes

$$\ln \frac{\gamma_1^\dagger}{\gamma_2^\dagger} - \ln \frac{\gamma_1}{\gamma_2} = \ln \frac{y_1^\dagger}{y_2^\dagger} - \ln \frac{y_1}{y_2} + \ln \frac{\Phi_1^\dagger}{\Phi_2^\dagger} - \ln \frac{\Phi_1}{\Phi_2}$$

or

$$\delta \ln \frac{\gamma_1}{\gamma_2} = \delta \ln \frac{y_1}{y_2} + \delta \ln \frac{\Phi_1}{\Phi_2} \tag{6-105}$$

This is an exact relation among residuals. A more useful form results from approximation. In particular, the final term involving only the secondary functions Φ_1 and Φ_2 is inherently of lower order than the other two, and may be neglected. Moreover

$$\delta \ln \frac{y_1}{y_2} \simeq \frac{y_2}{y_1} \delta \left(\frac{y_1}{y_2} \right) = \frac{\delta y_1}{y_1} - \frac{\delta y_2}{y_2}$$

Since $\delta y_2 = -\delta y_1$, this becomes

$$\delta \ln \frac{y_1}{y_2} \simeq \frac{\delta y_1}{y_1 y_2}$$

and by Eq. (6-105)

$$\delta \ln \frac{\gamma_1}{\gamma_2} \simeq \frac{\delta y_1}{y_1 y_2} \tag{6-106}$$

Thus, the residual $\delta \ln (\gamma_1/\gamma_2)$ is unrelated to δP, at least to a good approximation.

An expression for evaluation of this residual results when we eliminate γ_1 and γ_2 from Eq. (6-104) by Eq. (6-83):

$$\delta \ln \frac{\gamma_1}{\gamma_2} = \ln \frac{\gamma_1^\dagger}{\gamma_2^\dagger} - \ln \frac{y_1 P \Phi_1 / x_1 P_1^{sat}}{y_2 P \Phi_2 / x_2 P_2^{sat}}$$

or

$$\delta \ln \frac{\gamma_1}{\gamma_2} = \ln \frac{\gamma_1^\dagger}{\gamma_2^\dagger} + \ln \frac{y_2 x_1 \Phi_2}{y_1 x_2 \Phi_1} + \ln \frac{P_1^{sat}}{P_2^{sat}} \tag{6-107}$$

Minimization of the objective function $\sum [\delta \ln (\gamma_1/\gamma_2)]^2$ is a mechanism for carrying out the data-reduction procedure discussed in connection with Eq. (6-90). Here too, the equilibrium pressure P appears only in the secondary functions Φ_1 and Φ_2, and we require only a subset of x_1, y_1 data. Pressures are calculated from the correlation.

However, this data-reduction procedure is subject to an abstruse constraint. We multiply Eq. (6-107) by dx_1, and integrate between the limits $x_1 = 0$ to $x_1 = 1$:

$$\int_0^1 \delta \ln \frac{\gamma_1}{\gamma_2} \, dx_1 = \int_0^1 \ln \frac{\gamma_1^\dagger}{\gamma_2^\dagger} \, dx_1 + \int_0^1 \ln \frac{y_2 x_1 \Phi_2}{y_1 x_2 \Phi_1} \, dx_1 + \int_0^1 \ln \frac{P_1^{sat}}{P_2^{sat}} \, dx_1 \tag{6-108}$$

The first integral on the right is necessarily zero; this follows from Eq. (6-89) written as

$$dg^\dagger = \ln \frac{\gamma_1^\dagger}{\gamma_2^\dagger} \, dx_1$$

This equation is valid only when the $\ln \gamma_1^\dagger$ and $\ln \gamma_2^\dagger$ values satisfy the Gibbs-Duhem equation. Since these values are calculated from the correlating equation for $g^\dagger$, they necessarily conform with this requirement, as demonstrated in Example 3-6. Integrating the preceding equation, we get

$$\int_{g^\dagger(x_1=0)}^{g^\dagger(x_1=1)} dg^\dagger = \int_0^1 \ln \frac{\gamma_1^\dagger}{\gamma_2^\dagger} \, dx_1$$

The integral on the left is evaluated simply as

$$g^\dagger(x_1 = 1) - g^\dagger(x_1 = 0) = 0$$

a result which follows from the fact that any excess function based on Lewis-Randall standard states is zero at the composition limits. Thus, the integral of interest is always zero, and Eq. (6-108) becomes

$$\int_0^1 \delta \ln \frac{\gamma_1}{\gamma_2} \, dx_1 = \int_0^1 \ln \frac{y_2 x_1 \Phi_2}{y_1 x_2 \Phi_1} \, dx_1 + \ln \frac{P_1^{sat}}{P_2^{sat}} \tag{6-109}$$

where the last term merely reflects the fact that P_1^{sat} and P_2^{sat} are constant for constant temperature.

The terms on the right-hand side of Eq. (6-109) bear no relation whatever to the correlating equation for $g^\dagger$. Thus, the value of the integral on the left is independent of the correlating equation and of how well it fits the data. For a given data set and given ancillary data (such as the virial coefficients), this integral is of fixed value, represented approximately as the net area on a plot of the residuals $\delta \ln (\gamma_1/\gamma_2)$ versus x_1. Thus, minimization of the objective function $\sum [\delta \ln (\gamma_1/\gamma_2)]^2$ is constrained to yield residuals that satisfy Eq. (6-109). If the data set and ancillary data are such that the terms on the right-hand side of this equation exactly cancel, then data reduction yields residuals $\delta \ln (\gamma_1/\gamma_2)$ that scatter around zero. This is, however, rarely the case, and then data reduction yields values of $\delta \ln (\gamma_1/\gamma_2)$, which when plotted versus x_1, show bias from zero, and tend to scatter about a horizontal line representing the mean value of $\delta \ln (\gamma_1/\gamma_2)$ consistent with the fixed value of the integral:

$$\int_0^1 \delta \ln \frac{\gamma_1}{\gamma_2} \, dx_1 = \left(\delta \ln \frac{\gamma_1}{\gamma_2} \right)_{mean} \Delta x_1 = \left(\delta \ln \frac{\gamma_1}{\gamma_2} \right)_{mean}$$

Any other fit of the data provides a correlation that yields the same value of the integral and the same mean value, but the distribution is skewed with respect to the mean value.

Example 6-13 The data set for chloroform(1)/ethanol(2) treated in Example 6-12 is here reduced by minimization of $\sum [\delta \ln (\gamma_1/\gamma_2)]^2$. The residuals are calculated from

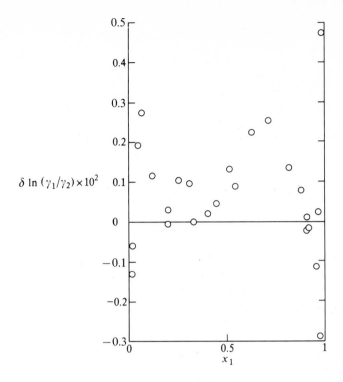

Figure 6-10 Residuals $\delta \ln (\gamma_1/\gamma_2)$ resulting from a fit of the four-parameter Margules equation to VLE data for chloroform(1)/ethanol(2) at 45°C. Fit based on minimization of $\sum [\delta \ln (\gamma_1/\gamma_2)]^2$. See Example 6-13.

Eq. (6-107) with $\gamma_i^\dagger$ values from the four-parameter Margules equation. The ancillary data are as before.

The parameters determined by this procedure are listed in Table 6-3. Figure 6-10 is a plot of the residuals $\delta \ln (\gamma_1/\gamma_2)$ versus x_1. Clearly, they do not scatter about zero, but have positive bias. This is a result of the constraint inherent in this data-reduction procedure. The same positive bias appears in the residuals δy_1, as shown by Fig. 6-11. This is inevitable, because Eq. (6-106) gives

$$\delta y_1 \simeq y_1 y_2 \, \delta \ln \frac{\gamma_1}{\gamma_2}$$

Thus, the pattern of δy_1 residuals is very like that shown by the $\delta \ln (\gamma_1/\gamma_2)$ values, the influence of the factor $y_1 y_2$ becoming evident primarily near the edges of the figure where y_1 or y_2 is very small. Nevertheless, this procedure does not give quite the best possible fit of the y_1 values. The residuals δy_1 scatter more or less randomly around an average value of 0.0012; on the other hand, the residuals δP, which do not influence the fit, are systematically negative. These values are also plotted in Fig. 6-11.

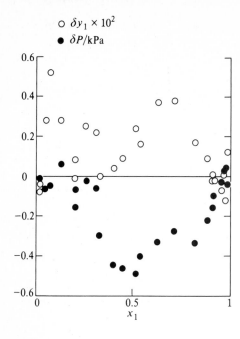

$\circ\ \delta y_1 \times 10^2$

$\bullet\ \delta P/kPa$

Figure 6-11 Residuals δy_1 and δP resulting from a fit of the four-parameter Margules equation to VLE data for chloroform(1)/ethanol(2) at 45°C. Fit based on minimization of $\sum [\delta \ln (\gamma_1/\gamma_2)]^2$. See Example 6-13.

Examples 6-12 and 6-13 illustrate the difficulties encountered when one tries to achieve a fit of the dependent variables P and y_1 through data reduction based on residuals in thermodynamic functions. We consider now procedures which separately fit one or the other of these measured variables through direct minimization of either $\sum (\delta P)^2$ or $\sum (\delta y_1)^2$. The means is provided by Eqs. (6-98) and (6-99):

$$P^\dagger = \frac{x_1 \gamma_1^\dagger P_1^{\text{sat}}}{\Phi_1} + \frac{x_2 \gamma_2^\dagger P_2^{\text{sat}}}{\Phi_2} \qquad (6\text{-}98)$$

and

$$y_1^\dagger = \frac{x_1 \gamma_1^\dagger P_1^{\text{sat}}}{P^\dagger \Phi_1} \qquad (6\text{-}99)$$

For minimization of $\sum (\delta P)^2$, one calculates values of $P^\dagger$ by Eq. (6-98); values of δP then follow from the definition

$$\delta P \equiv P^\dagger - P$$

The y_1 values enter only in the secondary functions Φ_1 and Φ_2, and as explained in connection with Eq. (6-94), experimental values are not needed. This procedure implements Barker's method.

For minimization of $\sum (\delta y_1)^2$, $y_1^\dagger$ values come from Eq. (6-99) with $P^\dagger$ values again provided by Eq. (6-98). By definition

$$\delta y_1 \equiv y_1^\dagger - y_1$$

In this procedure, experimental pressures are not required. The Φ_1 and Φ_2 values can be evaluated from $P^\dagger$ values.

Example 6-14 With the same data set and ancillary data as in the two preceding examples, we illustrate application of the procedures which provide separately direct fits of the x_1, P data and the x_1, y_1 data. The parameters which minimize $\sum (\delta P)^2$ and those which minimize $\sum (\delta y_1)^2$ are listed in Table 6-3. Figure 6-12 shows the residuals δy_1 and δP which result when the objective function is $\sum (\delta P)^2$. There is no doubt here that the fitting procedure accomplishes its purpose. The δP values scatter closely about zero. The root-mean-square value of δP is 0.07 kPa for pressures between 24 and 61 kPa. This is convincing evidence that the four-parameter Margules equation is indeed an appropriate correlating expression for this data set. The y_1 values, unused in this data-reduction procedure, are not so well represented, with the δy_1 values showing positive bias from zero. The root-mean-square value of δy_1 is 0.0030, whereas experimental y_1 values are reported to four decimal places.

Figure 6-13 shows the residuals δy_1 and δP which result when the objective function is $\sum (\delta y_1)^2$. Not only are the δP residuals systematically negative, with values up to about 0.6 kPa, but the δy_1 residuals are biased from zero, scattering around an average value of about 0.0012. The reason lies with the constraint of Eq. (6-109). Replacing $\delta \ln (\gamma_1 / \gamma_2)$ in this equation by $\delta y_1 / y_1 y_2$ in accord with Eq. (6-106), we get

$$\int_0^1 \frac{\delta y_1}{y_1 y_2} \, dx_1 \simeq \int_0^1 \ln \frac{y_2 x_1 \Phi_2}{y_1 x_2 \Phi_1} \, dx_1 + \ln \frac{P_1^{\text{sat}}}{P_2^{\text{sat}}} \tag{6-110}$$

The approximation is in fact excellent. When the terms on the right do not cancel, the integral on the left has a finite value, and so also does the integral

$$\int_0^1 \delta y_1 \, dx_1$$

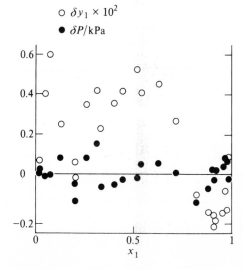

Figure 6-12 Residuals δy_1 and δP resulting from a fit of the four-parameter Margules equation to VLE data for chloroform(1)/ethanol(2) at 45°C. Fit based on minimization of $\sum (\delta P)^2$. See Example 6-14.

which represents approximately the net area on a plot of δy_1 versus x_1. Unless this quantity, as determined by the data set and ancillary data, is zero, no data-reduction procedure can produce a set of unbiased δy_1 residuals. Moreover, no data-reduction procedure can yield a fit for which $\sum (\delta y_1)^2$ is less than that given by direct minimization of this quantity. Thus, in this example, we have determined the two sets of parameters for the four-parameter Margules equation that produce on the one hand the best possible fit of the experimental pressures and on the other the best possible fit of the experimental vapor compositions.

The data set of Examples 6-12 through 6-14 is unusual only in its quality. Most such data sets, when similarly reduced, are characterized by residuals larger than those of our examples. Even with a very good data set, we have evident difficulty. Four different data-reduction procedures have produced four different correlations, with results as summarized in Table 6-3.

As illustrated in Example 6-14, one can always minimize $\sum (\delta P)^2$ to provide a correlation for which the δP residuals scatter about zero. This merely requires a correlating equation of adequate flexibility. Had we in Example 6-14 used the Margules equation with two parameters rather than four, then the δP residuals would have shown systematic deviation from zero, an unacceptable result. A consequence of this data-reduction procedure with an equation of adequate flexibility is that *all* systematic error in the data, of whatever origin, is transferred to the δy_1 residuals. Thus, the systematic deviation from zero of the δy_1 residuals of Fig. 6-12 is a consequence of systematic error in one or more of the variables. This method of data reduction therefore provides a single criterion for the *existence* of systematic error in the data and a clear test of whether the data are *thermodynamically consistent*. Such a test is possible because more data are available than the minimum required to provide a correlating expression for g.

The other procedure of data reduction illustrated in Example 6-14 minimizes $\sum (\delta y_1)^2$. However, unlike minimization of $\sum (\delta P)^2$, this minimization is constrained by Eq. (6-110), and systematic error may be reflected as systematic deviation from zero in *both* the δy_1 and δP residuals. However, systematic error in the measurement of the equilibrium pressure P is reflected only in the δP residuals, because the δy_1 residuals do not depend on the values of P. Thus, with accurate ancillary data, bias in the δy_1 residuals reflects systematic error in the measured values of x_1 or y_1, an incorrect value of the ratio P_1^{sat}/P_2^{sat}, or some combination of these. Particularly to be noted is that errors in the P_i^{sat} values degrade the results in a systematic way. Careful measurements of these values should always be made with the same lots of chemicals used for the rest of the data, and the measured values should be reported as part of the data set. The δy_1 residuals of Fig. 6-13 are systematically positive; the data set of our examples therefore contains systematic error such that the terms on the right-hand side of Eq. (6-110) do not sum to zero. Had we used a correlating equation of inadequate flexibility, these residuals would have been skewed with respect to their average value instead of scattering around it. Thus, the δy_1 residuals from minimization of $\sum (\delta y_1)^2$ provide an incomplete test of thermodynamic consistency, one that should always be accompanied by examination of the δP residuals or by a test based on the δy_1 residuals from minimization of $\sum (\delta P)^2$. Data which yield δy_1 residuals from minimization of $\sum (\delta y_1)^2$ that scatter around zero cannot be regarded as consistent unless they also yield δP residuals that scatter around zero, or, alternatively, δy_1 residuals from minimization of $\sum (\delta P)^2$ that scatter around zero.

Most data sets when reduced by minimization of $\sum (\delta P)^2$ and minimization of $\sum (\delta y_1)^2$ yield δy_1 residuals from both procedures that demonstrate some departure from thermodynamic consistency, as illustrated by Figs. 6-12 and 6-13. In fact, few sets of data prove to be as nearly consistent as the one treated here. When data exhibit a lack of thermodynamic consistency, it is impossible to find a data-reduction procedure that combines the goodness of fit for P given by minimization of $\sum (\delta P)^2$ with the goodness of fit for y_1 given by minimization of $\sum (\delta y_1)^2$. These represent limits, and all other procedures yield some kind of compromise. The procedures of Examples 6-12 and 6-13, based on minimization of $\sum (\delta g)^2$ and $\sum [\delta \ln (\gamma_1/\gamma_2)]^2$, produce such compromise fits, but not necessarily very good ones. The most direct compromise results from simultaneous minimization of the pressure and composition residuals. However, these residuals must be normalized if they are to be compatible for simultaneous treatment.

Letting w_P and w_y represent normalizing factors, we write the objective function as

$$S = \sum \left(\frac{\delta P}{w_P}\right)^2 + \sum \left(\frac{\delta y_1}{w_y}\right)^2 \qquad (6\text{-}111)$$

One reasonable normalization results when w_P is set equal to the root-mean-square value of δP resulting from minimization of $\sum (\delta y_1)^2$ and w_y is set equal to

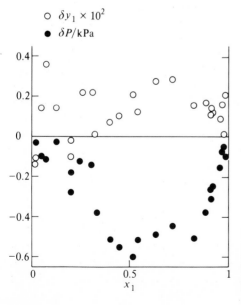

○ $\delta y_1 \times 10^2$
● $\delta P/kPa$

Figure 6-13 Residuals δy_1 and δP resulting from a fit of the four-parameter Margules equation to VLE data for chloroform(1)/ethanol(2) at 45°C. Fit based on minimization of $\sum (\delta y_1)^2$. See Example 6-14.

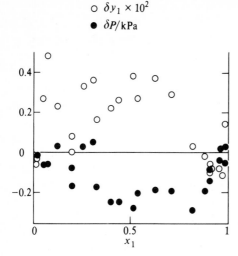

Figure 6-14 Residuals δy_1 and δP resulting from a fit of the four-parameter Margules equation to VLE data for chloroform(1)/ethanol(2) at 45°C. Fit based on minimization of the objective function given by Eq. (6-111).

the root-mean-square value of δy_1 resulting from minimization of $\sum (\delta P)^2$. For the present case, Table 6-3 lists these values as

$$w_P = 0.33 \qquad \text{and} \qquad w_y = 0.0030$$

Minimization of the objective function of Eq. (6-111) then yields the results given by the last column of Table 6-3. The δy_1 and δP residuals from this compromise fit are plotted in Fig. 6-14.

The chloroform/ethanol data set at 45°C clearly contains systematic error, and there is no way to know which data-reduction procedure yields the correlation closest to being correct. One therefore chooses subjectively. If all of the data are considered equally reliable, then the compromise fit based on the objective function of Eq. (6-111) is a reasonable choice. If there is reason to believe that the measured values of P are more reliable than those of y_1 (and this is often likely), then one is justified in choosing $\sum (\delta P)^2$ as objective function. If the procedure based on $\sum (\delta y_1)^2$ as objective function yields δy_1 residuals that scatter about zero, whereas the procedure based on $\sum (\delta P)^2$ yields δy_1 residuals that do not, then one may justify the choice of $\sum (\delta y_1)^2$ as objective function. For the rare data set that satisfies all consistency tests, all procedures should yield satisfactory results.

Vapor/liquid equilibrium data reduction can be accomplished by more-sophisticated techniques than those described here. In these, the objective function always includes weighting factors w_j:

$$S = \sum \frac{(\delta Y_j)^2}{w_j} \tag{6-112}$$

where index j identifies data points. Appropriate weighting factors are provided by a statistical theory known as the principle of maximum likelihood. A definitive treatment of statistically oriented computational techniques appropriate to VLE data reduction is given by Kemény et al. (1981). The validity of these techniques rests on the presumptions that the data set is free of systematic error and that the correlating equation does not itself introduce error. These two preconditions reflect the primary difficulties of data collection and correlation: inaccurate data and inadequate empirical equations. Once these are overcome, the *major* problems are solved. The remaining problem of how best to fit data, correct to within random error, by an inherently adequate equation is the only one solved by statistical methods. Its contribution to the accuracy of a correlation is relatively minor. When the preconditions to statistical treatment are not closely met, and they seldom are, one can do little further harm by setting $w_j = 1$ in Eq. (6-112). Moreover, improper application of statistical methods produces misleading results. Since these methods distribute systematic error over all measured variables, the error is divided among the possible sources, giving the appearance of minimal error, without increasing the reliability of the correlation. There is, in fact, *no* way to reduce bad data so as to produce a reliable correlation.

In the foregoing discussion of alternative procedures for VLE data reduction and of thermodynamic consistency, we have presumed availability of a full set of x_1, P, y_1 data at constant temperature. Such data are almost always taken with equilibrium stills. With only a subset of x_1, P data, taken with an equilibrium cell, one has only a choice of the algorithm in a single data-reduction procedure and no opportunity to test for consistency. This is often cited as a disadvantage of the equilibrium-cell method of data measurement. The logic is that if a full set of x_1, P, y_1 data is found self-consistent, then it is also most likely accurate. The problem is that such sets of data almost always prove not be be consistent, and are therefore inaccurate. The experimental effort expended for production of the extra data needed for consistency tests is better directed toward insuring accuracy in the *essential* data. The simplicity of the measurements required to produce a subset of x_1, P data with an equilibrium cell make such data susceptible to whatever degree of refinement is necessary to assure accuracy. Given accuracy, consistency is assured.

The P_i^{sat} values included with a subset of x_1, P data can, in fact, be tested for consistency with the rest of the data set. This very restricted test is an incidental result of a useful data-reduction procedure for high-quality isothermal x_1, P data. The vapor pressures P_1^{sat} and P_2^{sat} which appear on the right-hand side of Eq. (6-98)

$$P^\dagger = \frac{x_1 \gamma_1^\dagger P_1^{\text{sat}}}{\Phi_1} + \frac{x_2 \gamma_2^\dagger P_2^{\text{sat}}}{\Phi_2} \tag{6-98}$$

are treated as physical constants. On the other hand, the P_i^{sat} values are simply part of the data set to which Eq. (6-98) is applied in the data-reduction procedure. As limiting values of P for $x_i = 1.0$, the P_i^{sat} values are of no greater importance than any other value of P, and are equally subject to measurement error. Their special significance enters through the terms on the right-hand side of Eq. (6-98); here they interact with all data points of the set, and measurement errors influence the results in a systematic way.

We need to treat the P_i^{sat} values in their role as physical constants separately from the P values at $x_i = 1.0$, which are simply data points. This separation is accomplished when each P_i^{sat} is treated as a parameter to be evaluated in the data-reduction process along with the parameters in the correlating expression for g. The measured values of P at $x_i = 1.0$ are included in the data set, but are not identified as the P_i^{sat} values. Once evaluated, the P_i^{sat} values also represent the predicted values of the pressure $P^\dagger$ at $x_i = 1.0$ in any comparison of predicted and experimental values.

In this procedure, the *parameters* P_1^{sat} and P_2^{sat} are not intended to preempt the role assigned to the parameters in the correlating expression for g. They must not act as primary curve-fitting parameters; therefore, one first fixes P_1^{sat} and P_2^{sat} at their measured values and, in preliminary data reductions, determine the form of a correlation capable of fitting the data to within the experimental uncertainty. Only then can one properly include the P_i^{sat} as additional parameters.

An example of appropriate application of this procedure is provided by x_1, P data for 1-propanol(1)/n-heptane(2) at 60°C (Van Ness and Abbott, 1977). The data set of 13 points is of high precision and includes measurements at $x_1 = 0.0$ and $x_1 = 1.0$. The composition dependence of g for this system is complex, but preliminary reduction demonstrates the suitability of Eq. (5-97), with $\mathcal{M} \equiv g/x_1 x_2$:

$$\frac{g}{x_1 x_2} = A_{21}x_1 + A_{12}x_2 - \frac{\alpha_{12}\alpha_{21}x_1 x_2}{\alpha_{12}x_1 + \alpha_{21}x_2 + \eta x_1 x_2}$$

With this five-parameter "modified Margules" equation, we get the following results:

$$A_{21} = 1.9388 \qquad A_{12} = 2.9568$$

$$\alpha_{12} = 6.9903 \qquad \alpha_{21} = 1.4495 \qquad \eta = 2.1594$$

$$P_1^{sat}/kPa = 20.334 \qquad P_2^{sat}/kPa = 28.112$$

$$P(x_1 = 1.0)/kPa = 20.326 \qquad P(x_1 = 0.0)/kPa = 28.131$$

$$RMS \; \delta P/kPa = 0.041$$

The P_i^{sat} values determined by data reduction are clearly consistent with the corresponding values of P at $x_i = 1$ to well within the root-mean-square value of δP. Further discussion and additional examples are given by Abbott and Van Ness (1977).

Most data sets taken for binary systems with equilibrium stills consist of values for x_1, T, and y_1 taken at fixed *pressure*, often at 1.013 bar (1 atmosphere). Isobaric data are subject to reduction by procedures analogous to those for isothermal data. However, rigorous implementation of any procedure requires prior knowledge of at least the approximate temperature dependence of G^E or g, as discussed in Sec. 6-5 and illustrated in Example 6-8.

For isobaric data, the dependent variables are T and y_1, and the primary residuals are therefore δT and δy_1. As with isothermal data, there is no advantage to treatment of any but the primary residuals. For VLE in binary systems, Eqs. (6-91) and (6-95) are again the key thermodynamic relationships. Here, however, P is the fixed experimental pressure, and we want to find predicted values of the equilibrium temperature $T^\dagger$. Temperature, unfortunately, does not appear explicitly in either equation, but enters through the temperature dependence of the γ_i and P_i^{sat}. The secondary functions Φ_i also depend on temperature; however, their influence is small, and we assume they can be satisfactorily evaluated from the experimental values T and y_1. This approximation is by no means necessary, but it simplifies treatment, and has only a minor effect on results. We therefore write Eqs. (6-91) and (6-95) as

$$P = \frac{x_1 \gamma_1^\dagger (P_1^{sat})^\dagger}{\Phi_1} + \frac{x_2 \gamma_2^\dagger (P_2^{sat})^\dagger}{\Phi_2} \tag{6-113}$$

and

$$y_i^\dagger = \frac{x_i \gamma_i^\dagger (P_i^{sat})^\dagger}{\Phi_i P} \tag{6-114}$$

Values of $\gamma_1^\dagger$ and $\gamma_2^\dagger$ are calculated by Eqs. (6-93), now rewritten as

$$\gamma_1^\dagger = \exp\left[g^\dagger + x_2 \left(\frac{\partial g^\dagger}{\partial x_1}\right)_T\right] \tag{6-115a}$$

and

$$\gamma_2^\dagger = \exp\left[g^\dagger - x_1 \left(\frac{\partial g^\dagger}{\partial x_1}\right)_T\right] \tag{6-115b}$$

Here, $g^\dagger \equiv (G^E/RT)^\dagger$ is given by an expression, such as the four-parameter Margules equation [Eq. (6-63)], in which the parameters are functions of temperature [Eqs. (6-64)]. In the simplest case, where $C_{21} = C_{12} = 0$ and $A_{21} = A_{12} = A$, the expression reduces to the one-parameter Margules equation:

$$g^\dagger = A x_1 x_2$$

Assuming a very simple temperature dependence for A, we write this as

$$g^\dagger = \left(\frac{A_0}{T^\dagger} + A_1\right) x_1 x_2$$

where A_0 and A_1 are constants, independent of $T^\dagger$ and x. The presumption here is that the heat of mixing is given by the equation

$$\left(\frac{H^E}{RT}\right)^\dagger = \frac{A_0}{T^\dagger} x_1 x_2$$

This follows immediately from Eq. (6-55), written as

$$\left(\frac{H^E}{RT}\right)^\dagger = -T^\dagger \left(\frac{\partial g}{\partial T}\right)_x^\dagger$$

Thus

$$\left(\frac{H^E}{R}\right)^\dagger = A_0 x_1 x_2$$

and the heat of mixing is independent of temperature. Given data at one temperature, we can evaluate A_0. This leaves only A_1 in the equation for $g^\dagger$ to be evaluated by VLE data reduction.

Application of Eqs. (6-115) gives

$$\gamma_1^\dagger = \exp\left[\left(\frac{A_0}{T^\dagger} + A_1\right)x_2^2\right]$$

and

$$\gamma_2^\dagger = \exp\left[\left(\frac{A_0}{T^\dagger} + A_1\right)x_1^2\right]$$

In addition, we must express $(P_1^{sat})^\dagger$ and $(P_2^{sat})^\dagger$ as functions of temperature. Suitable equations are given in Example 4-2; the most widely used is the Antoine equation, Eq. (4-13), here written

$$(P_i^{sat})^\dagger = \exp\left(a_i - \frac{b_i}{T^\dagger + c_i}\right)$$

We presume the constants a_i, b_i, and c_i known. Substitution of these expressions into Eqs. (6-113) and (6-114) gives

$$P = \frac{x_1}{\Phi_1}\exp\left[a_1 - \frac{b_1}{T^\dagger + c_1} + \left(\frac{A_0}{T^\dagger} + A_1\right)x_2^2\right]$$

$$+ \frac{x_2}{\Phi_2}\exp\left[a_2 - \frac{b_2}{T^\dagger + c_2} + \left(\frac{A_0}{T^\dagger} + A_1\right)x_1^2\right] \quad (6\text{-}116)$$

and

$$y_1^\dagger = \frac{x_1}{\Phi_1 P}\exp\left[a_1 - \frac{b_1}{T^\dagger + c_1} + \left(\frac{A_0}{T^\dagger} + A_1\right)x_2^2\right] \quad (6\text{-}117)$$

The objective of VLE data reduction is to find the value of A_1 that minimizes either $\sum(\delta T)^2$ or $\sum(\delta y_1)^2$, where

$$\delta T \equiv T^\dagger - T \quad \text{and} \quad \delta y_1 \equiv y_1^\dagger - y_1$$

The procedure is inherently more difficult than for the corresponding treatment of isothermal x_1, P, y_1 data, because one cannot, even in this simplest case, solve explicitly for $T^\dagger$. Thus, each step of the regression procedure for A_1 must incorporate an iterative scheme to yield the value of $T^\dagger$. Newton's method (Appendix E) is well suited to this purpose. The steps of the data-reduction procedure are outlined as follows:

1. For each x_1, T, y_1 data point, evaluate Φ_1 and Φ_2. These are here taken as fixed values for use in all subsequent steps. (In a more sophisticated treatment, they would be continually recalculated with current values of $T^\dagger$ and $y_1^\dagger$. The results are little different.)
2. Pick a starting value for A_1. For *each* experimental value of x_1 and for the fixed value of P, solve Eq. (6-116) by Newton's method for $T^\dagger$, and evaluate $y_1^\dagger$ by Eq. (6-117).
3. Calculate the sets of values of δT and δy_1. One set or the other, depending on whether $\sum (\delta T)^2$ or $\sum (\delta y_1)^2$ is being minimized, is used in the regression scheme to provide a new value of A_1.
4. With this value of A_1, repeat steps 2 and 3. Iteration continues until the objective function chosen changes between consecutive iterations by less than some preset tolerance. The result is a value of A_1 which minimizes the objective function and yields sets of final values for δT and δy_1.

When the correlating equation is less simple, the expressions for $\gamma_1^\dagger$ and $\gamma_2^\dagger$ resulting from Eqs. (6-115) are more complex, but the general procedure is unchanged. For example, Eq. (6-63) contains four parameters, each expressed as a function of temperature by Eqs. (6-64). The constants in these equations which multiply a function of temperature are predetermined from whatever heat-of-mixing data are available; the remaining constants A_{211}, A_{121}, C_{211}, and C_{121} are then found by regression from the VLE data. One clearly must use a computer, and must have available a flexible program for nonlinear regression.

Newton's method is based on Eq. (E-2) of App. E; applied here to solution for $T^\dagger$, it becomes

$$T_{j+1}^\dagger = T_j^\dagger - \frac{Y_j}{(dY/dT^\dagger)_j}$$

The expression for Y follows from Eq. (6-113):

$$Y \equiv P - \frac{x_1 \gamma_1^\dagger (P_1^{\text{sat}})^\dagger}{\Phi_1} - \frac{x_2 \gamma_2^\dagger (P_2^{\text{sat}})^\dagger}{\Phi_2}$$

An initial value for $T^\dagger$ is provided by the experimental temperature T; iteration continues until Y is reduced to a small preset value. The required derivative is given by

$$\frac{dY}{dT^\dagger} = - \frac{x_1 \gamma_1^\dagger (P_1^{\text{sat}})^\dagger}{\Phi_1} \left[\frac{d \ln \gamma_1^\dagger}{dT^\dagger} + \frac{d \ln (P_1^{\text{sat}})^\dagger}{dT^\dagger} \right]$$
$$- \frac{x_2 \gamma_2^\dagger (P_2^{\text{sat}})^\dagger}{\Phi_2} \left[\frac{d \ln \gamma_2^\dagger}{dT^\dagger} + \frac{d \ln (P_2^{\text{sat}})^\dagger}{dT^\dagger} \right]$$

The derivatives $d \ln \gamma_i^\dagger / dT^\dagger$ are evaluated at constant x from expressions deriving from the correlating equation, and $d \ln (P_i^{\text{sat}})^\dagger / dT^\dagger$ from expressions for the temperature dependence of the vapor pressures. For the simple case represented by Eq. (6-116), we have

$$\ln \gamma_1^\dagger = \left(\frac{A_0}{T^\dagger} + A_1\right)x_2^2 \quad \text{and} \quad \ln \gamma_2^\dagger = \left(\frac{A_0}{T^\dagger} + A_1\right)x_1^2$$

from which

$$\frac{d \ln \gamma_1^\dagger}{dT^\dagger} = -A_0\left(\frac{x_2}{T^\dagger}\right)^2 \quad \text{and} \quad \frac{d \ln \gamma_2^\dagger}{dT^\dagger} = -A_0\left(\frac{x_1}{T^\dagger}\right)^2$$

From the Antoine equation for vapor pressures, one gets

$$\frac{d \ln (P_i^{\text{sat}})^\dagger}{dT^\dagger} = \frac{b_i}{(T^\dagger + c_i)^2}$$

In the differentiation $dY/dT^\dagger$ we have held the secondary functions Φ_1 and Φ_2 constant, thus avoiding the added complication of evaluating $d\Phi_i/dT^\dagger$. The presumption is that Φ_i values calculated from experimental temperatures and vapor compositions are adequate approximations. One can of course refine the procedure in the final stages of regression by recalculating the Φ_i with current values of $T^\dagger$ and $y_1^\dagger$.

Example 6-15 The VLE data compilation of Gmehling and Onken (1977) includes three data sets for acetone(1)/ethanol(2) at 1.013 bar that are in reasonable agreement with each other. We combine these three sets for data reduction. Correlation of heat-of-mixing data for this system in Example 6-8 provides values for the constants of Eqs. (6-67), which express the temperature dependence of the parameters in Eq. (6-65). These same constants apply as well to Eqs. (6-64), which give the temperature dependence of the parameters in Eq. (6-63), the four-parameter Margules equation for $g \equiv G^E/RT$. Combining Eqs. (6-64) with Eq. (6-63) and substituting values of the constants found from heat-of-mixing data, we get:

$$\frac{g^\dagger}{x_1 x_2} = \left(\frac{413.14}{T^\dagger} + A_{211} - 0.6902 \ln T^\dagger\right)x_1$$

$$+ \left(\frac{-380.76}{T^\dagger} + A_{121} - 3.1568 \ln T^\dagger\right)x_2$$

$$- \left[\left(\frac{1817.88}{T^\dagger} + C_{211} + 5.2825 \ln T^\dagger\right)x_1\right.$$

$$\left. + \left(\frac{-389.24}{T^\dagger} + C_{121} - 1.9422 \ln T^\dagger\right)x_2\right]x_1 x_2$$

This equation incorporates both the temperature and composition dependence of $g^\dagger$, and includes four undetermined constants to be evaluated by reduction of the VLE data at 1.013 bar. The numerical constants in the equation were found from H^E data at 25 and 50°C. This implies a linear relation of H^E to temperature, a relation assumed to hold upon extrapolation to the temperature range of the VLE data, 56 to 78°C.

The activity coefficients are most easily found from the equation for $g^\dagger/x_1 x_2$ by application of Eqs. (5-76). Making the identifications

$$\bar{M}_i^E \equiv \ln \gamma_i^\dagger \qquad \text{and} \qquad \mathcal{M} \equiv \mathcal{G}^\dagger \equiv \frac{g^\dagger}{x_1 x_2}$$

we get

$$\gamma_1^\dagger = \exp\left\{x_2^2\left[\mathcal{G}^\dagger + x_1\left(\frac{\partial \mathcal{G}^\dagger}{\partial x_1}\right)_T\right]\right\}$$

and

$$\gamma_2^\dagger = \exp\left\{x_1^2\left[\mathcal{G}^\dagger - x_2\left(\frac{\partial \mathcal{G}^\dagger}{\partial x_1}\right)_T\right]\right\}$$

We express the vapor pressures of acetone and ethanol as functions of temperature by Antoine equations:

$$\ln \left(P_1^{\text{sat}}\right)^\dagger/\text{kPa} = 14.3665 - \frac{2{,}773.86}{T^\dagger/\text{K} - 44.68}$$

and

$$\ln \left(P_2^{\text{sat}}\right)^\dagger/\text{kPa} = 16.8969 - \frac{3{,}803.98}{T^\dagger/\text{K} - 41.68}$$

The first equation is given by Ochi and Lu (1978), and the second by Reid et al. (1977).

For evaluation of Φ_i by Eq. (6-85), we need virial coefficients as a function of temperature. One procedure is to evaluate B_{11}, B_{22}, and B_{12}, at several temperatures in the interval of interest by a correlation, such as that of Hayden and O'Connell (1975). Values at other temperatures are then found by suitable interpolation.

The results of correlation based on minimization of $\sum (\delta T)^2$ are shown by Fig. 6-15. Clearly, the experimental temperatures are well represented by the correlation; the δT residuals scatter closely about zero. The δy_1 residuals, however, show systematic deviation from zero, with values up to 0.03. The data are seriously inconsistent. Although the three sets of data, indicated by the three different open symbols, are in excellent agreement, they evidently all incorporate equivalent systematic error.

Figure 6-16 displays the results based on minimization of $\sum (\delta y_1)^2$. The δy_1 residuals, with an average value of about 0.002, themselves show some positive bias. As with isothermal data, this minimization procedure is constrained. The constraining equation is analogous to Eq. (6-110), but is more complicated. In the present example, the δy_1 residuals give an indication of only minor inconsistency, whereas the δT residuals reveal major inconsistency.

These two data-reduction procedures yield limiting results: the best possible fit of the x_1, T data and the best possible fit of the x_1, y_1 data. Compromise correlations, which represent neither T nor y_1 so well, are achieved with an objective function analogous to that of Eq. (6-111):

$$S = \sum \left(\frac{\delta T}{w_T}\right)^2 + \sum \left(\frac{\delta y_1}{w_y}\right)^2 \qquad (6\text{-}118)$$

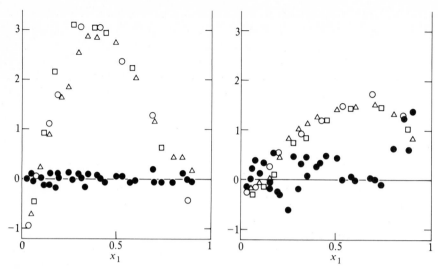

Figure 6-15 Residuals δy_1 and δT resulting from a fit of the four-parameter Margules equation to VLE data for acetone(1)/ethanol(2) at 1.013 bar. Fit based on minimization of $\sum (\delta T)^2$. Solid circles represent $\delta T/K$; open symbols, $\delta y_1 \times 10^2$.

Figure 6-16 Residuals δy_1 and δT resulting from a fit of the four-parameter Margules equation to VLE data for acetone(1)/ethanol(2) at 1.013 bar. Fit based on minimization of $\sum (\delta y_1)^2$. Solid circles represent $\delta y_1 \times 10^2$; open symbols, $\delta T/K$.

The normalizing factors w_T and w_y are appropriately taken as the root-mean-square values of δT and δy_1 found by minimization of $\sum (\delta y_1)^2$ and $\sum (\delta T)^2$ respectively. These values are here

$$w_T = 1.01 \text{ K} \qquad \text{and} \qquad w_y = 0.020$$

Tabulated results for all three data reductions are given in Table 6-4. They contain no clue as to which correlation is most nearly correct.

Table 6-4 Results of VLE data reduction for acetone(1)/ethanol(2) at 1.013 bar

Objective function	$\sum (\delta T)^2$	$\sum (\delta y_1)^2$	Eq. (6-118)
Parameter			
A_{211}	3.3769	2.8261	3.2298
A_{121}	20.1343	20.2774	20.2972
C_{211}	-36.2567	-37.2258	-36.3178
C_{121}	12.4957	12.7122	12.9647
RMS $\delta T/K$	0.09	1.01	0.43
RMS δy_1	0.020	0.005	0.010

Isobaric VLE data reported in the literature more often than not exhibit the serious thermodynamic inconsistency illustrated in the preceding example. However, good data do exist, as we demonstrate with the following example.

Example 6-16 A set of x_1, T, y_1 data at 1.013 bar for acetone(1)/methanol(2) is reported by Ochi and Lu (1978). This is the second system considered in Example 6-8, where a correlation of heat-of-mixing data at 50°C by the four-parameter Margules equation is given. Since H^E data are known for just one temperature, we assume that H^E is independent of T. This leads to the equation

$$\frac{G^E}{x_1 x_2 RT} = \left(\frac{A_{210}}{T} - A_{211}\right)x_1 + \left(\frac{A_{120}}{T} - A_{121}\right)x_2$$
$$- \left[\left(\frac{C_{210}}{T} - C_{211}\right)x_1 + \left(\frac{C_{120}}{T} - C_{121}\right)x_2\right]x_1 x_2$$

In Example 6-8 we evaluated the first constants of the terms in parentheses from H^E data at 50°C and the second constants from G^E data at 50°C. Here, we adopt the same first-constant set, but evaluate the second-constant set from the VLE data at 1.013 bar. Thus, our expression for $g^\dagger$ is

$$\frac{g^\dagger}{x_1 x_2} = \left(\frac{445.27}{T^\dagger} - A_{211}\right)x_1 + \left(\frac{333.14}{T^\dagger} - A_{121}\right)x_2$$
$$- \left[\left(\frac{14.15}{T^\dagger} - C_{211}\right)x_1 + \left(\frac{88.51}{T^\dagger} - C_{121}\right)x_2\right]x_1 x_2$$

Calculating $\gamma_1^\dagger$ and $\gamma_2^\dagger$ values from this equation, $(P_i^{sat})^\dagger$ values from the Antoine equations given by Ochi and Lu, and second virial coefficients by the Hayden-O'Connell correlation, we carry out data reduction through Eqs. (6-113) and (6-114) with objective functions $\sum (\delta T)^2$ and $\sum (\delta y_1)^2$ and with the compromise function given by Eq. (6-118). All results are presented in Table 6-5. All three correlations provide excellent representations of the entire data set. Note that the experimental y_1 values are reported to just three decimal places and the T values to two decimal places. Since the data clearly satisfy the requirements of thermodynamic consistency,

Table 6-5 Results of VLE data reduction for acetone(1)/methanol(2) at 1.013 bar

Objective function	$\sum (\delta T)^2$	$\sum (\delta y_1)^2$	Eq. (6-118)
Parameter			
A_{211}	−0.7640	−0.7642	−0.7621
A_{121}	−0.3614	−0.3966	−0.3836
C_{211}	−0.0054	−0.0404	−0.0044
C_{121}	−0.1679	−0.3147	−0.2669
RMS $\delta T/K$	0.017	0.037	0.024
RMS δy_1	0.0015	0.0006	0.0009

one here certainly chooses the compromise fit, which makes effective use of all the data.

In view of the excellence of all three correlations represented in Table 6-5, it is perhaps surprising that the parameter sets are not in closer agreement. The reason is that with empirical fitting equations a strong correlation may exist between one or more pairs of parameters. The objective function is then nearly minimized for a spectrum of parameter sets, and many sets can yield nearly equivalent correlations of the data.

The approximation introduced by the assumption that H^E is independent of temperature should in this case introduce negligible error, because the temperature range of the data, 55.3 to 64.5°C, is both small and little displaced from the temperature of 50°C to which the H^E data strictly apply.

Vapor/liquid equilibrium data for some systems are well represented by two-parameter equations, and for many systems such equations provide approximations adequate for practical purposes. Two-parameter equations have a special appeal because of their relative simplicity; moreover, the parameters can be evaluated from minimal data.

The two classical examples are the van Laar equation, Eq. (5-87), and the two-parameter Margules equation, Eq. (5-92). With $\mathcal{M} \equiv g/x_1 x_2$, these two equations and their associated activity coefficients from Eqs. (5-76) are:

van Laar equation

$$\frac{g}{x_1 x_2} = \frac{A'_{12} A'_{21}}{A'_{12} x_1 + A'_{21} x_2} \tag{6-119}$$

$$\ln \gamma_1 = A'_{12}\left(1 + \frac{A'_{12} x_1}{A'_{21} x_2}\right)^{-2} \tag{6-120a}$$

$$\ln \gamma_2 = A'_{21}\left(1 + \frac{A'_{21} x_2}{A'_{12} x_1}\right)^{-2} \tag{6-120b}$$

Margules equation

$$\frac{g}{x_1 x_2} = A_{21} x_1 + A_{12} x_2 \tag{6-121}$$

$$\ln \gamma_1 = x_2^2 [A_{12} + 2(A_{21} - A_{12}) x_1] \tag{6-122a}$$

$$\ln \gamma_2 = x_1^2 [A_{21} + 2(A_{12} - A_{21}) x_2] \tag{6-122b}$$

In the limit of infinite dilution, Eqs. (6-120) and (6-122) yield:

van Laar equation

$$\ln \gamma_1^\infty = A'_{12} \quad \text{and} \quad \ln \gamma_2^\infty = A'_{21}$$

Margules equation

$$\ln \gamma_1^\infty = A_{12} \quad \text{and} \quad \ln \gamma_2^\infty = A_{21}$$

In fact, the subscripts on the parameters reflect these results; the subscript 12 indicates a parameter associated with species 1 infinitely dilute in species 2, whereas subscript 21 suggests a parameter with the opposite association.

A modern equation of great popularity, proposed by Wilson (1964b), also contains just two parameters:

$$g = -x_1 \ln (x_1 + x_2 \Lambda_{12}) - x_2 \ln (x_2 + x_1 \Lambda_{21}) \qquad (6\text{-}123)$$

$$\ln \gamma_1 = -\ln (x_1 + x_2 \Lambda_{12}) + x_2 \left[\frac{\Lambda_{12}}{x_1 + x_2 \Lambda_{12}} - \frac{\Lambda_{21}}{x_2 + x_1 \Lambda_{21}} \right] \qquad (6\text{-}124a)$$

$$\ln \gamma_2 = -\ln (x_2 + x_1 \Lambda_{21}) - x_1 \left[\frac{\Lambda_{12}}{x_1 + x_2 \Lambda_{12}} - \frac{\Lambda_{21}}{x_2 + x_1 \Lambda_{21}} \right] \qquad (6\text{-}124b)$$

For infinite dilution, Eqs. (6-124) become

$$\ln \gamma_1^\infty = -\ln \Lambda_{12} + 1 - \Lambda_{21}$$

and

$$\ln \gamma_2^\infty = -\ln \Lambda_{21} + 1 - \Lambda_{12}$$

Although the parameters Λ_{12} and Λ_{21} are not individually associated with a particular limiting value, knowledge of $\ln \gamma_1^\infty$ and $\ln \gamma_2^\infty$ allows simultaneous solution of these equations for both parameters.

We now consider the relation of infinite-dilution activity coefficients to the experimental variables of VLE. For a binary system of species i and j, the activity coefficient of species i is given by Eq. (6-83):

$$\gamma_i = \frac{y_i P \Phi_i}{x_i P_i^{sat}}$$

In the limit as $x_i \to 0$, $y_i \to 0$, $P \to P_j^{sat}$, and this becomes

$$\gamma_i^\infty = \Phi_i^\infty \frac{P_j^{sat}}{P_i^{sat}} \lim_{\substack{x_i \to 0 \\ y_i \to 0}} \frac{y_i}{x_i}$$

Evaluating the limit by l'Hôpital's rule, we get

$$\boxed{\gamma_i^\infty = \Phi_i^\infty \frac{P_j^{sat}}{P_i^{sat}} \left(\frac{dy_i}{dx_i} \right)^\infty} \qquad (6\text{-}125)$$

This equation shows that the infinite-dilution value of an activity coefficient is directly related to the limiting slope of the y_i-versus-x_i curve for VLE. It is applicable to either isothermal or isobaric data.

For isothermal data the derivative $(dy_i/dx_i)_T^\infty$ is directly related to $(dP/dx_i)_T^\infty$. This follows from the coexistence equation for binary VLE, Eq. (6-82). For constant T, we write this equation as

$$\frac{(V^E)^v + x_1 V_1^v + x_2 V_2^v - V^l}{RT} = (y_1 - x_1) \frac{d \ln (\gamma_1/\gamma_2)^v}{dP} + \frac{y_1 - x_1}{y_1(1 - y_1)} \frac{dy_1}{dP}$$

In the limit as $x_1 \to 0$, $y_1 \to 0$, $(V^E)^v \to 0$, and $V^l \to V^l_2$. Thus, for infinite dilution of species 1, we have

$$\frac{V^v_2 - V^l_2}{RT} = \left(\frac{dy_1}{dP}\right)^\infty_T \lim_{\substack{x_1 \to 0 \\ y_1 \to 0}} \left(\frac{y_1 - x_1}{y_1}\right)$$

Application of l'Hôpital's rule gives

$$\lim_{\substack{x_1 \to 0 \\ y_1 \to 0}} \left(\frac{y_1 - x_1}{y_1}\right) = \lim_{\substack{x_1 \to 0 \\ y_1 \to 0}} \left(\frac{dy_1/dx_1 - 1}{dy_1/dx_1}\right)_T = \lim_{\substack{x_1 \to 0 \\ y_1 \to 0}} \left(\frac{dy_1/dP - dx_1/dP}{dy_1/dP}\right)_T$$

or

$$\lim_{\substack{x_1 \to 0 \\ y_1 \to 0}} \left(\frac{y_1 - x_1}{y_1}\right) = \frac{(dy_1/dP)^\infty_T - (dx_1/dP)^\infty_T}{(dy_1/dP)^\infty_T}$$

Therefore

$$\frac{V^v_2 - V^l_2}{RT} = \left(\frac{dy_1}{dP}\right)^\infty_T - \left(\frac{dx_1}{dP}\right)^\infty_T$$

or

$$\left(\frac{dy_1}{dP}\right)^\infty_T = \left(\frac{dx_1}{dP}\right)^\infty_T + \frac{\Delta V^{lv}_2}{RT}$$

For species 2 as a saturated liquid or vapor, the compressibility factor is given by $Z_2 = P^{sat}_2 V_2 / RT$. Therefore

$$\frac{\Delta V^{lv}_2}{RT} = \frac{\Delta Z^{lv}_2}{P^{sat}_2}$$

and

$$\left(\frac{dy_1}{dP}\right)^\infty_T = \left(\frac{dx_1}{dP}\right)^\infty_T + \frac{\Delta Z^{lv}_2}{P^{sat}_2} \tag{6-126}$$

Since $dy_1/dP = (dy_1/dx_1)(dx_1/dP)$, this equation may be rewritten as

$$\left(\frac{dy_1}{dx_1}\right)^\infty_T = 1 + \frac{\Delta Z^{lv}_2}{P^{sat}_2}\left(\frac{dP}{dx_1}\right)^\infty_T \tag{6-127}$$

Equation (6-126) relates the initial slopes of the P-versus-x_1 and P-versus-y_1 curves at constant temperature, whereas Eq. (6-127) relates the initial slopes of the y_1-versus-x_1 and P-versus-x_1 curves. Analogous equations apply at infinite dilution of species 2.

Substitution of Eq. (6-127) into Eq. (6-125), written for isothermal data and for $i = 1$, gives

$$\gamma^\infty_1 = \Phi^\infty_1 \frac{P^{sat}_2}{P^{sat}_1}\left[1 + \frac{\Delta Z^{lv}_2}{P^{sat}_2}\left(\frac{dP}{dx_1}\right)^\infty_T\right] \tag{6-128a}$$

Similarly,

$$\gamma_2^\infty = \Phi_2^\infty \frac{P_1^{sat}}{P_2^{sat}} \left[1 + \frac{\Delta Z_1^{lv}}{P_1^{sat}} \left(\frac{dP}{dx_2} \right)_T^\infty \right] \tag{6-128b}$$

If the two-term virial equation applies, Φ_i^∞ is evaluated by Eq. (6-85), which becomes

$$\Phi_i^\infty = \exp \left[\frac{(B_{ii} - V_i)(P_j^{sat} - P_i^{sat}) + P_j^{sat}\, \delta_{ij}}{RT} \right] \tag{6-129}$$

Approximate forms of Eqs. (6-128) result when we assume the vapor phase an ideal gas and the liquid volume negligible. Then, $\Phi_i = 1$, $\Delta Z_i^{lv} = 1$, and Eqs. (6-128) become

$$\gamma_1^\infty \simeq \frac{1}{P_1^{sat}} \left[P_2^{sat} + \left(\frac{dP}{dx_1} \right)_T^\infty \right] \tag{6-130a}$$

and

$$\gamma_2^\infty \simeq \frac{1}{P_2^{sat}} \left[P_1^{sat} + \left(\frac{dP}{dx_2} \right)_T^\infty \right] \tag{6-130b}$$

Completely analogous treatment of the coexistence equation for the constant-pressure case is possible; however, a simpler procedure takes advantage of the fact that for VLE in a binary system there are but two degrees of freedom, two independent variables. Thus, as pointed out by Null (1970), we can write

$$f(P, x_1, T) = 0$$

It follows from Eq. (A2-5) of the Appendix that

$$\left(\frac{\partial P}{\partial x_1} \right)_T = - \left(\frac{\partial P}{\partial T} \right)_{x_1} \left(\frac{\partial T}{\partial x_1} \right)_P$$

For infinite dilution of species 1, we therefore write

$$\left(\frac{dP}{dx_1} \right)_T^\infty = - \frac{dP_2^{sat}}{dT} \left(\frac{dT}{dx_1} \right)_P^\infty \tag{6-131}$$

Substitution of this result into Eq. (6-128a) gives

$$\gamma_1^\infty = \Phi_1^\infty \frac{P_2^{sat}}{P_1^{sat}} \left[1 - \frac{\Delta V_2^{lv}}{RT} \left(\frac{dP_2^{sat}}{dT} \right) \left(\frac{dT}{dx_1} \right)_P^\infty \right] \tag{6-132a}$$

Similarly,

$$\gamma_2^\infty = \Phi_2^\infty \frac{P_1^{sat}}{P_2^{sat}} \left[1 - \frac{\Delta V_1^{lv}}{RT} \left(\frac{dP_1^{sat}}{dT} \right) \left(\frac{dT}{dx_2} \right)_P^\infty \right] \tag{6-132b}$$

Since Eq. (4-6), the Clapeyron equation, may be written

$$\Delta V_i^{lv} \left(\frac{dP_i^{sat}}{dT} \right) = \frac{\Delta H_i^{lv}}{T}$$

Eqs. (6-132) have an alternative form involving the latent heat of vaporization.

Approximate values of γ_1^∞ are given by the expression obtained when Eq. (6-131) is combined with Eq. (6-130a):

$$\gamma_1^\infty \simeq \frac{1}{P_1^{sat}} \left[P_2^{sat} - \frac{dP_2^{sat}}{dT} \left(\frac{dT}{dx_1} \right)_P^\infty \right] \qquad (6\text{-}133a)$$

Similarly

$$\gamma_2^\infty \simeq \frac{1}{P_2^{sat}} \left[P_1^{sat} - \frac{dP_1^{sat}}{dT} \left(\frac{dT}{dx_2} \right)_P^\infty \right] \qquad (6\text{-}133b)$$

Example 6-17 The following VLE data at high dilution of species 1 and 2 are available for the acetone(1)/methanol(2) system at 50°C:

x_1	P/kPa	x_2	P/kPa
0.0000	55.654 (P_2^{sat})	0.0000	81.963 (P_1^{sat})
0.0206	57.633	0.0196	82.364

From these data we wish to estimate the parameters A_{21} and A_{12} in the Margules equation by application of Eqs. (6-128). Supplementary data are as follows (cm^3 mol^{-1}):

$$B_{11} = -1445 \qquad V_1 = 77$$

$$B_{22} = -1598 \qquad V_2 = 42$$

$$B_{12} = -1072$$

$$\delta_{12} = 2B_{12} - B_{11} - B_{22} = 899$$

The virial coefficients are from the Hayden-O'Connell (1975) correlation. By Eq. (6-129), we have

$$\Phi_1^\infty = \exp \left[\frac{(-1445 - 77)(55.654 - 81.963) + (55.654)(899)}{(8314)(323.15)} \right]$$

$$\Phi_1^\infty = 1.0341$$

and

$$\Phi_2^\infty = \exp \left[\frac{(-1598 - 42)(81.963 - 55.654) + (81.963)(899)}{(8314)(323.15)} \right]$$

$$\Phi_2^\infty = 1.0114$$

Evaluation of $\Delta Z_i^{lv} = Z_i^v - Z_i^l$ is as follows:

$$Z_i^v = 1 + \frac{B_{ii} P_i^{sat}}{RT}$$

$$Z_1^v = 1 - \frac{(1,445)(81.963)}{(8,314)(323.15)} = 0.9559$$

$$Z_2^v = 1 - \frac{(1,598)(55.654)}{(8,314)(323.15)} = 0.9669$$

$$Z_i^l = \frac{P_i^{sat} V_i}{RT}$$

$$Z_1^l = \frac{(81.963)(77)}{(8,314)(323.15)} = 0.0023$$

$$Z_2^l = \frac{(55.654)(42)}{(8,314)(323.15)} = 0.0009$$

$$\Delta Z_1^{lv} = 0.9559 - 0.0023 = 0.9536$$

$$\Delta Z_2^{lv} = 0.9669 - 0.0009 = 0.9660$$

Finally, we require values for the derivatives $(dP/dx_1)_T^\infty$ and $(dP/dx_2)_T^\infty$. These are estimated from the given data:

$$\left(\frac{dP}{dx_1}\right)_T^\infty \simeq \frac{P - P_2^{sat}}{x_1 - 0.0} = \frac{57.633 - 55.654}{0.0206} = 96.07 \text{ kPa}$$

and

$$\left(\frac{dP}{dx_2}\right)_T^\infty \simeq \frac{P - P_1^{sat}}{x_2 - 0.0} = \frac{82.364 - 81.963}{0.0196} = 20.46 \text{ kPa}$$

These estimates are probably low, because the slopes most likely decrease in the interval from $x_i = 0$ to $x_i \simeq 0.02$. We have now evaluated all quantities for substitution into Eqs. (6-128); thus,

$$\gamma_1^\infty = (1.0341)\left(\frac{55.654}{81.963}\right)\left[1 + \left(\frac{0.9660}{55.654}\right)(96.07)\right] = 1.8730$$

and

$$\gamma_2^\infty = (1.0114)\left(\frac{81.963}{55.654}\right)\left[1 + \left(\frac{0.9536}{81.963}\right)(20.46)\right] = 1.8441$$

From these results, we get

$$A_{12} = \ln \gamma_1^\infty = 0.6276 \qquad A_{21} = \ln \gamma_2^\infty = 0.6120$$

and the two-parameter Margules equation is written

$$\frac{g}{x_1 x_2} = 0.6120 x_1 + 0.6276 x_2$$

This is in reasonable agreement with the equation cited in Example 6-8:

$$\frac{g}{x_1 x_2} = 0.6369 x_1 + 0.6523 x_2$$

As anticipated, the parameters are a bit low. Equations (6-130), which introduce further approximations, lead to values which are still lower:

$$A_{12} = 0.6158 \quad \text{and} \quad A_{21} = 0.6100$$

Experimental data for calculation of γ_i^∞ values are best taken with equipment designed specifically for this purpose. One technique involves the direct measurement of pressure *differences* between two static cells at the same temperature, one cell containing pure species j and the other very dilute solutions of species i. The resulting data are directly applicable to Eqs. (6-128). A second technique compares the equilibrium temperatures, measured at the same pressure, of pure j and of very dilute solutions of i in j. These data are pertinent to Eqs. (6-132). In addition, one must measure dP_i^{sat}/dT for each species. The measurement of boiling temperatures is called ebulliometry.

Schreiber and Eckert (1971) have shown that data for a variety of systems are well correlated by two-parameter equations, most notably the Wilson equation [Eq. (6-123)], when the parameters are determined solely from values of the infinite-dilution activity coefficients. Application of Eq. (5-58) to the state of infinite dilution gives the effect of temperature on γ_i^∞:

$$\frac{d \ln \gamma_i^\infty}{dT} = -\frac{(\bar{H}_i^E)^\infty}{RT^2} \tag{6-134}$$

As throughout this section, we presume negligible influence of pressure. Thus, given a value of γ_i^∞ at one temperature, heat-of-mixing data provide the means for calculation of values at other temperatures. Depending on the data available, $(\bar{H}_i^E)^\infty$ is usually assumed independent of T or linear in T for integration of Eq. (6-134) over modest temperature intervals.

The experimental effort required for measurement of VLE data increases rapidly in the progression from binary to ternary to multicomponent systems. Indeed, one cannot hope to have direct measurements for the multitude of complex systems of practical interest. The emphasis here is on prediction through molecular theory or through empirical correlations inspired by molecular theory. All predictive methods presume the availability of a large and accurate VLE data base for binary systems; the emphasis put on binary systems is therefore not misplaced. However, such data are insufficient. Predictions must approximate reality; accurate data are required against which to compare the results of prediction. Ternary mixtures are by far the easiest to treat experimentally, and clearly represent the most appropriate testing ground for predictive models.

Subsets of x, P data at constant temperature for ternary systems are readily measured in an equilibrium cell. For a system of species i, j, and k, one loads the cell with a binary mixture of i and j, and adds incremental amounts of species k. Runs therefore follow paths of constant mole ratio x_i/x_j, and data are collected along lines such as those shown by Fig. 6-17.

Data reduction is by Barker's method, based on Eq. (6-96). The functions Φ_i are evaluated by Eq. (6-84) written for a ternary system. A convenient correlating expression for g is based on an equation proposed by Wohl (1953):

$$g_{123} = g_{12} + g_{13} + g_{23} + (C_0 + C_1 x_1 + C_2 x_2) x_1 x_2 x_3 \qquad (6\text{-}135)$$

The quantities g_{12}, g_{13}, and g_{23} represent predetermined correlating expressions for the constituent binary systems, with parameters evaluated from data for these systems. Only the "ternary" parameters C_0, C_1, and C_2 are found by regression of the data for the ternary mixtures. The procedure is illustrated and evaluated by Abbott et al. (1975).

Examples of results obtained by this procedure are shown in Figs. 6-18 through 6-25. Two systems are represented: acetone/1,4-dioxane/water (Loehe et al., 1981) and acetone/chloroform/methanol (Abbott et al., 1975), both at 50°C.

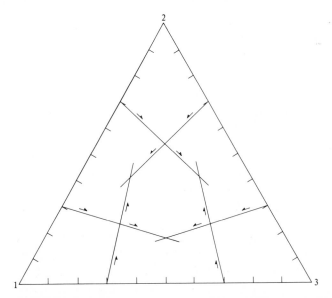

Figure 6-17 Diagram showing data paths on a grid of liquid mole fraction for a ternary system of species 1, 2, and 3. Each path is a straight line representing mixtures formed from the binary at its origin and the pure species of the opposite apex.

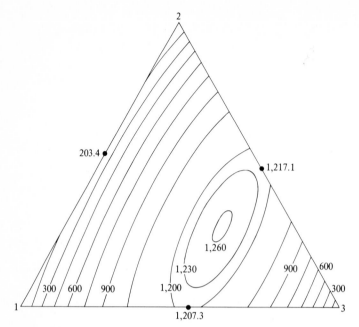

Figure 6-18 Contours of $G^E/\text{J mol}^{-1}$ for acetone(1)/1,4-dioxane(2)/water(3) at 50°C.

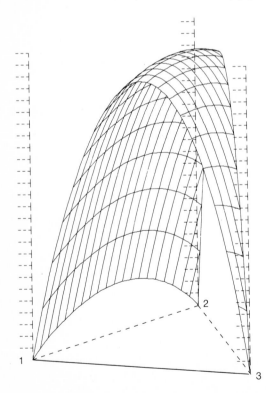

Figure 6-19 Oblique view of G^E surface for acetone(1)/1,4-dioxane(2)/water(3) at 50°C.

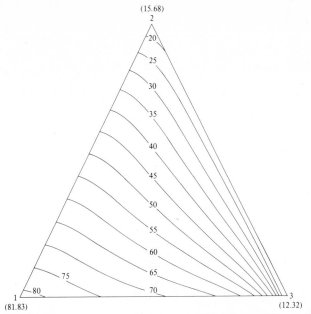

Figure 6-20 Isobars (P in kPa) for acetone(1)/1,4-dioxane(2)/water(3) at 50°C.

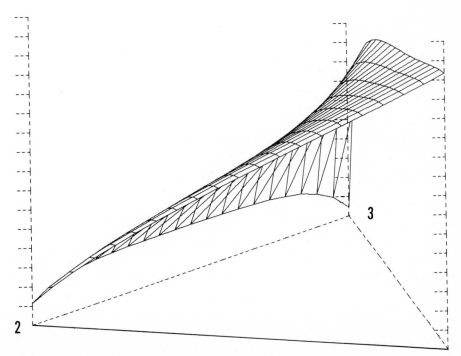

Figure 6-21 Oblique view of pressure surface for acetone(1)/1,4-dioxane(2)/water(3) at 50°C.

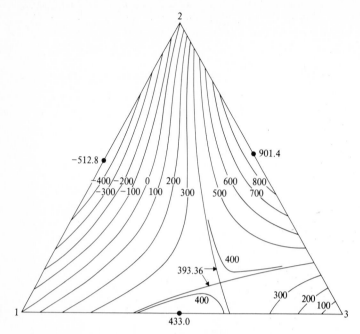

Figure 6-22 Contours of $G^E/\text{J mol}^{-1}$ for acetone(1)/chloroform(2)/methanol(3) at 50°C.

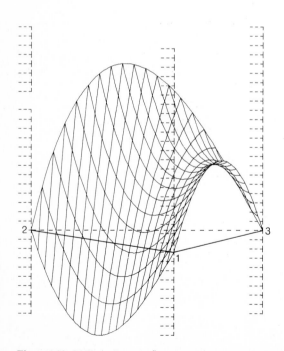

Figure 6-23 Oblique view of G^E surface for acetone(1)/chloroform(2)/methanol(3) at 50°C.

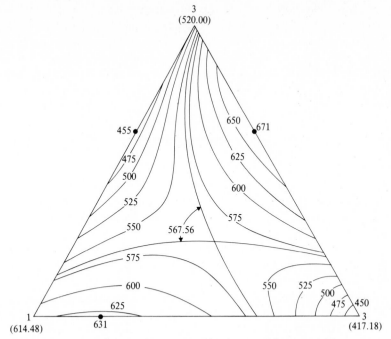

Figure 6-24 Isobars (P in torr) for acetone(1)/chloroform(2)/methanol(3) at 50°C.

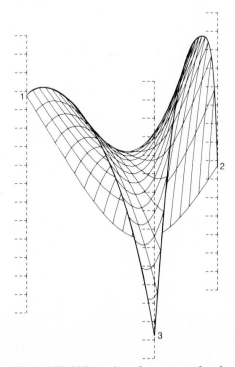

Figure 6-25 Oblique view of pressure surface for acetone(1)/chloroform(2)/methanol(3) at 50°C.

In each case, we show two contour diagrams on a triangular grid representing liquid-phase mole fractions. One has lines of constant G^E, and the other, isobars. Each is actually a projection of a surface whose elevation above or below the triangular surface represents G^E or P. With a suitable computer program and the correlating equation for g_{123}, one can generate views of either surface as seen from any vantage point. Oblique views of each surface are shown for both systems.

Figures 6-18 through 6-21 for acetone/1,4-dioxane/water are typical of many systems, showing no great complexity. Figures 6-22 through 6-25 for acetone/chloroform/methanol exhibit less-common behavior. The G^E surface contains a saddle point, marked by the intersecting contours of Fig. 6-22, and regions of both positive and negative values. The pressure surface shows a pronounced saddle point, the features of which are clear in Fig. 6-25. At this point, all derivatives dP/dx_i are zero, just as they are at the crest of an elevation or at the bottom of a depression. The saddle point is, in fact, a crest when approached from the valley and a bottom when approached along the ridge. Crests, bottoms, and saddle points all mark ternary azeotropes, where the P-x surface and the corresponding P-y surface are tangent to each other and to a horizontal surface. Each of the constituent binaries of this system, represented along the edges of the triangular diagram, also exhibits an azeotrope. Two are maximum-pressure azeotropes, and the other, minimum-pressure. These are entirely independent of the ternary saddle-point azeotrope.

6-8 LOW-PRESSURE VLE FROM THERMODYNAMIC CORRELATIONS

Expressions for $g \equiv G^E/RT$ as functions of composition and temperature store concisely much information for liquid mixtures. Given such an expression, we require methods for solution of the four principal VLE problems cited at the beginning of Sec. 6-3. Solutions to these problems are illustrated for the case where Raoult's law applies in parts (c) through (f) of Example 6-3. For the general case considered here, we follow exactly the same procedures, but with equations of greater complexity. In all cases Eq. (6-51) provides the basis of calculation, written either as

$$y_i = \frac{x_i \gamma_i P_i^{\text{sat}}}{\Phi_i P} \qquad (6\text{-}136)$$

or as

$$x_i = \frac{y_i \Phi_i P}{\gamma_i P_i^{\text{sat}}} \qquad (6\text{-}137)$$

Since both $\sum y_i$ and $\sum x_i$ must be unity, we also have

$$1 = \sum \frac{x_i \gamma_i P_i^{sat}}{\Phi_i P}$$

or

$$P = \sum \frac{x_i \gamma_i P_i^{sat}}{\Phi_i} \tag{6-138}$$

and

$$1 = \sum \frac{y_i \Phi_i P}{\gamma_i P_i^{sat}}$$

or

$$P = \frac{1}{\sum y_i \Phi_i / \gamma_i P_i^{sat}} \tag{6-139}$$

We presume knowledge of an Antoine equation for each species, giving P_i^{sat} as a function of T, of an expression for g as a function of x and T from which to evaluate the γ_i, and of all information necessary for calculation of the Φ_i by Eq. (6-84). We consider first mixtures of just two species $(i = 1, 2)$, and then generalize the results to multicomponent systems.

The simplest problem is calculation of vapor composition and pressure, given the liquid composition and temperature. This is the BUBL P calculation considered in Sec. 6-4. For a binary system, the problem is to calculate y_1 and P, given x_1 and T. The Raoult's-law counterpart is illustrated in part (d) of Example 6-3. Its relative simplicity derives from the fact that T and x_1 are given, and this allows immediate evaluation of P_1^{sat}, P_2^{sat}, γ_1, and γ_2 for use in all subsequent calculations. Equation (6-138) here becomes

$$P = \frac{x_1 \gamma_1 P_1^{sat}}{\Phi_1} + \frac{x_2 \gamma_2 P_2^{sat}}{\Phi_2} \tag{6-140}$$

and the only undetermined quantities on the right are Φ_1 and Φ_2. We set them equal to unity, and calculate an initial value for P. Initial values of y_1 and y_2 come from Eq. (6-136); with these, we evaluate Φ_1 and Φ_2 by Eq. (6-85). A return to Eq. (6-140) now gives a new value for P, and the procedure is repeated until the change in P between iterations is less than some small tolerance.

The DEW P calculation, which yields x_1 and P from given values of y_1 and T, is similar, but is based on Eq. (6-139) written for a binary system:

$$P = \frac{1}{y_1 \Phi_1 / \gamma_1 P_1^{sat} + y_2 \Phi_2 / \gamma_2 P_2^{sat}} \tag{6-141}$$

Although we can immediately determine P_1^{sat} and P_2^{sat}, we cannot initially evaluate γ_1 and γ_2. Calculations therefore start with

$$\gamma_1 = \gamma_2 = \Phi_1 = \Phi_2 = 1$$

Thus, initial calculation of P by Eq. (6-141) and of x_1 and x_2 by Eq. (6-137) yields the Raoult's-law values, as in part (f) of Example 6-3. With these, we evaluate γ_1, γ_2, Φ_1, and Φ_2, and return to Eq. (6-141) to start the next iteration. Again, the process continues to convergence.

Still less direct are the BUBL T and DEW T calculations, in which temperature, the essential variable, is not given. A reasonable initial value is found from the saturation temperatures or boiling points of the pure species at the given pressure. These are provided by the Antoine equation, Eq. (4-13), written as

$$T_i^{\text{sat}} = \frac{B_i}{A_i - \ln P} - C_i \tag{6-142}$$

The initial estimate of T is then taken as a mole-fraction-weighted average of these values.

For the BUBL T calculation, where we find y_1 and T from given values of x_1 and P, Eq. (6-140) is recast as

$$P = P_2^{\text{sat}} \left[\frac{x_1 \gamma_1}{\Phi_1} \left(\frac{P_1^{\text{sat}}}{P_2^{\text{sat}}} \right) + \frac{x_2 \gamma_2}{\Phi_2} \right]$$

or

$$P_2^{\text{sat}} = \frac{P}{(x_1 \gamma_1 / \Phi_1)(P_1^{\text{sat}} / P_2^{\text{sat}}) + x_2 \gamma_2 / \Phi_2} \tag{6-143}$$

Although $P_1^{\text{sat}} / P_2^{\text{sat}}$ depends on temperature only, the dependence is weak. This ratio is therefore not much in error even for poor estimates of T. The same principle was applied in part (c) of Example 6-3. For an initial estimate of T we here set

$$T = x_1 T_1^{\text{sat}} + x_2 T_2^{\text{sat}}$$

and for this temperature evaluate γ_1, γ_2, and the ratio $P_1^{\text{sat}} / P_2^{\text{sat}}$. With $\Phi_1 = \Phi_2 = 1$, Eq. (6-143) yields a value of P_2^{sat}, and Eq. (6-136) provides y_2. Furthermore, a new value of T is provided by the Antoine equation for species 2:

$$T = \frac{B_2}{A_2 - \ln P_2^{\text{sat}}} - C_2$$

Reevaluation of γ_1, γ_2, Φ_1, Φ_2, and $P_1^{\text{sat}} / P_2^{\text{sat}}$ leads us back to Eq. (6-143) for a second iteration. The process continues until the change in T between iterations is less than some small tolerance.

The DEW T calculation of x_1 and T for given values of y_1 and P is similar, but is based on Eq. (6-141), written as

$$P = \frac{P_1^{\text{sat}}}{y_1 \Phi_1 / \gamma_1 + (y_2 \Phi_2 / \gamma_2)(P_1^{\text{sat}} / P_2^{\text{sat}})}$$

or

$$P_1^{sat} = P\left[\frac{y_1\Phi_1}{\gamma_1} + \frac{y_2\Phi_2}{\gamma_2}\left(\frac{P_1^{sat}}{P_2^{sat}}\right)\right]$$ (6-144)

The initial estimate of T is here taken as

$$T = y_1 T_1^{sat} + y_2 T_2^{sat}$$

We now evaluate Φ_1, Φ_2, and P_1^{sat}/P_2^{sat}, and, with $\gamma_1 = \gamma_2 = 1$, calculate P_1^{sat} by Eq. (6-144) and x_1 by Eq. (6-137). A new value of T is provided by the Antoine equation:

$$T = \frac{B_1}{A_1 - \ln P_1^{sat}} - C_1$$

Following reevaluation of γ_1, γ_2, Φ_1, Φ_2, and P_1^{sat}/P_2^{sat}, we return to Eq. (6-144) and repeat the process to convergence. The Raoult's-law counterpart of this calculation is illustrated in part (e) of Example 6-3.

Example 6-18 The correlations given in Example 6-8 provide expressions for g as a function of x_1 and T for both the acetone/ethanol and acetone/methanol systems. In the case of acetone/ethanol, values are given for all the constants of Eqs. (6-64); substitution of these equations into Eq. (6-63) provides an expression for g from which γ_1 and γ_2 values may be found for any value of x_1 and for any temperature within the stated range. With the Antoine equations given in Example 6-15 and with the same virial coefficients, we make BUBL T calculations of y_1 and T for a pressure of 1.013 bar and for each value of x_1 in the data sets treated in that example. The result is a synthetic data set of y_1 and T values which are directly comparable with measured values. The temperatures are in reasonable agreement, but the y_1 values are not, with root-mean-square differences of $\delta T = 0.17°C$ and $\delta y_1 = 0.018$. The inconsistency of the experimental data evident in the results of Example 6-15 is therefore probably caused largely by systematic error in the y_1 measurements. The synthetic data set is inherently consistent, and in all probability more accurate than the measured data.

This conclusion is reinforced by consideration of the acetone/methanol system, for which the data set treated in Example 6-16 proved consistent. A correlation for g as a function of x_1 and T for this system is written in full near the end of Example 6-8. Again we do a BUBL T calculation of y_1 and T for this system at 1.013 bar for the same x_1 values as given in the data set referenced in Example 6-16. The Antoine equations and virial coefficients used in that example are also used in these calculations. The computed and experimental values are here in excellent agreement, with root-mean-square differences of $\delta y_1 = 0.0015$ and $\delta T = 0.11°C$.

The calculations described for binary systems are no different in principle for multicomponent systems. One must simply contend with more variables and greater computational complexity. A correlating equation of the functional form

$$g = g(T, x_1, x_2, \ldots)$$

must be known. Some of the options available are considered later. Antoine (or equivalent) equations must be available to provide the temperature dependence of each P_i^{sat}, and virial coefficients (and of far less importance, liquid volumes) are needed for evaluation of the Φ_i by Eq. (6-84). Given the required information, computer calculations are entirely practical with procedures that generalize those described for binary systems. In the following paragraphs, we present and discuss the block diagrams which represent the calculational procedures appropriate to solution of each of the principal VLE problems.

BUBL P: Calculation of $\{y_i\}$ and P, given $\{x_i\}$ and T

The procedure here is simple and direct. One reads and stores T, the set $\{x_i\}$, the constants in the expression for g, the Antoine constants, the virial coefficients, and the liquid volumes. Evaluation of the sets $\{P_i^{sat}\}$ and $\{\gamma_i\}$ follows immediately. Equations (6-138) and (6-136) are then solved for P and the set $\{y_i\}$. This allows evaluation of the set $\{\Phi_i\}$. Simple iteration leads to final values for P and $\{y_i\}$. The process ends when the change in pressure δP between iterations is less than a tolerance ε, set to a value of order 0.00005 kPa. The calculation process is represented by the block diagram of Fig. 6-26.

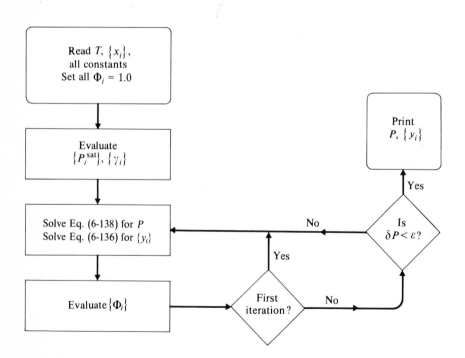

Figure 6-26 Block diagram for the calculation BUBL P.

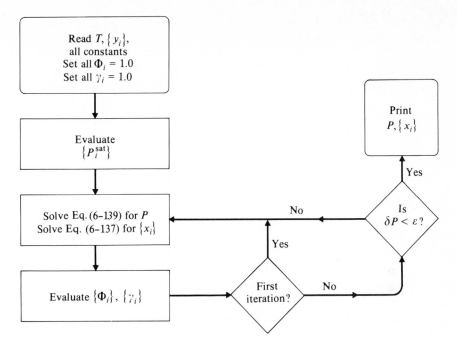

Figure 6-27 Block diagram for the calculation DEW P.

DEW P: Calculation of $\{x_i\}$ and P, given $\{y_i\}$ and T

This calculation is similar to BUBL P, but is based on alternative forms of the basic equations. The other difference is that we cannot here evaluate the set $\{\gamma_i\}$ from the given information. Figure 6-27 shows the block diagram for this calculation.

BUBL T: Calculation of $\{y_i\}$ and T, given $\{x_i\}$ and P

Equation (6-143), the basis of iteration for the BUBL P calculation for binary systems, is generalized to multicomponent systems as

$$P_k^{\text{sat}} = \frac{P}{\sum (x_i \gamma_i / \Phi_i)(P_i^{\text{sat}} / P_k^{\text{sat}})} \tag{6-145}$$

Subscript k identifies a particular species and the summation is over all species including k. The identity of species k is arbitrary and immaterial. Once Eq. (6-145) is solved for P_k^{sat}, the corresponding temperature is given by the Antoine equation for species k:

$$T = \frac{B_k}{A_k - \ln P_k^{\text{sat}}} - C_k \tag{6-146}$$

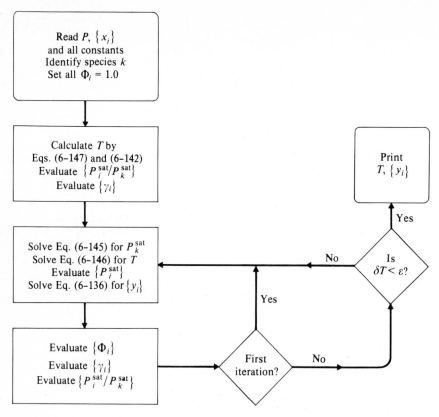

Figure 6-28 Block diagram for the calculation BUBL T.

For an initial value of T, we use the molar average boiling point:

$$T = \sum x_i T_i^{\text{sat}} \tag{6-147}$$

where the T_i^{sat} values come from Eq. (6-142). Iteration is controlled by T, and ends when the change δT between iterations is less than a tolerance ε, set to a value of order 0.0005 K. The block diagram of Fig. 6-28 outlines the procedure.

DEW T: Calculation of $\{x_i\}$ and T, given $\{y_i\}$ and P

This calculation is similar to BUBL T, but is based on a generalization of Eq. (6-144):

$$P_k^{\text{sat}} = P \sum \frac{y_i \Phi_i}{\gamma_i} \left(\frac{P_k^{\text{sat}}}{P_i^{\text{sat}}} \right) \tag{6-148}$$

Again species k is arbitrarily chosen and is included in the summation. An initial value of T is here provided by the equation:

$$T = \sum y_i T_i^{\text{sat}} \tag{6-149}$$

The complete calculational scheme appears as a block diagram in Fig. 6-29.

An additional VLE problem of general interest is the flash calculation, discussed in connection with Raoult's law in Sec. 6-3. In App. G we present a general algorithm for solution of the problem. However, the presumption is that the K_i values are known. In general, they are given by

$$K_i \equiv \frac{y_i}{x_i} = \frac{\gamma_i P_i^{\text{sat}}}{\Phi_i P} \tag{6-150}$$

an exact relationship which follows from Eq. (6-136). The difficulty, of course, is that the γ_i values depend on $\{x_i\}$ and the Φ_i values on $\{y_i\}$, the unknowns in a flash calculation. Again we resort to iteration, starting with Raoult's law $(\gamma_i = \Phi_i = 1)$. The flash calculation provides first sets of compositions $\{x_i\}$ and

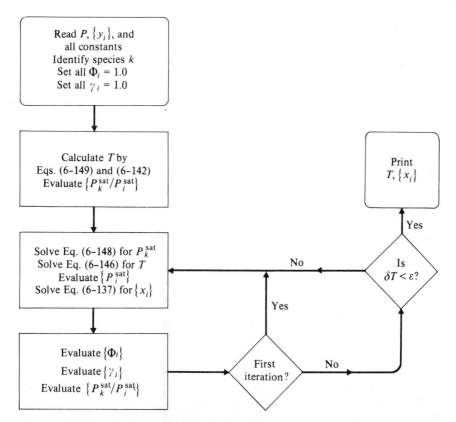

Figure 6-29 Block diagram for the calculation DEW T.

$\{y_i\}$ with which $\{\gamma_i\}$ and $\{\Phi_i\}$ are evaluated. The K_i values are then recomputed by Eq. (6-150), and the flash calculation is repeated. The process continues until successive sets $\{x_i\}$ and $\{y_i\}$ agree to within prescribed tolerances.

Throughout the general treatment of VLE calculations, we have assumed availability of a suitable correlating equation for g as a function of composition and temperature. In fact, data for multicomponent systems are almost never available for correlation, and the equation used for g is almost always predictive in character. One such equation results from simple combination of equations for the binary systems made up of species in the multicomponent system taken in pairs:

$$g = \sum_{\substack{\text{all} \\ \text{pairs}}} g_{ij} \tag{6-151}$$

This is an extension of Eq. (6-135) for ternary systems, but with no "ternary" parameters. It is only of approximate validity, but often suffices for practical purposes.

The concept of "local composition" was introduced into solution theory by G. M. Wilson (1964b) with publication of Eq. (6-123). Equations based on this concept are readily generalized to multicomponent systems; the Wilson equation is written

$$g = -\sum_i \left[x_i \ln \left(\sum_j x_j \Lambda_{ij} \right) \right] \tag{6-152}$$

Activity coefficients are then given as

$$\ln \gamma_i = 1 - \ln \left(\sum_j x_j \Lambda_{ij} \right) - \sum_k \left(\frac{x_k \Lambda_{ki}}{\sum_j x_j \Lambda_{kj}} \right) \tag{6-153}$$

In both Eqs. (6-152) and (6-153) all summations are over all species, with $\Lambda_{ij} = 1$ for $i = j$.

Local-composition theory takes into account only bimolecular interactions, and the equations for multicomponent systems therefore contain only parameters characteristic of the binary solutions formed by pairs of the constituent species. Thus, only binary-solution data are required for parameter determination. The resulting equations thus provide only approximate representation of solution properties, but one usually adequate for practical purposes.

Local-composition theory also provides the approximate temperature dependence of the parameters. Thus, for the Wilson equation,

$$\Lambda_{ij} = \frac{V_j}{V_i} \exp \left(\frac{-A_{ij}}{RT} \right) \qquad (i \neq j) \tag{6-154}$$

where V_j and V_i are the molar volumes at temperature T of the pure liquids j and i, and A_{ij} is a constant independent of composition and temperature. By far the most extensive source of parameters A_{ij} is the work of Gmehling and Onken, "Vapor-Liquid Equilibrium Data Collection," a series of volumes (appearing first in 1977) which summarize the world's published VLE data for low to moderate pressures and provide parameters for the Wilson as well as other equations.

Since the advent of Wilson's equation, others based on local-composition theory have been developed, most notably the NRTL (non-random two-liquid) equation (Renon and Prausnitz, 1968) and the UNIQUAC (universal quasi-chemical) equation (Abrams and Prausnitz, 1975). Both are discussed in the book by Reid, Prausnitz, and Sherwood (1977), and parameters for both are given by Gmehling and Onken.

In addition to the calculation of activity coefficients from correlating expressions for g, estimation procedures have been developed which rely on group-contribution methods. The two procedures in common use are the ASOG (analytical-solution-of-groups) method and the UNIFAC (UNIQUAC functional-group activity coefficients) method. Both are reviewed by Reid, Prausnitz, and Sherwood (1977), but exhaustive treatments are available in monographs devoted to each method: Kojima and Tochigi (1979) for ASOG, and Fredenslund, Gmehling, and Rasmussen (1977) for UNIFAC. The calculational procedures BUBL P, etc., are unchanged. One simply evaluates activity coefficients by calling a prescribed computer program that returns values calculated from a group-contribution method for any given temperature and liquid composition. Parameters relevant to all groups that make up the species must, of course, be available.

6-9 REDUCTION AND CORRELATION OF GAS-SOLUBILITY DATA

Up to now we have mainly considered VLE for cases in which the temperature is well below the critical temperature of each constituent species. It often happens, however, that at least one of the components, say species k, is near or above its critical temperature. When the liquid-phase mole fraction x_k is small and the equilibrium vapor-phase mole fraction y_k is large (near unity), it is conventional to call species k a "dissolved gas," and to label the physical situation one of "gas solubility." Such a designation is somewhat arbitrary. (Does the phase behavior of methane illustrated in Fig. 6-7 represent gas solubility?) Nevertheless, the classical thermodynamic treatment of this subject differs in important respects from the developments of the last two sections. We present here a brief discussion of gas solubility for single-solute/single-solvent systems. In what follows, species 1 is the dissolved gas (the *solute*), species 2 is the major component of the liquid phase (a subcritical *solvent*), and the liquid-phase mole fraction x_1 is the solubility of gaseous solute 1 in liquid solvent 2.

Our basis is the gamma/phi approach introduced in Sec. 6-5. Since the solute may be supercritical, we define its liquid-phase activity coefficient with respect to Henry's constant. Thus by Eq. (6-44) we have for species 1 that

$$y_1 P \Phi_1^* = x_1 (\gamma_1^*)^+ k_1^+ \qquad (6\text{-}155)$$

where $(\gamma_1^*)^+$ and k_1^+ are evaluated at reference conditions T^+ and P^+. Gas solubilities are normally reported or computed at isothermal conditions, and it is therefore convenient to set $T^+ = T$, in which case Eq. (6-46) provides the following expression for Φ_1^*:

$$\Phi_1^* = \hat{\phi}_1 \exp \int_P^{P^+} \frac{\overline{V}_1}{RT} \, dP \tag{6-156}$$

As before, $\hat{\phi}_1$ here refers to the vapor phase and $\overline{V}_1$ to the liquid phase.

Species 2 is by assumption below its critical temperature, and we define its liquid-phase activity coefficient with respect to the fugacity of pure liquid 2. We then have by Eq. (6-38) for species 2 that

$$\boxed{y_2 P\Phi_2 = x_2 \gamma_2^+ P_2^{\text{sat}}} \tag{6-157}$$

Again we set $T^+ = T$, and find from Eq. (6-42) an expression for Φ_2:

$$\Phi_2 = \frac{\hat{\phi}_2}{\phi_2^{\text{sat}}} \exp \left[\int_P^{P^+} \frac{\overline{V}_2^E}{RT} \, dP - \int_{P_2^{\text{sat}}}^{P} \frac{V_2}{RT} \, dP \right] \tag{6-158}$$

Equations (6-155) through (6-158) provide a rigorous framework for the computation of the gas solubility x_1, and for reduction of *isothermal* gas-solubility data.

Example 6-19 Similar to the derivation of Raoult's law presented in Sec. 6-3, one may develop for the case at hand a pair of equilibrium equations useful under certain idealized but well-defined conditions. Thus, if the vapor phase is an ideal-gas mixture, then $\hat{\phi}_1 = \hat{\phi}_2 = \phi_2^{\text{sat}} = 1$. Moreover, if the gas solubility is small, then $(\gamma_1^*)^+ \simeq \gamma_2^+ \simeq 1$. Finally, if the effect of pressure on liquid-phase fugacities is negligible, or, equivalently, if the integrals of Eqs. (6-156) and (6-158) are effectively zero, then the superscript on k_1^+ becomes superfluous. Under these conditions, Eqs. (6-155) and (6-157) simplify to the familiar recipes

$$y_1 P = x_1 k_1 \tag{6-159}$$

and

$$y_2 P = x_2 P_2^{\text{sat}} \tag{6-160}$$

Equation (6-159) is often called "Henry's law"; Eq. (6-160) is of course Raoult's law for solvent species 2.

Noting that $y_2 = 1 - y_1$ and that $x_2 = 1 - x_1$, we solve Eqs. (6-159) and (6-160) for the equilibrium mole fractions:

$$x_1 = \frac{P - P_2^{\text{sat}}}{k_1 - P_2^{\text{sat}}} \tag{A}$$

$$x_2 = \frac{k_1 - P}{k_1 - P_2^{\text{sat}}} \tag{B}$$

$$y_1 = \frac{k_1}{P} \left(\frac{P - P_2^{\text{sat}}}{k_1 - P_2^{\text{sat}}} \right) \tag{C}$$

$$y_2 = \frac{P_2^{sat}}{P}\left(\frac{k_1 - P}{k_1 - P_2^{sat}}\right) \tag{D}$$

The last two equations are often written as expressions for the vapor-phase *partial pressures* $(P_i \equiv y_i P)$:

$$P_1 = k_1\left(\frac{P - P_2^{sat}}{k_1 - P_2^{sat}}\right) \tag{E}$$

$$P_2 = P_2^{sat}\left(\frac{k_1 - P}{k_1 - P_2^{sat}}\right) \tag{F}$$

For very large k_1, Eqs. (A), (C), and (E) yield a set of further approximations often used for the solute species:

$$x_1 = \frac{P_1}{k_1} \tag{6-161}$$

$$y_1 = 1 - \frac{P_2^{sat}}{P} \tag{6-162}$$

$$P_1 = P - P_2^{sat} \tag{6-163}$$

With k_1 large, any finite x_1 makes P much larger than P_2^{sat}, and Eq. (6-161) becomes

$$x_1 = \frac{P}{k_1}$$

This approximation provides qualitative information about the effects of P and T on gas solubility. Writing the last equation as

$$\ln x_1 = \ln P - \ln k_1$$

we have that

$$\left(\frac{\partial \ln x_1}{\partial P}\right)_T = \frac{1}{P} - \left(\frac{\partial \ln k_1}{\partial P}\right)_T$$

and

$$\left(\frac{\partial \ln x_1}{\partial T}\right)_P = -\left(\frac{\partial \ln k_1}{\partial T}\right)_P$$

Consistent with the assumptions already stated, we treat k_1 as approximately a function of temperature only. Then,

$$\left(\frac{\partial \ln x_1}{\partial P}\right)_T \simeq \frac{1}{P} \tag{6-164}$$

Equation (5-135) provides an expression for the derivative of $\ln k_1$ with respect to T:

$$\left(\frac{\partial \ln k_1}{\partial T}\right)_P = \frac{H_1' - \bar{H}_1^\infty}{RT^2}$$

Therefore

$$\left(\frac{\partial \ln x_1}{\partial T}\right)_P \simeq -\left(\frac{H_1' - \bar{H}_1^{\infty}}{RT^2}\right) \tag{6-165}$$

We may now make some qualitative generalizations. First, Eq. (6-161) shows that for fixed T and P the solubility x_1 of a gas is inversely proportional to the value of Henry's constant. Second, Eq. (6-164), written as

$$d \ln x_1 \simeq d \ln P \qquad (\text{const } T)$$

shows that an increase in pressure at constant T increases the solubility of a gas. Finally, we conclude from Eq. (6-165) that the directional effect of temperature on x_1 is determined by the sign of the group $H_1' - \bar{H}_1^{\infty}$. When this group is positive (the usual case), increasing T *decreases* the solubility of a gas in a liquid. However, for very sparingly soluble gases (e.g., those at high reduced temperature), $H_1' - \bar{H}_1^{\infty}$ may actually be negative, and in this case the gas solubility *increases* with increasing T.

Example 6-20 The approximations for the P and T derivatives of $\ln x_1$ provided by Eqs. (6-164) and (6-165) are often inappropriate for quantitative work. Exact results are found by application of the binary coexistence equation; however, since x_1 (not y_1) is now the favored dependent composition variable, Eq. (6-82) is unsuitable and we return to Eq. (6-78), letting $\alpha \equiv v$ and $\beta \equiv l$. As in Example 6-11, we exclude species 2 from the sums $\sum'$, and find after some manipulation that

$$-\psi \, dP + \Omega \, dT = (y_1 - x_1) \, d \ln (\gamma_1^*/\gamma_2) + \frac{y_1 - x_1}{1 - x_1} \, d \ln x_1 \tag{6-166}$$

where, by Eqs. (6-79c) and (6-80c), since $(y_2 - x_2) = -(y_1 - x_1)$,

$$\psi \equiv \frac{-(V^v - V^l) + (y_1 - x_1)(\bar{V}_1^{\infty} - V_2^l)}{RT} \tag{6-167}$$

and

$$\Omega \equiv \frac{-(H^v - H^l) + (y_1 - x_1)(\bar{H}_1^{\infty} - H_2^l)}{RT^2} \tag{6-168}$$

Here, the activity coefficients are for species in the *liquid* phase, as are $\bar{V}_1^{\infty}$ and $\bar{H}_1^{\infty}$. Since γ_1^* and γ_2 each depend in general on x_1, P, and T, we may write also that

$$d \ln (\gamma_1^*/\gamma_2) = x_1 \left[\frac{\partial \ln (\gamma_1^*/\gamma_2)}{\partial x_1}\right]_{T,P} d \ln x_1 + \left[\frac{\partial \ln (\gamma_1^*/\gamma_2)}{\partial P}\right]_{T,x_1} dP$$
$$+ \left[\frac{\partial \ln (\gamma_1^*/\gamma_2)}{\partial T}\right]_{P,x_1} dT$$

Substitution of this equation into Eq. (6-166) and solution for $d \ln x_1$ then gives

$$d \ln x_1 = \left(\frac{\partial \ln x_1}{\partial P}\right)_T dP + \left(\frac{\partial \ln x_1}{\partial T}\right)_P dT$$

where

$$\left(\frac{\partial \ln x_1}{\partial P}\right)_T = \frac{1 - x_1}{(y_1 - x_1)X} \left\{-\psi - (y_1 - x_1)\left[\frac{\partial \ln (\gamma_1^*/\gamma_2)}{\partial P}\right]_{T,x_1}\right\} \tag{A}$$

and

$$\left(\frac{\partial \ln x_1}{\partial T}\right)_P = \frac{1 - x_1}{(y_1 - x_1)X}\left\{\Omega - (y_1 - x_1)\left[\frac{\partial \ln (\gamma_1^*/\gamma_2)}{\partial T}\right]_{P,\,x_1}\right\} \tag{B}$$

with

$$X \equiv 1 + x_1(1 - x_1)\left[\frac{\partial \ln (\gamma_1^*/\gamma_2)}{\partial x_1}\right]_{T,\,P} \tag{6-169}$$

Simplifications of Eqs. (A) and (B) are possible. Thus we have by Eqs. (5-59) and (5-58):

$$\left[\frac{\partial \ln (\gamma_1^*/\gamma_2)}{\partial P}\right]_{T,\,x_1} = \frac{(\bar{V}_1^l - \bar{V}_1^\infty) - (\bar{V}_2^l - V_2^l)}{RT} \tag{C}$$

$$\left[\frac{\partial \ln (\gamma_1^*/\gamma_2)}{\partial T}\right]_{P,\,x_1} = \frac{-(\bar{H}_1^l - \bar{H}_1^\infty) + (\bar{H}_2^l - H_2^l)}{RT^2} \tag{D}$$

Combination of Eqs. (A), (6-167), and (C), and of Eqs. (B), (6-168), and (D), yields on reduction the remarkably simple results

$$\left(\frac{\partial \ln x_1}{\partial P}\right)_T = \frac{(1 - x_1)(V^v - y_1 \bar{V}_1^l - y_2 \bar{V}_2^l)}{(y_1 - x_1)XRT} \tag{6-170}$$

and

$$\left(\frac{\partial \ln x_1}{\partial T}\right)_P = -\frac{(1 - x_1)(H^v - y_1 \bar{H}_1^l - y_2 \bar{H}_2^l)}{(y_1 - x_1)XRT^2} \tag{6-171}$$

Equations (6-170) and (6-171), with function X defined by Eq. (6-169), are *rigorous* counterparts of the approximate Eqs. (6-164) and (6-165), to which they reduce under appropriate conditions.

When both species of a binary system are subcritical, VLE data include the pure-component vapor pressures P_i^{sat} as part of the data set, and the primary purpose of data reduction is to provide values for parameters in a correlating expression for $g \equiv G^E/RT$, or at least to provide numerical values of g. With gas-solubility data, on the other hand, where k_1^+ replaces P_1^{sat} as a pure-component property, the goal of data reduction is evaluation of both k_1^+ and the correlating parameters. They may be determined either *sequentially* or *simultaneously*. Sequential procedures require the initial evaluation of k_1^+, and in the next few paragraphs we develop techniques for extraction of Henry's constant from a set of isothermal gas-solubility data.

Henry's constant for species 1, as defined by Eq. (3-95), is

$$k_1 = \lim_{x_1 \to 0} \left(\frac{\hat{f}_1}{x_1}\right) \tag{6-172}$$

For a system in VLE, $\hat{f}_1$ may be considered the fugacity of species 1 in either the liquid or vapor phase. Convenience usually dictates the choice, $\hat{f}_1 = \hat{f}_1^v$. By definition of the fugacity coefficient, we then have $\hat{f}_1 = \hat{\phi}_1 y_1 P$, and Eq. (6-172) becomes

$$k_1 = \lim_{x_1 \to 0} \left(\frac{\hat{\phi}_1 y_1 P}{x_1}\right) \tag{6-173a}$$

Substituting the partial pressure P_1 for $y_1 P$ gives the equivalent expression

$$k_1 = \lim_{x_1 \to 0} \left(\frac{\hat{\phi}_1 P_1}{x_1} \right) \qquad (6\text{-}173b)$$

In the limit as $x_1 \to 0$, $y_1 \to 0$, and therefore $P_1 \equiv y_1 P \to 0$. Moreover, $P \to P_2^{\text{sat}}$. Thus, the content of Eq. (6-173b) is more completely expressed by

$$k_1(P_2^{\text{sat}}) = \lim_{\substack{x_1 \to 0 \\ P_1 \to 0}} \left(\frac{\hat{\phi}_1 P_1}{x_1} \right) \qquad (6\text{-}174)$$

The notation $k_1(P_2^{\text{sat}})$ draws attention to the fact that P_2^{sat} is the pressure at which k_1 is evaluated. If this pressure is chosen as the reference pressure P^+, as it often is, then $k_1(P_2^{\text{sat}}) = k_1^+$. Thus, Henry's constant is the *intercept* on a plot of $\hat{\phi}_1 P_1 / x_1$ versus x_1 or versus P_1.

Expressions alternative to Eq. (6-174) relate $k_1(P_2^{\text{sat}})$ to limiting *slopes*. As $x_1 \to 0$, both y_1/x_1 and P_1/x_1 become indeterminate, suggesting application of l'Hôpital's rule. Designating by superscript ∞ the limiting value of a quantity as $x_1 \to 0$ and $y_1 \to 0$, we obtain from Eqs. (6-173) the additional expressions:

$$k_1(P_2^{\text{sat}}) = \hat{\phi}_1^{\infty} P_2^{\text{sat}} \left(\frac{dy_1}{dx_1} \right)^{\infty} \qquad (6\text{-}175a)$$

$$k_1(P_2^{\text{sat}}) = \hat{\phi}_1^{\infty} \left(\frac{dP_1}{dx_1} \right)^{\infty} \qquad (6\text{-}175b)$$

$$k_1(P_2^{\text{sat}}) = \left[\frac{d(\hat{\phi}_1 P_1)}{dx_1} \right]^{\infty} \qquad (6\text{-}175c)$$

A fourth expression depends on the limiting value of the x_1 derivative of the *total* pressure P. According to Eq. (6-127)

$$\left(\frac{dy_1}{dx_1} \right)^{\infty} = 1 + \frac{\Delta Z_2^{lv}}{P_2^{\text{sat}}} \left(\frac{dP}{dx_1} \right)^{\infty}$$

and substitution into Eq. (6-175a) gives

$$k_1(P_2^{\text{sat}}) = \hat{\phi}_1^{\infty} \left[P_2^{\text{sat}} + \Delta Z_2^{lv} \left(\frac{dP}{dx_1} \right)^{\infty} \right] \qquad (6\text{-}175d)$$

All derivatives in Eqs. (6-175) are written as *ordinary* derivatives because T is presumed fixed, and we have chosen x_1 as the single remaining independent thermodynamic variable.

Equations (6-174) and (6-175), and variations on them, provide rigorous bases for extraction of Henry's constant from gas-solubility data. Significantly, some require a full set of x_1, P, y_1 data; however, only x_1, y_1, or x_1, P data subsets are needed for Eqs. (6-175a) and (6-175d), in addition to the value of P_2^{sat}. In all cases, $\hat{\phi}_1$ or $\hat{\phi}_1^{\infty}$ must be calculated with an equation of state for the vapor phase. Limiting values, intercepts in the case of Eq. (6-174) and slopes in the case of Eqs. (6-175), are found either graphically or analytically from the appropriate quantities as functions of x_1 or P_1.

The effect of pressure on Henry's constant is given in general by Eq. (5-136):

$$\left(\frac{\partial \ln k_1}{\partial P}\right)_T = \frac{\bar{V}_1^\infty}{RT}$$

In particular, if the reference pressure P^+ is different from P_2^{sat}, a value of $k_1(P_2^{\text{sat}})$ calculated from experimental data may be corrected to a reference pressure by

$$k_1^+ = k_1(P_2^{\text{sat}}) \exp \int_{P_2^{\text{sat}}}^{P^+} \frac{\bar{V}_1^\infty}{RT} \, dP \qquad (6\text{-}176)$$

The quantity $\bar{V}_1^\infty$ is the partial molar volume at infinite dilution of the solute species in the liquid phase, a property for which experimental data are frequently lacking. It is often of the same order of magnitude as the saturation liquid volume of pure 1 at its normal boiling point, and its pressure dependence is usually safely neglected.

The second step in a sequential reduction of gas-solubility data is the determination of values for $(\gamma_1^*)^+$, or, equivalently, the extraction of values for parameters in an assumed correlating expression for the excess Gibbs function. The classical procedures presume the availability of a *complete* set of isothermal solubility data (i.e., of a set consisting of values of x_1 and y_1 for various values of the total pressure P), and the basis for the procedures is the equilibrium equation for the solute species, obtained by combination of Eqs. (6-155) and (6-156). Several equivalent expressions of this equation are possible, and we list them here for reference:

$$x_1(\gamma_1^*)^+ k_1^+ = y_1 \hat{\phi}_1 P \exp \int_P^{P^+} \frac{\bar{V}_1}{RT} \, dP \qquad (6\text{-}177a)$$

$$\frac{y_1 \hat{\phi}_1 P}{x_1} = k_1^+ (\gamma_1^*)^+ \exp \int_{P^+}^P \frac{\bar{V}_1}{RT} \, dP \qquad (6\text{-}177b)$$

$$\ln\left(\frac{y_1 \hat{\phi}_1 P}{x_1}\right) = \ln k_1^+ + \ln (\gamma_1^*)^+ + \int_{P^+}^P \frac{\bar{V}_1}{RT} \, dP \qquad (6\text{-}177c)$$

Once k_1^+ is available, one may in principle compute a value of $(\gamma_1^*)^+$ for each data point, e.g., from Eq. (6-177a). In addition to the data themselves, an equation of state for the vapor phase is required for calculation of $\hat{\phi}_1$, and partial molar volumes for the liquid phase are needed for evaluation of the integral. When a set of values for $(\gamma_1^*)^+$ has been determined, these values are correlated with liquid-phase mole fraction by an appropriate equation. The value of Henry's constant k_1^+ and the correlating equation for $(\gamma_1^*)^+$ are the final results of data reduction.

In VLE data reduction, the choice of a suitable correlating equation for the liquid-phase activity coefficients is critical but necessarily subjective; this is as true for the case of gas solubility as it is for conventional low-pressure VLE.

Although $\ln \gamma_1^*$ is a partial molar property with respect to $g^* \equiv (G^E/RT)^*$ defined according to the *unsymmetric* convention [see Eq. (5-125) and the accompanying discussion], correlating equations for $\ln \gamma_1^*$ are conventionally rationalized from expressions for g defined according to the *symmetrical* convention. A rigorous connection between $\ln \gamma_1^*$ and the symmetrical g is easily established for *binary* systems, as shown in the following paragraph.

By Eq. (5-129), γ_1^* and γ_1 are related through the infinite-dilution activity coefficient γ_1^∞:

$$\ln \gamma_1^* = \ln \gamma_1 - \ln \gamma_1^\infty \tag{5-129}$$

But $\ln \gamma_1$ is a partial molar property with respect to g, and thus, for a binary system [see, e.g., Eq. (6-93a)],

$$\ln \gamma_1 = g + x_2 \frac{dg}{dx_1} \qquad \text{(const } T, P) \tag{6-178}$$

Now, as $x_1 \to 0$, $x_2 \to 1$ and $g \to 0$. Therefore Eq. (6-178) yields the limit

$$\ln \gamma_1^\infty = \left(\frac{dg}{dx_1} \right)^\infty \tag{6-179}$$

This last result also follows directly from Eq. (6-89). Combination of Eqs. (5-129), (6-178), and (6-179) yields the required result:

$$\boxed{\ln \gamma_1^* = g + x_2 \frac{dg}{dx_1} - \left(\frac{dg}{dx_1} \right)^\infty} \qquad \text{(const } T, P) \tag{6-180}$$

Here, we are dealing with isothermal solubility data at a fixed reference pressure P^+. Equation (6-180) is therefore appropriate for derivation of recipes for $\ln (\gamma_1^*)^+$ from expressions giving g as a function of x_1 only. Parameters in these expressions determined from data reduction are thus for a *particular* $T^+ (= T)$ and P^+.

We illustrate the use of Eq. (6-180) by a simple example, a generalization of the numerical exercise done in Example 5-8. Suppose that $g (\equiv G^E/RT)$ is given by the one-parameter equation

$$g = A^+ x_1 x_2 = A^+ (x_1 - x_1^2)$$

Then

$$\frac{dg}{dx_1} = A^+ (1 - 2x_1)$$

and

$$\left(\frac{dg}{dx_1} \right)^\infty = A^+$$

Substituting these expressions into Eq. (6-180) and noting that $x_2 = 1 - x_1$, we find on rearrangement the recipe

$$\ln (\gamma_1^*)^+ = A^+ (x_2^2 - 1) \qquad (6\text{-}181)$$

Equation (6-181) is frequently used for correlation of $(\gamma_1^*)^+$ values over modest ranges of x_1. When gas-solubility data cover a wide range of x_1, the quality of the correlation becomes more sensitive to the functional form assumed for $g(x_1)$, and more comprehensive expressions, containing more parameters, may be required.

Example 6-21 Many of the expressions presented in this section are *rigorous*, subject at most to the (realistic) constraint of constant temperature. However, in application one inevitably must introduce approximations. We illustrate here by numerical example some of the features of gas-solubility data reduction, describing the most common approximations. We choose the $CO_2(1)$/water(2) system, for which Houghton et al. (1957) present an extensive compilation of smoothed data, in the form of isothermal partial pressures for CO_2 as a function of liquid-phase mole fraction x_1. The data at 50°C are given in the first two columns of Table 6-6; the third column contains values for ϕ_1, the vapor-phase fugacity coefficient of pure CO_2, computed by Houghton et al. from a high-precision equation of state.

Table 6-6 Gas-solubility data for $CO_2(1)$ in $H_2O(2)$ at 50°C, as compiled by Houghton et al. (1957). Values of $P_1(\text{calc})$ are determined from the correlation of Example 6-21.

P_1/bar	$x_1 \times 10^3$	ϕ_1	$\dfrac{\phi_1 P_1}{x_1}$/bar	$P_1(\text{calc})$/bar
1.013	0.342	0.99602	2,951	1.013
2.027	0.683	0.99208	2,943	2.031
4.053	1.354	0.98424	2,947	4.058
6.080	2.02	0.97646	2,938	6.103
8.106	2.66	0.96876	2,953	8.102
10.13	3.30	0.96112	2,951	10.13
12.16	3.93	0.95352	2,951	12.17
14.19	4.55	0.94596	2,950	14.20
16.21	5.15	0.93844	2,955	16.21
18.24	5.75	0.93098	2,953	18.25
20.27	6.34	0.92350	2,952	20.29
22.29	6.91	0.91606	2,956	22.30
24.32	7.47	0.90866	2,958	24.32
26.35	8.03	0.90124	2,957	26.37
28.37	8.57	0.89384	2,959	28.40
30.40	9.10	0.88644	2,961	30.42
32.42	9.62	0.87902	2,963	32.45
34.45	10.13	0.87160	2,964	34.49
36.48	10.63	0.86417	2,966	36.53

A reduction of the data is required. If this is done sequentially, the first step is a determination of $k_1(P_2^{sat})$. We have at our disposal at least six rigorous procedures, based on any one of Eqs. (6-174) or (6-175a,b,c,d). However, each of these procedures presumes the availability of fugacity coefficients $\hat{\phi}_1$ for CO_2 in vapor *mixtures*, whereas we only have values of ϕ_1, for *pure* CO_2. We therefore assume that

$$\hat{\phi}_1 \simeq \phi_1 \qquad (A)$$

Equation (A) is justified if vapor mixtures of CO_2 and H_2O are *ideal solutions*; physicochemically this is probably a bad assumption. However, if the vapor phase contains mostly CO_2, Eq. (A) can be rationalized from the property of $\hat{\phi}_i$ that

$$\lim_{y_i \to 1} \hat{\phi}_i = \phi_i$$

Since vapor compositions are not given in the data set, we must obtain estimates of the magnitude of y_1 by other means. The approximate Eqs. (6-162) and (6-163) of Example 6-19 are useful for this purpose. Solving Eq. (6-163) for P and substituting the result into Eq. (6-162), we find that

$$y_1 \simeq \frac{P_1}{P_1 + P_2^{sat}} \qquad (B)$$

At 50°C, the vapor pressure P_2^{sat} of water is 0.1233 bar, and Eq. (B) yields, for $P_1 = 1.013$ bar,

$$y_1 \simeq \frac{1.013}{1.013 + 0.1233} = 0.8915$$

Thus the vapor phase contains approximately 90 mol percent CO_2 at the lowest partial pressure for which data are given; at the higher partial pressures it contains considerably more. Hence, for $P_1 \simeq 1$ bar or greater, y_1 is close enough to unity to justify Eq. (A).

We now determine $k_1(P_2^{sat})$. As noted earlier, this determination can be based either on intercepts or on limiting slopes. According to Eq. (6-174) and Eq. (A)

$$k_1(P_2^{sat}) \simeq \lim_{\substack{x_1 \to 0 \\ P_1 \to 0}} \left(\frac{\phi_1 P_1}{x_1} \right) \qquad (C)$$

and thus we require values for the group $\phi_1 P_1/x_1$. These are computed from the data and the given values of ϕ_1, and are entered in the fourth column of Table 6-6. Although these entries show slightly erratic behavior at the lower partial pressures, a value of $k_1(P_2^{sat}) = 2,950$ bar, obtained by graphical extrapolation to $x_1 = 0$ (or $P_1 = 0$) is *consonant* with the data.

The evaluation of Henry's constants from limiting slopes depends on Eqs. (6-175). Since neither y_1 nor P, but only their product P_1, is given, Eqs. (6-175b) and (6-175c) are both appropriate. Consistent with Eq. (A), we write Eq. (6-175c) in the approximate form

$$k_1(P_2^{sat}) \simeq \left[\frac{d(\phi_1 P_1)}{dx_1} \right]^{\infty} \qquad (D)$$

The fugacity coefficient appearing in Eq. (6-175b) is $\hat{\phi}_1^{\infty}$. We cannot rationalize its replacement by ϕ_1 on the basis that the vapor phase is mostly CO_2, for in fact

$y_1 \to 0$. However, when $x_1 \to 0$, $P \to P_2^{sat}$, and this pressure is so low (~ 0.12 bar) that the vapor phase is safely assumed an ideal solution. In this event, $\hat{\phi}_1^\infty = \phi_1(P_2^{sat})$, where the notation $\phi_1(P_2^{sat})$ indicates the fugacity coefficient of pure CO_2 vapor at 50°C and at $P_2^{sat} = 0.1233$ bar. The data of Table 6-6 clearly show that at such a low pressure the fugacity coefficient is very nearly unity. We therefore write the approximate form of Eq. (6-175b) as

$$k_1(P_2^{sat}) \simeq \left(\frac{dP_1}{dx_1}\right)^\infty \tag{E}$$

Plots of P_1 versus x_1 and $\phi_1 P_1$ versus x_1 are shown on Fig. 6-30. Although both plots yield the same limiting derivatives, the trend of $\phi_1 P_1$ with x_1 is much more nearly linear, permitting an easier determination of $k_1(P_2^{sat})$. The value so obtained, as the slope of the straight line, is 2,950 bar, in agreement with the number found earlier by Eq. (C).

The second step in data reduction is the determination and correlation of liquid-phase departures from ideal-solution behavior, as manifested in $(\gamma_1^*)^+$. [Here, since

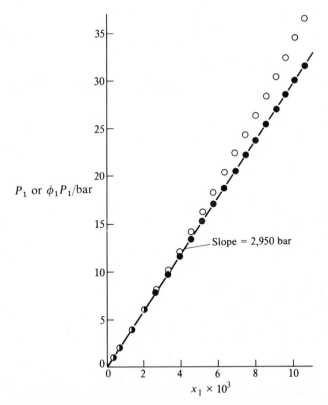

Figure 6-30 P_1 (open circles) and $\phi_1 P_1$ (closed circles) as a function of x_1 for $CO_2(1)$ dissolved in $H_2O(2)$ at 50°C. See Example 6-21.

$k_1^+ = k_1(P_2^{sat})$, the reference pressure P^+ is $P_2^{sat} = 0.1233$ bar.] Superficial consideration of the linearity of the $\phi_1 P_1$-versus-x_1 plot suggests that $(\gamma_1^*)^+ = 1.0$, because
Eq. (6-177b) yields as a limiting case the simple proportionality

$$\hat{\phi}_1 P_1 \simeq \phi_1 P_1 = k_1^+ x_1 \tag{F}$$

However, the validity of Eq. (F) rests also on the assumption that

$$\int_{P^+}^{P} \frac{\bar{V}_1}{RT} dP \simeq 0$$

and this assumption must be tested before one can conclude that $(\gamma_1^*)^+ = 1.0$. Parkinson and DeNevers (1969) determined liquid-phase partial molar volumes of CO_2 in
water, and found for temperatures between 5 and 40°C and for $x_1 < 0.008$ that

$$\bar{V}_1 \simeq \bar{V}_1^{\infty} = \text{const} = 37.6 \text{ cm}^3 \text{ mol}^{-1}$$

The maximum solubility in Table 6-6 is $x_1 = 0.0106$, and it is therefore probably
and excellent assumption for these 50°C data that the $\bar{V}_1^{\infty}$ value of Parkinson and
DeNevers in constant in evaluation of the integral. Thus, taking $\bar{V}_1 = \bar{V}_1^{\infty}$, we have

$$\int_{P^+}^{P} \frac{\bar{V}_1}{RT} dP = \int_{P_1^{sat}}^{P} \frac{\bar{V}_1}{RT} dP \simeq \frac{\bar{V}_1^{\infty}(P - P_2^{sat})}{RT}$$

But, by Eq. (6-163), $P - P_2^{sat} \simeq P_1$, giving finally

$$\int_{P^+}^{P} \frac{\bar{V}_1}{RT} dP \simeq \frac{\bar{V}_1^{\infty} P_1}{RT} \tag{G}$$

The approximation provided by Eq. (G) is commonly employed in the reduction of
gas-solubility data, and in the calculation of gas solubilities at high pressures. When
combined with Eq. (6-177c), with the additional assumption that $(\gamma_1^*)^+ = 1$, it yields
the *Krichevsky-Kasarnovsky equation* (1935):

$$\ln \left(\frac{\hat{\phi}_1 P_1}{x_1} \right) = \ln k_1^+ + \frac{\bar{V}_1^{\infty} P_1}{RT} \tag{H}$$

Equation (H) was used for many years for the extraction of infinite-dilution partial
molar volumes from gas-solubility data; unfortunately, if the range of P_1 is sufficient
for the second term on the right to be significant, the values of x_1 are also often large
enough for liquid-phase nonidealities to be important. Values of $\bar{V}_1^{\infty}$ determined this
way may therefore be unreliable.

For the present case, the values of the integral in Eq. (G) *are* significant, and we
conclude that the linearity of the $\phi_1 P_1$-versus-x_1 plot does *not* imply that $(\gamma_1^*)^+ =$
1.0. In fact, the "pressure effect" represented by Eq. (G) and the "composition
effect" embodied in the activity coefficient interact so as to cancel each other almost
exactly. Thus we must consider both terms. A graphical reduction of the data is
facilitated by Eq. (6-177c), which yields, on combination with Eq. (G),

$$\ln \left(\frac{\hat{\phi}_1 \mathbf{P}_1}{x_1} \right) = \ln k_1^+ + \ln (\gamma_1^*)^+ + \frac{\bar{V}_1^{\infty} P_1}{RT} \tag{I}$$

If we assume the simplest nontrivial expression for $\ln (\gamma_1^*)^+$, Eq. (6-181), then Eq. (I) becomes the *Krichevsky-Ilinskaya equation* (1945):

$$\ln \left(\frac{\hat{\phi}_1 P_1}{x_1} \right) = \ln k_1^+ + A^+(x_2^2 - 1) + \frac{\bar{V}_1^\infty P_1}{RT} \tag{J}$$

Setting $\hat{\phi}_1 = \phi_1$ in accordance with Eq. (A) and rearranging, we obtain from Eq. (J)

$$\mathcal{I} \equiv \frac{\bar{V}_1^\infty P_1}{RT} - \ln \left(\frac{\phi_1 P_1}{x_1 k_1^+} \right) = -A^+(x_2^2 - 1)$$

If $\bar{V}_1 = \bar{V}_1^\infty = \text{const}$ is a valid assumption, and *if* Eq. (6-181) is a valid expression for $\ln (\gamma_1^*)^+$, then a plot of $\mathcal{I}$ versus $-(x_2^2 - 1)$ must yield a straight line passing through the origin, with slope equal to A^+. Figure 6-31 depicts such a plot, for which deviations from linearity obtain only at the highest partial pressures. The slope of the straight line shown is 2.10, and this is the numerical value of A^+ at 50°C and 0.1233 bar.

The results of data reduction may be summarized briefly. For $CO_2(1)$ dissolved in liquid $H_2O(2)$ at 50°C, the VLE is adequately described by the expression

$$P_1 = \frac{x_1 k_1^+}{\phi_1} \exp \left[A^+(x_2^2 - 1) + \frac{\bar{V}_1^\infty P_1}{RT} \right] \tag{K}$$

Here, $k_1^+ = 2,950$ bar, $\bar{V}_1^\infty = 37.6$ cm^3 mol^{-1}, and $A^+ = 2.10$; the reference pressure P^+ is 0.1233 bar. Values of P_1 computed from this correlation are listed in the last column of Table 6-6. The average discrepancy between experimental and correlated values of P_1 is only about 0.1 percent, with a maximum difference of about 0.4 percent.

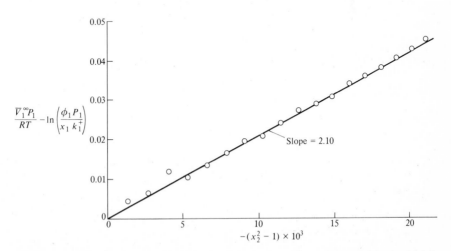

Figure 6-31 Plot of $\bar{V}_1^\infty P_1/RT - \ln (\phi_1 P_1/x_1 k_1^+)$ versus $-(x_2^2 - 1)$ for $CO_2(1)$ dissolved in $H_2O(2)$ at 50°C. See Example 6-21.

The above example treated the *sequential* reduction of a set of isothermal gas-solubility data, in which Henry's constant was determined prior to the correlation of liquid-phase deviations from ideal-solution behavior. *Simultaneous* determination of k_1^+ and of a correlation for $(\gamma_1^*)^+$ is also possible if one knows in advance the functional form for the composition dependence of g^*. For example, for the case just treated we could have rearranged Eq. (J) to the form (with $\hat{\phi}_1 = \phi_1$)

$$\mathcal{K} \equiv \frac{\bar{V}_1^\infty P_1}{RT} - \ln\left(\frac{\phi_1 P_1}{x_1}\right) = -\ln k_1^+ - A^+(x_2^2 - 1)$$

according to which a plot of $\mathcal{K}$ versus $-(x_2^2 - 1)$ yields $-\ln k_1^+$ as the intercept and A^+ as the slope. Graphical analysis is of course unnecessary if one has available a computer and a flexible program for nonlinear regression. Again referring to the last example, we write

$$P_1 = \frac{x_1 k_1^+}{\phi_1} \exp\left[A^+ x_1(x_1 - 2) + \frac{\bar{V}_1^\infty P_1}{RT}\right] \qquad (6\text{-}182)$$

Treating P_1 as the dependent variable and x_1 as the independent variable, one seeks the values of k_1^+ and A^+ which minimize the objective function $\sum (\delta P_1)^2$, where δP_1 is the difference between the value of P_1 calculated by Eq. (6-182) and the experimental value. Since P_1 appears on both sides of the equation, a multiply iterative procedure is required.

The compilation of Houghton et al. (1957) contains additional isothermal solubility data for CO_2 in water at temperatures other than 50°C; regression of these data at seven temperatures by Eq. (6-182) produces the values of k_1^+ and A^+ shown on Figure 6-32. In each case, the reference pressure P^+ is P_2^{sat} for the indicated temperature. However, the vapor pressure of water is so small in this temperature range that P^+ may, for all practical purposes, be treated as constant and essentially zero. Thus the trends shown on Fig. 6-32 represents pure temperature effects. The signs and magnitudes of the derivatives of the smooth curves drawn through the points admit interpretation. For example, we have by Eq. (5-135) that

$$H_1' - \bar{H}_1^\infty = RT^2\left(\frac{\partial \ln k_1}{\partial T}\right)_P$$

and hence

$$H_1' - \bar{H}_1^\infty = -R\left[\frac{\partial \ln k_1^+}{\partial(1/T)}\right]_P$$

Since $\ln k_1^+$ in this case decreases with $1/T$, we conclude that the difference $H_1' - \bar{H}_1^\infty$ is positive and decreases with increasing T, from about 33,500 J mol^{-1} at 0°C to about 17,500 J mol^{-1} at 50°C. Similarly, we have by Eq. (L) of Example 5-9 that

$$H^E = -RT^2\left[\frac{\partial(G^E/RT)}{\partial T}\right]_{P,x}$$

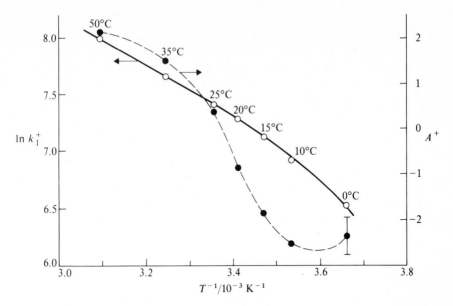

Figure 6-32 Plots of $\ln k_1^+$ (open circles) and A^+ (closed circles) versus $1/T$ for the $CO_2(1)/H_2O(2)$ system at several temperatures; k_1^+ is in bar, and T in K. See Eq. (6-182) and the accompanying discussion.

and thus

$$H^E = R\left[\frac{\partial g}{\partial(1/T)}\right]_{P,\,x}$$

where $g \equiv G^E/RT$. Since the source of our correlation of $(\gamma_1^*)^+$ is the expression

$$g = A^+ x_1 x_2$$

we have by the last two equations that

$$H^E = x_1 x_2 R\left[\frac{\partial A^+}{\partial(1/T)}\right]_P$$

According to the observed trends of A^+ with $1/T$, H^E is near zero or even slightly positive at the lowest temperatures, becomes increasingly negative as T increases, and then increases to a small negative value as T approaches 50°C. [The excess enthalpy is here identified with the heat of mixing for a process in which pure liquid water is combined with (hypothetical) liquid CO_2 at constant T and P^+ to produce liquid solutions of CO_2 and water.]

In the preceding developments we have made little or no use of the equilibrium equation for solvent species 2, because this is common practice in the *reduction* of gas-solubility data. However, *calculation* of gas solubilities requires the equilibrium equations for both species. Moreover, a full isothermal x_1, P, y_1

data set contains redundant information, and it is not necessary that all of this information be incorporated in a data-reduction procedure. We have from Eq. (6-155) that

$$y_1 P = x_1 (\gamma_1^*)^+ k_1^+ / \Phi_1^*$$

and similarly, from Eq. (6-157),

$$y_2 P = x_2 \gamma_2^+ P_2^{sat} / \Phi_2$$

from which, by addition, we obtain the analog of Eq. (6-91):

$$P = \frac{x_1 (\gamma_1^*)^+ k_1^+}{\Phi_1^*} + \frac{x_2 \gamma_2^+ P_2^{sat}}{\Phi_2} \qquad (6\text{-}183)$$

The activity coefficients in Eq. (6-183) may be eliminated in favor of g and its derivatives by Eqs. (6-180) and (6-93b), giving

$$P = \frac{x_1 k_1^+}{\Phi_1^*} \exp \left[g + x_2 \frac{dg}{dx_1} - \left(\frac{dg}{dx_1} \right)^\infty \right] + \frac{x_2 P_2^{sat}}{\Phi_2} \exp \left[g - x_1 \frac{dg}{dx_1} \right] \qquad (6\text{-}184)$$

Equation (6-184) is the analog of Eq. (6-94), and the procedures described earlier (e.g., Barker's method) for extraction of a correlation for g from isothermal $P - x_1$ data apply in principle also to Eq. (6-184). Implementation of these procedures is probably best done sequentially, with a prior determination of k_1^+ by Eqs. (6-175d) and (6-176).

In this section, we have treated the phenomenon of gas solubility as a special case of VLE. However, the subject has a vast literature of its own, with many conventions and notations peculiar to the area. Good entries to the literature are provided by a series of review papers by Battino and coworkers (Battino and Clever, 1966; Wilhelm and Battino, 1973; and Wilhelm et al., 1977), wherein are given descriptions of experimental methods, compilations of correlated data, and extensive bibliographies.

6-10 LIQUID/LIQUID AND VAPOR/LIQUID/LIQUID EQUILIBRIA

It is a matter of experience that some pairs of pure liquids, when mixed in appropriate proportions at certain temperatures and pressures, do not produce a single homogeneous liquid phase but instead form two liquid phases of different compositions. If the phases are at thermodynamic equilibrium, the phenomenon is an example *liquid/liquid equilibrium,* or "LLE."

The thermodynamic description of LLE is based on the same criteria used for VLE, namely, uniformity of T, P, and of the fugacity $\hat{f}_i$ for each chemical species in both phases. Designating the equilibrium liquid phases by the symbols

α and β, we therefore write the criterion for LLE in an N-component system of uniform T and P as

$$\hat{f}_i^\alpha = \hat{f}_i^\beta \qquad (i = 1, 2, \ldots, N)$$

or, introducing activity coefficients, as

$$x_i^\alpha \gamma_i^\alpha (f_i^\circ)^\alpha = x_i^\beta \gamma_i^\beta (f_i^\circ)^\beta \qquad (i = 1, 2, \ldots, N)$$

We assume that all species exist as pure liquids at the temperature of the system, and define all activity coefficients with respect to Lewis-Randall standard states. Then $(f_i^\circ)^\alpha = (f_i^\circ)^\beta = f_i$ for each component, and the last equation becomes

$$\boxed{x_i^\alpha \gamma_i^\alpha = x_i^\beta \gamma_i^\beta} \qquad (i = 1, 2, \ldots, N) \qquad (6\text{-}185)$$

Equation (6-185), the governing equation for LLE, is sometimes written in the equivalent form

$$\boxed{\hat{a}_i^\alpha = \hat{a}_i^\beta} \qquad (i = 1, 2, \ldots, N) \qquad (6\text{-}186)$$

where $\hat{a}_i$ is the *activity* of species i [see Sec. 5-5 and Eq. (J) of Example 5-9].

In Eq. (6-185), the activity coefficients γ_i^α and γ_i^β derive from the *same function* $g \equiv G^E/R\dot{T}$; thus they are functionally identical, distinguished mathematically only by the mole fractions to which they apply. For a liquid/liquid system containing N chemical species

$$\gamma_i^\alpha = \gamma_i(x_1^\alpha, x_2^\alpha, \ldots, x_{N-1}^\alpha, T, P) \qquad (6\text{-}187a)$$

and

$$\gamma_i^\beta = \gamma_i(x_1^\beta, x_2^\beta, \ldots, x_{N-1}^\beta, T, P) \qquad (6\text{-}187b)$$

According to Eqs. (6-185) and (6-187), we have N equilibrium equations and $2N$ intensive variables (T, P, and $N - 1$ independent mole fractions for each phase). Solution of the equilibrium equations for LLE therefore requires prior specification of numerical values for N of the intensive variables. This is in accord with the phase rule, Eq. (6-2), which gives $F = 2 - \pi + N - s = 2 - 2 + N - 0 = N$, the same result obtained for VLE with no special constraints on the equilibrium state.

The case just described is the *general* LLE problem, for which any number of species may be present, and for which pressure is a significant variable. Our concern here is with a simpler (but important) special case, that of *binary* LLE either at constant pressure or at reduced temperatures low enough that the effect of pressure on the activity coefficients may be ignored. There is then but one independent mole fraction per phase, and Eq. (6-185) gives

$$x_1^\alpha \gamma_1^\alpha = x_1^\beta \gamma_1^\beta \qquad (6\text{-}188a)$$

and

$$(1 - x_1^\alpha)\gamma_2^\alpha = (1 - x_1^\beta)\gamma_2^\beta \qquad (6\text{-}188b)$$

with

$$\gamma_i^\alpha = \gamma_i(x_1^\alpha, T) \tag{6-189a}$$

and

$$\gamma_i^\beta = \gamma_i(x_1^\beta, T) \tag{6-189b}$$

Here we have two equations and three variables (x_1^α, x_1^β, and T); fixing one of the variables allows solution of Eqs. (6-188) for the remaining two. Since $\ln \gamma_i$, rather than γ_i, is a more natural thermodynamic function, application of Eqs. (6-188) often proceeds from the rearrangements

$$\ln \left(\gamma_1^\alpha / \gamma_1^\beta \right) = \ln \left(\frac{x_1^\beta}{x_1^\alpha} \right) \tag{6-190a}$$

and

$$\ln \left(\gamma_2^\alpha / \gamma_2^\beta \right) = \ln \left(\frac{1 - x_1^\beta}{1 - x_1^\alpha} \right) \tag{6-190b}$$

For conditions of constant pressure, or when pressure effects are negligible, binary LLE is conveniently displayed on a *solubility diagram*, a plot of T versus x_1. Figure 6-33 shows binary solubility diagrams of three types. The first (Fig. 6-33a) is the most inclusive of the three. Curves defining the "island" on this diagram (*binodal curves*) represent the compositions of coexisting phases: curve UAL, those of the α phase, and curve UBL, those of the β phase. (Throughout this section, we define the α liquid phase as the one rich in component 2, and the β liquid phase as the one rich in component 1.) Equilibrium compositions x_1^α and x_1^β at a particular T are defined by the intersections of a horizontal *tie line*

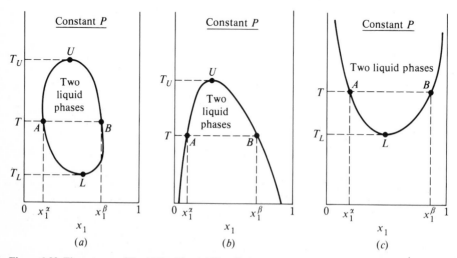

Figure 6-33 Three types of liquid/liquid solubility diagram.

with the binodal curves. Temperature T_L is a lower *consolute temperature*, or lower *critical solution temperature* (LCST); temperature T_U is an upper consolute temperature, or upper critical solution temperature (UCST). At temperatures between T_L and T_U, LLE is possible; for $T < T_L$ and $T > T_U$, a single liquid phase is obtained for the full range of compositions. The consolute points are analogous to the liquid/gas critical point of a pure fluid; they are limiting states of two-phase equilibrium for which all properties of the two equilibrium phases are identical.

Actually, the behavior shown on Fig. 6-33a is infrequently observed; the LLE binodal curves are often interrupted by curves for yet another phase transition. When the binodal curves intersect the freezing curve, only a UCST can exist (Fig. 6-33b); when they intersect the VLE liquidus curve, only an LCST can exist (Fig. 6-33c); when they intersect both, no consolute point exists, and a fourth type of behavior is observed.

Thus it is apparent that real systems exhibit a diversity of LLE behavior. The thermodynamic basis for calculation or correlation of LLE is an expression for g, and the suitability of a particular expression is determined by its ability to accommodate the various features illustrated by Fig. 6-33. That this is a *severe* test of an expression for g should be obvious, for, unlike their role in low-pressure VLE applications where they represent corrections to Raoult's law, the liquid-phase activity coefficients constitute the *only* thermodynamic contribution to an LLE calculation.

Example 6-22 An important limiting case of binary LLE is that for which the α phase is extremely dilute in species 1 and the β phase is extremely dilute in species 2. In this event, we have approximately

$$\gamma_1^\alpha \simeq \gamma_1^\infty$$

$$\gamma_2^\alpha \simeq 1$$

$$\gamma_1^\beta \simeq 1$$

and

$$\gamma_2^\beta \simeq \gamma_2^\infty$$

Substitution into the equilibrium equations, Eqs. (6-188), gives

$$x_1^\alpha \gamma_1^\infty \simeq x_1^\beta$$

and

$$1 - x_1^\alpha \simeq (1 - x_1^\beta)\gamma_2^\infty$$

and solution for the mole fractions yields the approximate equations

$$x_1^\alpha = \frac{\gamma_2^\infty - 1}{\gamma_1^\infty \gamma_2^\infty - 1} \tag{A}$$

and

$$x_1^\beta = \frac{\gamma_1^\infty (\gamma_2^\infty - 1)}{\gamma_1^\infty \gamma_2^\infty - 1} \tag{B}$$

Alternatively, we may solve for the γ_i^∞, obtaining

$$\gamma_1^\infty = \frac{x_1^\beta}{x_1^\alpha} \tag{C}$$

and

$$\gamma_2^\infty = \frac{1 - x_1^\alpha}{1 - x_1^\beta} \tag{D}$$

Equations (A) and (B) can be used for order-of-magnitude estimates of equilibrium compositions from two-parameter expressions for g, where the γ_i^∞ are usually related to the parameters in a simple way. Equations (C) and (D) serve the opposite function; they provide simple explicit expressions for the γ_i^∞ in terms of measurable equilibrium compositions.

It is apparent from Eqs. (C) and (D) that positive deviations from ideal-solution behavior (in the sense of the Lewis-Randall rule) promote LLE, for

$$\gamma_1^\infty \simeq \frac{1}{x_1^\alpha} > 1$$

and

$$\gamma_2^\infty \simeq \frac{1}{x_2^\beta} > 1$$

The extreme example of binary LLE is that of *complete* immiscibility of the two species, for which case it is required by Eq. (6-188) that

$$\gamma_1^\alpha = \gamma_2^\beta = \infty$$

Strictly speaking, probably no two liquids are completely immiscible. However, actual solubilities may be so small (e.g., for some hydrocarbon/water systems) that the idealizations $x_1^\alpha = x_2^\beta = 0$ provide suitable approximations for practical calculations. (See Example 6-28.)

Example 6-23 The simplest expression for $g \equiv G^E/RT$ capable of predicting LLE is the one-parameter equation

$$g = Ax_1x_2 \tag{A}$$

for which

$$\ln \gamma_1 = Ax_2^2 = A(1 - x_1)^2$$

and

$$\ln \gamma_2 = Ax_1^2$$

Specializing the last two equations to the α and β phases and substituting into Eqs. (6-190), we obtain

$$A[(1 - x_1^\alpha)^2 - (1 - x_1^\beta)^2] = \ln\left(\frac{x_1^\beta}{x_1^\alpha}\right) \tag{B}$$

and

$$A[(x_1^\alpha)^2 - (x_1^\beta)^2] = \ln\left(\frac{1 - x_1^\beta}{1 - x_1^\alpha}\right) \tag{C}$$

Given a value of parameter A, one finds the equilibrium compositions x_1^α and x_1^β as solutions to Eqs. (B) and (C).

Solubility curves implied by Eq. (A) are in fact symmetrical about $x_1 = 0.5$, for substitution of the relation

$$x_1^\beta = 1 - x_1^\alpha \tag{D}$$

into Eqs. (B) and (C) reduces them both to the *same* equation, viz.,

$$A(1 - 2x_1) = \ln\left(\frac{1 - x_1}{x_1}\right) \tag{E}$$

Equation (E) has the trivial solution $x_1 = 1/2$ for *all* values of A. When $A > 2$, the equation has three real roots: $x_1 = 1/2$, $x_1 = r$, and $x_1 = 1 - r$, where $0 < r < 1/2$. The latter two roots are the *equilibrium* compositions (x_1^α and x_1^β). At $A = 2$, the three roots become identical and equal to 1/2, and for $A < 2$ only the trivial solution exists. Liquid/liquid equilibrium thus obtains only if $A \geq 2$; the case $A = 2$ corresponds to a consolute point. Table 6-7 contains values of A computed from Eq. (E) for various values of $x_1^\alpha(= 1 - x_1^\beta)$. Particularly to be noted is the extreme sensitivity of x_1^α and x_1^β to small changes in A near the consolute point.

The actual shape of a solubility curve predicted from an expression for g depends on the temperature dependence of the parameters in the expression. To illustrate this, we assume that parameter A in Eq. (A) varies with T according to

$$A = \frac{a}{T} + b - c \ln T \tag{F}$$

Table 6-7 Liquid-liquid equilibrium compositions implied by $g = Ax_1x_2$ for various values of A. (See Example 6-23.)

A	$x_1^\alpha(= 1 - x_1^\beta)$
2.0	0.5
2.0067	0.45
2.0273	0.4
2.0635	0.35
2.1182	0.3
2.1972	0.25
2.3105	0.2
2.4780	0.15
2.7465	0.1
3.2716	0.05
4.6889	0.01
5.3468	0.005
6.9206	0.001

where a, b, and c are constants. By Eqs. (6-60) and (6-61), this implies that C_P^E is independent of T and that H^E varies linearly with T:

$$C_P^E = Rcx_1 x_2 \qquad \text{(G)}$$

$$H^E = R(a + cT)x_1 x_2 \qquad \text{(H)}$$

The temperature dependence of A is directly related to the excess enthalpy, for, by Eq. (F),

$$\frac{dA}{dT} = -\frac{1}{T^2}(a + cT)$$

and combination of this equation with Eq. (H) gives

$$\frac{dA}{dT} = -\frac{H^E}{x_1 x_2 RT^2}$$

Thus parameter A decreases with increasing T for an endothermic system (positive H^E), and increases with increasing T for an exothermic system (negative H^E). We have shown that $A = 2$ corresponds to a consolute point. If A is *decreasing* with increasing T (negative dA/dT) as it passes through 2.0, the consolute temperature is clearly a UCST; conversely, if A is *increasing* with increasing T (positive dA/dT) as it passes through 2.0, then the consolute temperature is an LCST. Hence a system described by Eqs. (A) and (F) exhibits a UCST if endothermic at the consolute point and an LCST if exothermic at the consolute point.

The above-described features are best illustrated by numerical example. We treat hypothetical binary systems for which LLE obtains in the temperature range 250 to 450 K, and for which constant c of Eq. (F) is numerically equal to 3.0. This implies a positive excess heat capacity, independent of T, for which by Eq. (G) the maximum value (at $x_1 = x_2 = 0.5$) is

$$C_P^E(\text{max}) = 8.314 \times 3.0 \times \tfrac{1}{4} = 6.24 \text{ J mol}^{-1} \text{ K}^{-1}$$

Realistic values are assigned to constants a and b, such that consolute points obtain between 250 and 450 K. Three cases are examined, with A given by the equations

$$A = \frac{-975}{T} + 22.4 - 3 \ln T \qquad \text{(I)}$$

$$A = \frac{-540}{T} + 21.1 - 3 \ln T \qquad \text{(J)}$$

and

$$A = \frac{-1,500}{T} + 23.9 - 3 \ln T \qquad \text{(K)}$$

Consolute points occur when $A = 2$, or by Eq. (F), when

$$T \ln T = \frac{a}{c} - \left(\frac{2 - b}{c}\right)T \qquad \text{(L)}$$

Depending on the values of a, b, and c, Eq. (L) is solved by zero, one, or two values of T. For the case represented by Eq. (I), we find *two* solutions, corresponding to an LCST and a UCST:

$$T_L = 272.9 \text{ K}$$

and

$$T_U = 391.2 \text{ K}$$

Values of A are plotted on Fig. 6-34a, and the solubility curve [computed from Eq. (E)] is shown on Fig. 6-34b. This case—that of a closed solubility loop—is of the type shown in Fig. 6-33a. It requires that H^E *change sign* in the temperature interval for which LLE obtains.

For the second case, with A given by Eq. (J), Eq. (L) is solved by only *one* value of T in the range 250 to 450 K:

$$T_U = 346.0 \text{ K}$$

This is a UCST, because Eq. (H) gives a positive H^E at 346.0 K. Values of A and the corresponding solubility curve are given by Fig. 6-35.

The third case is similar to the second, there being only one T (339.7 K) that solves Eq. (L) for $250 \text{ K} \leq T \leq 450 \text{ K}$. However, this is an LCST, because H^E is now negative. Numerical results computed from Eqs. (K) and (E) are displayed on Fig. 6-36.

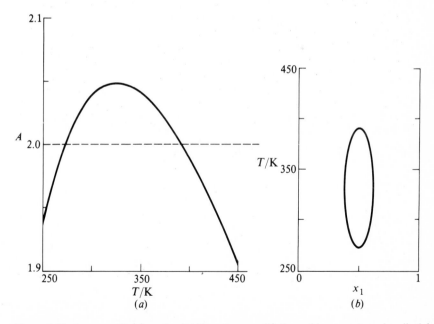

Figure 6-34 A versus T (a) and solubility diagram (b) for a binary system described by $g = A x_1 x_2$ with $A = -975/T + 22.4 - 3 \ln T$. (See Example 6-23.)

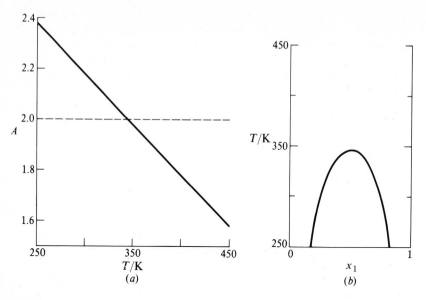

Figure 6-35 A versus T (a) and solubility diagram (b) for a binary system described by $g = Ax_1 x_2$ with $A = -540/T + 21.1 - 3 \ln T$. (See Example 6-23.)

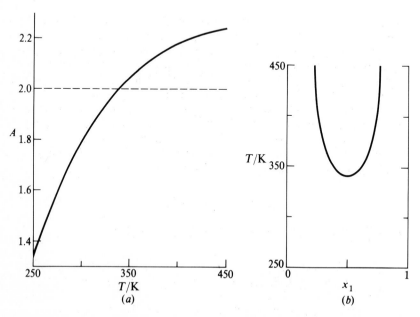

Figure 6-36 A versus T (a) and solubility diagram (b) for a binary system described by $g = Ax_1 x_2$ with $A = -1500/T + 23.9 - 3 \ln T$. (See Example 6-23.)

Example 6-24 Liquid/liquid equilibrium data may be used for estimation of parameters in an expression for g. In particular, Eqs. (6-190) and one (x_1^α, x_1^β) data point are sufficient in principle for determination of both parameters in a two-parameter expression for g, provided of course that the equation is capable of describing LLE. The *temperature dependence* of the parameters may also be estimated from a *set* $\{x_1^\alpha, x_1^\beta\}$ of solubility data as a function of T.

As an example, we consider the two-parameter Margules equation, Eq. (6-121), for which

$$\ln \gamma_1 = x_2^2[A_{12} + 2(A_{21} - A_{12})x_1] \qquad (6\text{-}122a)$$

and

$$\ln \gamma_2 = x_1^2[A_{21} + 2(A_{12} - A_{21})x_2] \qquad (6\text{-}122b)$$

Specializing Eqs. (6-122) to the α and β phases and substituting the results into Eqs. (6-190), we find on rearrangement that

$$[(x_2^\beta)^2(x_2^\beta - x_1^\beta) - (x_2^\alpha)^2(x_2^\alpha - x_1^\alpha)]A_{12}$$
$$+ 2[x_1^\beta(x_2^\beta)^2 - x_1^\alpha(x_2^\alpha)^2]A_{21} = \ln\left(\frac{x_1^\alpha}{x_1^\beta}\right) \qquad (A)$$

and

$$2[x_2^\beta(x_1^\beta)^2 - x_2^\alpha(x_1^\alpha)^2]A_{12} + [(x_1^\beta)^2(x_1^\beta - x_2^\beta)$$
$$- (x_1^\alpha)^2(x_1^\alpha - x_2^\alpha)]A_{21} = \ln\left(\frac{1 - x_1^\alpha}{1 - x_1^\beta}\right) \qquad (B)$$

Equations (A) and (B) are linear in parameters A_{12} and A_{21}; given values of the equilibrium compositions x_1^α ($= 1 - x_2^\alpha$) and x_1^β ($= 1 - x_2^\beta$), one easily solves for both A_{12} and A_{21}.

Suppose, for example, that $x_1^\alpha = 0.2$ and $x_1^\beta = 0.9$ at some temperature. Then $x_2^\alpha = 1 - 0.2 = 0.8$ and $x_2^\beta = 1 - 0.9 = 0.1$, and substitution into Eqs. (A) and (B) gives

$$[(0.1)^2(0.1 - 0.9) - (0.8)^2(0.8 - 0.2)]A_{12}$$
$$+ 2[(0.9)(0.1)^2 - (0.2)(0.8)^2]A_{21} = \ln\left(\frac{0.2}{0.9}\right)$$

and

$$2[(0.1)(0.9)^2 - (0.8)(0.2)^2]A_{12} + [(0.9)^2(0.9 - 0.1)$$
$$- (0.2)^2(0.2 - 0.8)]A_{21} = \ln\left(\frac{0.8}{0.1}\right)$$

or

$$-0.392A_{12} - 0.238A_{21} = -1.5040773$$

and

$$0.098A_{12} + 0.672A_{21} = 2.0794415$$

from which

$$A_{12} = 2.1484 \qquad \text{and} \qquad A_{21} = 2.7811$$

Thus, at the temperature for which the solubility data are given, we have determined that

$$g \equiv \frac{G^E}{RT} = (2.7811x_1 + 2.1484x_2)x_1x_2 \tag{C}$$

This empirical expression is in effect an *extrapolation* device for estimating g in the ranges $0 \le x_1 \le 0.2$ and $0.9 \le x_1 \le 1.0$. Other two-parameter expressions [e.g., the van Laar equation, Eq. (6-119)], with parameters determined from the given solubilities, provide somewhat different extrapolations outside the two-liquid region. Only a functionally appropriate equation for g can yield *proper* extrapolated values; unfortunately, there is no single two-parameter equation known to be suitable for all binary systems.

Example 6-23 shows that the expression $g = Ax_1x_2$ cannot predict LLE for values of $A < 2$; for such values of A, use of this equation presumes that for all compositions a binary liquid solution is *stable* with respect to separation into two other liquid phases (phase splitting). Moreover, as demonstrated later (Example 6-26), the Wilson equation predicts stability with respect to phase splitting for *all* parameter values, and is therefore not a suitable correlating expression for systems of limited miscibility. We are thus led to the question of what fundamental mathematical condition is satisfied by an expression for $g \equiv G^E/RT$ when it is consistent with the stability of a single liquid phase.

In Sec. 6-2, we found that the equilibrium state of a closed, multiphase, PVT system is that state for which the total Gibbs function G^t attains a minimum at constant T and P. However, in developing alternative equilibrium criteria from this statement, we have, explicitly or implicitly, based the derivations solely on the equation

$$dG^t_{T,P} = 0 \tag{6-11}$$

which merely requires that the equilibrium state occur at an *extremum* in G^t. Determination that such a state actually corresponds to a *minimum* requires examination of the higher-ordered differentials of G^t. Specifically, if the first nonvanishing differential is the second, then we must have

$$\boxed{d^2G^t_{T,P} > 0} \tag{6-191}$$

General treatment of the consequences of application of this equation to multiphase, multicomponent systems is an example of *thermodynamic stability analysis*. Stability analysis is a mathematically complex subject, and we do not here develop it in depth; elementary treatments are given by Callen (1960), Münster (1970), and Modell and Reid (1974). We consider only the special case of direct importance to this section: the stability of a binary liquid phase with respect to phase splitting at constant T and P.

For this special case, if the equilibrium state in a closed system at fixed T and P is in fact a single homogeneous phase (rather than a pair of phases), then the inequality (6-191) must be satisfied for all perturbations around this state that lead to inhomogeneities in composition. Thus, for purposes of analysis, we imagine the phase divided into two regions, r and s, which are not separate phases but which undergo differential variations in composition as the result of "interregion" mass transfer. If the original phase is stable (i.e., if it cannot separate into two phases), then the inequality (6-191) is satisfied for all such variations. Our purpose is to determine the implications of stability on the behavior of thermodynamic functions other than G^t.

The independent variables subject to change in regions r and s as a result of mass transfer are n_1^r, n_2^r, n_1^s, and n_2^s, the mole numbers of the two species in the two regions. The second differential of G^t accompanying this hypothetical transfer of mass is, by definition,

$$
\begin{aligned}
d^2 G_{T,P}^t &= (d^2 G_{T,P}^t)^r + (d^2 G_{T,P}^t)^s \\
&= \left(\frac{\partial^2 G^t}{\partial n_1^2}\right)^r (dn_1^r)^2 + 2\left(\frac{\partial^2 G^t}{\partial n_1 \, \partial n_2}\right)^r dn_1^r \, dn_2^r + \left(\frac{\partial^2 G^t}{\partial n_2^2}\right)^r (dn_2^r)^2 \\
&\quad + \left(\frac{\partial^2 G^t}{\partial n_1^2}\right)^s (dn_1^s)^2 + 2\left(\frac{\partial^2 G^t}{\partial n_1 \, \partial n_2}\right)^s dn_1^s \, dn_2^s + \left(\frac{\partial^2 G^t}{\partial n_2^2}\right)^s (dn_2^s)^2 \quad (6\text{-}192)
\end{aligned}
$$

Here, all derivatives are evaluated for the original equilibrium state at conditions of constant T and P. Moreover, they are related to the composition derivatives of the chemical potentials. Thus, since μ_1 and μ_2 at constant T and P are functions of x_1 only, we find from Eq. (2-21) that

$$
\frac{\partial^2 G^t}{\partial n_1^2} = \frac{\partial \mu_1}{\partial n_1} = \left(\frac{\partial x_1}{\partial n_1}\right)\frac{d\mu_1}{dx_1} = \frac{x_2}{n}\frac{d\mu_1}{dx_1} \tag{6-193}
$$

$$
\frac{\partial^2 G^t}{\partial n_1 \, \partial n_2} = \frac{\partial \mu_1}{\partial n_2} = \left(\frac{\partial x_1}{\partial n_2}\right)\frac{d\mu_1}{dx_1} = \frac{-x_1}{n}\frac{d\mu_1}{dx_1} \tag{6-194}
$$

and

$$
\frac{\partial^2 G^t}{\partial n_2^2} = \frac{\partial \mu_2}{\partial n_2} = \left(\frac{\partial x_1}{\partial n_2}\right)\frac{d\mu_2}{dx_1} = -\frac{x_1}{n}\frac{d\mu_2}{dx_1}
$$

However, by the Gibbs-Duhem equation,

$$
x_1 \frac{d\mu_1}{dx_1} + x_2 \frac{d\mu_2}{dx_1} = 0
$$

Combination of the last two equations gives

$$
\frac{\partial^2 G^t}{\partial n_2^2} = \frac{x_1^2}{x_2 n}\frac{d\mu_1}{dx_1} \tag{6-195}
$$

Equations (6-193) through (6-195) are now specialized to regions r and s, and substituted into Eq. (6-192). The result is greatly simplified if we note that, since the derivatives of G^t are evaluated at the original equilibrium state, all intensive properties appearing in these derivatives are the same for regions r and s. Thus we obtain

$$d^2G^t_{T,P} = \frac{1}{x_2}\frac{d\mu_1}{dx_1}\left\{ x_2^2\left[\frac{(dn_1^r)^2}{n^r} + \frac{(dn_1^s)^2}{n^s}\right] - 2x_1x_2\left(\frac{dn_1^r\ dn_2^r}{n^r} + \frac{dn_1^s\ dn_2^s}{n^s}\right)\right.$$

$$\left. + x_1^2\left[\frac{(dn_2^r)^2}{n^r} + \frac{(dn_2^s)^2}{n^s}\right]\right\} \quad (6\text{-}196)$$

Here, n^r and n^s are the (arbitrary) total numbers of moles in regions r and s. Since the system is closed, we have (in the absence of chemical reactions) the material-balance equations

$$n_i^r + n_i^s = n_i = \text{const} \qquad (i = 1, 2)$$

from which

$$dn_i^s = -dn_i^r \qquad (i = 1, 2) \tag{6-197}$$

and thus

$$dn_i^s\ dn_j^s = dn_i^r\ dn_j^r \qquad (i, j = 1, 2) \tag{6-198}$$

Substitution of Eqs. (6-197) and (6-198) into Eq. (6-196) gives finally, on simplification,

$$d^2G^t_{T,P} = \frac{d\mu_1}{dx_1}\left[\frac{n^r + n^s}{x_2 n^r n^s}(x_2\ dn_1^r - x_1\ dn_2^r)^2\right] \tag{6-199}$$

By inequality (6-191), the right-hand side of Eq. (6-199) must be positive for stability. But the group in brackets is necessarily positive, and we conclude that the inequality is satisfied when

$$\frac{d\mu_1}{dx_1} > 0 \qquad (\text{const } T, P) \tag{6-200}$$

Inequality (6-200) is a *necessary* condition for stability of a two-component, homogeneous mixture. That is, if such a mixture is stable with respect to phase splitting, then the inequality is obeyed. On the other hand, if

$$\frac{d\mu_1}{dx_1} < 0 \qquad (\text{const } T, P) \tag{6-201}$$

for a given value of x_1, then the mixture is unstable for this value of x_1 and phase splitting occurs. The borderline case

$$\frac{d\mu_1}{dx_1} = 0 \qquad (\text{const } T, P) \tag{6-202}$$

implies that $d^2 G'_{T,P} = 0$; a system may be stable or unstable for this condition, depending on the sign of the first nonvanishing higher-order differential $d^m G'_{T,P}$, where $m \geq 3$.

It should be carefully noted that inequality (6-200) is not a *sufficient* condition for stability with respect to phase splitting (at least in the sense that the word "stable" is commonly applied), for there may exist states for which the inequality is satisfied, but which are unstable with respect to *large* perturbations. Such states, which are observed experimentally, are called *metastable*. One may of course broaden the concept of stability to include metastable states, in which case inequality (6-200) becomes (by definition) a sufficient as well as necessary condition for *intrinsic stability*. This in fact is standard practice, according to which both inequalities (6-191) and (6-200) are labeled as *criteria* for intrinsic stability. If a system is intrinsically stable as a single phase, it may or may not form two phases as a result of perturbations, depending on whether the perturbations are large or small. If it is intrinsically unstable, it is *absolutely* unstable to perturbations of any magnitude, and single-phase behavior cannot even in principle be obtained.

Many expressions alternative to inequality (6-200) are possible. For example, we have by the Gibbs-Duhem equation that

$$\frac{d\mu_1}{dx_1} = -\frac{x_2}{x_1}\frac{d\mu_2}{dx_1} = \frac{x_2}{x_1}\frac{d\mu_2}{dx_2} \qquad \text{(const } T, P)$$

and thus (6-200) is generalized to apply to both species:

$$\boxed{\frac{d\mu_i}{dx_i} > 0} \qquad i = 1, 2 \qquad \text{(const } T, P) \tag{6-203}$$

Also, since $\mu_1 \equiv \bar{G}_1$, then, by Eq. (3-12a),

$$\mu_1 = G + x_2 \frac{dG}{dx_1}$$

from which

$$\frac{d\mu_1}{dx_1} = \frac{dG}{dx_1} - \frac{dG}{dx_1} + x_2 \frac{d^2G}{dx_1^2} = x_2 \frac{d^2G}{dx_1^2}$$

Hence, by inequality (6-200),

$$\frac{d^2G}{dx_1^2} > 0 \qquad \text{(const } T, P)$$

This inequality is also generalizable to both species:

$$\frac{d^2G}{dx_i^2} > 0 \qquad i = 1, 2 \qquad \text{(const } T, P) \tag{6-204}$$

Other equivalent inequalities are easily derived, and we list some here for reference:

$$\boxed{\frac{d^2(\Delta G/RT)}{dx_i^2} > 0}$$ (6-205)

$$\frac{d^2(G^E/RT)}{dx_i^2} > -\frac{1}{x_1 x_2}$$ (6-206)

$$\frac{d \ln \gamma_i}{dx_i} > -\frac{1}{x_i}$$ (6-207)

$$\frac{d \ln \hat{a}_i}{dx_i} > 0$$ (6-208)

$$\frac{d\hat{f}_i}{dx_i} > 0$$ (6-209)

In inequalities (6-205) through (6-209), as in (6-203) and (6-204), index i refers to either species 1 or 2 in a binary system, and to conditions of constant T and P.

Example 6-25 We found in Example 6-23 that LLE is predicted by the expression $g = A x_1 x_2$ only when $A \geq 2$. This result is also easily obtained from the intrinsic stability criterion. For example, inequality (6-206) provides the requirement

$$\frac{d^2 g}{dx_1^2} > -\frac{1}{x_1 x_2}$$

Since

$$\frac{d^2 g}{dx_1^2} = \frac{d^2(A x_1 x_2)}{dx_1^2} = -2A$$

we must also have

$$2A < \frac{1}{x_1 x_2}$$

The minimum value of the right-hand side of this inequality is 4, obtained for $x_1 = x_2 = 1/2$; thus $A < 2$ yields stability of single-phase mixtures over the entire composition range. Conversely, if $A > 2$, then binary mixtures described by $g = A x_1 x_2$ form two liquid phases over some part of the composition range.

Example 6-26 Some expressions for g are incapable of representing LLE. One such expression is the Wilson equation:

$$g = -x_1 \ln (x_1 + x_2 \Lambda_{12}) - x_2 \ln (x_2 + x_1 \Lambda_{21})$$ (6-123)

If LLE is never predicted by Eq. (6-123), then the criterion for intrinsic stability is satisfied for all values of Λ_{12}, Λ_{21}, and x_1. That this is the case is most easily seen by examination of the derivative $d \ln \hat{a}_1/dx_1$. An expression for $\ln \gamma_1$ was given earlier for the Wilson equation as Eq. (6-124a). Since $\hat{a}_1 = x_1 \gamma_1$, addition of $\ln x_1$ to both sides of Eq. (6-124a) yields

$$\ln \hat{a}_1 = -\ln \left(1 + \frac{x_2}{x_1} \Lambda_{12}\right) + x_2 \left[\frac{\Lambda_{12}}{x_1 + x_2 \Lambda_{12}} - \frac{\Lambda_{21}}{x_2 + x_1 \Lambda_{21}}\right]$$

from which we obtain

$$\frac{d \ln \hat{a}_1}{dx_1} = \frac{x_2 \Lambda_{12}^2}{x_1(x_1 + x_2 \Lambda_{12})^2} + \frac{\Lambda_{21}^2}{(x_2 + x_1 \Lambda_{21})^2}$$

All quantities on the right-hand side of this equation are positive, and thus

$$\frac{d \ln \hat{a}_1}{dx_1} > 0$$

for all x_1 and for all nonzero Λ_{12} and Λ_{21}. (Λ_{12} and Λ_{21} are positive *definite*, because $\Lambda_{12} = \Lambda_{21} = 0$ yields infinite values for γ_1^∞ and γ_2^∞.) Thus inequality (6-208) is always satisfied, and LLE cannot be represented by the Wilson equation.

Some of the intrinsic stability criteria for binary systems admit simple algebraic or geometric interpretation. For example, by inequality (6-209)

$$\frac{d\hat{f}_i}{dx_i} > 0 \qquad i = 1, 2 \qquad (\text{const } T, P)$$

and we see that the fugacity of a species in a stable binary system must be *monotone increasing* in the mole fraction of the species. This feature was noted in Sec. 3-8 in connection with the discussion of Fig. 3-7. Also, by inequality (6-205)

$$\frac{d^2(\Delta G/RT)}{dx_i^2} > 0 \qquad i = 1, 2 \qquad (\text{const } T, P)$$

and thus a graph of $\Delta G/RT$ versus x_i for a stable binary system is *concave upward*. This feature of the $\Delta G/RT$-versus-x_i plot merits further discussion.

The Gibbs function change of mixing ΔG (defined with respect to Lewis-Randall standard states) is necessarily negative (except at $x_1 = 0$ and $x_1 = 1$, where it is zero), because G^t for the mixture equilibrium state must be lower than that for the unmixed fluids. Otherwise,

$$G^t(\text{mixture}) \geq G^t(\text{unmixed fluids}) \qquad (\text{const } T, P)$$

and $G^t(\text{mixture})$ could not be a minimum at constant T and P, as required by the second law. Since $\Delta G \leq 0$ for all x_1, there is therefore *some* part of the composition range for which inequality (6-205) is satisfied. In fact, it is easily shown that

$$\lim_{x_1 \to 0} \frac{d^2(\Delta G/RT)}{dx_1^2} = +\infty$$

and

$$\lim_{x_1 \to 1} \frac{d^2(\Delta G/RT)}{dx_1^2} = +\infty$$

and thus the stability criterion is satisfied at the ends of the diagram. Violations of the criterion, if they happen, must occur on the open interval $0 < x_1 < 1$.

Figure 6-37 shows plots of $\Delta G/RT$ for two cases; they derive from

$$\frac{\Delta G}{RT} = \frac{G^E}{RT} + \frac{\Delta G^{id}}{RT} = g + x_1 \ln x_1 + x_2 \ln x_2$$

with $g \equiv G^E/RT$ given by the two-parameter Margules equation

$$g = (A_{21}x_1 + A_{12}x_2)x_1 x_2$$

In case A, the parameters are assigned the values $A_{12} = 1.0$ and $A_{21} = 1.5$; for case B, $A_{12} = 2.1484$ and $A_{21} = 2.7811$, the values determined in Example 6-24 for solubility limits $x_1^\alpha = 0.2$ and $x_1^\beta = 0.9$.

The $\Delta G/RT$ curve for case A is unremarkable; it is concave upward for all x_1, and thus stable single-phase behavior obtains for the entire composition range. The corresponding curve for case B, on the other hand, is concave downward for part of the composition range, and thus liquid/liquid phase splitting occurs. Compositions x_1^α and x_1^β of the equilibrium liquid phases are determined by the tangent construction shown, as we now demonstrate.

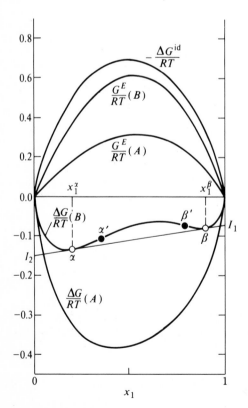

Figure 6-37 $\Delta G/RT$ for a binary system. For case A, stable single-phase mixtures obtain at all compositions. For case B, two phases are formed over part of the compositon range.

By the method of tangent intercepts (see Fig. 3-1 and the accompanying discussion), the intercepts I_1 and I_2 produce values for partial molar properties:

$$I_1 = \overline{\Delta G_1}/RT$$

and

$$I_2 = \overline{\Delta G_2}/RT$$

But the tangent is common to points α and β, and thus

$$(\overline{\Delta G_1}/RT)^\alpha = (\overline{\Delta G_1}/RT)^\beta$$

and

$$(\overline{\Delta G_2}/RT)^\alpha = (\overline{\Delta G_2}/RT)^\beta$$

From the last column of Table 5-2, we have

$$\ln \hat{a}_i = \overline{\Delta G_i}/RT$$

and $\ln \hat{a}_i$ is a partial molar property with respect to $\Delta G/RT$. Thus, the states α and β defined by the tangent construction have the property that

$$(\ln \hat{a}_1)^\alpha = (\ln \hat{a}_1)^\beta$$

and

$$(\ln \hat{a}_2)^\alpha = (\ln \hat{a}_2)^\beta$$

or that

$$\hat{a}_1^\alpha = \hat{a}_1^\beta$$

and

$$\hat{a}_2^\alpha = \hat{a}_2^\beta$$

These are just the equilibrium criteria of Eq. (6-186) written for a binary system. In this case, the tangent construction yields equilibrium compositions $x_1^\alpha = 0.2$ and $x_1^\beta = 0.9$.

Points α' and β' (at $x_1 = 0.3537$ and $x_1 = 0.7902$) are points of inflection, where

$$\frac{d^2(\Delta G/RT)}{dx_1^2} = 0$$

Clearly, these points, which define the limits of intrinsic stability, do *not* define the two-phase equilibrium compositions x_1^α and x_1^β; neither do the local minima, where

$$\frac{d(\Delta G/RT)}{dx_1} = 0$$

The segments $\alpha\alpha'$ and $\beta\beta'$ represent states of metastable equilibrium, where single-phase behavior can obtain in principle. However, such states are unstable to large perturbations. Segment $\alpha'\beta'$, for which

$$\frac{d^2(\Delta G/RT)}{dx_1^2} < 0$$

defines a region of *absolute* instability, for which single-phase behavior is impossible in principle.

Frequently, the curve representing LLE intersects the VLE bubble-point curve, giving rise to the phenomenon of vapor/liquid/liquid equilibrium (VLLE). Two types of isobaric Txy diagrams for binary systems exhibiting VLLE are shown by Fig. 6-38. For both types, states of three phases in equilibrium fall on a horizontal line because, as explained below, there is but a single degree of freedom.

The first type of behavior (Fig. 6-38a) is characterized by the presence of a *heterogeneous azeotrope of the first kind* (point C). This is not an azeotrope in the strict sense of the word—vapor of composition y_1^* is not in equilibrium with a single liquid phase of the same composition—but it exhibits the "constant-boiling-temperature" phenomenon characteristic of a true (*homogeneous*) azeotrope. That is, a two-phase liquid system with overall composition between $(x_1^\alpha)^*$ and $(x_1^\beta)^*$, if supplied with sufficient heat, will boil at temperature T^*, giving off vapor of the same constant composition y_1^* until one or both of the liquid phases disappears.

For the second type of VLLE (Fig. 6-38b), one observes a *heterogeneous azeotrope of the second kind*. Here, the composition y_1^* of the vapor in equilibrium with two liquids does not lie between the compositions of the two liquids;

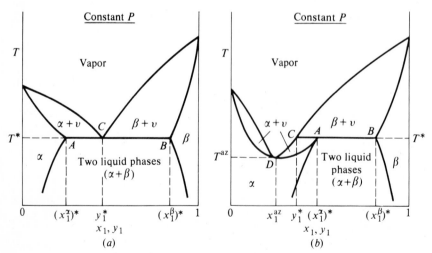

Figure 6-38 Two types of VLLE. In (a), we show a heterogeneous azeotrope of the *first* kind; in (b) a heterogeneous azeotrope of the *second* kind, as well as a homogeneous azeotrope.

moreover, y_1 is less than x_1 for all states to the right of point D. [Compare this behavior with that of Fig. 6-38a, where $y_1 > x_1$ for $x_1 < (x_1^z)^*$, but $y_1 < x_1$ for $x_1 > (x_1^\beta)^*$.] However, the constant-boiling-temperature phenomenon still occurs, and we therefore classify the behavior as azeotropy. Figure 6-38b also shows a *homogeneous* azeotrope (state D); however, azeotropy to the left of the three-phase line CAB does not *necessarily* occur. (Note that the details of Fig. 6-38b to the left of point C are exaggerated in scale as an aid to comprehension.)

Thermodynamic description of VLLE is based on the equal-fugacity criterion:

$$\hat{f}_i^z = \hat{f}_i^\beta = \hat{f}_i^v \qquad (i = 1, 2, \dots, N)$$

At low pressures, the gamma/phi approach used for VLE is equally appropriate to VLLE. Referring liquid-phase activity coefficients to Lewis-Randall standard states, we can write [see Eq. (6-38)]:

$$x_i^z(\gamma_i^+)^z P_i^{\text{sat}} = y_i \Phi_i P \qquad (i = 1, 2, \dots, N) \tag{6-210a}$$

and

$$x_i^\beta(\gamma_i^+)^\beta P_i^{\text{sat}} = y_i \Phi_i P \qquad (i = 1, 2, \dots, N) \tag{6-210b}$$

where Φ_i is defined rigorously by Eq. (6-42). By Eqs. (6-210) we have $2N$ equilibrium equations, and there are $N - 1$ intensive variables (T, P, and $N - 1$ independent mole fractions for each of the three phases). Thus, for multicomponent VLLE, solution of the equilibrium equations requires prior specification of numerical values for $N - 1$ of the intensive variables. For the simplest case (the only one treated here), that of a binary system, $N - 1 = 1$ and there is only one degree of freedom. Unlike LLE at low reduced temperatures, pressure is a significant variable in VLLE calculations because of the presence of the vapor phase. Its effect on *liquid-phase* properties however is often safely ignored.

To illustrate the nature of VLLE calculations, we assume that the vapor phase is an ideal gas and ignore the effect of pressure on liquid properties. Under these conditions, for a reference temperature T^+ equal to the system temperature, $\Phi_i = 1$ and the superscript $(+)$ on the γ_i is superfluous. Equations (6-210) then become, for a binary system,

$$x_1^z \gamma_1^z P_1^{\text{sat}} = y_1 P \tag{6-211a}$$

$$x_1^\beta \gamma_1^\beta P_1^{\text{sat}} = y_1 P \tag{6-211b}$$

$$(1 - x_1^z)\gamma_2^z P_2^{\text{sat}} = (1 - y_1)P \tag{6-211c}$$

and

$$(1 - x_1^\beta)\gamma_2^\beta P_2^{\text{sat}} = (1 - y_1)P \tag{6-211d}$$

The vapor compositions can be eliminated by adding appropriate pairs of equations. Four possible expressions result:

$$x_1^\alpha \gamma_1^\alpha P_1^{sat} + (1 - x_1^\alpha)\gamma_2^\alpha P_2^{sat} = P \tag{6-212a}$$

$$x_1^\alpha \gamma_1^\alpha P_1^{sat} + (1 - x_1^\beta)\gamma_2^\beta P_2^{sat} = P \tag{6-212b}$$

$$x_1^\beta \gamma_1^\beta P_1^{sat} + (1 - x_1^\alpha)\gamma_2^\alpha P_2^{sat} = P \tag{6-212c}$$

and

$$x_1^\beta \gamma_1^\beta P_1^{sat} + (1 - x_1^\beta)\gamma_2^\beta P_2^{sat} = P \tag{6-212d}$$

Each of these equations is satisfied at equilibrium, but one is more useful than the others. Consider the limiting case of completely immiscible liquids. Then (see Example 6-22)

$$x_1^\alpha = 0 \qquad \gamma_1^\alpha = \infty \qquad \gamma_2^\alpha = 1$$

and

$$x_1^\beta = 1 \qquad \gamma_1^\beta = 1 \qquad \gamma_2^\beta = \infty$$

from which

$$x_1^\alpha \gamma_1^\alpha \to (0)(\infty)$$

and

$$(1 - x_1^\beta)\gamma_2^\beta \to (0)(\infty)$$

That is, the products $x_1^\alpha \gamma_1^\alpha$ and $(1 - x_1^\beta)\gamma_2^\beta$ become indeterminate. Only Eq. (6-212c) does not contain either of these products, and we select it as one of our working equations:

$$x_1^\beta \gamma_1^\beta P_1^{sat} + (1 - x_1^\alpha)\gamma_2^\alpha P_2^{sat} = P \tag{6-212c}$$

Two more equations result when we equate the left-hand sides of Eqs. (6-211a) and (6-211b) and the left-hand sides of Eqs. (6-211c) and (6-211d):

$$x_1^\alpha \gamma_1^\alpha = x_1^\beta \gamma_1^\beta \tag{6-213}$$

and

$$(1 - x_1^\alpha)\gamma_2^\alpha = (1 - x_1^\beta)\gamma_2^\beta \tag{6-214}$$

This is the usual pair of equations for LLE; along with Eq. (6-212c), they provide three of the four equations required for description of VLLE. Since none includes y_1, the fourth equation must be an expression for this variable. Any *one* of Eqs. (6-211) will do; for example, Eq. (6-211b) gives

$$y_1 = \frac{x_1^\beta \gamma_1^\beta P_1^{sat}}{P} \tag{6-215}$$

Equations (6-212c) and (6-213) through (6-215) constitute a set of four equations in five variables: x_1^α, x_1^β, y_1, T, and P. Fixing one of the variables allows solution for the remaining four. The simplest case is that of specified temperature. Since by assumption the γ_i depend on T and composition only, Eqs. (6-213) and (6-214) are first solved for the liquid compositions x_1^α and x_1^β. The vapor pressures P_i^{sat} depend on T only, and the total pressure is therefore next computed from Eq. (6-212c). Finally, the vapor composition is found from Eq. (6-215).

Example 6-27 We illustrate the calculation of isothermal VLLE for a binary system for which $g = 2.2x_1 x_2$ and for which the pure-component vapor pressures are (a) $P_1^{\text{sat}} = 25$ kPa, $P_2^{\text{sat}} = 50$ kPa; (b) $P_1^{\text{sat}} = 25$ kPa, $P_2^{\text{sat}} = 150$ kPa; and (c) $P_1^{\text{sat}} = 25$ kPa, $P_2^{\text{sat}} = 300$ kPa, and prepare the isothermal Pxy diagrams for all three cases.

(a) The expression for g is of the form $Ax_1 x_2$, with $A = 2.2$. We assume A independent of pressure, and therefore liquid compositions at *all* pressures for which LLE (or VLLE) obtain are found from Eq. (E) of Example 6-23:

$$2.2(1 - 2x_1) = \ln \left(\frac{1 - x_1}{x_1} \right) \tag{A}$$

Solution of Eq. (A) gives $x_1^\alpha = 0.2485$ and $x_1^\beta = 0.7515$. The corresponding values of γ_1^β and γ_2^α are (see Example 6-23)

$$\gamma_1^\beta = \exp\left[2.2(1 - x_1^\beta)^2\right] = \exp\left[2.2(0.2485)^2\right] = 1.1455$$

and

$$\gamma_2^\alpha = \exp\left[2.2(x_1^\alpha)^2\right] = \exp\left[2.2(0.2485)^2\right] = 1.1455$$

The pressure P^* for three-phase equilibrium is found from Eq. (6-212c):

$$P^* = x_1^\beta \gamma_1^\beta P_1^{\text{sat}} + (1 - x_1^\alpha)\gamma_2^\alpha P_2^{\text{sat}}$$

$$= (0.7515)(1.1455)(25) + (0.7515)(1.1455)(50)$$

or

$$P^* = 21.521 + 43.042 = 64.563 \text{ kPa}$$

Finally, the vapor composition for VLLE is determined from Eq. (6-215):

$$y_1^* = \frac{x_1^\beta \gamma_1^\beta P_1^{\text{sat}}}{P^*} = \frac{21.521}{64.563}$$

or

$$y_1^* = 0.3333$$

Thus y_1^* lies between $x_1^\alpha (= 0.2485)$ and $x_1^\beta (= 0.7515)$, and the system forms a heterogeneous azeotrope of the first kind.

Conventional VLE obtains for a range of pressures below $P^* = 64.563$ kPa. Here, the bubble- and dew-point curves have two branches, both described by the usual equations for low-pressure VLE:

$$x_1 \gamma_1 P_1^{\text{sat}} + x_2 \gamma_2 P_2^{\text{sat}} = P \tag{B}$$

and

$$y_1 = \frac{x_1 \gamma_1 P_1^{\text{sat}}}{P} \tag{C}$$

Determination of the curves is straightforward, for the vapor pressures are given, and the γ_i at constant T depend on x_1 only:

$$\gamma_1 = \exp\left[2.2(1 - x_1)^2\right] \qquad (D)$$

and

$$\gamma_2 = \exp\left(2.2x_1^2\right) \qquad (E)$$

One merely specifies a value of x_1 ($0 \le x_1 < 0.2485$ and $0.7515 < x_1 \le 1$), computes P from Eqs. (B), (D), and (E), and then finally determines the corresponding value of y_1 from Eq. (C).

The complete isothermal Pxy diagram is shown in Fig. 6-39; it is analogous to the isobaric Txy diagram of Fig. 6-38a.

(b) Since the expression for g is unchanged, the equilibrium *liquid* compositions for LLE and VLLE are the same as for part (a): $x_1^\alpha = 0.2485$ and $x_1^\beta = 0.7515$. However, the three-phase-equilibrium pressure and vapor composition, which depend on the P_i^{sat}, are different.

$$P^* = x_1^\beta \gamma_1^\beta P_1^{\text{sat}} + (1 - x_1^\alpha)\gamma_2^\alpha P_2^{\text{sat}} = (0.7515)(1.1455)(25) + (0.7515)(1.1455)(150)$$

or

$$P^* = 21.521 + 129.126 = 150.647 \text{ kPa}$$

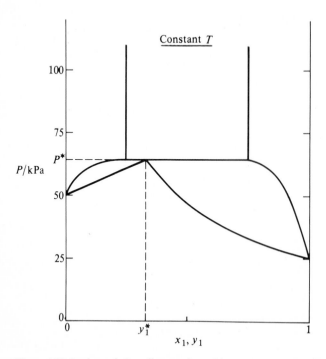

Figure 6-39 Isothermal Pxy diagram for a binary system with $g(\text{liquid}) = 2.2x_1 x_2$ and with $P_1^{\text{sat}} = 25$ kPa, $P_2^{\text{sat}} = 50$ kPa. [See Example 6-27, part (a).]

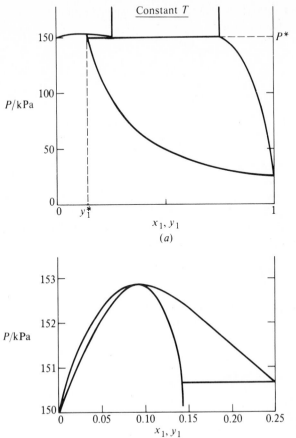

Figure 6-40 Isothermal Pxy diagram for a binary system with $g(\text{liquid}) = 2.2x_1 x_2$ and with $P_1^{\text{sat}} = 25$ kPa, $P_2^{\text{sat}} = 150$ kPa. Complete diagram is drawn to scale in (a); (b) is the region of homogeneous azeotropy drawn to an expanded scale [See Example 6-27, part (b).]

and

$$y_1^* = \frac{x_1^\beta \gamma_1^\beta P_1^{\text{sat}}}{P^*} = \frac{21.521}{150.647}$$

or

$$y_1^* = 0.1429$$

Here, y_1^* does *not* lie between x_1^γ and x_1^β, and heterogeneous azeotropy of the second kind is observed. In addition, a *homogeneous* azeotrope is found from Eqs. (B) through (E), at a mole fraction $x_1^{\text{az}} = y_1^{\text{az}} = 0.0928$ and at a pressure $P^{\text{az}} = 152.868$ kPa.

The complete Pxy diagram is shown in Fig. 6-40a, with the region of homogeneous azeotropy drawn to an expanded scale in Fig. 6-40b. Figure 6-40 is an isothermal analog of the schematic isobaric Txy diagram of Fig. 6-38b. Especially to be noted is the extremely small range of pressures obtained in the region of homogeneous azeotropy. A similarly small range of temperatures is observed on an isobaric diagram drawn to scale.

(c) The calculations here are similar to those of part (b). We find

$$P^* = x_1^\beta \gamma_1^\beta P_1^{sat} + (1 - x_1^\alpha)\gamma_2^\alpha P_2^{sat}$$

$$= (0.7515)(1.1455)(25) + (0.7515)(1.1455)(300)$$

or

$$P^* = 21.521 + 258.253 = 279.774 \text{ kPa}$$

and

$$y_1^* = \frac{x_1^\beta \gamma_1^\beta P_1^{sat}}{P^*} = \frac{21.521}{279.774}$$

or

$$y_1^* = 0.0769$$

Again, $y_1^* < x_1^\alpha < x_1^\beta$, and we obtain heterogeneous azeotropy of the second kind. However, there is no homogeneous azeotrope in this case because of the extreme difference in pure-component vapor pressures ($P_2^{sat}/P_1^{sat} = 300/25 = 12$). The complete Pxy diagram is shown in Fig. 6-41.

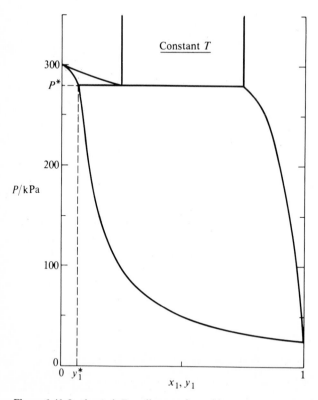

Figure 6-41 Isothermal Pxy diagram for a binary system with $g(\text{liquid}) = 2.2x_1 x_2$ and with $P_1^{sat} = 25$ kPa, $P_2^{sat} = 300$ kPa. [See Example 6-27, part (c).]

Example 6-28 The preceding example illustrates the diversity of behavior possible for systems exhibiting VLLE, and shows that very simple models can generate relatively complicated Pxy diagrams. Particularly simple equilibrium diagrams are obtained for an approximation of considerable practical importance: that of *complete immiscibility* of the pure liquids. For this idealized case,

$$x_1^\alpha = 0 \qquad \gamma_2^\alpha = 1$$

and

$$x_1^\beta = 1 \qquad \gamma_1^\beta = 1$$

and Eq. (6-212c) becomes

$$P = P_1^{sat} + P_2^{sat} \tag{A}$$

from which, by Eq. (6-215),

$$y_1 = \frac{P_1^{sat}}{P_1^{sat} + P_2^{sat}} \tag{B}$$

Equations (A) and (B) determine the state of three-phase equilibrium. States of VLE are computed from the equation

$$y_i P = x_i \gamma_i P_i^{sat}$$

For vapor in equilibrium with pure liquid 2, $x_2 = 1$ and $\gamma_2 = 1$, and

$$y_2 P = (1 - y_1)P = P_2^{sat}$$

or

$$y_1 = 1 - \frac{P_2^{sat}}{P} \tag{C}$$

Similarly, for vapor in equilibrium with pure liquid 1, $x_1 = 1$ and $\gamma_1 = 1$, and

$$y_1 P = P_1^{sat}$$

or

$$y_1 = \frac{P_1^{sat}}{P} \tag{D}$$

We consider application of these equations to the n-octane(1)/water(2) system, for which pure-component vapor pressures are given in Table 6-8. At a *constant temperature* of 100°C, the vapor pressures are constant at the values

$$P_1^{sat} = 0.4683 \text{ bar}$$

and

$$P_2^{sat} = 1.0133 \text{ bar}$$

By Eq. (A), the three-phase equilibrium pressure is

$$P^* = 0.4683 + 1.0133 = 1.4816 \text{ bar}$$

and by Eq. (B) the three-phase equilibrium vapor composition is

$$y_1^* = \frac{0.4683}{1.4816} = 0.3161$$

Table 6-8 Vapor-pressure data for the n-octane(1)/water(2) system. (See Example 6-28.)

$t/°C$	P_1^{sat}/bar	P_2^{sat}/bar	$P_1^{sat} + P_2^{sat}/bar$
85	0.2803	0.5780	0.8583
90	0.3345	0.7011	1.0356
95	0.3969	0.8454	1.2423
100	0.4683	1.0133	1.4816
105	0.5497	1.2081	1.7578
110	0.6420	1.4327	2.0747
115	0.7463	1.6908	2.4371
120	0.8635	1.9853	2.8488
125	0.9948	2.3211	3.3159
130	1.1413	2.7016	3.8429

For pressures above P^* (region III in Fig. 6-42a), pure liquid octane is in equilibrium with pure liquid water. At pressures below P^*, there are two regions of VLE. In region I, vapor is in equilibrium with pure liquid octane, with compositions given by Eq. (D):

$$y_1(I) = \frac{P_1^{sat}}{P} = \frac{0.4683}{P}$$

In region II, vapor is in equilibrium with pure liquid water, with compositions given by Eq. (C):

$$y_1(II) = 1 - \frac{P_2^{sat}}{P} = 1 - \frac{1.0133}{P}$$

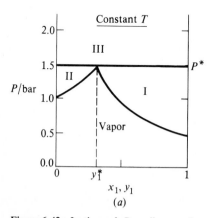

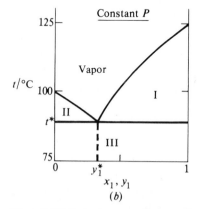

Figure 6-42a Isothermal Pxy diagram for a binary system with two immiscible liquids. The system and conditions are described in Example 6-28.

Figure 6-42b Isobaric txy diagram for a binary system with two immiscible liquids. The system and conditions are described in Example 6-28.

Region I (see Fig. 6-42a) extends from y_1^* and P^* to $y_1 = 1$, at a pressure of 0.4683 bar; region II extends from $y_1 = 0$, at a pressure of 1.0133 bar, to y_1^* and P^*. Isothermal Pxy diagrams for other temperatures are constructed similarly.

In constructing isobaric txy diagrams, we use the same equations, but temperature is now the quantity sought. Suppose we require a txy diagram for a total pressure of 1 bar. The three-phase equilibrium temperature t^* is determined from Eq. (A):

$$P = P_1^{sat} + P_2^{sat} = 1 \text{ bar}$$

The fourth column of Table 6-8 contains values of the sum $P_1^{sat} + P_2^{sat}$ for various temperatures, and by inspection, we see that t^* lies between 85 and 90°C. Interpolation gives

$$t^* = 89.02°C$$

at which temperature we also find, by interpolation,

$$P_1^{sat}(t^*) = 0.3245 \text{ bar}$$

and

$$P_2^{sat}(t^*) = 0.6755 \text{ bar}$$

Thus, by Eq. (B),

$$y_1^* = \frac{0.3245}{1.0000} = 0.3245$$

For temperatures below t^* (region III in Fig. 6-42b), pure liquid octane is in equilibrium with pure liquid water. At temperatures above t^*, there are two regions of VLE. In region I, vapor is in equilibrium with pure liquid octane, with compositions given by Eq. (D):

$$y_1(\text{I}) = \frac{P_1^{sat}}{P} = \frac{P_1^{sat}}{1.0000}$$

In region II, vapor is in equilibrium with pure liquid water, with compositions given by Eq. (C):

$$y_1(\text{II}) = 1 - \frac{P_2^{sat}}{P} = 1 - \frac{P_2^{sat}}{1.0000}$$

Region I (see Fig. 6-42b) extends from y_1^* and t^* to $y_1 = 1$ at $t = 125.13°C$, the saturation temperature of pure n-octane at 1 bar. Similarly, region II extends from $y_1 = 0$ at $t = 99.63°C$ (the saturation temperature for pure water at 1 bar) to y_1^* and t^*.

It should be carefully noted that n-octane and water do in fact exhibit finite (but small) mutual solubilities as liquids, and that the approach to calculation of VLLE adopted in this example is therefore not strictly correct. For applications requiring high accuracy, the more rigorous gamma/phi approach described earlier would be appropriate.

We have considered in this section LLE and VLLE mainly for binary systems, because for such systems the thermodynamic principles are most easily exposed. In practical applications, however (particularly those involving LLE), multicomponent systems containing three or more species are frequently encountered. In a series of comprehensive review articles, Sørensen et al. (1979, 1980) treat the retrieval and correlation of binary *and* multicomponent LLE data, and also the prediction of LLE by the UNIFAC group-contribution method. Prausnitz and coauthors [Prausnitz et al. (1980)] similarly discuss computation procedures and the reduction of data for binary and multicomponent LLE; a comprehensive compilation of available data is given by Sørensen and Arlt (1979, 1980).

MATHEMATICAL TECHNIQUES FOR SOLUTION THERMODYNAMICS

A-1 EXACT DIFFERENTIALS AND STATE FUNCTIONS

Mathematical descriptions of the changes which occur in physical systems often lead to differential expressions of the form:

$$C_1 \, dX_1 + C_2 \, dX_2 + \cdots + C_n \, dX_n \equiv \sum C_i \, dX_i \tag{A1-1}$$

where the X_i are *independent* variables, and the C_i are functions of the X_i. When it is possible to set the differential expression (A1-1) equal to dY, the differential of a *function* Y, where

$$Y = Y(X_1, X_2, \ldots, X_n)$$

then the differential expression (A1-1) is said to be *exact*, and we can write:

$$dY = C_1 \, dX_1 + \cdots + C_n \, dX_n \equiv \sum C_i \, dX_i \tag{A1-2}$$

Mathematics provides a *definition* for the differential of such a function:

$$dY = \left(\frac{\partial Y}{\partial X_1}\right)_{X_j} dX_1 + \left(\frac{\partial Y}{\partial X_2}\right)_{X_j} dX_2 + \cdots + \left(\frac{\partial Y}{\partial X_n}\right)_{X_j} dX_n \equiv \sum \left(\frac{\partial Y}{\partial X_i}\right)_{X_j} dX_i$$

where the subscript X_j on the partial derivatives indicates that all X_i are held constant except the one in the derivative considered. Since the X_i are *independent*, this last equation and Eq. (A1-2) may be equated term by term to give:

$$C_1 = \left(\frac{\partial Y}{\partial X_1}\right)_{X_j}, \ldots, C_n = \left(\frac{\partial Y}{\partial X_n}\right)_{X_j} \quad \text{or} \quad C_i = \left(\frac{\partial Y}{\partial X_i}\right)_{X_j} \tag{A1-3}$$

From this we see that when the differential expression, Eq. (A1-1), is exact, the C_i are interpreted as partial differential coefficients in the defining equation for dY, and each C_i and its corresponding X_i are said to be *conjugate* to each other.

If Y and its derivatives are continuous, then for any pair of independent variables X_k and X_l, we have the mathematical requirement that

$$\frac{\partial^2 Y}{\partial X_k \, \partial X_l} = \frac{\partial^2 Y}{\partial X_l \, \partial X_k}$$

From Eq. (A1-3) we have

$$C_k = \left(\frac{\partial Y}{\partial X_k}\right)_{X_j} \quad \text{and} \quad C_l = \left(\frac{\partial Y}{\partial X_l}\right)_{X_j}$$

Therefore

$$\left(\frac{\partial C_k}{\partial X_l}\right)_{X_j} = \frac{\partial^2 Y}{\partial X_l \, \partial X_k} \quad \text{and} \quad \left(\frac{\partial C_l}{\partial X_k}\right)_{X_j} = \frac{\partial^2 Y}{\partial X_k \, \partial X_l}$$

and as a result we get the important equation:

$$\boxed{\left(\frac{\partial C_k}{\partial X_l}\right)_{X_j} = \left(\frac{\partial C_l}{\partial X_k}\right)_{X_j}} \tag{A1-4}$$

Equation (A1-4) is a *reciprocity relation*. It holds for any two pairs of conjugate variables (C_k, X_k) and (C_l, X_l) in an exact differential expression, and represents a condition that is both necessary and sufficient for the exactness of Eq. (A1-1).

The simplest application of Eq. (A1-4) is to a system which can be fully described by fixing just two independent state variables, say x and y. If a third variable z is a *function* of x and y, then we may write

$$dz = M \, dx + N \, dy \tag{A1-5}$$

where

$$M \equiv \left(\frac{\partial z}{\partial x}\right)_y \quad \text{and} \quad N \equiv \left(\frac{\partial z}{\partial y}\right)_x$$

Application of Eq. (A1-4) to Eq. (A1-5) then yields the single reciprocity relation

$$\boxed{\left(\frac{\partial M}{\partial y}\right)_x = \left(\frac{\partial N}{\partial x}\right)_y} \tag{A1-6}$$

Equation (A1-6) finds use in the derivation of the *Maxwell equations* for constant-composition PVT systems (see Sec. 2-5).

There are several other characteristics of exact differentials in addition to the exactness criterion of Eq. (A1-4) that are important in thermodynamics. If $dY = \sum (C_i \, dX_i)$ is an exact differential expression, then

I. The value of the integral $\Delta Y = \int_A^B \sum C_i \, dX_i$ is independent of the path followed from point A to point B.
II. The integral around any closed path $\oint dY = \oint \sum C_i \, dX_i$ is identically zero.
III. The function Y, defined only by $dY = \sum C_i \, dX_i$, can be determined only to within an additive constant.

The attributes characterized in items I and II are shared by all proper thermodynamic functions, and the differentials of all such functions are known from experiment and experience to be exact. These functions are variously called *state functions*, *state properties*, *variables of state*, or *point functions*. Item III states the limit to which purely mathematical considerations can aid in the deduction of values for a thermodynamic function Y defined by means of Eq. (A1-2). It does not rule out the existence of absolute values for Y, but implies that such values must be otherwise obtained.

A-2 TRANSFORMATION RELATIONSHIPS FOR SYSTEMS OF TWO INDEPENDENT VARIABLES

This section is devoted to the development of some useful relationships among first partial derivatives for the thermodynamically important case of a system which can be fully specified by fixing two state variables. If these variables are designated x and y, then any other state function z is related to x and y by an equation having the functional form

$$f(x, y, z) = 0$$

Since any pair of the three variables may be selected as independent, this functional relationship may be expressed in three additional alternative forms

$$x = x(y, z) \qquad y = y(x, z) \qquad z = z(x, y)$$

Arbitrarily selecting the first two of these, we may write expressions for the total differentials dx and dy:

$$dx = \left(\frac{\partial x}{\partial y}\right)_z dy + \left(\frac{\partial x}{\partial z}\right)_y dz \tag{A2-1}$$

$$dy = \left(\frac{\partial y}{\partial x}\right)_z dx + \left(\frac{\partial y}{\partial z}\right)_x dz \tag{A2-2}$$

Elimination of the differential dy between Eqs. (A2-1) and (A2-2) gives

$$\left[\left(\frac{\partial x}{\partial y}\right)_z \left(\frac{\partial y}{\partial x}\right)_z - 1\right] dx + \left[\left(\frac{\partial x}{\partial y}\right)_z \left(\frac{\partial y}{\partial z}\right)_x + \left(\frac{\partial x}{\partial z}\right)_y\right] dz = 0 \tag{A2-3}$$

Since x and z are independently variable, the coefficients of dx and dz must be identically zero if Eq. (A2-3) is to be generally valid. Hence

$$\boxed{\left(\frac{\partial x}{\partial y}\right)_z = \left(\frac{\partial y}{\partial x}\right)_z^{-1}} \tag{A2-4}$$

and

$$\left(\frac{\partial x}{\partial z}\right)_y = -\left(\frac{\partial x}{\partial y}\right)_z\left(\frac{\partial y}{\partial z}\right)_x$$

which, in view of Eq. (A2-4) can be written,

$$\boxed{\left(\frac{\partial x}{\partial y}\right)_z = -\left(\frac{\partial x}{\partial z}\right)_y\left(\frac{\partial z}{\partial y}\right)_x} \tag{A2-5}$$

If Eq. (A2-1) is divided through by the differential of a fourth state variable, dw, then

$$\frac{dx}{dw} = \left(\frac{\partial x}{\partial y}\right)_z\frac{dy}{dw} + \left(\frac{\partial x}{\partial z}\right)_y\frac{dz}{dw}$$

Restriction of this equation to constant z reduces it to

$$\left(\frac{\partial x}{\partial w}\right)_z = \left(\frac{\partial x}{\partial y}\right)_z\left(\frac{\partial y}{\partial w}\right)_z$$

from which

$$\boxed{\left(\frac{\partial x}{\partial y}\right)_z = \left(\frac{\partial x}{\partial w}\right)_z\left(\frac{\partial w}{\partial y}\right)_z} \tag{A2-6}$$

If x is now taken to be a function of y and w, then

$$dx = \left(\frac{\partial x}{\partial y}\right)_w dy + \left(\frac{\partial x}{\partial w}\right)_y dw$$

Division of this equation by dy with restriction to constant z gives

$$\boxed{\left(\frac{\partial x}{\partial y}\right)_z = \left(\frac{\partial x}{\partial y}\right)_w + \left(\frac{\partial x}{\partial w}\right)_y\left(\frac{\partial w}{\partial y}\right)_z} \tag{A2-7}$$

The equations of this section, or variations on them, provide the basis for many of the transformations employed in the thermodynamics of PVT systems of constant composition.

A-3 LEGENDRE TRANSFORMATIONS

The fundamental property relation for a single-phase PVT system was developed in Sec. 2-1:

$$d(nU) = T\,d(nS) - P\,d(nV) + \sum \mu_i\,dn_i \tag{2-7}$$

This equation implies that nU is always a function of nS, nV, and the n_i in a single-phase, open, PVT system. However, the choice of nS, nV, and the n_i as independent variables is not always convenient. Other sets of variables are often advantageously employed. It is therefore useful to define new functions related to nU, and whose total differentials are consistent with Eq. (2-7), but for which the natural independent variables are sets other than nS, nV, and the n_i. A standard mathematical method exists for the systematic definition of functions of the kind required: the Legendre transformation.

Recall the exact differential expression presented earlier:

$$dY = C_1\,dX_1 + C_2\,dX_2 + \cdots + C_n\,dX_n \tag{A1-2}$$

Legendre transformations define Y-related functions for which the sets of variables contain one or more of the C_i in place of the conjugate X_i. For a total differential expression exhibiting n variables there are $2^n - 1$ possible Legendre transformations, namely:

$$
\left.
\begin{aligned}
\mathcal{T}_1 &= \mathcal{T}_1(C_1, X_2, X_3, \ldots, X_n) \equiv Y - C_1 X_1 \\
\mathcal{T}_2 &= \mathcal{T}_2(X_1, C_2, X_3, \ldots, X_n) \equiv Y - C_2 X_2 \\
&\;\;\vdots \qquad\qquad \vdots \qquad\qquad \vdots \\
\mathcal{T}_n &= \mathcal{T}_n(X_1, X_2, X_3, \ldots, C_n) \equiv Y - C_n X_n \\
\mathcal{T}_{1,2} &= \mathcal{T}_{1,2}(C_1, C_2, X_3, \ldots, X_n) \equiv Y - C_1 X_1 - C_2 X_2 \\
\mathcal{T}_{1,3} &= \mathcal{T}_{1,3}(C_1, X_2, C_3, \ldots, X_n) \equiv Y - C_1 X_1 - C_3 X_3 \\
&\;\;\vdots \qquad\qquad \vdots \qquad\qquad \vdots \\
\mathcal{T}_{1,\ldots,n} &= \mathcal{T}_{1,\ldots,n}(C_1, C_2, C_3, \ldots, C_n) \equiv Y - \sum C_i X_i
\end{aligned}
\right\} \tag{A3-1}
$$

Each $\mathcal{T}$ in Eqs. (A3-1) represents a new *function*, and in each case the independent variables, shown in parentheses, are the *canonical* variables for that function. Thus Eqs. (A3-1) provide recipes for the definition of a set of new functions consistent with a particular exact differential expression, and they identify the variables which are unique to each function. These have the following special property: when a transformation function $\mathcal{T}$ is known as a function of its n canonical variables, then the remaining n variables among those appearing in the original exact differential expression (the X_i and their conjugate C_i) can be recovered by differentiation of $\mathcal{T}$. This is not in general true for arbitrarily chosen sets of variables.

For example, if $Y = Y(X_1, X_2, X_3)$ then

$$dY = C_1\, dX_1 + C_2\, dX_2 + C_3\, dX_3 \tag{A}$$

From Eqs. (A3-1), $\mathcal{T}_1(C_1, X_2, X_3) \equiv Y - C_1 X_1$. To simplify notation, we let this function be Z. Thus

$$Z \equiv Y - C_1 X_1 \tag{B}$$

Differentiating $Z = Z(C_1, X_2, X_3)$ we have

$$dZ = \left(\frac{\partial Z}{\partial C_1}\right)_{X_2,\, X_3} dC_1 + \left(\frac{\partial Z}{\partial X_2}\right)_{C_1,\, X_3} dX_2 + \left(\frac{\partial Z}{\partial X_3}\right)_{C_1,\, X_2} dX_3 \tag{C}$$

The differential dZ can also be found from (B):

$$dZ = dY - C_1\, dX_1 - X_1\, dC_1$$

and substitution for dY by (A) gives:

$$dZ = -X_1\, dC_1 + C_2\, dX_2 + C_3\, dX_3 \tag{D}$$

Comparison of (C) and (D) shows that

$$X_1 = -\left(\frac{\partial Z}{\partial C_1}\right)_{X_2,\, X_3} \qquad C_2 = \left(\frac{\partial Z}{\partial X_2}\right)_{C_1,\, X_3} \qquad C_3 = \left(\frac{\partial Z}{\partial X_3}\right)_{C_1,\, X_2}$$

Thus from the original variables X_1, X_2, and X_3 and their conjugates C_1, C_2, and C_3 in the differential expression (A), we have Z as a function of C_1, X_2, and X_3, and the remaining variables X_1, C_2, and C_3 are given by derivatives of Z.

A-4 EULER'S THEOREM ON HOMOGENEOUS FUNCTIONS

A function F is *homogeneous of degree m* in the variables z_1, z_2, ... if, for any value of the parameter α,

$$\boxed{F(\alpha z_1, \alpha z_2, \ldots) = \alpha^m F(z_1, z_2, \ldots)} \tag{A4-1}$$

There follows from Eq. (A4-1) an important relationship connecting F with its partial derivatives with respect to the z_i.

Consider a differential change in $F(\alpha z_1, \alpha z_2, \ldots)$ resulting from a differential change in α, at constant values of all of the z_i. By Eq. (A4-1)

$$dF(\alpha z_1, \alpha z_2, \ldots) = m\alpha^{m-1} F(z_1, z_2, \ldots)\, d\alpha \qquad (\text{const } z_1, z_2, \ldots)$$

from which

$$\left[\frac{\partial F(\alpha z_1, \alpha z_2, \ldots)}{\partial \alpha}\right]_z = m\alpha^{m-1} F(z_1, z_2, \ldots) \tag{A4-2}$$

where subscript z denotes constancy of all of the z_i. However, by application of the chain rule we can also write that

$$\left[\frac{\partial F(\alpha z_1, \alpha z_2, \ldots)}{\partial \alpha}\right]_z = \sum_i \left[\frac{\partial F(\alpha z_1, \alpha z_2, \ldots)}{\partial (\alpha z_i)}\right]_{\alpha z_j} \left[\frac{\partial (\alpha z_i)}{\partial \alpha}\right]_z$$

or

$$\left[\frac{\partial F(\alpha z_1, \alpha z_2, \ldots)}{\partial \alpha}\right]_z = \sum_i z_i \left[\frac{\partial F(\alpha z_1, \alpha z_2, \ldots)}{\partial (\alpha z_i)}\right]_{\alpha z_j} \tag{A4-3}$$

where subscript αz_j denotes constancy of all of the αz_j, except for $j = i$.

Equating the right-hand sides of Eqs. (A4-2) and (A4-3), we get

$$m\alpha^{m-1}F(z_1, z_2, \ldots) = \sum_i z_i \left[\frac{\partial F(\alpha z_1, \alpha z_2, \ldots)}{\partial (\alpha z_i)}\right]_{\alpha z_j}$$

But this expression must hold for any value of α. In particular, it must hold for $\alpha = 1$, for which case it becomes

$$mF(z_1, z_2, \ldots) = \sum_i z_i \left[\frac{\partial F(z_1, z_2, \ldots)}{\partial z_i}\right]_{z_j}$$

or, more concisely,

$$\boxed{mF = \sum_i z_i \left(\frac{\partial F}{\partial z_i}\right)_{z_j}} \tag{A4-4}$$

Equation (A4-4) is *Euler's theorem on homogeneous functions*.

The important applications of Eq. (A4-4) in solution thermodynamics are to functions that are homogeneous of the zeroth or first degree in the mole numbers at conditions of constant T and P. We consider first the *molar properties M* of a phase. If the mole numbers n_1, n_2, ... are each increased by the same factor α, then the composition of the phase (as measured by the mole fractions x_i) remains unchanged. If this process is carried out at constant T and P, then it is a matter of experience (see Postulate 1.4) that M also remains unchanged. Thus, at constant T and P, M is homogeneous of degree *zero* in the mole numbers n_i, and, by Eq. (A4-4),

$$0 = \sum_i n_i \left(\frac{\partial M}{\partial n_i}\right)_{n_j} \qquad (\text{const } T, P)$$

or, equivalently,

$$\boxed{\sum_i n_i \left(\frac{\partial M}{\partial n_i}\right)_{T, P, n_j} = 0} \tag{A4-5}$$

We consider next the *total properties nM* of a phase. If the mole numbers n_1, n_2, ... are each increased by the same factor α at constant T and P, then it is a matter of experience that the value of nM increases by the same factor α. Thus, at constant T and P, nM is homogeneous of the *first* degree in the mole numbers n_i, and, by Eq. (A4-4),

$$nM = \sum_i n_i \left[\frac{\partial(nM)}{\partial n_i}\right]_{n_j} \qquad (\text{const } T, P)$$

or, equivalently,

$$nM = \sum_i n_i \left[\frac{\partial(nM)}{\partial n_i}\right]_{T, P, n_j} \qquad (A4-6)$$

But the derivative is by definition the partial molar property $\bar{M}_i$. Thus Eq. (A4-6) may be written in a form presented in Chap. 3:

$$nM = \sum_i n_i \bar{M}_i \qquad (3-5)$$

or, equivalently,

$$M = \sum_i x_i \bar{M}_i \qquad (3-6)$$

Actually, independent derivation of Eqs. (A4-5) and (A4-6) is unnecessary. Either equation follows from the other if one invokes the identity

$$\left[\frac{\partial(nM)}{\partial n_i}\right]_{T, P, n_j} = M + n\left(\frac{\partial M}{\partial n_i}\right)_{T, P, n_j} \qquad (A4-7)$$

For example, substitution of Eq. (A4-7) into Eq. (A4-6) gives

$$nM = \sum n_i M + n \sum n_i \left(\frac{\partial M}{\partial n_i}\right)_{T, P, n_j}$$

But $\sum n_i M = M \sum n_i = nM$, and thus Eq. (A4-5) is recovered.

Explicit use of Euler's theorem is in fact unnecessary for the derivation of Eq. (3-6). We illustrate an alternative procedure in the following paragraphs. For a differential change in state of a phase, we have by Eq. (3-4) that

$$d(nM) = n\left(\frac{\partial M}{\partial T}\right)_{P, x} dT + n\left(\frac{\partial M}{\partial P}\right)_{T, x} dP + \sum \bar{M}_i \, dn_i \qquad (3-4)$$

But $d(nM) = n\, dM + M\, dn$, or, equivalently,

$$d(nM) = n\, dM + \sum M\, dn_i$$

Combination of the last equation with Eq. (3-4) gives, on rearrangement,

$$dM = \left(\frac{\partial M}{\partial T}\right)_{P, x} dT + \left(\frac{\partial M}{\partial P}\right)_{T, x} dP + \sum (\bar{M}_i - M)\frac{dn_i}{n} \qquad (A4-8)$$

Now, $n_i = x_i n$, where x_i is the mole fraction of species i. It follows that $dn_i = n\, dx_i + x_i\, dn$, or that

$$\frac{dn_i}{n} = dx_i + x_i \frac{dn}{n} \qquad \text{(A4-9)}$$

Therefore, the summation in Eq. (A4-8) may be written

$$\sum (\bar{M}_i - M)\frac{dn_i}{n} = \sum (\bar{M}_i - M)\, dx_i + \sum x_i(\bar{M}_i - M)\frac{dn}{n}$$

or

$$\sum (\bar{M}_i - M)\frac{dn_i}{n} = \sum \bar{M}_i\, dx_i - M \sum dx_i + \left(\sum x_i\bar{M}_i\right)\frac{dn}{n} - M\left(\sum x_i\right)\frac{dn}{n}$$

But $\sum x_i = 1$ and $\sum dx_i = 0$, and the last equation reduces to

$$\sum (\bar{M}_i - M)\frac{dn_i}{n} = \sum \bar{M}_i\, dx_i + \left(\sum x_i\bar{M}_i - M\right)\frac{dn}{n}$$

Combination of this expression with Eq. (A4-8) then gives an alternative relationship:

$$dM = \left(\frac{\partial M}{\partial T}\right)_{P,\,x} dT + \left(\frac{\partial M}{\partial P}\right)_{T,\,x} dP + \sum \bar{M}_i\, dx_i + \left(\sum x_i\bar{M}_i - M\right)\frac{dn}{n}$$
$$\text{(A4-10)}$$

Equation (A4-10) is valid for any differential change in equilibrium state undergone by a phase. We consider now a *particular* differential change of state, in which each of the mole numbers is increased by the same relative amount, at constant T and P. For this case

$$\frac{dn_1}{n_1} = \frac{dn_2}{n_2} = \cdots = \frac{dn_N}{n_N}$$

or

$$dn_i = \frac{n_i}{n_N}\, dn_N \quad (i = 1, 2, \ldots, N)$$

and

$$dn = \sum dn_i = \left(\sum n_i\right)\frac{dn_N}{n_N} = \frac{n}{n_N}\, dn_N$$

Since N can be any species i, it follows from Eq. (A4-9) that

$$dx_i = 0$$

and thus Eq. (A4-10) becomes

$$dM = \left(\sum x_i\bar{M}_i - M\right)\frac{dn_N}{n_N} \qquad \text{(const } T, P, x) \qquad \text{(A4-11)}$$

But by Postulate 1.4, M must remain *constant*:

$$dM = 0 \qquad (\text{const } T, P, x) \qquad \text{(A4-12)}$$

Since dn_N/n_N is arbitrary, Eqs. (A4-11) and (A4-12) can be identical only if

$$\sum x_i \bar{M}_i - M = 0,$$

i.e., if

$$M = \sum x_i \bar{M}_i$$

which is Eq. (3-6).

CONVERSION FACTORS AND VALUES OF THE GAS CONSTANT

Because standard reference books contain data in diverse units, we include Tables B-1 and B-2 to aid the conversion of values from one set of units to another. Those units having no connection with the SI system are enclosed in parentheses. The following definitions are noted:

(ft) $\equiv$ U.S. National Bureau of Standards defined foot $\equiv 3.048 \times 10^{-1}$ m

(in) $\equiv$ U.S. National Bureau of Standards defined inch $\equiv 2.54 \times 10^{-2}$ m

$(lb_m) \equiv$ U.S. National Bureau of Standards defined pound mass (avoirdupois) $\equiv 4.5359237 \times 10^{-1}$ kg

$(lb_f) \equiv$ force to accelerate 1 (lb_m) 32.1740 (ft) s^{-2}

(atm) $\equiv$ standard atmospheric pressure

(psia) $\equiv$ pounds force per square inch absolute pressure

(torr) $\equiv$ pressure exerted by 1 mm mercury at 0°C and standard gravity

(cal) $\equiv$ thermochemical calorie

(Btu) $\equiv$ international steam table British thermal unit

(lb mol) $\equiv$ mass in pounds mass with numerical value equal to the molar mass (molecular weight)

(R) $\equiv$ absolute temperature in Rankines

The conversion factors of Table B-1 are referred to a single basic or derived unit of the SI system. Conversions between other pairs of units for a given quantity are made as in the following example:

$$1 \text{ bar} = 0.986923 \text{ (atm)} = 750.061 \text{ (torr)}$$

Thus

$$1 \text{ (atm)} = \frac{750.061}{0.986923} = 760.00 \text{ (torr)}$$

Table B-1 Conversion Factors

Quantity	Conversion
Length	$1 \text{ m} = 100 \text{ cm}$ $= 3.28084 \text{ (ft)}$ $= 39.3701 \text{ (in)}$
Mass	$1 \text{ kg} = 10^3 \text{ g}$ $= 2.20462 \text{ (lb}_m\text{)}$
Force	$1 \text{ N} = 1 \text{ kg m s}^{-2}$ $= 10^5 \text{ (dyne)}$ $= 0.224809 \text{ (lb}_f\text{)}$
Pressure	$1 \text{ bar} = 10^5 \text{ N m}^{-2}$ $= 10^5 \text{ Pa}$ $= 10^2 \text{ kPa}$ $= 10^6 \text{ (dyne) cm}^{-2}$ $= 0.986923 \text{ (atm)}$ $= 14.5038 \text{ (psia)}$ $= 750.061 \text{ (torr)}$
Volume	$1 \text{ m}^3 = 10^6 \text{ cm}^3$ $= 35.3147 \text{ (ft)}^3$
Density	$1 \text{ g cm}^{-3} = 10^3 \text{ kg m}^{-3}$ $= 62.4278 \text{ (lb}_m\text{) (ft)}^{-3}$
Energy	$1 \text{ J} = 1 \text{ N m}$ $= 1 \text{ m}^3 \text{ Pa}$ $= 10^{-5} \text{ m}^3 \text{ bar}$ $= 10 \text{ cm}^3 \text{ bar}$ $= 9.86923 \text{ cm}^3 \text{ (atm)}$ $= 10^7 \text{ (dyne) cm}$ $= 10^7 \text{ (erg)}$ $= 0.239006 \text{ (cal)}$ $= 5.12197 \times 10^{-3} \text{ (ft)}^3 \text{ (psia)}$ $= 0.737562 \text{ (ft) (lb}_f\text{)}$ $= 9.47831 \times 10^{-4} \text{ (Btu)}$

Table B-2 Values of the Universal Gas Constant

$R = 8.314 \text{ J mol}^{-1} \text{ K}^{-1} = 8.314 \text{ m}^3 \text{ Pa mol}^{-1} \text{ K}^{-1}$

$= 83.14 \text{ cm}^3 \text{ bar mol}^{-1} \text{ K}^{-1} = 8{,}314 \text{ cm}^3 \text{ kPa mol}^{-1} \text{ K}^{-1} = 82.06 \text{ cm}^3 \text{ (atm) mol}^{-1} \text{ K}^{-1}$

$= 62{,}356 \text{ cm}^3 \text{ (torr) mol}^{-1} \text{ K}^{-1}$

$= 1.987 \text{ (cal) mol}^{-1} \text{ K}^{-1} = 1.986 \text{ (Btu) (lb mol)}^{-1} \text{ (R)}^{-1}$

$= 0.7302 \text{ (ft)}^3 \text{ (atm) (lb mol)}^{-1} \text{ (R)}^{-1} = 10.73 \text{ (ft)}^3 \text{ (psia) (lb mol)}^{-1} \text{ (R)}^{-1}$

$= 1545 \text{ (ft) (lb}_f\text{) (lb mol)}^{-1} \text{ (R)}^{-1}$

CALCULATION OF RESIDUAL FUNCTIONS FROM EQUATIONS OF STATE

Given a PVT equation of state valid from $P = 0$ to arbitrary pressure P, one may determine expressions for $\ln \phi$ and for the residual functions $\Delta M'$. Equations of state may be explicit in either volume or pressure, however, and the favored volumetric variable may be either the molar volume V or the molar density ρ. The use of different types of equations of state requires the use of different formulas for the derived functions. We present in this appendix a compendium of general formulas for $\Delta H'$, $\Delta S'$, $\ln \phi$, and $\Delta C_P'$ (or $\Delta C_V'$), suitable for application to PVT equations of state of six functional types:

$$V = V(T, P)$$

$$Z = Z(T, P)$$

$$P = P(T, V)$$

$$Z = Z(T, V)$$

$$P = P(T, \rho)$$

$$Z = Z(T, \rho)$$

The formulas, valid for either a pure substance or for a constant-composition mixture, are summarized in Tables C-1 through C-4. The following paragraphs contain outlines of their derivations.

Table C-1 Formulas for the residual enthalpy

Form of equation of state	$\Delta H'$	
$V = V(T, P)$	$\int_0^P \left[T\left(\dfrac{\partial V}{\partial T}\right)_P - V \right] dP$	(2-85)
$Z = Z(T, P)$	$RT^2 \int_0^P \left(\dfrac{\partial Z}{\partial T}\right)_P \dfrac{dP}{P}$	(4-17)
$P = P(T, V)$	$-\int_\infty^V \left[T\left(\dfrac{\partial P}{\partial T}\right)_V + V\left(\dfrac{\partial P}{\partial V}\right)_T \right] dV$	(C-4)
$Z = Z(T, V)$	$-RT^2 \int_\infty^V \left(\dfrac{\partial Z}{\partial T}\right)_V \dfrac{dV}{V} - RT(Z - 1)$	(C-9)
$P = P(T, \rho)$	$\int_0^\rho \left[T\left(\dfrac{\partial P}{\partial T}\right)_\rho - \rho\left(\dfrac{\partial P}{\partial \rho}\right)_T \right] \dfrac{d\rho}{\rho^2}$	(C-13)
$Z = Z(T, \rho)$	$RT^2 \int_0^\rho \left(\dfrac{\partial Z}{\partial T}\right)_\rho \dfrac{d\rho}{\rho} - RT(Z - 1)$	(4-67)

Volume-explicit equations of the form $V = V(T, P)$ are treated in Secs. 2-11 and 4-3, where expressions for $\Delta H'$, $\Delta S'$, and $\Delta C'_P$ are given as Eqs. (2-85), (2-86), and (4-24). The corresponding formula for $\ln \phi$ is obtained by combination of Eqs. (2-85) and (2-86) with Eq. (4-22):

$$\ln \phi = \frac{\Delta S'}{R} - \frac{\Delta H'}{RT} \tag{4-22}$$

Table C-2 Formulas for the residual entropy

Form of equation of state	$\Delta S'$	
$V = V(T, P)$	$\int_0^P \left[\left(\dfrac{\partial V}{\partial T}\right)_P - \dfrac{R}{P} \right] dP$	(2-86)
$Z = Z(T, P)$	$R \int_0^P \left[T\left(\dfrac{\partial Z}{\partial T}\right)_P + Z - 1 \right] \dfrac{dP}{P}$	(4-18)
$P = P(T, V)$	$-\int_\infty^V \left[\left(\dfrac{\partial P}{\partial T}\right)_V + \dfrac{R}{P}\left(\dfrac{\partial P}{\partial V}\right)_T \right] dV$	(C-5)
$Z = Z(T, V)$	$-R \int_\infty^V \left[T\left(\dfrac{\partial Z}{\partial T}\right)_V + Z - 1 \right] \dfrac{dV}{V} - R \ln Z$	(C-10)
$P = P(T, \rho)$	$\int_0^\rho \left[\left(\dfrac{\partial P}{\partial T}\right)_\rho - \dfrac{R\rho^2}{P}\left(\dfrac{\partial P}{\partial \rho}\right)_T \right] \dfrac{d\rho}{\rho^2}$	(C-14)
$Z = Z(T, \rho)$	$R \int_0^\rho \left[T\left(\dfrac{\partial Z}{\partial T}\right)_\rho + Z - 1 \right] \dfrac{d\rho}{\rho} - R \ln Z$	(4-68)

Table C-3 Formulas for $\ln \phi$

Form of equation of state	$\ln \phi$	
$V = V(T, P)$	$\dfrac{1}{RT}\displaystyle\int_0^P \left(V - \dfrac{RT}{P}\right) dP$	(C-1)
$Z = Z(T, P)$	$\displaystyle\int_0^P (Z - 1)\dfrac{dP}{P}$	(C-2)
$P = P(T, V)$	$\dfrac{1}{RT}\displaystyle\int_\infty^V \left(V - \dfrac{RT}{P}\right)\left(\dfrac{\partial P}{\partial V}\right)_T dV$	(C-6)
$Z = Z(T, V)$	$Z - 1 - \ln Z - \displaystyle\int_\infty^V (Z - 1)\dfrac{dV}{V}$	(C-11)
$P = P(T, \rho)$	$\dfrac{1}{RT}\displaystyle\int_0^\rho \left(1 - \dfrac{\rho RT}{P}\right)\left(\dfrac{\partial P}{\partial \rho}\right)_T \dfrac{d\rho}{\rho}$	(C-15)
$Z = Z(T, \rho)$	$Z - 1 - \ln Z + \displaystyle\int_0^\rho (Z - 1)\dfrac{d\rho}{\rho}$	(4-69)

The result is

$$\ln \phi = \frac{1}{RT}\int_0^P \left(V - \frac{RT}{P}\right) dP \qquad \text{(C-1)}$$

Equation (C-1) also follows directly on integration of Eq. (3-82) from $P = 0$ to arbitrary pressure. Here we note that $\ln \phi = 0$ for $P = 0$, and that $\Delta V' \equiv V' - V = RT/P - V$.

Table C-4 Formulas for residual heat capacities

Form of equation of state	Residual heat capacity	
$V = V(T, P)$	$\Delta C'_P = T \displaystyle\int_0^P \left(\dfrac{\partial^2 V}{\partial T^2}\right)_P dP$	(4-24)
$Z = Z(T, P)$	$\Delta C'_P = RT \displaystyle\int_0^P \left[T\left(\dfrac{\partial^2 Z}{\partial T^2}\right)_P + 2\left(\dfrac{\partial Z}{\partial T}\right)_P\right]\dfrac{dP}{P}$	(4-25)
$P = P(T, V)$	$\Delta C'_V = -T \displaystyle\int_\infty^V \left(\dfrac{\partial^2 P}{\partial T^2}\right)_V dV$	(C-7)
$Z = Z(T, V)$	$\Delta C'_V = -RT \displaystyle\int_\infty^V \left[T\left(\dfrac{\partial^2 Z}{\partial T^2}\right)_V + 2\left(\dfrac{\partial Z}{\partial T}\right)_V\right]\dfrac{dV}{V}$	(C-12)
$P = P(T, \rho)$	$\Delta C'_V = T \displaystyle\int_0^\rho \left(\dfrac{\partial^2 P}{\partial T^2}\right)_\rho \dfrac{d\rho}{\rho^2}$	(C-16)
$Z = Z(T, \rho)$	$\Delta C'_V = RT \displaystyle\int_0^\rho \left[T\left(\dfrac{\partial^2 Z}{\partial T^2}\right)_\rho + 2\left(\dfrac{\partial Z}{\partial T}\right)_\rho\right]\dfrac{d\rho}{\rho}$	(4-70)

Volume-explicit equations of the form $Z = Z(T, P)$ are treated in Sec. 4-3, where expressions for $\Delta H'$, $\Delta S'$, and $\Delta C_p'$ are given as Eqs. (4-17), (4-18), and (4-25). The corresponding formula for $\ln \phi$ is found by combination of Eqs. (4-17), (4-18), and (4-22); the result is

$$\ln \phi = \int_0^P (Z - 1)\frac{dP}{P} \tag{C-2}$$

Equation (C-2) also follows from integration of Eq. (3-82), or as a generalization of Eq. (3-70).

The basis for derivation of expressions for $\Delta H'$ and $\Delta S'$ from pressure-explicit equations of state is the following equation, valid for any residual function $\Delta M'$ whose value approaches zero as $V \to \infty$ (i.e., as $P \to 0$):

$$\Delta M' = \int_\infty^V \left(\frac{\partial \Delta M'}{\partial V}\right) dV \qquad (\text{const } T, x)$$

But

$$\left(\frac{\partial \Delta M'}{\partial V}\right)_T = \left(\frac{\partial \Delta M'}{\partial P}\right)_T \left(\frac{\partial P}{\partial V}\right)_T$$

and combination of these equations gives

$$\Delta M' = \int_\infty^V \left(\frac{\partial \Delta M'}{\partial P}\right)_T \left(\frac{\partial P}{\partial V}\right)_T dV \tag{C-3}$$

From Eq. (2-85)

$$\left(\frac{\partial \Delta H'}{\partial P}\right)_T = T\left(\frac{\partial V}{\partial T}\right)_P - V$$

Also, by Eq. (A2-5),

$$\left(\frac{\partial V}{\partial T}\right)_P \left(\frac{\partial P}{\partial V}\right)_T = -\left(\frac{\partial P}{\partial T}\right)_V$$

and thus Eq. (C-3) yields, for $\Delta M' \equiv \Delta H'$,

$$\Delta H' = -\int_\infty^V \left[T\left(\frac{\partial P}{\partial T}\right)_V + V\left(\frac{\partial P}{\partial V}\right)_T\right] dV \tag{C-4}$$

Similarly, by Eq. (2-86),

$$\left(\frac{\partial \Delta S'}{\partial P}\right)_T = \left(\frac{\partial V}{\partial T}\right)_P - \frac{R}{P}$$

and thus Eq. (C-3) yields, for $\Delta M' \equiv \Delta S'$,

$$\Delta S' = -\int_\infty^V \left[\left(\frac{\partial P}{\partial T}\right)_V + \frac{R}{P}\left(\frac{\partial P}{\partial V}\right)_T\right] dV \tag{C-5}$$

A formula for $\ln \phi$ is determined by combination of Eqs. (C-4), (C-5), and (4-22):

$$\ln \phi = \frac{1}{RT} \int_{\infty}^{V} \left(V - \frac{RT}{P} \right) \left(\frac{\partial P}{\partial V} \right)_T dV \qquad \text{(C-6)}$$

The natural residual heat capacity for a pressure-explicit equation of state is $\Delta C_V'$, not $\Delta C_P'$. It is known that C_V for a real gas approaches its ideal-gas value C_V^* as $V \rightarrow \infty$ (i.e., as $P \rightarrow 0$). Moreover, by Eqs. (2-56) and (2-56) *ideal*,

$$\left(\frac{\partial C_V}{\partial V} \right)_T = T \left(\frac{\partial^2 P}{\partial T^2} \right)_V$$

and

$$\left(\frac{\partial C_V^*}{\partial V} \right)_T = 0$$

Thus,

$$\left(\frac{\partial \Delta C_V'}{\partial V} \right)_T = -T \left(\frac{\partial^2 P}{\partial T^2} \right)_V$$

and integration from $V = \infty$ to finite V gives

$$\Delta C_V' = -T \int_{\infty}^{V} \left(\frac{\partial^2 P}{\partial T^2} \right)_V dV \qquad \text{(C-7)}$$

Equations (C-4) through (C-7) apply to a pressure-explicit equation of state of the form $P = P(T, V)$. Extension of these results to an equation of the form $Z = Z(T, V)$ is made by use of the following substitutions:

$$\left(\frac{\partial P}{\partial V} \right)_T = \frac{RT}{V} \left(\frac{\partial Z}{\partial V} \right)_T - \frac{ZRT}{V^2} \qquad \text{(2-78)}$$

$$\left(\frac{\partial P}{\partial T} \right)_V = \frac{RT}{V} \left(\frac{\partial Z}{\partial T} \right)_V + \frac{ZR}{V} \qquad \text{(2-79)}$$

$$\left(\frac{\partial^2 P}{\partial T^2} \right)_V = \frac{RT}{V} \left(\frac{\partial^2 Z}{\partial T^2} \right)_V + \frac{2R}{V} \left(\frac{\partial Z}{\partial T} \right)_V \qquad \text{(C-8)}$$

Thus we find that

$$\Delta H' = -RT^2 \int_{\infty}^{V} \left(\frac{\partial Z}{\partial T} \right)_V \frac{dV}{V} - RT(Z - 1) \qquad \text{(C-9)}$$

$$\Delta S' = -RT \int_{\infty}^{V} \left(\frac{\partial Z}{\partial T} \right)_V \frac{dV}{V} - R \int_{\infty}^{V} (Z - 1) \frac{dV}{V} - R \ln Z \qquad \text{(C-10)}$$

$$\ln \phi = Z - 1 - \ln Z - \int_{\infty}^{V} (Z - 1)\frac{dV}{V} \tag{C-11}$$

and

$$\Delta C_V' = -RT \int_{\infty}^{V} \left[T\left(\frac{\partial^2 Z}{\partial T^2}\right)_V + 2\left(\frac{\partial Z}{\partial T}\right)_V \right]\frac{dV}{V} \tag{C-12}$$

We treat finally pressure-explicit equations of state of the forms $P = P(T, \rho)$ or $Z = Z(T, \rho)$. Expressions for the derived functions follow immediately from Eqs. (C-4) through (C-7) or from Eqs. (C-9) through (C-12) if one notes that, by definition,

$$\rho \equiv V^{-1}$$

Thus, Eqs. (C-4) through (C-7) become Eqs. (C-13) through (C-16) in Tables C-1 through C-4. Similarly, Eqs. (C-9) through (C-12) yield Eqs. (4-67) through (4-70), a set of formulas presented without proof in Sec. 4-5.

Given an expression for $\Delta C_V'$, one may readily find the corresponding formula for $\Delta C_P'$. From the definitions of $\Delta C_P'$ and $\Delta C_V'$, we have

$$\Delta C_P' = \Delta C_V' + (C_P' - C_V') - (C_P - C_V)$$

But, by Eq. (2-57) *ideal*,

$$C_P' - C_V' = R$$

and from Eq. (2-57)

$$C_P - C_V = T\left(\frac{\partial V}{\partial T}\right)_P\left(\frac{\partial P}{\partial T}\right)_V = -T\left(\frac{\partial P}{\partial T}\right)_V^2\left(\frac{\partial P}{\partial V}\right)_T^{-1}$$

Combination of these equations gives a result suitable for use with Eq. (C-7) and a pressure-explicit equation of state of the type $P = P(T, V)$:

$$\Delta C_P' = \Delta C_V' + R + T\left(\frac{\partial P}{\partial T}\right)_V^2\left(\frac{\partial P}{\partial V}\right)_T^{-1} \tag{C-17}$$

For equations of state of the type $Z = Z(T, V)$, we combine Eqs. (C-17), (2-78), and (2-79), obtaining

$$\Delta C_P' = \Delta C_V' + R + R\frac{[T(\partial Z/\partial T)_V + Z]^2}{[V(\partial Z/\partial V)_T - Z]} \tag{C-18}$$

with $\Delta C_V'$ given by Eq. (C-12). Finally, elimination of V in favor of ρ in Eqs. (C-17) and (C-18) yields

$$\Delta C_P' = \Delta C_V' + R - \frac{T(\partial P/\partial T)_\rho^2}{\rho^2(\partial P/\partial \rho)_T} \tag{C-19}$$

and

$$\Delta C_P' = \Delta C_V' + R - R\frac{[T(\partial Z/\partial T)_\rho + Z]^2}{[\rho(\partial Z/\partial \rho)_T + Z]} \tag{C-20}$$

Equations (C-19) and (C-16) are used with equations of state of the form $P = P(T, \rho)$, and Eqs. (C-20) and (4-70) with equations of state of the type $Z = Z(T, \rho)$.

D

CRITICAL CONSTANTS AND ACENTRIC FACTORS

	T_c/K	P_c/bar	$V_c/$ $10^{-6}\,\text{m}^3\,\text{mol}^{-1}$	Z_c	ω
Paraffins:					
Methane	190.6	46.0	99.	0.288	0.008
Ethane	305.4	48.8	148.	0.285	0.098
Propane	369.8	42.5	203.	0.281	0.152
n-Butane	425.2	38.0	255.	0.274	0.193
Isobutane	408.1	36.5	263.	0.283	0.176
n-Pentane	469.6	33.7	304.	0.262	0.251
Isopentane	460.4	33.8	306.	0.271	0.227
Neopentane	433.8	32.0	303.	0.269	0.197
n-Hexane	507.4	29.7	370.	0.260	0.296
n-Heptane	540.2	27.4	432.	0.263	0.351
n-Octane	568.8	24.8	492.	0.259	0.394
Monoolefins:					
Ethylene	282.4	50.4	129.	0.276	0.085
Propylene	365.0	46.2	181.	0.275	0.148
1-Butene	419.6	40.2	240.	0.277	0.187
1-Pentene	464.7	40.5	300.	0.31	0.245
Miscellaneous organic compounds:					
Acetic acid	594.4	57.9	171.	0.200	0.454
Acetone	508.1	47.0	209.	0.232	0.309
Acetonitrile	547.9	48.3	173.	0.184	0.321
Acetylene	308.3	61.4	113.	0.271	0.184
Benzene	562.1	48.9	259.	0.271	0.212

	T_c/K	P_c/bar	$V_c/$ $10^{-6}\ m^3\ mol^{-1}$	Z_c	ω
1,3-Butadiene	425.0	43.3	221.	0.270	0.195
Chlorobenzene	632.4	45.2	308.	0.265	0.249
Cyclohexane	553.4	40.7	308.	0.273	0.213
Dichlorodifluoromethane					
(Freon-12)	385.0	41.2	217.	0.280	0.176
Diethyl ether	466.7	36.4	280.	0.262	0.281
Ethanol	516.2	63.8	167.	0.248	0.635
Ethylene oxide	469.	71.9	140.	0.258	0.200
Methanol	512.6	81.0	118.	0.224	0.559
Methyl chloride	416.3	66.8	139.	0.268	0.156
Methyl ethyl ketone	535.6	41.5	267.	0.249	0.329
Toluene	591.7	41.1	316.	0.264	0.257
Trichlorofluoromethane					
(Freon-11)	471.2	44.1	248.	0.279	0.188
Trichlorotrifluoroethane					
(Freon-113)	487.2	34.1	304.	0.256	0.252
Elementary gases:					
Argon	150.8	48.7	74.9	0.291	0.0
Bromine	584.	103.	127.	0.270	0.132
Chlorine	417.	77.	124.	0.275	0.073
Helium 4	5.2	2.27	57.3	0.301	-0.387
Hydrogen	33.2	13.0	65.0	0.305	-0.22
Krypton	209.4	55.0	91.2	0.288	0.0
Neon	44.4	27.6	41.7	0.311	0.0
Nitrogen	126.2	33.9	89.5	0.290	0.040
Oxygen	154.6	50.5	73.4	0.288	0.021
Xenon	289.7	58.4	118.	0.286	0.0
Miscellaneous inorganic					
compounds:					
Ammonia	405.6	112.8	72.5	0.242	0.250
Carbon dioxide	304.2	73.8	94.0	0.274	0.225
Carbon disulfide	552.	79.	170.	0.293	0.115
Carbon monoxide	132.9	35.0	93.1	0.295	0.049
Carbon tetrachloride	556.4	45.6	276.	0.272	0.194
Chloroform	536.4	55.	239.	0.293	0.216
Hydrazine	653.	147.	96.1	0.260	0.328
Hydrogen chloride	324.6	83.	81.	0.249	0.12
Hydrogen cyanide	456.8	53.9	139.	0.197	0.407
Hydrogen sulfide	373.2	89.4	98.5	0.284	0.100
Nitric oxide (NO)	180.	65.	58.	0.25	0.607
Nitrous oxide (N_2O)	309.6	72.4	97.4	0.274	0.160
Sulfur dioxide	430.8	78.8	122.	0.268	0.251
Sulfur trioxide	491.0	82.	130.	0.26	0.41
Water	647.3	220.5	56.	0.229	0.344

References: A. P. Kudchadker, G. H. Alani, and B. J. Zwolinski, *Chem. Rev.*, **68**: 659 (1968); J. F. Mathews, *Chem. Rev.*, **72**: 71 (1972); R. C. Reid, J. M. Prausnitz, and T. K. Sherwood, "The Properties of Gases and Liquids," 3d ed., McGraw-Hill, New York, 1977; C. A. Passut and R. P. Danner, *Ind. Eng. Chem. Process Des. Develop.*, **12**: 365 (1974).

NEWTON'S METHOD

Thermodynamic problems must sometimes be solved by numerical techniques. In such cases, one often needs an iteration procedure to generate a sequence of approximations which rapidly approach as a limit the exact solution to an equation. One procedure is *Newton's method*, a technique for finding a root $X = X_s$ of the algebraic equation

$$Y(X) = 0 \qquad\qquad (\text{E-1})$$

The basis for the method is illustrated graphically on Fig. E-1, a sketch of Y versus X in a region near $Y(X) = 0$. Let $X = X_1$ be an initial estimate of a

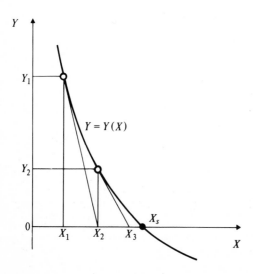

Figure E-1 Graphical illustration of Newton's method for finding a root X_s of the equation $Y(X) = 0$.

solution to Eq. (E-1). By construction, we identify the corresponding value of Y, $Y_1 = Y(X_1)$, and a tangent drawn to the curve at (X_1, Y_1) determines by its intersection with the X axis a second estimate X_2 of the solution $X = X_s$. The value for X_2 is easily found if one notes that the slope of the tangent line is equal to the first derivative of Y with respect to X. Thus, at (X_1, Y_1), we may write

$$\left(\frac{dY}{dX}\right)_1 = \frac{0 - Y_1}{X_2 - X_1}$$

from which

$$X_2 = X_1 - \frac{Y_1}{(dY/dX)_1} \qquad \text{(A)}$$

A second application of this procedure yields a third estimate X_3 of the solution $X = X_s$. Thus, at (X_2, Y_2) we may write

$$\left(\frac{dY}{dX}\right)_2 = \frac{0 - Y_2}{X_3 - X_2}$$

from which

$$X_3 = X_2 - \frac{Y_2}{(dY/dX)_2} \qquad \text{(B)}$$

and, by induction, we obtain as a generalization of Eqs. (A) and (B) the following recursive formula:

$$\boxed{X_{j+1} = X_j - \frac{Y_j}{(dY/dX)_j}} \qquad \text{(E-2)}$$

Equation (E-2) is the mathematical statement of Newton's method. Given an estimate X_j of a solution to Eq. (E-1), it provides a rational basis for a better estimate X_{j+1} of a solution to the same equation. The procedure is applied repeatedly until computed values of Y differ from zero to within some prescribed tolerance. The method presumes the availability of an analytical expression for Y as a function of X; the derivative on the right-hand side of Eq. (E-2) may be evaluated analytically, or may be approximated numerically as a ratio of finite differences. In thermodynamics, dY/dX is often given by a relatively simple expression, making the analytical treatment straightforward.

The virtue of Newton's method is that it converges *quadratically* (i.e., quickly); its major disadvantage derives from the presence of the derivative in the *denominator* of Eq. (E-2). At an extremum or point of horizontal inflection in Y, $dY/dX = 0$, and the right-hand side of Eq. (E-2) becomes infinite or indeterminate. Cases requiring the traversal of such points demand special consideration, or the use of other iterative procedures. Fortunately, many thermodynamic problems involve functions $Y(X)$ that are monotonic in X; for such cases, Newton's method is usually appropriate.

SUMMARY OF GENERAL EQUATIONS
FOR G^E AND RELATED FUNCTIONS

In the upper left quadrant of Table F-1 we list a number of important equations which follow from specializations of Eq. (3-4):

$$d(nM) = n\left(\frac{\partial M}{\partial T}\right)_{P,\,x} dT + n\left(\frac{\partial M}{\partial P}\right)_{T,\,x} dP + \sum \bar{M}_i \, dn_i \qquad (3\text{-}4)$$

Each is labeled with an equation number that indicates its original location. Each may also be written for the special case for which $n = 1$ and $n_i = x_i$; in such equations the x_i are subject to the constraint that $\sum x_i = 1$.

For one mole of a constant-composition solution or for one mole of a pure fluid, Eq. (3-4) becomes

$$dM = \left(\frac{\partial M}{\partial T}\right)_{P,\,x} dT + \left(\frac{\partial M}{\partial P}\right)_{T,\,x} dP \qquad (\text{const } x) \qquad (\text{F-1})$$

Specializations of this equation appear in the upper right quadrant of Table F-1. With the exception of Eq. (F-3) all appear in the text.

The analogy discussed in Sec. 3-4 applies to the properties considered here, and allows us to write the analog of Eq. (F-1) as

$$d\bar{M}_i = \left(\frac{\partial \bar{M}_i}{\partial T}\right)_{P,\,x} dT + \left(\frac{\partial \bar{M}_i}{\partial P}\right)_{T,\,x} dP \qquad (\text{const } x) \qquad (\text{F-2})$$

Specializations of this equation are given in the lower left quadrant of Table F-1, where Eqs. (F-4) and (F-5) appear for the first time.

Table F-1

General equations for an open system

$$d(nG) = -nS\,dT + nV\,dP + \sum \mu_i\,dn_i \tag{2-17}$$

$$d\left(\frac{nG}{RT}\right) = -\frac{nH}{RT^2}dT + \frac{nV}{RT}dP + \sum \frac{\mu_i}{RT}dn_i \tag{3-32}$$

$$d(n\ln f) = \frac{n\Delta H'}{RT^2}dT + \frac{nV}{RT}dP + \sum \ln\frac{\hat{f}_i}{x_i}\,dn_i \tag{3-83}$$

$$d(n\ln\phi) = \frac{n\Delta H'}{RT^2}dT - \frac{n\Delta V'}{RT}dP + \sum \ln\hat{\phi}_i\,dn_i \tag{3-84}$$

$$d\left(\frac{n\Delta G}{RT}\right) = -\frac{nH^E}{RT^2}dT + \frac{nV^E}{RT}dP + \sum \ln\hat{a}_i\,dn_i \tag{5-50}$$

$$d\left(\frac{nG^E}{RT}\right) = -\frac{nH^E}{RT^2}dT + \frac{nV^E}{RT}dP + \sum \ln\gamma_i\,dn_i \tag{5-54}$$

Equations for one mole (constant composition)

$$dG = -S\,dT + V\,dP \tag{2-29}$$

$$d\left(\frac{G}{RT}\right) = -\frac{H}{RT^2}dT + \frac{V}{RT}dP \tag{3-34}$$

$$d\ln f = \frac{\Delta H'}{RT^2}dT + \frac{V}{RT}dP \tag{3-87}$$

$$d\ln\phi = \frac{\Delta H'}{RT^2}dT - \frac{\Delta V'}{RT}dP \tag{3-88}$$

$$d\left(\frac{\Delta G}{RT}\right) = -\frac{H^E}{RT^2}dT + \frac{V^E}{RT}dP \tag{F-3}$$

$$d\left(\frac{G^E}{RT}\right) = -\frac{H^E}{RT^2}dT + \frac{V^E}{RT}dP \tag{5-56}$$

Equations for partial molar properties (constant compositon)

$$d\bar{G}_i = d\mu_i = -\bar{S}_i\,dT + \bar{V}_i\,dP \tag{3-28}$$

$$d\left(\frac{\bar{G}_i}{RT}\right) = d\left(\frac{\mu_i}{RT}\right) = -\frac{\bar{H}_i}{RT^2}dT + \frac{\bar{V}_i}{RT}dP \tag{F-4}$$

$$d\ln\frac{\hat{f}_i}{x_i} = d\ln\hat{f}_i = \frac{H_i' - \bar{H}_i}{RT^2}dT + \frac{\bar{V}_i}{RT}dP \tag{3-89}$$

$$d\ln\hat{\phi}_i = \frac{H_i' - \bar{H}_i}{RT^2}dT - \frac{V_i' - \bar{V}_i}{RT}dP \tag{3-90}$$

$$d\left(\frac{\overline{\Delta G_i}}{RT}\right) = d\ln\hat{a}_i = -\frac{\bar{H}_i^E}{RT^2}dT + \frac{\bar{V}_i^E}{RT}dP \tag{F-5}$$

$$d\left(\frac{\bar{G}_i^E}{RT}\right) = d\ln\gamma_i = -\frac{\bar{H}_i^E}{RT^2}dT + \frac{\bar{V}_i^E}{RT}dP \tag{5-57}$$

Gibbs-Duhem equations

$$-S\,dT + V\,dP = \sum x_i\,d\bar{G}_i = \sum x_i\,d\mu_i \tag{3-25}$$

$$-\frac{H}{RT^2}dT + \frac{V}{RT}dP = \sum x_i\,d\left(\frac{\mu_i}{RT}\right) \tag{3-33}$$

$$\frac{\Delta H'}{RT^2}dT + \frac{V}{RT}dP = \sum x_i\,d\ln\frac{\hat{f}_i}{x_i} = \sum x_i\,d\ln\hat{f}_i \tag{3-85}$$

$$\frac{\Delta H'}{RT^2}dT - \frac{\Delta V'}{RT}dP = \sum x_i\,d\ln\hat{\phi}_i \tag{3-86}$$

$$-\frac{H^E}{RT^2}dT + \frac{V^E}{RT}dP = \sum x_i\,d\ln\hat{a}_i \tag{5-51}$$

$$-\frac{H^E}{RT^2}dT + \frac{V^E}{RT}dP = \sum x_i\,d\ln\gamma_i \tag{5-55}$$

Another equation of major importance is the Gibbs-Duhem equation, which in its general form is given by Eq. (3-15):

$$\left(\frac{\partial M}{\partial T}\right)_{P,\,x} dT + \left(\frac{\partial M}{\partial P}\right)_{T,\,x} dP = \sum x_i\, d\bar{M}_i \qquad (3\text{-}15)$$

We list the various specializations of Eq. (3-15) along with their identifying equation numbers in the lower right quadrant of Table F-1. These equations may be multiplied directly by n.

In using this table, one should recall the equalities:

$$H^E = \Delta H \qquad \bar{H}_i^E = \overline{\Delta H}_i$$

and

$$V^E = \Delta V \qquad \bar{V}_i^E = \overline{\Delta V}_i$$

The great utility of the equations listed in Table F-1 is that they represent most concisely a large body of information. One may by inspection reduce them to particular cases, write down partial derivatives, and develop the reciprocal relations that follow from the fact that they are exact differential expressions.

VLE FLASH CALCULATIONS
(SINGLE LIQUID PHASE)

A physical basis for a T-P flash calculation is shown schematically in Fig. G-1. We consider F moles of a feed mixture with overall composition given by the set of N mole fractions $\{z_i\} \equiv z_1, z_2, \ldots, z_N$. The feed is introduced into a separator, where there are formed L moles of liquid and V moles of vapor at some specified T and P. The compositions of these phases are designated by the sets of mole fractions $\{x_i\} \equiv x_1, x_2, \ldots, x_N$ and $\{y_i\} \equiv y_1, y_2, \ldots, y_N$.

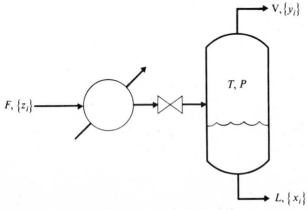

Figure G-1 Physical basis for a T-P flash calculation.

Without loss of generality, we may let $F = 1$; then L is the molar *fraction* of liquid formed in the separator, and V is the molar *fraction* of vapor. Thus,

$$L + V = 1 \tag{G-1}$$

A component material balance gives

$$z_i = Lx_i + Vy_i \qquad (i = 1, 2, \dots, N) \tag{G-2}$$

where, by definition, the y_i are related to the x_i through the "K values" K_i:

$$y_i \equiv K_i x_i \qquad (i = 1, 2, \dots, N) \tag{G-3}$$

In a flash calculation, the sets $\{z_i\}$ and $\{K_i\} \equiv K_1, K_2, \dots, K_N$ are presumed known.

Equations (G-1) through (G-3) may be combined and solved to produce four expressions—two for x_i and two for y_i:

$$x_i = \frac{z_i}{K_i + (1 - K_i)L} \tag{G-4}$$

$$x_i = \frac{z_i}{1 + (K_i - 1)V} \tag{G-5}$$

$$y_i = \frac{K_i z_i}{K_i + (1 - K_i)L} \tag{G-6}$$

$$y_i = \frac{K_i z_i}{1 + (K_i - 1)V} \tag{G-7}$$

The goal of a flash calculation is to find a value of L or V $[0 < (L, V) < 1]$ for which $\sum x_i = 1$ and $\sum y_i = 1$, or by Eqs. (G-4) through (G-7), for which

$$F_1(L) \equiv \sum \frac{z_i}{K_i + (1 - K_i)L} - 1 = 0 \tag{G-8}$$

$$F_2(V) \equiv \sum \frac{z_i}{1 + (K_i - 1)V} - 1 = 0 \tag{G-9}$$

$$F_3(L) \equiv \sum \frac{K_i z_i}{K_i + (1 - K_i)L} - 1 = 0 \tag{G-10}$$

$$F_4(V) \equiv \sum \frac{K_i z_i}{1 + (K_i - 1)V} - 1 = 0 \tag{G-11}$$

Equations (G-8) through (G-11) are all equivalent, and any *one* of them can serve as the algebraic basis for a flash calculation (see, e.g., Example 6-5). However, the four functions F_1 through F_4 are highly nonlinear in L or V, and moreover exhibit extrema on the range $0 < (L, V) < 1$. The latter feature requires that one take special precautions when devising numerical methods for solving the equations.

King (1980) reviews flash-calculation techniques, and summarizes results of published studies. For numerical work, a procedure proposed by Rachford and Rice (1952) is recommended. Subtraction of Eq. (G-9) from Eq. (G-11) defines a new function $\mathscr{F}(V)$ and produces a new equation:

$$\mathscr{F}(V) \equiv \sum \frac{z_i(K_i - 1)}{1 + (K_i - 1)V} = 0 \qquad \text{(G-12)}$$

Function $\mathscr{F}(V)$ is better behaved than either $F_2(V)$ or $F_4(V)$. For example, it is *monotonic* in V, as the first derivative is always negative:

$$\frac{d\mathscr{F}}{dV} = -\sum \frac{z_i(K_i - 1)^2}{[1 + (K_i - 1)V]^2} \qquad \text{(G-13)}$$

Equations (G-12) and (G-13) are particularly convenient for application of Newton's method to a flash calculation (see App. E).

One must know before starting a flash calculation if two phases actually exist for given sets $\{z_i\}$ and $\{K_i\}$. This is readily determined by examination of the numerical values of $\mathscr{F}(V)$ at the limits $V = 0$ and $V = 1$. By the definition of $\mathscr{F}(V)$, we have

$$\mathscr{F}(0) \equiv \sum z_i K_i - 1$$

and

$$\mathscr{F}(1) \equiv 1 - \sum (z_i / K_i)$$

Consideration of the properties of $\mathscr{F}(V)$ reveals that two phases exist (that is, $0 < V < 1$) if

$$\mathscr{F}(0) > 0$$

and

$$\mathscr{F}(1) < 0$$

If $\mathscr{F}(0) > 0$ and $\mathscr{F}(1) = 0$, then the mixture is at its *dew point* (saturated vapor); if $\mathscr{F}(0) = 0$ and $\mathscr{F}(1) < 0$, it is at its *bubble point* (saturated liquid). Cases for which $\mathscr{F}(0) < 0$ or $\mathscr{F}(1) > 0$ correspond to subcooled liquid or superheated vapor, respectively.

The above characteristics are summarized in Table G-1, and Fig. G-2 shows representative plots of $\mathscr{F}(V)$ versus V for the various cases. The system is the one treated in Example 6-5: benzene(1)/toluene(2)/ethylbenzene(3) at 100°C, with $z_1 = 0.45$, $z_2 = 0.35$, and $z_3 = 0.20$, and with K values given by Raoult's law. Curves 2 and 4 represent $\mathscr{F}(V)$ versus V for the dew-point and bubble-point

Table G-1 Characteristics of limiting values of the function

$$\mathscr{F}(V) \equiv \sum \frac{z_i(K_i - 1)}{1 + (K_i - 1)V}$$

[The behavior of $\mathscr{F}(V)$ for each case is illustrated in Fig. G-2.]

Case	Physical state	$\mathscr{F}(0)$ $[\equiv \sum z_i K_i - 1]$	$\mathscr{F}(1)$ $[\equiv 1 - \sum (z_i/K_i)]$
1	Superheated vapor	>0	>0
2	Saturated vapor (dew point)	>0	$=0$
3	Two phases (liquid + vapor)	>0	<0
4	Saturated liquid (bubble point)	$=0$	<0
5	Subcooled liquid	<0	<0

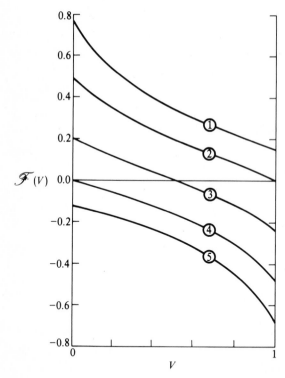

Figure G-2 Plots of

$$\mathscr{F}(V) \bigg| \equiv \sum \frac{z_i(K_i - 1)}{1 + (K_i - 1)V} \bigg|$$

versus V. Individual curves are representative of the cases listed in Table G-1; the particular system and conditions are described in the text.

pressures (0.7659 bar and 1.1383 bar, respectively); curve 3 for two-phase behavior is evaluated for 0.9521 bar, the average of the dew- and bubble-point pressures. It crosses the $\mathscr{F}(V) = 0$ axis at $V = 0.505$, the value obtained by trial in Example 6-5. Curves 1 and 5 are for pressures of 0.65 bar (superheated vapor) and 1.30 bar (subcooled liquid) respectively.

LITERATURE CITATIONS

Abbott, M. M.: "Cubic Equations of State," *AIChE J.*, **19**: 596–601, 1973.

———: "Cubic Equations of State: An Interpretive Review," *Equations of State in Engineering and Research*, K. C. Chao and R. L. Robinson, Jr., ed., Adv. in Chem. Series 182, pp. 47–70, Am. Chem. Soc., Washington, D.C., 1979.

——— J. K. Floess, G. E. Walsh, and H. C. Van Ness: "Vapor-Liquid Equilibrium: Part IV. Reduction of *P-x* Data for Ternary Systems," *AIChE J.*, **21**: 72–76, 1975.

——— and H. C. Van Ness: "An Extension of Barker's Method for Reduction of VLE Data," *Fluid Phase Equilibria*, **1**: 3–11, 1977.

——— and ———: "Vapor-Liquid Equilibrium: Part III. Data Reduction with Precise Expressions for G^E," *AIChE J.*, **21**: 62–71, 1975.

Abrams, D. S., and J. M. Prausnitz: "Statistical Thermodynamics of Liquid Mixtures: A New Expression for the Excess Gibbs Energy of Partly or Completely Miscible Systems," *AIChE J.*, **21**: 116–128, 1975.

Asselineau, L., G. Bogdanic, and J. Vidal: "A Versatile Algorithm for Calculating Vapor-Liquid Equilibria," *Fluid Phase Equilibria*, **3**: 273–290, 1979.

Barker, J. A.: "Determination of Activity Coefficients from Total Pressure Measurements," *Austral. J. Chem.*, **6**: 207–210, 1953.

Barner, H. E., R. L. Pigford, and W. C. Schreiner: "A Modified Redlich-Kwong Equation of State," paper (Preprint No. 38-66) presented at 31st Midyear API Meeting, Houston, Texas, 1966.

Battino, R., and H. L. Clever: "The Solubility of Gases in Liquids," *Chem. Rev.*, **66**: 395–463, 1966.

Bender, E.: "An Equation of State for Predicting Vapor-Liquid Equilibria of the System N_2–Ar–O_2," *Cryogenics*, **13**: 11–18, 1973.

Benedict, M., G. B. Webb, and L. C. Rubin: "An Empirical Equation for Thermodynamic Properties of Light Hydrocarbons and Their Mixtures. I. Methane, Ethane, Propane, and *n*-Butane," *J. Chem. Phys.*, **8**: 334–345, 1940.

——— ——— and ———: "An Empirical Equation for Thermodynamic Properties of Light Hydrocarbons and Their Mixtures. II. Mixtures of Methane, Ethane, Propane, and *n*-Butane," *J. Chem. Phys.*, **10**: 747–758, 1942.

Beret, S., and J. M. Prausnitz: "Perturbed Hard-Chain Theory: An Equation of State for Fluids Containing Small or Large Molecules," *AIChE J.*, **21**: 1123–1132, 1975.

Berthelot, D. J.: *J. de Phys.* **8**: 263, 1899.

Bett, K. E., J. S. Rowlinson, and G. Saville: *Thermodynamics for Chemical Engineers*, The MIT Press, Cambridge, Massachusetts, 1975, pp. 172–174.

Callen, H. P.: *Thermodynamics*, Wiley, New York, 1960, chap. 8.

Carnahan, N. F., and K. E. Starling: "Equation of State for Non-attracting Rigid Spheres," *J. Chem. Phys.*, **51**: 635–636, 1969.

———— and ————: "Intermolecular Repulsions and the Equation of State for Fluids," *AIChE J.*, **18**: 1184–1189, 1972.

Chaudhry, M. M., H. C. Van Ness, and M. M. Abbott: "Excess Thermodynamic Functions for Ternary Systems. 6. Total-Pressure Data and G^E for Acetone-Ethanol-Water at 50°C," *J. Chem. Eng. Data*, **25**: 254–257, 1980.

Chueh, P. L., and J. M. Prausnitz: "Third Virial Coefficients of Nonpolar Gases and Their Mixtures," *AIChE J.*, **12**: 896–902, 1967a.

———— and ————: "Vapor-Liquid Equilibria at High Pressures: Calculation of Partial Molar Volumes in Nonpolar Liquid Mixtures," *AIChE J.*, **13**: 1099–1106, 1967b.

———— and ————: "Vapor-Liquid Equilibria at High Pressures: Vapor-Phase Fugacity Coefficients in Nonpolar and Quantum Gas Mixtures," *Ind. Eng. Chem. Fundam.*, **6**: 492–498, 1967c.

Clausius, R.: *Ann. Phys. Chem.*, **IX**: 337, 1880.

Curl, R. F., Jr., and K. S. Pitzer: "Volumetric and Thermodynamic Properties of Fluids—Enthalpy, Free Energy, and Entropy," *Ind. Eng. Chem.*, **50**: 265–274, 1958.

De Santis, R., and B. Grande: "An Equation for Predicting Third Virial Coefficients of Nonpolar Gases," *AIChE J.*, **25**: 931–938, 1979.

Donohue, M. D., and J. M. Prausnitz: "Perturbed Hard Chain Theory for Fluid Mixtures: Thermodynamic Properties for Mixtures in Natural Gas and Petroleum Technology," *AIChE J.*, **24**: 849–860, 1978.

Dymond, J. H., and E. B. Smith: *The Virial Coefficients of Pure Gases and Mixtures—A Critical Compilation*, Clarendon Press, Oxford, 1980.

Evans, R. B., III, and G. M. Watson: "Compressibility Factors of Nitrogen—*n*-Butane Mixtures in the Gas Phase," *Chem. Eng. Data Series*, **1**: 67–71, 1956.

Fredenslund, A., J. Gmehling, and P. Rasmussen: *Vapor-Liquid Equilibria using UNIFAC*, Elsevier, Amsterdam, 1977.

Gibbs, J. W.: *The Scientific Papers of J. W. Gibbs*, Dover, New York, 1961, vol. I, pp. 55–349.

Gibbs, R. E., and H. C. Van Ness: "Vapor-Liquid Equilibria from Total-Pressure Measurements. A New Apparatus," *Ind. Eng. Chem. Fundam.*, **11**: 410–413, 1972.

Gmehling, J., D. D. Liu, and J. M. Prausnitz: "High-Pressure Vapor-Liquid Equilibria for Mixtures Containing One or More Polar Components. Application of an Equation of State which Includes Dimerization Equilibria," *Chem. Eng. Sci.*, **34**: 951–958, 1979.

———— and U. Onken: *Vapor-Liquid Equilibrium Data Collection*, DECHEMA, Frankfurt/Main, 1977, vol. I, part 2a, pp. 321, 322, and 326.

Hála, H., J. Pick, V. Fried, and O. Vilim: *Vapor-Liquid Equilibrium*, 2d ed., Pergamon, Oxford, 1967.

Hayden, J. G., and J. P. O'Connell: "A Generalized Method for Predicting Second Virial Coefficients," *Ind. Eng. Chem. Proc. Des. Dev.*, **14**: 209–216, 1975.

Hilsenrath et al.: *Tables of Thermal Properties of Gases*, U.S. National Bureau of Standards Circular 564, Washington, D.C., 1955.

Horvath, A. L.: "Redlich-Kwong Equation of State: Review for Chemical Engineering Calculations," *Chem. Eng. Sci.*, **29**: 1334–1340, 1974.

Houghton, G., A. M. McLean, and P. D. Ritchie: "Compressibility, Fugacity, and Water-Solubility of Carbon Dioxide in the Region 0–36 Atm and 0–100°C," *Chem. Eng. Sci.*, **6**: 132–137, 1957.

Huron, M.-J., and J. Vidal: "New Mixing Rules in Simple Equations of State for Representing Vapor-Liquid Equilibria of Strongly Non-ideal Mixtures," *Fluid Phase Equilibria*, **3**: 255–271, 1979.

Kalra, H., D. B. Robinson, and T. R. Krishnan: "The Equilibrium Phase Properties of the Ethane-Hydrogen Sulfide System at Subambient Temperatures," *J. Chem. Eng. Data*, **22**: 85–88, 1977.

Kang, T. L., L. J. Hirth, K. A. Kobe, and J. J. McKetta: "Pressure-Volume-Temperature Properties of Sulfur Dioxide," *J. Chem. Eng. Data*, **6**: 220–226, 1961.

Kay, W. B.: "Density of Hydrocarbon Gases and Vapors," *Ind. Eng. Chem.*, **28**: 1014–1019, 1936.

Keenan, J. H., F. G. Keyes, P. G. Hill, and J. G. Moore: *Steam Tables (International Edition—Metric Units)*, Wiley, New York, 1969.

Kemény, S., S. Skjold-Jørgensen, J. Manczinger, and K. Tóth: "Reduction of Thermodynamic Data by Means of the Multiresponse Maximum Likelihood Principle," *AIChE J.*, in press.

King, C. J.: *Separation Processes*, 2d ed., McGraw-Hill, New York, 1980, p. 75.

Kojima, K., and T. Tochigi: *Prediction of Vapor-Liquid Equilibria by the ASOG Method*, Elsevier, Amsterdam, 1979.

Krichevsky, I. R., and A. A. Ilinskaya: "Partial Molar Volumes of Gases Dissolved in Liquids," *Acta Physicochimica, URSS*, **20**: 327–348, 1945.

——— and J. S. Kasarnovsky: "Thermodynamical Calculation of Solubilities of Nitrogen and Hydrogen in Water at High Pressures," *J. Am. Chem. Soc.*, **57**: 2168–2171, 1935.

Larkin, J. A., and R. C. Pemberton: "Thermodynamic Properties of Mixtures of Water + Ethanol between 298.15 and 383.15 K," *Report Chem. 43*, National Physical Laboratory, January 1976.

Lee, B.-I, J. H. Erbar, and W. C. Edmister: "Prediction of Thermodynamic Properties for Low Temperature Hydrocarbon Process Calculations," *AIChE J.*, **19**: 349–356, 1973.

——— and M. G. Kesler: "A Generalized Thermodynamic Correlation Based on Three-Parameter Corresponding States," *AIChE J.*, **21**: 510–527, 1040, 1975.

Leland, T. W., Jr., and P. S. Chappelear: "The Corresponding States Principle. A Review of Current Theory and Practice," *Ind. Eng. Chem.*, **60**(7): 15–43, 1968.

Loehe, J. R., H. C. Van Ness, and M. M. Abbott: "Excess Thermodynamic Functions for Ternary Systems. 7. Total-Pressure Data and G^E for Acetone/1,4-Dioxane/Water at 50°C," *J. Chem. Eng. Data*, **26**: 178–181, 1981.

Maher, P. J., and B. D. Smith: "A New Total Pressure Vapor-Liquid Equilibrium Apparatus. The Ethanol + Aniline System at 313.15, 350.81, and 386.67 K," *J. Chem. Eng. Data*, **24**: 16–22, 1979.

Malanowski, S.: *Równowaga Ciecz-Para*, Państwowe Wydawnictwo Naukowe, Warszawa, 1974, sec. 2.6.

Marsh, K. N.: "A General Method for Calculating the Excess Gibbs Free Energy from Isothermal Vapor-Liquid Equilibria," *J. Chem. Thermodynamics*, **9**: 719–724, 1977.

———: "The Measurement of Thermodynamic Excess Functions of Binary Liquid Mixtures," *Chemical Thermodynamics*, vol. 2, The Chemical Society, London, 1978, pp. 1–45.

Martin, J. J.: "Cubic Equations of State—Which?," *Ind. Eng. Chem. Fundam.*, **18**: 81–97, 1979.

———: "Equations of State," *Ind. Eng. Chem.*, **59**: 34–52, 1967.

——— and Y.-C. Hou: "Development of an Equation of State for Gases," *AIChE J.*, **1**: 142–151, 1955.

Martinez-Ortiz, J. A., and D. B. Manley: "Direct Solution of the Isothermal Gibbs-Duhem Equation by an Iterative Method for Binary Systems," *AIChE J.*, **23**: 393–395, 1977.

Mason, E. A., and T. H. Spurling: *The Virial Equation of State*, Pergamon, New York, 1969.

Michelsen, M. L.: "Calculation of Phase Envelopes and Critical Points for Multicomponent Mixtures," *Fluid Phase Equilibria*, **4**: 1–10, 1980.

Mixon, F. O., B. Gumowski, and B. H. Carpenter: "Computation of Vapor-Liquid Equilibrium Data from Solution Vapor Pressure Measurements," *Ind. Eng. Chem. Fundam.*, **4**: 455–459, 1965.

Modell, M., and R. C. Reid: *Thermodynamics and its Applications*, Prentice-Hall, Englewood Cliffs, N.J., 1974, Chap. 7.

Morris, J. W., P. J. Mulvey, M. M. Abbott, and H. C. Van Ness: "Excess Thermodynamic Functions for Ternary Systems. 1. Acetone-Chloroform-Methanol at 50°C," *J. Chem. Eng. Data*, **20**: 403–405, 1975.

Münster, A.: *Classical Thermodynamics*. Wiley-Interscience, London, 1970, Chap. VI.

Nicolaides, G. L., and C. A. Eckert: "Experimental Heats of Mixing of Some Miscible and Partially Miscible Nonelectrolyte Systems," *J. Chem. Eng. Data*, **23**: 152–156, 1978.

Null, H. R.: *Phase Equilibrium in Process Design*, Wiley-Interscience, New York, 1970, p. 134.

Ochi, K., and B. C.-Y. Lu: "Determination and Correlation of Binary Vapor-Liquid Equilibrium Data," *Fluid Phase Equilibria*, **1**: 185–200, 1978.

Parkinson, W. J., N. De Nevers: "Partial Molal Volume of Carbon Dioxide in Water Solutions," *Ind. Eng. Chem. Fundam.*, **8**: 709–713, 1969.

Pemberton, R. C., and C. J. Mash: "Thermodynamic Properties of Aqueous Non-electrolyte Mixtures. II. Vapor Pressures and Excess Gibbs Energies for Water + Ethanol at 303.15 to 363.15 K Determined by an Accurate Static Method," *J. Chem. Thermodyn.*, **10**: 867–888, 1978.

Peng, D.-Y., and D. B. Robinson: "A New Two-Constant Equation of State," *Ind. Eng. Chem. Fundam.*, **15**: 59–64, 1976.

Pitzer, K. S.: "The Volumetric and Thermodynamic Properties of Fluids. I. Theoretical Basis and Virial Coefficients," *J. Am. Chem. Soc.*, **77**: 3427–3433, 1955.

—— and R. F. Curl, Jr.: "The Volumetric and Thermodynamic Properties of Fluids. III. Empirical Equation for the Second Virial Coefficient," *J. Am. Chem. Soc.*, **79**: 2369–2370, 1957.

—— D. Z. Lippmann, R. F. Curl, Jr., C. M. Huggins, and D. E. Peterson: "The Volumetric and Thermodynamic Properties of Fluids. II. Compressibility Factor, Vapor Pressure, and Entropy of Vaporization," *J. Am. Chem. Soc.*, **77**: 3433–3440, 1955.

Prausnitz, J. M.: *Molecular Thermodynamics of Fluid-Phase Equilibria*, Prentice-Hall, Englewood Cliffs, N.J., 1969, Chap. 5.

—— T. F. Anderson, E. A. Grens, C. A. Eckert, R. Hsieh, and J. P. O'Connell: *Computer Calculations for Multicomponent Vapor-Liquid and Liquid-Liquid Equilibria*, Prentice-Hall, Englewood Cliffs, N.J., 1980, Chaps. 4 and 7.

—— C. A. Eckert, R. V. Orye, and J. P. O'Connell: *Computer Calculations for Multicomponent Vapor-Liquid Equilibria*, Prentice-Hall, Englewood Cliffs, N.J., 1967, Chap. 5.

Rachford, H. H., Jr., and J. D. Rice: "Procedure for use of Electronic Digital Computers in Calculating Flash Vaporization Hydrocarbon Equilibrium," *J. Petrol. Technol.*, **4**(10): Sec. 1, p. 19 and Sec. 2, p. 3, October, 1952.

Rea, H. E., C. F. Spencer, and R. P. Danner: "Effect of Pressure and Temperature on the Liquid Densities of Pure Hydrocarbons," *J. Chem. Eng. Data*, **18**: 227–230, 1973.

Redlich, O., and A. T. Kister: "Algebraic Representation of the Thermodynamic Properties and the Classification of Solutions," *Ind. Eng. Chem.*, **40**: 345–348, 1948.

—— and J. N. S. Kwong: "On the Thermodynamics of Solutions. V. An Equation of State. Fugacities of Gaseous Solutions," *Chem. Reviews*, **44**: 233–244, 1949.

Reid, R. C., J. M. Prausnitz, and T. K. Sherwood: *The Properties of Gases and Liquids*, 3d ed., McGraw-Hill, New York, 1977.

—— and T. K. Sherwood: *The Properties of Gases and Liquids*, 2d ed., McGraw-Hill, New York, 1966.

Renon, H., and J. M. Prausnitz: "Local Compositions in Thermodynamic Excess Functions for Liquid Mixtures," *AIChE J.*, **14**: 135–144, 1968.

Sage, B. H., and W. N. Lacey: *Some Properties of the Lighter Hydrocarbons, Hydrogen Sulfide, and Carbon Dioxide*, American Petroleum Institute, New York, 1955.

—— and ——: *Thermodynamic Properties of the Lighter Hydrocarbons and Nitrogen*, American Petroleum Institute, New York, 1950.

Sayegh, S. G., and J. H. Vera: "Model-Free Methods for Vapor-Liquid Equilibria Calculations. Binary Systems," *Chem. Eng. Sci.*, **35**: 2247–2256, 1980.

Scatchard, G., and C. L. Raymond: "Vapor-Liquid Equilibrium. II. Chloroform-Ethanol Mixtures at 35, 45, and 55°C," *J. Am. Chem. Soc.*, **60**: 1278–1287, 1938.

Schreiber, L. B., and C. A. Eckert: "Use of Infinite-Dilution Activity Coefficients with Wilson's Equation," *Ind. Eng. Chem. Process Des. Develop.*, **10**: 572–576, 1971.

Soave, G.: "Equilibrium Constants from a Modified Redlich-Kwong Equation of State," *Chem. Eng. Sci.*, **27**: 1197–1203, 1972.

Sørensen, J. M., and W. Arlt: *Liquid-Liquid Equilibrium Data Collection*, DECHEMA Chemistry Data Series, Frankfurt/Main, vol. V, pt. 1, 1979, pts. 2 and 3, 1980.

———— T. Magnussen, P. Rasmussen, and A. Fredenslund: "Liquid-Liquid Equilibrium Data: Their Retrieval, Correlation and Prediction. Part I: Retrieval; Part II: Correlation; Part III: Prediction," *Fluid Phase Equilibria*, **2**: 297–309, 1979; **3**: 47–82, 1979; **4**: 151–163, 1980.

Spencer, C. F., and S. B. Adler: "A Critical Review of Equations for Predicting Liquid Density," *J. Chem. Eng. Data*, **23**: 82–89, 1978.

————and R. P. Danner: "Improved Equation for Prediction of Saturated Liquid Density," *J. Chem. Eng. Data*, **17**: 236–241, 1972.

Starling, K. E., and J. E. Powers: "Enthalpy of Mixtures by Modified BWR Equation," *Ind. Eng. Chem. Fundam.*, **9**: 531–537, 1970.

Steele, K., B. E. Poling, and D. B. Manley: "Vapor Pressures for the System 1-Butene, Isobutane, and 1,3-Butadiene," *J. Chem. Eng. Data*, **21**: 399–403, 1976.

Su, G. J.: "Modified Law of Corresponding States for Real Gases," *Ind. Eng. Chem.*, **38**: 803–806, 1946.

Tarakad, R. R., and R. P. Danner: "An Improved Corresponding-States Method for Polar Fluids: Correlation of Second Virial Coefficients," *AIChE J.*, **23**: 685–695, 1977.

Tomlins, R. P., and K. N. Marsh: "A New Apparatus for Measuring the Vapor Pressure of Liquid Mixtures. Excess Gibbs Free Energy of Octamethylcyclotetrasiloxane + Cyclohexane at 308.15 K," *J. Chem. Thermodynamics*, **8**: 1185–1194, 1976.

Tsonopoulos, C.: "An Empirical Correlation of Second Virial Coefficients," *AIChE J.*, **20**: 263–272, 1974.

————: "Second Virial Coefficients of Polar Haloalkanes," *AIChE J.*, **21**: 827–829, 1975.

————: "Second Virial Coefficients of Water Pollutants," *AIChE J.*, **24**: 1112–1115, 1978.

van der Waals, J. D.: Doctoral Dissertation, Leiden, Holland, 1873.

Van Ness, H. C.: "On Integration of the Coexistence Equation for Binary Vapor-Liquid Equilibrium," *AIChE J.*, **16**: 18–22, 1970.

———— and M. M. Abbott: *Int. DATA Ser., Selec. Data Mixtures, Ser. A,* **1977**: pp. 7–9, 1977.

———— and ————: *Int. DATA Ser., Selec. Data Mixtures, Ser. A,* **1978**: 59–61, 1978*b*.

———— and ————: *Int. DATA Ser., Selec. Data Mixtures, Ser. A,* **1978**: 65, 1978*c*.

———— and ————: "A Procedure for Rapid Degassing of Liquids," *Ind. Eng. Chem. Fundam.*, **17**: 66–67, 1978*a*.

———— and ————: "Vapor-Liquid Equilibrium. Part VI. Standard State Fugacities for Supercritical Components," *AIChE J.*, **25**: 645–653, 1979.

———— and R. V. Mrazek: "Treatment of Thermodynamic Data for Homogeneous Binary Systems," *AIChE J.*, **5**: 209–212, 1959.

Vidal, J.: "Mixing Rules and Excess Properties in Cubic Equations of State," *Chem. Eng. Sci.*, **33**: 787–791, 1978.

Wilhelm, E., and R. Battino: "Thermodynamic Functions of the Solubilities of Gases in Liquids at 25°C," *Chem. Rev.*, **73**: 1–9, 1973.

————, ———— and R. J. Wilcox: "Low-Pressure Solubility of Gases in Liquid Water," *Chem. Rev.*, **77**: 219–262, 1977.

Wilson, G. M.: "Vapor-Liquid Equilibria; Correlation by Means of a Modified Redlich-Kwong Equation of State," *Adv. Cryog. Eng.*, **9**: 168–176, 1964*a*.

————: "Vapor-Liquid Equilibrium. XI. A New Expression for the Excess Free Energy of Mixing," *J. Am. Chem. Soc.*, **86**: 127–130, 1964*b*.

Winnick, J., and J. Kong: "Excess Volumes of Liquids Containing Polar Liquids," *Ind. Eng. Chem. Fundam.*, **13**: 292–293, 1974.

Wohl, K.: "Thermodynamic Evaluation of Binary and Ternary Liquid Systems," *Chem. Eng. Progr.*, **49**: 218–219, 1953.

I

PROBLEMS

2-1 The following statement is a general criterion for thermodynamic equilibrium: The equilibrium state of an isolated system is that state for which the entropy is a maximum. Consider an isolated, multiphase $(p = \alpha, \beta, ..., \pi)$, multicomponent $(i = 1, 2, ..., N)$ system in which no chemical reactions occur. Show that the following equalities result from this statement and must therefore be satisfied for phase equilibrium:

$$T^\alpha = T^\beta = \cdots = T^\pi$$

$$P^\alpha = P^\beta = \cdots = P^\pi$$

$$\mu_i^\alpha = \mu_i^\beta = \cdots = \mu_i^\pi \qquad (i = 1, 2, ..., N)$$

2-2 Figure I2-2 depicts an isolated composite system comprising two binary fluid mixtures separated by a *rigid* microporous partition. The partition is a perfect heat conductor, and is permeable to species 1 but not to species 2. Show that at thermodynamic equilibrium

$$T^\alpha = T^\beta$$

and

$$\mu_1^\alpha = \mu_1^\beta$$

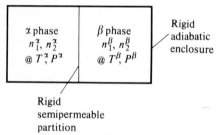

α phase
n_1^α, n_2^α
@ T^α, P^α

β phase
n_1^β, n_2^β
@ T^β, P^β

Rigid adiabatic enclosure

Rigid semipermeable partition

Figure I2-2

but that neither the pressures P^α and P^β nor the chemical potentials μ_2^α and μ_2^β need be equal. (*Hint:* Use the entropy-maximization principle of Prob. 2-1, incorporating two special constraints on the equilibrium state.)

2-3 For certain reversible processes in closed systems Q or W may be identified with a particular property change. For example

$$\Delta U = Q_{\text{rev}} \qquad (\text{const } V)$$

$$\Delta U = W_{\text{rev}} \qquad (\text{const } S)$$

$$\Delta H = Q_{\text{rev}} \qquad (\text{const } P)$$

Can similar identifications be made for the property changes ΔA and ΔG?

2-4 Equation (2-7) may be rewritten as

$$d(nS) = \frac{1}{T} d(nU) + \frac{P}{T} d(nV) - \sum \frac{\mu_i}{T} dn_i \qquad \text{(A)}$$

This is the *entropy formulation* of the fundamental property relation. Repeat the developments of Secs. 2-3 and 2-4, defining a new set of primary functions related to the entropy and developing a set of alternative forms of the fundamental property relation represented by Eq. (A).

2-5 Show that

$$\mu_i = -T\left[\frac{\partial(nS)}{\partial n_i}\right]_{nU, nV, n_j} = P\left[\frac{\partial(nV)}{\partial n_i}\right]_{nU, nS, n_j}$$

where μ_i is the chemical potential of species i.

2-6 It is clear from Eqs. (2-26) through (2-29) that T, P, V, and S serve as natural independent variables in the thermodynamic description of constant-composition mixtures. In what important respects does S differ from T, P, and V?

2-7 The suggestion has been made that the definition of G for a pure fluid can be rationalized by an integration of Eq. (2-26) at constant T and P. Comment on this.

2-8 Show that

$$X - Y\left(\frac{\partial X}{\partial Y}\right)_W = -Y^2\left[\frac{\partial(X/Y)}{\partial Y}\right]_W$$

Using this result, prove for a constant-composition solution that

(a)
$$U = -P^2\left[\frac{\partial(H/P)}{\partial P}\right]_S = -T^2\left[\frac{\partial(A/T)}{\partial T}\right]_V$$

(b)
$$H = -V^2\left[\frac{\partial(U/V)}{\partial V}\right]_S = -T^2\left[\frac{\partial(G/T)}{\partial T}\right]_P$$

(c)
$$A = -P^2\left[\frac{\partial(G/P)}{\partial P}\right]_T = -S^2\left[\frac{\partial(U/S)}{\partial S}\right]_V$$

(d)
$$G = -V^2\left[\frac{\partial(A/V)}{\partial V}\right]_T = -S^2\left[\frac{\partial(H/S)}{\partial S}\right]_P$$

Note that the second relation of (b) is the Gibbs-Helmholtz equation, Eq. (3-30).

2-9 For a constant-composition solution prove that:

(a)
$$U = G - P\left(\frac{\partial G}{\partial P}\right)_T - T\left(\frac{\partial G}{\partial T}\right)_P$$

(b)
$$H = A - V\left(\frac{\partial A}{\partial V}\right)_T - T\left(\frac{\partial A}{\partial T}\right)_V$$

(c)
$$A = H - P\left(\frac{\partial H}{\partial P}\right)_S - S\left(\frac{\partial H}{\partial S}\right)_P$$

(d)
$$G = U - V\left(\frac{\partial U}{\partial V}\right)_S - S\left(\frac{\partial U}{\partial S}\right)_V$$

2-10 Each of the primary thermodynamic properties U, H, A, and G for a pure substance may be expressed as a function of its canonical variables, yielding a canonical equation of state. From such an equation, one can evaluate the remaining thermodynamic properties in terms of the primary property, its canonical variables, and the derivatives of the primary property with respect to its canonical variables. Find relations from which one may develop expressions for the following properties:

(a) P, T, Z, H, A, G, β, κ, C_P, C_V, given $U = U(S, V)$.
(b) V, T, Z, U, A, G, β, κ, C_P, C_V, given $H = H(S, P)$.
(c) P, S, Z, U, H, G, β, κ, C_P, C_V, given $A = A(T, V)$.
(d) V, S, Z, U, H, A, β, κ, C_P, C_V, given $G = G(T, P)$.

For what areas of application would you expect each of these canonical equations to be particularly useful?

2-11 A TS diagram is useful for analysis of idealized processes because reversible heat transfer is given as the area under a curve on the diagram. Show that on a TS diagram

(a) *Isobars have slopes* $= TC_P^{-1}$
(b) *Isochores have slopes* $= TC_V^{-1}$
(c) *Isenthalps have slopes* $= T(1 - \beta T)C_P^{-1}$.

2-12 The *Mollier diagram* (a plot of H versus S) is useful for engineering applications because *isenthalps* describe horizontal lines and *isentropes* vertical lines on such a diagram. Show that on a Mollier diagram

(a) *Isobars have slopes* $= T$.
(b) *Isotherms have slopes* $= T - \beta^{-1}$.
(c) *Isochores have slopes* $= T + (\gamma - 1)\beta^{-1}$.

Here, γ is the ratio of heat capacities C_P/C_V. What is the behavior of these slopes in the region of high superheat?

2-13 The *adiabatic compressibility* κ_S is an experimentally accessible quantity, related to the soundspeed of a fluid. By definition

$$\kappa_S \equiv -\frac{1}{V}\left(\frac{\partial V}{\partial P}\right)_S$$

Derive the following equations connecting κ_S with other observable quantities:

$$\kappa_S = \kappa \frac{C_V}{C_P}$$

$$\kappa_S = \kappa - \frac{\beta^2 T V}{C_P}$$

2-14 Verify that an ideal gas with constant heat capacities obeys the following *canonical equations of state*:

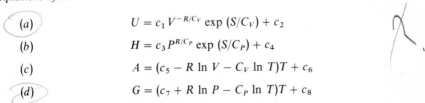

(a)	$U = c_1 V^{-R/C_V} \exp\left(S/C_V\right) + c_2$
(b)	$H = c_3 P^{R/C_P} \exp\left(S/C_P\right) + c_4$
(c)	$A = (c_5 - R \ln V - C_V \ln T)T + c_6$
(d)	$G = (c_7 + R \ln P - C_P \ln T)T + c_8$

In these equations the c_i are constants. In what important sense is the content of these equations different from that of Eq. (2-60)?

2-15 One mole of an ideal gas undergoes a reversible process for which P and V are related by the equation

$$PV^\delta = \text{const}$$

Here δ is an empirical constant. Define an *apparent heat capacity* C' by the equation

$$dQ_{\text{rev}} \equiv C' \, dT$$

and determine an expression relating C' to R, δ, and the heat-capacity ratio γ.

Answer: $C' = R(\delta - \gamma)/(\delta - 1)(\gamma - 1)$.

2-16 Prove that

$$(\partial\beta/\partial P)_T = -(\partial\kappa/\partial T)_P$$

2-17 The pseudovolume fraction, defined as

$$\Phi_i \equiv \frac{x_i V_i}{\sum x_j V_j}$$

is sometimes used as a measure of liquid composition. However, because the pure-component molar volumes V_j depend on T and P, so does Φ_i. Derive the following expression for the T dependence:

$$\left(\frac{\partial\Phi_i}{\partial T}\right)_{P,\,x} = \Phi_i(\beta_i - \sum \Phi_j\beta_j)$$

2-18 Derive the following expressions for the *Joule-Thomson coefficient* μ:

$$\mu = \frac{RT^2}{PC_P}\left(\frac{\partial Z}{\partial T}\right)_P$$

$$\mu = \frac{V(\beta T - 1)}{C_P}$$

2-19 Any total extensive property M^t for a phase may be normalized with respect to the total volume V^t, thus defining a *density function*:

$$\tilde{M} \equiv \frac{M^t}{V^t}$$

Develop the following expressions for the T and P dependence of a density function for a constant-composition solution:

$$\left(\frac{\partial \ln \tilde{M}}{\partial T} \right)_{P, x} = \left(\frac{\partial \ln M}{\partial T} \right)_{P, x} - \beta$$

$$\left(\frac{\partial \ln \tilde{M}}{\partial P} \right)_{T, x} = \left(\frac{\partial \ln M}{\partial P} \right)_{T, x} - \kappa$$

2-20 The *incompressible fluid* is a model substance for which V is a constant, independent of T and P. Show that for this substance

(a) $C_P = C_V$.
(b) U, S, and A depend on T only.
(c) H and G are functions of both T and P.

What interpretation can be given to the derivative $(\partial P/\partial T)_V$ for an incompressible fluid?

2-21 One finds in the literature a quantity called a *departure function*, defined as

$$\Delta M'' \equiv M'(P^\circ, T) - M(P, T)$$

where P° is a *fixed reference pressure*. This quantity is clearly defined differently from a residual function:

$$\Delta M' \equiv M'(P, T) - M(P, T)$$

Develop an equation relating $\Delta M''$ to $\Delta M'$. For what properties are the two quantitites different?

2-22 Calculate ΔS^t when 10^6 kJ are added to 25 kg mol of methane initially at 250°C in a flow process at 1 bar. For methane:

$$\frac{C_P}{R} = 1.702 + 9.081 \times 10^{-3} T - 2.164 \times 10^{-6} T^2 \qquad (T = \text{K})$$

3-1 (a) Show that the partial molar mass of species i in solution is equal to its molar mass (molecular weight).

(b) Show that a partial *specific* property is obtained by division of the partial *molar* property by the molecular weight of the species.

3-2 Given an empirical expression for the molar density of a binary mixture, e.g.,

$$\rho = a_0 + a_1 x_1 + a_2 x_1^2 + \cdots$$

find the corresponding expressions for $\bar{V}_1$ and $\bar{V}_2$.

3-3 Consider the class of *density functions* defined in Prob. 2-19. Determine an expression relating the usual partial molar property $\bar{M}_i$ to V, $\bar{V}_i$, and the corresponding partial molar density function. Check your result against that of Example 3-9 for the special case $M^t = n$.

3-4 Given that

$$M = \sum_j x_j(M_j + \ln x_j) - \sum_j \left[x_j \ln \left(\sum_k x_k \Lambda_{jk} \right) \right]$$

for some dimensionless molar property M of a multicomponent system, where the Λ's depend on T and P only, determine an expression for the partial molar property $\bar{M}_i$.

3-5 Given that

$$M = \sum_j x_j M_j + \frac{1}{2} \sum_j \sum_k \frac{A_{jk} A_{kj} x_j x_k}{A_{jk} x_j + A_{kj} x_k}$$

for some molar property M of a multicomponent system, where the A's depend on T and P only, determine an expression for the partial molar property $\bar{M}_i$.

3-6 Suppose that the partial molar property $\bar{M}_1$ of species 1 in a binary system is represented by a polynomial expression in x_2:

$$\bar{M}_1 = M_1 + \sum_{n=2}^{m} a_n x_2^n$$

Here, M_1 and the coefficients a_n depend on T and P only. Determine the corresponding polynomial expression for $\bar{M}_2$.

3-7 (a) Prove that for a binary system at constant T and P the derivatives $d\bar{M}_1/dx_1$ and $d\bar{M}_2/dx_1$ are equal in magnitude but opposite in sign when $x_1 = x_2 = 0.5$.

(b) Is it possible for partial-molar-property data to satisfy the area tests of Eqs. (3-21) or (3-22), but not the slope tests of Eqs. (3-19) or (3-20)? What about the converse situation? Devise examples illustrating your conclusions.

3-8 A quantity called the *apparent molar volume*, defined for species 1 in a binary liquid mixture by

$$\mathscr{V}_1 = \frac{\rho_2 - \rho}{m_1 \rho \rho_2} + \frac{\mathscr{M}_1}{\rho}$$

is sometimes used for smoothing volumetric data at low concentrations of species 1. Here,

ρ = mass density of the mixture
ρ_2 = mass density of pure species 2 at the mixture T and P
m_1 = concentration of species 1 in moles per unit mass of solution
$\mathscr{M}_1$ = molecular weight of species 1

(a) Prove that

$$\mathscr{V}_1 = \frac{V}{x_1}\left(1 - \frac{\mathscr{M} V_2}{\mathscr{M}_2 V}\right) + \frac{\mathscr{M}_1}{\mathscr{M}} V$$

where x_1 = mole fraction of species 1
$\mathscr{M} = x_1 \mathscr{M}_1 + x_2 \mathscr{M}_2$
V = molar volume of mixture
V_2 = molar volume of pure species 2 at the mixture T and P

(b) Prove that

$$\lim_{x_1 \to 0} \mathscr{V}_1 = \bar{V}_1^\infty$$

3-9 A certain class of substances is described by the canonical equation

$$G = \sum x_k \Gamma_k + RT \sum x_k \ln x_k P$$

where the Γ_k depend on T only. Derive formulas for the following properties of such substances:

(a) G_i (b) S_i (c) H_i (d) U_i (e) C_{P_i}
(f) C_{V_i} (g) V_i (h) $\bar{G}_i$ (i) $\bar{S}_i$ (j) $\bar{V}_i$

3-10 It is a matter of experience that many liquid-phase properties at temperatures well below the critical depend only weakly on pressure. Explain why this is *not* true for the liquid-phase compressibility factor Z^l and fugacity coefficient ϕ^l.

3-11 The following equation is valid for certain residual functions for real-gas mixtures:

$$\Delta M' = \sum y_i M_i' - M$$

For what properties M does it *not* apply?

3-12 Suppose that, in the definition of the fugacity $\hat{f}_i$, Eq. (3-57) were abandoned and replaced by

$$\lim_{P \to 0} (\hat{f}_i / x_i^m P) = 1$$

where m is some number other than unity. Examine the implications of this new definition.

3-13 A ternary gas mixture contains 30 mol % A, 10 mol % B, and 60 mol % C. At a pressure of 50 bar and a temperature of 350 K the fugacity coefficients of A, B, and C in the mixture are 0.7, 0.8, and 0.9. What are the fugacity and fugacity coefficient of the mixture?

3-14 Prove that

(a) $$\phi = \prod \hat{\phi}_i^{x_i}$$

(b) $$f = \prod (\hat{f}_i / x_i)^{x_i}$$

3-15 The logarithm of a function can have no units in dimensionally consistent equations, such as those resulting from thermodynamic theory. Thus, one might expect the argument of a logarithm in such equations to be a dimensionless number. In Eqs. (3-75), (3-76), and (3-83), for example, we find logarithms of fugacity, which always has dimensions of pressure. How is this explained?

3-16 The behavior of electrolyte solutions differs significantly from that of nonelectrolytes. Consider a system consisting of a dissociable electrolyte solute E dissolved in a nonelectrolyte solvent S. Experimental results indicate that

$$\lim_{x_E \to 0} \frac{\hat{f}_E}{x_E^v} = k_E \tag{A}$$

(a) Show that Eq. (A) implies

$$\lim_{x_S \to 1} \frac{\hat{f}_S}{x_S^v} = f_S \tag{B}$$

(b) Suppose there exists a mole-fraction scale $\tilde{x}$ such that

$$\lim_{x_E \to 0} \frac{\hat{f}_E}{\tilde{x}_E^v} = k_E' \tag{C}$$

and

$$\lim_{x_S \to 1} \frac{\hat{f}_S}{\tilde{x}_S} = f_S \tag{D}$$

Writing the Gibbs-Duhem equation as

$$x_E \frac{d \ln \hat{f}_E}{d\tilde{x}_E} + x_S \frac{d \ln \hat{f}_S}{d\tilde{x}_E} = 0 \tag{E}$$

determine from Eqs. (C), (D), and (E) algebraic expressions which *define* $\tilde{x}_E$ and $\tilde{x}_S$ in terms of x_E (and/or x_S) and v.

(c) Give a physical interpretation to your answers to part b.

4-1 The following table contains data for the known triple points of water. Prepare a schematic **PT** diagram for H_2O. (*Note:* There is no ice IV.)

Phases in equilibrium	P/bar	T/K
Ice I/liquid/vapor	0.006105	273.16
Ice I/liquid/ice III	2,074	251.2
Ice I/ice II/ice III	2,130	238.5
Ice II/ice III/ice V	3,440	248.9
Ice III/liquid/ice V	3,460	256.2
Ice V/liquid/ice VI	6,260	273.31
Ice VI/liquid/ice VII	22,000	354.8

4-2 For a pure fluid, show that

$$\Delta U^{lv} = \left(T \frac{dP^{sat}}{dT} - P^{sat} \right) \Delta V^{lv}$$

and

$$\Delta A^{lv} = -P^{sat} \Delta V^{lv}$$

4-3 Let P_1^{sat} and P_2^{sat} be values of the saturation vapor pressure of a pure liquid at absolute temperatures T_1 and T_2. Justify the following interpolation formula for estimation of the vapor pressure P^{sat} at temperature T ($T_1 < T < T_2$):

$$\ln P^{sat} = \ln P_1^{sat} + \frac{T_2(T - T_1)}{T(T_2 - T_1)} \ln \frac{P_2^{sat}}{P_1^{sat}}$$

4-4 (a) A "3-minute egg" takes more than three minutes in Denver or Mexico City. Why?

(b) Explain the principle of operation of a pressure cooker.

(c) Why do ice-skates work? What other substances besides ice might be candidates for a skating surface?

4-5 Prove that the slope of the sublimation curve (P^{sat} versus T) of a pure substance at the solid/liquid/vapor triple point is greater than that of the vaporization curve at the same point.

4-6 We define the *saturation heat capacity* C_σ by analogy with Eqs. (2-41) and (2-50):

$$C_\sigma \equiv T\left(\frac{dS}{dT}\right)^{\text{sat}} = T\frac{dS^{\text{sat}}}{dT}$$

This is the heat capacity of a saturated liquid or vapor, and, in general, it is equal neither to C_P or C_V nor to dH^{sat}/dT or dU^{sat}/dT. Show instead that

$$C_\sigma = C_V + \frac{T\beta}{\kappa}\frac{dV^{\text{sat}}}{dT} = \frac{dU^{\text{sat}}}{dT} + P\frac{dV^{\text{sat}}}{dT}$$

and

$$C_\sigma = C_P - T\beta V\frac{dP^{\text{sat}}}{dT} = \frac{dH^{\text{sat}}}{dT} - V\frac{dP^{\text{sat}}}{dT}$$

where β and κ are defined by Eqs. (2-62) and (2-63).

Assuming that $dX/dY \simeq \Delta X/\Delta Y$ for closely spaced states and taking data from a table of properties for saturated steam, show that outside the critical region:

(a) $C_\sigma \simeq C_P$ for saturated liquid.
(b) $C_\sigma < 0$ for saturated vapor.

4-7 The entropy changes accompanying the familiar first-order phase transformations which occur upon heating a pure substance are always positive (except at the liquid/vapor critical state, where $\Delta S^{lv} = 0$). Offer a simple explanation based on molecular considerations for this observation. Figure 4-2a illustrates a **PT** diagram for a substance that expands on melting and shows the fusion curve with positive slope. How would the figure be different for water, which expands on *freezing*?

4-8 The "order" of a phase transition is equal to the order of the lowest derivative of G showing a discontinuity on the transition line. Thus, the liquid/vapor transition of a pure fluid is *first* order, because both $S[=-(\partial G/\partial T)_P]$ and $V[=(\partial G/\partial P)_T]$ change discontinuously from the liquid to the vapor state. In a *second*-order transition, G, S, and V are all continuous on the transition line, but the three second derivatives $(\partial^2 G/\partial T^2)_P$, $(\partial^2 G/\partial T\ \partial P)$, and $(\partial^2 G/\partial P^2)_T$ are all discontinuous. For this case, the Clapeyron equation in the form of Eq. (4-10) remains valid, but indeterminate: $dP^{\text{sat}}/dT = 0/0$. Show for a second-order transition between states a and b that

(a) There is no "latent-heat" effect.

(b) $$\frac{dP^{\text{sat}}}{dT} = \frac{1}{TV}\frac{\Delta C_P^{ab}}{\Delta\beta^{ab}} = \frac{\Delta\beta^{ab}}{\Delta\kappa^{ab}}$$

where β and κ are defined by Eqs. (2-62) and (2-63).

4-9 Draw careful sketches of M versus T for equilibrium states of a pure fluid traversing the subcooled-liquid, liquid/vapor, and superheated-vapor regions for:

(a) $M \equiv G$
(b) $M \equiv S$
(c) $M \equiv V$
(d) $M \equiv C_P$

How would these sketches be different if the liquid/vapor transition were second order rather than first order? (See Prob. 4-8.)

4-10 Some corresponding-states correlations employ the critical compressibility factor Z_c, rather than the acentric factor ω, as a third parameter. The two types of correlations (one based on T_c, P_c, and Z_c, the other on T_c, P_c, and ω) would be equivalent were there a one-to-one correspondence between Z_c and ω. The data of App. D allow a test of this correspondence. Prepare a plot of Z_c versus ω to show how well Z_c correlates with ω.

4-11 The following conversation was overheard in the corridors of a large engineering firm:

New engineer: "Hi boss. Why the big smile?"

Old-timer: "I finally won a wager with Harry Carey, from Research. He bet me a buck that I couldn't come up with a quick but accurate estimate for the molar volume of argon at 300 K and 300 bar. Nothing to it! I plugged into the ideal-gas equation, and out she fell: about 83 cm³ mol⁻¹. Harry shook his head, but he paid up. What do you think about that?"

New engineer: "Hope your luck continues."

Argon at the stated conditions is *not* an ideal gas. Why did the old-timer win his wager?

4-12 *Trouton's rule* (1884) states that ΔS^{lv} evaluated at the normal boiling point is approximately the same (about 85 J mol⁻¹ K⁻¹) for all normal (e.g., nonpolar) fluids. *Hildebrand's rule* (1915) states that ΔS^{lv} is approximately the same for all normal fluids when evaluated at temperatures for which the fluids have the same molar volume as saturated vapors. Is either of these rules consistent with the theorem of corresponding states? If not, what characteristic of fluid behavior in each case would divide fluids into classes such that each rule would be consistent with the theorem for a given class?

4-13 The *solubility parameter* of a species is defined as

$$\delta_i \equiv \left(\frac{\Delta U_i^{lv}}{V_i^l}\right)^{1/2}$$

Assuming that V_i^l may be taken as the molar volume of species i as a saturated liquid at the system temperature, show that δ_i should be correlatable within the corresponding-states framework as

$$\delta_i = P_{c_i}^{1/2} F(T_{r_i}; \pi_i)$$

Here, F is some function of T_{r_i} and of a third parameter π_i. Such a correlation was developed by Lyckman et al. [*Chem. Eng. Sci.*, **20**: 703 (1965)] with $\pi_i \equiv \omega_i$, the acentric factor.

4-14 Derive *Edmister's formula* for estimation of the acentric factor:

$$\omega = \frac{3}{7}\left(\frac{\theta}{1-\theta}\right)\log_{10} P_c - 1$$

where $\theta \equiv T_b/T_c$ and T_b is the normal boiling point. ($P_c = $ atm.)

4-15 Is the theorem of corresponding states an appropriate basis for correlation of ideal-gas heat capacities? Of Joule-Thomson coefficients? Of thermodynamic soundspeeds? Why or why not?

4-16 The dependent variable in corresponding-states correlations is normally a reduced, or dimensionless, quantity. Yet one also finds such correlations for $\Delta S'$ and ΔS^{lv} in absolute entropy units, for example, J mol⁻¹ K⁻¹. Why is this permissible within the corresponding-states framework?

4-17 Although use of the common logarithm ($\log_{10}$) seems firmly entrenched in some of the sciences, the universal availability of cheap electronic calculators has removed any advantage this function once enjoyed over the more fundamental natural logarithm ($\ln \equiv \log_e$). Devise a corresponding-states parameter equivalent to Pitzer's acentric factor, but incorporating the *natural* logarithm in its definition.

4-18 The basis for the Pitzer correlations is Eq. (4-27)

$$Z = Z^0 + \omega Z^1$$

in which the simple fluid with zero acentric factor is chosen as a *reference substance* with respect to which the properties of nonsimple fluids are correlated. Extensions of this technique are possible in which additional or alternative reference substances are used.

(a) Introducing a second reference substance R with acentric factor ω_R, deduce the correlating expression

$$Z = Z^0 + \frac{\omega}{\omega_R}(Z^R - Z^0)$$

This equation is the basis for the correlation of Lee and Kesler [*AIChE J.*, **21**: 510 (1975)].

(b) Introducing *two* reference substances R1 and R2 with acentric factors ω_{R1} and ω_{R2}, deduce the correlating expression

$$Z = Z^{R1} + \left(\frac{\omega - \omega_{R1}}{\omega_{R2} - \omega_{R1}}\right)(Z^{R2} - Z^{R1})$$

Equations of this type have been proposed by Teja and Sandler [*AIChE J.*, **26**: 337, 341 (1980)].

(c) Examine the possibilities of extended correlations of the Pitzer type if instead of Eq. (4-27) one proceeds from an expression *quadratic* in acentric factor:

$$Z = Z^0 + \omega Z^1 + \omega^2 Z^2$$

4-19 Given a corresponding-states correlation of the Pitzer type, with

$$\omega_p = \sum x_i \omega_i$$

and with quadratic pseudocritical rules

$$T_{pc} = \sum_i \sum_j x_i x_j T_{c_{ij}} \quad \text{and} \quad P_{pc} = \sum_i \sum_j x_i x_j P_{c_{ij}}$$

determine an expression for $\ln \hat{\phi}_i$. (See Example 4-4).

4-20 Show that the density-series virial equation yields linear isochores when each virial coefficient $\mathscr{B}_n$ varies with T according to

$$\mathscr{B}_n = a_n - \frac{b_n}{T}$$

where a_n and b_n are constants.

4-21 Show that the 3-term virial equation in density, Eq. (4-79), when subjected to the classical critical derivative conditions, Eqs. (4-1), yields the following estimates for the second and third virial coefficients at the critical temperature:

$$B_c = -\frac{RT_c}{3P_c} \qquad C_c = \frac{R^2 T_c^2}{27 P_c^2}$$

Determine by analysis of data from the literature whether these estimates are reasonable.

4-22 The vapor-phase molar volume of a particular compound is reported as 23,000 cm^3 mol^{-1} at 300 K and 1 bar. No other data are available. Without assuming ideal-gas behavior, determine a reasonable estimate of the molar volume of the vapor at 300 K and 5 bar.

4-23 J. J. Martin [*Chem. Eng. Progr. Symp. Ser.*, vol. 59, no. 44, pp. 120–126, 1963] has published a thorough study of the thermodynamic properties of the "real ideal gas." For example, he shows for a real gas that

$$\lim_{V \to \infty} \left(\frac{\partial U}{\partial V} \right)_T = 0$$

whereas

$$\lim_{V \to \infty} \left(\frac{\partial U}{\partial \rho} \right)_T = -RT^2 \frac{dB}{dT}$$

and that

$$\lim_{V \to \infty} \left(\frac{\partial C_V}{\partial V} \right)_T = 0$$

whereas

$$\lim_{V \to \infty} \left(\frac{\partial C_V}{\partial \rho} \right)_T = -RT \left(2 \frac{dB}{dT} + T \frac{d^2 B}{dT^2} \right)$$

Here B is the density-series second virial coefficient. Verify these expressions. Why should the infinite-volume limits of the derivatives with respect to molar volume be different from those with respect to molar density?

4-24 YO-YO HYDROCARBONS CORPORATION

To: Mable MacAroon, Engineering Division
From: Ned Meddler, Legal Department
Re: The Great Butane Mystery

As you have probably heard, we are engaged in a major hassle with the Mucho Gaz Corporation over apparent short-shipments of liquified *n*-butane for our utilities people.

We buy butane in railroad tank cars. Each tanker has a 120-m^3 capacity, and contains saturated liquid butane in equilibrium with its vapor at 25°C. Mucho Gaz claims that the tankers are 99 percent (by volume) full of liquid when they leave their plant. On receipt at our installations, the tankers are weighed, the liquid is pumped out, and the tankers are weighed again. The mass of liquid is found by difference.

Unfortunately, the amount of liquid determined in this way does not agree with what we pay for, i.e., the mass calculated on the basis of 99 volume percent. In fact, we always seem to get short-changed by about 700 kg per tanker. The utilities people assure us that the tankers are leakproof, and that there is only about 0.1 volume percent liquid left in the tankers after pump-out. They also tell us that the temperature of the tankers is controlled at 25°C, both during filling and during pump-out.

Before we go any farther with the legal aspects of this problem, I would like your engineers to look at it and see if there's some subtle technical point that we've missed. Mucho Gaz has a generally good reputation, and I find it hard to believe that they're roasting us to the tune of 700 kg of butane per tanker. Also Sammy Bloat of Utilities wants you to estimate the heat-transfer requirement to keep the tanker contents at 25°C during pump-out. He needs the number for sizing a standby generator to power the heaters in case of a blackout.

Incidentally, I'm told that the vapor pressure of liquid n-butane is given by the equation:

$$\ln P(\text{kPa} = 13.66323 - \frac{2154.90}{238.73 + t/^\circ\text{C}}$$

4-25 What result is obtained when Eq. (4-126) is applied to the case where $M \equiv V$?

4-26 Derive an expression for $\bar{V}_i$ for a component of a mixture described by the two-term virial equation in density, Eq. (4-77). Compare your result with the analogous equation based on Eq. (4-78).

4-27 Verify Eqs. (4-105), (4-115), (4-116), and (4-117).

4-28 Offer convincing arguments to explain the observation that many useful equations of state are of *odd* order (i.e., cubic, quintic, etc.) in molar volume or density.

4-29 The van der Waals equation of state is given by Eq. (4-137).
Prove that for a pure fluid obeying this equation

(*a*)   Isochores are linear.
(*b*) C_V depends on T only.
(*c*) U varies linearly with V^{-1} at constant T.

4-30 The quantities $T(\partial P/\partial T)_V$ and $(\partial U/\partial V)_T$ are sometimes called the "thermal pressure" and the "internal pressure" of a fluid. Rationalize the origins of these names, and determine expressions for the two quantities that apply to

(*a*) An ideal gas.
(*b*) A van der Waals fluid.
(*c*) A Redlich-Kwong fluid.

4-31 In 1900, Berthelot [*Comptes rendus*, **130**: 69 (1900)] published a two-constant cubic equation that represented an improvement over the earlier equation of van der Waals. Consider the cubic equation

$$P = \frac{RT}{V - b} - \frac{a}{V^2 + mbV + nb^2} \tag{A}$$

where a, b, m, and n are constants, and impose the following conditions:

(i) Equations (4-1a) and (4-1b) must be satisfied.
(ii) The values of m and n must be chosen so that

$$\frac{P_c V_c}{R T_c} = \frac{9}{32} \tag{B}$$

and

$$\frac{b P_c}{R T_c} = \frac{3}{32} \tag{C}$$

Conditions (B) and (C) are simple and more realistic than the corresponding values of 3/8 and 1/8 implied by the van der Waals equation, but other constraints might be equally satisfactory. Reconstruct Berthelot's derivation, and show that

$$m = \frac{8}{3} \qquad n = -\frac{35}{12} \qquad \frac{a P_c}{R^2 T_c^2} = \left(\frac{13}{16}\right)^3$$

4-32 The general cubic equation, Eq. (4-136), can be written in an alternative form (R. L. Robinson, Jr., personal communication to M. M. Abbott, September, 1977):

$$P = \frac{RT(V^2 + \alpha V + \beta)}{V^3 + \lambda V^2 + \mu V + \nu}$$

As in Eq. (4-136), all five parameters may be functions of temperature and composition. Show that Robinson's equation is equivalent to Eq. (4-136), i.e., find relations among the parameters in the two expressions that make them identical.

4-33 E. M. Holleran [*J. Chem. Phys.*, **47**: 5318 (1967)] finds that temperature and molar density are related linearly for the states of unit compressibility factor:

$$\rho = a + bT \qquad (Z = 1)$$

Find an equation of state that represents this behavior.

4-34 The following empirical equation of state has been proposed for representation of gas and liquid volumes:

$$P = \frac{RT}{V - c_1 V^{1/2}} - \frac{c_2}{V^{9/5}}$$

Here, c_1 and c_2 are positive empirical constants. Comment on the suitability of this expression for representing the *detailed* behavior of gases at low to moderate pressures. In particular, what are the second and third virial coefficients implied by this equation?

4-35 The *Dieterici* equation of state is

$$P = \frac{RT}{V - b} \exp\left(-a/RTV\right)$$

where a and b are constants. Verify that this equation, when constrained to satisfy the critical derivative conditions of Eqs. (4-1a, b), yields the following results:

$$\frac{P_c V_c}{R T_c} = \frac{2}{e^2} = 0.27067$$

$$\frac{b P_c}{R T_c} = \frac{1}{e^2} = 0.13534$$

$$\frac{a P_c}{R^2 T_c^2} = \frac{4}{e^2} = 0.54134$$

where $e = 2.71828\ldots$ is the base for natural logarithms.

4-36 Determine from the general cubic equation, Eq. (4-136):

(a) An expression for $\ln \phi$.
(b) Expressions for the density-series virial coefficients B, C, and D.

4-37 When the quadratic mixing rule, Eq. (4-186), is used for estimation of parameter θ in a cubic equation of state for ternary or higher-order mixtures, what (roughly speaking) is being assumed about the nature of molecular interactions?

4-38 Specific mixing rules for parameters a and b in the original Redlich-Kwong equation are implied if the pseudocritical parameters T_{pc} and P_{pc} are given by Kay's rules,

Eqs. (4-35a) and (4-35b). Starting with Eqs. (C) and (D) of Example 4-17, show that these mixing rules are:

$$a = \frac{[\sum x_i(a_i/b_i)^{2/3}]^{5/2}}{\sum x_i(a_i^2/b_i^5)^{1/3}}$$

and

$$b = \frac{\sum x_i(a_i/b_i)^{2/3}}{\sum x_i(a_i^2/b_i^5)^{1/3}}$$

4-39 Determine expressions for the density-series virial coefficients B, C, and D implied by the BWR equation of state, Eq. (4-199).

4-40 (a) The differential *Tait equation of state* for liquids is

$$-\left(\frac{\partial V}{\partial P}\right)_T = \frac{A}{P + \pi(T)}$$

Here, A is a constant for a given fluid and parameter π depends on temperature only. Determine from the Tait equation expressions for V, β, and κ.

(b) The reduced *Rackett equation of state* for saturated liquids is

$$V_r^{\text{sat}} = Z_c^{(1 - T_r)^a}$$

Here, a is a constant. Determine from the Rackett equation an expression for β_σ, the *volume expansivity at saturation*:

$$\beta_\sigma \equiv \frac{1}{V^{\text{sat}}} \frac{dV^{\text{sat}}}{dT}$$

What additional information is required for determination of κ_σ, the *isothermal compressibility at saturation*?

4-41 New empirical equations of state are sometimes developed from old ones through deviation functions. Thus, for the compressibility factor,

$$Z = Z_R + \delta Z \tag{A}$$

where δZ is the deviation function and Z_R is given by the reference equation. This technique was used by Gray et al. [*AIChE. J.*, **16**: 991 (1970)] and by Redlich [*Ind. Eng. Chem. Fundam.*, **14**: 257 (1975)] to improve particular equations of state. Show that the fugacity coefficient derived from Eq. (A) can be represented as

$$\ln \phi = \ln \phi_R + \delta \ln \phi$$

where for a given temperature

$$\delta \ln \phi \equiv \delta Z + \ln Z_R - \ln (Z_R + \delta Z) + \int_0^\rho \delta Z \frac{d\rho}{\rho} \tag{B1}$$

or

$$\delta \ln \phi \equiv \int_0^P \delta Z \frac{dP}{P} \tag{B2}$$

depending on whether δZ is a function of T and ρ or of T and P. What limitations do Eqs. (A) and (B) impose on the dependence of δZ on density or on pressure? Assume here that Z_R has the attributes of a well-behaved equation of state.

4-42 The equation of Carnahan and Starling [*J. Chem. Phys.*, **51**: 635 (1969)] presented in Sec. 4-9 is based on the virial expansion for hard spheres:

$$Z = 1 + 4y + 10y^2 + 18.36y^3 + 28.2y^4 + 39.5y^5 + \cdots$$

Here $y \equiv b/4V$, where b is a parameter and V is molar volume. Carnahan and Starling noticed that if all coefficients of the y^n are made integers, then

$$Z = 1 + 4y + 10y^2 + 18y^3 + 28y^4 + 40y^5 + \cdots \tag{A}$$

and the coefficients are given by

$$C_n = n^2 + 3n$$

Thus

$$Z = 1 + 3 \sum_{n=0}^{\infty} ny^n + \sum_{n=0}^{\infty} n^2 y^n$$

Noting that

$$\sum_{n=0}^{\infty} y^n = (1 - y)^{-1}$$

and that

$$\sum_{n=0}^{\infty} n^k y^n = y \frac{d}{dy} \sum_{n=0}^{\infty} n^{k-1} y^n$$

show that Eq. (A) is reproduced by the rational function

$$Z = \frac{(1 + y + y^2 - y^3)}{(1 - y)^3}$$

which is the equation of Carnahan and Starling.

4-43 Modern treatments of the critical state deal with *critical exponents* λ, defined as follows. Let ε be a dimensionless independent thermodynamic variable referred to the critical state:

$$\varepsilon \equiv \left| \frac{X - X_c}{X_c} \right|$$

Here, for example, X might be T or ρ. Consider the behavior of some dependent variable Y as the critical state is approached along a particular path p, and assume that this behavior is asymptotically represented by

$$Y_p \sim \varepsilon^\lambda F(\varepsilon) \qquad \text{as } \varepsilon \to 0$$

If $F(\varepsilon)$ is an analytic function of ε, then λ is calculable from experimental data by the recipe

$$\lambda = \lim_{\varepsilon \to 0} \left(\frac{\ln Y_p}{\ln \varepsilon} \right)$$

 (*a*) Verify this equation.
 (*b*) Assuming for purposes of illustration that $F(\varepsilon) = 1$, examine the asymptotic behavior of Y_p for $\lambda = -1$, $-1/2$, $1/2$, and 1.

(c) Suppose that $\lambda = 0$. Then the asymptotic behavior of Y_p is determined by $F(\varepsilon)$. Examine two cases of this type, with $F(\varepsilon) = A + B\varepsilon$ and with $F(\varepsilon) = A + B \ln \varepsilon$.

(d) The following sets of assignments for Y and X characterize (in part) the behavior of real pure fluids:

    (1) $Y_p \equiv P - P_c$ along the critical isotherm, with $X \equiv \rho$ and $F(\varepsilon)$ analytic.
    (2) $Y_p \equiv \rho^l - \rho^v$ along the liquid/vapor coexistence curve, with $X \equiv T$ and $F(\varepsilon)$ analytic.
    (3) $Y_p \equiv C_V$ along the critical isochore, with $X \equiv T$ and $F(\varepsilon)$ analytic.

What values of λ are implied for each of these items by the van der Waals equation, Eq. (4-137)? How do these values compare with experiment? [For hints, see the entertaining and informative review article by J. M. H. Levelt Sengers in *Physica*, **73**: 73 (1974).]

5-1 (a) The property changes of mixing defined with respect to the standard mixing process (see Sec. 5-1) presume equal temperatures *and pressures* before and after mixing. One may, however, define a class of property changes of mixing for which temperature *and volume* remain constant. Designating the former property change by ΔM_P and the latter one by ΔM_V, show that the two quantities are approximately related by the expression

$$\Delta M_V \simeq \Delta M_P + \frac{1}{\kappa V}\left(\frac{\partial M}{\partial P}\right)_T \Delta V_P$$

Here, κ, V, and $(\partial M/\partial P)_T$ refer to the *mixture*.

(b) Modeling of solution behavior frequently provides an expression for ΔA_V, whereas ΔG_P is actually sought. Show that

$$\Delta G_P \simeq \Delta A_V$$

(c) Since $\Delta G_P = \Delta H_P - T \Delta S_P$ and $\Delta A_V = \Delta U_V - T \Delta S_V$, the result of part b might suggest that $\Delta H_P \simeq \Delta U_V$ and $\Delta S_P \simeq \Delta S_V$. Show that this is *not* generally the case.

5-2 The shapes of the ΔM-versus-x_1 curves of Figs. 5-3 through 5-5 suggest the possible use of trigonometric functions to represent property changes of mixing (or of excess functions) for binary systems. Explore this possibility, considering also the implied expressions for the partial properties.

5-3 For a particular binary system at constant T and P, the molar enthalpy change of mixing is given by

$$\Delta H = \sum x_i A_i(1 - x_i) \qquad (i = 1, 2)$$

where the x_i are mole fractions and the A_i are constants. Since this equation is of the form of Eq. (5-2),

$$\Delta M = \sum x_i \overline{\Delta M_i}$$

one is tempted to make the identification

$$\overline{\Delta H_i} = A_i(1 - x_i)$$

Derive expressions for $\overline{\Delta H_1}$ and $\overline{\Delta H_2}$ to show whether or not this is true. In addition, combine your expressions according to Eq. (5-2) to show that the original equation for ΔH is recovered.

5-4 Figures 5-7 and 5-13 show curves for $\overline{\Delta H_i}$ versus x_1 for a binary system at constant T and P crossing just once. Is there any thermodynamic reason why curves of $\overline{\Delta M_i}$ (or

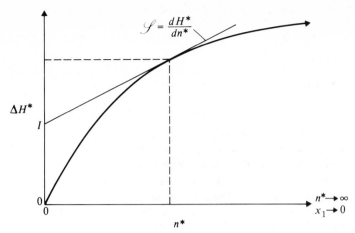

Figure I5-5

$\bar{M}_i^E$) should cross just once? What features of a ΔM (or M^E)-versus-x_1 plot determine where curves of the partial properties cross?

5-5 Figure I5-5 shows a plot of ΔH^* versus n^* for a binary system. Here, ΔH^* is the heat of mixing *per mole of solute* and n^* is the moles of solvent per mole of solute. Prove that the construction shown yields:

(a) $$\overline{\Delta H}_1 = I$$

(b) $$\overline{\Delta H}_2 = \mathscr{S}$$

(c) $$\lim_{n^* \to \infty} I = \overline{\Delta H}_1^\infty$$

$$\lim_{n^* \to \infty} \mathscr{S} = 0$$

$$\lim_{n^* \to \infty} \Delta H^* = \overline{\Delta H}_1^\infty$$

Species 1 is the solute, and species 2 the solvent.

5-6 A naive approximation for the molar density of a mixture is provided by the expression

$$\rho = \sum x_i \rho_i$$

where ρ_i is the molar density of pure species i at the mixture T and P. Is this expression consistent with the ideal-solution model (Lewis-Randall standard states)? If not, find an expression in density that is.

5-7 Expressions for the *molar* properties M^{id} of an ideal solution are summarized in Table 5-1. Which, if any, of these expressions also apply as they stand to *specific* properties of an ideal solution? For this case x_i is a mass fraction, M^{id} and M_i are specific properties, and R is based on a unit *mass* of solution.

5-8 One intuitively expects the entropy to increase as the result of the increased disorder brought about by a mixing process. How is it that ΔS, the entropy change of mixing at constant T and P, is observed to be negative for some real mixtures?

5-9 Consider a binary liquid solution comprising species 1 and 2. Species 1 is known to behave ideally over the entire composition range, i.e.,

$$\ln \gamma_1 = 0 \quad \text{for all} \quad x_1, 0 \le x_1 \le 1$$

Is it possible for species 2 to behave nonideally over any part of the composition range? Explain.

5-10 Assume that the following equation is valid:

$$\frac{G^E}{RT} = x_1 \ln\left(\frac{1}{x_1 + x_2 A}\right) + x_2 \ln\left(\frac{1}{x_2 + x_1 B}\right)$$

where A and B are parameters independent of the mole fractions x_1 and x_2, and are therefore constants at constant T and P. Since this equation has the form $M^E = x_1 \bar{M}_1^E + x_2 \bar{M}_2^E$ it might be true that

$$\frac{\bar{G}_1^E}{RT} = \ln\left(\frac{1}{x_1 + x_2 A}\right) \quad \text{and} \quad \frac{\bar{G}_2^E}{RT} = \ln\left(\frac{1}{x_2 + x_1 B}\right)$$

Prove whether or not this is the case.

5-11 From the molecular point of view, Eq. (5-28), the expression for ΔS^{id}, is regarded as the entropy change of *random mixing*, i.e., the formation of a solution in which the molecules are distributed randomly both in position and in orientation. In this event $S^E = 0$. For many real mixtures, S^E is known to be positive, suggesting that they are more random than random. How can this be explained?

5-12 Determine general expressions for the property changes of mixing ΔG, ΔV, ΔH, and ΔS as functions of composition and the activities $\hat{a}_i$ and their derivatives.

5-13 Prepare sketches of the activities $\hat{a}_1$ and $\hat{a}_2$ as functions of x_1 at constant T and P for the two species in a binary solution. Assume Lewis-Randall standard states and consider *three* cases: ideal-solution behavior, positive deviations from ideal-solution behavior, and negative deviations from ideal-solution behavior.

5-14 A particular class of solutions is described by the equation

$$\frac{G^E}{RT} = A x_1 x_2$$

where A depends on T and P only. Moreover, for this class of solutions, V^E and H^E are independent of pressure. Determine expressions for H^E and V^E consistent with these requirements.

5-15 The development of expressions for G^E ("modeling") sometimes proceeds from Eq. (5-63):

$$G^E = H^E - TS^E$$

With this approach, expressions proposed separately for H^E and for S^E are combined to provide an expression for G^E. However, given this expression for G^E, Eqs. (5-61) and (5-62) should reproduce the expressions proposed for H^E and S^E. What relation between the temperature derivatives of the expressions for H^E and S^E guarantees that this will be so?

5-16 "Enthalpic" and "entropic" effects combine through Eq. (5-63) to determine the behavior of the excess Gibbs function: $G^E = H^E - TS^E$. For example, the sign of G^E is determined by the signs and relative magnitudes of H^E and S^E. The table illustrates the various possibilities for cases where H^E and S^E each have but a single sign. Find in the literature, if you can, examples of all six combinations of signs. Also, find examples where values of H^E and S^E of the same sign combine so as to produce nearly zero values of G^E.

Sign of H^E	Sign of S^E	Sign of G^E
+	+	+, −
+	−	+
−	−	−, +
−	+	−

5-17 Under the assignments

$$\mathcal{M} \equiv G^E/x_1 x_2 RT$$

$$\tau_{12} = -\frac{1}{\alpha} \ln G_{12}$$

and

$$\tau_{21} = -\frac{1}{\alpha} \ln G_{21}$$

the four-parameter expression, Eq. (5-99), reduces to the three-parameter *NRTL equation* for G^E [H. Renon and J. M. Prausnitz, *AIChE J.*, **14**: 135 (1968)]. Determine the corresponding expressions for $\ln \gamma_1$ and $\ln \gamma_2$.

5-18 Derive Eqs. (5-79) and (5-80).

5-19 The *Flory-Huggins* equation for ΔS of a polymer(1)/solvent(2) mixture is

$$\Delta S/R = -x_1 \ln \Phi_1 - x_2 \ln \Phi_2$$

Here, Φ_1 and Φ_2 are volume fractions, defined as

$$\Phi_1 \equiv \frac{sx_1}{sx_1 + x_2} \qquad \Phi_2 \equiv \frac{x_2}{sx_1 + x_2}$$

where s is the number of polymer segments having the same size as a molecule of the solvent. Show that the excess entropy S^E of such a mixture is always *positive*, approaching zero in the limit as $s \to 1$.

5-20 The composition dependence of function $\mathcal{M}$ for a binary system is given by

$$\mathcal{M} = a_0 + a_1 x_1 + a_2 x_1^2 + a_3 x_1^3 + a_4 x_1^4$$

We wish to convert this to an equation of the Margules form:

$$\mathcal{M} = A_{21} x_1 + A_{12} x_2 - (C_{21} x_1 + C_{12} x_2) x_1 x_2 + D x_1^2 x_2^2$$

Show that

$$A_{21} = a_0 + a_1 + a_2 + a_3 + a_4$$

$$A_{12} = a_0$$

$$C_{21} = a_2 + 2a_3 + 3a_4$$

$$C_{12} = a_2 + a_3 + a_4$$

$$D = a_4$$

5-21 The question has arisen as to whether it is possible to have *un*symmetrical expressions for G^E/RT (Lewis-Randall standard states) for which the activity coefficients at infinite dilution are *equal*; it is in fact possible. Devise an expression for G^E/RT for a binary system, unsymmetrical under the transformation $x_1 \leftrightarrow x_2$, but for which $\gamma_1^\infty = \gamma_2^\infty$.

5-22 Your boss requires a quick estimate of the heat of mixing for a 75 mole percent solution of noxone(1) in water(2) at 25°C. A hasty search of the literature provides only one citation: an abstract of an article from an obscure and unavailable journal, in which it is claimed that the maximum value of ΔH for this system is 1160 J mol^{-1}, at a temperature of 300 K and a mole fraction of 0.45 noxone. Stating carefully any assumptions you make, determine a reasonable estimate of ΔH at $x_1 = 0.75$ and $t = 25$°C.

5-23 Offer simple explanations based on molecular principles for the following observations:

(a) For alcohol(1)/hydrocarbon(2) systems, the limiting value of $\mathscr{H} \equiv H^E/x_1 x_2$ as $x_1 \to 0$ is very large ($\sim 23,000$ J mol^{-1}).

(b) The excess Gibbs function G^E is positive for the chloroform/ethanol system, but negative for the chloroform/acetone system.

5-24 (a) Some binary systems (e.g., mixtures of benzene with hexafluorobenzene) show mixed deviations from ideal-solution behavior, i.e., $\mathscr{G}$ ($\equiv G^E/x_1 x_2 RT$) is negative over part of the composition range but positive over the remainder. Demonstrate that the van Laar equation, Eq. (5-87), is incapable of representing this behavior.

(b) Some binary systems (e.g., mixtures of chloroform with methanol and with ethanol) exhibit a change of sign in the curvature of a plot of $\mathscr{G}$ versus x_1. Demonstrate that the four-parameter modified Margules equation, Eq. (5-96), is incapable of representing this behavior.

5-25 A commonly used equation for representation of the composition dependence of excess functions for binary systems is

$$M^E = x(1 - x) \sum_{j=0}^{n-1} a_j(1 - 2x)^j$$

An entirely equivalent equation may be written:

$$M^E = x(1 - x) \sum_{j=0}^{n-1} b_j x^j$$

Handa and Benson [*Fluid Phase Equilibria,* **3**: 185 (1979)] give the relation between the two sets of coefficients as

$$b_k = \frac{(-2)^k}{k!} \sum_{j=k}^{n} \frac{a_j j!}{(j - k)!}$$

Verify this equation for $x \equiv x_1$.

5-26 Efficient computerized reduction of VLE data requires comprehensive empirical recipes for $g \equiv G^E/RT$ which combine the features of many simpler expressions. One such recipe for binary systems is a combination of the Margules and modified Margules equations, Eqs. (5-90) and (5-97):

$$\frac{g_{ij}}{x_i x_j} = A_{ji} x_i + A_{ij} x_j - (C_{ji} x_i + C_{ij} x_j) x_i x_j$$

$$+ (D_{ji} x_i + D_{ij} x_j) x_i^2 x_j^2 - \frac{\alpha_{ij} \alpha_{ji} x_i x_j}{\alpha_{ij} x_i + \alpha_{ji} x_j + \eta_{ij} x_i x_j} \quad (A)$$

(a) Determine expressions for $\ln \gamma_1$ and $\ln \gamma_2$ for a 1/2 binary system described by Eq. (A).

(b) Consider a 1/2/3 ternary system for which $g_{123} \equiv G_{123}^E/RT$ is represented by Eq. (5-109):

$$g_{123} = g_{12} + g_{13} + g_{23} + x_1 x_2 x_3 F(x)$$

Here, $F(x)$ is an arbitrary function of composition, and each of the binaries is described by Eq. (A). Determine expressions for $\ln \gamma_1$, $\ln \gamma_2$, and $\ln \gamma_3$.

5-27 (a) Two types of "chemical" effect are frequently invoked as explanations for the behavior of liquid solutions: *association* and *solvation*. Explain how each of these mechanisms could influence the signs or magnitudes of excess functions, and find examples from the literature illustrating your points. How are chemical effects incorporated into expressions for the excess functions?

(b) Chemical effects are also used to explain the behavior of gases and their mixtures. Explain how *association* or *decomposition* could affect the value of the compressibility factor Z for a nominally pure gas. How are chemical effects incorporated into expressions for Z?

5-28 The following equation has been proposed:

$$g \equiv \frac{G^E}{RT} = Ax_1 x_2 + B \ln (1 + Cx_1 x_2)$$

where parameters A, B, and C depend on T and P only. Determine:

(a) The implied expression for $\ln \gamma_1$ (Lewis-Randall standard state).

(b) The implied expression for $\ln \gamma_1^*$ (Henry's-law standard state).

5-29 For a binary system of species 1 and 2, we can write Eq. (5-126) as

$$g = x_1 \ln \gamma_1 + x_2 \ln \gamma_2$$

where $g \equiv G^E/RT$.

(a) For given T and P, show that

$$\frac{dg}{dx_1} = \ln \frac{\gamma_1}{\gamma_2}$$

(b) What are the limiting values of $\ln (\gamma_1/\gamma_2)$ at $x_1 = 0$ and at $x_1 = 1$ when the standard states for both species are based on the Lewis-Randall rule?

(c) What is the limiting value of $\ln (\gamma_1/\gamma_2)$ at $x_1 = 0$ when the standard state for species 1 is based on Henry's law and that for species 2 on the Lewis-Randall rule?

(d) For given T and P, show that

$$\frac{d^2 g}{dx_1^2} = \frac{d \ln (\gamma_1/\gamma_2)}{dx_1} = \frac{1}{x_2} \frac{d \ln (\hat{f}_1/x_1)}{dx_1}$$

Do values of this quantity depend on the choice of standard states?

5-30 For a given T and P the fugacity of component 1 in a binary liquid mixture is given by

$$\ln \frac{\hat{f}_1}{x_1} = 2 - 3x_1^2 + 2x_1^3$$

where x_1 is the mole fraction of component 1. Determine:
- (a) The fugacity of pure component 1, f_1.
- (b) Henry's constant, k_1.
- (c) An expression for $\ln \gamma_1$ (LR standard states).
- (d) An expression for $\ln \gamma_1^*$ (HL standard states).
- (e) The value of γ_1 at $x_1 = 1$.
- (f) The value of γ_1^∞.
- (g) The value of γ_1^* at $x_1 = 1$.
- (h) The value of γ_1^* at $x_1 = 0$.
- (i) An expression for $d \ln \gamma_1 / dx_1$.
- (j) An expression for $\ln \gamma_2$.
- (k) An expression for G^E/RT.

5-31 Figure I5-31 is taken from an article on Henry's constants; it is intended to demonstrate the uncertainties inherent in extrapolating observed fugacity behavior for dissolved supercritical gases. The system is a binary, the circles represent data, and the figure is drawn for conditions of constant T and P. Comment on the thermodynamic reasonableness of the extrapolated portions of the $\ln (\hat{f}_1/x_1)$-versus-x_1 curve represented by the dashed lines.

5-32 For a particular binary liquid solution at a fixed T and P, the fugacity of the solution is given by:

$$\ln f = 1.8x_1 + 0.5x_2 + 1.1x_1 x_2$$

where f is in bar and x_1 and x_2 are mole fractions.

I. Determine:
- (a) Values for f_1 and f_2 in bar.
- (b) Expressions for $\ln (\hat{f}_1/x_1)$ and $\ln (\hat{f}_2/x_2)$ as functions of x_1 and x_2.
- (c) Values for $\ln (\hat{f}_1/x_1)^\infty$ and $\ln (\hat{f}_2/x_2)^\infty$ and for Henry's constants k_1 and k_2 in bar.
- (d) Values for $d \ln (\hat{f}_1/x_1)/dx_1$ and $d \ln (\hat{f}_2/x_2)/dx_1$ at both $x_1 = 0$ and $x_1 = 1$.
- (e) Expressions for $\hat{f}_1$ and $\hat{f}_2$ in bar as functions of x_1 and x_2.

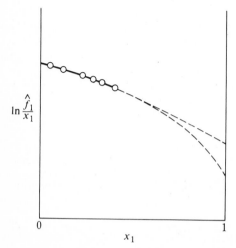

Figure I5-31.

(f) Values for $d\hat{f}_1/dx_1$ and $d\hat{f}_2/dx_1$ at both $x_1 = 0$ and $x_1 = 1$.

Prepare two graphs on which are plotted:

(1) $f, \hat{f}_1$, and $\hat{f}_2$ in bar versus x_1. In addition show lines for the Lewis-Randall rule and for Henry's law.

(2) $\ln f$, $\ln(\hat{f}_1/x_1)$ and $\ln(\hat{f}_2/x_2)$ versus x_1. Superimpose lines representing $\ln f^{id} = x_1 \ln f_1 + x_2 \ln f_2$ and $\ln f^{id} = x_1 \ln k_1 + x_2 \ln f_2$.

II. Determine from the expression for $\ln f$:

(a) Expressions for $\ln \gamma_1$ and $\ln \gamma_2$ as functions of x_1 and x_2.

(b) Values for $\ln \gamma_1^\infty$ and $\ln \gamma_2^\infty$.

(c) An expression for $\ln \gamma_1^*$, where $\gamma_1^* = \hat{f}_1/x_1 k_1$.

(d) Expressions for $G^E/RT = x_1 \ln \gamma_1 + x_2 \ln \gamma_2$; $(G^E/RT)^* = x_1 \ln \gamma_1^* + x_2 \ln \gamma_2$; and $\Delta \ln f = \ln f - \ln f^{id}$ (both cases) all as functions of x_1 and x_2.

Prepare a graph on which are plotted $\ln \gamma_1$, $\ln \gamma_1^*$, $\ln \gamma_2$, G^E/RT, and $(G^E/RT)^*$ versus x_1.

6-1 (a) Extend the mathematical statement of the phase rule, Eq. (6-2), to include systems in which there occur r independent chemical reactions. What is the significance of "independence" in this context? How does one determine r?

(b) Application of Duhem's theorem to a phase-equilibrium situation requires that one know the overall composition z_i of each component present. What analogous quantities must be known for application of Duhem's theorem to a single-phase, multicomponent, chemically reactive system?

6-2 A closed, nonreactive system contains species 1 and 2 in VLE. Species 2 is a light gas, essentially insoluble in the liquid phase. Some extra moles of species 2 are added to the system, which is then restored to its initial T and P. As a result of this process, does the total number of moles of liquid increase, decrease, or remain the same?

6-3 For the triple-point, solid/liquid/vapor equilibrium of a specified amount of pure substance, fixing which of the following pairs of variables does not allow complete determination of the equilibrium state?

(a) T, P (b) H, V (c) H, S (d) T, V
(e) U, V (f) U, S (g) G, V (h) A, V

Note that A, G, H, S, U, and V are molar properties for the system taken as a whole.

6-4 Models of solution behavior which provide approximate expressions for the composition dependence of G^E, H^E, and S^E are in general observed to represent experimental data for G^E better than for H^E and S^E. Indeed, relatively simple models, which furnish acceptable expressions for G^E, often fail to yield useful expressions for H^E and S^E. This apparent insensitivity of G^E to model imperfections is no accident, as has been explained by Hildebrand and Scott (The Solubility of Nonelectrolytes, 3d ed., pp. 135–136, Dover, New York, 1965).

Consider the total properties of a closed system G^t, H^t, and S^t. Suppose that a single modeling variable π is available for adjustment, and that the value of π which gives correct results is π'. Then, for fixed values of T, P, and all other variables, we may relate an incorrect value of property M^t to the correct value $(M^t)'$ through a Taylor expansion about $\pi = \pi'$. Thus,

$$\delta M^t = \left(\frac{\partial M^t}{\partial \pi}\right)' \delta\pi + \left(\frac{\partial^2 M^t}{\partial \pi^2}\right)' (\delta\pi)^2 + \cdots$$

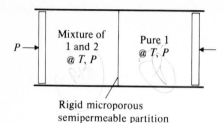

Rigid microporous
semipermeable partition

Figure I6-5.

where $\delta M^t \equiv M^t - (M^t)'$, $\delta \pi \equiv \pi - \pi'$, and all derivatives are evaluated at $\pi = \pi'$. Show that, because of the criterion of thermodynamic equilibrium, errors in G^t vary approximately as the square of the error in π, whereas errors in H^t and S^t vary directly with the error in π. Hence, for small $\delta \pi$, G^t (and thus G^E) is less sensitive to errors in π.

6-5 Consider the physical situation represented by Fig. I6-5. A chamber is divided into two compartments by a rigid porous partition. The left compartment contains a binary solvent(1)/solute(2) liquid mixture, and the right contains pure liquid solvent; the partition is permeable to species 1 only. Movable pistons permit independent adjustment of the pressures in the two compartments.

When both pressures are the same, a nonequilibrium situation exists (why?), and solvent diffuses spontaneously from right to left. However, if the pressure on the left is increased (that on the right being held constant), then equilibrium can be achieved (why?). Designating the pressure *increase* on the left by π, and proceeding from the equilibrium criterion that

$$\hat{f}_1(T, P + \pi, x_1) = f_1(T, P)$$

derive the following implicit expression for the *osmotic pressure* π:

$$\int_P^{P+\pi} \frac{\bar{V}_1}{RT} \, dP = -\ln (x_1 \gamma_1)$$

Here, γ_1 is the activity coefficient of species 1 at conditions T, P, and x_1. Suppose that the solution is very dilute in species 2, and that the effect of pressure on liquid volumes is negligible. Then show that

$$\pi \simeq \frac{x_2 RT}{V_1} \simeq \frac{C_2 RT}{\mathcal{M}_2}$$

where $\mathcal{M}_2$ is the molecular weight of species 2, and C_2 is its mass concentration.

6-6 For a multicomponent mixture of composition z_i with VLE described by Raoult's law, show that the bubble-point pressure P_B and dew-point pressure P_D are given by the expressions

$$P_B = \sum z_i P_i^{\text{sat}}$$

$$P_D = \left(\sum z_i / P_i^{\text{sat}} \right)^{-1}$$

6-7 If standard states based on the Lewis-Randall rule are adopted for the liquid-phase activity coefficients, show that the equal-fugacity requirement for VLE may be expressed as

$$x_i \gamma_i \phi_i^l = y_i \hat{\phi}_i^v \qquad (i = 1, 2, \ldots, N)$$

This equation is the basis for the *Chao-Seader method* for calculation of VLE [K. C. Chao and J. D. Seader, *AIChE J.*, **7**: 598 (1961)].

6-8 Most VLE problems are formulated through Eq. (6-12):

$$\hat{f}_i^l = \hat{f}_i^v$$

Is it also generally true that the *mixture* fugacities f^l and f^v are equal at equilibrium? Is it ever true?

6-9 Consider a binary system in VLE at sufficiently low pressures that Eq. (6-16) applies:

$$y_i P = x_i \gamma_i P_i^{\text{sat}} \qquad (i = 1, 2)$$

(a) Prove that
$$\lim_{x_1 \to 0} \alpha_{12} = \frac{\gamma_1^\infty P_1^{\text{sat}}}{P_2^{\text{sat}}}$$

and
$$\lim_{x_1 \to 1} \alpha_{12} = \frac{P_1^{\text{sat}}}{\gamma_2^\infty P_2^{\text{sat}}}$$

where α_{12} is relative volatility.

(b) Show how the results of part a can be used to check for azeotrope formation in a binary system. Is this check both a sufficient *and* a necessary test for binary azeotropy? Explain.

6-10 The relative volatility is introduced in Example 6-3. By definition, it is a measure of the relative "lightness" of one distributed species with respect to another:

$$\alpha_{ij} \equiv \frac{y_i/x_i}{y_j/x_j} = \frac{x_j y_i}{x_i y_j}$$

(a) Demonstrate that, for a multicomponent system, knowing each of the α_{ij} as a function of liquid composition is equivalent to knowing all of the y_i as functions of liquid composition. (Here, j represents any *particular* reference species chosen as a basis for the definition of the α_{ij}.) Specifically, prove that

$$y_i = \frac{\alpha_{ij} x_i}{\sum \alpha_{lj} x_l}$$

where the sum is taken over *all* species.

(b) The reference species j with respect to which α_{ij} is defined is arbitrary. Suppose that instead of particular species j, species k is chosen for reference. Then show that α_{ij} and α_{ik} are related by

$$\alpha_{ij} = \alpha_{kj} \alpha_{ik}$$

6-11 Given the K values K_1 and K_2 for a binary system in VLE, with K_1 and K_2 defined by Eq. (6-20),

$$K_i \equiv y_i/x_i \qquad (i = 1, 2)$$

demonstrate that if two phases are actually present, then one K value is greater than or equal to 1.0, and the other less than or equal to 1.0. For a *multicomponent* system in VLE, are there similar conditions on the magnitudes of the K values? What special states are represented by cases for which all K values are equal to 1.0?

6-12 A rare type of low-pressure binary VLE behavior is that of *multiple azeotropy*, in which the dew- and bubble-point curves are S-shaped, thus yielding at different compositions both a minimum-pressure and a maximum-pressure azeotrope. A well-documented

example is given by Gaw and Swinton [*Trans. Faraday Soc.*, **64**: 2023 (1968)]. Assuming the applicability of Eq. (6-16), determine under what circumstances multiple azeotropy is likely to occur. Does thermodynamics suggest any limits on the number of azeotropes that can obtain at a given T or P in a binary system?

6-13 Consistent with Eq. (6-16), the following equation may be written for the composition dependence of $\ln \alpha_{12}$ in a binary system:

$$\frac{d \ln \alpha_{12}}{dx_1} = \frac{\partial \ln (\gamma_1/\gamma_2)}{\partial x_1} + \left[\frac{\bar{H}_2^E - \bar{H}_1^E}{RT^2} + \frac{d \ln (P_1^{sat}/P_2^{sat})}{dT}\right]\frac{dT}{dx_1}$$

Derive this expression, and apply it separately to the special cases of constant T and constant P. For the isobaric case, under what special circumstances can one assume that

$$\frac{d \ln \alpha_{12}}{dx_1} \simeq \frac{\partial \ln (\gamma_1/\gamma_2)}{\partial x_1}$$

Under what conditions would you expect a plot of $\ln \alpha_{12}$ versus x_1 to be *linear*?

6-14 A *regular* solution is one for which $S^E = V^E = 0$. What are the implications of "regularity" on the behavior of the other excess functions? On the activity coefficients?

6-15 An engineer arrives home tired and thirsty, only to find that her husband has drunk the last can of cold beer. Undaunted, she puts a six-pack in the freezer, sits down to watch TV, and promptly falls asleep. Later that evening the husband, on finding the beer in the freezer, shakes a can to see if the beer is frozen. It is not. He then opens the can, with the expected result. Moreover, the remaining beer is solid. Why?

6-16 A very small amount of nonelectrolyte solute species 1 is dissolved in liquid solvent 2.

(*a*) Assuming the liquid solution in equilibrium with pure vapor species 2, show that the *differential boiling-point elevation* due to the presence of species 1 is approximately

$$\frac{dT}{dx_1} = \frac{RT^2}{\Delta H_2^{lv}}$$

(*b*) Assuming the liquid solution in equilibrium with pure solid species 2, show that the *differential freezing-point depression* is approximately

$$\frac{dT}{dx_1} = -\frac{RT^2}{\Delta H_2^{sl}}$$

In both cases apply an appropriate form of the coexistence equation. Why does one find that the differential freezing-point depression is numerically larger than the boiling-point elevation? If the solute species were a dissociable electrolyte, would these effects be smaller, larger, or the same? Explain.

6-17 Through application of Eqs. (6-74) and (4-6) show that for a system exhibiting an azeotrope in VLE the change in P^{az} with T is given by

$$\frac{d \ln P^{az}}{dT} = \sum x_i^{az} \frac{d \ln P_i^{sat}}{dT}$$

provided the vapor phase is an ideal gas, H^E for the liquid phase is zero, and V^l is negligible compared with V^v.

6-18 Provide rationalizations for the following qualitative generalizations of azeotrope behavior in binary systems. Where necessary, assume applicability of the two expressions:

$$x_i \gamma_i P_i^{\text{sat}} = y_i P \qquad (i = 1, 2)$$

and

$$\frac{G^E}{RT} = A x_1 x_2 \qquad (A = \text{const})$$

(a) The P-x_1 curve for a system exhibiting maximum-pressure azeotropy is relatively flat at the top.

(b) The more nearly equal P_1^{sat} and P_2^{sat}, the more likely is azeotropy.

(c) The more nearly equal P_1^{sat} and P_2^{sat}, the more rapidly x_1^{az} changes with temperature.

(d) A maximum-pressure azeotrope is richer in the lower-boiling species; the converse is true for a minimum-pressure azeotrope.

(e) An increase of T (or of P) for a maximum-pressure azeotrope increases x_i^{az} for the species whose P_i^{sat} is the more sensitive to T; the converse is true for a minimum-pressure azeotrope.

6-19 For VLE in a binary system, define the *heat of solution* of species 1 as

$$\overline{\Delta H}_1^{\text{soln}} \equiv \overline{H}_1^l - \overline{H}_1^v$$

Derive the following rigorous expression for $\overline{\Delta H}_1^{\text{soln}}$ [See A. E. Sherwood and J. M. Prausnitz, *AIChE J.*, **8**: 519 (1962)]:

$$\frac{\overline{\Delta H}_1^{\text{soln}}}{R} = \left[1 + \left(\frac{\partial \ln \hat{\phi}_1^v}{\partial \ln y_1} \right)_{T, P} \right] \left[\left(\frac{\partial \ln y_1}{\partial(1/T)} \right)_P - \left(\frac{\partial \ln y_1}{\partial \ln x_1} \right)_T \left(\frac{\partial \ln x_1}{\partial(1/T)} \right)_P \right]$$
$$+ (\overline{Z}_1^v - \overline{Z}_1^l) \left(\frac{\partial \ln P}{\partial \ln x_1} \right)_T \left(\frac{\partial \ln x_1}{\partial(1/T)} \right)_P$$

Note that derivatives with only one variable held constant are evaluated from VLE data at constant T *or* at constant P.

6-20 In general one cannot integrate even the simplified coexistence equation, Eq. (6-92), analytically. However, for the very special case where

$$P = a + b x_1 \qquad (a, b = \text{const})$$

direct integration is possible. Determine for this case the resulting expression for y_1 as a function of x_1. To what special case of VLE does this result apply?

6-21 In some binary systems, $\ln \gamma_i$ for one of the species exhibits a maximum with respect to composition at constant T and P. [Chloroform(1)/ethanol(2) at 50°C is an example; $\ln \gamma_1$ shows a maximum at a low chloroform concentration.] Show that

(a) A maximum in $\ln \gamma_1$ implies a minimum in $\ln \gamma_2$ at the same composition.

(b) Neither the van Laar equation, Eq. (6-119), nor the Wilson equation, Eq. (6-123), is capable of representing such behavior for finite values of the parameters.

(c) The two-parameter Margules equation, Eq. (6-121), necessarily yields a maximum in one $\ln \gamma_i$ if the parameters are positive and their ratio is less than 0.5 or greater than 2.

6-22 For binary VLE, any single T, P, x, y data point (except the end points where $x_1 = 0$ or $x_2 = 0$) can in principle be used for evaluation of the parameters in any two-parameter expression for G^E. In particular, data for an azeotropic state are sometimes employed for this purpose.

(a) What experimental considerations lead one to prefer an azeotropic state (provided it exists) to some other single state of VLE?

(b) Mueller and Kearns [J. Phys. Chem., **62**: 1441 (1958)] report the following values for the azeotropic state of acetone(1)/chloroform(2) at 50°C:

$$x_1^{az} = 0.3740 \qquad P^{az} = 0.6068 \text{ bar}$$

For the same temperature, they give

$$P_1^{sat} = 0.8120 \text{ bar} \qquad P_2^{sat} = 0.6913 \text{ bar}$$

Determine from these data estimates of the parameters in the two-parameter Margules, van Laar, and Wilson equations. Prepare on a single graph sketches of $\mathscr{G} \equiv G^E/x_1 x_2 RT$ versus x_1 for these equations. Assume the validity of Eq. (6-16).

(c) Repeat part b for acetone(1)/n-heptane(2) at 50°C, for which Pluddemann and Schaefer [Z. Elektrochem., **63**: 1024 (1959)] report

$$x_1^{az} = 0.9183 \qquad P^{az} = 0.8249 \text{ bar}$$

$$P_1^{sat} = 0.8143 \text{ bar} \qquad P_2^{sat} = 0.1883 \text{ bar}$$

(d) Comment on the advisability of basing a thermodynamic correlation on a single data point.

6-23 (a) Develop an efficient numerical procedure for determination of parameters Λ_{12} and Λ_{21} in Wilson's equation from given values of γ_1^∞ and γ_2^∞.

(b) Find values of Λ_{12} and Λ_{21} from the following pairs of infinite-dilution activity coefficients:

(1) $\gamma_1^\infty = \gamma_2^\infty = 1.5$
(2) $\gamma_1^\infty = 4.0 \qquad \gamma_2^\infty = 5.5$
(3) $\gamma_1^\infty = 0.5 \qquad \gamma_2^\infty = 0.3$

In case 3, three possible solutions exist. [See A. J. Ladurelli, C. H. Eon, and G. Guiochon, Ind. Eng. Chem. Fundam., **14**: 191 (1975).] For each, plot $\ln \gamma_1$ and $\ln \gamma_2$ versus x_1. Does one set of parameters yield results which seem more reasonable (or more likely) than the others?

6-24 The following is a set of VLE data for acetonitrile(1)/benzene(2) at 45°C [I. Brown and F. Smith: Austn. J. Chem., **8**: 62 (1955)]:

x_1	y_1	P/kPa
0.0000	0.0000	29.819
0.0455	0.1056	31.957
0.0940	0.1818	33.553
0.1829	0.2783	35.285
0.2909	0.3607	36.457
0.3980	0.4274	36.996
0.5069	0.4885	37.068
0.5458	0.5098	36.978
0.5946	0.5375	36.778
0.7206	0.6157	35.792
0.8145	0.6913	34.372
0.8972	0.7869	32.331
0.9573	0.8916	30.038
1.0000	1.0000	27.778

(a) This set of data is reasonably well correlated by an equation of the form

$$g \equiv \frac{G^E}{RT} = Ax_1 x_2$$

Assuming the validity of Eq. (6-16), determine a suitable value for A using: (1) the $x_1 - y_1$ data only; (2) the $x_1 - P$ data only; (3) all of the data.

(b) Repeat part a using Eq. (6-83) together with Eq. (6-85).

(c) Is the correlation improved when g is represented by the two-parameter Margules equation, Eq. (6-63) with $C_{21} = C_{12} = 0$? By the three-parameter Margules equation, Eq. (6-63) with $C_{21} = C_{12} = C$? Are the data consistent?

6-25 The following is a set of data for acetonitrile(1)/benzene(2) at 101.33 kPa (1 atm) [Krishna et al.: *J. Chem. Eng. Data,* **25**: 11 (1980)]:

x_1	y_1	$t/°C$
0.080	0.199	76.3
0.210	0.320	74.4
0.233	0.343	74.0
0.287	0.374	73.8
0.335	0.400	73.4
0.419	0.455	73.2
0.4706	0.4706	73.0
0.487	0.481	73.2
0.560	0.515	73.4
0.620	0.551	73.7
0.629	0.562	73.8
0.701	0.607	74.4
0.758	0.645	74.9
0.824	0.707	76.0
0.923	0.835	78.0
0.935	0.853	78.5
0.944	0.875	79.0
0.973	0.938	80.4
0.980	0.952	80.6

The authors, unfortunately, give no data for the vapor pressures of the pure species. The following Antoine equations come from Item 11, Appendix J:

$$\ln P_1^{\text{sat}}/\text{kPa} = 14.2724 - \frac{2945.47}{T/\text{K} - 49.15}$$

$$\ln P_2^{\text{sat}}/\text{kPa} = 13.8858 = \frac{2788.51}{T/\text{K} - 52.36}$$

Data for this system should be well fit by the three-parameter (or possibly the two-parameter) Margules equation.

(a) Since the temperature spread is less than 10°C and since the H^E values for this system are not large, assume the parameters in your expression for g are independent of T, and evaluate them by minimizing $\sum (\delta T)^2$. How well do the y_1 values calculated from your correlation agree with the experimental values? What is the effect of setting $\Phi_i = 1$ in Eq. (6-83) in comparison with evaluating it by Eq. (6-85)?

(b) Values of H^E for this system at 25 and 41.2°C are given by DiCave [J. Chem. Eng. Data, 25: 70 (1980)]. Using these data repeat part a with temperature-dependent parameters in your correlating equation for g.

(c) Using the correlation for g developed in part c of Prob. 6-24 together with the H^E data of DiCave, predict the VLE data for this system at 101.33 kPa and compare your predicted values of T and y_1 with the experimental values.

6-26 (a) Locate a suitable set of binary isothermal P-x-y data in the literature.

(b) Investigate the values reported or used for P_1^{sat} and P_2^{sat} by searching the literature for other values for comparison.

(c) Calculate the virial coefficients B_{11}, B_{22}, and B_{12} by an appropriate generalized correlation. Compare your results with those reported.

(d) To get an idea of the general quality of the data and of the complexity required in a correlating equation, calculate $G^E/x_1 x_2 RT$ for all data points and plot versus x_1.

(e) Find a correlating equation for $g \equiv G^E/RT$ which fits the P-x data by minimization of $\sum (\delta P)^2$. From your correlating equation, calculate values of P and y_1 for comparison with the experimental values. Plot δP and δy_1 versus x_1 as in Fig. 6-12. Are the data consistent?

(f) Reevaluate the parameters in your correlating equation for g by minimizing $\sum (\delta y_1)^2$. Calculate values of δy_1 and δP and plot versus x_1, as in Fig. 6-13. Are the data consistent?

(g) Determine a suitable compromise fit of the data, and prepare a plot similar to Fig. 6-14.

6-27 Locate in the literature a set of binary isobaric T-x-y data and enough H^E data for the same system to allow a thermodynamic analysis of the VLE data. Carry out the calculations illustrated in Examples 6-15 and 6-16.

6-28 In the older literature x, y data for binary VLE are sometimes represented by smoothing equations of the form

$$\alpha_{12} = \frac{1 + a_{12}x_2 + a_{122}x_2^2}{1 + a_{21}x_1 + a_{211}x_1^2} \tag{A}$$

where α_{12} is relative volatility and the a's are empirical constants.

(a) What are advantages and disadvantages of this approach to VLE-data correlation, as compared with the methods of Secs. 6-5 through 6-8.

(b) Hála et al. [Vapour-Liquid Equilibrium Data at Normal Pressures, Pergamon, Oxford, 1968, p. 439] give the following values of the constants in Eq. (A) for the carbon disulfide(1)/acetone(2) system at 35.17°C:

$$a_{12} = 7.1875 \qquad a_{122} = -2.4064$$

$$a_{21} = 1.4685 \qquad a_{211} = 2.5891$$

At 35.17°C, the vapor pressures of the pure species are approximately

$$P_1^{sat} = 0.698 \text{ bar} \qquad P_2^{sat} = 0.469 \text{ bar}$$

Using only the data given here, determine good estimates for γ_1^∞, γ_2^∞, and the azeotrope composition at 35.17°C.

6-29 Construct the P-x_1-y_1 diagram for acetonitrile(1)/methyl acetate(2) at 50°C from the following data:

$$\frac{G^E}{RT} = (0.239x_1 + 0.271x_2)x_1x_2$$

$$P_1^{sat} = 33.85 \text{ kPa}$$

$$P_2^{sat} = 79.29 \text{ kPa}$$

Vapor-phase nonidealities may be neglected.

6-30 Construct T-x_1 and y_1-x_1 diagrams for the cyclohexanone(1)/phenol(2) system at 30 kPa. Available data are as follows:

$$\frac{G^E}{RT} = -2.1x_1x_2 \qquad (\text{independent of } T \text{ and } P)$$

$$\ln P_1^{sat}/\text{kPa} = 15.0886 - \frac{4093.3}{t/°C + 236.12}$$

$$\ln P_2^{sat}/\text{kPa} = 14.4130 - \frac{3490.885}{t/°C + 174.569}$$

Vapor-phase nonidealities may be neglected.

6-31 The data of Goodwin and Newsham [*J. Chem. Eng. Data*, **19**: 363 (1974)] for cyclohexanone(1)/cyclohexanol(2) can be correlated by the equation

$$g \equiv \frac{G^E}{RT} = Ax_1x_2$$

where

$$A = 0.0013043\,T/\text{K} - 1.452 \ln T/\text{K} + 8.37694$$

The vapor pressures of the pure species are given by

$$\ln P_1^{sat}/\text{kPa} = 15.0886 - \frac{4093.3}{t/°C + 236.12}$$

$$\ln P_2^{sat}/\text{kPa} = 14.1918 - \frac{3035.96}{t/°C + 156.60}$$

Select a pressure between 4 and 100 kPa, and construct the t-x_1-y_1 diagram for this system. *Note*: Goodwin and Newsham give data for 30, 100, 200, 395, and 750 torr.

6-32 The *Scatchard-Hildebrand equation* for G^E for a binary liquid system is

$$G^E = (x_1 V_1^l + x_2 V_2^l)\Phi_1\Phi_2(\delta_1 - \delta_2)^2 \tag{A}$$

Here, the V_i^l are molar volumes, the Φ_i are apparent volume fractions, defined as

$$\Phi_i \equiv \frac{x_i V_i^l}{\sum x_j V_j^l}$$

and the δ_i are *solubility parameters*, defined as

$$\delta_i \equiv \left(\frac{\Delta U_i^{lv}}{V_i^l}\right)^{1/2} \tag{B}$$

Show that Eq. (A) is equivalent to the van Laar equation, Eq. (6-119), with

$$A'_{ij} \equiv \frac{V_i^l(\delta_i - \delta_j)^2}{RT}$$

Equation (A) is readily extended to multicomponent systems:

$$G^E = \sum x_k V_k^l (\delta_k - \bar{\delta})^2$$

where

$$\bar{\delta} \equiv \sum \Phi_k \delta_k$$

Show for species i in a multicompnent system that

$$\ln \gamma_i = \frac{V_i^l}{RT}(\delta_i - \bar{\delta})^2$$

6-33 The product gases from a methanol-synthesis reactor have the following composition in mole fractions:

$$CH_3OH: \ 0.045$$
$$H_2O: \ 0.033$$
$$H_2: \ 0.809$$
$$CO: \ 0.028$$
$$CO_2: \ 0.057$$
$$N_2: \ 0.028$$

The gas stream at 100 bar is cooled to 38°C to condense most of the methanol and water. What is the equilibrium composition of the gas stream leaving the condenser? What fraction of the entering methanol leaves in the gas stream? Assume that the condensate is a binary mixture of methanol(1) and water(2) for which

$$\frac{G^E}{RT} = (0.3857x_1 + 0.7377x_2)x_1 x_2$$

at 100 bar and 38°C and that the Redlich-Kwong equation adequately represents the properties of the gas phase.

6-34 The *absolute humidity* $\mathscr{H}$ is defined as the mass of water vapor in a unit mass of dry air. Show that at low pressures where the ideal-gas law provides a reasonable equation of state

$$\mathscr{H} = \frac{\mathscr{M}_w}{\mathscr{M}_a} \frac{P_w}{P - P_w}$$

Here, $\mathscr{M}_w$ and $\mathscr{M}_a$ are the molecular weights of water and of air, and P_w is the partial pressure of water vapor. The *saturation humidity* $\mathscr{H}_s$ is the value of $\mathscr{H}$ when moist air is in phase equilibrium with a large body of pure liquid water. Show by a VLE argument that to a good approximation

$$\mathscr{H}_s = \frac{\mathscr{M}_w}{\mathscr{M}_a} \frac{P_w^{sat}}{P - P_w^{sat}}$$

The *percentage relative humidity* $\mathscr{H}_r$ is defined as

$$\mathscr{H}_r \equiv 100 \frac{P_w}{P_w^{sat}}$$

Show that

$$\mathscr{H}_r = 100 \frac{\mathscr{H} \mathscr{M}_w + \mathscr{M}_a \mathscr{H}_s}{\mathscr{H}_s \mathscr{M}_w + \mathscr{M}_a \mathscr{H}}$$

6-35 The development of Eqs. (6-170) and (6-171) in Example 6-20 omits most of the details of derivation. Supply the missing steps, and show that these equations reduce to Eqs. (6-164) and (6-165) under appropriate conditions.

6-36 Determine expressions for $\ln \gamma_1^*$ for binary liquid solutions described by

(a) The van Laar equation, Eq. (6-119).
(b) The two-parameter Margules equation, Eq. (6-121).
(c) The Wilson equation, Eq. (6-123).

6-37 Extensive gas-solubility data are available for the ammonia(1)/water(2) system. Locate some, and reduce them at several temperatures by the methods of Sec. 6-9. Note that liquid-mixture densities are available, and that independent estimation of $\bar{V}_1$ is therefore possible. Are the observed effects of temperature on k_1^+ and $(\gamma_1^*)^+$ consistent with what you would expect from available enthalpy data for this system?

6-38 Plots of valid data for $\Delta H/RT$ and $\Delta S/R$ versus x_1 at constant T and P are made on a single graph for a binary system of miscible liquids. Both property changes of mixing are based on Lewis-Randall standard states. Is there any thermodynamic limit to the number of times these curves can cross?

6-39 The limiting behavior of binary liquid systems exhibiting large positive deviations from ideal-solution behavior is complete immiscibility of the two pure liquids. What is the limiting behavior of systems exhibiting large *negative* deviations from ideal-solution behavior?

6-40 Consider the idealized ternary LLE situation where solute species 1 is distributed between two liquid phases α and β containing completely immiscible solvent species 2 and 3. Assuming the availability of expressions for G_{12}^E and G_{13}^E of the two liquid phases, show how values for the *distribution coefficient* $K_1 \equiv x_1^\alpha/x_1^\beta$ of the solute are obtained. What complications are introduced if one can *not* ignore the mutual solubilities of the solvents?

6-41 Starting with the coexistence equation for binary two-phase equilibrium, show that the slope of the "α-side" of the LLE solubility diagram is given by the equation

$$\frac{dT}{dx_1^\alpha} = \frac{-(x_1^\beta - x_1^\alpha)XRT^2}{x_1^\alpha x_2^\alpha[x_1^\beta(\bar{H}_1^\beta - \bar{H}_1^\alpha) + x_2^\beta(\bar{H}_2^\beta - \bar{H}_2^\alpha)]}$$

where

$$X \equiv 1 + x_1^\alpha x_2^\alpha \left[\frac{\partial \ln (\gamma_1/\gamma_2)^\alpha}{\partial x_1^\alpha} \right]_{T,P}$$

6-42 Figures 6-34, 6-35, and 6-36 are based on Eqs. (A), (I), (J), and (K) of Example 6-23, with C_P^E assumed *positive* and given by $C_P^E/R = 3x_1x_2$. Graph the corresponding figures for the following cases, in which C_P^E is assumed *negative*:

(a) $A = \dfrac{975}{T} - 18.4 + 3 \ln T$

(b) $A = \dfrac{540}{T} - 17.1 + 3 \ln T$

(c) $A = \dfrac{1500}{T} - 19.9 + 3 \ln T$

6-43 It has been suggested that a value for G^E of at least $0.5RT$ is required for liquid/liquid phase splitting in a binary system. Offer some justification for this statement.

6-44 Example 6-24 illustrated the determination of parameters in the Margules equation from an LLE data point. Repeat the numerical exercise of that example for the two-parameter van Laar equation, Eq. (6-119). Compare the detailed behavior of the two equations on a plot of $\mathscr{G}(\equiv G^E/x_1 x_2\, RT)$ versus x_1.

6-45 Prepare sketches of $\hat{a}_i$ versus x_1 and of $\hat{f}_i$ versus x_1 for both species in a binary system exhibiting LLE. Illustrate on these graphs constructions which determine the equilibrium compositions x_1^α and x_1^β.

6-46 It was demonstrated in Example 6-26 that the Wilson equation for G^E is incapable of representing LLE. Show that the simple modification of Wilson's equation given by

$$G^E/RT = -C[x_1 \ln (x_1 + x_2 \Lambda_{12}) + x_2 \ln (x_2 + x_1 \Lambda_{21})]$$

can represent LLE. Here, C is a constant.

6-47 Under conditions such that isothermal VLE in a binary system is properly described by Eq. (6-16),

$$y_i P = x_i \gamma_i P_i^{\text{sat}}$$

show that

$$\left(\frac{dP}{dx_1}\right)_{x_1 = 0} \geq -P_2^{\text{sat}}$$

and

$$\left(\frac{dP}{dx_1}\right)_{x_1 = 1} \leq P_1^{\text{sat}}$$

Under the same conditions, show that for positive azeotropy

$$P^{\text{az}} < P_1^{\text{sat}} + P_2^{\text{sat}}$$

6-48 Consider the representation of mixture fugacities for a binary liquid system by the equation

$$\ln f = A + Bx_1 - Cx_1^3$$

where parameters A, B, and C depend on T and P only. Determine:

(a) The expression for G^E/RT (Lewis-Randall standard states) implied by this equation.

(b) A numerical inequality constraint for positive values of C that guarantees intrinsic stability for all $x_1 (0 \leq x_1 \leq 1)$.

6-49 Derive Eqs. (6-205) through (6-209).

6-50 A Pxy diagram for a binary system at constant T is shown in Figure I6-50. For each of the indicated pressure levels, sketch on a single graph the Gibbs function G versus composition relation for a vapor phase, both where it is stable and where it is not. The curves should be of proper shape and should lie in correct relation to one another. Assuming G for a liquid phase to be independent of P, sketch the G-versus-composition curve for this phase, showing its proper location in relation to the curves for vapor. Also, draw in the tie line connecting the phases in equilibrium for $P = P_C$.

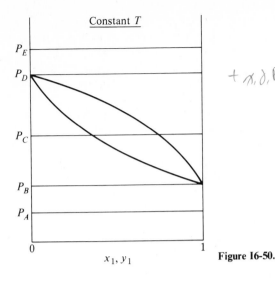

Constant T

Figure 16-50.

6-51 In Example 6-22 we developed from the LLE *equilibrium* equations a plausibility argument demonstrating that positive deviations from ideal-solution behavior are conducive to liquid/liquid phase splitting.

(*a*) Use one of the binary intrinsic stability criteria to reach this same conclusion.

(*b*) Is it possible *in principle* for a system exhibiting negative deviations from ideality to form two liquid phases?

6-52 For a binary system in VLE described by Eq. (6-16), prove that the slope of the bubble-point curve at constant T is given by

$$\frac{dP}{dx_1} = \left(1 + x_1 \frac{d \ln \gamma_1}{dx_1}\right)(\gamma_1 P_1^{sat} - \gamma_2 P_2^{sat})$$

At a homogeneous azeotrope, $\gamma_1 P_1^{sat} = \gamma_2 P_2^{sat}$, and thus $dP/dx_1 = 0$. For what other condition does $dP/dx_1 = 0$, and what is its significance? Show also that

$$\frac{d^2 P}{dx_1^2} = \frac{\gamma_1 P_1^{sat}}{x_2}\left(1 + x_1 \frac{d \ln \gamma_1}{dx_1}\right)\frac{d \ln \gamma_1}{dx_1}$$

at a homogeneous azeotrope, and discuss the implications of this equation.

6-53 Choosing a criterion of equilibrium involving only extensive quantities, derive for a pure fluid the following conditions for *mechanical* and *thermal* stability:

$$\left(\frac{\partial P}{\partial V}\right)_T < 0 \quad \text{and} \quad C_V > 0$$

[Eq. (6-200) and its consequences represent conditions for *diffusional* stability in a binary mixture.]

6-54 A binary vapor mixture of composition y_1^* coexists in a state of three-phase equilibrium with two binary liquid mixtures of compositions x_1^α and x_1^β. Derive an expression relating the *overall* composition z_1 of such a three-phase system to y_1^*, x_1^α, x_1^β, and the relative molar amounts of each phase. (This expression is the three-phase analog of the lever rule for binary two-phase equilibrium.)

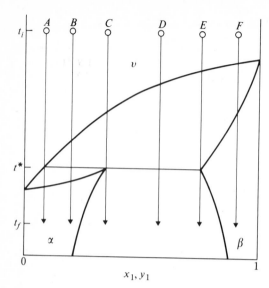

Figure I6-55.

6-55 Figure I6-55 depicts an isobaric txy diagram for a binary system exhibiting VLLE. Vapor mixtures of six different compositions are cooled from the same initial temperature t_i to the same final temperature t_f along the paths shown. Describe the sequences of physical states assumed by each mixture during each cooling process.

6-56 Figures 6-2, 6-3, and 6-39 through 6-41 illustrate seven kinds of isothermal VLE or VLLE. Prepare an isothermal y_1-x_1 diagram corresponding to each of these cases. To facilitate comparison of the various types of behavior, assume for each case that $P_1^{sat} < P_2^{sat}$.

6-57 Vapor sulfur hexafluoride SF_6 at pressures of about 1,600 kPa is used as a dielectric in large primary circuit breakers for electric transmission systems. As liquids, SF_6 and H_2O are essentially immiscible, and it is therefore necessary to specify a low enough moisture content in the vapor SF_6 so that if condensation occurs in cold weather a liquid-water phase will not form first in the system. For a preliminary determination, assume the vapor phase an ideal gas and prepare the phase diagram (see Fig. 6-42b) for $H_2O(1)/SF_6(2)$ at 1,600 kPa in the composition range up to 1,000 parts per million of water (mole basis). The following approximate equations for vapor pressures are adequate:

$$\ln P_1^{sat}/kPa = 19.1478 - \frac{5,363.70}{T/K}$$

$$\ln P_2^{sat}/kPa = 14.6511 - \frac{2,048.97}{T/K}$$

6-58 Signor et al. [Helv. Chim. Acta, **52**: 2347 (1969)] report the following VLLE data for diethyl ether(1)/water(2), a system of limited miscibility. At 25°C:

x_1	P/kPa	y_1	x_1	P/kPa	y_1
0.000	3.168	0.000	$0.9502(x_1^\beta)$	$71.89(P*)$	$0.956(y_1^*)$
0.002	17.27	0.817	0.960	71.87	0.963
0.004	27.26	0.884	0.970	71.85	0.970
0.006	35.90	0.912	0.980	71.82	0.978
0.008	43.73	0.928	0.990	71.70	0.988
0.010	51.04	0.938	1.000	71.45	1.000
0.012	58.16	0.946			
0.014	65.23	0.952			
$0.0159(x_1^\alpha)$	$71.89(P*)$	$0.956(y_1^*)$			

(a) Prepare a Pxy diagram of the data similar to Fig. 6-40; include an expanded-scale representation of the region for $x_1 > 0.95$.

(b) Determine from the solubility limits, x_1^α and x_1^β, values of the parameters in the two-parameter Margules equation. (See Example 6-24.) With this equation and assuming the validity of Eq. (6-16), calculate values of P and y_1 corresponding to the x_1 values of the data set. How well do the calculated values compare with the experimental values of P and y_1?

(c) Repeat part b with the van Laar equation.

(d) An alternative procedure sometimes used for prediction of Pxy behavior from solubility data $(x_1^\alpha, x_1^\beta, P*)$ and the P_1^{sat} and P_2^{sat} values is to assume that Henry's law applies to the dilute component (i),

$$y_i P = k_i x_i$$

and that Raoult's law is valid for the concentrated component (j),

$$y_j P = P_j^{sat} x_j$$

Then

$$P = k_i x_i + P_j^{sat} x_j$$

throughout the regions of miscibility. Henry's constant k_i is determined from the solubility data; for example

$$k_1 = \frac{P* - P_2^{sat} x_2^\alpha}{x_1^\alpha}$$

Making these assumptions, calculate P and y_1 values corresponding to the x_1 values of the data set. How do these results compare with the data? Are they significantly better or worse than the results of parts b and c?

(e) Calculate experimental values of γ_1 and γ_2 for each data point and plot versus x_1. How good an assumption is Raoult's law for the concentrated component? What are the values of γ_1^∞ and γ_2^∞? Writing Eq. (5-128) as $k_i = P_i^{sat} \gamma_i^\infty$ (why?), calculate the true values of Henry's constants for the species at infinite dilution. How do these compare with the values found in part d? How good an assumption is Henry's law for the dilute species over the full solubility range?

(f) Can you devise a correlation based on all the data that represents them reasonably well?

DATA SOURCES AND BIBLIOGRAPHIES

1. Boublik, T., V. Fried, and E. Hála: *The Vapor Pressures of Pure Substances*, Elsevier, Amsterdam, 1973.
2. Fredenslund, A., J. Gmehling, and P. Rasmussen: *Vapor-Liquid Equilibria Using UNIFAC*, Elsevier, Amsterdam, 1977. (For a revised version of the UNIFAC parameter tables, see Skjold-Jørgensen et al: *Ind. Eng. Chem. Process Des. Dev.*, **18**: 714 (1979). Further revisions will most likely appear periodically in the literature.)
3. Gmehling, J., and U. Onken: *Vapor-Liquid Equilibrium Data Collection*, DECHEMA, Frankfurt/Main, vol. I, pts. 1 and 2a, 1977. (Remaining 10 parts published in subsequent years.)
4. Handa, Y. P., and G. C. Benson: "Volume Changes on Mixing Two Liquids: A Review of the Experimental Techniques and the Literature Data," *Fluid Phase Equilibria*, **3**: 185-249 (1979).
5. Hicks, C. P. (ed.): "A Bibliography of Thermodynamic Quantities for Binary Fluid Mixtures," chap. 9, *Chemical Thermodynamics*, vol. 2, The Chemical Society, London, 1978.
6. Hirata, M., S. Ohe, and K. Nagahama: *Computer Aided Data Book of Vapor-Liquid Equilibria*, Elsevier, Amsterdam, 1975.
7. Kehiaian, H. V.: "Thermodynamics of Organic Mixtures," chap. 5, *MTP International Review of Science, Physical Chemistry, Thermochemistry and Thermodynamics*, ser. 1, vol. 10, pp. 121-158, Butterworths, London, 1972.
8. Kojima, K., and T. Tochigi: *Prediction of Vapor-Liquid Equilibria by the ASOG Method*, Elsevier, Amsterdam, 1979.
9. Ohe, S.: *Computer Aided Data Book of Vapor Pressure*, Data Book Publishing Co., Tokyo, 1976.
10. Prausnitz, J. M., T. F. Anderson, E. A. Grens, C. A. Eckert, R. Hsieh, and J. P. O'Connell: *Computer Calculations for Multicomponent Vapor-Liquid and Liquid-Liquid Equilibria*, Prentice-Hall, Englewood Cliffs, N.J., 1980, App. C. (In particular, Apps. C-1 and C-4 contain the data required to apply the Hayden-O'Connell correlation for second virial coefficients.)
11. Reid, R. C., J. M. Prausnitz, and T. K. Sherwood: *The Properties of Gases and Liquids*, 3d ed., Appendix A, " Property Data Bank," McGraw-Hill, New York, 1977.
12. Sørensen, J. M., and W. Arlt: *Liquid-Liquid Equilibrium Data Collection*, DECHEMA Chemistry Data Series, Frankfurt/Main, vol. V, pt. 1, 1979, pts. 2 and 3, 1980.

13. Wichterle, I., J. Linek, and E. Hála: *Vapor-Liquid Equilibrium Data Bibliography*, Elsevier, Amsterdam, 1973. Supplement I, 1976; Supplement II, 1979.
14. Wisniak, J., and A. Tamir: *Mixing and Excess Thermodynamic Properties. A Literature Source Book*, Elsevier, Amsterdam, 1978.
15. *Bulletin of Chemical Thermodynamics*, an annual publication of Thermochemistry, Inc., Oklahoma State University, Stillwater, Oklahoma 74074.
16. *Selected Values of Properties of Chemical Compounds*, Thermodynamics Research Center Data Project, and *Selected Values of Properties of Hydrocarbons and Related Compounds*, American Petroleum Institute Research Project 44, serial publications of the Thermodynamics Research Center, College Station, Texas 77843.
17. *Technical Data Book-Petroleum Refining*, 3d ed., American Petroleum Institute, Washington, 1977.
18. *International DATA Series, Selected Data on Mixtures, Series A. Thermodynamic Properties of Nonreacting Binary Systems of Organic Substances*, a periodical publication of the Thermodynamics Research Center, College Station, Texas 77843.
19. *International Data Series B, Thermodynamic Properties of Aqueous Organic Systems*, a periodical publication of Engineering Sciences Data Unit, 251–259 Regent St., London W1R 7AD.

INDEX